The Coptic Encyclopedia

Editors and Consultants

The Coptic Encyclopedia

Aziz S. Atiya
EDITOR IN CHIEF

Volume 2

Macmillan Publishing Company
NEW YORK
Collier Macmillan Canada
TORONTO
Maxwell Macmillan International
NEW YORK · OXFORD · SINGAPORE · SYDNEY

Macmillan Publishing Company
866 Third Avenue, New York, NY 10022

Collier Macmillan Canada, Inc.
1200 Eglinton Avenue East, Suite 200, Don Mills, Ontario M3C 3N1

Library of Congress Catalog Card No.: 90-23448

Printed in the United States of America

printing number
1 2 3 4 5 6 7 8 9 10

Library of Congress Cataloging-in-Publication Data

The Coptic encyclopedia / Aziz S. Atiya, editor-in-chief.
p. cm.
Includes bibliographical references and index.
ISBN 0-02-897025-X (set)
1. Coptic Church—Dictionaries. 2. Copts—Dictionaries.
I. Atiya, Aziz S., 1898–
BX130.5.C66 1991 90-23448
281'.7'03—dc20 CIP

The preparation of this volume was made possible in part by a grant from the National Endowment for the Humanities, an independent federal agency.

Photographs on pages 567, 736, 754, 755, 790, 791, 876–878, 1284, 1311, and 2168 are reproduced courtesy of the Metropolitan Museum of Art. Photography by the Egyptian Expedition.

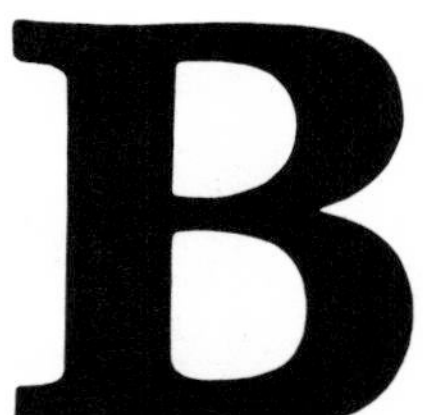

BABĪJ, Arabic name of an Egyptian town in the province of Gharbiyyah now known as Abbīj. It lies in the western Delta about 5 miles (8 km) northwest of Kafr al-Zayyāt. Muslim authors of the Middle Ages mentioned the town often. IBN ḤAWQAL, writing in the tenth century, said there were many churches and a mosque there. The existence of "many churches" in the tenth century suggests that the place must have had great importance for Christians in earlier centuries.

From Kellia al-Muna there is extant the gravestone of a monk named Goutinos, the son of Niamin, from Pebidj. The stone is probably to be dated to the sixth or seventh century and may have reference to the Babīj that is now Abbīj. It is possible that this town is also the Babīj given in a colophon as the abode of the scribe of a manuscript dated to 1255 (Vatican Library, Arabic no. LX, fol. 125v).

BIBLIOGRAPHY

Timm, S. *Das christlich-koptische Ägypten in arabischer Zeit,* Vol. 1, pp. 274–75. Wiesbaden, 1984.

RANDALL STEWART

BABLUHIYYAH. *See* Tanis.

BABYLON, the oldest part of the city of Cairo. Babylon is situated on the east bank of the Nile, to some extent on the border between Upper and Lower Egypt. The same spot marks the mouth of a canal, originally cut about 600 B.C., which connected the Nile to the Red Sea. The city was widely regarded among ancient writers (Diodorus Siculus 1.56. 3; Strabo *Geography* 17. 1.30) as having been built by the Babylonians of Mesopotamia. More probably, however, the name goes back to the Old Egyptian *Pr-h'pj-n-Jwnw* ("Nile house of Heliopolis"), which sounded like "Babylon" to the Greeks (Gardiner, 1947, p. 143).

In late antiquity "Babylon" designated the settled country between Heliopolis and the Roman fortress situated to the south. Today it refers to what is left of the Roman fortress itself. The Arabs named this fort QAṢR AL-SHAMʿ (Palace of Candles), a designation difficult to explain. In the Roman period one of the three legions controlling Egypt was stationed in the fort, which was the most important bastion in the country. From here as late as the seventh century was conducted the decisive battle against the Arabs, into whose hands it fell on 9 April 641 after a seven-month siege. A bishop of Babylon called Cyrus is mentioned in the first half of the fifth century. His residence, however, like that of his immediate successors and of course all other remaining civilians, was situated outside the fortress.

The Fortress

The present fortress (Butler, 1914; Toy, 1937, pp. 52–78), which conventionally dates from the period of the emperor Trajan in the second century, is, according to the sources, a reconstruction of a fortress that goes back to the Persian period (Josephus 2.15, 1). Of this, however, there is no certain knowledge.

Although the Roman fortress was used as a quarry down to the end of the nineteenth century, it must be regarded as one of the best-preserved fortress structures from the Roman period. Certainly one can still recognize the course of the curtain wall with its numerous half-rounded bastions and

Foreground: Fort of Babylon (Old Cairo). Background: entrance to the Coptic Museum. *Courtesy Arab Republic of Egypt.*

flights of stairs. On the west side, where the fortress was bordered immediately by the river, there was a river gate flanked by two remarkably strong, fully circular towers, a rare feature in the layout of Roman fortresses. A second gate faced south with a door between two half-rounded towers opening out in traditional fashion from an inner court and functioning as a land gate. Almost certainly there was at least a second land gate on the north side of the fortress. Ruins of the buildings within the fortress are not visible.

After the conquest of the fortress, the victorious Arab army created the new city of al-Fusṭāṭ to the north of Babylon around the mosque, named after the commander-in-chief ʿAmr ibn al-ʿĀṣ. The native, mostly Christian population, who had probably lost most of their houses, settled in the razed fortress, where they had already taken up quarters during the siege.

Churches Within the Fortress

The oldest churches within the fortress also belong to this Arab period. The oldest foundation that is known is the Church of Saint Sergius (Abū Sarjah), which exists to this day (Butler, 1884, pp. 181ff.; Middleton, 1885, pp. 397ff.). It is the episcopal church in the city and was built at the turn of the seventh to the eighth century in the period of ʿAbd al-Malik under the patriarchate of JOHN III. It is a basilica with a gallery built over columns with a western return aisle and tripartite sanctuary, which was presumably separated from the nave by a narrow room now no longer in existence.

There is a crypt beneath the sanctuary with wall niches arranged crosswise. At a later date it was given a three-aisle form by the insertion of two rows of columns. Because of its structural connection with the upper church, the crypt could have been built only after the construction of the church. Since the later Middle Ages, the legend has circulated that the Holy Family found shelter in this crypt during the flight to Egypt. Al-MAQRĪZĪ, writing in the fifteenth century, is the first serious historian to give an account of it. Earlier references are found in some reports of pilgrims from the west (listed in Coquin, 1974, p. 97), but these simply reiterate the accounts of the local dragomans. Nevertheless, the crypt of Saint Sergius is never mentioned in descriptions of the various stops of the Holy Family in the large historical works of the Coptic church.

The Church of Sitt Barbārah (Monneret de Villard and A. Patricolo, 1922) is a sister building of the Church of Saint Sergius. It comes from the same period and likewise was designed as a basilica with galleries, although it is substantially less well preserved. Extensive restoration work was carried out at the beginning of the twentieth century, and at the same time the opportunity was taken to adapt the building to the demands of modern worship, which above all required more altar rooms. As a result, the *khūrus*, originally situated in front of the sanctuary, was sacrificed. The side chapel on the south side may belong, at least in outline, to the original building, but the row of chapels attached to the north side was first built at the beginning of the twentieth century. The rooms originally situated in this area had quite a different shape.

The Church of Sitt Maryam (al-ʿAdhrā'), called al-Muʿallaqah (the Suspended One), was for a time the church of the patriarchate in the city (Butler, 1914, Vol. 1, pp. 206ff.). It is constructed over the south gate of the Roman fortress and consequently can only have been built after the Arab conquest. It is first mentioned in literature in the period of the

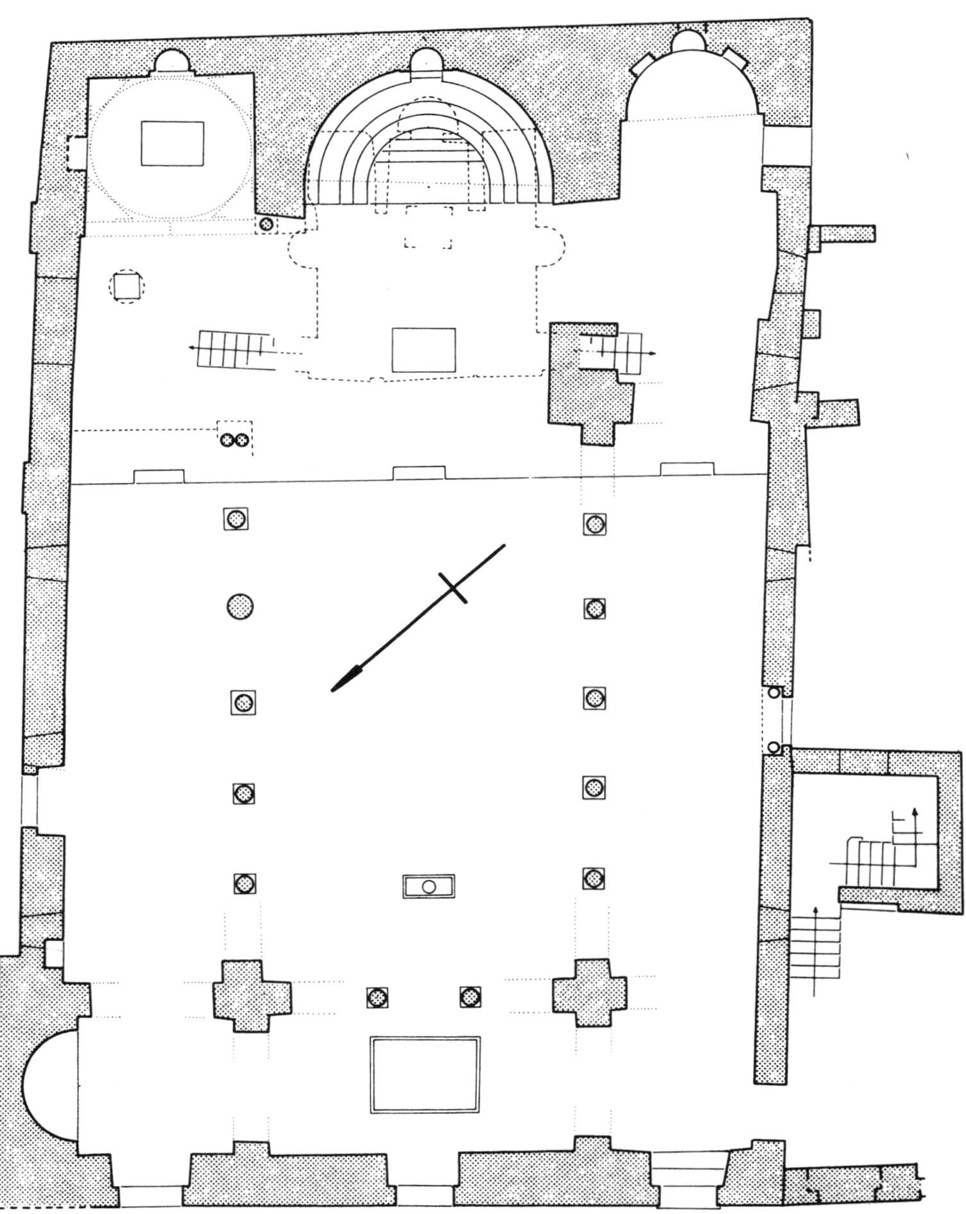

Plan of the Church of Saint Sergius. *Courtesy Peter Grossmann.*

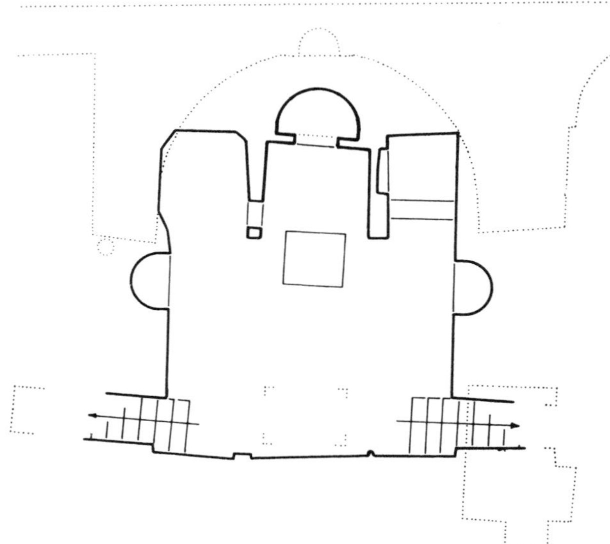

Plan of the crypt beneath the sanctuary of the Church of Saint Sergius. *Courtesy Peter Grossmann.*

ninth-century patriarch YUSĀB I in a report dealing with the destruction of the gallery. In its original outline, the church appears to have been a columned structure with a nave and two aisles built in the traditional manner with a narthex and tripartite sanctuary. Attached to it was an additional chapel constructed over the southeast tower of the Roman fortress and connected to the actual basilica by a colonnade, once open. In the late tenth century, MICHAEL IV extended the upper floor of this side chapel in order to provide accommodation for the patriarchs. During the last restoration, it was erroneously turned into an additional chapel. What is left of the Church of Sitt Maryam in its original state is confined to the area of this side chapel. The basilica itself, however, was inexpertly restored in the nineteenth century, whereby a church with a nave and four aisles came into being, and in the process the gallery was removed.

The Greek Church of Saint George, which like its predecessor was built over the north tower of the former river gate of the Roman fortress, was rebuilt after a devastating fire on 4 August 1903. In its structural outline, it comprises a double-shelled rotunda with a concentric inner colonnade supporting an elevated cupola. The eastern section of the ambulatory is occupied by the sanctuary. The entrance to the church lies to the north. How far this arrangement corresponds to the original outline, which was already destroyed once before in the course of the disturbances of the year 1882, can no longer be ascertained from the present state of the building. The church may be regarded as old, even though mention of it in the sources does not go back very far. The earliest mention is by Ibn Duqmāq in the fourteenth century. At that time the church was connected with a nunnery.

Other churches are not significant. The Coptic Church of Saint George, belonging clearly to the four-pillar type of building, was burned down in the middle of the nineteenth century and was rebuilt without cupolas at the end of the century. To the same complex belongs a Qā'at al-'Irsān (Wedding House), a small palace of the Mamluk period. The Church of the Virgin, Qaṣrīyyat al-Rīḥān, mentioned in the late ninth century, was substantially a late-eighteenth-century construction and with its two inner pillars comprised, to an extent, a reduced form of the late medieval four-pillar building in Egypt. In the spring of 1979 the church fell victim to a fire. The church of the Coptic nunnery dedicated to Saint George (Dayr al-Banāt) originally functioned as a Mamluk palace. The synagogue of Banī Ezra was originally a Coptic church but was sold in the ninth century to the Jewish community, who converted the building into a synagogue. Today the shape of the original church can no longer be seen.

Churches Outside the Fortress

The preserved parts of the Church of Mār Mīnā go back to its foundation in the first half of the eighth century. It was preceded by a small chapel of unknown date that was destroyed in 725. This eighth-century building was presumably a basilica with a nave and two aisles with galleries in the traditional manner. Of this only sections of the sanctuary of remarkable depth, together with the southern outer wall, have survived. In the eleventh or early twelfth century, the church was furnished with a *parekklesion*, but in the present state of rebuilding, only scarcely identifiable remains on the south side have survived. Judging by its present shape, it would appear that we are dealing with an oblong church with cupolas characteristic of Upper Egypt.

Churches in Dayr Abū Sayfayn

The most important church in Dayr Abū Sayfayn and the largest ancient church in the area of ancient Babylon is dedicated to Saint Mercurius (Marqūriyūs). Of the original building, the foundation walls, a part of the present outer wall, and the eastern section of the sanctuary are best preserved.

They give a picture of a wide church of generous proportions with a northern annex–perhaps used as a baptistery–on the level of the sanctuary. In this form, the church is perhaps the only church building left standing that goes back to a pre-Muslim foundation. At an unknown point in time, the church was partly destroyed and subsequently secularized. In the late tenth century Patriarch Abraham had the church rebuilt, making extensive use of the existing building. In that building the area of the *khūrus* is clearly proved to be a later installation. The windows in the south wall and the rows of pillars on both sides of the nave originate from the time of Abraham. The dome over the *khūrus* goes back to a reconstruction after a conflagration in the second half of the twelfth century, when only the chapel of Saint George situated at the east end of the south gallery is reported to have remained intact.

In the northeast corner, the church has two extra chapels, which were probably added in the twelfth century. The one situated closer to the church follows the model of a reduced four-column construction. Its spatial irregularities result from its architectural fusion with the remains of the north annex of the original construction.

A few steps south of the Church of Mercurius lies the Church of Saint Sinuthius (Anbā Shinūdah), which is mentioned as early as the middle of the eighth century and certainly had an existence be-

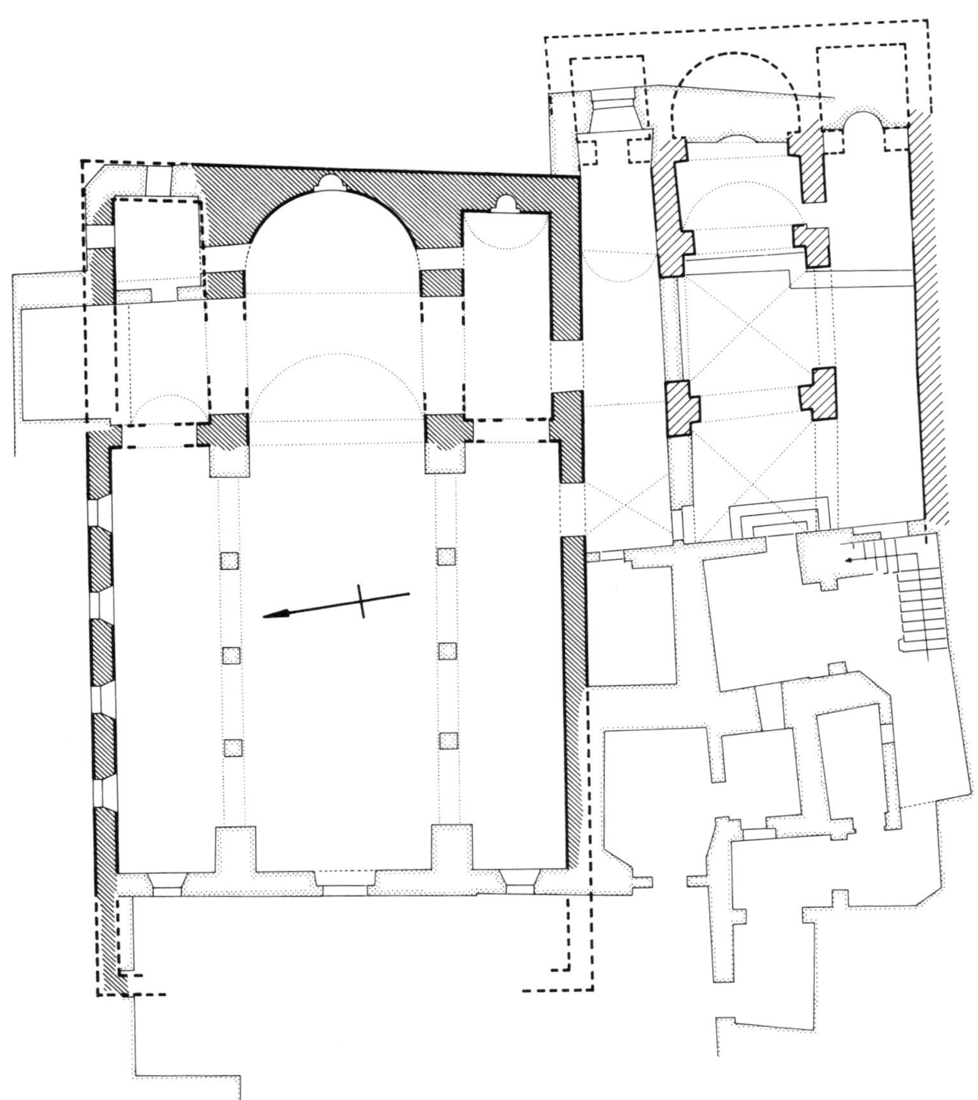

Plan of the Church of Mār Mīnā. *Courtesy Peter Grossmann.*

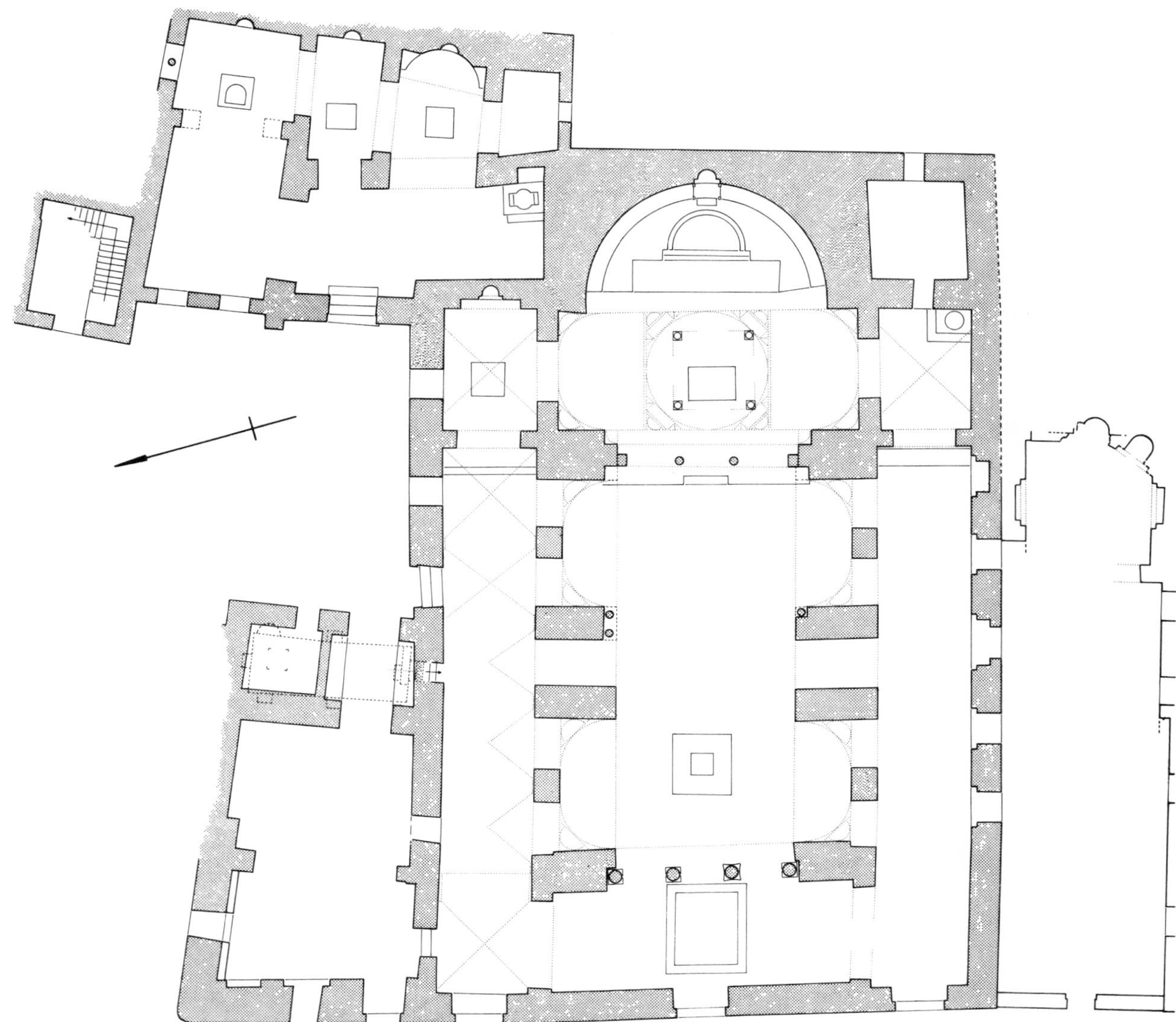

Plan of the church complex dedicated to Saint Mercurius. *Courtesy Peter Grossmann.*

fore that time. In its present form the church is a basilica with an often reconstructed gallery and a subsequently extended sanctuary and a later *khūrus*. It is no longer possible to determine exactly the original shape of the sanctuary, but it seems that it had the conventional tripartite division. In the Middle Ages the entrance lay on the south side of the church, where today the epiphany tank and the remains of a columned portico are preserved. In modern times the entrance was shifted back to the west side.

The third church in Dayr Abū Sayfayn is dedicated to the Virgin Mary, called al-Damshīriyyah. It is mentioned by al-Kindī in the tenth century among the new buildings torn down by ʿAli ibn Sulaymān al-ʿAbbāsī in the eighth century. Whether there are vestiges of the eighth century in the present structure remains doubtful, although on account of the irregularities of its shape, the possibility cannot be ruled out absolutely. It gives the appearance of a sturdily reconstructed basilica with several reused columns. The sanctuary has the usual tripartite division. The apse side chamber on the north was transformed in more recent times into a BAYT AL-NISĀʾ (area for women to receive communion).

The al-ʿAdhrāʾ church in ḤĀRIT ZUWAYLAH was mentioned in the early twelfth century when it was used to consecrate a bishop. In the second half of the twelfth century the church was apparently taken over by the Armenians. Today it belongs to a women's convent.

The building itself has been very badly reconstructed, and none of the walls seems to be older than the eighteenth century. However, because of the incorporation of the older foundations, one can recognize roughly some of the outlines of its original structure. They suggest that the original building had the outline of a transept basilica. In comparison with other examples of this type, the size of this building is remarkably small, despite the multiaisled transept. An origin in the early Christian period has thus clearly to be excluded. The sanctuary certainly had a central semicircular apse, and it appears that only this apse had a *khūrus* in front of it. One cannot recognize the original appearance of the side rooms from their present state. Only reused columns were utilized as supports.

Churches in the Monasteries South of the Fortress

The Church of the Virgin in Babylon al-Daraj is first mentioned under the patriarch ZACHARIAS in the eleventh century, and since the late eleventh century was considered to be one of the sites where the Holy Family stopped during the flight to Egypt. Architecturally it is a basilica, whose nave at present is covered by a barrel roof. Apart from this, the only original elements are preserved in the west part of the church with the walled-in columns of the western row of supports.

Dayr al-Amīr Tādrus contains two churches that are arranged on the two sides of an inner court. The one on the south side, dedicated to Saint Theodorus (Tādrus), is first mentioned in the second half of the eleventh century and still contains remains of a centralized building with an ambulatory originally constructed around four corner pillars. Otherwise its present construction is substantially from the eighteenth century. Characteristic are the large semicircular sanctuaries and the absence of a *khūrus*.

The church on the north side is dedicated to Saint Cyrus and Saint John, and its earliest mention is by Ibn Duqmāq in the fourteenth century. Inside are preserved the remains of a powerful *khūrus* dividing wall. On the outside the church has been completely reconstructed so that it is no longer possible to recognize its original form.

The Church of Saint Michael is the most southerly of the Babylon churches and, according to a note in the *History of the Patriarchs*, was built at the beginning of the eleventh century. Indeed, all that survives of the original layout of the church are a couple of pillars concealed in the later surrounding wall and also possibly a few sections of the original outer walls. They indicate that the building was once a basilica. Today the church shows all the signs of various reconstructions with numerous alterations and additions on all sides.

BIBLIOGRAPHY

Butler, A. J. *The Ancient Coptic Churches of Egypt*, Vol. 1. Oxford, 1884.

______. *Babylon of Egypt*. Oxford, 1914.

Coquin, C. *Les édifices chrétiens du Vieux Caire*. Bibliothèque d'études coptes 11. Cairo, 1974.

Gardiner, A. H. *Ancient Egyptian Onomastica*, Vol. 2. London, 1947.

Grossmann, P. "Zur christlichen Baukunst in Ägypten." *Enchoria* 8 (1978):141, plate 16b.

______. *Mittelalterliche Langhauskuppelkirchen und verwandte Typen in Oberägypten*. Glückstadt, 1982.

Middleton, J. H. "On the Coptic Churches of Old Cairo." *Archaeologia* 48 (1885):397ff.

Monneret de Villard, U. "Note storiche sulle chiese di al-Fusṭāṭ." *Rendiconti della Reale Accademia Nationale dei Lincei* 5, ser. 6 (1929):286ff.

Monneret de Villard, U., and M. A. Patricolo. *La chiesa di S. Barbara*. Florence, 1922.

Patricolo, M. A. "Monuments coptes." *Comptes rendus du Comité de conservation des monuments de l'art arabe* 32 (1915–1919):192ff.

Toy, S. "Babylon of Egypt." *Journal of the British Archaeological Association* 3, ser. 1 (1937):52–78.

PETER GROSSMANN

BACHATLY, CHARLES (1909–1957), secretary of the SOCIETY OF COPTIC ARCHAEOLOGY from its establishment in 1934 until his death. He laid the foundations for the society's program of activity and for its library. He also designed its main series of publications. In 1944 he organized at Cairo a successful exhibition of Coptic art, which was probably the first anywhere in the world. In 1948 and 1949 he directed the society's excavations at DAYR APA PHOIBAMMON in Upper Egypt.

BIBLIOGRAPHY

Ghali, Mirrit Boutros. Obituary of Charles Bachatly. *Bulletin de la Société d'archéologie copte* 14 (1950–1957):249–51.

Khater, A. "Bibliographie de Charles Bachatly." *Bulletin de la Société d'archéologie copte* 14 (1950–1957):227–28.

MIRRIT BOUTROS GHALI

BACHEUS, fictitious figure in Coptic literature to whom at least two homilies are attributed. He is mentioned in a homily *In Praise of the Cross* attributed to CYRIL OF JERUSALEM (ed. Campagnano, 1980, pp. 84–100); this seems to be the oldest text in which he is named. According to this text, Bacheus was a presbyter and archimandrite of a small monastery near Aschalon in Palestine. Because he worked a miracle related to the Cross, a Samaritan named Isaac was converted to Christianity. The period in which the episode is supposed to have occurred is that of Cyril of Jerusalem (d. 387).

Thus we can place Bacheus in the fourth century. However, elements gleaned from the homily attributed to Cyril indicate the sixth century, when the construction of the homiletic and hagiographical CYCLES began. It is probable that shortly afterward, perhaps the beginning of the seventh century, Bacheus was detached from the cycle of Cyril and a cycle dedicated to him personally was started.

Documentation of this is found in the title of one of the two homilies attributed to him, conserved in an unpublished fragment in very poor condition (University Library, Oslo, 217). Here Bacheus has become bishop of Maiuma (Gaza), a particularly important center in the period of the Chalcedonian controversies, and near to Aschalon. It is also stated specifically that "he converted Isaac the Samaritan. . . ." The homily in question is *In Honor of the Twelve Apostles,* and at present only eight (unpublished) folios of it are known (National Library, Naples, IB13, 31–8: cat. Zoega no. 265). They contain an "autobiographical" passage and a passage that speaks of the apostles as judges in the Valley of Josaphat.

At present, eight folios from the same codex are known of the other homily (National Library, Naples, IB13, 24–30: cat. Zoega no. 264; and Coptic Museum, Cairo, cat. 9232); however, they do not contain the beginning nor, therefore, the title. The content, nevertheless, suggests that this is an *Encomium of the Three Young Men of Babylon,* who are praised and whose history is related. Here, too, Bacheus names himself "autobiographically" and hence the attribution is certain. In this case he states he is the disciple of the famous martyr James the Persian or JAMES INTERCISUS, and that he intends going to visit his martyrium in Egypt.

BIBLIOGRAPHY

Campagnano, A., ed. *Ps. Cirillo di Gerusalemme, Omelie copte sulla passione, sulla Croce e sulla Vergine.* Testi e documenti per lo studio dell'antichità, Serie Copta, Vol. 65. Milan, 1980.

Zoega, G. *Catalogus Codicum Copticorum Manuscriptorum qui in Museo Borgiano Velitris Adservantur.* Roma, 1810; Hildesheim, 1973.

TITO ORLANDI

BADĀRĪ, AL-. *See* Pilgrimages.

BADR AL-JAMĀLĪ, Fatimid vizier at the time of al-Mustanṣir (1035–1094). Badr al-Jāmālī was born at the beginning of the eleventh century. He was an Armenian slave of the Syrian amir Jamāl al-Dawlah ibn ʿAmmār. He began his career in Syria, where he was governor of Damascus twice, then of ʿAkkā. Although not always successful in his political career—he was expelled from his post in Damascus twice—he had, thanks to the Armenian troops that formed the nucleus of his army, won considerable fame by his struggle against the armies of the Saljūqs. When al-Mustanṣir was hard pressed from without by the attacks of the Saljūqs and from within by famine, mismanagement, and the continuing struggle between his slaves and the Turkish troops led by Badr's arch enemy Nāṣir al-Dawlah ibn Ḥamdān, he was finally deprived of all authority. It was to Badr that he turned for help.

In the winter of A.H. 466/A.D. 1073 Badr put to sea from ʿAkkā and unexpectedly turned up in Egypt, where he rapidly started mastering the situation by doing away with his enemies in one stroke and restoring law and order to the terror-stricken country. As a consequence, he was appointed commander-in-chief of the army, whence his title *amīr al juyūsh* (by which he was known henceforth), vizier, chief justice (*qāḍī al-quḍāh*), and chief propagandist of the Ismāʿīlī faith (*dāʿī al-duʿāh*).

With his investiture, a decisive change took place in the office of the vizierate and the position of the vizier. The early Fatimids up to al-Muʿizz had conferred executive tasks to officials called *muwaqqiʿ* (protector) or *mudabbir* (director). According to the unanimous witness of the sources, Yaʿqūb ibn Killis was the first to bear the title of vizier (*wazīr*). His vizierate was a "vizierate of execution" (*wizārat al-*

tanfīdh) or "vizierate of the pen" (*wizārat al-qalam*). The holder of this office "was he who, depending on the imam's opinion and guidance, acted as a mediator between the latter and the people" (al-Qalqashandī, *Subḥ* V, 449). From Ibn Killis's death to the appointment of al-Jarjarā'ī, the caliph's first minister held the title of *wāsiṭah*, which according to al-Qalqashandī denoted a slightly lower rank. From al-Jarjarā'ī to Badr's appointment, which was preceded by the total decline of the vizierate, the viziers were again "viziers of execution."

With Badr's accession to power, matters changed fundamentally. Badr was no longer executor of the will of a sovereign caliph. On the contrary, al-Mustanṣir authorized him to run the affairs of the state entirely at his own discretion. His position was no longer that of a vizier of execution but of a vizier of authorization (*wazīr al-tafwīḍ*) and as his power extended to the civil as well as to the military administration, that of a vizier of the sword and the pen (*wazīr al-sayf wa al-qalam*).

During the years after his appointment, Badr successfully extended his power to the rest of Egypt, which he brought back to Fatimid authority, whereas he could not prevent Syria from gradually being lost to the Fatimids under his reign. In 1076, Damascus was taken by the Saljūqs and, in spite of several attempts to regain it (1078–1079, 1085–1086, 1098–1090), never became Fatimid again. In 1076 an attempt of a Saljūq army to conquer the Egyptian capital was repelled. As a consequence, Badr fortified the city with a new wall and three gates, the Bāb Zuwaylah, the Bāb al-Naṣr, and the Bāb al-Futūḥ, making use of the considerable increase of tax revenue realized under his regime.

Throughout these events, Badr's appearance on the Egyptian scene had a considerable influence on the situation of the Christian communities of Egypt. First of all, it marked the beginning of what is generally called the "Armenian period" of the Fatimid empire. Badr brought with him his Armenian picked troops on whom he could rely firmly in all his undertakings. He allotted them comfortable quarters in Cairo and took care that they had enough places of worship, sometimes at the expense of the Copts. In Tulunid times, there had been single Armenian detachments in the Egyptian army. After Basileios I in 1021 had deprived the Armenian prince Baspurakan of his territories and had given him Cappadocia in exchange, the Armenians had rapidly spread over Cilicia and Syria and had also come from there to Egypt. Badr, a son of Christian parents, was tolerant. He encouraged the immigration of Armenians to Egypt. In 1075–1076 the Armenian Catholicos Gregor II Vkayaser (Martyrophilos) paid a visit to Egypt. He was not only received with highest honors by the court but was also given permission to consecrate his nephew, whose name was also Gregor, as Armenian Catholicos of Egypt.

The Coptic church, too, benefited from Badr's benevolent attitude toward his former coreligionists. They were allowed to build and restore their churches, although they occasionally lost a church to the Armenian community. The Coptic patriarch CYRIL II (1078–1092) was treated respectfully by the vizier at his enthronement in 1078, although there is no proof that he held an especially influential position with the latter. On one occasion Badr settled a controversy among the clergy concerning problems of the moral qualification of some ecclesiastical dignitaries by referring them to their own legislation. The vizier's leniency reached its limit, however, as soon as financial affairs were involved. Thus, in 1086 he increased the poll tax (JIZYAH) and, along with this measure, reintroduced the distinctive dress regulations for non-Muslims that had fallen into disuse for years. In the same year, a number of bishops had to pay a fine for allegedly having embezzled money deposited with them by the rebels during the preceding riots.

Another point of dispute concerned the relations between the Coptic see of Alexandria and the Coptic church of Nubia and Ethiopia. These relations had been viewed with suspicion by the state as early as al-Ḥākim's time, who finally cut them off altogether. In later times they were resumed again, but under the strict control of the court in Cairo. The court tried to influence the election of metropolitans for the southern regions to get some influence on the church affairs of the area, which they could make use of for improving the situation of the Muslims living in those Christian-dominated countries. In this Badr made no exception. It was with this in view that he, on two occasions under the patriarchates of CHRISTODOULOS (1047–1077) and Cyril II, interfered with the enthronement and administration of metropolitans in the south, putting the patriarch and the bishops under hard pressure to enforce his intentions. Badr died in 1094, after he had installed his son, al-Afḍal Shahanshāh, in the vizierate.

BIBLIOGRAPHY

Canard, M. "Un Vizier chrétien à l'époque fāṭimite." *Annales de l'Institut d'études orientales* 12

(1954):84–113.

______. "Notes sur les Arméniens en Egypte à l'époque fāṭimite." *Annales de l'Institut d'Études orientales* 13 (1955):143–57.

Dhahabi, al-. *Kitāb duwal al-Islām*, Vol. 1, pp. 206, 208, 209. Hyderabad, A.H. 1377/(1957).

Ibn Khallikān, ed. *Muḥyi 'd-Dīn 'Abd al-Ḥamīd*, (Biographical Dictionary), trans. William MacGuckin Baron Slane. Cairo, 1948–1949.

Ibn Muyassar. *Annales d'Egypte*. Publications de l'Institut français d'Archéologie orientale, ed. H. Massé, pp. 15–16, 20, 22–28, 30–31. Cairo, 1919.

Ibn al-Qalānsī. *Ḍail Ta'rīḥ Dimishq*, ed. H. F. Amedroz, pp. 84, 93–97, 109–110. Leiden, 1908.

Lane-Poole, S. *A History of Egypt in the Middle Ages*. London, 1901.

Mājid, A. M. *Al-Imām al-Mustansir bi'llāh al-Fāṭimī*. Cairo, 1960.

O'Leary, D. *A Short History of the Fatimid Khalifate*. London, 1923.

Qalqashandī, Aḥmad ibn 'Alī al. *Ṣubḥ al-A'shā*, 14 vols. Cairo, 1913.

Wüstenfeld, F. *Geschichte der Fatimiden-Chalifen*. Göttingen, 1881.

SUBHI Y. LABIB

BAGAWĀT, AL-. [*This entry consists of three articles. The first discusses the location, the grave sites, and the architecture. The second catalogues and discusses the Greek inscriptions. Coptic inscriptions are the subject of the third article.*]

Location and Architecture

Al-Bagawāt is an early Christian necropolis of the ancient town of Hibis (modern Khargah). The graves of the pagan period were arranged as rock tombs on the north and west slopes of the cliff lying to the east opposite the former town area (on the general situation, see Winlock, 1941, pl. 29), or gradually climbed higher. The later graves, predominantly deriving from the Christian period, spread out on the height of the cliff itself and gradually moved from there farther to the east. Almost in the middle and at the same time in a commanding position is a large building (chapel 180) with extremely thin walls, originally constructed as a courtyard building, which in the archaeological literature is frequently described as a church (Hauser, 1932, p. 40; Fakhry, 1951, pp. 157–59). Inside, a western portico and an open triconch directed toward the east are situated exactly opposite one another on the two sides of the inner court. Later the interior was transformed into a three-aisle BASILICA and provided with an external peristyle running all round. Functionally the building served for the holding of meals for the dead (*cenae funebres*). In the side aisles and also in the area of the outside peristyle, the couches (*klinai*), arranged in a semicircle, are still preserved at several places, and in some cases the masonry tables are preserved as well. They must have been reserved by the poorer families, who in their graves could not provide for any room of their own for the purpose.

The graves themselves are either flat oblong hollows in the ground with a low superstructure built of bricks or quarrystone, or underground hypogea accessible only by a vertical shaft and sometimes containing several grave chambers. Over the entrance to the shaft there is usually a mausoleum. In several cases the *klinai* for the meals for the dead, here also arranged in a semicircle, have also survived outside these mausoleums.

While there are several rotundas, the great majority of the mausoleums are constructed as tetrapyla built upon four corner supports. The side openings are, however, everywhere closed up, or at most give room for a small niche. The roofing above almost always consists of a dome. In numerous cases these tetrapyla have been provided on the entrance side with a row of applied columns, which are evidently meant to feign the existence of a propylon (the propyla at chapels 23 and 166). In addition, several have a walled forecourt (chapels 150, 199, 211, 233). In some cases an apse is added on the east side of the mausoleum (chapels 205, 206), and this was occasionally expanded into a rotunda-like (chapels 69, 192, 259) or octagonal form (chapel 213). In not a few cases, the mausoleums are connected with a small church (chapels 9, 24, 90), or have themselves assumed the form of a church through the addition of corresponding cultic rooms (chapels 25, 66, 130). Of particular importance is a building complex lying in the northern area (chapels 23–29), which started out from a three-aisle double hall, repeatedly provided with further buildings, some of them ecclesiastical (chapels 24 and 25 are unmistakably churches). Presumably this double hall, like the latter so-called church, was a building for holding meals for the dead.

BIBLIOGRAPHY

Bock, W. de. *Matériaux pour servir à l'archéologie de l'Egypte chrétienne*, pp. 7–38. St. Petersburg, 1901.

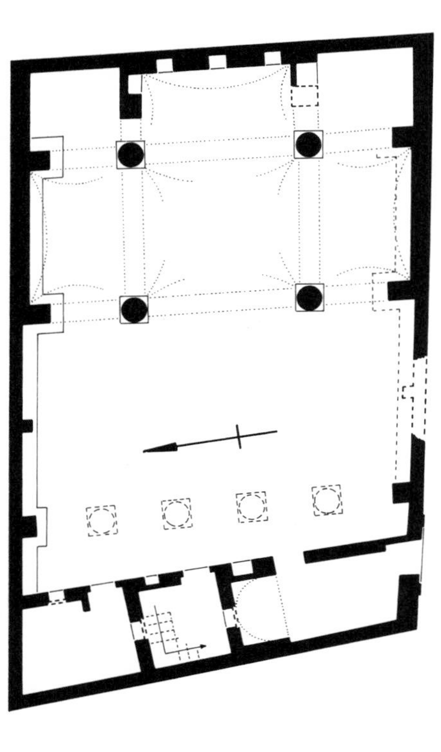

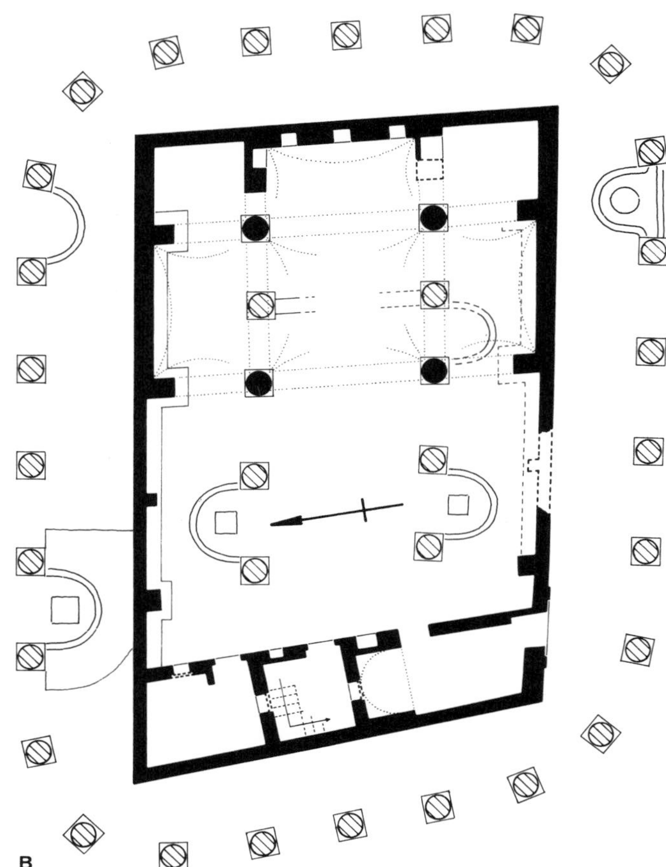

Plan of Chapel 180 at al-Bagawāt. A. The original courtyard building. B. The later three-aisled basilica with external peristyle. *Courtesy Peter Grossmann.*

Fakhry, A. *The Egyptian Deserts: The Necropolis of El-Bagawāt in Kharga Oasis.* Cairo, 1951.

Grossmann, P. *Mittelalterliche Langhauskuppelkirchen und verwandte Typen in Oberägypten.* Glückstadt, 1982.

Hauser, W. "The Christian Necropolis in Khargeh Oasis." *Bulletin of the Metropolitan Museum of Art* (1932):38–50.

Kaufmann, C. M. *Ein altchristliches Pompeji.* Mainz, 1902.

Winlock, H. E. *The Temple of Hibis in el Khargeh Oasis I.* New York, 1941.

PETER GROSSMANN

Greek Inscriptions

Among nearly 400 Coptic or Greco-Coptic graffiti, one may count at al-Bagawāt scarcely twenty-five Greek inscriptions or graffiti, to which must be added a dozen funerary stelae discovered in recent years in situ. A fundamental distinction must be made between graffiti by visitors and graffiti or drawings that may be called original to the site. It is among the latter that we rank several liturgical texts, a *trisagion* (a short hymn of response), some prayers, or simple quotations of sacred texts. In this respect, appeals to the divine pity are most frequent. The God of the Old Testament, Christ, and the Holy Trinity are invoked impartially. Even Saint Paul is quoted. In the tomb of the young Petechon, a long acrostic poem on the name of the deceased informs us that he left his earthly fiancée to become a partaker of the spirit. With some epitaphs, only the surrounding decoration and the general context give reason for thinking them Christian. So it is with the epitaph of a soldier from Hermonthis; for that of Aytheio, no doubt also a soldier who came from far away, since he was a native of the region of Bostra; and for that of Tis, which recalls that his mausoleum cost forty *artabae* (of wheat). Passing visitors address themselves to Christ, to enter into his kingdom, or to God, the one who succors. There are also naturally slaves of Jesus Christ, who have left only a signature. Some of the Greek texts

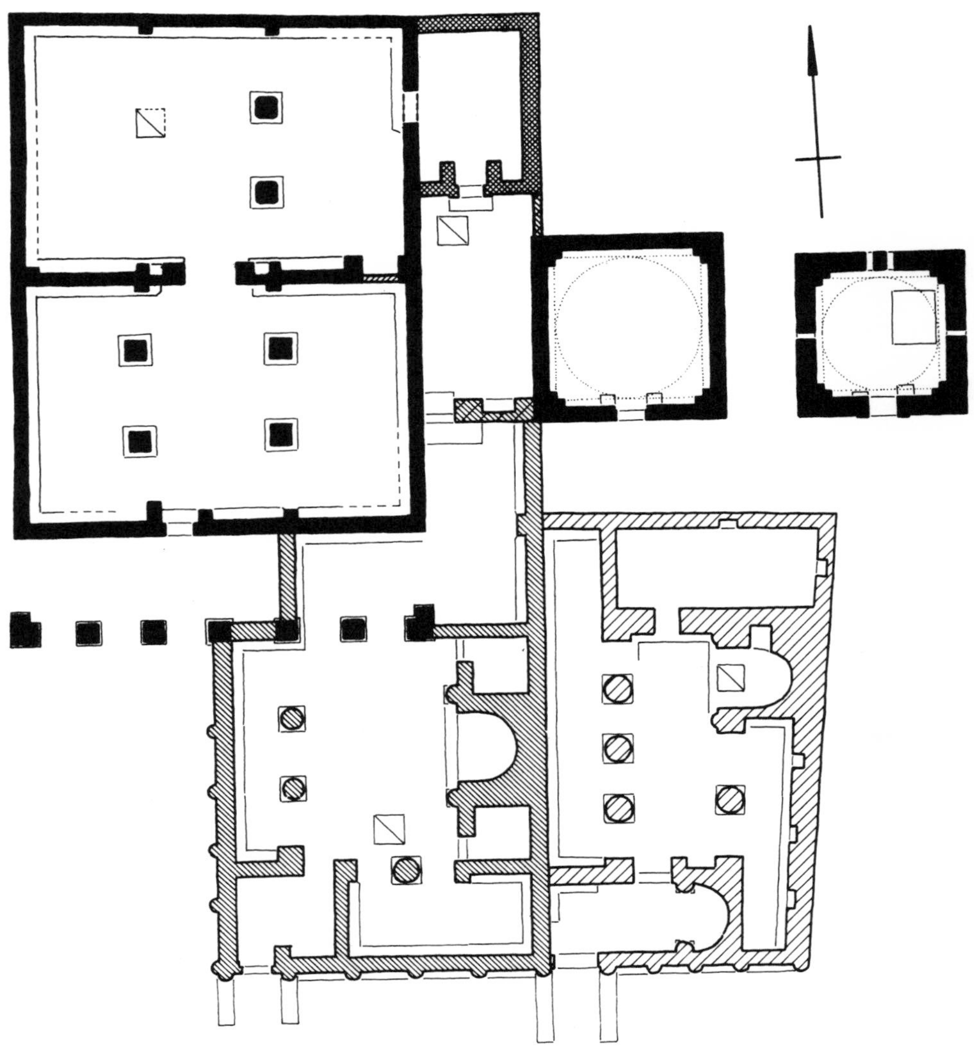

Plan of the complex in the northern area of al-Bagawāt. *Courtesy Peter Grossmann.*

of al-Bagawāt go back to the fourth century. They are naturally indigenous; transient visitors wrote there in Greek down to the sixth and seventh centuries and perhaps beyond. The known funerary stelae from al-Bagawāt are all late, and in general contain only the name of the deceased. They are those of Sarapammon, Apollōn, Senamounis, Psenpnouthes, Timouthis, Horus, Thlatos, Tephatis, and Ploua.

BIBLIOGRAPHY

Roquet, G. "Les graffites coptes de Bagawāt (Oasis de Kharga). Remarques préliminaires." *Bulletin (trimestriel) de la Société française d'études mariales* 76 (1976):25–49.

GUY WAGNER

Coptic Inscriptions

Of the 263 chapels in the cemetery of al-Bagawāt counted by Fakhry (1951), a considerable number are covered with Arabic graffiti of all periods; the historical importance of some of them has been opportunely underlined by I. M. Haggagi (1978). Thirty-five chapels contain Greek and Coptic graffiti, numbering nearly 400. Recently (Roquet, 1976) the history of the exploration of the site has been recalled, and the interest of the documentation collected made plain. Some graffiti are simple signatures, a name, a family connection, a visitor's identity card. Others are elaborate, incised or painted, sometimes carefully done: a prayer, an appeal to the invited visitor to pray for the signatory, imitating the usual formulas of the colophons of manuscripts. Other graffiti are anecdotal. With others, we follow the itinerary of some persons in their visiting of the chapels and in their devotion. Some writers are monks or clergy—so they say—but others are more unexpected: local officers, such as a *lashane* (village magistrate); a *lamashe* (warrior, champion); an amir's courier. If the visitor prides himself on his birthplace, a place name is preserved. Few texts are dated. From 1013, however, there are two graffiti by the same visitor, written in Bohairic. The local speech shows traces or remainders of its affinities with the Lycopolitan dialect. In sum, everything seems to indicate that the frequenting of the site at al-Bagawāt by Coptic speakers was spaced out between the sixth and eleventh centuries.

BIBLIOGRAPHY

Fakhry, A. *The Egyptian Deserts: The Necropolis of El-Bagawāt in Kharga Oasis.* Cairo, 1951.

Haggagi, I. M. "Graffites arabes de Bagawāt." In *Annales islamologiques* 14 (1978):271–87, pls. 21–22.

Roquet, G. "Les graffites coptes de Bagawāt (Oasis de Kharga). Remarques préliminaires." *Bulletin (trimestriel) de la Société française d'études mariales* 76 (1976):25–49.

G. ROQUET

BAGHĀM IBN BAQŪRAH AL-ṢAWWĀF,

eleventh-century Copt from Old Cairo/Babylon and the nephew of Anbā Jirjā, bishop of Misārah. His father had connections with one of the influential personalities in the court of the Fatimid caliph al-Mustanṣir (1035–1094). For some time he was contemporary with Pope CHRISTODOULOS (1047–1077).

After his conversion to Islam at age twenty-two, he was rejected and disowned by both his parents. It happened thereafter that he decided to be rebaptized. Because Islamic law prohibits apostasy and inflicts the penalty of death on the apostate, some of the monks of the Monastery of Abū Maqār—whom he had met during his solitude in the Church of Mīkhā'īl al-Mukhtārah for a few days—advised him to accompany them to that monastery to join it. Baghām rejected the offer, for he yearned to confess Christ on the same spot where he denied Him.

He then departed from the monks and girded his waist with a girdle, which distinguished him as a submissive Copt in accordance with the pledge of 'Umar ibn al-Khaṭṭāb. He walked in this fashion throughout the markets of Old Cairo. When the Muslims noticed the girdle round his waist, they seized him and led him to the police, who arrested him.

When his father received the news, he immediately offered a large sum of money to a friend, a Muslim who worked in the caliph's court, and entreated him to save his son from death. But the Muslim friend refused to interfere in this delicate matter unless the father convinced his son to feign madness, so that when witnesses were brought to him in prison to examine his case, they would confirm his insanity. Thus, he would not be considered responsible for what he had done, his life would be spared, and he would be set free, despite the fact that he was a Copt.

By coincidence, there was in prison a Syrian monk who undertook to counsel him and explain to him that he was proceeding toward martyrdom. Baghām, however, considered death in Christ's name as "sweeter than honey." In this way, he started to yearn for martyrdom and to prefer it to life. When the Muslim prosecutors went to Baghām in prison, they started to interrogate him to verify his case. It became evident to them that he was thoroughly sane. In addition, he declared before them that Coptic Christianity was the only true faith.

According to formalities, the governor of Egypt sent the prosecutors to the minister to whom they submitted the case, and explained to him the conclusions they reached concerning Baghām.

In conformity with the terms of Islamic law, whether Sunnite or Shi'ite, and in the light of Baghām's confession, there was no way to avoid sentencing him to death. The minister gave orders for his execution.

The HISTORY OF THE PATRIARCHS by SĀWĪRUS IBN AL-MUQAFFA' records in full the details of the story of the martyrdom of this young Copt until his decapitation. The Fatimid caliph al-Mustanṣir had ordered his body to be handed over to his family to bury it wherever they wanted. Baghām's father carried the body to the Church of Mīkhā'īl al-Mukhtārah and buried his son outside its door. When on the third day Anbā Christodoulus came from Dayr al-Sham' to the church, he objected to Baghām's burial outside the church, saying that the martyr should be interred within the church. When he opened the coffin to kiss the martyr, he found that his blood had not dried. He dipped his finger into it and signed the cross with it on his garment. Afterward, the body was interred in the sanctuary, which was dedicated to his name.

SUBHI Y. LABIB

BAHĪJ, a small village inhabited solely by bedouins, with a weekly market. It is located west of Alexandria (the last railway station before Burj al-'Arab) on the south shore of Lake Maryūt. The mounds of debris north of Bahīj (Kom Bahīj) contain ceramics of the Late Period. Possibly this is to be identified with the fortress of Psammetich I mentioned by Herodotus. In the area of the cemetery south of the railway line there are traces of a small settlement of late antiquity with the remains of a pillared structure that probably can be identified as a church. During excavations by the Egyptian Antiquities Organization in the spring of 1969 some buildings were found, as well as the remains of a wine press. The site is perhaps identical with the ancient Philoxenite on the south shore of Lake Maryūt, which is frequently mentioned in the miracle stories of Saint Menas as the landing place for pilgrims traveling to ABŪ MĪNĀ (Drescher, 1946, fols. 13.3, 27.1, 6).

BIBLIOGRAPHY

Drescher, J., ed. and trans. *Apa Mena: A Selection of Coptic Texts Relating to St. Menas.* Cairo, 1946.

PETER GROSSMANN

BAHJŪRAH, village in the Nag Hammadi district of Upper Egypt on the left bank of the Nile and the site of two monasteries, that of Saint Bīdabā, which is still in existence, and that of Mār Jirjis. The first mention of the latter seems to have been made by the Capuchin fathers Protais and François in the seventeenth century. Their text is reproduced by S. Sauneron (1973, p. 95). It was copied by J. de Thévenot, then by J. Vansleb, who could not go beyond Jirjā (1677, p. 413; 1678, p. 247).

S. Clarke, in his index of the churches of Egypt, indicated two churches dedicated to Mār Jirjis in this region and still extant, no doubt corresponding to the monastery noticed by the seventeenth-century travelers, that of Bahjūrah and that of Nāḥiyat al-Jabal (1912, p. 214, nos. 44–45).

BIBLIOGRAPHY

Clarke, S. *Christian Antiquities in the Nile Valley.* Oxford, 1912.

Sauneron, S. *Villes et légendes d'Egypte.* Cairo, 1973.

The Travels of Monsieur de Thévenot. Eng. trans. London, 1687.

Vansleb, J. *Nouvelle relation en forme de journal d'un voyage fait en Egypte en 1672 et 1673.* Paris, 1677. Translated as *The Present State of Egypt.* London, 1678.

RENÉ-GEORGES COQUIN
MAURICE MARTIN, S.J.

BAHNASĀ, AL-, modern name of the city that was known in Greek as Oxyrhynchus and in Coptic as Pemdje. The city is located on the western edge of the Nile Valley about 10 miles (16 km) northwest of Banī Mazār in the province of Minyā.

Although al-Bahnasā is best known today as the site of one of the largest finds of Greek papyri ever made (see OXYRHYNCHUS PAPYRI), the area has a long and rich Christian tradition. Coptic-Arabic hagiographic literature mentions the city often as the birthplace of various saints and the place where many martyrs died during the persecutions of DIOCLETIAN in the early fourth century. The SYNAXARION indicated that al-Bahnasā was the seat of a bishop by the beginning of the fourth century.

Monasticism also made an early appearance in the city. The HISTORIA MONACHORUM IN AEGYPTO states that in the latter part of the fourth century the monasteries around al-Bahnasā were so numerous that they virtually constituted a city of their own. Not only did the city have twelve churches but monks also inhabited the buildings that had previously been pagan temples and shrines. The work goes on to say that there were some 5,000 monks within the city and an even greater number in the surrounding monasteries. Subject to the bishop of the diocese were 10,000 monks and 20,000 nuns.

BIBLIOGRAPHY

Amélineau, E. *La Géographie de l'Egypte à l'époque copte,* pp. 90–93. Paris, 1893.

Timm, S. *Das christlich-koptische Ägypten in arabischer Zeit,* Vol. 1, pp. 283–300. Wiesbaden, 1984.

RANDALL STEWART

BAJŪRĪ, SHAYKH IBRĀHĪM, AL- (1784–1860), noted Azhar professor who became *Shaykh* *al-Islam* in July 1847. He authored many works on Islamic jurisprudence, logic, and Arabic grammar, as well as works of religious commentary. He is noted for his resistance to 'Abbās I's attempts to exile all Copts from Egypt.

Al-Bajūrī became the imam of the Islamic community (*Shaykh al-Islām*) in the latter years of Muḥammad Alī's reign (1805–1849) and during the regency of his son Ibrāhīm (1849), as well as in the reign of his grandson and successor 'Abbās I (1849–1854). During the rule of both Muḥammad 'Alī and Ibrāhīm, the Copts enjoyed a great deal of influence and occupied principal posts in the administration of the state of Egypt, notably in finance and taxation.

However, with the accession of 'Abbās, the situation began to change radically. The new khedive is known to have been an outspoken bigot. Besides being out of humor with all of Egypt and having no sympathy for Egyptians, he especially hated Christians and aimed to rid the state of them. He dismissed the French officials who had been engaged by his grandfather, and was restrained from the wholesale dismissal of the Copts from the government because of their importance in the financial machinery of the state.

During his administration he once contemplated exiling all Copts from Egypt to the Upper Sudan. But such a drastic and massive enterprise could not be undertaken without a religious *fatwā* (juristic consultation) issued by the highest Muslim authority. Shaykh Ibrahim al-Bajūri, who was asked to issue such a *fatwā*, rejected 'Abbās's scheme by saying, "If you mean by your project the people of the Covenant who are the dwellers of the land and its owners, then grace be to Allah, no change has occurred to the Islamic Covenant and no breach thereof to incur their victimization and they must be left under the Covenant to the day of doom."

'ABD AL-RAḤĪM

BAKHĀNIS-TMOUSHONS, village situated on the left bank of the Nile, in the Nag Hammadi district, about 4 miles (7 km) to the northeast of FARSHŪṬ. The ancient Arabic spelling was Makhānis, under which it is easy to recognize the Coptic name Tmoushons, the Coptic article T having been dropped and the *sh* sound having evolved into the Arabic *kha,* a development already perceptible in the Greek transcription Mouchonsis (Halkin, 1932, p. 462). The equivalence of these name forms is attested by the Coptic-Arabic scalae (Munier, 1939, p. 222; Ramzī, 1963, p. 196).

The fourth establishment of PACHOMIUS is placed at Tmoushons by both the Greek and the Coptic Lives. In fact, it was a certain Jonas, the superior of this monastery, who sought, and obtained, for himself and his monks affiliation with the Pachomian community (Halkin, 1932, p. 37; Lefort, 1943, pp. 116, 246). The identification of Tmoushons with Bakhānis is provided by the Arabic version, a faithful translation of the Sahidic recension S^5, preserved in Vatican Manuscript Arabic 172, fol. 37^{r-v}; it can also be deduced from the fact that the Arabic Life of Shenute speaks of "Jonas, master of the laura of Bakhānis, who loves the pure community" (Amélineau, 1886–1888, p. 460). When one went there on foot from PBOW (Fāw al-Qiblī), one passed by Sheneset (Chenoboskion or Qaṣr al-Ṣayyād), and there crossed the river on a ferryboat (Lefort, 1943, pp. 160–64).

Lefort (1939, pp. 399–401) wanted to place Tmoushons at the present site of Dayr Anbā Bīḏābā, or 1.25 miles (2 km) west of Nag Hammadi and hence more than 6 miles (10 km) to the south of the present Bakhānis. Apart from the fact that the Arabic place-name clearly derives from the Coptic Tmoushons, the interpretation that Lefort gives of a single passage in the Coptic lives of Pachomius is forced: one cannot conclude from it that Tmoushons was only a six hours' walk from Pbow.

BIBLIOGRAPHY

Amélineau, E. *Monuments pour servir à l'histoire de l'Egypte chrétienne aux IVe, Ve, VIe et VIIe siècles.* Mémoires publiés par les Membres de la Mission archéologique Française au Caire 4. Paris, 1886–1888.

______. *La Géographie de l'Egypte à l'époque copte.* Paris, 1893, pp. 515–17.

Coquin, R. G. "Un Complément aux vies sahidiques de Pachôme: Le Manuscrit IFAO Copte 3." *Bulletin de l'Institut français d'Archéologie orientale* 79 (1979):209–47.

Halkin, F. *Sancti Pachomii Vitae Graecae.* Subsidia Hagiographica 19. Brussels, 1932.

Lefort, L. T. "Les Premiers monastères pachômiens: Exploration topographique." *Muséon* 52 (1939):379–407.

______. *Les Vies coptes de saint Pachôme.* Bibliothèque du Muséon 16. Louvain, 1943.

Ramzī, M. *Al-Qāmūs al-Jughrāfī fī al-Bilād al-Miṣriyyah,* Vol. 2, pt. 4. Cairo, 1963.

Munier, H. "La Géographie de l'Egypte d'après les listes coptes-arabes." *Bulletin de la Société d'archéologie copte* 5 (1939):201–243.

RENÉ-GEORGES COQUIN

BALDACHIN, originally a supported "canopy" of rich silk material supported on four or six columns, named after the city of Baghdad where this material was made. The old Italian form of the name is Baldacco, from which is derived the diminutive *baldacchino*. Since the beginning of the seventeenth century, this term had been borrowed by other European languages. Functionally the baldachin served as the emblem of rank of secular rulers and spiritual dignitaries as well as for the visual identification and display of relics, inner sanctums, and altars. It could be carried or erected only for use on special occasions or be set permanently in a fixed position. It is related to the ciborium and differs from it in principle only in its lack of stability. Inevitably the baldachin appears frequently as a substitute for it. But whereas the ciborium was open on all sides, the baldachin, especially as of a throne or statue, could also stand in front of a pillar or wall and consequently be open only on three sides. In this form it also shows architectural affinities with the aedicula. In Arabic texts the baldachin in most cases is simply called QUBBAH, which denotes a cupola and thus cannot be distinguished from the ciborium or tabernacle.

BIBLIOGRAPHY

Klauser, T. "Ciborium." *Reallexikon für Antike und Christentum* 3 (1957), cols. 68–86.

Schramm, P. E. *Herrschaftszeichnen und Staatssymbolik*, Vol. 3, pp. 722ff. Stuttgart, 1956.

PETER GROSSMANN

BALESTRI, GIUSEPPE (1866–1940), Italian Coptologist and a member of the Augustinian order. He is best known for his publication of the Sahidic folios of the New Testament presently in the Borgia Museum (*Sacrorum Bibliorum Fragmenta Copto-Sahidica Musei Borgiani*, Vol. 3, *Novum Testamentum*, Rome, 1904). With H. Hyvernat he also edited the acts of the Coptic martyrs, *Acta Martyrum* 1–2 (Paris, 1907–1924; repr., Louvain, 1953, 1961).

BIBLIOGRAPHY

Vosté, J.-M. "Giuseppe Balestri, coptologo e biblista." *L'osservatore romano*, 29/30 April 1940, p. 3.

MARTIN KRAUSE

BALLANA KINGDOM AND CULTURE. The breakup of the Sudanese empire of KUSH in the fourth century was the signal for major population movements in the Nile Valley. Both Nubian-speaking tribes (see NUBIANS) and BEJA TRIBES took possession of different territories that had formerly been under the rule of Kush. In the far north of NUBIA there appeared a kind of hybrid culture that combined some of the old traditions of Kush with new influences from Greco-Roman Egypt. The Meroitic written language of Kush disappeared, to be replaced on a very limited scale by Greek.

When the post-Kushite culture of lower Nubia was first discovered by archaeologists early in the twentieth century, it was given the designation "X-Group" because of uncertainty as to who the newcomers were. Some scholars identified them with the Blemmye people, today known as Beja, who are often mentioned in classical texts, while others preferred an identification with the Nubian-speaking Nobatae (see NOBATIA) mentioned by Procopius. More recent investigation has suggested that the X-Group culture was not unique to either group but was common to the two of them. From this altered viewpoint, the term X-Group is seen to be inappropriate, and there has been a tendency to replace it with the designation "Ballana culture."

The discovery in the 1930s of spectacular royal tombs at Ballana and Quṣtul, near the Egyptian-Sudanese border, revealed that the Ballana people had been subject to a very powerful monarchy. The kings and queens were buried in chamber tombs under great earthen tumuli, together with an astonishing array of their accumulated wealth as well as sacrificial animals and human retainers. The mortuary ritual was generally, though not absolutely, similar to that followed by the earlier rulers of Kush, and in particular the Ballana royal crowns retained the familiar Kushite emblems of authority.

The Ballana monarchy, as reflected in the royal tombs, is believed to have endured from about 350 to 550. The kings and their subjects evidently kept up the worship of the old Egyptian deities, especially Isis, even though Egypt by this time was officially Christian and the cult of the earlier deities had been suppressed. Christian ideas were also beginning to make some headway among the Nubians, to judge from the votive lamps and other Christian paraphernalia found in the Ballana tombs.

Very few textual records from the Ballana period have survived. There are, however, two complete royal texts, both in highly eccentric Greek, found at Kalabsha and at QAṢR IBRĪM. One is the victory proclamation of King Silko of the Nobatae and the other is a letter that makes reference to the same king. Since Silko appears to have been a strong ruler and to have extended his rule over a considerable territory, there is reason to suppose that he may be one of the kings buried at Ballana. If so, the Ballana rulers are to be identified specifically with the Nobatae rather than with the Blemmye, and the Ballana kingdom is none other than the historical kingdom of Nobatia, whose conversion to Christianity in the sixth century was recorded by John of Ephesus (see NUBIA, EVANGELIZATION OF). The Ballana culture was in any case the immediate forerunner of the Christian civilization of medieval Nubia.

BIBLIOGRAPHY

Adams, W. Y. *Nubia, Corridor to Africa,* pp. 390–424. Princeton, N.J., 1977.
Emery, W. B. *Nubian Treasure.* London, 1948.
———. *Egypt in Nubia,* pp. 232–47. London, 1965.
Kirwan, L. P. "A Survey of Nubian Origins." *Sudan Notes and Records* 29 (1937):47–62.
———. "Studies in the Later History of Nubia." *University of Liverpool Annals of Archaeology and Anthropology* 24 (1937):69–105.
———. "The X-Group Enigma." In *Vanished Civilisations,* ed. E. Bacon. London, 1963.
Monneret de Villard, U. *Storia della Nubia cristiana,* pp. 36–60. Orientalia Christiana Analecta 118. Rome, 1938.
Vantini, G. *Christianity in the Sudan,* pp. 24–32. Bologna, 1981.

WILLIAM Y. ADAMS

BALLĀṢ, AL-, town located in the province of Qenā on the west side of the Nile about 3 miles (5 km) northwest of QIFṬ. In Coptic documents the name of the town appears as ⲡⲁⲗⲗⲁⲥ (Pallas).

This town may have been the birthplace of Apa NOB the Confessor. Although the SYNAXARION for 23 Ba'ūnah says he was born in Bala'ūs (also referred to as Balanās), an Arabic manuscript (National Library, Paris, no. 154) states that al-Ballāṣ was his birthplace. There was a church of Apa Sansno in al-Ballāṣ, and Muslim authors of the Middle Ages often mention a monastery in the area. Some sources call the monastery Dayr Kahmas and others Dayr Markis, but it is not known whose monastery this was.

BIBLIOGRAPHY

Amélineau, E. *La Géographie de l'Egypte à l'époque copte,* pp. 81–82. Paris, 1893.
Timm, S. *Das christlich-koptische Ägypten in arabischer Zeit,* Vol. 1, pp. 306–307. Wiesbaden, 1984.

RANDALL STEWART

BALYANĀ, AL-, city in the province of Jirjā in middle Egypt. It is located on the west side of the Nile roughly between Akhmīm and Nag Hammadi.

Christian-Arabic literature makes few references to al-Balyanā. However, as indicated by the account of the struggle of Patriarch SHENUTE I (858–880) with the heretical views of a bishop from al-Balyanā, the city was the seat of a bishopric at least as early as the middle of the ninth century. In the eleventh century, Mark, a bishop of al-Balyanā, participated in an unsuccessful plot instigated by John, bishop of Sakhā, to depose the patriarch CHRISTODOULOS.

The city is also mentioned on two gravestones. From the year 932 comes the tombstone of Kyra Susinne, whose father Psate was from al-Balyanā (Stern, 1878, pp. 26ff.). The Fitzwilliam Museum in Cambridge preserves the tombstone of Apa Theodorus, son of Mose, a presbyter from al-Balyanā. The inscription was made in 939 (Crum, 1904, p. 43, plate XXXVIII).

BIBLIOGRAPHY

Amélineau, E. *La Géographie de l'Egypte à l'époque copte,* pp. 93–94. Paris, 1893.
Crum, W. E. "Coptic Graffiti, etc." In *The Osireion at Abydos,* ed. M. A. Murray, pp. 38–43. Publications of the British School of Archaeology in Egypt 9. London, 1904.
Stern, L. "Sahidische Inschriften an alten Denkmälern." *Zeitschrift für Ägyptische Sprache und Altertumskunde* 16 (1878):9–28.
Timm, S. *Das christlich-koptische Ägypten in arabischer Zeit,* Vol. 1, pp. 312–14. Wiesbaden, 1984.

RANDALL STEWART

BANĀ, a city in the province of Gharbiyyah in the middle of the Egyptian Delta, located about 6 miles (9.5 km) south of Samannūd and 3 miles (5 km) south of Abūṣīr Banā. In Greek the place was known as lower Kynopolis (in Upper Egypt there was also a Kynopolis, now known as al-Qays). In Coptic documents the city's name appears as ⲡⲁⲛⲁⲩ (Panau).

Kynopolis/Banā has a long Christian tradition. The city has had a bishop since at least as early as the first quarter of the fourth century. In a list of bishops given to ATHANASIUS in 325, MELITIUS names Bishop Hermaion "in Kyno and Bousiris" (Munier, 1943, p. 3). Apparently the city also had an orthodox bishop at that time, for in a document (now lost, but quoted by Sozomen) Athanasius wrote that a Bishop Harpokration of Kynopolis attended the

Council of NICAEA in 325. This Kynopolis was undoubtedly the city in the Delta rather than the town of the same name in Upper Egypt, for the Coptic and Arabic lists of the participants in the council indicate that the Kynopolis represented by Bishop Adamantius was known in Coptic as Koeis and in Arabic as al-Qays (Munier, 1943, p. 4).

Around 459 Bishop Marion of Kynopolis joined with other bishops in condemning Eutychius and his heresies (Munier, 1943, p. 23). The fact that all the other bishops who took part in this action were from cities in the Delta is an indication that the Kynopolis administered by Marion was the Delta city and not the Kynopolis in Upper Egypt. The last bishop of Kynopolis/Banā of whom we have a record is Bishop Mark, who met together with a number of other bishops in the Muʿallaqah Church in Cairo in 1240 (Munier, 1943, p. 31).

During the patriarchate of ALEXANDER II (705–730) the heretical church in Banā was one of those that John of Ṣā reunited with the Coptic patriarchate. Under authorization from the Muslim administration, John had threatened these churches with double taxes if they remained separate from the main Coptic church. Although submission dispelled the immediate threat of a greater tax burden, just a few years later increased taxes and forced labors imposed by ʿUbayd Allāh, the governor of Egypt, led to bloody battles between Christians and Muslims in Banā, Ṣā, and Samannūd.

The patriarchs COSMAS I (730–731) and JOHN IV (775–799) were from Banā.

BIBLIOGRAPHY

Amélineau, E. *La Géographie de l'Egypte à l'époque copte,* pp. 84–85. Paris, 1893.

Munier, H. *Recueil des listes épiscopales de l'église copte.* Cairo, 1943.

Timm, S. *Das christlich-koptische Ägypten in arabischer Zeit,* pt. 1, pp. 318–24. Wiesbaden, 1984.

RANDALL STEWART

BANĀWĀN, AL-,

BANĀWĀN, AL-, town located in the province of Gharbiyyah in the Egyptian Delta, some 9 miles (14 km) northwest of al-Maḥallah al-Kubrā.

The SYNAXARION for 25 Abīb tells the story of the martyr Apa Krajon who hailed from al-Banāwān. A church was built for him in his hometown after his death. On the basis of this account it can be deduced that al-Banāwān knew Christianity at least as early as the fourth century. However, for the first few centuries after the ARAB CONQUEST OF EGYPT there are no witnesses to Christianity in the town. Nonetheless, the town appears in the medieval Coptic-Arabic registers and in a list of Coptic bishoprics. Historical sources speak of a bishop in the town as early as 1078, when Bishop Mena from al-Banāwān attended the synod in Cairo that chose a successor to Patriarch CHRISTODOULOS.

BIBLIOGRAPHY

Amélineau, E. *La Géographie de l'Egypte à l'époque copte,* pp. 86–87, 349. Paris, 1893.

Timm, S. *Das christlich-koptische Ägypten in arabischer Zeit,* Vol. 1, pp. 327–30. Wiesbaden, 1984.

RANDALL STEWART

BANĪ ḤASAN AND SPEOS ARTEMIDOS, two groups of tombs dug into the rock about 8 miles (13 km) south of the town of Minyā. The first group consists of hypogea of the eleventh and twelfth dynasties and derives its name from the neighboring village, Banī Ḥasan, which perpetuates the name of an Arabic tribe that established itself there before spreading throughout the region.

The second group is about 2 miles (3 km) from the first, in a valley called Valley of the Anchorites. Its mouth is close to a temple built by Thutmose III and known as Speos Artemidos since the Hellenistic period. (A general introduction is provided by Martin, 1971, pp. 61–64, and Meinardus, 1965, pp. 261–62, and 1977, pp. 368–69.)

At Banī Ḥasan, the Greek and Coptic inscriptions and the graffiti were noted by the traveler F. Granger (1745, p. 130). They were brought to the notice of the public by two English archaeologists, A. H. Sayce (1881–1882, pp. 112–23) and P. E. Newberry (1894, pp. 65–68). An account of the monastic installations in these tombs is given by A. Badawy (1953, pp. 66–89). The tomb of Nuternekht (tomb 23) has on the north wall a Coptic alphabet, and for this reason it has been thought that it perhaps served as a school. Tomb 28 was once a church, for it bears on the ceiling and on the east wall the traces of an apse. A door has been opened up to effect communication between this and tomb 30.

At Speos Artemidos, we must distinguish the *speos* itself and the tombs or quarries that surround it from a wadi about a mile to the south, the caves of which were inhabited by a colony of anchorites. The former has been described by J. Capart (1930, p. 180). The graffiti inscribed on these walls were published by R. Holthoer (1976, pp. 97–99) and M. Martin (Martin, et al. 1971, pp. 79–81). Martin estimates that the colony of monks came to install itself in Speos Artemidos and the neighborhood at the beginning of the fifth century, by reason of the form of the crosses engraved on the walls.

The installations in the wadi are perfectly preserved, with traces of the external constructions. It is difficult to decide whether they were used by cenobites or hermits.

BIBLIOGRAPHY

Badawy, A. "Les Premiers établissements chrétiens dans les anciennes tombes d'Egypte." In *Tome commémoratif du millénaire de la Bibliothèque patriarcae d'Alexandrie.* Alexandria, 1953.

Capart, J. "Coins ignorés d'Egypte." *Chronique d'Egypte* 10 (1930):180ff.

Granger, F. *Relation du voyage fait en Egypte, par le sieur Granger, en l'année 1730.* Paris, 1745.

Holthoer, R. "Coptic Graffiti in Speos Artemidos." *Studia Orientalia* 45 (1976):97–99.

Martin, M., et al. *La Laure de Der al-Dik à Antinoé.* Bibliothèque d'études coptes 8. Cairo, 1971.

Meinardus, O. *Christian Egypt, Ancient and Modern.* Cairo, 1965; 2nd ed., 1977.

Newberry, P. E. *Beni Hasan,* Vol. 2. London, 1894.

Sayce, A. H. "Coptic Inscriptions of Beni Hasan and Deir el-Medineh." *Proceedings of the Society of Biblical Archaeology* 4 (1881–1882):117–23.

RENÉ-GEORGES COQUIN
MAURICE MARTIN, S.J.

BANĪ KALB, village, today called Banī Majdā, situated on the left bank of the Nile 3 miles (5 km) west of Manfalūṭ (north of ASYŪṬ). Al-Maqrīzī (1853, Vol. 2, p. 506; 1845, pp. 42 [text], 101 [trans.]) mentioned a monastery there, uninhabited in his time (fifteenth century) but serving as a church for the Christians of Manfalūṭ. According to him, it was consecrated to the archangel Gabriel. However, J. Vansleb (1677, p. 361; 1678, p. 217) wrote that it is dedicated to the archangels Gabriel and Raphael. S. Clarke (1912, p. 209, no. 2), who reproduced the official list of the patriarchate, gives Saint MICHAEL as patron of the church. Such permutations among the titulary archangels of churches are very common.

BIBLIOGRAPHY

Clarke, S. *Christian Antiquities in the Nile Valley.* Oxford, 1912.

Vansleb, J. *Nouvelle Relation en forme de journal d'un voyage fait en Egypte en 1672 et 1673.* Paris, 1677. Translated as *The Present State of Egypt.* London, 1678.

RENÉ-GEORGES COQUIN
MAURICE MARTIN, S.J.

BANĪ MURR. *See* Pilgrimages.

BANĪ SUEF, capital of the province of Banī Suef and situated on the west bank of the Nile about 22 miles (35 km) south of the Fayyūm. Until the nineteenth century, Banī Suef belonged to the ancient province of BAHNASĀ (Oxyrhynchus), which was famous for its Coptic heritage. The origin of the name Banī Suef is difficult to trace, but Arab medieval geographers called it Banmasawayh and in the sixteenth century it became known as Banī Suwayf or Suef.

Many old churches and monasteries are to be found in the immediate vicinity of Banī Suef, although documents do not attest to the existence of an early bishopric in the city itself. Nonetheless, in the twentieth century Banī Suef became the seat of a bishop. It now has a convent and a church built on the site of an older church whose columns are still lying in sight. A museum built in the mid-twentieth century contains manuscripts, stones, and artifacts from Coptic ruins in the surrounding area.

BIBLIOGRAPHY

Timm, S. *Das christlich-koptische Ägypten in arabischer Zeit,* Vol. 1, p. 336. Wiesbaden, 1984.

RAGAI MAKAR

BANŪ AL-KANZ (colloquially, Banī Kanz), originally a warrior tribe of mixed Arab and BEJA ancestry. They established de facto control over the Aswan area in Fatimid times, and one of their rulers was rewarded with the title Kanz al-Dawlah (treasure of the state) for his service to the Fatimid caliph. From then on the title was treated as hereditary by the successive chiefs of the Banū al-Kanz.

The Ayyubids inaugurated their rule in Upper Egypt by driving out the Banū al-Kanz, who retreated into the most northerly portion of Nubia. Here they amalgamated with already settled Nubian elements and in time adopted a Nubian dialect. They are the ancestors of the Kanuz Nubians of today (see NUBIANS).

In Nubia, the Banū al-Kanz established a quasi-independent Muslim principality within what was nominally the territory of NOBATIA. The Kanz al-Dawlah, even though a Muslim, became a figure of importance within the Christian Nubian kingdom, and may even at times have held the traditional office of eparch of Nobatia. Eventually he and his family became allied by marriage with the ruling house of MAKOURIA itself, and it was through that connection that in 1323 the Kanz al-Dawlah succeeded to the throne of the Christian kingdom.

The Banū al-Kanz had apparently lost control of the Nubian throne again by 1365, and thereafter they reverted to their outlaw ways. They plundered Aswan and the surrounding districts repeatedly in the fourteenth and fifteenth centuries, and were largely responsible for destroying the overland trade between Upper Egypt and ʿAydhāb on the Red Sea. They also played a significant part in the weakening and final destruction of the Christian kingdoms of Nubia. Their depredations ended only with the imposition of Ottoman rule in Egypt and Nubia in the sixteenth century. No trace of their warrior tradition survives among the Kanuz Nubians of today, who are peacefully resettled in the area around Kom Ombo.

BIBLIOGRAPHY

Adams, W. Y. *Nubia, Corridor to Africa*, pp. 524–31. Princeton, N.J., 1977.

Hasan, Y. F. *The Arabs and the Sudan*, pp. 58–60. Edinburgh, 1967.

MacMichael, H. A. *A History of the Arabs in the Sudan*, Vol. 1, pp. 149–51. London, 1922.

WILLIAM Y. ADAMS

BAPTISM. [*This entry consists of two articles. The first discusses the origin, features, and administration of the sacrament, and the second focuses on infant baptism.*]

Origin, Features, and Administration of Baptism

Baptism is the sacrament by which the recipient is regenerated through triple immersion in water in the name of the Father, the Son, and the Holy Spirit, enters into union with Christ and the body of the church, and receives the gift of the Holy Spirit. Baptism is regarded as the first and principal sacrament, without which none of the other sacraments can be administered. Its primary importance is manifest in the words of Jesus Christ: "unless one is born of water and the Spirit, he cannot enter the kingdom of God" (Jn. 3:5).

This sacrament was instituted by Christ following His Resurrection, when He said to the disciples, "All authority in heaven and on earth has been given to me. Go therefore and make disciples of all nations, baptizing them in the name of the Father and of the Son and of the Holy Spirit" (Mt. 28:18–19), and, "He who believes and is baptized will be saved; but he who does not believe will be condemned" (Mk. 16:16). Christ's words indicate the universal nature of the sacrament of baptism and its prerequisite importance for salvation.

Before Christ's institution of baptism as a sacrament, other baptismal forms had existed, such as that performed by John the Baptist, which was by divine command (Mt. 21:25; Mk. 11:30). The disciples, too, used to baptize people during the life of Christ on earth, before His Resurrection and the fulfillment of divine ransom. However, in contrast with Christian baptism, carried out in accordance with Christ's teaching and recommendations, those earlier forms of baptism had no sacramental qualities. They were merely acts of immersion in water as an expression of repentance on the part of penitent Jews and their belief in the imminent fulfillment of the messianic hope and the coming of Christ. The sacrament of Christian baptism, on the other hand, is administered in the name of the Father, the Son, and the Holy Spirit, to all believers without distinction, for the purpose of penitence and the forgiveness of sins, and for the gift of the Holy Spirit. It is, furthermore, an expression of belief in Christ who has already come, while the earlier baptism was nothing but a prelude to a fuller and more efficacious baptism by One greater than John and the disciples, One who would baptize with the Holy Spirit (Mk. 1:8).

This basic distinction between Christian baptism and earlier baptisms was clearly brought out in the writings of the early fathers. According to Tertullian (c. 160–c. 220), "in the Acts of the Apostles, we find that men who had 'John's baptism,' had not received the Holy Spirit, whom they knew not even by hearing. . . . And so, 'the baptism of repentance' was dealt with as if it were a candidate for the remission and sanctification shortly about to follow in Christ: for in that John used to preach 'baptism for the remission of sins,' the declaration was made with reference to a future remission . . . that repentance is antecedent, remission subsequent; and this is 'preparing the way'" (Tertullian, *On Baptism*).

Similar interpretations permeate the writings of other Fathers, such as ATHANASIUS of Alexandria (c. 296–373) in the *Treatise on Matthew* 3, CYRIL OF JERUSALEM (c. 315–386) in *Catechetical Lecture* 3 and 4, and Augustine (354–430) in *Epistle 51*.

The effect of baptism in purification, remission of sins, and spiritual regeneration makes it an essential, indispensable element for salvation. This inherent feature was also amply expounded by several of the fathers, such as Saint Justin Martyr (c. 100–c. 165), Saint CLEMENT OF ALEXANDRIA (c. 150–c. 215), Saint Cyril of Jerusalem (c. 315–386), Saint BASIL THE GREAT (c. 330–379), and Saint John Chrysostom (c. 347–407).

Baptism imparts the following graces to the baptized: (1) spiritual regeneration, as explained by Christ to Nicodemus (Jn. 3:3–8); (2) purification and remission of sins (Acts 2:38; 1 Pt. 3:21; Eph. 5:25–27; 1 Cor. 6:11); (3) membership in the one body of Christ (Gal. 3:26–29; 1 Cor. 12:13; Acts 2:41; Rom. 6:3–5); and (4) release from the punishment of sins (Mk. 16:16; Ti. 3:5–7; 1 Pt. 1:3, 4).

As ordained by Christ in teaching and put into practice through His baptism in the waters of the Jordan, the visible element used in administering the sacrament of baptism has always been water, by trine immersion in the name of the three hypostases of the Holy Trinity. Full immersion is symbolic of Christ's burial, hence Saint Paul's words, "Therefore we are buried with Him by baptism into death, that like as Christ was raised up from the dead by the glory of the Father, even so we also should walk in newness of life. For if we have been planted together in the likeness of His death, we shall be also in the likeness of His resurrection" (Rom. 6:4, 5). These principles receive ample attention in the writings of the church fathers.

Once baptism is validly administered, it cannot be repeated. Hence the reaffirmation in the Nicene-Constantinopolitan Creed: "We confess one baptism for the remission of sins." A repetition of the baptismal rite would therefore be sacrilegious, for the following considerations. Since baptism is an act of spiritual birth, no one person can be born twice; in its symbolic nature and sacramental representation of Christ's death, burial, and resurrection, it should take place only once; according to the concept of baptism, it has an indelible, ineffaceable character on the soul of the baptized, which renders its repetition utterly otiose. In the case of those persons seeking reconciliation with the church after having been baptized by heretics or schismatics, the sacrament is administered to them on the grounds that the earlier baptism was null and void. Hence the stipulation of Apostolic Canon 47, "Let a bishop or presbyter who shall baptize again one who has rightly received baptism, or who shall not baptize one who has been polluted by the ungodly, be deposed, as despising the cross and death of the Lord, and not making a distinction between the true priests and the false."

The issue of rebaptism was one of the vexed questions that troubled the church in the third century, giving rise to a prolonged and serious dispute between Saint Cyprian, bishop of Carthage (d. 258), and Pope Stephen of Rome (254–257). The former maintained the urgency of rebaptism in certain cases, the latter held that any baptism in the name of Christ or the three Persons of the Trinity should not be repeated. The Council of Carthage (255) ruled that heretics and those whom they baptized had to be rebaptized, while those who had been baptized in the church but lapsed were not to be baptized. According to Canon 19 of the first Council of NICAEA (325): "Concerning the Paulianists who have flown for refuge to the Catholic church, it has been decreed that they must by all means be rebaptized; and if any of them who in past time have been numbered among their clergy should be found blameless and without reproach, let them be rebaptized and ordained by the bishop of the Catholic church . . ." (*The Canons of the 318 Holy Fathers*). Likewise Canon 8 of the synod of Laodicea (between 343 and 381) decreed that: "Persons converted from the heresy of those who are called Phrygians, even should they be among those reputed by them as clergymen, and even should they be called the very chiefest, are with all care to be both instructed and baptized by the bishops and presbyters of the church."

The principle of the noniteration of baptism receives particular stress in the writings of John Chrysostom: "Baptism is a cross, and 'our old man was crucified with Him' for we were made conformable to the likeness of His death' [Rom. 6:5; Phil. 3:10], and again, 'we were buried therefore with Him by baptism into death' [Rom. 6:4]. Wherefore as it is not possible that Christ should be crucified a second time, for that is to 'put Him to an open shame' [Heb. 6:6], so neither is it possible to be baptized a second time" (*Homilies on Hebrews* 9.6).

The authority to baptize was conferred by Christ to the apostles (Mt. 28:19) who, in turn, gave it to the bishops who succeeded them and to the presbyters. Deacons and deaconesses who assist the bishop or presbyter do not exercise the right of administering the sacrament.

Since the apostolic age, baptism has been administered at any time of the year, upon condition that the candidate is deemed worthy to receive it. There were, however, certain occasions on which large numbers of people were usually baptized, such as on Easter Eve, Pentecost, and Epiphany. "Pascha [i.e., Easter] affords a more than usually solemn day for baptism; when, withal, the Lord's passion, in which we are baptized, was completed. . . . After that, Pentecost is a most joyous space for conferring baptisms" (Tertullian, *De Baptismo* 19).

In the Coptic church many baptisms are usually carried out on the Eve of Epiphany (11 Ṭūbah) in commemoration of Jesus' baptism, and also on the sixth Sunday of the great Lent, known as Christening Sunday.

Believers who were martyred for the sake of Jesus Christ without having been baptized are said to have gained an extraordinary baptism of blood, or martyrdom. It is recognized by the church through the commemoration of the martyrdom of the Holy Innocents, those children of Bethlehem who were massacred by order of Herod in his attempt to kill the Infant Jesus (Mt. 2:16–18). It also applies to martyrs who died during the times of persecution without having previously received the sacrament.

Before a person is baptized, it is essential that he or she have a firm belief in Jesus Christ the Redeemer (Mk. 16:16; Acts 16:31) and a genuine feeling of repentance (Acts 11:38; 3:9), make an explicit confession of faith, and repeat after the priest the formula of the renunciation of the devil. In the case of children, their sponsors make these commitments on their behalf.

Infant Baptism

Since the apostolic age, the baptism of infants has been recognized as a common and by no means premature practice. Male infants were due for baptism forty days and females eighty days after birth, when the mother had completed her purification days. In cases of illness or fear that an infant might not survive this prescribed period, he or she could be taken to church by another woman who acted on this occasion as sponsor. Hence the obligation that the church places on parents, requiring them to have their offspring baptized at the first available opportunity after the aforementioned duration of time.

The reasons for this practice are several. First, baptism is a sacrament of purification, cleansing from original sin, and spiritual regeneration. Second, baptism is a prerequisite for salvation and entry into the kingdom of God. To deny it to infants is to deprive them of this grace. The argument that at this age children are still immature and lacking in the ability to understand matters of faith is refuted on the basis that they are to be baptized in accordance with their parents' or their sponsors' faith, just as in the Old Testament circumcision on the eighth day after birth was routine ritual not dependent on the age of discretion. Baptism in the New Testament is the counterpart of circumcision in the Old.

Third, we learn from the Acts of the Apostles that the apostles administered baptism to entire families, grown-ups as well as youngsters. Peter baptized Cornelius the centurion, one of the early converts to Christianity, and his household (Acts 10:44–48). Paul baptized the family of Lydia the dealer in purple fabric (16:14–15); the jailer at Philippi and his whole family (16:33); Crispus, who held high office in the synagogue at Corinthus, and his family (18:8); and the household of Stephanas (1 Cor. 1:16).

Fourth, the fathers placed particular emphasis on infant baptism. Origen (185–253), the "greatest scholar of Christian antiquity," wrote: "The church received from the apostles the tradition of giving baptism even to infants. For the apostles, to whom were committed the secrets of divine mysteries, knew that there is in everyone the innate stain of sin, which must be washed away through water and the Spirit."

Similarly clear views are expressed by a host of other fathers, such as Clement of Alexandria, Tertullian, Saint John Chrysostom, Saint Augustine, and many others.

The issue was also debated in church councils, and the church's decision was given its definitive form in the provisions stipulated by canon 110 of the Council of Carthage (419): ". . . whosoever denies that infants newly from their mothers' wombs should be baptized, or says that baptism is for remission of sins, but that they derive from Adam no original sin, which needs to be removed by the laver of regeneration, from whence the conclusion follows, that in them the form of baptism for the remission of sins, is to be understood as false and not true, let him be anathema" (*Canons of the 217 Blessed Fathers*).

BIBLIOGRAPHY

De Pressensé, E. *The Early Years of Christianity*, Vol. 1. London, 1880.

Evetts, B. T. A. *The Rites of the Coptic Church.*

London, 1888.
Ḥabīb Jirjis. *Asrār al-Kanīsah al-Sab'ah,* 2nd ed., pp. 30–58. Cairo, 1950.
Jurgens, W. A., ed. and trans. *The Faith of the Early Fathers,* Vol. 1, Collegeville, Minn., 1970; Vols. 2 and 3, Collegeville, Minn., 1979.
Kelly, J. N. D. *Early Christian Doctrines,* 5th ed. San Francisco, 1978.
Lebreton, J., and J. Zeiller. *L'Eglise primitive.* Paris, 1964.
Neunheusser, B. *Baptême et confirmation.* Paris, 1966.
Stone, D. *Holy Baptism,* 4th ed. London, 1905.
Wooley, R. M. *Coptic Offices.* London, 1930.
Yūḥannā Salāmah. *Kitāb al-La'ālī' al-Nafīsah fī Sharḥ Ṭuqūs wa-Mu'taqadāt al-Kanīsah,* Vol. 2, pp. 38–40. Cairo, 1909.

ARCHBISHOP BASILIOS

BAPTISM, INFANT. *See* Baptism.

BAPTISM, LITURGY OF. The office of holy baptism comprises four sections: (1) absolution of the woman; (2) renunciation of the devil; (3) sanctification of the water of the font; and (4) loosening of the girdle of the baptized.

The Absolution of the Woman

When a woman has given birth to a male child, at the end of forty days the priest begins the prayers by saying: "Have mercy upon us, O God, Father Almighty. All-Holy Trinity, have mercy upon us. Lord God of powers, be with us, for we have no help in our tribulations and afflictions, save Thee." Then follows the Lord's Prayer and the prayer of thanksgiving, after which incense is offered. The Epistle (Heb. 1:8–12) is read, the *Trisagion* is chanted. The priest says the prayer of the Gospel. Psalm 31:1–2 is read, then the Gospel (Lk. 2:21–35), then the three greater intercessions (peace of the church, the fathers, and the congregation). Then the Creed is recited, and the priest says the next prayer: "Lord God Almighty, Father of our Lord, our God and our Savior Jesus Christ, . . . who came to us in the flesh through the Holy Theotokos and the Holy Spirit, healer and physician of our nature. . . . For the sake of man whom Thou didst form and the creature of woman whom Thou didst produce from him, to be his assistant, after the dispensation of canonical marriage, Thou didst bless the fruit of the lawful offspring of the image of Thy likeness. . . . Wherefore, O Lord, Thou hast purified our nature, and delivered us through the inward personal reconciliation in mystical fellowship. . . . We pray Thee to look upon Thy handmaid. May she be renewed in body, in soul, and in spirit. Absolve her from all accusations, all her acts and forgive her all her trespasses. . . ." The Lord's Prayer follows, then the three absolutions and the benediction.

When a woman has given birth to a female child, at the end of eighty days the prayers remain the same as in the case of a male child, but the readings from the scriptures differ. The epistle is from 1 Corinthians 7:12–14, the Psalm versicle is 44:9, and the Gospel is according to Luke 10:38–42.

After this, the priest anoints the mother with oil, and she enters the church to receive Holy Communion.

The Renunciation of the Devil

The priest says the prayer of absolution over the mother of the child, which, after a reference to the ordinance of the purification according to God's command to Moses, includes the following: "May she be worthy of the communion of Thy holy mysteries, without falling into judgment."

Then follows the intercession of the catechumens, "O lover of men, have mercy on Thy servants the catechumens, who have received instruction. . . . Strengthen them in Thy faith . . . show them the way in which they ought to walk, instruct them in the grace of Thy Holy Spirit. . . . Bestow upon them remission of their sins, and grant them by Thy grace that they may be made worthy of the holy baptism of the new birth."

Here the priest prays over the oil of the catechumens. Taking the vessel of oil, he says: "Lord God Almighty . . . we pray and beseech Thy goodness . . . to look upon this oil, give it power to cast out devils, magic, sorcery and all idolatry; change it and manifest it as an oil for the anointing of catechumens and imparting of faith to the soul, through Christ Jesus our Lord."

Then follows another prayer over the oil, beginning with the words, "Lord God Almighty, Father of our Savior Jesus Christ, who was crucified for us under Pontius Pilate, when He had made the good confession; send Thy holy power upon this oil . . . for the overthrow of all evil acts."

At this point the priest removes all rings, earrings, ornaments, or bracelets from those children who will be baptized, and takes the vessel of oil and proceeds to anoint them, the males first and then the females. He anoints the forehead, saying "Thou

[name] art anointed in the name of the Father and of the Son and of the Holy Ghost, One God, [with] oil of catechumens in the holy only catholic and apostolic church of God, Amen." Then he anoints the child's chest, his right hand, and his left hand, saying: "May this oil make all assaults of the adversary void. Amen."

He continues to pray that God may grant His servants growth in His faith, and remission of their sins, preparing them to be temples of the Holy Spirit, worthy to obtain the grace for which they were presented, and to be cleansed from the sin and corruption of the world. Then they kneel down, and the priest prays over them saying, "Let us pray that God may open the ears of their hearts, and kindle within them a light of knowledge, . . . to grant them a saving purity, and eternal redemption, to beget them a second time by the new birth of the laver and remission of their sins."

After this the priest lays hands upon them and prays for their delivery from all demons, darkness, and uncleanliness (this last section is partly a prayer of exorcism).

Then the person to be baptized, looking toward the west, with the left hand outstretched, repeats after the priest, "I renounce thee, Satan, and all thy unclean works, and all thy wicked angels and all thy evil demons, and all thy power, and all thy abominable service, and all thy evil cunning and error, and all thy host, and all thy authority, and all the rest of thy impieties." Then the following sentence is repeated thrice: "I renounce thee." The priest breathes upon the face of the candidate, and says thrice "Come forth, unclean spirit."

After this, turning to the east, and with both hands uplifted, the person to be baptized says, "I join myself to Thee, O Christ my God, and all Thy laws which are for salvation, all Thy life-giving service, all Thy vivifying works." Then follows the confession of faith, in the following words: "I believe in one God, God the Father almighty, and His only-begotten Son, Jesus Christ our Lord, and the Holy life-giving Spirit, and the resurrection of the flesh, and the one only, holy, catholic, apostolic church. Amen."

The priest here asks the candidate thrice, "Do you believe?" and he answers, "I believe." Thereupon the priest prays that God may "establish their faith, and let His power dwell in them that they turn not back again to those things they have left, . . . to renew their life, to fill them with the power of the Holy Spirit unto oneness and union with His only-begotten Son."

While the candidate kneels, the priest resumes his prayer over him, saying: "Master, our Savior, the beneficent Lover of man, to Thee alone is this mystery performed . . . we beseech Thee, enlighten the eyes of their understanding with the light of knowledge . . . all traces of idolatry and unbelief cast out of their heart. Prepare their souls for the reception of Thy Holy Spirit. Let them be worthy of the new birth of the laver."

The priest takes the oil of joy or gladness and anoints the person to be baptized on his forehead, his heart, his arms, his back (opposite the heart), and in the middle of his two hands in the sign of the cross, saying, "Thou [Name] art anointed with the oil of gladness, availing against all workings of the adversary, unto thy grafting into the sweet olive tree of the holy catholic apostolic church of God. Amen."

The priest says the first prayer of laying on of hands: "Let them be sheep of the flock, and sons of Thy heavenly bride chamber, and heirs of Thy imperishable and eternal kingdom." In a second prayer he asks that God may "open the eyes of their heart, that they may be enlightened with the light of the gospel of Thy kingdom. Let the angels of light have part in their life, to save them from all attacks of the adversary and from all evil assaults . . . And make them sheep of the fold of Thy Christ, . . . purified vessels, sons of the light, heirs of Thy kingdom."

Unction is performed thirty-six times before the actual baptism, and the same number of times with the holy chrism immediately after baptism. There is a strong symbolic reference to the fragrant oil that the woman poured over Christ's head at Bethany, and to our Lord's words, "She has done it to prepare me for burial" (Mt. 26:12), since the very act of baptizing resembles the death and burial of Jesus Christ. "We were buried therefore with him by baptism into death, so that as Christ was raised from the dead by the glory of the Father, we too might walk in newness of life" (Rom. 6:4).

The use of oil prior to baptism was also mentioned in the *Apostolic Constitutions;* "concerning baptism, O bishop, or presbyter, we have already given direction, and we now say. . . . But thou shalt beforehand anoint the person with the holy oil, and afterward baptize him with water, and in the conclusion shalt seal him with the ointment."

Sanctification of the Water of the Font

The priest enters the baptistery, takes the pure (unmixed) oil, and pours it into the font in the form of the cross, saying, "In the Name of the Father, the

Son and the Holy Spirit, one God. Blessed be God the Father almighty, Amen. Blessed be His only-begotten Son, Jesus Christ, our Lord, Amen. Blessed be the Holy Spirit, the Comforter, Amen." He says inaudibly the prayer "Our Master, call Thy servants to Thy holy light. Make them worthy of this great grace of holy baptism." Then follows the prayer of thanksgiving, and he offers the incense. The Pauline Epistle (Ti. 2:11; 3:7) is read, and the priest says the prayer of Paul, beginning, "O Lord of knowledge and Dispenser of wisdom, . . . who in Thy goodness didst call Paul who was once a persecutor to be a chosen vessel, etc." Then follows the Catholic Epistle (1 Jn. 5:5–13) and its prayer, beginning: "O Lord our God, who through Thy holy apostles didst reveal unto us the mystery of the glorious Gospel of Thy Christ. . . ." The priest says the prayer of absolution, addressed to the Father, beginning: "Lord God Almighty, the Healer of our souls, our bodies, and our spirits, etc." Acts 8:26–39 follows, and after this the *Trisagion*, the intercession of the Gospel, the psalm-versicle (32:1–2), and the Gospel (Jn. 3:1–21).

Then the seven great prayers are said: for the sick; for travelers; for the waters (sowings, or the weather); for the ruler; for the dead (those who have fallen asleep); for the offerings; and for the catechumens.

The priest then prays on behalf of the persons to be baptized: "O God of the prophets and Lord of the apostles, who didst proclaim the coming of Thy Christ through Thy holy prophets, and didst send John the prophet and forerunner before Him, we pray that Thou sendst Thy holy power that it may come upon this baptism, give power to Thy servants and prepare them to receive the holy baptism of the new birth, unto the remission of their sins and the hope of incorruption, etc." He also prays an invocation inaudibly that God may enable him to fulfil the ministry of the great mystery of baptism that was first constituted in heaven.

After this the priest says the three great intercessions for the peace, the fathers, and the congregation, and then the creed. He then pours the oil into the baptismal font three times in the form of the cross, saying, "In the name of the Father, etc." and "Blessed, etc." as he had done earlier with the unmixed oil. He then says the following prayer: "Creator of the waters, Maker of the universe, we call upon Thy holy and eternal power. . . . We pray Thee, our Master, for Thy servants, change them, transform them, hallow them, give them power, that through this water and this oil, all adverse powers may be brought to nought, etc." Here he breathes thrice upon the water in the form of the cross, saying, "Sanctify this water and this oil that they may become a laver of the new birth, Amen; unto eternal life, Amen; a garment of incorruption, Amen; a grace of sonship, Amen; a renewing of the Holy Spirit, Amen, . . ." He seals the water thrice with the cross, in the name of the Father and of the Son and of the Holy Spirit.

The deacon says, "Pray for perfect peace and love and the holy salutation of the apostles." The people say, "Through the intercessions of the holy Theotokos Mary, O Lord, bestow upon us the forgiveness of our sins. . . ."

The rest of the liturgy of baptism is conducted with various interpositions by the deacon and responses from the congregation. The priest then takes the holy chrism and pours a little of it in the baptismal font three times in the form of the cross, repeating what he previously said in the course of the consecration of the unmixed oil. He also says the Alleluia and the following portions of the Psalms while stirring the water: Psalm 29:3, 4; 34:5, 11; 66:12; 51:7–10; 132:13. The people sing Psalm 150.

At this point the deacon leads the person to be baptized from the west and brings him to the east against the font, to the left of the priest, who asks him his name, and immerses him thrice. At each immersion he raises him up and breathes in his face. At the first immersion he says, "I baptize thee [Name] in the name of the Father," at the second immersion, "and of the Son," and at the third immersion, "and of the Holy Spirit. Amen." Then, taking the holy chrism and praying over it, saying, "Lord, who alone art mighty . . . , bestow the Holy Spirit in the pouring out of the holy chrism. Let it be a living seal and a confirmation to Thy servants." Then he anoints the baptized person with the holy unction thirty-six times in the sign of the cross, during which he says, "In the name of the Father, and of the Son, and of the Holy Spirit. An unction of the grace of the Holy Spirit, Amen. An unction of a pledge of the kingdom of heaven, Amen. An unction of a fellowship of life eternal and immortal, Amen. A holy unction of Christ our God, and an indissoluble seal, Amen. Thou [Name] art anointed with holy chrism in the name of the Father, and of the Son, and of the Holy Spirit, Amen."

Then the priest lays his hand upon the baptized person and says, "May thou be blessed with the blessing of the heavenly ones, and the blessing of the angels. . . ." He breathes over his face saying, "Receive the Holy Spirit, and be a purified vessel through Christ Jesus our Lord. . . ."

After this prayer, the priest clothes him in a white garment, saying, "A garment of life eternal and incorruptible, Amen." Then he says a prayer, "Lord God Almighty . . . who commanded that Thy servants be born through the laver of the new birth, and bestowed upon them forgiveness of their sins, the garment of incorruption and the grace of sonship. . . ." Afterward the baptized are clothed with the rest of their garments, and the priest says a prayer over the crowns and the girdle, "Lord God almighty, . . . who hast bestowed crowns upon Thy holy apostles, Thy prophets and Thy martyrs . . . , do Thou again bless these crowns which we have prepared to bestow on Thy servants who have received holy baptism, that they may be unto them crowns of glory and honour, Amen; crowns of blessing and glory, Amen; crowns of virtue and righteousness, Amen; crowns of wisdom and understanding, Amen; give them strength to fulfil Thy commandments and Thy ordinances, that they may attain to the benefits of the Kingdom of heaven."

The priest girds the baptized with a girdle in the form of the cross, and sets the crown on the head of each one of them, saying, "Set, O Master, Lord God, upon Thy servants crowns from heaven, Amen; crowns of glory, Amen; crowns of faith invincible, Amen; crowns of confirmation, Amen; crowns of righteousness, Amen, Grant that Thy servants be filled with the grace of the Holy Spirit."

Then follows an address by the priest to the parents and spiritual sponsors of the baptized, emphasizing their commitments toward them. Holy Communion is then administered to those who have been baptized, and the priest lays his hand upon them saying, "Make Thy servants, O God, grow in Thy wisdom; give them understanding in Thy fear; bring them to maturity; bestow upon them the knowledge of the truth; keep them undefiled in faith, through the intercessions of the Lady of us all, the Holy Theotokos, the Virgin Mary, the baptist forerunner John, and all the choir of the saints, the prophets, the apostles, the martyrs and the crossbearers, Amen."

A unique feature of the Coptic baptismal rite ensures that the water, to which a few drops of the holy chrism have been added, is properly disposed of at the end of the baptismal service. The priest pours water over his hands in the font, and washes its surroundings as well as the cross. Then he says a prayer for the release of the water. The priest allows the water to be drained away, either into the well beneath the font or elsewhere, making sure that none of it is put to any other use.

Loosening of the Girdle of the Newly Baptized

This service is performed eight days after baptism. The priest says the prayer of thanksgiving over a basin containing some fresh water and surrounded with lighted candles. Then he offers incense, and the Pauline Epistle (1 Cor. 10:1–4) is read, followed by the *Trisagion,* the intercession to the Gospel, the psalm versicle (32:1–2) and the Gospel (Mt. 3:1–6). After this the priest prays the three great intercessions (peace, the fathers, and the congregation), and the people recite the Creed and the Lord's Prayer. The priest says the absolution prayers, makes the sign of the cross over the water three times while saying: "One is the Holy Father, One is the Holy Son, One is the Holy Spirit, Amen." Then the people sing Psalm 150. After this the child is bathed in the water, and his girdle and baptismal robe are also washed in it, before it is disposed of in the sea, the river, or a field.

BIBLIOGRAPHY

Burmester, O. H. E. "The Baptismal Rite of the Coptic Church, a Critical Study." *Bulletin de la Société d'archéologie Copte* 11 (1947):27–86.

Evetts, B. T. A. *The Rites of the Coptic Church, the Order of Baptism and the Order of Matrimony,* trans. from Coptic manuscripts. London, 1888.

Percival, H. R. *Excursus on the Worship of the Early Church. In A Select Library of the Nicene and Post-Nicene Fathers,* 2nd ser., ed. P. Schaff and H. Wace. Grand Rapids, Mich., 1956.

William Sulaymān Qelādah. *Kitāb al-Disqūlayah Ta'ālīm al-Rusul,* chaps. 38–41, pp. 488–97. Cairo, 1979.

Woolley, R. M. *Coptic Offices.* London, 1930.

Yūḥannā Salāmah. *Kitāb al-La'āli' al-Nafīsah fī Sharḥ Ṭuqūs wa-Mu'taqadāt al-Kanīsah,* Vol. 2, pp. 9–54. Cairo, 1909.

ARCHBISHOP BASILIOS

BAPTISM OF CHRIST. *See* Christian Subjects in Coptic Art.

BAPTISTERY. *See* Architectural Elements of Churches.

BAPTISTERY, CONSECRATION OF. After the consecration of a new church and its altar, the bishop, together with the clergy and deacons carrying crosses and lighted candles, proceeds to consecrate the baptismal font. There exist two versions of the consecration liturgy. In the more widely used ceremony the bishop starts with the Prayer of Thanksgiving, followed by a Pauline epistle (Eph. 2:13, 3:12). The deacons sing the *Trisagion* and a priest says the Intercession of the Gospel. The Gospel reading, preceded by Psalm 25:4, is taken from John 3:1–17, the key verse being Christ's words to Nicodemus: "Unless one is born anew, he cannot see the kingdom of God." The three Great Intercessions follow, namely, peace, the church fathers, and the congregations, after which all recite the creed.

The bishop then reads the baptismal prayer, which has for its theme the regenerative power of baptism. The words of the prayer come from a translation of a Coptic and Arabic manuscript presented by Patriarch CYRIL V (1874–1927) to the bishop of Salisbury, England, in 1898.

The people recite the Lord's Prayer, and the bishop says the absolutions. Afterward he pours water into the font from the jars previously used in the consecration of the church, washes it, and wipes it dry, while the deacons sing Psalms 26:1, 8; 26:4; and 43:3–4. He takes the chrism and signs five crosses, on its four sides and base, saying, "We consecrate this font for the name of Saint John the Baptist in the name of the Father and Son and Holy Spirit." A few psalms are then read, the font is covered, and the bishop says the benediction. Once again the people recite the Lord's Prayer, after which the bishop, clergy, and deacons return to the church to celebrate the liturgy.

A second, lengthier version is given in a copy of the Euchologion printed in Rome in 1762. It comprises the following sections:

1. seven psalms: 122, 127, 132, 133, 134, 135, 136
2. three Old Testament prophecies: Genesis 28:10–22; Isaiah 1:16–27; Ezekiel 40:1–23
3. Psalm 117 and the Hymn of the Golden Censer
4. Ephesians 4:1–10
5. 1 Peter 3:13–22
6. Acts of the Apostles 19:1–10
7. the *Trisagion*
8. Gospel intercession and lection: Matthew 17:1–5; John 5:1–18
9. *Kyrie eleison* (ten times)
10. the Seven Great Intercessions: travelers, the sick, the ruler, the water (or plants, or fruit), the dormants, the oblations, and the catechumens
11. *Kyrie eleison* (a hundred times)
12. the Three Great Intercessions: peace, church fathers, and congregations.

Then follows the baptismal prayer and the subsequent sections as mentioned in the first version of the ceremony.

BIBLIOGRAPHY

Horner, G. *The Service for the Consecration of a Church and Altar, According to the Coptic Rite.* London, 1902.

ARCHBISHOP BASILIOS

BAQṬ TREATY. The *Baqṭ* was a negotiated agreement between ʿAbdallāh ibn Saʿīd ibn Abī Sarḥ, the Umayyad governor of Egypt, and the Nubian king of MAKOURIA. It was concluded at DONGOLA in A.D. 632 following an unsuccessful Muslim attempt to subjugate the Nubian kingdom. The name *baqṭ* is presumed to be derivative from Greek *pakton* (agreement), and is unique to this one document; no other covenant made by the medieval Arabs was given the same designation. This reflects the fact that the agreement itself was in many ways unique in the annals of Arab foreign relations, since it exempted the Nubians from the *dār al-harb* (the community of nations at war with Islam) without including them in the *dār al-Islam* (the community of Islam).

Several different versions of the *Baqṭ* have been recorded by different authors. Most of them wrote at a time when the agreement was still nominally in force but long after the original date of its execution. The earliest written account of the *Baqṭ* appears to be that of Al-Balādhūri (d. 892), who merely states that the Nubians were exempted from paying JIZYAH (poll tax) but agreed to furnish annually a gift of 300 slaves in exchange for the equivalent value in food. Later writers mention various other conditions, such as provision of horses by the Nubians and of wine and various kinds of cloth by the Egyptians. The fullest recorded version of the agreement is that in al-MAQRĪZĪ's *al-Khiṭaṭ* (Plans), written more than 700 years after the actual date of the treaty. According to al-Maqrīzī, the Egyptians and the Nubians promised not to make war on one another, and each agreed to guarantee safe conduct of the other's citizens when traveling. In addition, the Nubians were to return any runaway slaves or Muslim outlaws who fell into their hands, to look after a mosque that the Muslims had built at Dongola, and to furnish an annual tribute of 360 slaves. In al-Maqrīzī's text there is no mention of any quid pro quo on the part of the Egyptians.

Doubts have been cast on the authenticity of al-Maqrīzī's and other late versions of the *Baqṭ*, written as they were several centuries after the fact. However, a letter found at QAṢR IBRĪM in 1972 confirms the accuracy of many of the treaty provisions reported by al-Maqrīzī. In the letter, which bears the date A.H. 141/A.D. 758, the Abbasid governor Mūsā ibn Ka'b complains to the king of Makouria about various Nubian transgressions of the *Baqṭ*. Among his specific complaints were that the Nubians were not making the annual payment of slaves, were harboring runaway slaves, were protecting Egyptian fugitives, and were mistreating Egyptian merchants and diplomats.

The one provision of the *Baqṭ*, as reported by al-Maqrīzī, that appears to be clearly anachronistic relates to a mosque at Dongola. There was certainly no mosque at Dongola in 632, or even 300 years later, when IBN SALĪM AL-ASWĀNĪ visited the place. He and his followers were obliged to retire to the desert to perform the sacrifice of 'Id al-Aḍḥāh, as he reported in his *Kitāb Akhbār al-Nūbah* (Reports on Nubia).

Because of its unusual provisions, the status of the *Baqṭ* was disputed by Muslim jurists themselves. The annual payment of slaves was regarded by some as a kind of tribute, but most commentators characterized it as a gift *(hadiyyah)*. The agreement itself was sometimes designated as a *ṣulḥ*, or imposed settlement, but in fact the Nubians had not been militarily defeated or subjugated. Consequently, other writers rejected the term *ṣulḥ*, and referred to the *Baqṭ* as a truce *(hudnah)* or neutralization *(muwāda'ah)*.

The *Baqṭ* remained at least nominally in force for more than 600 years, and it largely shaped the course of Egyptian–Nubian relations in the Middle Ages. After its signing, the Egyptians never again attempted the conquest of Makouria, although they often complained of the Nubians' failure to abide by the terms of the treaty. In 835 the annual payment of slaves had apparently not been met for fourteen years, and the newly installed Caliph al-Mu'taṣim sent an urgent demand that the full arrears be made up. Such a demand was far beyond the resources of the Nubian king Zacharias, and consequently his son George went as an envoy to Baghdad to negotiate with the caliph. According to historians the royal envoy was received with honor and was sent home loaded with gifts. The fourteen-year arrears were forgiven and the Nubian quota of slaves was made payable every three years instead of every year. Some minor changes were made in the provisions of exchange; among other things, wine was excluded from the Egyptian payment.

The advent of Fatimid rule in Egypt in 969 was accompanied by a renewed demand for payment of the *Baqṭ*, which was evidently once again in arrears. This was the occasion for the famous diplomatic mission of Ibn Salīm al-Aswānī, who went to Dongola to present the Fatimid demand directly to the king of Makouria. His mission resulted in the establishment of exceptionally cordial relations between the Nubians and the Fatimids, even though the *Baqṭ* payment seems to have lapsed. There is no further mention of it either in Fatimid or in Ayyubid times.

The coming of Mamluk rule in 1260 was accompanied by an immediate demand for a resumption of the *Baqṭ*. The Mamluks, unlike their predecessors, evidently looked upon the agreement as a *ṣulḥ*, and upon the Nubians as vassals. Consequently, they were quite ready to back up their demands by military force. Mamluk armies invaded Nubia eight times between 1276 and 1323, usually for the purpose of installing a puppet king who would acknowledge Mamluk suzerainty and would resume the *Baqṭ* payment. Nevertheless, they were outmaneuvered by the Muslim BANŪ AL-KANZ, who eventually obtained the throne of Makouria for themselves. With the accession of a Muslim ruler at Dongola in 1323, the requirement of the *Baqṭ* payment was formally declared to be at an end.

BIBLIOGRAPHY

Adams, W. Y. *Nubia, Corridor to Africa*, pp. 451–58. Princeton, N.J., 1977.

Burckhardt, J. L. *Travels in Nubia*, pp. 511–16. London, 1819.

Forand, P. "Early Muslim Relations with Nubia." *Der Islam* 48 (1971):111–21.

Hinds, M., and H. Sakkout. "A Letter from the Governor of Egypt to the King of Nubia and Muqurra Concerning Egyptian–Nubian Relations in 141/758." In *Studia Arabica et Islamica*, ed. Wadad al-Qadi. Beirut, 1981.

Vantini, G. *Christianity in the Sudan*, pp. 65–70. Bologna, 1981.

WILLIAM Y. ADAMS

BARAMŪN, AL-, city located in the Egyptian Delta about 6 miles (10 km) northeast of al-Manṣūrah in the province of Daqahliyyah. The city was a bishopric by 1257, when Bishop Mīkhā'īl of al-Baramūn was present at the consecration of the holy chrism (Munier, 1943, p. 34). A medieval list of churches in Egypt indicates that there was a church of al-Malāk Mīkhā'īl in al-Baramūn (see Amélineau, 1893, pp. 578, 580).

BIBLIOGRAPHY

Amélineau, E. *La Géographie de l'Egypte à l'époque copte*, p. 88. Paris, 1893.

Munier, H. *Recueil des listes épiscopales de l'église copte*. Cairo, 1943.

Timm, S. *Das christlich-koptische Ägypten in arabischer Zeit*, Vol. 1, pp. 340–41. Wiesbaden, 1984.

RANDALL STEWART

BARARI, AL-. *See* Pilgrimages.

BARDENHEWER, OTTO (1851–1935), German ecclesiastical historian specializing in patristic studies. He was born at Munich-Gladbach and educated at Bonn and Würzburg. He lectured on exegesis of both the Old and the New Testament at Munich and Münster. His one-volume *Patrologie* (Freiburg, 1894) appeared in numerous editions and was translated into English by T. J. Shahan (St. Louis, 1908). Later he published a much more extensive work entitled *Geschichte der altkirchlichen Literatur* (5 vols., Freiburg, 1902–1932). This work is the most complete on the subject to date. It deals with the Greek literature associated with the church fathers from Alexandria in Volume 4 and Syrian literature in Volumes 4 and 5.

BIBLIOGRAPHY

Sickenbeger, J. *Erinnerungen an Otto Bardenhewer*. Freiburg, 1937.

AZIZ S. ATIYA

BAR HEBRAEUS (Ibn al-'Ibrī), Orthodox Syrian, born at Malaṭiyyah in 1226. His full name was Abū al-Faraj Jamāl al-Dīn ibn Tāj al-Dīn Hārūn ibn Tūmā al-Malaṭī. He came from a family of Christian (not Jewish, as has sometimes been maintained) origin. He studied medicine and philosophy with his father, and then emigrated to Antioch in 1243 after the Mongol invasion. In 1244 he became a monk, and under the name of Gregorius was consecrated bishop of Gubos on 12 September, 1246, and then bishop of Aleppo in 1252. In 1264, he became *maphrian* (consecrator) of Cilicia at Sīs (and hence head of the Eastern Jacobites). He made his home in Mosul, but often journeyed to Tabrīz and Marāghah, capital of the Mongol forces, where he died on 30 July 1286. The greatest thinker of the Syrian church in the Middle Ages, he composed numerous works in Syriac concerning nearly every religious topic.

He is known in Arabic for his *Mukhtaṣar Tārīkh al-Duwal* (Short History of the World), which was published in Oxford in 1663 by E. Pococke with a Latin translation; it was reedited and translated many times thereafter. This history, a résumé of his great chronicle written in Syriac, was composed at the request of Muslim scholars in one month's time in 1285, shortly before his death. It is divided into ten great ages, beginning with the creation of the world, ending with the death of the Mongol Ilchan Arghūn (1285), and covering the Medes, Greeks, Franks, Byzantines, and Arabs.

None of Ibn al-'Ibrī's works was mentioned by any Copt in the Middle Ages, not even Abū al-Barakāt ibn Kabar, probably because Ibn al-'Ibrī came too late in relation to the Coptic Golden Age. However, a detailed research into the catalogs of Arabic manuscripts shows that he was already known to the Copts of the fourteenth century. In fact, a manuscript in the National Library, Paris (Arabe 296), which contains the *History of the Dynasties*, was copied by an anonymous Copt in the fourteenth century, and the same may be said of a manuscript in the Laurenziana, Florence (Oriental 93). Later, in 1693, Yūsuf ibn 'Aṭiyyah, known by the name of Quzmān, copied this same text (National Library, Paris, Arabe 299). At the end of the seventeenth century, an anonymous Copt also made a copy of this text for the Orientalist Fourmont; a fragment of this copy survives (Paris, Arabe 809). At the end of the eighteenth century, still another copy was made in Egypt by Mīkhā'īl al-Ṣabbāgh (Munich, Arabic 377). Among the thirty-five manuscripts of this history thus far identified some probably originated in Cairo, but information about this is lacking in the catalogs.

Bar Hebraeus' liturgical work, *Manārat al-Aqdās* (Lamp of the Sanctuary), seems to have been unknown to the Copts before the eighteenth century. However, it is attested in two manuscripts at the Coptic Patriarchate in Cairo: (1) the Theology 337 (Simaykah, no. 434), copied in 1799 by both the priest Jirjis al-Isnāwī and by Ibrāhīm Abū Ṭabl ibn Sim'ān al-Khawānkī; and (2) the Theology 323, copied by the latter in 1813.

BIBLIOGRAPHY

Baumstark, A. *Geschichte der syrischen Literatur mit Anschluss der christlich-palästinensischen Texte,* pp. 312–20. Bonn, 1922.

Kawerau, P. *Das Christentum des Ostens,* pp. 63–82. Cologne and Mainz, 1972.

Nau, F. "Bar Hébraeus, Grégoire Abulfarage." In *Dictionnaire de théologie catholique,* Vol. 2, cols. 401–406. Paris, 1932.

Ortiz de Urbino, I. *Patrologia syriaca,* pp. 207ff. Rome, 1958.

Segal, J. B. "Ibn al-'Ibrī." In *The Encyclopaedia of Islam,* Vol. 3, pp. 804–805. New edition, Leiden, 1971.

KHALIL SAMIR, S.J.

BARLĀM AND YUWĀṢAF, a collection of fables widely diffused in the Christian East; it is also known among Buddhists, Muslims, and Jews.

In Arabic, these fables are found from the beginning of the ninth century. Other recensions or reworkings of the lost Arabic original are known. Two of these are in Georgian, and these gave rise to the Greek metaphrastic version. The early Christian Arabic version known to us probably derives from the Greek, and was no doubt made in the eleventh century. The earliest known manuscript of this version (Sinai Arabic 540) can be dated to the twelfth century.

The Arabic version soon spread among the Copts. We find it in a thirteenth-century manuscript (Coptic Patriarchate, Cairo, History 43; Graf, no. 530; Simaykah, no. 605). At the end of the thirteenth century, the Coptic encyclopedist Abū al-Barakāt IBN KABAR (d. 1324) mentions the *Kitāb Barlām* or *Barla'ām al-Nāsik wa-Yuwāṣaf* in his Christian Arabic bibliography, among the Coptic medieval works.

Indeed, two fourteenth-century Arabic manuscripts of Coptic provenance attribute this novel to a certain Yūhannā of Dayr Mār Mūsā. This is probably the monastery mentioned by ABŪ AL-MAKĀRIM beside Dahshūr, opposite Ḥilwān. This might be the name of the author of a reworking, or else simply a Coptization of Melchite traditions that attribute this novel to Yūḥannā of the Monastery of Saint Sabas, or to Yūḥannā al-Dimashqī, or to Yūḥannā of Mount Sinai. This question has not yet been studied. There are at least three manuscripts giving this attribution, all of them Coptic (Coptic Patriarchate, Cairo, History 41, Graf, no. 566, Simaykah, no. 647, fourteenth century; National Library, Paris, Arabe 271, also fourteenth century; and Arabe 272, copied in 1643).

In the seventeenth century another attribution to "a monk of the Mount of Gethsemane" (al-Jasmāniyyah) made its appearance among the Copts. This is found in three manuscripts, all of Coptic origin (Coptic Patriarchate, Cairo, History 4, Graf, no. 565, Simaykah, no. 619, copied in 1605; National Library, Paris, Arabe 273, copied in 1752 and restored in 1763; Arabe 274, copied in 1778).

Other Arabic manuscripts of this novel are of Coptic provenance, witnessing to the diffusion of this text up to the modern period (Coptic Patriarchate, Cairo, History 42, Simaykah, no. 604, copied in the fourteenth century or at the beginning of the fifteenth century; Coptic Patriarchate, Cairo, History 86, Simaykah, no. 669, first text, dating unknown, but bequeathed to the patriarchate in 1814; National Library, Paris, Arabe 4792, copied in the nineteenth century; Arabe 4891, copied in 1864). At the beginning of the twentieth century, two Copts, Wahbā Bey and Ḥabīb Jirjis, edited the only published Arabic version.

The Melchites often illuminated the text of this novel with numerous miniatures (see, for example, the Paris Arabe manuscripts 273 and 274, the Vatican Arabic manuscript 692, the Dayr al-Sha'īr 953, etc.); we know of only one illuminated Coptic manuscript, however (Coptic Patriarchate, Cairo, History 19, Graf, no. 531, Simaykah, no. 611, copied in the sixteenth century with some clumsy illuminations: "poorly designed pictures of people," according to Simaykah).

Last, from the Arabic recension of the Copts, an Ethiopian translation was made, under Sarṣa Dengel (1563–1597), the work of 'Enbākōm, or Habaqqūq, an Ethiopian of Yemenite origin. One of the manuscripts of this translation (British Library, London, Ethiopian 275), copied between 1746 and 1755, mentions Barṣawmā ibn Abī al-Faraj as the author of the Arabic recension. This person is otherwise unknown.

BIBLIOGRAPHY

Dodge, B. *The Fihrist of al-Nadīm,* Vol. 1, pp. 260, 359. New York, 1970.

Gimaret, D. "Traces et parallèles du Kitāb Bilawhar wa-Būdasaf dans la tradition arabe." *Bulletin d'é-*

tudes orientales 24 (1971):97–133.

———. *Le livre de Bilawhar et Būdāsaf selon la version arabe ismaélienne.* Geneva and Paris, 1971.

———. *Kitāb Bilawhar wa-Būdasf.* Recherches de l'Institut de lettres orientales de Beyrouth A6. Beirut, 1972.

Kamil, M. "Translations from Arabic in Ethiopic Literature." *Bulletin de la Société d'Archéologie copte* 7 (1941):61–71.

Nadīm, al-. *Kitāb al-Fihrist,* ed. Riḍā Tajaddud, pp. 132, 186. Tehran, 1971.

Nasrallah, J. *Histoire du mouvement littéraire dans l'église melchite du Ve au XXe siècle,* Vol. 3, pt. 1 (969–1250), pp. 178–86. Louvain and Paris, 1983.

Wahbā Bey and Habīb Jirjis. *Sīrat Barlām wa-Yuwāṣaf.* Cairo, 1909.

KHALIL SAMIR, S.J.

BARNS, JOHN WINTOUR BALDWIN (1912–1974), British Egyptologist and papyrologist, born in Bristol. He was educated at the University of Bristol and at Oxford. There he studied under C. H. Roberts and B. Gunn. He was a Lady Wallis Budge research fellow in Egyptology at University College, Oxford (1945–1953), lecturer in papyrology at Oxford (1953–1965), and professor of Egyptology at Oxford (1965–1974). He was ordained in the Church of England in 1956.

Although he published comparatively little in the field of Coptic studies, his strength lay in his teaching of the language and literature. Apart from his papyrological studies and articles, his works include *The Ashmolean Ostracon of Sinuhe* (London, 1952); *Five Ramesseum Papyri* (Oxford, 1956); *Four Martyrdoms from the Pierpont Morgan Coptic Codices,* with E. A. Raymond (Oxford, 1973); and *Nag Hammadi Codices: Greek and Coptic Papyri from the Cartonnage of the Covers,* with G. M. Browne and J. C. Shelton (Leiden, 1981). He died in Oxford.

BIBLIOGRAPHY

Davies, W. V. "John Wintour Baldwin Barns." *Journal of Egyptian Archeology* 60 (1974):243–46.

Lloyd-Jones, H. Editorial Foreword. *Journal of Egyptian Archaeology* 60 (1974):3.

Maher, E. "Rev. John Wintour Baldwin Barns 1912–1974." *Bulletin de la Société d'archéologie copte* 21 (1971–1973):219–22.

"Nécrologie." *Bulletin de la Société française d'égyptologie* 69 (1974):4.

M. L. BIERBRIER

BARONIUS, CESARE (1538–1607), Italian ecclesiastical historian and churchman. He was elevated to the cardinalate in 1596 and, the next year, became prefect of the Vatican Library. He missed becoming pope because of Spanish opposition. His major work as a historian is the monumental but unfinished *Annales Ecclesiastici.* He planned it as a complete chronological record of the history of the Catholic church. By his death, he had reached the year 1198, and others tried to continue his work, though unsuccessfully. In his lifetime, he published twelve folio-size volumes (Rome, 1588–1593). The work was reedited by J. D. MANSI in thirty-five volumes (Lucca, 1738–1759). A new edition (ed. A. Theiner, 1864–1883) with all continuations (37 vols., Bar-le-Duc and Paris, 1864–1883) was originally planned in fifty volumes but was never completed. Baronius reproduced numerous extensive selections from the original sources, and excerpts from the *Annales* appeared in French, Italian, German, Polish, and Arabic. This ambitious enterprise, however, fell short of modern standards of research and was rather defective when it came to Eastern Christendom. Here his information was insufficient, as he saw the events from a strictly Roman Catholic point of view.

BIBLIOGRAPHY

Calenzio, G. *La vita e gli scritti del Cardenale Cesare Baronio.* Rome, 1907.

Libero, G. de. *Cesare Baronio, padre della storia ecclesiastica.* Alba, 1939.

AZIZ S. ATIYA

BARSANUPHIANS, one of several Alexandrian splinter groups of those Monophysites who, because they had rejected the communion of their patriarch, were known as *Acephaloi* (headless). They separated themselves from the Jacobites in the latter part of the fifth century under Emperor Zeno. In the patriarchate of ALEXANDER II (705–730), John of Ṣā converted the Barsanuphians at al-Munā to orthodoxy. At the beginning of the ninth century MARK II, patriarch of Alexandria, baptized the two leaders of the Barsanuphians, George and his son Abraham, at the Church of the Martyr Saint Menas at Maryūt. The rest of the Barsanuphians then followed their leaders back into the communion of the church.

The Barsanuphius from whom the sect derived its

name was not BARSANUPHIUS the Anchorite monk but a pretender to the episcopal rank.

BIBLIOGRAPHY

Neale, J. M. *A History of the Holy Eastern Church: The Patriarchate of Alexandria*, Vol. 2, pp. 22, 137. London, 1847.

RANDALL STEWART

BARSANUPHIUS, SAINT, fifth–sixth century anchorite. Although he is not mentioned in the Coptic SYNAXARION, Barsanuphius deserves a place of honor because of his outstanding holiness and the exceptional influence he exercised in the history of Christian spirituality. He was of Egyptian origin, and his mother tongue was Coptic. We know nothing of his youth or life until we find him as a hermit in a monastery founded near Gaza at the end of the fifth century by Seridos. "The Grand Old Man," as he was called, never left his cell and saw nobody except Seridos, who acted as his secretary. Barsanuphius was not only the spiritual director of the monks of the community of Seridos and the superior but was also consulted by a host of monks, priests, laymen, and bishops of the region. All these exchanges were carried out in writing through the intermediary of Seridos, who passed on the requests and replies, the latter being written down by him in Greek to the dictation of the Grand Old Man or the "alter ego" of Barsanuphius, "the other Old Man," John, a hermit in a neighboring cell.

About 850 letters from this correspondence, collected by a monk of the community, have been preserved and were published by Nicodemus the Hagiographer at Venice in 1816. A good many of these letters were translated into Arabic and Georgian. The *Garden of the Monks*, published in Cairo, contains long extracts from them. Multiple editions in Slavonic and Russian appeared in the eighteenth and nineteenth centuries.

This dossier of undisputed authenticity is the only document of this kind that informs us about the practice of spiritual direction in ancient monasticism. Brought up on the Bible and the apothegms of the fathers, which he quoted constantly, Barsanuphius was indeed in the line of his Egyptian masters by reason of his rigorous asceticism and deep spiritual life. He also emulated them in his humility and the extraordinary gifts with which God endowed him. Among his most famous disciples at least two names well known in Oriental hagiography must be mentioned: Dorotheus and Dositheus.

BIBLIOGRAPHY

ΒΙΒΛΟΣ . . . ΒΑΡΣΑΝΟΥΦΙΟΥ ΚΑΙ ΙΩΑΝΝΟΥ, ed. Nikodemos Hagiorita. Venice, 1816. Second ed., Soterios N. Schoinas. Volos, 1960.

Chitty, D. J. *Barsanuphius and John, Questions and Answers.* PO 31, pt. 3. Paris, 1966.

Hausherr, I. "Barsanuphe." In *Dictionnaire de spiritualité*, Vol. 1, cols. 1255–62. Paris, 1937.

Regnault, L. *Maîtres spirituels au désert de Gaza.* Solesmes, 1967.

Regnault, L.; P. Lemaire; and B. Outtier. *Barsanuphe et Jean de Gaza, Correspondance.* Solesmes, 1972.

LUCIEN REGNAULT

BARSŪM THE NAKED, SAINT. Numerous sources assure us of Barsūm's historicity and give us some details of his life. He was born to a well-to-do family in Cairo at an unstated date. He lost his parents while he was young, and his maternal uncle became his guardian. When the uncle squandered his ward's inheritance, Barsūm refused to take him to court. He became secretary to the regent Shajar al-Durr, widow of the sultan al-Malik al-Ṣāliḥ, in 1250. (Christians were not unusual in the administration.) When he decided to live as a hermit he took up residence in a small, gloomy cave that was inhabited by a serpent. The cave is still shown today in the Church of Saint Mercurius (ABŪ SAYFAYN) in Old Cairo. He lived there for twenty years (the Arabic Synaxarion speaks of fifteen years, and the Ethiopian, of thirty-three), but when a period of oppression of Christians came, he climbed to the roof of the church, where he remained, enduring there the cold and the heat. This was reported to the chief of police of Cairo and several Muslim authorities, for it was forbidden for anyone to live night and day in a public building. As a result, he was put in prison, where, according to the Synaxarion, he remained less than a week. When he came out, it was to take refuge in the monastery of DAYR SHAHRĀN, to the south of Cairo, a monastery that was dedicated to Saint Mercurius and received his name after his death. According to the testimony of Ibn al-Suqāʿī, Barsūm remained there for seventeen years, from 1300, living in a courtyard on a heap of dust and ashes. Because he wore hardly any garments, he was called "the Naked." He died on 5 Nasī A.M. 1033/28 August A.D. 1317. He was buried in front of the door of the church of the monastery. Numerous miracles were attributed to him, as the Arabic life recounts.

He was greatly renowned, and the Muslim historian al-Maqrīzī mentions him in speaking of the Monastery of Shahrān (1853, Vol. 2, p. 501).

BIBLIOGRAPHY

Budge, E. A. W. *The Book of the Saints of the Ethiopian Church,* 4 vols. Cambridge, 1928.

Crum, W. E. "Barsauma the Naked." *Proceedings of the Society of Biblical Archeology* 29 (1907):135–49, 187–206.

Troupeau, G. "Compte-rendu d'Ibn al-Ṣuqā'ī." *Arabica* 33 (1976):330–31.

RENÉ-GEORGES COQUIN

BARTALOMEWOS. *See* Ethiopian Prelates.

BASHBĪSH, a town in Egypt said by medieval Muslim authors to be the forerunner of Niṣf Awwal Bashbīsh and Niṣf Thanī Bashbīsh, located in the Gharbiyyah province.

The HISTORY OF THE PATRIARCHS mentions Bashbīsh in passing as a geographical reference point. During the patriarchate of ZACHARIAS (1004–1032), a conflict arose between the bishop of Ṭānah and the bishop of Samannūd over which bishopric could rightfully claim al-Kom Sandara. According to the account, this place lay between Bashbīsh and Shubrā Damānah. It is uncertain whether this Bashbīsh is the same city spoken of by the Muslim authors.

BIBLIOGRAPHY

Timm, S. *Das christlich-koptische Ägypten in arabischer Zeit,* Vol. 1, pp. 353–54. Wiesbaden, 1984.

RANDALL STEWART

BASHMŪR, AL-, an area in Egypt in which the Christian inhabitants revolted against Arab rule in the eighth and ninth centuries (see BASHMURIC REVOLTS).

Christianity in the area suffered greatly as a result of the Bashmurites' final defeat by the Arabs, but it was not quashed completely, as evidenced by the visit of a presbyter from al-Bashmūr in Cairo around 1200.

The exact boundaries of al-Bashmūr are uncertain because the medieval sources are discrepant. The HISTORY OF THE PATRIARCHS says that the area was most easily accessible from Tida and Shubrā. This statement would place al-Bashmūr in the northern Delta, just south of Lake Burullus. ABŪ ṢĀLIḤ THE ARMENIAN averred that in a later period at least the inhabitants of al-Bashmūr and the inhabitants of al-Bashrūd were the same people. The exact location of al-Bashrūd is similarly uncertain, but it appears to have been northwest of Sakhā (Timm, 1984, p. 360). IBN ḤAWQAL stated that the lake in Nastarūh was also called Buḥayrat al-Bashmūr (in Maspero and Wiet, 1914–1919, p. 36), suggesting that the region of the Bashmurites was near Nastarūh, that is, north of the cities known today as Disūq and Kafr al-Shaykh. Abū al-Fidā, however, placed al-Bashmūr between the Dumyāṭ arm of the Nile and Ashmūn Ṭanāḥ (Maspero and Wiet, p. 44).

It is possible that the boundaries of al-Bashmūr have not been constant throughout the centuries. Perhaps from the mid-eighth to the mid-ninth century, al-Bashmūr encompassed the entire marsh region northeast of Fuwwah extending as far to the east as just north of Dikirnis. Later it may have been limited to the eastern part of this area. The name al-Bashmūr survives in this region as the name of a Nile canal that breaks off about 4.5 miles (7 km) east of al-Manṣūrah by al-Salamūn and runs through the area between the Damietta arm of the Nile and Dikirnis before emptying into the al-Sirw canal some 3.5 miles (5.5 km) south of Daqahlah.

BIBLIOGRAPHY

Maspero, J., and G. Wiet. *Matériaux pour servir à la géographie de l'Egypte.* Cairo, 1914–1919.

Timm, S. *Das christlich-koptische Ägypten in arabischer Zeit,* Vol. 1, pp. 354–56. Wiesbaden, 1984.

RANDALL STEWART

BASHMURIC. *See Appendix.*

BASHMURIC REVOLTS. In the seventh, eighth, and ninth centuries Copts revolted a number of times against the Arabic administration in different parts of Egypt and were rapidly crushed. Only in the Bashmuric region (see BASHMŪR, AL-) were Copts able to resist for a relatively long period against repeated attacks of the Arabic army by land and by sea and to inflict heavy losses on their oppressors while enduring lengthy sieges.

Though Arabic geographers are not consistent in their delineation of the borders of al-Bashmūr, it appears that the Bashmurites lived in the marshy regions that lay near the Mediterranean coast in the northern part of the Delta between the Rosetta and Damietta branches of the Nile close to the lake of Idkū. The region had a history of intransigence; through the centuries its inhabitants had revolted against their Egyptian, Roman, and Byzantine masters. This was also the last region in Egypt to submit to the Arabs, years after the rest of the country had been conquered.

The marshy land of al-Bashmūr with its low-lying sandy banks offered two major advantages: security and economic self-sufficiency. Access to the inhabited parts of the region was through sandy banks that were sometimes too narrow to admit the passage of more than one person, and the marshes with their thickets of reeds served as cover for revolutionary operations. Thus nature offered this region protection from intrusion and natural cover, elements denied all other parts of Egypt where the flatness of the land afforded easy access to inhabited places, with no forests or hills to hide insurgents. The Bashmuric region was the only part of Egypt where the Arabic authorities could not apply their policy of settling Arabic tribes among the native population to prevent revolts.

The economic infrastructure of the region also aided the Bashmurites. While they did not possess the kind of fertile fields that gave rise elsewhere in Egypt to widespread civilization and later to foreign occupation, they did have space for limited agriculture, which, in combination with the region's richness in fish and fowl, provided enough food to withstand any siege. These conditions rendered the Bashmurites far less vulnerable than the fellahin in other parts of Egypt, who depended on an intricate irrigation network that could be easily cut by the army in case of revolt.

Arabic historians viewed the Bashmuric uprisings as a reaction to the heavy fiscal demands placed on the Copts, a view that seems to have influenced the conclusions of quite a few modern historians. However, one can discern a relationship between an increase in Arabic intolerance and the beginning of the Bashmuric revolts. One notes a difference between the attitude of the Bashmurites and the passive acquiescence of other Copts in the face of this growing intolerance.

The difficulty in defining the exact limits of the region occupied by the Bashmurites makes it impossible to date precisely the beginning of the series of Bashmuric revolts. The recorded anti-Arab revolts that were a reaction against the growing hardening of the Arabic policy from the second part of the seventh century began to occur as early as the close of that century, first in the eastern part of the Delta and later extending to the whole Delta as well as to Upper Egypt. The topography of the Bashmurite region and the reluctance of the army to operate there suggest that the revolts may have begun in this area before extending to the neighboring areas of the Delta. One should also bear in mind that it was in the northern part of the Delta that Byzantines landed for a short time in 720, which could mean that the area was already in agitation or even in open revolt.

Revolts flared up in the last years of the Umayyads, perhaps because the caliph Marwān could not tolerate trouble in Egypt, his last stronghold. SĀWĪRUS IBN AL-MUQAFFA' provides precious information about the dramatic last operation against the Bashmurites before the arrival of the Abbasids in Egypt. It seems that Hawthara, Marwān's governor in Egypt, had already failed to end the revolt, in spite of his repeated expeditions by land and by sea. When Marwān arrived in Egypt to deal with the uprising personally, he proposed an armistice, probably to consolidate his position in front of the advancing Abbasids. When the Copts refused the treaty, Marwān joined the army he had brought from Damascus to the troops already fighting the Copts in Egypt. As further pressure upon the Copts, Hawthara took KHĀ'ĪL I (744–767), the Coptic patriarch, hostage, transported him to Rashīd (Rosetta), which was a government stronghold, and threatened to kill him if the Bashmurites did not end the hostilities. Far from being intimidated by this step, the Copts avenged it by not only attacking the besieging army, which had to evacuate its positions, but also by destroying Rashīd. Marwān responded by ordering his troops to sack the villages, churches, and monasteries they encountered.

The arrival of the Abbasids did not improve the situation, as the political disorder between them and the Umayyads encouraged revolts by the Copts and by the Arabic settlers. Arabic historians speak about the Bashrūds (a corruption of Bashmurites), who joined the revolt of 767, which flared up in the Delta. The expedition sent by the governor Yazīd ibn Ḥātem against them was defeated, his local high officials were killed, and the army retreated to al-Fusṭāṭ (Old Cairo).

In 830, the caliph al-Ma'mūn, desiring to quash the rebellions in the Delta, sent a strong army to the area under the command of the Turkish general Afshīn. The army destroyed the rebels in the eastern part of the Delta and in Alexandria, but was helpless against the Bashmurites. Afshīn approached the patriarch and asked him to use his influence to stop the revolts. The patriarch agreed to intervene, but his letters to the insurgents were fruitless and his envoys achieved no success.

Finally Afshīn asked the caliph to come in person. Al-Ma'mūn arrived in Egypt accompanied by Dionysus of Tell Mahre, the patriarch of Antioch, who was to help in negotiations with the Coptic patriarch. When the two patriarchs were unable to obtain any positive results, the caliph took command of the army and launched a systematic attack on the rebels. Losses were great on both sides. To stop the slaughter, the caliph offered the Bashmurites an armistice. The insurgents accepted the offer. The temporary success of this rebellion did not achieve any amelioration of the conditions that had made the Bashmurites revolt. Some of them were deported to Iraq; others were sent to Syria and were sold as slaves in Damascus. The army destroyed and burned the entire area to wipe out all possibility of further revolts.

Thus ended the last revolt of the Copts in Egypt. Without any real political plan or any national leadership, without any organized armed force, and in the face of a strong, experienced army, these spasmodic revolts were an indication of desperate courage. Not only did they achieve nothing but they drained the force and pride of the Copts. Nonetheless, these revolts are important for Coptic history, as they shed light on the character of the Coptic masses.

BIBLIOGRAPHY

Abbot, N. *The Kurrah Papyri from Aphrodito in the Oriental Institute.* Chicago, 1938.

Atiya, A. S. "Kibt." In *The Encyclopaedia of Islam,* Vol. 5, ed. C. E. Bosworth; E. van Donzel; B. Lewis; and C. Pellat, pp. 90–95. New ed., Leiden, 1985.

Becker, C. *Beiträge zur Geschichte Ägyptens unter dem Islam.* Strasbourg, 1902–1903. Repr. Philadelphia, 1977.

Bell, H. I. *Greek Papyri in the British Museum,* Vol. 5. London, 1917.

Butler, A. J. *The Arab Conquest of Egypt and the Last Thirty Years of the Roman Dominion,* 2nd ed. Oxford, 1978.

Cahen, C. "Ḍarība." In *The Encyclopaedia of Islam,* Vol. 2, ed. B. Lewis; C. Pellat; and J. Schacht, pp. 142–45. New ed. Leiden, 1965.

Quatremère, E. *Recherches critiques et historiques.* Paris, 1808.

Tritton, A. S. *The Califs and Their Non-Muslim Subject.* Oxford, 1930.

Wüstenfeld, H. F. *Die Statthälter von Ägypten zur Zeit der Chalifen.* Göttingen, 1875–1876.

MOUNIR MEGALLY

BASHRUDAT, AL-. *See* Bashmūr, al-.

BASHRUT. *See* Bashmūr, al-.

BASIL, SAINT, CANONS OF. *See* Canons of Saint Basil.

BASIL THE GREAT, archbishop of Caesarea in Cappadocia (330–379). Basil supported the tradition of ATHANASIUS in continuing the defense of orthodoxy against ARIANISM, particularly in Asia Minor. He was an active theologian, but was able to connect theological work with ascetic practice.

Basil's background and education were Hellenistic. The descendant of a rich and longtime Christian family, he began his studies with fifteen years in Caesarea in Cappadocia, continued in Constantinople, and moved to Athens in 351. Although Basil considered classical learning profane and took a critical point of view toward it, he made good use of his knowledge of the old writers and of the classical world.

As a Christian, he was foremost an ascetic and a monk, a founder of monasteries who gathered persons of like spirit around him. But he also became involved in church practice and church politics, became a presbyter, and in 370 archbishop of Caesarea. Basil was renowned as an eloquent preacher of ethics.

He once visited the monasteries of Egypt, where his principles of asceticism and orthodox theology were well accepted along the Nile. As a result we find Basil's name in Coptic literature, although not every homily transmitted under his name is authentic. A complete corpus of Basil's works in Coptic translations does not exist—a situation true in Greek literature as well. Both traditions erroneously handed down the homilies of Basil under the name of Basilios. Illustrative of Basil's popularity in Egypt, the homily on the wedding of Cana of Patriarch Benjamin I includes a quotation by Basil; this is not yet verified.

Some specific homilies attributed to Basil follow.

A homily on Noah's Ark (Vatican Library, Codex Copticus 68, fols. 33–52^{v}) is almost certainly of Greek origin, but is not found in Basil's Greek works and lacks Basilian theological viewpoints. Although this homily is extant in Coptic (Bohairic), Coptic rhetoric is missing. The author's view of the world points to a source in northern Syria and Mesopotamia about 550 to 600. Perhaps this homily came to Egypt via the Syrian colony, since Bohairic appears to be the original translation. It waxes strong in biblical and ethical exhortations. Another homily exists in Sahidic (two versions) about the generation according to the flesh of Our Lord Jesus Christ delivered on 29 Kiyahk. This is attributed in Greek to JOHN CHRYSOSTOM and is dated about the fifth century. Another homily in Bohairic (Vatican Library, Codex 58, fols. 178–94^{v}) treats the important problem of fasting. The Greek original has been found in the Greek works of Basil. However, the Coptic (two manuscripts exist) is an adaptation and revision of the Greek original according to Egyptian requirements. Also, the homilies on the subjects of the end of the world, Solomon's temple, and the parting of the body and soul seem to have been composed by Basil and obviously stem from a Greek origin.

As a preacher, Basil's eloquence revolved around the ideas of God's creation, sin and its consequences, and Mary as a more honorable temple than Solomon's (British Museum, Or. 5001, fols. 130b–162a: Sahidic-Coptic).

A homily that shows that God was not the author of evil can be found in a Bohairic codex containing the works of John Chrysostom. But in Greek the homily is ascribed to Basil. The Coptic version contains some discrepancies when compared to the Greek (Vatican Library, Codex Copticus 57, fols. 74–89^{v}).

Two other homilies delivered in the church of the Archangel Saint Michael exist, as well as some Sahidic *Wonders of the Holy Mercurius,* all under the name of Basil. Basil's Greek introduction to the monastic orders is extant in Sahidic.

Well known in Egypt was a catechesis about the THEOTOKOS, the Virgin Mary, pronounced by Basil on the occasion of the dedication of the church built by Eumenios on 21 Ba'ūnah. This catechesis concerns ethical problems, probably the reason for its popularity in Egypt. It is doubtful that this writing is from Basil. Manuscript and fragments are transmitted in Bohairic and show that different recensions existed (Vatican Library, Codex Copticus 67, fols. 69–89^{v}).

In summary, it is clear that Basil was one of the Greek church fathers most quoted in Coptic literature. His complete works in Coptic are not yet known, but surely the Egyptians translated directly his most popular Greek and Syrian homilies, or revised them, or translated them from existing revisions. Those not known to be authentic were probably translated directly from a Greek original that bears the marks of Basilian philosophy. Such works comprised biblical homilies, or catechetical admonitions about ethics, or eulogies of asceticism.

Finally, we should not forget that the greatest part of the Basilian heritage in the Syrian language must have been transmitted to Egypt through the Syrian colony, whose labors in this field must not be undervalued. The *Anaphora* of Saint Basil, whose best versions appear in Greek and Coptic in the Nile Valley, demonstrate also the popularity and renown of Basil in Egypt (see also ANAPHORA OF SAINT BASIL).

BIBLIOGRAPHY

Budge, E. A. W. *Coptic Homilies in the Dialect of Upper Egypt.* London, 1910; New York, 1977.

Campenhausen, H. Freiherr von. *Griechische Kirchenväter,* pp. 86–100. Urban-Bücher 14. Stuttgart, 1955.

Capelle, D. B., O.S.B. "Les Liturgies basiliennes et saint Basile." In *Un témoin archaique de la liturgie copte de S. Basile,* ed. J. Doresse and Dom E. Lanne, pp. 45–74. Louvain, 1960.

Doresse, J., and D. E. Lanne. *Un Témoin archaique de la liturgie copte de S. Basile.* Bibliothèque du Muséon 47. Louvain, 1960.

Hauschild, W. D. "Basilius von Cäsarea," In *Theologische Realenzyklopädie,* Vol. 5, pp. 301–313. Berlin and New York, 1980.

Hebbelynck, A. and A. van Lantschoot. *Codices Coptici Vaticani, Barberiniani, Borgiani, Rossiani,* Vol. 1. Vatican City, 1937.

Khalil, S., S.J. "La Version arabe du Basile alexandrin (codex Kacmarcik)." *Orientalia Christiana Periodica* 44 (1978):342–90.

Lucchesi, E., and P. Devos. "Un Corpus basilien en copte." *Analecta Bollandiana* 99 (1987):95–100.

Müller, C. D. G. "Die alte koptische Predigt (Versuch eines Überblicks)." Dissertation, Heidelberg 1953; Darmstadt, 1954.

______. "Einige Bemerkungen zur Lars praedicandi der alten koptischen Kirche." *Le Muséon* 67 (1954):231–70.

Orlandi, T. *Elementi di Lingua e Letteratura copta,* p. 116. Milan, 1970.

Vis, H. de. *Homélies coptes de la Vaticane,* Vol. 2, pp. 203–241. Copenhagen, 1929.

C. DETLEF G. MÜLLER

BASILICA, a building type of classical and medieval architecture.

The Non-Christian Basilica

In ancient Rome the basilica was a covered, mostly rectangular, public building with entrances usually on the long sides (one of the few exceptions is the famous basilica at Pompei). Frequently, and especially in the older buildings, the outer walls are even opened up into continuous colonnades. These buildings thus lack an external termination in the strict sense.

The division of the interior into multiple aisles seems to have become common at an early date (Vitruvius, *De aedificiis* 5. 1, 5). Few provincial basilicas were constructed with a single nave. It was not required that the nave should be higher than the side aisles, although examples can be found where this is the case.

One of the requirements of the basilica was that it should be suitable for commercial exchanges and occasional judicial proceedings. From passages in ancient literature that contain references to the function of the basilica (collected by Ohr, 1973, pp. 162ff.), it emerges that it was designed primarily for the more prominent type of business activities. That is, it concerned above all the entrepreneurs and great merchants, whereas retail trade took place in the shops and stalls along the columned streets. To fulfill its function, the basilica had to be spacious and to be located at a central and easily accessible position within the town. In this regard the area around the forum was particularly suitable (Vitruvius, 5. 1, 4).

In its interior, the basilica contained a podium mostly located at one of the end walls for municipal officials, who performed certain notarial functions at the conclusion of contracts and at court decisions.

Because of the great importance of the basilica for ancient commercial activity, a basilica could be found in nearly every Roman municipium. For the most part they were made possible by large endowments from individual citizens, who also spared no expense on their sumptuous furnishings. Famous examples are the Basilica Ulpia in the Forum Traiani in Rome (Macdonald, 1965, pp. 67ff., pl. 74) and the basilica of Septimius Severus at Leptis Magna in North Africa (Apollonj-Ghetti, 1976).

The origins of the basilica are as yet obscure. Even the name ("royal") is a problem: it derives from Greek, but appears in a form that is not attested in contemporary Greek. The form is Latin and current only in the Latin West in this form. Because Vitruvius—though in a very different context—compares the basilica to so-called Egyptian halls (6. 3, 8–10), attempts have been made to derive it from the hypostyle hall prevalent in pharaonic temple architecture, such halls being in several instances furnished with a raised middle section. But this is unconvincing. The two have in common only a very small external and even dispensable feature, whereas they do not correspond at all in regard to their general architectural outline function (see Haeny, 1970, pp. 78–80). Generally speaking, one inclines today toward the assumption that the Greek stoa belonged to the forerunners of the Roman basilica. At any rate, it has the same function, and not infrequently goes back to royal endowments. An important link is provided by the five-aisled stoa in the dock quarter of Delos dating from the end of the third century B.C. (Leroux, 1909). This stoa is different from the Roman basilica only in its structural design, in that the Roman basilica had no need for a central row of columns.

The Christian Basilica

The adoption of the term "basilica" for the Christian house of worship is attested quite early. In its ecclesiastical sense, the word is nevertheless not restricted to a particular structural type. It is rather a label of rank, and may refer to a longitudinal-plan building as well as to a central-plan structure. What is important is that it has to do with a large, conspicuous edifice, as a rule, a cathedral. In the history of art and in archaeology the term basilica means a rectangular, longitudinal-plan structure, normally covered by a wooden roof, and subdivided into several aisles (mostly three or five). Certain North African basilicas exhibit an even larger number of aisles. The breadth of the nave normally exceeds by far that of the side aisles, and it is also considerably loftier, so as to provide room for a row of windows, the clerestory, in the zone of wall above the colonnades on each side, thus clear of the roofs of the side aisles. The roof of the early Christian basilica is, as a rule, a wooden saddleback roof. In some regions where wood was scarce, a barrel-vault roofing has been adopted at an early stage. The roofs of the side aisles are for the most part built as shed roofs, but they may also be constructed as flat roofs—particularly in regions with little rainfall as, for example, in Egypt.

In gallery churches the aisles often possess two floors. Such churches are common in the Eastern countries, and presumably originated mainly from the requirement of keeping the sexes of the believers apart. The necessary stairs are for the most part located at the short sides of the *narthex,* which in Syria led to the development of a kind of double tower facade. Otherwise the narthex is a kind of entrance hall, which ordinarily spans the full width of the church and very frequently opens outward into a continuous series of *columns.* The narthex also occurs in the same form with central-plan edifices.

The ritual center of the basilica, finally, is the *sanctuary* at the eastern end. It exhibits a variety of designs, in accordance with the various liturgical ordinances in the different parts of the Christian *oikoumene* (world). In the West and in Asia Minor, the basilica normally ends in a semicircular *apse* that as a rule protrudes from the otherwise straight east wall as a simple cylinder-shaped and occasionally polygonally encased part of the building. In Egypt and Syria, the apse, from the early fifth century onward, is flanked on both sides by two lateral chambers (so-called pastophorias), designed for subsidiary liturgical functions. The place where the altar stands is usually (apart from some churches of Syria and Palestine) not inside the apse but in front of it, in a section enclosed by low cancelli (presbytery) and in many cases raised above the floor of the nave by at least one step. In terms of spatial architecture this presbytery actually belongs to the area of the nave.

A special development of the basilica is represented by the transept basilica in which the section of the nave in front of the sanctuary was expanded on both sides. Since the introduction of such a feature to the building was accompanied by a change in the orientation of the beams, and consequently, also, in the ridge line, it is referred to as a transept. It may have one or more aisles. A pseudotransept occurs when only the exterior profile of the basilica in front of the apse is extended, while in the interior only the number of aisles in this part is increased, as is the case with the Leonidas Basilica in Lechaion at Corinth and the Old Church at Old Dongola.

Besides these variations in the design of the basilica caused by the geographical position and by different local building traditions, further divergences arise from the distinct evolution of the basilica in each region. In the Greek sphere, as well as in Syria (presumably by way of Constantinople), additional side chapels were required. Here, in the seventh or eighth century, the so-called templon became fully established. This is a higher rising screen the upper zone of which was shut by curtains. Its original function was to separate more emphatically the sanctuary from the part of the church where the laity stayed and to guard the acts performed in the sanctuary from the view of the believers. A similar development is to be recorded for almost the entire East. On the contrary, in Western architecture the region of the altar remains open and visible. Notable here is the development of the tower facade of the basilica. In the East the multiplication of altars led, furthermore, to a remarkable elaboration of the ritual.

The construction of basilicas came to an end in Eastern architecture at the beginning of the Middle Byzantine period, around the middle of the tenth century. Before that date the basilica had been the most widespread building type, despite the construction of numerous central-plan edifices. In the West the basilica was used almost without interruption until the time of the Renaissance. During this time, it underwent several modifications of style, but nonetheless never lost its specific shape.

The question of the origins of the Christian basilica is also still an obscure one. Attempts have been made to derive it from the pagan market basilica, from the columned streets common in the East Roman Empire, or from the basilica-like throne halls that can be found in some imperial palaces. Occasionally the theory is also advocated that it was preceded by a hypaethral type of building, the so-called *basilica discoperta,* which was thought to be attested in Salona (Dyggve, 1940, pp. 415–31). All these hypotheses face as many objections. Moreover, they all share the same error of seeking to establish a single type of building as the model of the Christian basilica. Today the view begins to gain renewed acceptance that the furnishing of the Christian basilica with several aisles should be regarded as simply a method of enlarging the covered space when the need for increased space arose. Some pagan places of worship were constructed with three aisles as well, like the Baccheion in Athens and the "Sacellum delle tre navate" in Ostia Antica, which was probably a Mithraeum. The Jewish communities designed their houses of worship (synagogues) with three aisles at about the same time as the Christians. In other respects, the Christian house of worship was shaped according to the pattern commonly used at the period for assembly buildings: a rectangular room equipped for the performance of the religious ceremonies, with a section at one of the end walls. Also the word "basilica" seems not to have referred initially to a particular structural type but to the Christian church as such. According to the suggestive conjecture of A. von Gerkan (1953, pp. 129ff.), the name derives from the usage of the early church before the official acknowledgment of the Christian religion, when the liturgy was still celebrated in the most prominent room of a private house. This room likewise bore the name basilica (Vituvius, *De aedificiis* 6. 3, 8–10), and the name may have been taken over from here.

The Christian Basilica in Egypt

Compared with the general shape of the basilica, the Egyptian basilica exhibits certain peculiarities. Here, as in Syria, a sanctuary with several rooms and a straight wall toward the east is well established at an early date. There existed a predilection, particularly in Upper Egypt, for furnishing the apse with several niches and an inner circle of columns. Furthermore, in a considerable number of cases, the apse has been replaced by a *triconch*. The lateral rooms in these cases received an angular shape. Moreover, an additional row of columns was set up in front of the entrance to the triconch, which for structural reasons was relatively narrow, so as to enrich the interior aspect of the eastern end of the nave. Subsequently this was adopted for churches with a simple semicircular apse as well, whenever the apse happened to be particularly narrow (Grossmann, 1973, pp. 167ff.). As regards the subdivision of the naos, the Egyptian basilica contains certain peculiarities in the design of the western section. Whereas in the rest of the Christian world the side aisles continue as far as the west end of the basilica, in Egypt they are, with few exceptions (ABŪ MĪNĀ), connected by a transverse section of the same design as these, the so-called return aisle. The aisles thereby acquire the appearance of an ambulatory going around three sides. The origin of the return aisle is probably to be sought in the demands created by the gallery church. Above the return aisle was a kind of bridge that connected the galleries of both sides, so that only a single staircase was required. Subsequently, however, the return aisle could also be found in churches that surely were not furnished with galleries. For the location of the gallery staircase, there is no fixed rule. It is frequently built as an external addition at the southwest corner of the basilica.

The walls of the Egyptian basilica—with the exception of some edifices in Lower Egypt—are provided with numerous niches. They are the cause of the often remarkably strong walls of Egyptian basilicas and should, it seems, be considered a peculiarity of mud brick construction. An *atrium* occurs only rarely in Egyptian basilicas. Nevertheless, there are exceptions to this in Abū Mīnā and al-Ashmūnayn. In the early medieval period, that is, during the time following the Arab conquest, the Egyptian basilica at first changed very little. The edifices, nevertheless, became smaller and more modest in their design. In addition, in the seventh century a special transverse wall was inserted between the sanctuary and the nave, serving a function similar to that of the templon, and out of this the iconostasis developed in the Greek church. Unlike these, however, the transverse wall is constructed to reach the ceiling of the basilica. At first it produced a small transverse passage in front of the sanctuary; later this passage widened out into a full room, the *khūrus*. Since the apse opening itself, on the other hand, kept its traditional form as an arch spanning its full width, the architectural opportunity presented itself to combine both rooms into the overriding form of the triconch, whereby a familiar idea from early Christian architecture came to be reapplied.

A further change of the Egyptian basilica took place with the introduction of vault constructions during the Fatimid period, by a development parallel to that which occurred in Islamic architecture. In Upper Egypt the preference was to place two *domes* one behind the other as a roofing of the nave. This subsequently led to the gradual abandonment of the basilica because the two domes were structurally incompatible with its basic design. In Lower Egypt, on the other hand, the basilica was covered with a continuous barrel vault. This did not interfere with the longitudinal design of the basilica; thus it retained its characteristic shape even into the Mamluk period.

[*See also:* Architectural Elements of Churches.]

BIBLIOGRAPHY

Apollonj-Ghetti, B. M. *Il foro e la basilica severiana di Leptis Magna*. Rome, 1976.

Calza, G., and G. Becatti. *Ostia*. Rome, 1954.

Clarke, S. *Christian Antiquities in the Nile Valley*. Oxford, 1912.

Deichmann, F. W. "Basilika." *Reallexikon für Antike und Christentum* 1 (1950):1249–59.

Delvoye, C. "Basilika." *Reallexikon der byzantinischen Kunst* 1 (1966):514–67.

Dyggve, E. "Basilica discoperta." *Atti IV Congresso internazionale Archeologia christiana* 1 (1940):415–31.

Gartkiewicz, P. M. "New Outline of the History of Nubian Church Architecture." *Bulletin Antieke Beschaving* 55 (1980):137–60.

Gerkan, A. von. "Die profane und die kirchliche Basilika." *Römische Quartalschrift für christliche Altertumskunde und Kirchengeschichte* 48 (1953):129ff.

Grossmann, P. "Die von Somers Clarke in Ober-Anṣinā entdeckten Kirchenbauten." *Mitteilungen des Deutschen Archäologischen Instituts, Abteilung Kairo* 24 (1969):144–68.

______. "Eine vergessene frühchristliche Kirche beim Luxor-Tempel." *Mitteilungen des Deutschen Archäologischen Instituts, Abteilung Kairo* 29 (1973):167–81.

______. "Zur christlichen Baukunst in Ägypten." *Enchoria* 8 (1978):135–46.

Haeny, G. *Basilikale Anlagen in der ägyptischen Baukunst des Neuen Reiches* (1970).

Langlotz, E. *Der architekturgeschichtliche Ursprung der christlichen Basilika*. Opladen, 1972.

Leroux, J. *La Salle hypostyle*. Explorations archéologiques de Délos 2. Paris, 1909.

Macdonald, W. L. *The Architecture of the Roman Empire*. London, 1965.

Ohr, K. F. *Die Basilika in Pompeji*. Karlsruhe, 1973.

Travlos, J. *Pictorial Dictionary of Ancient Athens*. London, 1971. Originally published in German trans. Tübingen.

PETER GROSSMANN

BASILIDES, second-century Alexandrian Gnostic teacher. According to CLEMENT OF ALEXANDRIA (*Stromata* vii.106.4), Basilides taught in Alexandria during the reign of Hadrian (117–138) and Antoninus Pius (138–161). EUSEBIUS OF CAESAREA gives the precise date of A.D. 132 (Jerome, 1846, cols. 619–20). He would seem to be the earliest of the three leading Gnostic teachers in Alexandria. The others were Valentinus (c. 140–160) and HERACLEON (170–180).

Basilides appears to have claimed Glaukias, "Peter's interpreter," as his teacher (Clement *Stromata* vii.106.4), which also points to an early date for his activities. He and his son, Isidore, were prodigious workers. They are credited with compiling the first full-scale Christian commentary on any of the Gospels (perhaps Luke), the twenty-four-book *Exegetica* (Eusebius *Historia ecclesiastica* iv.7.7). In addition, they were responsible for works on Oriental prophecy, "The Exposition of the Prophet Parchor" (Clement *Stromata* vi.53.2); on Platonic philosophy, "On the Inseparable Soul"; on ethics; and on poetry. They ranged widely over theology, theosophy, ethics, exegesis, and mysticism, seeking to relate Christianity to the general religious experience of mankind.

Unfortunately, very little of Basilides' work has survived. Clement of Alexandria quotes from it verbatim and must be preferred as a primary source. Irenaeus and Hippolytus, who also seek to refute him, fail to agree, though in places Hippolytus stands nearer to Clement's sources than does Irenaeus. Hegemonius, writing the *Acta Archelai* early in the fourth century, tends to overemphasize the dualism in Basilides' system and relate it to that of Mani (*Acta Archelai* 67.4).

Both Hippolytus and Irenaeus agree that for Basilides, God was the origin of all things. According to Irenaeus, He was "unborn" (*Adversus haereses* 1.24.3); for Hippolytus, "God came from nothingness" (*Refutation of All Heresies* vii.23.2). Creation "out of nothing," in opposition to current Hebrew-Christian affirmations that "in the beginning was God" (cf. Gen. 1:1), is one of Basilides' claims to originality as a thinker.

Hippolytus records that Basilides believed that God made the world out of nonexistents (*Refutation of All Heresies* vii.23.4) through a "world seed" created out of nothing. Irenaeus is more explicit. To him, Basilides thought in terms of progressive emanations, which Hippolytus denies (*Refutation of All Heresies* vii.22.2): Mind (*Nous*), followed by Reason (*Logos*) and then, in descending order, Prudence, Wisdom, and Power. Thus the Stoic virtues are placed at the summit of Basilides' scale of values. From these divine forces emanated "the powers, principalities and angels that are also called the first, and by them the first heaven was made" (*Adversus haereses* 1.24.3). From their emanations, other angelic powers emanated until 365 separate heavens had come into existence, corresponding to the number of days in the year. The angels who possessed the last heaven were responsible for creating the earth and the nations inhabiting it. The chief ruler of the nations was Yahweh, the God of the Jews, whom Basilides described as an aggressive god whose aim was to subject all other nations to himself, an aim opposed by all the other guardian deities. "For this reason the other nations were alienated from this nation" (the Jews), says Basilides (*Adversus haereses* 1.24.3), doubtless echoing the extreme anti-Jewish feeling of Alexandria at the time.

At this point God sent *Nous* to appear to mankind in human form, as Jesus of Nazareth, to bestow deliverance from Yahweh. Naturally, the Crucifixion was not a real act, as *Nous* could not suffer; the

Jews crucified Simon of Cyrene, who had carried the cross, believing him to be Jesus, while Jesus, taking the form of Simon, stood by, laughing at them.

The key to this system was that each of the high deities believed himself to be God and was ignorant of the existence of the heavens above his own sphere. Thus, Yahweh thought that he was God and ruler of the universe, and hence had no answer to the message of salvation preached by *Nous* through Jesus. Man had the means of saving his immortal soul by accepting this message. "He had," Basilides declared (Clement *Stromata* iv.12.86), "one fragment of the will of God to love everything," and hence could apprehend the divine message. However, belief only in the literal message of the Gospels implied that such a believer was still a slave of Yahweh. True religion was wholly spiritual, attuned to *Nous* and not to any intermediary power.

Basilides, however, was not concerned only with cosmogony. Another fragment of the *Exegetica* (bk. 23) preserved by Clement shows him to have been a deep-thinking moral theologian concerned with the nature of evil and of suffering (*Stromata* iv.12.81.1–83.1). He aimed at answering objections to Christianity concerned with why God did not intervene to protect confessors, and why martyrs had to suffer if God was good and compassionate. All suffering, Basilides replied, was the result of sin. Confessors may not have been grievous offenders, but they possessed the capacity and the desire to sin—perhaps they were even being punished for sins committed in a previous life. Martyrdom cleansed them from all guilt. Even Jesus, as the temptations showed, possessed the possibility to sin, since through his incarnation he had become man.

Though Clement of Alexandria recoiled from these ideas as "atheistic" (*Stromata* iv.12.85.1), they were founded on the conviction that God could not be the author of evil. Basilides accepted the Platonic view of Providence: that in no sense could it be responsible for evil (*Stromata* iv.82.2). Evil was due, rather, to the influence of the archons, chief of whom was Yahweh.

Basilides was the first Christian theologian to interpret the New Testament allegorically. Plato and Homer, as well as Paul, aid in the elucidation of the divine message contained in the Gospels. Basilides reveals himself as a thinker of boldness and speculative power. Though he may have been influenced by some pre-Christian Gnostic writing, such as the PARAPHRASE OF SHEM, he was the first to see that a Christianity that relied so heavily on the Old Testament for its understanding of God could hardly be the real saving religion for mankind. If many of his ideas proved unacceptable to orthodox Christians, Basilides nonetheless helped to free Christianity from subjection to the prevalent apocalyptic and millenarian concepts. He saw that a universal religion must draw on the wisdom of all mankind, and that if the end was a mystical faith, the way to that end lay through understanding the message of the great philosophers and poets, in particular Plato and Homer. The emergence of an authentically gentile Christianity owes much to Basilides.

Basilides' views seem almost certainly to have influenced VALENTINUS; and there are reminiscences of his ideas, such as the ignorance of the Great Archon (Yahweh) and crucifixion of a substitute for Christ, in the *Second Treatise of the Great Seth*. Isidore is mentioned in the Nag Hammadi Codex, tractate IX. Much of the Gnostic view of the origins of creation, and man's relation to it and to God, may be said to have originated with Basilides. He is part of the Alexandrian Jewish and Christian philosophical tradition that produced PHILO, Valentinus, Clement, and ORIGEN.

BIBLIOGRAPHY

Förster, W. "Das System des Basilides." *New Testament Studies* 9 (1962–1963):233–55.

———, ed. *Die Gnosis,* trans. and ed. R. McL. Wilson, Vol. 1. Oxford, 1972.

Hegemonius. *Acta Archelai,* ed. H. Beeson. Die griechischen christlichen Schriftsteller der ersten drei Jahrhunderte 16. Leipzig, 1906.

Hort, F. J. "Basilides." In DCB 1, pp. 268–81. Repr. New York, 1974.

Jerome. *S. Hieronymi interpretatio Chronicae Eusebii Pamphili.* In PL 27, cols. 34–676. Paris, 1846.

May, G. *Schöpfung aus Nichts,* pp. 63–86. Berlin, 1978.

Mülenberg, E. "Basilides." In *Theologische Realenzyklopädie,* Vol. 5, pp. 296–301. Berlin and New York, 1980. Discussion in detail of Basilides' system.

Nautin, P. "Les fragments de Basilide sur la souffrance." In *Mélanges offerts en honneur de H. C. Puech,* pp. 393–403. Paris, 1974.

Quispel, G. "L'homme gnostique: la doctrine de Basilide." *Eranos Jahrbuch* 16 (1948):89–193.

Robinson, J. M., ed. *The Nag Hammadi Library.* San Francisco, 1977.

Waszink, J. H. "Basilides." In *Reallexikon für Antike und Christentum,* Vol. 1, cols. 1217–25. Stuttgart, 1950.

W. H. C. FREND

BASILIOS I. *See* Jerusalem, Coptic See of.

BASILIOS II, archbishop of Jerusalem (1818–1899). Basilios was born in the village of Al-Ḍabbah in the governorate of Qenā. When he was twenty-five he entered the monastery of Saint Antony (DAYR ANBA ANṬŪNIYŪS) in the Eastern Desert. After six years he was ordained priest, and was made archpriest three years later. He was then chosen to be head of the monastery.

In 1856 he became archbishop of the see of Jerusalem during the time of Patriarch CYRIL IV (1854–1861), taking the name Basilios. The archbishop of Jerusalem was also considered head of the monastery of Anbā Basilios. He renovated the monastery, which is next to the Holy Sepulcher, and built a church and a building for the patriarchate, as well as rooms for pilgrims and other visitors. The monastery and Church of Saint George in Jerusalem were also restored. The archbishop took pains to preserve the church's sacred objects, especially in DAYR AL-SULṬĀN in Jerusalem. In Jaffa, he bought a large orchard where he built a church and monastery for Coptic visitors.

He had many other churches built in different places and restored others. He was well known for his charitable nature and his concern for the poor. He was renowned for his broad-mindedness, honesty, good counsel, and love for the church and his people. Despite ill health, Basilios continued to look after his diocese and its people until his death on 26 March 1899 at the age of eighty-two. He was buried in the bishops' shrine near the Coptic church that he had built in Jaffa.

ARCHBISHOP BASILIOS

BASILIOS III, archbishop of Jerusalem (?–1935). Basilios came from the town of Akhmīm and became a monk at DAYR ANBĀ ANTŪNIYŪS before serving in Jerusalem. When, after the death of TIMOTHEOS I, the diocese was divided into two parts, he was appointed to the newly created see of Jerusalem, which consisted of the governorates of the Canal, Sharqiyyah, and Sinai, plus Jerusalem itself, and changed his name from Jacob Antony to Basilios III. He was consecrated archbishop in 1925. He remained archbishop for ten years until his death on 1 Bashans A.M. 1651. He is buried in the monastery of Saint Antony in Jaffa next to Basilios II.

ARCHBISHOP BASILIOS

BASILIOS, ARCHIVE OF. The archive of Basilios, pagarch of Aphrodito in the time of Governor Qurrah ibn Sharīk (698–722), is the largest and most notable of the collections of the early Arab period. Found at Kom Ishqāw in 1901, the papyri were acquired mainly by the British Museum, though substantial collections are in Paris (the Louvre), Tbilisi, Cairo, and other cities. (The earlier archive from Aphrodito, that of Dioscoros, from the age of Justinian, was published by J. Maspero in *Papyrus grecs d'époque byzantine,* with further items in *Greek Papyri in the British Museum* [hereafter P. Lond.], Vol. 5.) The majority, acquired by the British Museum in 1903, were published by H. I. Bell in Volume 4 of P. Lond. (also containing the Coptic pieces, published by W. E. Crum). The purely Arabic texts were published by Becker in 1907 (hereafter PAF); some of the Greek and Arabic texts represent two versions of the same document (for instance, P. Lond. 1346 [PAF IV]; 1349 (probably) *Papyri Schott-Reinhardt* I; 1345—or more probably 1359 [PAF III]).

Basilios was the pagarch of the pagarchy of which Aphrodito was the administrative center. The correspondence, which consists largely of letters from Qurrah to Basilios (written between 708 and 711), sheds much light both on the administration of the pagarchy in the twenty years around the turn of the eighth century and on the general nature and principles of Umayyad rule in relation to the provincial population of Egypt and to the provincial administration. Basilios, though occupying the same rank as his contemporary Papas, pagarch of Apollōnos Anō (Idfū), evidently enjoyed a more privileged status, for whereas the communications of the latter are with the *dux* of the Thebaid or his *topoteretes* (representatives), stationed at Antinoopolis, those of Basilios, as preserved, are exclusively from Qurrah, the governor of Egypt, residing at al-Fusṭāṭ (Old Cairo). Whether the explanation of this privileged correspondence lies in the greater importance of the pagarchy of Aphrodito, or in personal relations between Basilios and high-ranking Egyptian officials, is not clear, but because of it we learn more about the policy of the Umayyad government from this archive than from that of Papas.

It has been generally remarked that the picture of Qurrah drawn from this correspondence does not bear out the highly colored and unfavorable account of the greed and brutality of Walīd's governor that is found particularly in the HISTORY OF THE PATRIARCHS and in other non-Muslim Arabic sources; it shows him to have been a firm and determined administrator, more anxious for the welfare of his subjects than for the well-being of his officials (see particularly P. Lond. 1349, 1356, 1380, 1393 [republished in full in *Journal of Egyptian Archeology* 12 (1926):275ff.]; and, for an Arabic example, the strongly worded no. IV in Abbott's *The Kurrah Papyri;* cf. *History of the Patriarchs,* Vol. 1, pt. 3, pp. 57ff., esp. p. 64, for the hostile view).

The direct link between Basilios and the authorities at al-Fusṭāṭ (or, on occasion, Alexandria) is shown above all by the fact that, in addition to the letters and orders that passed from one to the other, all monies, taxes, and exactions required by the governor were sent to him directly, and the amir of the Thebaid was bypassed. In the Papas archive, on the other hand, all payments in money and requisitions in kind are centrally collected at Antinoopolis and forwarded by the amir or his representative. Basilios had a permanent agent at al-Fusṭāṭ to whom his contributions were delivered.

In addition to the letters from Qurrah to Basilios (P. Lond. 1332–1407, and in other collections), the archive includes a few *entagia* (P. Lond. 1408–11), accounts and registers of the utmost importance, drawn up for fiscal purposes. These cover all the many forms of taxation applied by the government to the pagarchy in this period: poll tax, land tax, and numerous minor and extraordinary imposts (P. Lond. 1412–61). The correspondence also covers a characteristic range of official demands for laborers, notably caulkers, to be employed in the shipyards at Babylon and, particularly, Clysma, and for work on the new mosques being built at al-Fusṭāṭ, Jerusalem, and Damascus, the Umayyad capital. If the pagarchy of Aphrodito can be regarded as typical, there can be no doubt that Egyptian labor was heavily drawn upon for these major architectural undertakings of the Umayyads. In addition there are continuous and pressing demands for speed in the provision of manpower and in the payment of taxes —and it is quite clear that Basilios, like Papas at Apollōnopolis, dragged his feet as much as he dared on numerous occasions.

Another major subject covered is the tracing and registration of fugitives who repeatedly moved from pagarchy to pagarchy. The Muslim authorities found it difficult to keep track of such fugitives because of their concealment and other ruses (see Cadell, 1967, no. 5, with introduction). The clearest guide to the study of the complex accounts (P. Lond. 1412ff.) is in D. C. Dennett's *Conversion and the Poll Tax in Early Islam* (Cambridge, Mass., 1950; repr. in Dennett's *Islamic Taxation: Two Studies* [New York, 1973]). The author shows by an analysis of the relevant registers and by a comparison with the terms of the capitulation given in the Arab chroniclers and in JOHN OF NIKIOU that the principle applied was one of individual taxation, in the form of poll tax and land tax in particular, and not of an overall tribute based on a central assessment. Dennett's study corrects the account given by Bell in the introduction to P. Lond. (vol. 4) and in the introduction to numbers 1412ff., which was based on the conclusion that the figures were quotas required for an overall payment of tribute (as also in Bell's article in *Byzantion* 28 [1928]:278ff.).

BIBLIOGRAPHY

Abbott, N. *The Kurrah Papyri from Aphrodito in the Oriental Institute.* Studies in Ancient Oriental Civilization 15. Chicago, 1938.

Becker, Z. F. "Arabische Papyri des Aphroditofundes." *Zeitschrift für Assyriologie* 20 (1907):68–94.

______. *Der Islam,* Vol. 2, pp. 245–68. Strasbourg, 1911.

Butler, A. J. *The Arab Conquest of Egypt,* 2nd ed., ed. P. M. Fraser. Oxford, 1978.

Cadell, H. "Nouveaux fragments de la correspondance de Kurrah ben Sharik." *Recherches de Papyrologie* 4 (1967):107–160. On pp. 142–50 is a dated list of all Greek and Arabic papyri from Qurrah.

Greek Papyri in the British Museum, ed. F. G. Kenyon and H. I. Bell, 5 vols. London, 1893–1917.

Grohmann, A. *Arabic Papyri in the Egyptian Library,* Vol. 1. Cairo, 1934.

Papyri russischer und georgischer Sammlungen, ed. G. Zereteli, O. Kruger, and P. Jernstedt, 5 vols. Tiflis, 1925–1935; repr. 1965. Some items complete papyri in P. Lond., Vol. 4.

Papyrus grecs d'époque byzantine, ed. J. Maspero, 3 vols. Cairo, 1911–1916.

Sammelbuch griechischer Urkunden aus Ägypten, ed. F. Preisigke, F. Bilabel, and E. Kiessling, nos. 10453–80. Strasbourg, Heidelberg, and Wiesbaden, 1916–.

Veröffentlichungen aus der Heidelberger Papyrussammlung (P. Heid), Vol. 3, *Papyri Schott-Reinhardt* I, ed. C. H. Becker. Heidelberg, 1906.

P. M. FRASER

BASILIUS (Bey) (d. 1847), eldest of three sons of Muʿallim Ghālī who was killed by Ibrāhīm Pasha, son of MUḤAMMAD ʿALĪ, at the city of Ziftā. Muḥammad ʿAlī appointed Basilius to succeed his father in the administration of finances and thus he became the first Copt to be granted the title of bey. Moreover, to reconcile the Ghālī family, the viceroy appointed the other brothers, Doss and Ṭubyā, to two principal posts in the government administration. Basilius remained in charge of the general finances of Egypt until his death in November 1847.

MOUNIR SHOUCRI

BASIL OF OXYRHYNCHUS, sixth-century author of the homily *In Honor of Longinus* (*hegumenos* of ENATON), found complete in a codex now in New York (Pierpont Morgan Library, M 579, fols. 103–110, unpublished). According to the title of the homily, Basil was bishop of Pemje (Oxyrhynchus). He delivered the homily on the occasion of the consecration of a church dedicated to LONGINUS in the Monastery of Salamites on Mount Thone.

No information concerning Basil can be gleaned from the content of the homily; this is a powerful argument in favor of its authenticity, because works composed *a posteriori* during the period of the CYCLES usually contain elements of purported autobiography. However, stylistic criteria point to the period of Damian (end of the sixth century) for Basil, as the structure of the encomium is similar to that of PSEUDO-PISENTIUS OF QIFṬ, *In Honor of Onophrius;* other themes recall the encomia of CONSTANTINE of Asyūṭ, *In Honor of Athanasius.*

The homily begins with a eulogy to the virginity of the ascetic life in the figure of John the Baptist. One of those who imitated the saint was Longinus, together with his companion Lucius. There follows an exhortation to the people to pay careful heed to the commemoration, since this attention is a useful exercise of moral edification. In this connection, the author cites the example of Joshua in relation to the life of Moses. Reference is then made to the miracles worked by Longinus. This would seem to be based on the *Life of Longinus (and Lucius),* which may be assigned to the period of the "plerophoriai" (fifth and sixth centuries; see LITERATURE, COPTIC). This text is found in the same manuscript.

After this comes the final peroration in which the faithful are invited to follow the example of Longinus.

BIBLIOGRAPHY

Cotelier, J. B. *Apophthegmata Patrum.* In PG 65, cols. 71–440. Paris, 1864.

TITO ORLANDI

BASIN AND EWER. *See* Liturgical Vestments.

BASSET, RENÉ (1855–1924), French Arabist and specialist in Berber. He was born at Lunéville. He was dean of the Faculté des Lettres of Algiers and a corresponding member of the Académie des Inscriptions et Belles-Lettres. He died in Algeria. As editor, he published the works of his friend Father Charles Foucauld (*Grammar,* 1908, 1922; *Dictionary,* 1918–1921), and among other works, he wrote *Les Documents arabes sur l'expédition de Charlemagne en Espagne* (1904) and *Recherches sur la religion des Berbères* (1910). His principal work is his edition of the Coptic *Synaxaire arabe-jacobite,* PO 3, 13, 56, 78, 84, and 100, which appeared between 1905 and 1928.

BIBLIOGRAPHY

Coignet, J. "Basset, René." In *Dictionnaire d'histoire et de géographie ecclésiastiques,* col. 1268. Paris, 1932.

Furlani, J. "Basset, René." In *Enciclopedia cattolica,* pp. 984–85. Vatican City, 1949.

FRANÇOIS GRAFFIN, S.J.

BASṬAH, city located in the Eastern Delta just south of al-Zaqāzīq in the province of Sharqiyyah. In Egyptian the city was known as Per-Bastet (the domain of Bastet, the lion goddess).

A powerful political center, Basṭah provided the kings of the Twenty-second Dynasty (945–712 B.C.) and served as the capital of the eighteenth Lower Egyptian nome during the Late Period (712–332 B.C.). The Greek historian Herodotus, writing in the fifth century, knew the city as Boubastis and referred to it often, describing its temples and other sights. At the location of the ancient Egyptian settlement, excavators have uncovered temples of Bastet, Keti, Hori, Pepy, Atum, and Mihos, as well as tombs and cat cemeteries.

Coptic sources, which give the name of the city as Bouasti or Pouasti, record a long Christian tradition for the place. Athanasius mentions that the city had a Melitian bishop as early as A.D. 325 (*Apologia Secunda* II.71, in *Athanasius Werke,* Vol. 2, p. 150). Other sources speak of orthodox bishops in this early period also (see Timm, 1984, p. 363).

Basṭah is mentioned often in accounts of martyrs from the period before 640. The martyr Shenute, who was imprisoned in Antinoopolis, came from Basṭah (Hyvernat, 1886–1887, p. 100). Apa Apoli was put to death there during the governorship of Ptolemaios (see Evelyn-White, 1926, pp. 87–93).

Given the area's Christian tradition it is surprising

that Basṭah does not appear in the medieval Coptic-Arabic scales, but the city is included in a medieval list of Egyptian bishoprics (Munier, 1943, pp. 47–54), and various bishops of Basṭah are attested. Bishop Pahom from Basṭah was present at the conflict between Patriarch YŪSĀB I (830–849) and Muḥammad ibn 'Abd Allāh, where he took sides against the patriarch. In 1078, Bishop Gabriel of Basṭah attended the synod at DAYR ANBĀ MAQĀR in Wādī al-Natrun where CYRIL II (1078–1092) was selected as the sixty-seventh patriarch (Munier, 1943, p. 26). One of the three bishops who ordained John as bishop of Cairo in 1118 was John "bishop of al-Khandaq," and the see of Basṭah assisted Patriarch MARK III (1167–1189) and Bishop John of Tamwayh in the dedication of a church in al-Basātīn.

Coptic tradition holds that Basṭah was the first stopping place in Egypt of the family of Jesus on the FLIGHT INTO EGYPT. When the inhabitants of Basṭah would not receive Jesus and Mary, they pitched their tent outside the city, where a spring was made to flow for them. Later the people of Basṭah revered this spot. A church dedicated to the Virgin Mary was built on the site in 1185.

BIBLIOGRAPHY

Amélineau, E. *La Géographie de l'Egypte à l'époque copte,* p. 89. Paris, 1893.

Athanasius Werke, ed. H.-G. Opitz. Berlin, 1934–.

Baines, J., and J. Málek. *Atlas of Ancient Egypt,* pp. 174–75. New York, 1980.

Evelyn-White, H. G. *The Monasteries of the Wadi 'n Natrun,* pt. 1. New York, 1926.

Hyvernat, H. *Les Actes des martyrs de l'Egypte.* Paris, 1886–1887.

Munier, H. *Recueil des listes épiscopales de l'église copte.* Cairo, 1943.

Timm, S. *Das christlich-koptische Ägypten in arabischer Zeit,* pt. 1, pp. 362–65. Wiesbaden, 1984.

RANDALL STEWART

BATANŪN, AL-,

BATANŪN, AL-, a city located some 10 miles (16 km) south of Ṭanṭā in the province of al-Minūfiyyah. It was known in Coptic times as Pathanon.

Al-Batanūn was the birthplace of Patriarch SHENUTE I (858–880) and the place to which the remains of the FORTY-NINE MARTYRS of Scetis were brought for a time after having been stolen from their resting place in Scetis, probably at the beginning of the seventh century. In al-Batanūn the remains were kept in the church of Apa Onophrius (Zoega, 1810, pp. 95–97).

Muslim authors in the medieval period mention al-Batanūn, but they give no information about Christians or churches in the town.

There are today two churches in al-Batanūn, one of Sarapammon, built around 1897, and one of the Virgin Mary.

BIBLIOGRAPHY

Amélineau, E. *La Géographie de l'Egypte à l'époque copte,* pp. 306–307. Paris, 1893.

Timm, S. *Christliche Stätten in Ägypten,* p. 63. Wiesbaden, 1979.

———. *Das christlich-koptische Ägypten in arabischer Zeit,* pt. 1, pp. 372–74. Wiesbaden, 1984.

Zoega, G. *Catalogus codicum copticorum manuscriptorum qui in Museo Borgiano Velitris adservantur.* Rome, 1810.

RANDALL STEWART

BAṬN AL-ḤAJAR (belly of stones), the name popularly given to an especially rocky and inhospitable area of Nubia, extending southward for about 80 miles (120 km) from the Second Cataract of the Nile. Here the Nile flows through a denuded landscape of granite outcrops and boulders, with very little floodplain on either side of the river. The river channel itself is impeded by many small cataracts, the best known of which are those of Semna and Dal. Because of these impediments, upriver and downriver navigation is possible only at the peak of the Nile flood.

The Baṭn al-Ḥajar had few inhabitants or resources, but it was strategically important because it lay on the frontier between Lower and Upper Nubia. It served for a long time as a barrier both to the southward penetration of Egyptians and to the northward movement of Nubians, and it was here that the pharaohs of the Twelfth Dynasty built an imposing chain of frontier fortifications.

During the Middle Ages, the Baṭn al-Ḥajar lay within the territory of NOBATIA. It was, however, a kind of economic frontier, for the region to the north was freely open to trade and settlement by Muslims, while to the south all trade was a royal monopoly. To enforce this policy there were two customs posts, one at Takoa at the lower end of the Baṭn al-Ḥajar and one at a place (the "upper *maqs*") near its upper end.

After traversing the Baṭn al-Ḥajar, the tenth-century visitor IBN SALĪM AL-ASWĀNĪ wrote:

These are the worst parts of Nubia which I have seen, owing to the difficulty and narrowness of the ground and the fatiguing road. The river is constantly interrupted by rapid falls and projecting mountains, so that it is precipitated down the rocks, and is in some places not above fifty cubits wide from one bank to the other. The country abounds in high mountains, narrow passes, and roads along which you cannot proceed mounted. . . . These mountains are the strongholds of the Nubians, and among them the inhabitants of the districts bordering on the Muslim country take refuge.

This function as a refuge and sanctuary became even more significant in the disturbed political and military conditions of the later Middle Ages. There was a rapid growth of population, apparently fleeing southward from the depredations of the BANŪ AL-KANZ in Lower Nubia, and fortified settlements as well as miniature castles were built on many of the islands of the Baṭn al-Ḥajar. Except for the Middle Kingdom fortresses, nearly all of the known archaeological remains of the region date from the later medieval period. It was undoubtedly because of this fortress quality that the Baṭn al-Ḥajar and the adjoining part of Lower Nubia were the last outposts of Christianity in the Sudan, surviving even after the kingdom of MAKOURIA had succumbed to Arab rule.

A number of the fortress sites in the Baṭn al-Ḥajar were excavated in the period between 1960 and 1970, but the results have not yet been published in detail.

[*See also:* Nubian Archaeology, Medieval.]

BIBLIOGRAPHY

Adams, W. Y. "The University of Kentucky Excavations at Kulubnarti, 1969." In *Kunst und Geschichte Nubiens in christlicher Zeit,* ed. E. Dinkler. Recklinghausen, 1970.

______. *Nubia, Corridor to Africa,* pp. 26–28, 511–16, 580–83. Princeton, 1977.

Burckhardt, J. L. *Travels in Nubia,* pp. 494–95. London, 1819.

Chittick, H. N. "Antiquities of the Batn el Hajjar." *Kush* 5 (1957):42–48.

Dinkler, E. "Die deutschen Ausgrabungen auf den Inseln Sunnarti, Tangur und in Kulb 1968–69." In *Kunst und Geschichte Nubiens in christlicher Zeit,* ed. E. Dinkler. Recklinghausen, 1970.

Mills, A. J. "The Archaeological Survey from Gemai to Dal—Report on the 1965–1966 Season." *Kush* 15 (1973):200–210.

Mills, A. J., and H.-A. Nordström. "The Archaeological Survey from Gemai to Dal. Preliminary Report on the Season 1964–65." *Kush* 14 (1966):1–15.

WILLIAM Y. ADAMS

BĀWĪṬ. [*This entry consists of three articles:* History; Archaeology, Architecture, and Sculpture; *and* Paintings.]

History

The town of Bāwīṭ is located between Dayrūṭ and Asyūṭ. The site is famous through the excavations carried out there at the beginning of the twentieth century, the results of which were important for the history of Coptic art. From the numerous inscriptions discovered there, it is known that it was dedicated to a Saint Apollo, who seems to have been its founder. Unfortunately, the literary witnesses—a life of Phif (or PHIB), companion and friend of Apollo (Orlandi and Campagnano, 1975), and Greek papyri (Gascou, 1981, p. 220)—speak of an Apollo of another monastery, very near at Titkois (Greek) or Titkooh (Coptic). Other texts speak of a Saint Apollo in the nome of Hermopolis Magna (today at al-ASHMŪNAYN) but without specifying the place, such as the HISTORIA MONACHORUM IN AEGYPTO, relating a pilgrimage by the hermits of Egypt during the winter of 394—395. In the Coptic fragments of the Life of PAUL OF ṬAMMAH, it is related that he visited an Apollo in this same region (Amélineau, 1888–1895, pp. 759ff.). Finally, the SYNAXARION, which commemorates Phib and his friend Apollo on 25 Bābah, speaks of a site called Jabal Ablūj. These texts have so many common elements that it appears probable that there was an Apollo who had a friend and companion named Phib who died twenty years before him, and another companion called Papohe. He was a monk and then no doubt superior at Titkois and, in his old age (perhaps eighty), founded a hermitage center at Bāwīṭ. The *Historia monachorum in Aegypto* relates that visitors were welcomed by the singing of psalms and that the hermits assembled daily for the Eucharist and a common meal and returned to their hermitages after hearing Apollo's teaching. This same scenario was followed when Paul of Ṭammah paid a visit to Apollo. Moreover, Paul noted that Apollo delivered his sermons sitting on a throne. The paintings found at Bāwīṭ present him sitting on a divan with

Phib and another monk named Anoup (Clédat, 1910).

It is very difficult to determine what kind of monastery Apollo founded, in view of the fact that only 5 percent of the site has been excavated and that it underwent many transformations between the founding and the abandonment of the monastery. It seems too much to affirm that the site is of Pachomian character with some "individual liberties" of an anchorite type (Torp, 1964, p. 185), for the excavations themselves have demonstrated the existence of cells outside the surrounding wall in the desert, and the numerous inscriptions attesting the cult of Apollo, which is always associated with Phib and Anoup, are found only on the walls of hermitages in Middle and Upper Egypt, at Wādī Sarjah, Dayr al-Bala'izah, and as far as Isnā, but never on the walls of a monastery known to have been Pachomian. It therefore seems more in conformity with what is known of Egyptian monasticism to think that the so-called *dayr* of Bawīṭ was, at least in its origins, a common center for surrounding hermitages. The only difference between this and similar establishments is that the hermits assembled there for the Eucharist and a common meal, followed perhaps by an address from the father of the monastery, not every week but daily, as both the *Historia monachorum* and the fragments of the Life of Paul of Tamma clearly show.

If the monastery was indeed founded toward the end of the fourth century, the excavations show that it had become prosperous by the sixth century and as late as the ninth, but was destroyed, it seems, in the second half of the twelfth century (Torp, 1965, pp. 153–77).

It must be added that an establishment for women adjoined it but does not seem to have existed at the beginning.

BIBLIOGRAPHY

Amélineau, E. *Monuments pour servir à l'histoire de l'Egypte chrétienne.* Paris, 1888.

Chassinat, E. *Fouilles à Baouit,* Vol. 1. Mémoires de l'Institut français d'Archéologie orientale 13. Cairo, 1911.

Clédat, J. "Recherches sur le kom de Baouit." *Comptes rendus de l'académie des inscriptions et belles lettres* (1902):525–46.

———. "Nouvelles recherches à Baouit." *Comptes rendus de l'Académie des inscriptions et belles lettres* (1904):517–26.

———. *Le Monastère et la nécropole de Baouit.* Mémoires de l'Institut français d'Archéologie orientale 12, 39. Cairo, 1904, 1916.

———. "Baouit." In *Dictionnaire d'archéologie chrétienne et de liturgie,* Vol. 2. Paris, 1910.

Coquin, R.-G. "Apollon de Titkooh ou Apollon de Bawiṭ?" *Orientalia* 46 (1977):436–66.

Drew-Bear, M. *Le Nome Hermopolite.* American Studies in Papyrology 21. Missoula, Mont., 1979.

Gascou, J. "Documents grecs relatifs au monastère d'abba Apollon de Titkois." *Anagennèsis* (Athens) 1 (1981):219–30.

Krause, M., and K. Wessel. "Bawit." *Reallexikon zur byzantinischen Kunst,* Vol. 1. Stuttgart, 1966.

Maspero, J., and E. Drioton. *Fouilles exécutées à Baouit.* Mémoires de l'Institut français d'Archéologie orientale 59. Cairo, 1931–1932.

O'Leary, De L. *The Saints of Egypt.* London and New York, 1937; repr. Amsterdam, 1974.

Orlandi, T., and A. Campagnano. *Vite dei monaci Phif e Longino.* Testi e documenti 51. Milan, 1975.

Torp, H. "Murs d'enceinte des monastères coptes primitifs et couvents-forteresses." *Mélanges d'Archéologie et d'Histoire* 76 (1964):173–200.

———. "La Date de la fondation du monastère de Baouit et de son abandon." *Mélanges d'Archéologie et d'Histoire* (Rome) 77 (1965):153–77.

Walters, C. C. *Monastic Archeology in Egypt,* Warminster, 1974.

René-Georges Coquin
Maurice Martin, S.J.

Archaeology, Architecture, and Sculpture

Architecture

The archaeological site lies about 1.25 miles (2 km) west of the village of Bāwīṭ and about 17 miles (28 km) south of al-Ashmūnayn. The ruins first became known in the last decade of the nineteenth century as a result of private digging, when investigations were made into the provenance of objects that came into the art trade. With the limited task of uncovering the buildings already visible and also finding out whether the *kom* (mound) contained any more monuments, J. Clédat, E. Chassinat, and C. Palanque between 1901 and 1904 and J. Maspero in 1913 cleared buildings and made several soundings. At the end of these activities, which in intention and execution were far removed from a regular excavation, the substance of the most important building, the so-called South Church, was destroyed by the removal of the architectural sculpture; a selection of wall paintings that had survived the excavation was removed as well. The finds thus carried off are today located in the Coptic Museum in Cairo and the Louvre in Paris (de Graviers, 1932, pp. 51ff.). The excavators produced preliminary reports and partial publications of the excavation in which, however, architecture and sculpture were largely neglected. Only plans of the individual campaigns were published. There is no overall plan recording all the excavated complexes (a hypothetical attempt, incorrect in details, is Torp, 1981, pl. 1). Since the soundings exposed only partial areas and the area of settlement was not systematically defined, we do not know the extent of the buildings, nor can we ascertain whether the main concentration of the total complex was then found and excavated. In conformity with the circumstances of these archaeological activities, there are for the monuments no datings assured by excavation data (stratigraphy, ceramics, coins). Since building phases and even rebuildings, which we can identify in many sections on the basis of old excavation photographs, were almost without exception not observed or even documented at the time, we have no clues as to the relative chronology of the complex.

The oldest chronological information in situ (from the beginning of the eighth century) was contained in painted inscriptions (cf. Krause and Wessel, 1966, cols. 570–71). They offer, however, only a terminus ante quem for the layer of plaster, but certainly not a reliable approximate estimate for the building concerned, which may have been considerably older, rebuilt, or put to new use.

It has now been shown beyond any doubt through inscriptions in the buildings of Bāwīṭ that the buildings excavated at that time belonged to the monastery of Apa Apollo, and a few published papyri of the ninth century from Bāwīṭ (Krause, 1958) give us detailed information about the conditions and financial transactions of that period in this monastery. The well-known wall paintings, most of which probably date from the seventh and eighth centuries, were certainly produced for the monastery.

We cannot, however, conclude from this that the early history of the monastery of Apa Apollo, known only through allusions and by no means clearly (see Timm, 1984, pp. 643–45), stands in causal relationship with the buildings of the *kom* of Bāwīṭ excavated at that time or that the original buildings on this ground were erected for the monastery of Apa Apollo. For example, clear evidence for activity in church building is lacking precisely from the critical period of the fifth century and the first half of the sixth. Imposing architectural remains deriving from this period are rather remarkably untypical for church architecture (see below). The history of early building in Bāwīṭ (perhaps fourth, fifth, and sixth centuries) has not yet been materially clarified. An investigation of this problem would be extremely valuable.

Similarly, the decline of the monastery cannot be dated with certainty. Estimates vary from the year 900 to the fourteenth century. In favor of a fairly early date for abandonment of the monastery is the fact that the Islamic authors of the Middle Ages knew the site but did not mention the monastery.

Architecture

The excavation of the so-called South Church led to publication of a volume of plates (Chassinat, 1911) but only a minimum of written information. No consideration was given to the fact that the architecture shows unusual features for a church building, that strong stylistic anomalies in the architectural sculpture found there cannot be denied, and that the structure was accepted for decades as a homogeneous church building of the sixth century because of some column capitals modeled on impost capitals. It has occasionally been considerably overvalued architecturally (e.g., the conjectured reconstruction of it as a domed basilica, untenable on static grounds alone, or the claim that it was the source of all the important architectural sculpture found in the surroundings of Bāwīṭ).

A critical examination of the excavation photographs (Severin, 1977, pls. 32–38) has revealed that the structure went through two building phases, characterized by different wall-building techniques. The older consists of ashlar work and the later of bricks, or at least a brick base. The building sections of the earlier phase contain original architectural sculpture, while those of the later phase show the insertion or reconstruction of heterogeneous decoration, some of it reused pieces of work that fit very badly. It has not yet been possible to determine the function of the parts belonging to the older phase. At any rate, they need not have been part of a church building. The provisional attribution of the older building sections to the fourth century has in the meantime been corrected to a date in the fifth century (Severin, 1986; cf. Effenberger, 1981, pp. 79ff.). The rebuilding, in which the thoroughly makeshift architecture of the South Church originated, must have been carried out at the earliest in the late sixth or even the seventh century.

Of the North Church, the excavators reported

Excavation of a room in the North Church at Bāwīṭ. Clédat Expedition. *Reprinted from* Monastères et la Nécropole de Bâwit, *Vol. 1, by Jean Clédat, Cairo, 1904–1906.*

only that it lay to the north of the so-called South Church, was simpler in form, and had cruciform pillars, columns, and a wooden ICONOSTASIS. Sun-dried and burnt bricks and limestone were used as building materials. Recently the ground plan of the structure uncovered has been established on the basis of three old, unpublished excavation photographs. In particular, it emerged that here, too, building phases were clearly to be distinguished in the architectural remains. At least the cruciform pillars in the transverse section and parts of the east wall derive from an older construction of the pre-Islamic period. That they are the remains of an original church building on this site is improbable. In a later phase, church architecture made its appearance through additions and reconstructions of brick wall work in compartments already existing and through the introduction of reused bases, columns, and capitals; the old excavation uncovered the ruins of this. The conversion of the early structure into a church can be dated at the earliest to the eighth century, as the existence of a proper *khūrus* (room between sanctuary and naos) shows.

Perhaps the North Church, built into older architectural remains, superseded the South Church, which for its part originated in reconstructions of the late sixth or seventh century.

Scattered throughout the area and surrounded by a wall that could be traced only in the northwest are several small buildings. Excavation has revealed that many of them were joined together to make up an irregular complex. Inscriptions indicate that some of them were dwellings (Krause, 1966, col. 569). The buildings, described as tomb chapels after the excavation by J. Clédat, were claimed to have been living quarters proper by J. Maspero in 1913 (Maspero and Drioton, 1931–1943, Vol. 5), who pointed out that no burials had been found and that the form of the buildings, the inscriptions, the iconography of the paintings, and the household goods found there spoke against their having been used for interments.

This is by no means the final word on the subject. It is beyond doubt that at the time of the oldest dated inscriptions (beginning of eighth century) the buildings were part of the Monastery of Apa Apollo and that the South Church came into being in the form of a rebuilding, at the latest in the seventh century. From the excavation photographs of many parts of the scattered building complexes, extensive reconstructions can be identified; this points to an architectural history marked by development and change. (An unfortunately arbitrary attempt to classify one of the building complexes into different phases is in Torp, 1981, ill. 2.) We ought to include in our reckoning the original structures in the area

Excavation of the passage between the North and South churches at Bāwīṭ. *Reprinted from* Monastères et la Nécropole de Bâwit, *Vol. 1, by Jean Clédat, Cairo, 1904–1906.*

of the South and North churches, the function of which is not yet clear but which certainly were originally not church buildings. Finally, one must not lose sight of the fact that only recently the entire picture of DAYR APA JEREMIAH, in terms of topography, history, and art history, had to be almost completely rewritten. Of building operations in the area of the *kom* of Bāwīṭ, at least in the fifth and sixth centuries, we know nothing for certain (extent, architectural form, and function), and therefore, for the time being, should rule out neither any future confirmation of the conventional interpretations nor the possibility of perhaps surprising new insights (such as the possibility that the first building phase was a necropolis).

Sculpture

The limestone and wood sculpture from Bāwīṭ (in the Coptic Museum in Cairo, the Louvre in Paris, the Early Christian and Byzantine Collection in East Berlin) is extraordinarily rich and stylistically varied. There are no firmly dated pieces. Many sculptures were indeed found in situ in the excavation, but a fairly large part of them were reused in the course of building, especially in the South Church. Hence, as a rule, we do not know for what position or for what type of architecture they were produced.

The high point of this local sculpture production in limestone was the fifth century and the first half of the sixth century, as in Saqqara, and in many cases there are quite astonishingly close similarities in the types and forms of the sculpture produced at the two sites. In the limestone sculpture of Bāwīṭ, as in Saqqara in the sixth century, there were also imitations of modern Constantinopolitan models (impost capitals, especially of the fold type), which in the particular case of a figurative and ornamental decorated pillar comes close to being a direct copy. Yet, on the whole, such pieces remain very rare and isolated. They are far outnumbered by the characteristic examples of a local and markedly provincial production. Taken as a whole, the limestone sculptures do not reveal a uniform local style. They fall into several groups that follow different classes of models.

Quite unique are the wood sculptures of Bāwīṭ, often works of very good quality. They were mostly wrought for architectural decoration and probably derive from between the fifth and ninth centuries (Rutschowscaya, 1986), but their datings are still influenced by outmoded ideas and datings associated with the architectural history of Bāwīṭ.

BIBLIOGRAPHY

Chassinat, E. *Fouilles à Baouit,* Vol. 1. Mémoires publiés par les membres de l'Institut français d'Archéologie orientale du Caire 13. Cairo, 1911.

Clédat, J. "Recherches sur le kom de Baouit." In *Comptes-rendus de l'Académie des inscriptions et belles-lettres,* pp. 525–46. Paris, 1902.

______. *Nouvelles Recherches à Baouit (Haute-*

Egypte): Campagnes 1903–1904, pp. 517–26. Académie des Inscriptions et Belles-Lettres: Comptes rendus des séances de l'année 1904. Paris, 1904.

———. "Bawit." In *Dictionnaire d'archéologie chrétienne et de liturgie*, Vol. 2, cols. 203–251. Paris, 1910.

———. *Le Monastère et la nécropole de Baouit*. Mémoires publiés par les membres de l'Institut français d'Archéologie orientale du Caire 12 and 39. Cairo, Vol. 1, 1904–1906; Vol. 2, pt. 1, 1916.

Effenberger, A. "Scultura e arte minore copta." *Felix Ravenna quarta serie Fascicolo* 1–2 (1981):65–102.

Graviers, J. de. "Inventaire des objets coptes de la Salle de Baouit au Louvre." *Rivista di archeologia cristiana* 9 (1932):50–102.

Krause, M. *Das Apa Apollo Kloster zu Bawit: Untersuchungen unveröffentlichter Urkunden als Beitrag zur Geschichte des ägyptischen Mönchtums*. Leipzig, 1958.

Krause, M., and K. Wessel. "Bawīt." In *Reallexikon zur byzantinischen Kunst*, Vol. 1, cols. 568–83. Stuttgart, 1966.

Maspero, J., and E. Drioton. *Fouilles exécutées à Baouit*. Mémoires publiés par les membres de l'Institut français d'Archéologie orientale du Caire 59. Cairo, 1931–1943.

Palanque, C. "Rapport sur les recherches effectuées à Baouit en 1903." *Bulletin de l'Institut français d'Archéologie orientale* 5 (1906):1–21.

Rutschowscaya, M. H. *Catalogue des bois de l'Egypte copte* (Musée du Louvre). Paris, 1986.

Severin, H. G. "Zur Süd-Kirche von Bawit." *Mitteilungen des deutschen archäologischen Instituts, Abteilung Kairo* 33 (1977):113–24.

———. *Gli scavi eseguiti ad Ahnas, Bahnasa, Bawit e Saqqara: Storia della interpretazioni e nuovi risultati (XXVIII Corso di Cultura sull'arte Ravennate e Bizantina)*, pp. 299–314. Ravenna, 1981.

———. "Beispiele der Verwendung spätantiker Spolien: Ägyptische Notizen." In *Studien zur spätantiken und byzantinischen Kunst F. W. Deichmann gewidmet*, ed. O. Feld and U. Peschlow, Vol. 2, pp. 101–104. Monographien des Römisch-Germanischen Zentralmuseums 10. Mainz, 1986.

Timm, S. "Dēr Anbā Abullū'." *Das christlich-koptische Ägypten in arabischer Zeit*, Vol. 2, pp. 643–53. Beihefte zum Tübinger Atlas des Vorderen Orients, series B nr. 41/2. Wiesbaden, 1984.

Torp, H. *The Carved Decorations of the North and South Churches at Bāwīṭ*. Kolloquium über spätantike und frühmittelalterliche Skulptur 2. Vortragstexte 1970, pp. 35–41. Mainz, 1972.

———. "Le Monastère copte de Baouit: Quelques notes d'introduction." *Acta ad archaeologiam et artium historiam pertinentia* 9 (1981):1–8.

HANS GEORG SEVERIN

Paintings

The extensive pictorial decor at the Monastery of Bāwīṭ is distinctive yet diverse in style. While a certain number of themes, subjects, or motifs may have parallels elsewhere, the Bāwīṭ pictures do maintain a distinctive character. Since there are multiple portrayals of the same idea in various places at the site, one finds notable variations in style (e.g., the group of Mary and the Apostles beneath the Triumph of Christ (Clédat, 1904), compared to the other examples of this theme). Some themes are narrative, in which case successive scenes may be fitted one within another (e.g., the Massacre of the Innocents); on the other hand, one scene may fill a single panel in a juxtaposed series of events (e.g., scenes of the life of David).

The subjects most frequently portrayed are Christ, His childhood, His baptism, His triumph, Mary, the angels, the apostles, Coptic saints, hunting, various symbols, and decorative elements, both plant and geometric.

There are four styles of pictorial decor at Bāwīṭ. The first—which rarely appears—derives directly from the Alexandrian "Graces and Divinities of Happiness" (e.g., the Triumph of Christ cited above). Even though this style is slightly mechanical because of the stereotyped movement of certain parts of the ensemble, it is balanced by other individual poses. Above all—in contrast to other examples of this theme at Bāwīṭ itself—the uniform turning of the heads toward Christ enthroned brings out a notable realism, and herein lies an important clue for dating it. Moreover, this is not a copy of the Hellenistic Graces but rather a Coptic interpretation thereof, as can be seen by the compression of the bodies, the slight enlarging of the pupils, and correction of the outline.

The second style evidences a completely different influence that is no less strong and indicates a sort of Byzantine implantation at Bāwīṭ. It is undeniably the work of very good Byzantine painters or talented Coptic students.

The most typical scene—unfortunately an isolated one—is that of the gazelle hunt, in which the clothing offers proof of Byzantine influence. While Clédat thought he detected therein a Persian influence, it can be more simply explained as a transmission of these clothing details through the Byzantine occupation of Egypt at Antinoopolis in the sixth and seventh century, as is evidenced by the silk fabrics excavated there. All doubt is excluded by the long blouse gathered at the waist over tight-legged pants, with its black borders and consistent dark-green color highlighted by bright reflection. The same may be said for the very harmonious composition found in the bodies and limbs of the human figures and the elegant forms of the gazelles. However, the vagueness of the facial features most likely indicates a Coptic artist.

Another scene, many times repeated, deserves mention. It consists of juxtaposed figures, two of them holding a key. They stand beside three other figures seated on a cushioned divan or decorated banquette, one of whom is facing front while the other two flank him in a three-quarter or profile position. The drape of the folds in the clothing—particularly in that of those seated—is closely related to the well-known drape common to Byzantine art in the sixth century. Here again, the faces are impersonal. Fortunately, however, the inscription of the names—collected and noted by Clédat—permits one to interpret these scenes as an homage to the great names of Coptic monasticism. A recourse to Coptic painters trained in the surrounding Byzantine classicism could be a confirmation of this.

The third style, the one most common at Bāwīṭ, takes its inspiration from the above and can be seen in groupings, usually consisting of monks juxtaposed and often identified or personalized by insignia that may be functional (a saint, a book, or a key, if not a lamp or vase) or perhaps historic. In addition to the study of the folds of their long, usually white robes, certain decorations indirectly provide a date for this style, which is the ninth century. For instance, in a monk's long tunic, one finds the motif of ribbons and rings against a violet background decorated with a plant having ascending or descending branches, all executed in ecru and outlined in the finest manner. The faces of this style, with their different coiffures and beards, show more realistic traits. The scenes of the Triumph of Christ, which are more conventional, also appear to belong to this period.

The last style is one in which convention has become the rule, with heavy bodies, folds of identical clothing, and faces that vary but reveal no attempt to portray the actual person.

Ornamentation followed the same evolution. As with the sculpture in relief, it became more and more "mechanical." Nonetheless, such ornamentation has the merit of providing frames to scenes depicting human figures, also introducing a fantastic element unusual to such conventional art, and thereby giving it great vitality.

The variety of subjects is enormous and covers a large part of Christian iconography. However, certain subjects of prime importance do not appear at all, such as the Passion, the cross, the Resurrection (not even in its Byzantine form of the Descent of Christ into Hell), and the Ascension (not to be confused with the Triumph of Christ, which appears frequently). Nonetheless, thanks to the scope of the monuments now excavated and the considerable number of frescoes brought to light, the sampling is complete enough to make such absences insignificant, counterbalanced as they are by the importance given to the Triumph of Christ and, consequently, His humanity as well as His divinity.

The subjects found at Bāwīṭ may be classified into two categories: first, themes about Christian personages, such as Christ, Mary, angels, prophets, saints, and monks; and second, decorative or symbolic themes, usually meant for liturgical use or having ornamental value with a more or less precise symbolism.

Christian Personages

Christ. The iconography of Christ is more important by the way it portrays God the Savior than by the variety or frequency of its use. Christ's life on earth is depicted in a certain number of scenes. Though each can be seen in only one example (save a few exceptions to be considered later), in discussing them, we cannot exclude the possibility that others may have been destroyed or have not as yet been discovered. One series for which there is a single example in each case is that of the childhood of Christ. Found in Chapel 51, it juxtaposes the Annunciation, the visitation and departure from Elizabeth's home, the Nativity, and finally, the massacre of the innocents (Clédat, 1904–1906, Vol. 1, pp. 524–25, pl. 4).

From the public life of Christ, there are three scenes: the Baptism of Christ (found in two strikingly different examples), the Miracle at Cana, and the Last Supper.

The identification of the Miracle at Cana in Bāwīṭ is hypothetical. The excavator, Clédat (Vol. 2, 1916, p. 6), thought it to be the Last Supper, and one should not underestimate his interpretation. Nonetheless, until there is further inquiry based on a more thorough documentation of the history of this excavation, it is clear that some essential elements of this scene have long since been destroyed, since one can see only a few personages reclining for a meal and eight amphorae in alignment, of which seven are painted blue and one red. The repetition of these amphorae and their differences in color seem to favor the identification with Cana. The richness of those elements that have survived from this scene would seem to date it from the sixth century.

The Last Supper occupied the back of the sanctuary of the South Church. The photography of this scene now extant is of bad quality, but it does portray the table at which Christ is seated, surrounded by His apostles. The poses of these figures denote a late date corresponding to the last years of the monastery.

No other portrayals of Christ's life on earth—not His miracles, preaching, or other events mentioned in the Gospels, including those of the Passion—have been revealed by the excavations. On the other hand, Christ in His celestial glory is portrayed at Bāwīṭ in a number of examples. These are of two types, one isolated and relatively simple, and the other more elaborate and complex.

The first is characterized by the pose of Christ facing front, sitting between an eagle and an ox (chapel 26). Christ, beardless, holds the Holy Book on His left arm while pointing to it with His right hand. The rather sumptuous and classical style dates this painting to the sixth century.

The second type of this theme, enriched with divers details, forms the upper half of a scene in which the lower level portrays Mary surrounded by two groups of figures facing front. Because of its greater complexity, this type clearly appears to have been inspired by a more Coptic style that can be recognized by its compressed character, in addition to certain other aspects, such as the coloring (thought to be inspired by the Ascension of the sixth-century Syrian Gospel of Rabula), that indicate a later date, probably the seventh century.

The general schema of the upper zone comprises the sun and moon placed in the corners, Christ enthroned beneath them, facing front, encircled by a mandorla that may be supported by the four evangelical symbols and flanked by two archangels, two local saints, or even by the four evangelists grouped two on each side. Christ, who may be pictured with or without a beard, is holding the Holy Book. The details above Christ in his glory may vary. The mandorla itself, of a wider almond shape than usual, tends to a perfect circle. In the group found in chapel 17, some of the heads—each framed in a medallion—are those of the evangelistic symbols, with the head of a man replacing that of a woman.

In the lower zone of this scene, the central figure is Mary, enthroned either with or without the Holy Child or else standing without the Child in an orant pose (Chapel 17, pl. 41). The groups of figures juxtaposed about her, augmented on the sides by one or two local saints, are most generally the apostles.

Superposing two zones whose figures are all juxtaposed and facing front does not indicate a simple dualistic concept. The ensemble forms one entity whose apparent line of separation conceals a close relationship between the figures of the lower zone, who mystically exalt Christ, and the divine inhabitant of the upper one. Although it distinguishes the earthly figures from Christ triumphant in glory, this scene abolishes the restrictions of time and makes the Eternal all-important. This transcendence is underscored in the scenes wherein the seated Virgin holds on her lap the infant Jesus, who, in such cases, is not also pictured in His celestial exaltation.

To these portrayals of Christ must be added a medium-sized medallion discovered in the excavations at Bāwīṭ by the Coptic Museum of Cairo and now on display there. Here Christ's figure is a bust flanked by two angels.

As can be judged from the above, the pictorial iconography of Christ at Bāwīṭ is rich despite the above-mentioned lacunae. While reflecting the reality of time as one indivisible entity, this iconography seems to emphasize Christ's human nature by portraying the cycle of His childhood and His baptism even as it shows His divinity by insisting on the theme of the Triumph of Christ.

Mary. Apart from the scenes of the Childhood of Christ cycle—which belong to the narrative genre and of which there is but one example known at Bāwīṭ—the portrayals of Mary at this site concern her divine motherhood and the homage paid her.

A realism that emphasizes the solemnity of this theme emerges from the *Galactotrophousa* (Mother nursing her child) found in a niche, wherein Mary is enthroned but as a bust with her child lying crosswise, whom she nurses at her right breast. The painting seems to belong to the fifth or sixth century.

The essential element of solemnity conferred upon her by the restricted movement is generally evidenced both by her enthronement and by the child seated facing front at her left side. There are some details, however, which modify this solemnity—notably, the figures added to the scene. Such additions might consist of an archangel followed by a deacon at each side of Mary's throne or a series of persons, as in chapel 7.

It is also in Chapel 3 that Mary, enthroned with Jesus at her side facing front, is flanked by two groups, each one consisting of many juxtaposed figures proceeding to the outer edge of the scene. The first two figures are saints standing, crowned with a halo, holding in one hand a diadem and in the other a staff that terminates in a red cross-bearing disk. Then follow two local saints (of whom one is named Apollo), prophets, and an archangel.

Another rather late development (ninth century, according to the figures' clothing) sets Mary enthroned between two angels, each holding in his right hand an incense burner while the right arm supports an incense box. Christ's importance is increased by the fact that He is seated in a small circular mandorla that Mary holds in her two hands in front of her breast.

The still more solemn and cosmic role given to Mary—either enthroned or alone and standing in an orant pose—appears in the scenes depicting the Triumph of Christ.

Holy Personages. The category of *holy personages* includes the saints and prophets of the Old Testament and Christian saints and monks.

In chapel 12, within a frame bordered by garlands of vines and twisted fringe, is a long line of prophets: Isaiah, Jeremiah, Ezekiel, Daniel, Hosea, Joel, Amos, Obadiah, Jonah, Micah, Nahum, Habakkuk, Zephaniah, Haggai, Zechariah, and Malachi. These figures are damaged more often than not, but if one may judge by two of the better conserved ones (Amos and Habakkuk), they are crowned with haloes and wearing a tunic held in at the waist by a belt, covered by a pallium at the shoulders and revealing beneath its hem the bottoms of tight pants and ornamented sandals. Each personage is holding an unrolled scroll upon which is inscribed a passage from his work. Between Haggai and Zechariah there is inserted a scene of a bow-and-arrow lion hunt. Beneath this high frieze there are figures representing the Virtues (busts), birds, marine animals, and putti (cherubs), all of which alternate and interlace with each other. These paintings, highly colored and well drawn, probably date from the beginning of the monastery.

Also in this category are pictures of the youth of David.

The apostles are not absent from Bāwīṭ, for they are depicted around Mary in the lower register of the Triumph of Christ. But they do not appear to have been portrayed individually, not even Peter or Paul.

Apparently no one has as yet identified either the pictures or saints' names among those figures often crowned with a halo and clothed in a long white tunic who are juxtaposed—frequently at a three-fourths angle—and whose lineup recalls the processions of the martyrs of Saint Apollinaris at Ravenna. They may perhaps be recognized as Copts by their short beards that terminate in a goatee. The only saints that seem to have been identified are VICTOR, PHOIBAMMON, and Sisinnios (see SAINTS, COPTIC).

Monks are often portrayed, but none of them can necessarily be identified even when his name, preceded by the title Apa (Father), is mentioned, for the same name is repeated for different monks. Their clothing consists primarily of a long tunic, a pallium, and sandals. The name of one monk has survived on a panel conserved at the Louvre, which identifies the personage as MENAS, who was once of the monastery of Bāwīṭ.

Certain local saints (one of whom is identified as Apollo) are placed standing on each side of Mary enthroned.

Angels, Archangels, and Demons. As is particularly suitable in Egypt, angels are to be found in all types of scenes and ornamentation. As in Byzantine art, they form the almost obligatory bodyguard of Mary. Often they are pictured in medallions as busts crowned with haloes and may be recognized both by their short haircut and bangs (a "Joan of Arc" haircut) and by the upper part of their wings protruding into the register above.

There are some instances in which an angel is the principal figure in a single scene. For example, there is the angel standing and holding against his bosom the Three Hebrew Children of Babylon, who, reduced to the size of infants, rest against his cloak. One also finds scenes in which, at the left of a row of monks proceeding from the center, there is an angel holding a staff that terminates in a cross, standing between two of the monks, who are also standing and holding a Holy Book. There is another scene with an angel holding a disk in one hand and a staff capped with a cross in the other, flanked by monks standing—one of whom is named Apollo—each carrying a Holy Book. An angel, flying above and behind Saint Phoibammon on horseback, is holding a circular crown ready to be placed on his head.

The three great archangels also have their place in the chapels of Bāwīṭ. Saint Gabriel is depicted at the right of the Virgin Mary in one of the pictures of her as the Mother of God. Saint Michael and Saint Raphael are portrayed elsewhere.

Demons are rarely pictured, and only—so it

seems—beneath a symbolic personage, whether it be the demoness Alabastria conquered by Saint Sisinnios or those animals that have traditionally been emblems of evil since pharaonic times: scorpions, serpents, crocodiles, ibis, and hippopotamuses, to which may be added the mummified owl depicted in the above-mentioned picture of Saint Sisinnios.

Without exception, angelic figures—who may be identified by their deeds—wear a long tunic with sleeves, which may be simple but is more often decorated, usually with stripes descending from the shoulder, a border around the hem and up the sides, squares or small circles (*orbicula*) that descend from the shoulder, and/or lateral ornaments with an interior design, either figurative or decorative. The demoness, on the other hand, has her upper torso bared.

Ornamentation and Symbols

With the exception of decorative motifs found in architecture using geometric designs or plants from nature as handed down from Hellenistic tradition, ornamentation may indicate sacred symbolism. In certain cases, the symbolism is Christian.

Plants. The acanthus is used profusely, as in the friezes and interlacings that are often inhabited by various creatures. One of these interlacings alternates circles and lozenges, with the circles containing the head of an angel or a saint (male or female), while the lozenges enclose birds (sometimes a peacock) along with fruits and plants. In the spaces between the circles and lozenges there is a basket of fruit; in another chapel there are interlacings containing busts of the allegorical Virtues, eagles, putti, and marine animals alternating with each other.

In chapel 3 the baseboard is composed of square parterres of flowers diagonally juxtaposed. These parterres differ from one another by their manner of displaying the flowerets; thus, some stand tall on their stems, whereas others show only the petals unfolding. However, each parterre shows but one single floral example repeated ad infinitum and set in a complex of intersecting lozenges. It is entirely possible that these imitation gardens may be—as in the catacomb paintings at Rome—an evocation of the Garden of Eden via the intermediary Elysian Fields.

A pomegranate tree and low plants at the foot of a mountain form the natural decor of a symbolic lion hunt.

Animals. There is an Elysian evocation in the positioning of poultry and garden birds, among which one may cite the peacock that inhabits the interlacings in chapel 18. The peacock, inherited from pharaonic times, succeeded the phoenix as a symbol of eternity. Thus, at Bāwīṭ it has not left its native habitat, though it appears in Hellenistic landscapes.

The eagle—which in Coptic art is sometimes confused with the peacock or dove—is well portrayed three times at Bāwīṭ, always facing front with wings outspread. It appears in chapel 12, where it alternates in the interlacings with divers other objects; chapel 27, where a medallion hangs from its neck; and chapel 32, where it is given a rich necklace terminating in a metallic crescent from which hangs a flower-shaped cross. The eagle is holding in its beak a Coptic cross.

A hind-shaped unicorn with front hooves hobbled takes shape near the monks of chapel 17. The elegance of the design and colors dates this scene to the fifth or sixth century. It is possible that it may already be a symbol of the Incarnation.

A bow-and-arrow lion hunt—highly colored, set in a decor of mountains near low plants and a pomegranate tree—separates the prophets Haggai and Zechariah in the Chapel of the Prophets. The feline is turning its head in the direction whence came the arrow, which has pierced its right eye and cranium. This may be an allusion to the freeing of Israel announced in Zechariah 11:3: "Hark, the roar of the lions, for the jungle of the Jordan is laid waste!" The feline, though somewhat stylized, is skillfully drawn and posed.

The same may be said for a bear with its tongue hanging out placed near a saint in chapel 17. The pose indicates a realistic portrayal, one carefully observed and well drawn.

To these scenes must be added the marine animals that alternate with other subjects in some interlacings.

A beardless soldier, perhaps an infantryman, is found in chapel 18. He is standing, clothed in a short tunic (with sleeves covering his arms to the wrist), of which the upper part—decorated on the shoulders and down the center by a colored stripe—recalls a Byzantine military uniform.

The Virtues of Faith, Hope, Charity, Patience, and the rest may be seen alternating with the other subjects noted above (eagle, putti, marine animals) in an interlacing placed in a register beneath the row of prophets.

At the Monastery of Bāwīṭ the cross may be depicted as such, with no symbolic overtones. It may be the Roman cross upon a cruciform pedestal, decorated with simple interlacings in the crosspiece, from which hang two lamps. One also finds the ansate cross, itself decorated in the empty spaces with precious stones. Finally, in chapel 1, one sees the cross supported by the branch of a laurel tree, which implies heroic overtones.

The cross may also appear as a Christian emblem on some objects. Such is the case of the Coptic cross found on vestments or on the picture of a bronze lamp.

Geometric Designs. A baseboard of juxtaposed squares enclosing a floweret, each separated by intersecting lozenges, has been discussed above with plants.

In the grand reception hall at Bāwīṭ, there was a rather high plinth about 4 feet (1.20 m) covered with approximately twenty colored squares set in succession, each showing various combinations of curved or straight lines to distinguish it from the next. The style recalls a genre of Byzantine ornamentation, but it is quite possible that the artist may have invented a new ornamentation here. It can be dated to the sixth or seventh century.

A liturgical lamp hanging by a chain from a sort of railing is painted in a scene clearly meant to be liturgical. The lamp is patterned after those bronze lamps that have an elongated body closed at one end and prolonged by a beak at the other. The belly, which is visible, is decorated with a Coptic cross between two vertical dotted lines. Also to be mentioned are two bronze lamps that hang from the crosspiece of a cross.

There survive only rare but important elements from Bāwīṭ. Some are located in the Coptic Museum at Cairo, and there is one painted panel in the Louvre. However, as can be seen, the photographs taken by Jean Clédat's mission at the site in 1903—with their colors often reproduced by Clédat's talented artist, François Daumas, and complemented by the excavator's research—provide a good survey of the most important items from what is perhaps the largest surviving collection of Coptic paintings.

BIBLIOGRAPHY

Chassinat, E. *Fouilles à Baouit.* Mémoires publiés par les membres de l'Institut français d'Archéologie orientale 13. Cairo, 1911.

Clédat, J. "Recherches sur le kom de Baouit." In *Comptes-rendus de l'Académie des inscriptions et belles lettres,* pp. 525–46. Paris, 1902.

______. "Nouvelles recherches à Baouit (Haute Egypte); Campagne 1903–1904." *Comptes-rendus de l'Académie des inscriptions et belles lettres,* pp. 517–20. Paris, 1904.

______. "Baouit." In *Dictionnaire d'archéologie chrétienne et de liturgie,* Vol. 2, pt. 1, cols. 203–251, ed. F. Cabrol. Paris, 1910.

______. *Le Monastère et la nécropole de Baouit.* Mémoires publiés par des membres de l'Institut français d'Archéologie orientale 12 and 39. Cairo, Vol. 1, 1904–1906, and Vol. 2, 1916.

Drioton, E. "Un Bas-relief copte des trois hébreux dans la fournaise." *Bulletin de la Société d'archéologie copte* 8 (1942):7.

Krause, M., and K. Wessel. "Bawīt." In *Reallexikon zur byzantinischen Kunst,* cols. 568–84. Stuttgart, 1966.

Maspero, J. *Fouilles exécutées à Baouit* (notes taken and edited by E. Drioton). Mémoires de l'Institut français d'Archéologie orientale 59. Cairo, 1932–1943.

Régnier de Crozals, F. *Eléments de base pour servir à l'étude de la vie quotidienne des moines au monastère de Baouit d'après les inscriptions et les monuments.* Mémoire de l'Ecole du Louvre. Paris, 1987.

PIERRE DU BOURGUET, S.J.

BAYAD AL-NAṢĀRĀ. *See* Pilgrimages.

BAYAHU, AL-. *See* Pilgrimages.

BAYT AL-ʿAJĪN (Arabic, House of Dough), the bakehouse for the preparation of the EUCHARISTIC BREAD. From the early Middle Ages *Bayt al-ʿAjīn* has formed an important element of every church complex in Egypt. Occasionally the room is also described as "Bethlehem" (Burmester, 1967, p. 81f.). In accordance with its importance, the *Bayt al-ʿAjīn* usually lies close to the entrance to the church, but is only rarely actually connected with the church buildings. As a rule it is a small smoke-blackened room containing a small baking oven, some storage space for wood for the fire, and the equipment necessary for the baking process.

BIBLIOGRAPHY

Burmester, O. H. E. *The Egyptian or Coptic Church.* Cairo, 1967.

Graf, G. *Verzeichnis arabischer kirchlicher Termini,* p. 77. Louvain, 1954.

PETER GROSSMANN

BAYT AL-NISĀ' (Arabic, House of the Women), an area within the church reserved for the women, which became usual only in modern church buildings in Egypt. The practice was incorrectly dated to the tenth century (in Butler, 1970, pp. 19ff.) on the basis of a wrong assessment of the Mercurius church at DAYR ABŪ SAYFAYN. Where possible, it has its own entrance from the outside. Thus, in more recent churches, the *Bayt al-Nisā'* takes over the function of the galleries of the early Christian and medieval BASILICA. There is a fine example in the al-'Adhrā' church (seventeenth–eighteenth century) of Banī Adyāḍ (south of Manfalūt), in which the *Bayt al-Nisā'* lies west of the naos proper and is separated from it by a wide arched opening with a lattice, and two lateral windows. The separate entrance is on the southern short side. In the old church of DAYR ABŪ ḤINNIS the *Bayt al-Nisā'* was added on the south side of the church, where at the same time several large arched openings had to be cut in the wall. In most cases the *Bayt al-Niṣa'* is separated from the church area only by a wooden lattice. Thus in the two monasteries at Suhāj the south conch today serves as a *Bayt al-Nisā'*. In the church of Dayr al-Naqlūn the northern side aisle was set apart as a *Bayt al-Nisā'*.

BIBLIOGRAPHY

Butler, A. J. *The Ancient Coptic Churches of Egypt*, Vol. 1, 2nd ed. Oxford, 1970.

PETER GROSSMANN

BEJA TRIBES. The nomadic and warlike Beja tribes have occupied the Red Sea hills of Egypt and the Sudan since very early times. In pharaonic days the tribes were known as the Medjay and were already regarded as a menace by the settled populations in the Nile Valley. One of the Egyptian frontier fortresses built in Nubia during the Twelfth Dynasty bore the name "Repelling the Medjay." Because of their fighting prowess, the nomads were sometimes recruited to serve as mercenaries in the pharaoh's palace guard. Later, under the name Blemmye, they are mentioned repeatedly in classical texts as the principal threat to Ptolemaic and Roman authority in NUBIA, as well as to the empire of KUSH, which lay to the south.

Medieval Arabic texts always give the name Beja rather than Blemmye. The earliest of these date from the eighth century, and there are a great many references to the Beja in documents from later centuries. Firsthand descriptions of them and of their country were written by IBN ḤAWQAL and by IBN SALĪM AL-ASWĀNĪ. At one time there was some uncertainty as to whether the Beja of medieval and modern times could be positively identified with the Blemmye of classical texts, but this has been resolved by documents recently found at QAṢR IBRĪM, in which the name is given as Blemmye in Coptic and as Beja in Arabic.

Both in late classical and in early medieval texts there are a number of references to Christianity among the Blemmye/Beja. Apparently their conversion was undertaken at the same time as was that of the Nubians (see NUBIA, EVANGELIZATION OF) in the middle of the sixth century. When the missionary LONGINUS was on his way to convert the Nubian kingdom of 'ALWĀ, he is reported to have traveled through the Blemmye country under the protection of the "king of the Blemmyes" himself. However, the transplant of Christianity evidently did not flourish among the nomads, who had no settled communities or permanent buildings. In the tenth century they were described by Ibn Salīm as having no religion, while others described them as worshippers of idols or of the stars.

Beginning in the ninth century the Beja were increasingly interpenetrated by Arab migrants from the Ḥijāz, who established a kind of feudal aristocracy among them. Through this agency the Beja were converted to Islam, and as soldiers of the new faith they became once again a menace to the settled populations of Christian Nubia, as well as to Upper Egypt. Beja attacks played a part in the weakening and final dissolution of the medieval kingdom of MAKOURIA.

There are four main Beja tribes today: the Bisharin, Amarar, Hadendowa, and Banī 'Āmīr. The first three speak languages of the Kushitic or Hamitic family, related to Galla and Somali, while the Banī 'Āmīr have adopted the Semitic Tigre language of Eritrea. The 'Ababdah, a fifth group, have lost their indigenous language and speak only Arabic, but still retain a sense of Beja identity and history.

[*See also:* Banūal-Kanz.]

BIBLIOGRAPHY

Adams, W. Y. *Nubia, Corridor to Africa*, pp. 56–60. Princeton, N.J., 1977.

Burckhardt, J. L. *Travels in Nubia*, pp. 503–511. London, 1819.

Kirwan, L. P. "Studies in the Later History of Nubia." *University of Liverpool Annals of Archaeology and Anthropology* 24 (1937):69–105.

MacMichael, H. A. *A History of the Arabs in the Sudan,* Vol. 1, pp. 35–51. London, 1922.
Paul, A. *A History of the Beja Tribes of the Sudan.* London, 1954.
Revillout, E. "Mémoire sur les Blemmyes, à propos d'une inscription copte." *Mémoires presentés par divers savants à l'Académie des inscriptions et belles-lettres,* Vol. 8, Pt. 2, Ser. 1. Paris, 1874. *Second mémoire sur les Blemmyes, d'après les inscriptions démotiques des Nubiens.* Paris, 1887.
Trimingham, J. S. *Islam in the Sudan,* pp. 10–16. London, 1949.
Vantini, G. *Christianity in the Sudan,* pp. 91–102. Bologna, 1981.
Woolley, C. L., and D. Randall-MacIver. *Karanog, the Romano-Nubian Cemetery.* University of Pennsylvania, Egyptian Department of the University Museum, Eckley B. Coxe Junior Expedition to Nubia, Vol. 3, 1910.

WILLIAM Y. ADAMS

BELL, HAROLD IDRIS (1879–1967), English pioneer of papyrology. He entered the Department of Manuscripts of the British Museum in 1903 and retired in 1944 as keeper of the department. He was a member of many learned societies and academies and a fellow of the British Academy and its president from 1946 to 1950. He published numerous Greek and some Coptic papyri and wrote many important articles about Egypt. His bibliography, compiled by J. David Thomas, is in *Journal of Egyptian Archaeology* 40, 1954, pp. 3–6, and 53, 1967, pp. 139–40.

BIBLIOGRAPHY

Skeat, T.-C. "Sir Harold Idris Bell." *Journal of Egyptian Archaeology* 53 (1967):131–39.

MARTIN KRAUSE

BELLEROPHON AND THE CHIMERA. *See* Mythological Subjects in Coptic Art.

BELLS. *See* Metalwork, Coptic; Music, Coptic: Musical Instruments.

BELTS. *See* Costume, Civil.

BENEVOLENT SOCIETIES, COPTIC, societies set up by voluntary organizations, which constitute an important element in the social fabric of Egypt. Their growing importance and the role they played were conducive to the creation of a Ministry of Social Affairs in 1952, with the express aim of supervising these societies, which multiplied throughout the country in both Muslim and Coptic communities. In 1930, the ministry issued a useful guide under the title *Directory of Social Societies and Organizations,* which included Coptic associations and defined their functions. A description of the most important and effective organizations follows.

The oldest and still the most important of these societies, founded in 1881, is the Benevolent Coptic Society, whose first president was Boutros Ghālī. Its achievements were detailed in a report issued on the occasion of its golden jubilee. Though initially it was founded to help the needy of the community, it developed into a huge organization by extending its projects to most fields of education and public health by the end of the nineteenth century. Apart from the establishment of schools and technical centers for both boys and girls, it was ultimately able to build its own hospital. Its role strongly motivated numerous emerging societies.

Next in importance and seniority, the Tawfīq Society was founded in 1891, and its name, which means "reconciliation," signified an aim that was essentially the coordination between the modern reform tendencies with what was best in the older systems. The society distinguished itself in the establishment of schools run by a highly proficient faculty. Parallel to the educational endeavor, this society attended to cultural interests, first, through the establishment of a public library and, second, by the foundation of a printing press, which published many books.

Jam'iyyat al-Nash'ah al-Qibṭiyyah, founded in 1896 at Hārit al-Saqqayīn in Cairo, had three main objectives: teaching the Coptic language, inculcating the principles of religion, and compiling a history of the Copts.

The society also published an annual calendar giving the Coptic, Gregorian, and Hegira dates in three separate columns, and details of fasts, feasts, and commemoration of saints, as well as agricultural information related to seasonal crops, sowing, irrigation, and harvesting.

Jam'iyyat Aṣdiqā' al-Kitāb al-Muqaddas, one of the most active Coptic societies, was founded in 1908 by Basīlī Buṭrus, who devoted a great deal of his energy toward its development. He remained as its president until his death in 1921. A graduate of the Clerical College, he spent his early years as a preacher in the Coptic churches of Suez, Bahjūrah, Minyā, and Ṭanṭā before settling down as a teacher of religious studies in the Coptic College, where he became interested in the service of Coptic youth and founded the aforementioned society. He then went to England in May 1910 to study English activities in this sphere.

Buṭrus devised a closely knit organization with several secretaries, committees, study circles, and a board of directors to watch over the fulfillment of the religious aims of the society. In 1932 summer camping grounds were provided on the shores of the Mediterranean at the Manderah seaside resort, east of Alexandria, for socioreligious gatherings. In 1953 the society established its own Saint Mark's chapel in Shubrā, and a noted educationist, Ḥāfiẓ Dawūd, was consecrated as its priest.

The society paid special attention to the young people living in the capital away from home, and in particular took care of girl students for whom a special branch was founded.

Jam'iyyat Thamarat al-Tawfīq was founded in Cairo in 1908 by Tadrus Mīkhā'īl as a charitable organization to provide free education to the poor. In 1909 it established a boys' school; a dispensary was founded in the following year. It is also worth noting that the society took an active part during the nationalist movement of 1919, and that SA'D ZAGHLŪL chose its premises to be a venue for his political speeches as a mark of Coptic-Muslim solidarity.

Jam'iyyat al-Ikhlāṣ was established in 1909 in Alexandria to carry out socioreligious reform and to support the Community Council in implementing its resolutions. Among its outstanding achievements were the building of the second church in Alexandria (dedicated to the Virgin Mary), a large hospital, a sewing and needlecraft center for girls, and an elementary school.

BIBLIOGRAPHY

Diamond Jubilee of al-Tawfīq Society Report. Cairo, 1967.

Directory of Social Societies and Organizations. The Regional Association of Societies in Cairo. Published by the Ministry of Social Affairs. Cairo, 1970.

FUAD MEGALLY
SULAYMĀN NĀSĪM

BENJAMIN I, thirty-eighth patriarch of the See of Saint Mark (622–661). He was born about 590 at Barshūṭ, a village in the province of Beheirah in the western Delta.

Benjamin was undoubtedly one of the greatest patriarchs of the Coptic church. He lived through the tremendous upheavals of the Persian invasion (619–629) and the ARAB CONQUEST OF EGYPT in 641. He was able to steer the church through these turbulent and confused times to a fresh beginning side by side with the emerging power of Islam.

The story of Benjamin's youth is obscure, although he came from a Coptic family with comfortable means. Since Alexandria was within reach of his village, it can be assumed that he had a measure of education in that capital city. No record of the size of his family exists, but it is known that he had one brother, Mennas, who was tortured with fire by the Byzantine patriarch, Cyrus, and brutally murdered by drowning in the Nile. This occurred because Mennas refused to accept the Chalcedonian profession of faith or to reveal the whereabouts of his fugitive brother, a demonstration of the steadfast character of his family in matters of faith and national pride.

Benjamin's early life was marked by ascetic habits, and in 620 at the rather mature age of thirty, he took the monastic vow at the monastery of Canopus, which had escaped destruction by the Persians because of its isolated geographical situation. Here he improved his asceticism under the prevailing Pachomian monastic rule within the complex of monastic settlements better known in the Lower Egyptian tradition. Here, too, Benjamin found his spiritual mentor in an old holy man by the name of Theonas who vested him with the *schema* or monastic garment. Theonas also instructed him in the virtues of monasticism—holiness, patience, and self-control—as well as in the study of the Holy Scriptures, which indicates that he was not illiterate. He is known to have concentrated on and memorized the Gospel of Saint John.

Theonas presented his pupil to the reigning patriarch, ANDRONICUS, who had become aware of Benjamin's piety and ability. Following a tradition of the Coptic church, Andronicus retained Benjamin in his service, ordained him as priest, and appointed him as his assistant, anticipating his possible succession to the patriarchate. The new position acquainted Benjamin with the conduct of church affairs as well as with the various elements of the community, whose high esteem he won. This paved the way for his election and succession to the patriarchate after the death of Andronicus.

Little is known about the early years of Benjamin's pontificate beyond the issuance of encyclicals to fix the date of Easter and to instruct the clergy in matters of doctrine. He managed to steer the church out of the difficult period of the Persian invasion. Though the originals of the encyclicals of his reign were lost, Benjamin is known to have collected fifteen and edited them in codex form.

In 631, Cyrus, or Kyros, the Chalcedonian bishop of Phasis in the Caucasus, was appointed by Emperor Heraclius both as Melchite patriarch of Egypt and as prefect in command of the military forces of the Byzantine province, with explicit orders to curb all religious separatism—by persuasion or, if necessary, by force of arms. The native Benjamin, now a rival patriarch, took to flight from his new enemy, and moved from desert monastery to monastery in order to foil his pursuing persecutors. A new chapter of merciless persecution of all those who refused to declare recognition of the Chalcedonian profession was inaugurated. It was at this time that Benjamin's brother, Mennas, joined the native rebels against Cyrus. Property of all clerics who followed the national patriarch in flight was confiscated and many churches were forcibly passed to Melchite hands.

It was at this juncture that ʿAmr ibn al-ʿĀṣ appeared with a relatively small army on the frontiers of Egypt. The Arab conquest of the province began on 12 December 639, and the fortress of Babylon fell into Arab hands on 9 April 641. The invasion of Alexandria took place on 17 September 642. It is not known whether the Copts played an active role in the invasion. What is certain is that they did not stand by the side of their Byzantine persecutors during the war.

In the meantime, ʿAmr issued a safe-conduct to Benjamin, who seems to have returned to the valley at a slow pace either at the end of 643 or the beginning of 644. Apparently Sanutius (or Shenute), the augustal duke of the Thebaid, who supported the Egyptian cause, gave Benjamin funds to restore the Church of Saint Mark before his departure after the Arab conquest.

Benjamin worked hard to rearrange the affairs of the church and bring back order to its devastated properties and to strengthen the morale of his demoralized people. Then the moment came for a face-to-face encounter with ʿAmr. In this historic meeting of universal importance, ʿAmr is quoted to have said that he had never seen such an impressive man of God as Benjamin (Butler, 1978, p. 442). Although the length and substance of the meeting are unknown, the first conference between the representatives of Egyptian Christianity and Islam was conducted with dignity, a situation that ʿAmr did not find in the Asian conquest. ʿAmr restored to Benjamin all the rights that the Byzantines had denied him, and recognized him as the sole representative of the Egyptian people. The patriarch prayed for ʿAmr, addressing him with admiration. The encounter was a full success for the patriarch.

Benjamin set out to restore the Egyptian church by renewing the policies of one of his great predecessors, DAMIAN. He also laid the foundations of an amicable relationship with the conquerors and ʿAmr, who honored the "People of the Book," although they were destined to struggle with emerging difficulties at later dates. This was true partly because of disunion between the Christians themselves, as some pockets of sectarians and Melchites had survived the Arab conquest. However, Benjamin was able in the long run to bring considerable unity to his church. Those who had fled to the Pentapolis began to return, and the bishops such as Cyrus of Nikiou and Victor of Phiom, who had apostatized to the Chalcedonian profession, were persuaded to come back to the mother church. It is said, however, that the Chalcedonians were too numerous, and that some of them clung to their beliefs, leaving a rift within the church. That fact provided some future Islamic authorities with opportunities to set one faction against another in an effort to extort financial benefits from the hard-pressed population.

However, for the time being, those same Islamic authorities were satisfied with Benjamin's efforts to maintain law and order in the country. He rigorously applied his judicial functions even in accordance with the Byzantine legal system.

The patriarch made pontifical visitations to the dioceses and to monasteries, restoring churches wherever restoration was needed. An impressive feat of his time was the recovery of Saint Mark's head, which the Greeks wanted to smuggle to Byzantium. In the end, it was probably deposited in the sanctuary bearing his name in the monastery of Saint Macarius (DAYR ANBĀ MAQĀR) between 28 December 645 and 3 January 646 (or 647). It was on this occasion that Benjamin issued his canons to the monks of Saint Macarius.

Benjamin's strong personality was felt during the governorship of ʿAmr's successor, ʿAbdallah ibn Saʿd ibn Abī-al-Sarḥ ibn al-Ḥārith al-ʿĀmirī (A.H. 25–35/A.D. 645–655), whose lust for money came at a time when agricultural products were depleted and people were impoverished. It was through his intercession that solace was brought to the oppressed subjects.

After a long and monumental career, the patriarch passed the last two years of his life stricken with severe illness. After suffering greatly, he died on 3 January 661. So deep was the impression of his long reign on the minds of his contemporaries that the legend was circulated among them that not only did the angels carry his noble soul to heaven but it was also escorted by Saint Athanasius the Apostolic, Saint Severus of Antioch, and Saint Theodosius. These legends attest to his immortal role in saving Egyptian orthodoxy.

BIBLIOGRAPHY

Brakmann, H. "Zum Pariser Fragment angeblich des koptischen Patriarchen Agathon. Ein neues Blatt der Vita Benjamin I." *Le Muséon* 93 (1980):299–309.

Coquin, R.-G. *Livre de la consécration du sanctuaire de Benjamin.* Bibliothèque d'Etudes Coptes 13. Cairo, 1975.

Girgis Daoud Girgis. "Abba Benjamin the Coptic Patriarch in the 7th Century." In *Nubia et Oriens Christianus: Festschrift für C. Detlef G. Müller zum 60. Geburtstag,* ed. P. O. Scholz and R. Stempel. Tübingen, 1987.

Müller, C. D. G. "Benjamin I, 38. Patriarch von Alexandrien." *Le Muséon* 69 (1956):313–40.

———. "Neues über Benjamin I, 38. Patriarchen von Alexandrien." *Le Muséon* 72 (1959):323–47.

———. *Die Homilie über die Hochzeit zu Kana und weitere Schriften des Patriarchen Benjamin I von Alexandrien.* Abhandlungen der Heidelberger Akademie der Wissenschaften, Philosophisch-historische Klasse. Heidelberg, 1968.

———. "Der Stand der Forschungen über Benjamin I, den 38. Patriarchen von Alexandrien." *Zeitschrift der deutschen morgenländischen Gesellschaft,* Supplement I 2 (1969):404–10.

———. *Grundzüge des christlich-islamischen Ägypten,* Vol. 11. Darmstadt, 1969.

Zotenberg, H. "Mémoire sur la chronique byzantine de Jean, évêque de Nikiou V." *Journal Asiatique,* ser. 7, no. 13 (1879):348–86.

C. DETLEF G. MÜLLER

BENJAMIN II, eighty-second patriarch of the See of Saint Mark (1327–1339). Benjamin's life before taking the monastic vow is utterly unknown beyond the fact mentioned by the HISTORY OF THE PATRIARCHS that he was a native of the town of Dimiqrāṭ south of Armant in Upper Egypt. Apparently his nomination was supported by a prophecy of one of the greatest saints of the day. Before his death in 1320, BARSŪM THE NAKED (al-'Iryan) from his solitary cell in the hills adjacent to the city of Ṭurah predicted the accession of the monk Benjamin. Thus, his selection and consecration found no opposition from the clergy or the laity. He was a contemporary of Sultan al-Nāṣir Muḥammad ibn Qalāwūn (1310–1341), during his third tenure of the Mamluk sultanate, when the tempestuous wave of persecution and pressures on the Copts began to subside. One factor that helped the return to peaceful coexistence between the Muslims and Copts was the advent of an embassy from the Ethiopian sovereign. The monarch pleaded on behalf of the Copts and requested permission to let them rebuild and restore their ruined churches. He threatened to destroy the Muslim mosques within his own kingdom if the Copts were not allowed to restore their churches. Apparently al-Nāṣir responded to that call and renewed the original terms of the Covenant of 'Umar ibn al-Khaṭṭāb, which guaranteed the survival of existing churches at this time, but forbade the construction of new ones. Benjamin started diligently to restore the churches that the mobs had destroyed in what the Islamic historian al-MAQRĪZĪ and others described as the "battle of the Christians" (*Wāqi'at al-Naṣārā*).

Benjamin oversaw the speedy restoration of the damaged churches and resumed the preparation of the CHRISM, which had been suspended during the patriarchate of JOHN IX. This operation was performed at the Monastery of Saint Macarius (DAYR ANBĀ MAQĀR) in Wādī al-Naṭrūn, in a full ecclesiastical assembly attended by twenty bishops from Lower and Upper Egypt. There, the bishops celebrated Easter after the completion of this important ecclesiastical function.

While in the wilderness of SHIHĀT in Wādī al-Naṭrūn, the patriarch was able to inspect the neighboring monasteries, and concentrated his attention on the ancient DAYR ANBĀ BISHOI, which he restored using his patriarchal funds. Further, he supplied its depleted residents with a new group of monks from other quarters.

During Benjamin's reign, Sultan al-Nāṣir appointed an Islamized Copt to the highest office in his court. This was Sharaf al-Dīn 'Abd al-Wahhāb ibn al-Tāj Faḍl Allāh, known in Islamic sources as al-Nushu'. It was expected that such an appointment might give the Copts favors or at least relief from repression. On the contrary, al-Nushu', according to the *History of the Patriarchs,* was very hard in his treatment of his former coreligionists, probably to prove the sincerity of his apostasy to the Muslim administration. The *History* records that al-Nushu' was able to amass immense wealth and that he imposed many hardships on the Copts and abused their women, monks, and nuns. It is said that the Lord punished him for these crimes. In fact, the Muslim sources and chroniclers such as al-Maqrīzī and Ibn Ḥajar al-ʿAsqalānī paint an eloquent picture of the downfall of al-Nushu'. He managed to infuriate the Mamluk amirs by his arrogance and his heavy-handedness to such an extent that they worked hard to poison al-Nāṣir's mind against him. The sultan dismissed him from office and killed him and his family, while confiscating the vast wealth he had accumulated. As additional humiliation, his body was buried in the Jewish cemetery in a shroud costing only four dirhams. However, his tomb was guarded by officers for a week to prevent the mob whom al-Nushu' had oppressed from desecrating his remains and stealing them for burning in the open. The *History of the Patriarchs* ascribes this sorry ending to his unforgivable treatment of the Copts.

Although the *History's* biography of Benjamin is only ten lines, the Islamic sources contain numerous details on the events of his age, including the names of many Copts who feigned apostasy to the Islamic faith. Benjamin II died after a reign of continuous struggles that lasted eleven years, seven months, and twenty-six days. He was buried in DAYR SHAHRĀN, and the patriarchal see remained vacant for a year after his death.

BIBLIOGRAPHY

Lane-Poole, S. *The Mohammadan Dynasties.* London, 1893; repr. New Delhi, 1986.

______. *History of Egypt in the Middle Ages.* London, 1901.

SUBHI Y. LABIB

BESA, fifth-century monk and third abbot of the White Monastery (DAYR ANBĀ SHINŪDAH), situated beside the ancient village of Atrīb in the region of Akhmīm, near Suhāj. The monastery was founded by PJOL in the middle of the fourth century, and Besa's immediate predecessor as abbot was SHENUTE. No Life of Besa exists, and any attempt to sketch his biography must be based on his own writings—his *Life of Shenute* and his *Letters and Sermons*—and on the occasional references to him that have survived in Coptic literature. Neither Besa's date of birth nor that of his death is known. If the date of Shenute's death is assumed to be 466, this is the year of Besa's succession as abbot of the White Monastery.

From a fragment of a manuscript leaf now in the British Library (Or. 3581B, 64), it appears that an Apa Besa had an interview with the emperor Zeno who came to the throne in 474. If the reading and identification of the two names are correct, it can be concluded that Besa lived until after 474. There is no doubt that Besa spent some time as a monk under Shenute and that during Shenute's lifetime he attained a position of trust and responsibility. In his old age, Shenute nominated him to be his successor. Like his predecessor, Besa was given the ecclesiastical title ARCHIMANDRITE. A fragment of a panegyric on Besa (Paris, National Library, 131.[7], 37) that has survived testifies that his memory was held in high esteem. An indirect testimony to Besa's reputation in monastic circles of later ages is the preservation and continued copying of his writings. His name is also remembered in the liturgy where it is coupled with that of Shenute in the *Memento* of the saints.

From Besa's writings it is clear that his life was devoted to the administration of the White Monastery and to the pastoral care of its monks and nuns. To teach and encourage them, to exhort and upbraid and, if necessary, to punish them was his daily duty. He had supreme authority not only over the community in which he lived but also over the daughter houses, both monasteries and convents, that formed part of the White Monastery. He assumed even wider responsibilities when, in time of famine, he gave refuge in the monastery to about 5,000 to 6,000 victims and saw to it that they were cared for by his monks. Food, baths, and medical treatment were provided, and those who died were buried. He is also on record as having given exhortation and advice to clergy and laymen of certain villages outside his monastery.

His inspiration for his own life of asceticism and for his teaching is primarily the Bible. Every page of his writings bears witness to his intimate knowledge of and respect for it. His admiration for Shenute and his loyalty to him are apparent not only in his *Life of Shenute* but also in references to him in his other writings. Although the Bible and Shenute were the two most active influences on Besa, his respect for monastic tradition is revealed by his frequent references to the commandments of "our fathers" as well as by quotations from ATHANASIUS and ANTONY.

While it is true that many of Besa's writings are provoked by the lapses of his monks and nuns, it must not be supposed that monasticism under him offered nothing more than a penal code to enable the individual to lead the good life. The ideal of fellowship and mutual advancement was alive in his communities. That his writings contain hardly any references to the doctrinal controversies of his day may, at least in part, be accounted for by the predominantly pastoral concerns displayed in them.

All his writings are in the Sahidic dialect with the exception of the *Life of Shenute*, which, in its entirety, has been preserved in Bohairic but which no doubt was composed originally in Sahidic. Besa's style is difficult to characterize. It is largely conditioned by the subject matter of his writings. In the *Life of Shenute*, he adopts the conventional style of the panegyric; in his moral exhortations he is often formal, stilted, and diffuse. Sometimes, however, when a problem engages his keen personal interest, his style becomes vivid and persuasive.

It is perhaps inevitable that the figure of Shenute should dwarf that of his successor. Nevertheless, this fact ought not to blind us to the many positive qualities of Besa. In his writings, he occasionally accuses himself of weakness, but it is clear that, in order to fulfill his manifold duties, this had to be overcome. His humility and utter sincerity shine through all his writings, and his moral earnestness and saintliness must have done much to strengthen the roots of monasticism and to encourage its growth.

BIBLIOGRAPHY

Cauwenbergh, P. van. *Etude sur les moines d'Egypte*, pp. 137ff. Paris, 1914.

Kuhn, K. H. "A Fifth Century Egyptian Abbot." *Journal of Theological Studies* 5 (1954):36–48, 174–187; 6 (1955):35–48.

______, ed. *Letters and Sermons of Besa. Textus*. In CSCO 157, Scriptores Coptici 21. Louvain, 1956.

______, ed. *Letters and Sermons of Besa, Versio*. In CSCO 158, Scriptores Coptici 22. Louvain, 1956.

Leipoldt, J., ed. *Sinuthii vita bohairice. Textus*. In CSCO 41, Scriptores Coptici 1. Louvain, 1906.

Wiesmann, H. *Sinuthii vita bohairice. Versio*. In CSCO 129, Scriptores Coptici 16. Louvain, 1951.

K. H. KUHN

BESAMON, SAINT, a martyr of the Basilidian CYCLE. Of his Passion there is only one Sahidic fragment left, which can be set at the beginning of the work (Till, 1935, pp. 42–48). The text begins with the advice to DIOCLETIAN to begin the persecution. The advice is accepted and Diocletian proclaims his famous edict. A boy named Besamon, son of the general BASILIDES, comes in and, ripping his clothes off, goes to the emperor to reproach him and to confess himself a faithful Christian. The text ends here. It is odd that Besamon is not mentioned in the other Passions belonging to the same Basilidian cycle.

BIBLIOGRAPHY

Till, W. C. *Koptische Heiligen- und Martyrerlegenden*, Vol. 1. Orientalia Christiana Analecta 102. Rome, 1935.

TITO ORLANDI

BESSARION, SAINT, fourth-century anchorite. According to the short series of apothegms attributed to Bessarion in the alphabetical collection of the APOPHTHEGMATA PATRUM, the saint (festal date, 25 Misrā) was a contemporary of JOHN OF LYCOPOLIS. He lived, therefore, for at least part of his life, in the second half of the fourth century, at SCETIS. He had a disciple called Doulas, who depicted his master as a powerful thaumaturgist who cured the possessed, walked on the water, made seawater drinkable, and could even stop the sun in its course. But Bessarion was also a great ascetic, capable of going forty days without rest and praying in an upright position for weeks at a time. He was, above all, eager for humility and judged himself the most guilty of sinners.

The last apothegm of the series presents Bessarion as one of God's perpetual wanderers, settling nowhere, but according to the best witnesses, it really refers to another anchorite, one named Serapion. It is also to the latter that should be attributed the famous anecdote of the little gospel that the anchorite always carried with him and with which he finally parted for the benefit of the poor. Bessarion is mentioned in the Alexandrian SYNAXARION.

BIBLIOGRAPHY

Cotelier, J. B., ed. *Apophthegmata Patrum*. In PG 65, pp. 137–44. Paris, 1864.

Grébaut, S. *Synaxaire éthiopien*. In PO 9, pp. 392–95. Paris, 1907ff.

LUCIEN REGNAULT

BETROTHAL CUSTOMS. In times past it was both the duty and the right of the parents to choose a spouse for their child. Today it is only required that they grant their approval to the match.

The Coptic betrothal ceremony consists of two events: the engagement and the official betrothal. The engagement (*shabkah*) takes place when, after the couple has obtained parental approval to wed, the future groom goes with his parents to the home of the bride-to-be and presents her with a gift of some value, befitting his financial situation. This is a private, family meeting, and a simple meal is served. There is no religious ceremony, and the engagement may be revoked at any time.

The official betrothal has a religious character, and is sealed by the church in a formal procedure, which can be broken only by its intervention. For this ceremony the home of the future bride is gaily decorated with small flags and colorful strings of lights outside and many flowers inside. Before commencing with the prayers, the priest must ascertain in writing that there are no legal obstacles to the marriage by checking the mutual agreement between the couple, the compatibility of their ages, and the size of the dowry to be paid by the fiancé. This custom is gradually disappearing. The date for the wedding ceremony is generally set at this time, providing that the couple have reached legal age (eighteen years for the boy, sixteen years for the girl). Having thus established the marriage contract, the priest dates the document and has it signed by all parties involved as well as certain notable guests.

Then, two wedding rings of gold or diamonds are wrapped, along with the wedding crowns, in a white veil that will cover the heads of the couple on their wedding day. The priest reads the contract, blesses the couple three times with his cross, and recites the Lord's Prayer in concert with all those present. Next, turning toward the East and baring his head, he says the Prayer of Thanksgiving, and offers up incense, while the choir of deacons sings to the accompaniment of triangles and cymbals. After appropriate lections from the Epistles, Gospels, and Psalms, the priest recites the three prayers of intercession, the Creed, and three special prayers for the betrothal contract. Once again he recites the Lord's Prayer, and says another prayer over the veil. Then taking one of the wedding rings, he places it upon the right hand of the future bridegroom, who, in turn, takes the other ring and places it upon the right hand of his bride-to-be.

BIBLIOGRAPHY

Burmester, O. H. E. *The Egyptian or Coptic Church*, pp. 131ff. Cairo, 1967.

CÉRÈS WISSA WASSEF

BIBLE, COPTIC VERSION. *See* Old Testament, Coptic Translation of; New Testament, Coptic Versions.

BIBLE MANUSCRIPTS, GREEK. The Hebrew text of the Old Testament was translated into Greek. The *Letter of Aristeas* gives a legendary account of this undertaking. The name of the translation, the Septuagint (LXX), comes from the number of the translators. The historical core of the legend may be that the Pentateuch was translated in Alexandria under Ptolemy II Philadelphus (285–246 B.C.), and the other writings of the Old Testament were translated later. The Christians of Egypt took over this Greek translation as Holy Scripture, and later it formed the basis for the translation of the Old Testament books into Coptic (see OLD TESTAMENT, COPTIC TRANSLATIONS OF THE).

The great parchment manuscripts of the fourth or fifth century, written in uncials—the codices Sinaiticus, Vaticanus, Alexandrinus, and Ephraemi Syri *rescriptus*—contain, with various lacunae, the Greek Old and New Testaments and some apocryphal writings. Still older are the papyrus codices of the Septuagint that were found in Egypt (place of discovery unknown) and are now in the Bodmer and Chester Beatty libraries. They date from between the first half of the second century (Numbers and Deuteronomy) and the fourth century. The Bodmer Library (see BODMER PAPYRI) has the major part of the Psalter, dating from the third/fourth century. The Chester Beatty Library has a greater number of Old Testament books (see CHESTER BEATTY BIBLICAL PAPYRI): Genesis in two incomplete copies, Numbers, Deuteronomy, Isaiah, Jeremiah, Ezekiel, Esther, Daniel, and Ecclesiastes. The copies of Genesis, though incomplete, are especially important because the book is missing in the codices Sinaiticus and Vaticanus. All of these manuscripts are of great value for the textual history of the Septuagint (see BIBLE TEXT, EGYPTIAN). To these we may add the HAMBURG PAPYRUS. It is unknown where this manuscript was discovered, but it was written about 400. It contains the Song of Solomon in Greek and Coptic, and also Ecclesiastes in both languages, while it presents only the Coptic version of the Lamentations of Jeremiah. The Coptic translations are written in the Old Fayyumic dialect. An edition by Diebner appeared in 1989).

The Greek-Coptic bilingual manuscripts of the Old Testament (Nagel, "Griechisch-koptische Bilinguen . . . ," pp. 246ff.) are also important for the history of the text. Through the allegorical interpretation of Scripture, the Old Testament played a great role in the church in Egypt, particularly in its early period. There are traces of the Old Testament also in Egyptian monasticism, especially Pachomian monasticism (Krause, 1981, p. 230 n. 48). Frequently whole Old Testament books, especially the Psalter, were memorized.

The books of the New Testament in the original Greek gradually came to Egypt with the missionaries who in the first century brought the Christian message, probably first to Alexandria and then to Egypt as a whole. In public worship the New Testament was read in Greek and—so far as this language was not understood by the Christians—translated orally into Coptic. Fixing the translations into the Coptic dialects in writing followed, at the latest, after the middle of the third century. Antony of Kome (b. 251/252) heard a reading from Matthew 19 in his home church about 272. Since he did not know Greek, the reading must have been in Coptic. Despite the translation of the New Testament into the Coptic dialects, further Greek manuscripts were copied in Egypt, as is shown by the manuscripts found there (survey in Aland, 1976; and Aland and Aland, pp. 106ff.). A papyrus fragment (P^{52}) containing John 18:31–33 and 37–38 (see Aland and Aland, p. 109) was written as early as about 125, some thirty years after the presumed date of the Fourth Gospel.

The New Testament papyri, especially the excellently preserved Greek manuscripts that reached the Chester Beatty collection in 1930–1931, and those that later were added to the Bodmer collection, together with the great parchment codices already mentioned above, which also contain New Testament writings, show first the Alexandrian and then the Egyptian text. P^{46} and P^{66}, dated about 200, contain the text of this time; P^{75}, that of the beginning of the third century; and P^{72}, that of the third/fourth century. P^{75} is so close to the Codex Vaticanus that the theory of a revision of the New Testament text in the fourth century must be abandoned. According to Aland and Aland (p. 103), in the "early" text we can distinguish alongside the "normal" text, which hands down the original text, a "free" text (represented, for example, by P^{45}, P^{46}, and P^{66}) with more variations than in the "normal" text, and a "firm" text (represented by P^{75}), which accurately transmits the original text.

BIBLIOGRAPHY

Aland, K. *Kurzgefasste Liste der griechischen Handschriften des Neuen Testaments.* Arbeiten zur neutestamentlichen Textforschung 1. Berlin, 1963.

———. *Die griechischen Handschriften des Neuen Testaments—Korrekturen und Ergänzungen zur "Kurzgefassten Liste." Materialien zur neutestamentlichen Handschriftenkunde,* Vol. 1. Arbeiten zur Neutestamentlichen Textforschung 3. Berlin, 1969.

———. *Repertorium der griechischen christlichen Papyri,* Vol. 1. Berlin, 1976.

Aland, K., and B. Aland. *Der Text des Neuen Testaments.* Stuttgart, 1982.

Diebner, B. J. *Hamburger Papyrus Bil. 1. Die alttestamentlichen Texte des Papyrus bilinguis 1 der Staats- und Universitätsbibliothek Hamburg.* Geneva, 1989.

Kenyon, F. G. *The Chester Beatty Biblical Papyri,* Vols. 1–3 and supplement. London, 1933–1937.

———. *The Text of the Greek Bible,* 3rd ed. London, 1975.

Krause, M. "Der Erlassbrief Theodors." In *Studies Presented to Hans Jakob Polotsky,* ed. D. W. Young. East Gloucester, Mass., 1981.

Metzger, B. M. *The Early Versions of the New Testament.* Oxford, 1977.

Nagel, P. "Studien zur Überlieferung des sahidischen Alten Testaments, Teil I: Der Stand der Wiederherstellung der alttestamentlichen Kodizes der Sammlung Borgia (Cod. I–XVI)." *Zeitschrift für ägyptische Sprache und Altertumskunde* 110 (1983):51–74.

———. "Griechisch-koptische Bilinguen des Alten Testaments." In *Graeco-coptica. Griechen und Kopten im byzantinischen Ägypten.* Wissenschaftliche Beiträge, Martin-Luther-Universität, Halle-Wittenberg, 1984.

———. "Studien zur Textüberlieferung des sahidischen Alten Testaments, Teil I B: Der Stand der Wiederherstellung der alttestamentlichen Kodizes der Sammlung Borgia (Cod. XVII–XXX)." *Zeitschrift für ägyptische Sprache und Altertumskunde* 111 (1984):138–64.

Treu, K. "Griechisch-koptische Bilinguen des Neuen Testaments." In *Koptologische Studien in der DDR.* Halle-Wittenberg, 1965.

MARTIN KRAUSE

BIBLE TEXT, EGYPTIAN, a group of Greek biblical texts originating in Alexandria, the site of the famous CATECHETICAL SCHOOL where Coptic and Greek theologians were busy with Christian religious studies, undoubtedly including texts of the Bible. It was here that ORIGEN compiled his famous Hexapla (see HEXAPLA AND TETRAPLA), and surely this tradition persisted at that school in the early centuries of Christianity. It is possible that its scholars collected all available texts of the Old and New

Testaments for study and collation of some authorized versions, as is evident from the CHESTER BEATTY PAPYRI, where emendations prove that there was research associated with their labor. The work on the Egyptian text was probably accelerated during the episcopate of HESYCHIUS, an Egyptian bishop and biblical scholar, whose recension of the Gospels is cited by Saint Jerome.

Hesychius was martyred in 311, two years before Constantine I declared Christianity the state religion by the issuance of the Edict of Milan. Modern scholarship has designated his work the Hesychian recension of the Gospels, which must have been utilized by later scribes. It is known that Constantine ordered the preparation of fifty copies of the Bible for distribution among the Christian churches of the empire. These were made at Alexandria or Caesarea or both, though Alexandria, with its concentration of theologians at the Catechetical School, appears to have been the natural center for handling this task. Of the Constantine Bibles, four somewhat incomplete texts have survived, all on vellum rather than papyrus. These are the CODEX VATICANUS, the CODEX SINAITICUS, the CODEX ALEXANDRINUS, and the CODEX EPHRAEMI SYRI. Together with the earlier Coptic papyri comprising the Chester Beatty Collection and the BODMER PAPYRI, these codices constitute the most valuable source of the Egyptian text of the Bible.

BIBLIOGRAPHY

Finegan, J. *Light from the Ancient Past,* 2nd ed. Princeton, 1950.

Gregory, C. R. *Canon and Text of the New Testament.* New York, 1907.

Kenyon, F. G. *Handbook of Textual Criticism of the New Testament,* 2nd ed. London, 1912.

______. *The Chester Beatty Biblical Papyri,* 8 vols. London, 1933–1958.

______. "Hesychius and the Text of the New Testament." In *Cinquantenaire de l'Ecole biblique et archéologique française de Jérusalem (15 novembre 1890–15 novembre 1940).*

______. *Our Bible and the Ancient MSS.* London, 1948; repr. New York, 1958.

Lake, K. *The Text of the New Testament,* 6th ed. London, 1928.

Lietzmann, H. *Einführung in die Textgeschichte der Paulusbriefe, An die Römer,* 4th ed. Handbuch zum Neuen Testament 8. Tübingen, 1933.

Milligan, G. *The New Testament Documents, Their Origin and Early History.* London, 1913.

______. *The New Testament and Its Transmission.* London, 1932.

Roberts, C. H. *The Biblical Papyri of the John Rylands Library.* Manchester, 1936.

Wilckens, U. *Die griechischen Papyrusurkunden.* Berlin, 1897.

AZIZ S. ATIYA

BIBLICAL SUBJECTS IN COPTIC ART.

[The term "biblical subjects" here designates subjects taken from the Old Testament; subjects from the New Testament are grouped with the Christian subjects as a whole (see CHRISTIAN SUBJECTS IN COPTIC ART).

Biblical subjects are far from rare in Coptic art, although they are not as frequent as they are, for example, in the Roman catacombs. Coptic art emphasizes Christian subjects, rather selectively chosen, and also certain themes or figures of pagan origin that have been given Christian interpretation (see MYTHOLOGICAL SUBJECTS IN COPTIC ART).

This entry consists of the following short articles by different authors:

Abraham and Isaac
Adam and Eve
Daniel in the Lion's Den
David at the Court of Saul
Demons
Jonah
Joseph
The Three Hebrews in the Furnace

Other Old Testament subjects are dealt with in other entries as follows:

Adam and Eve in Eden (see ART AND ARCHITECTURE, COPTIC)
Job (see ILLUMINATION)
Moses (see ILLUMINATION)]

Abraham and Isaac

The story of the patriarch Abraham, who was willing to sacrifice his cherished son, Isaac, in obedience to God's command, occupied an important place in Coptic iconography. Probably the oldest representation is in a wall painting discovered at Tell Idfū in 1923–1924 (Henne, 1925, pp. 25, 26, 30). The upper part has disappeared, leaving a headless man clothed in a short tunic. With his left hand he is grasping another, smaller person by the hair and prepares to pierce him with a sword. The remaining details correspond to the essentials of the known iconography of the scene, which are suggested by some unidentifiable traces on the right. This possibility, as well as the location of this mural in a quarter consisting of houses attributed to the Christian epoch (Henne, 1925, p. 25, n. 5), verifies the identification of the figure as Abraham. The linear style places this painting in the fourth century.

Abraham and Isaac stand out in relief in a niche under a broken pediment originally from DAYR APA JEREMIAH at Saqqara and now in the Coptic Museum, Cairo. Two sequences of scroll patterns with stylized leaves converge toward a central cross, surrounded by a leafy crown. The two figures are full-face. At the top left, the hand of God holds back the raised right arm of Abraham wielding the knife while Abraham's left hand grasps Isaac's head by the hair. Isaac slightly bends his knees. The ram, which God provided as a substitute sacrifice, stands in profile under the divine hand and the patriarch's upraised arm. A good study of this piece by J. Leibovitch locates it, perhaps a little too precisely, in the middle of the fifth century by reason of the special aspect of the pediment (Leibovitch, 1940). The symmetry of the composition, as well as the lifelike proportions of the figures and the naturalism of the vegetal elements, suggest a date at the beginning of the century.

Leaving aside possible examples that may have been destroyed, the theme reappears much later in two woven sleeve bands of the ninth century. One belongs to the Historic Museum of Textiles in Lyons and is in excellent condition. The other, in the Cooper-Hewitt Museum, New York, has loose threads in the center, somewhat to the detriment of Abraham and the ram. Both bands show the complete scene. They come from the same model and have the same composition. In the Cooper-Hewitt piece, for example, the scene fills a yellow ochre square, which is flanked by two panels decorated with red crossbars bearing a flower or a bird, the spread-out halves of flowers, and borders of overlapping leaves. In both bands Coptic letters are scattered near the heads of Abraham and Isaac, some of them forming part of the men's names. Both bands exhibit features characteristic of the ninth century—crossbars, spread flower-halves, flying-shuttle lines of unbleached thread, borders of overlapping leaves, and the defective transcription of the names (Du Bourguet, 1964, pp. 26–30, sec. F).

In painting, Abraham and Isaac appear again in the *haykal* (sanctuary) of the ancient church of DAYR ANBĀ ANṬŪNIYŪS near the Red Sea (Piankoff, 1958, pp. 156–59, pl. 1). This mural matches another sanctuary painting, of the meeting of Abraham and MELCHIZEDEK, in the traditional symbolism relating to the Eucharist. The general attitude of Abraham is the same as in the preceding examples, but his head is haloed, and he is clothed in a long decorated tunic with sleeves, caught at the waist by a green girdle. With his right hand he holds the hair of the kneeling Isaac, whose head is turned backward. With his left hand he prepares to pierce him with a long dagger. The style, no doubt influenced by Byzantium, which still maintained some contacts with the Fatimids, who ruled Egypt in the tenth to twelfth century, may place this painting at the end of the twelfth century.

In a wooden panel from the Fatimid period the scene appears in relief. Abraham is represented in profile, with his legs apart. He is clothed in a long robe with pleats; his haloed head is turned backward and upward toward that of a winged angel, who appears in the upper left corner. He turns his back to a tree whose foliage shelters a ram set in profile above the patriarch and his son. The latter is stretched on an altar, and his father is preparing to cut his throat. The reproduction of Abraham's clothing and the undulations of the foliage are fairly characteristic of the Coptic woodwork of the period (Beckwith, 1963, no. 140, and Rutschowscaya, 1986, nos. 355–58). Variety and fidelity clearly mark this panel which does credit to the originality of Coptic art down to its final period.

BIBLIOGRAPHY

Beckwith, J. *Coptic Sculpture 300–1300.* London, 1963.

Bourguet, P. du. *Musée National du Louvre. Catalogue des étoffes coptes.* Paris, 1964.

Henne, H. "Tell Edfou." Collection des fouilles de l'Institut Français d'Archéologie Orientale du Caire (1923–24) vol. 2, pt. 3. Cairo, 1925.

Leibovitch, J. "Un fronton de niche à scène biblique." *Bulletin de la Société d'Archéologie Copte* 6 (1940):169–75.

Pagan and Christian Egypt. Brooklyn Museum, New York, 23 January to 9 March 1941.

Piankoff, A. "Peintures au monastère de Saint Antoine." *Bulletin de la Société d'Archéologie Copte* 14 (1950–1957). (Cairo, 1958):151–63.

Rutschowscaya, M.-H. *Catalogue des bois de l'Egypte copte.* Paris, 1986.

PIERRE DU BOURGUET, S.J.

Adam and Eve

The story of Adam and Eve, the protoparents, who were expelled from the Garden of Eden for disobedience to God, seems to have inspired the Copts hardly at all. There is no portrayal extant in either sculpture or the minor arts. Painting alone occasionally reflects this theme. The oldest depictions are found at al-Bagawāt, near the Khargah oasis. In the fourth-century Chapel of the Exodus, Adam and Eve appear simply standing; Eve is called "Mother of All the Living." In the sixth-century Chapel of Peace, both Adam and Eve, hiding their nakedness with their hands, stand next to the Tree of Knowledge, around which winds the serpent-tempter. A tenth-century painting from Umm al-Barakāt in the Fayyūm now in the Coptic Museum, Cairo, presents two episodes from the biblical tale. In the first, on the right, near a luxuriant tree under which animals take shelter, Adam and Eve, nude and unashamed, are eating the forbidden fruit. In the other, on the left, Adam lifts an accusing arm toward Eve. Both of them, ashamed of their nudity, cover themselves with vine leaves. Finally, in Dayr Apa Apollo at Bāwīṭ, in Chapel 28, a lone man is called "Our Father Adam" (Clédat, 1904, p. 160 and pl. 106). A similar depiction was also found in an unnumbered chapel (Grabar, 1946).

BIBLIOGRAPHY

Clédat, J. *Le monastère et la nécropole de Baouît.* Cairo, 1904.

Grabar, A. *Martyrium, Récherches sur le culte des reliques et l'art chrétien antique* 2; *Iconographie.* Paris, 1946.

Simaykah, M. *Guide sommaire du Musée copte et des principales églises du Caïre,* pl. 103. Cairo, 1937.

MARGUERITE RASSART-DEBERGH

Adam and Eve. Tenth century. *Courtesy Coptic Museum, Cairo.*

Daniel in the Lion's Den

According to the book of Daniel, Daniel, a devout Jew at the Babylonian court of Nebuchadnezzar, is cast into a lion's den for his faith. This theme seems to have been illustrated rarely in Coptic art. The most ancient portrayal, dating from the fourth century, is a painting from the Chapel of the Exodus at al-Bagawāt. Here Daniel is pictured standing between two lions and praying; two centuries later the same subject was painted in the Chapel of Peace, also at al-Bagawāt. The theme then seems to disappear from painting. (According to H. G. Evelyn-White, the subject was depicted at DAYR ANBĀ MAQĀR in WĀDĪ AL-NAṬRŪN, but J. Leroy questions this identification [Leroy, 1982, pp. 45 and 78].) Nonetheless the prophet is evoked in Chapel 19 in Dayr Apa Apollo at Bāwīṭ, alongside the names of the Three Hebrews in the Furnace, another episode from the book of Daniel (Clédat, 1904).

Daniel is also found in sculpture and in the minor arts. Two reliefs present the story, each from a different aspect. In the one, Daniel, a heroic nude orant (praying figure), is surrounded by two lions threatening him with jaws gaping, fangs sharpened, and claws bared. The scene is framed by pillars carved in light relief and by draperies tied at the height of the hero's face. The second relief, in the Royal Museums of Art and History, Brussels, adopts a more classical iconography. Here the praying Daniel wears a traditional Middle Eastern costume: *anaxyrides* (close fitting trousers), boots, a belted tunic, a flowing cloak held by a fibula, and a small conical cap. The lions, completely subdued, are licking the feet of the man they should have devoured. The composition occupies the center of a niche under a pediment decorated with plants and peacocks. By its style and technique this relief is related to works of the fifth and sixth centuries (Rassart-Debergh, 1976, pp. 20–21). A third relief, from the seventh century, in the Coptic Museum, Cairo, links these two earlier representations: Daniel, dressed in a Middle Eastern costume, raises his arms; the lion on the left rears up threateningly while the one on the right places his muzzle on the feet of the hero (Effenberger, 1975, no. 51).

A similar scene is depicted on two pieces in wood dating from the fifth century in the State Museum of Berlin: a comb from AKHMĪM (Effenberger, 1975, no. 85), and a beam or girder perhaps from Bāwīṭ (Badawy, 1978, no. 3.83, p. 162). On the beam the hero and the lions—seated on their haunches and stretching their heads toward Daniel—are cut away from an architectural background. On an ivory pyx of the sixth century (in the Dumbarton Oaks Collection, Washington, D.C.), the lion's den is suggested by two low brick walls before which the lions are crouching (Badawy, 1978, no. 3.77, p. 158). Daniel, simply dressed, lifts his arms toward heaven while an angel approaches, closing the mouth of the lion on the right with his hand.

David at the Court of Saul

The early history of David, the shepherd boy chosen by the prophet Samuel to be king, the hero who killed the giant Goliath and played the harp for King Saul, is told in First Samuel. The appearance of David in scenes from this period of his life in wall paintings in several chapels at Dayr Apa Apollo at Bāwīṭ suggests that he was so honored at other sites in Egypt, although no evidence has survived. He was important in Christian iconography as both an ancestor of Christ and a prefiguration of Christ. Moreover, it is possible that the Coptic restriction of his story to his youth was inspired by its analogy at certain points to the story of Joseph at the court of pharaoh. Both youths, for example, served a ruler and were saviors of their people, and both prefigured Christ.

Several of the paintings of David could not be saved. Those that have been photographed or identified from various details present two isolated episodes and a decorative series.

In one isolated episode, in Chapel 34, Saul is shown in profile, seated upon a throne, and David appears as an interpreter of dreams (Clédat, 1916, pl. 13). In another, in Chapel 32, David appears as a cupbearer holding two amphorae under an imitation *arcosolium* (arched cell in a catacomb) (Clédat, pls. 6 and 9).

The decorative series runs at middle height on the walls of Chapel 3 (Clédat, 1904, pp. 10–20). It is a frieze consisting of 20-inch (50 cm) squares alternating between scenes and decorative areas divided into four linked swastikas. The scenes are episodes from the story of David: the rejection of David's brothers by Samuel, Samuel's choice of David, Saul equipping David for battle, David confronting Goliath, David slaying Goliath, David playing the lyre before Saul on his throne, who threatens him with a javelin, David and his friend Jonathan, and David at the house of the priest Ahimelech.

The style of the two sets of subjects is perceptibly different. The paintings of the isolated episodes are more richly decorated and their figures more sumptuously clothed than those in the decorative series. They appear to be earlier than the series, possibly from the sixth century. Several indications, including the beards of those watching David's fight with Goliath and the sketchy character of the design, suggest a date in the seventh or eighth century.

BIBLIOGRAPHY

Clédat, J. *Le Monastère et la nécropole de Baouît.* Mémoires des Membres de l'Institut français d'Archéologie orientale, Vol. 12 (1904) and Vol. 39 (1916).

PIERRE DU BOURGUET, S.J.

Demons

Malevolent spirits, or demons, had great importance in ancient Egypt and in the literature of the Coptic monasteries. Even accounting for the destruction of so much Coptic art, one would think that demons should have left traces in what has survived or been recorded. Such representations, however, are extremely rare.

Apart from the more than doubtful identification of a demon with a child in a mural in Chapel 17 of Dayr Apa Apollo at Bāwīṭ (Clédat, 1904, vol. 2, fasc. 2, pl. 46 and p. 78), there was in the same chapel (pl. 55) a fresco in which, amid magic symbols, Saint Sisinnios, pictured as a Byzantine horseman, pins to the ground the white-skinned female demon Alabastria. He also puts to flight a kind of winged siren, described as Alabastria's daughter, and finally a centaur holding a hook. These two figures also recall the race of demons, the siren by her serpent's tail and the centaur because the demon showed himself to Saint ANTONY THE GREAT in that form as described by Saint Jerome (cf. Jerome, 1898, p. 4). There are, however, representations of malevolent figures with dark skin, who may have some connection with demons, in some portrayals of the story of the patriarch Joseph (see below). Examples are some tenth-century textile decorations—*orbicula* (circles) perhaps for cushions, and *clavi* (bands framing the front opening) and sleeve bands for garments—and miniature paintings such as that of the Octateuch of the Seraglio, which portrays Joseph being sold to the Ishmaelites by his jealous brothers (Kitzinger, 1937–1938, pp. 266–68).

Possibly the rarity of demons in Coptic art was due to superstitious fear of their images, which could have been carried over from pharaonic to Christian times. The images just cited would have been accepted only because they exalted good over evil, that is, the power of Saint Sisinnios over demons and the victory of Joseph over the instruments of his brothers.

The dark color of the malevolent figures in the textiles and miniatures may be related to the fact that the black color given to demons in other parts of the Christian world was probably of Coptic origin. It must have been characteristic of politico-religious precursors in the pharaonic period transformed into Christian demons. Indeed, there is every reason to think that Coptic monastic stories were the vehicle for this iconographic detail, in the West as well as in the East. In such stories the demon is persistently presented as "the little black Ethiopian" or more simply either as "the little Ethiopian" or "the black one." No other description in early Christian literature or iconography specifies the color of the demon's skin.

The expressions "the black one" and "the Ethiopian" (and its synonym "the Nubian") go back to descriptions of the wicked god Seth, associated with the desert and sterility, in various Egyptian writings of the Ptolemaic period. A curse was laid upon Seth by Psamtik I in 660 B.C. to destroy even into the holy places any impulse of the black people of Nubia, who had killed his father, to ascend again the throne of pharoah. This curse was applied to the descendants of the Nubian kings of the Twenty-fifth Dynasty. The expressions were passed on through stories of the customs, monastic rules, and lives of the Coptic monks, including tales of frequent pillaging of their monasteries by the nomadic Blemmyes (see BEJA TRIBES), who came north from Nubia by way of the desert. Thus the black color associated with people so damaging to monastic life in Egypt could not but pass into the general iconography of the demons who opposed monastic asceticism in the wider Christian world.

BIBLIOGRAPHY

Clédat, J. *Le Monastère et la nécropole de Baouît.* Mémoires de l'Institut français d'Archéologie orientale 12 (1904).

Du Bourguet, P. "L'origine pharaonique d'un détail dans l'iconographie chrétienne: La Peau noire du démon." In *Proceedings of the XXVIIth International Congress of Orientalists,* Ann Arbor, Mich. 13–19 August 1967, ed. Denis Sinor et al. Wiesbaden, 1971.

Jerome (Eusebius Hieronymus). "Vie de Saint Paul de Thèbes." *Annales du Musèe Guimet* 25 (1898):4.

Kitzinger, E. "The Story of Joseph on a Coptic Tapestry." *London University Journal of the Warburg Institute* 1 (1937–1938):266–68.

PIERRE DU BOURGUET, S.J.

Jonah

According to the book of Jonah, the prophet Jonah tries to escape God's command to preach repentance in Nineveh by going to sea, but he is thrown overboard in a storm as a bearer of bad luck and swallowed by a great fish. After three days he is coughed up and eventually carries out his mission.

Apparently Coptic iconography uses nothing of the Jonah story except that he was regurgitated by a sea creature.

The theme appears in two works in the Louvre Museum, Paris—a decorative high-relief from the southern church of Dayr Apa Apollo of the fifth or sixth century and the lateral panel of a hanging made of an uncut bouclé fabric dating from the ninth century. In this panel Jonah rises vertically, in an attitude of prayer, from the mouth of the sea creature in the shelter of a castor oil plant. The fish mentioned in the Bible here takes the form of the *kētos,* a sea creature given two forepaws and sometimes two ears, which the Greeks used, from the fifth century B.C., to picture "cetaceans" and especially whales.

These two features—regurgitation by the sea creature and the presence of the castor oil plant (which evokes Yahweh's pity for the inhabitants of Nineveh)—were interpreted by Christians as symbols of the Resurrection of Christ.

BIBLIOGRAPHY

Badawy, A. *Coptic Art and Archaeology: The Art of the Christian Egyptian from the late Antique to the Middle Ages.* Cambridge, Mass., and London, 1978.

Bourguet, P. du "Deux pièces coptes de la fin de la période ommeyyade." *Revue du Louvre et des Musées de France* 19, 2 (1969):101–2.

PIERRE DU BOURGUET, S.J.

Jonah delivered from the whale beneath the turpentine tree. Limestone. Bāwīṭ. Sixth century. Height: 35cm. *Courtesy Louvre Museum, Paris.*

Joseph

The story of Joseph, son of the patriarch Jacob, who was sold into slavery by his jealous brothers but rose to favor with the Egyptian pharaoh and fed his hungry people, is told in Genesis 37. It is the only biblical theme that is widely depicted in Coptic art—on about fifty tapestry ornaments on Coptic textiles (Vikan, 1979, pp. 105f. note 4; Liberec-Kybalova, 1967, no. 83; Weitzman, 1979, no. 412; and Nauerth, 1978). Thus almost all the larger museum collections of Coptic textiles (see TEXTILES, ICONOGRAPHY OF COPTIC) possess one or more pieces reproducing pictures from the story of Joseph. The theme appears on the different forms of the trimming of tunics of late antiquity: *clavi,* sleeve bands, and above all *orbicula.* On these *orbicula,* large or small, the complete sequence of the scenes is most frequently and best documented. The cycle of nine pictures depicts the following: (1) pharaoh's dreams, which as a rule were presented in a central medallion, while the eight other episodes run around this medallion either clockwise or counter clockwise; (2) above the center, the picture of Jacob, who sits on a splendid bed and sends Joseph to his brothers; (3) Joseph meeting them in the field at Sichem (Vikan, 1979, p. 106, n. 9); (4) Joseph cast into a well (Vikan, 1979, p. 106, n. 10, notes an example in which Joseph is drawn out of the well); (5) Joseph's brothers dipping his coat in the blood of a slaughtered goat, although the thought that the brothers wish to murder Joseph, who is small and has a nimbus, probably plays some part in the picture (on the problem of this scene, see Nauerth, 1978, pp. 154f., and Vikan, 1979, p. 107, n. 43); (6) the sale of Joseph to the Ishmaelites; (7) his brother Reuben's grief at the empty well; (8) Joseph's journey to Egypt; and finally (9) the sale of Joseph to the Egyptian Potiphar. The scenes of an *orbiculum* could face to the right or to the left, a convention explained by the ancient custom of adorning tunics with two *orbicula,* showing the same or an opposing pattern, set opposite each other on the garment at the shoulders or at knee level.

The very close sequence of the pictures on the *orbicula* and the occasional contraction of scenes (e.g., scenes 1, 2, 3, 5) indicate that the origin of these illustrations is to be sought not in textile art but in book illustration. On the basis of an exact analysis of the individual scenes, G. Vikan has shown that the Coptic fabrics drew on the Sir Robert Cotton manuscript, whereas the Joseph scenes

Story of Joseph. Tapestry. Ninth–tenth century. Height: 26.5 cm.; width: 28 cm. *Courtesy Pushkin Museum, Moscow.*

on the Lens silk textile did not (Weitzmann, 1979, no. 413). This relationship at the same time provides a proof that the Cotton manuscript is of Egyptian origin. The fact that the illustrations in the Coptic manuscript are limited to Genesis 37 is still a problem, which is probably connected with the assessment of the figure of Joseph. His Egyptian career, for example, is not further represented (Weitzmann, 1979, p. 462; Vikan, 1976, pp. 99 and 108, with n. 62), although admittedly the chapter is in literary terms also a self-contained block between Genesis 36 and 38.

The original sequence of scenes was altered in manifold ways, often almost beyond recognition, by the omission of individual scenes or figures. This is especially observable on the sleeve bands, on which the mirror-image arrangement of individual elements still plays a special role. (Problems in detail are perhaps also technically conditioned, namely, by the use of weaving stencils; cf. Nauerth, 1978, pp. 158f).

BIBLIOGRAPHY

Liberec-Kybalova, M. *Die alten Weber am Nil.* Prague, 1967.

Nauerth, C. "Die Josefsgeschichte auf koptischen Stoffen." *Enchoria* 8, 2 (1978):151–59.

Vikan, G. *Illustrated Manuscripts of Pseudo-Ephraem's Life of Joseph and the Romance of Joseph and Aseneth.* Unpublished diss. Princeton, 1976.

———. "Joseph Iconography on Coptic Textiles." *Gesta* 18, 1 (1979):99–107.

Weitzmann, K. *Age of Spirituality,* catalog of the exhibition at the Metropolitan Museum of Art, 19 November 1977 to 12 February 1978. New York, 1979.

CLAUDIA NAUERTH

The Three Hebrews in the Furnace

The story of the three young Hebrews in the furnace, sometimes called the Three Holy Children, is told in the book of Daniel in the Septuagint and in the Apocrypha to the Bible. Exiles in Babylonia, they were thrown into a fiery furnace by the Babylonian king Nebuchadnezzar for refusing to worship an idol, but, praising God, they were rescued by an angel. Their names in Babylonian are Abednego, Shadrach, and Meshach (Azariah, Hananiah, and Mishael in Hebrew).

The theme of the three young men is abundantly illustrated from the earliest period of Christianity, except in Byzantine art, appearing in sculpture (on sarcophagi), in painting and the minor arts, and more rarely in mosaic. Two episodes in particular are represented: the appearance of the young men before Nebuchadnezzar, who points out the idol while they turn away in horror, and the three standing in the furnace, the flame of which is sometimes fanned by an attendant, either alone or accompanied by the angel who saves them. Sometimes the two episodes are associated with Nebuchadnezzar enthroned near the idol and witnessing their torment.

Coptic Egypt and Christian Nubia highly esteemed the subject, both in texts and in art. A special source of inspiration for them, rarely depicted in the West, was the point at which the angel descends from heaven to quell the flames.

A relief of the seventh century preserved in the Coptic Museum in Cairo shows the young men and the angel side by side. The three Hebrews raise their arms in the attitude of prayer. They are dressed in Parthian costume, consisting of a knee-length tunic with puffed sleeves closed at the wrist and tied at the waist; trousers; and a chlamys (cloak), fastened on the right shoulder by a clasp and covering the left shoulder and forearm. Contrary to what is normally seen, their feet are bare. They wear conical caps on their curling hair, which frames their beardless faces. The angel, whose long tunic reaches to his bare feet, raises his left arm in a gesture of protection; in his right hand he holds the long rod with which he has just stilled the flames.

Slightly different is the fourth-century representation in the Chapel of the Exodus at al-Bagawāt, near Khargah. Here, the furnace is depicted as a kind of hut of flames with an opening on the right, the name marked in Greek. Four people are standing in the flames—in the foreground three orants, identical in their attitude and their clothing (a tunic adorned with *clavi* descending over trousers and/or dark-colored boots), and in the background the angel of the Lord.

The three Hebrews are equally called to mind in the Chapel of Peace at al-Bagawāt, beside a sixth-century mural showing Daniel in the lions' den (see above). Some allegorical figures, carrying their name in Greek, allude to various episodes in the life of the prophet; among them *eukhē* ("prayer") recalls the song which the young men addressed to God.

In a sixth-century drawing, from a private house in Wādī Sarjah, now in the British Museum, London, the three Hebrews stand in the middle of a group of haloed busts in the posture of prayer amid flames that they trample down. In an effort to convey movement and perspective, their bodies are seen from the front, while the faces are shown in three-quarters view. Their gaze converges on a small haloed figure, wearing tunic and mantle and with bare feet, who stands above them. His left arm is raised to waist level, while his right hand holds the long rod with which he is quenching the flames. The inscription *angelos* leaves no doubt as to his identity. All three Hebrews wear tunics caught at the waist and swelling over trousers; the chlamys, fastened under the neck, is stirred by the wind, which will calm the flame. On their heads they wear Phrygian caps, and their feet are shod with slippers.

The theme also appeared in DAYR APA JEREMIAH on the east wall of cell F, to the left of the niche.

This mural, from the seventh century, no longer exists. In the early twentieth century, color had already disappeared and no more remained of the picture of the three Hebrews than an outline in red and black (Quibell, 1908). Nevertheless the scene remains legible; the three young men standing close together raise their arms. They are dressed in Parthian costume: tunic falling to the knees with three flaps, according to Quibell's drawing, long trousers, chlamys held by a heavy brooch fixed on the chest. The curls that frame their young and beardless faces do not seem to be topped by the usual Phrygian cap but are encircled by a large aureole. On their right, a little larger in size, the angel, bending slightly, is quenching the fire with his long rod ending in a cross. Flames surround the whole composition. A vertical element closes off the picture on the right. Unfortunately it is not possible to decide whether this was simply a thick line or a column on which the bust of Nebuchadnezzar was raised.

Perhaps there was another presentation of this theme in Room 773 of the monastery, where Jeremiah himself was accustomed to sit. The decoration of this apartment was peculiar to it; for example, a jeweled cross stands on a dais framed by columns and hangings. According to Quibell, "There were traces of human figures standing among flowers, then an inscription of Saints' names and beyond them on a white ground just the names ⲛⲉⲃⲱⲭⲟⲇⲟⲛⲟⲥⲟⲣ (Nebuchadnezzar) and ⲇⲟⲩⲗⲟⲥ (slave), evidently a description of a scene which has disappeared, destroyed when the buttresses were built" (Quibell, 1908, p. 11). Perhaps it was a picture of the young men being flung into the furnace tended by a slave, in the presence of Nebuchadnezzar.

The iconography of a seventh-century painting adorning Room 30 of Dayr Apa Apollo at Bāwīṭ is unique. An angel holds in his bosom three small figures clad in tunics and wearing boots. The idea of punishment has completely disappeared. The angel is lifting up those whom he has just snatched from their tormentor. This variant iconography might be explained by the importance accorded to the saving angel in the valley of the Nile in the Christian era.

From some centuries later comes the painting in the north sanctuary of Dayr Anbā Maqār in the Wādī al-Naṭrūn described by H. G. Evelyn-White: "In the space at the north end of the east wall are seen the upper parts of four figures rather less than life size, so severely scarred and battered that it is hopeless to describe them . . . . The identity of these figures is established by inscriptions painted in white on the red border above the scene: the first is labelled Ananias . . ., the fourth Misael . . ., the second and third are therefore Azarias and, probably, Michael" (Evelyn-White, 3, 1933, p. 103).

In Dayr Anbā Anṭūniyūs, among the numerous paintings—some of them dated with certainty to the first half of the thirteenth century—there is one in the choir that according to J. Leroy represents the theme of the three Hebrews. Today it is scarcely legible, but one can still distinguish the angel, holding in his right hand a long staff which passes in front of the three young men. All are clad in a tunic with a mantle fastened at the neck. On the ground and above the figures one can make out leaping flames.

At DAYR ANBĀ BŪLĀ, the same theme appears on a painting of the eighteenth century. Despite its recent date, this picture corresponds to the ancient pattern: the three Hebrews, represented as orants, are protected by the angel, who stands at their right; he stretches his left wing over their heads, while his right wing, folded, closes off the composition; with his right hand he holds in front of the young men the rod with which he has stilled the fire.

Two further pieces deserve mention, although strictly speaking one cannot call them Coptic. Both the Murano ivory in the National Museum of Ravenna and the icon of the Hebrews in the Monastery of Saint Catherine, Mount Sinai, share the iconography of the Coptic works cited above.

Thus, apart from the representations at al-Bagawāt and Bāwīṭ, we can demonstrate a large degree of unity in the iconography of the three Hebrews. They are praying, their arms raised to heaven, and the angel, sometimes in the midst of them but more often beside them, extinguishes the fire with his rod. It is not, as in early Christian art, their refusal that is portrayed, nor even their punishment, but that miraculous moment when the indomitable faith they have shown delivers them from martyrdom. This pattern will later be handed on to Christian Nubia, at FARAS, for example, or Sonqi Tino; here the angel will be identified as the archangel Michael.

BIBLIOGRAPHY

Evelyn-White, H. G. *The Monasteries of the Wadi'n Natrun.* Part 3: *The Architecture and Archeology.* New York, 1933.

Leroy, J. "Le Programme décoratif de l'église de Saint-Antoine du désert de la mer rouge." *Bulletin de l'Institut français d'archéologie orientale* 76 (1976):347–79.

Meinardus, O. "The XVIIIth Century Wall-Paintings in the Church of St. Paul, The Theban. Dair Anba Bula." *Bulletin de la société d'archéologie Copte* 19 (1967–1968); published in 1970:181–97.

Quibell, J. E. *Excavations at Saqqara 1906–1907.* Cairo, 1908.

Rassart-Debergh, M. "Les Trois hébreux dans la fournaise dans l'art paléochrétien. Iconographie." *Byzantion* 48 (1978):430–55.

MARGUERITE RASSART-DEBERGH

BIJIJ. *See* Jabal Khashm al-Qu'ud.

BILABEL, FRIEDRICH (1888–1948), German papyrologist. He was a professor at Heidelberg and edited nearly 150 papyri, including Coptic and Arabic papyri, publishing *Griechische, koptische und arabische Texte zur Religion und religiösen Literatur in Ägyptens Spätzeit,* with A. Grohmann (Heidelberg, 1934) and *Zwei Urkunden aus dem bischöf-*

lichen Archiv von Panopolis in Ägypten (Heidelberg, 1935). He also wrote many articles on Coptic ostraca (see *Aegyptus* 2, 1921, pp. 586–88, and 13, 1933, pp. 555–62).

BIBLIOGRAPHY

Dawson, W. R., and E. P. Uphill. *Who Was Who in Egyptology*. London, 1972.
Préaux, C. "Friedrich Bilabel." *Chronique d'Egypte* 23 (1948):247–50.

MARTIN KRAUSE

BILAD, town in Egypt, the location of which is now unknown. The SYNAXARION, under the commemoration of the martyr Anbā Bajūsh on 26 Ṭūbah, states that Bajūsh, a wealthy man, was from a place to the north of Bilad. Arianus, the Byzantine governor in Antinoopolis, interrogated and tortured Bajūsh, who was eventually martyred near Salmūn, west of Ṭimā, in the district of the city of Tkow. E. Amélineau theorizes that the Bilad mentioned in this account may be the modern Bilād al-Māl in the province of Qinā in Upper Egypt (1893, p. 100). This identification, however, is untenable since the orthography of the two place names is different and because Bilād al-Māl is not attested before the nineteenth century.

BIBLIOGRAPHY

Amélineau, E. *La Géographie de l'Egypte à l'époque copte*, p. 100. Paris, 1893.
Timm, S. *Das christlich-koptische Ägypten in arabischer Zeit*, pt. 1, pp. 391–92. Wiesbaden, 1984.

RANDALL STEWART

BILBEIS, city in the province of Sharqiyyah located at the junction of the Eastern Desert and the Delta about 30 miles (48 km) northeast of Cairo.

Though Bilbeis is seldom mentioned in Greek and Latin sources from the Roman-Byzantine era, it is apparent that the city existed prior to the ARAB CONQUEST OF EGYPT in 641 and that it had a bishop as early as the seventh century. The name of the city appears often in Coptic scales, which is an indication of an older tradition. Bilbeis also occurs in the lists of Egyptian bishoprics (Munier, 1943, pp. 47, 54, 63). The first bishop in Bilbeis whose name we know was Apa Abraham. The Coptic account of the FORTY-NINE MARTYRS of Scetis states that Abraham sought the remains of the martyrs when they lay in the cave of Piamoun. From this story one can reasonably assume that Abraham, who was a contemporary of John, Hegumenos of Scetis, was bishop in the pre-Arabic period (cf. Evelyn-White, 1932, pp. 270–71).

Another Abraham who served as bishop of Bilbeis was present at the synod held in Cairo in 744 to choose KHĀ'ĪL I as patriarch.

Under the direction of King Amalrich of Jerusalem, the Crusaders took Bilbeis in 1168, and some Copts lost their lives in the battles. However, by the fourteenth century, the city was once again the seat of a Coptic bishop. There is also evidence to suggest that Bilbeis boasted a Christian writing school at the beginning of the fourteenth century.

Coptic tradition says that Bilbeis was one of the stopping places of the family of Jesus during the FLIGHT INTO EGYPT.

BIBLIOGRAPHY

Amélineau, E. *La Géographie de l'Egypte à l'époque copte*, pp. 333–35. Paris, 1893.
Evelyn-White, H. *The Monasteries of the Wadi 'n Natrun*, pt. 2, *The History of the Monasteries of Nitria and of Scetis*. New York, 1932.
Munier, H. *Recueil des listes épiscopales de l'église copte*. Cairo, 1943.
Timm, S. *Christliche Stätten in Ägypten*, p. 64. Wiesbaden, 1979.
———. *Das christlich-koptische Ägypten in arabischer Zeit*, pt. 1, pp. 401–406. Wiesbaden, 1984.

RANDALL STEWART

BILJĀY, town located in the Egyptian Delta about 5 miles (8 km) south of al-Manṣūrah in the Daqahliyyah province. Biljāy takes its place in Christian history as the birthplace of the martyr DIOS who was killed during the reign of the emperor Maximian (Rossi, 1893).

BIBLIOGRAPHY

Amélineau, E. *La Géographie de l'Egypte à l'époque copte*, pp. 100–101. Paris, 1893.
Rossi, F. *Un nuovo codice copto del museo Egizio di Torino*, pp. 3–136. Rome, 1893.
Timm, S. *Das christlich-koptische Ägypten in arabischer Zeit*, pt. 4, pp. 1886–87. Wiesbaden, 1988.

RANDALL STEWART

BIMĪN. *See* Pamin, Saint.

BIRMĀ, town located in the Egyptian Delta about 7 miles (11 km) northwest of Tanta in the province of Gharbiyyah.

Although Birmā is listed in a number of Coptic-Arabic scales and in a list of Egyptian bishoprics (Munier, 1943, p. 64), the town is rarely referred to in Christian-Arabic literature and no bishop for the place is attested in any source. The earliest mention of Birmā in Coptic-Arabic literature is as a geographical reference point for the place where the amir al-Juyūsh defeated the Kurds in 1077.

Patriarch MATTHEW I (1378–1409) had the relics of Saint George that were venerated in Birmā brought to DAYR ANBĀ ṢAMŪ'ĪL of Qalamun in the Fayyūm. In 1424, Patriarch GABRIEL V (1409–1427) returned the relics to Birmā (Viaud, 1979, p. 30).

Birmā has two Coptic churches, both of which are dedicated to Saint George. One of these churches was built in 1206 and later abandoned; the other was erected in 1611 (Viaud, p. 30).

BIBLIOGRAPHY

Amélineau, E. *La Géographie de l'Egypte à l'époque copte,* pp. 101–102. Paris, 1893.

Munier, H. *Recueil des listes épiscopales de l'église copte.* Cairo, 1943.

Timm, S. *Das christlich-koptische Ägypten in arabischer Zeit,* pt. 1, pp. 407–409. Wiesbaden, 1984.

Viaud, G. *Les Pèlerinages coptes en Egypte.* From the notes of Jacob Muyser. Cairo, 1979.

RANDALL STEWART

BIRTH RITES AND CUSTOMS. Birth practices in Egypt are based on ancient, time-honored customs, and although they have tended to disappear among urban dwellers, especially since the twentieth century, they are still maintained as strongly as ever in rural society.

An expectant woman receives much attention from those about her, as they seek to satisfy her every craving for certain foods, for it is believed that they might otherwise appear on the body of the newborn. Another prevalent belief is that whatever comes into the prospective mother's view will influence the unborn child, and thus she is careful to surround herself with lovely sights, preferring to look upon those who are distinguished by their physical beauty or social prestige.

Among people of modest circumstances, it is customary that when a woman is about to give birth, she returns to her father's home. Under optimum conditions, a physician or a midwife attends the birth. During the forty days of confinement following the birth (practiced no more), the new mother was cared for by her mother, or in her absence, by neighborhood women who took turns at the bedside.

In the country, the placenta and umbilical cord are given particular attention, for it is believed that they protect the mother and assure long life to the child (see Blackman, 1916). Their importance may be traced to pharaonic Egypt, where a special priest would have cared for the royal placenta (Ayrout, 1952).

Because pregnancy and childbirth have left the new mother extremely weak and susceptible to infection, those attending her take great precautions to help her regain strength and to protect her from all evil. On the third day after the birth, she is purged with castor oil, and then she must literally gorge herself in order to restore her health and activate the mammary glands. Further, in order to spare her any anxiety that could dry up her milk or cause her to become sterile, all visitors are carefully screened. While those who might cause her trouble are not necessarily ill-intentioned, they may, under certain conditions, be innocent intermediaries for evil, for example, if they have just returned from a burial, or have the palms of their hands and soles of their feet covered with henna, or if they have just been circumcised, or are wearing antique gold pieces, precious stones, or pearls. However, should evil befall the recovering mother, there are numerous magical recipes to counteract this, one of which will surely be administered to her at once.

Because children are so highly prized, a sterile woman is regarded with great disfavor. She has an entire arsenal of recipes at her disposal to cure her infirmity. Fecundity is especially high in rural areas, and the rites are as numerous as they are varied. Considerable power is attributed to pharaonic objects (Ayrout, 1952, pp. 121–22), and thus barren women pay many visits to nearby necropolises and the Cairo Museum.

The Coptic Ceremony of the Seventh Day is celebrated seven days after the birth of a child and is attended by women only. It is a rather complex event that requires much preparation.

The preceding evening the family installs, in the bedroom of the mother and child, a large winnowing sieve, a mortar, a knife, and a basin filled with water, nuts, and soap. There is a tray near the baby's pillow upon which seven items have been placed to correspond to the seven days just past: wheat, broad beans, lentils, barley, corn or rice, artemisia or incense, and salt. On the wheat rests an egg that is to be cooked the next day and offered to someone advanced in years. This is to ensure the child's longevity. Nearby are a watch, inkstand, and pen for a boy, or scissors, a thimble, needle, and thread for a girl.

The midwife comes about noon. As the guests arrive, they slip coins into the water-filled basin for the midwife, which will be added to the fees paid by the father. The ceremony begins with the "Name Ritual." For this, a shallow silver or copper basin has been prepared that holds a large terra-cotta jug for a boy or, for a girl, a goglet richly decorated with flowers, silk scarves, and some jewels from the mother for her daughter. On the rim of the basin three candles have been placed, each one bearing a name chosen by the parents. The name attached to the candle that burns the longest is the one to be given the newborn child, for it is considered to be the most beneficent.

Holding the baby in her arms, the midwife takes the tray with its seven items and scatters these contents throughout the house. She is followed by the mother, clothed in white, with a brasier in one hand, casting incense. With the other hand, she casts salt into the air to combat the evil eye. These women are preceded by a procession of children who carry candles and chant wishes of longevity, prosperity, and fertility for the newborn. Once again in the bedroom, the midwife places the infant into the sieve; then she knocks inside the mortar seven times, and at each blow, the mother steps over the sieve. Next, the midwife takes the sieve, and gently shakes the child back and forth like grain three times. These acts are supposed to inure the child and develop his courage. The sieve is then filled with nuts, almonds, and chick peas which the midwife casts out into the room for the children in attendance. With each gesture, she clicks her tongue, "Chick, chick, chick," as if calling chickens. Next, she places the water-filled basin upon her knees, and offers a nut for good luck to each woman who gives her a bit of money. The donor plunges her hand into the water, called angel's water, and moistens her face while formulating wishes of longevity for the newborn. The parents of the new mother send her cakes baked for the event, and a variety of nuts.

The evening before this ceremony, a reception is given for the men of the family and friends of the father. Here they are served syrup, sweets, almonds, and the traditional *mughāt,* a warm drink made from the aromatic roots of *glossostemon bruguieri.* *Mughāt* is the relished drink offered to any visitor who calls to congratulate the new mother.

BIBLIOGRAPHY

Ayrout, H. H. *Fellahs d'Egypte.* Cairo, 1952.

Blackman, A. M. "The Pharaoh's Placenta and the Moon God Khons." *Journal of Egyptian Archeology* 3, series 1 (1916).

Blackman, W. S. *Les fellahs de Haute Egypte.* Paris, 1948.

Lane, W. E. *An Account of the Manners and Customs of the Modern Egyptians,* 2nd ed. London, New York, and Melbourne, 1890.

Leeder, S. H. *Modern Sons of the Pharaohs.* London, 1918.

Wassef, Cérès W. *Pratiques rituelles et alimentaires des Coptes.* Cairo, 1971.

CÉRÈS WISSA WASSEF

BISADAH. *See* Psoï.

BISHOP, a clergyman of the highest order, senior in rank to priests and deacons. The Coptic term (*episkopos*) and the Arabic (*usquf*) are derived from the Greek and Latin versions (*episkopos, episcopus*), which, etymologically, mean "overseer."

Bishops are successors to the apostles, and, from the historical point of view, the episcopate is a continuation of the apostolate. The Pastoral Epistles lay down in some detail the requisite qualities of a person worthy of being a good bishop (1 Tim. 3:1–7; Ti. 1:7–10), which can be summarized as follows. (1) As God's steward, a bishop must be above reproach. (2) As Saint Paul's successor, he must be a competent teacher, able to expound the true Christian doctrine, having a twofold duty: to fill the faithful with zeal, and to refute the arguments of those who hold unorthodox views. (3) As Christ's follower, he must be no lover of wealth. (4) He must be courteous, hospitable, and well thought of by Christians and non-Christians alike.

In addition to these Pauline qualifications, two further conditions were later imposed. (1) According to the *Constitutions of the Holy Apostles,* candidates for the bishopric should be at least fifty years of age, to ensure wisdom and sagacity. This rule, however, was sometimes waived in the case of outstanding persons who had special merits justifying their eligibility, as, for example, Saint ATHANASIUS, who was consecrated bishop of Alexandria at the age of twenty-three. (2) A candidate should already be ordained priest and protopriest (Connolly, 1929, chap. 3, p. 24).

Selection of Bishops

The DIDASCALIA stipulates the unanimous approval of the congregation of the chosen person. The *Constitutions of the Holy Apostles* also stresses that the person to be ordained bishop "is to be chosen by the whole people, who, when he is named and approved, let the people assemble with the presbytery and bishops that are present, on the Lord's day, and let them give their consent."

Some church authorities (Ibn Sabbāʿ and al-Ṣafī ibn al-ʿAssāl) add that the candidate had to be paraded before the congregation, so that if any person held anything against him he could publicly object to the candidate's eligibility, giving reasons for so doing. In that event, ordination was to be postponed for three months during which the matter would be thoroughly investigated in the presence of the said person and the candidate.

Canon 4 of the Council of NICAEA (325) insists upon the approval of the metropolitan and other bishops of the province: "It is most fitting that a bishop should be installed by all the bishops in his province. But if such a thing is difficult either because of the urgency of circumstances or because of the distance to be traveled, at least three should meet together somewhere and by their votes combined with those of the ones absent and joining in the election by letter they should carry out the ordination thereafter. But as for the ratification of the proceedings, let it be entrusted in each province to the metropolitan" (Cummings, 1957, p. 168).

Consecration of Bishops

According to the *Didascalia,* the consecration of a bishop should take place on a Sunday at the cathedral, in the presence of the clergy and the congregation, with at least two or three bishops officiating. Canon 6 of the Council of Nicaea attaches special importance to the consent of the pope, patriarch, or metropolitan: "Let the ancient customs in Egypt, Libya, and Pentapolis prevail, that the bishop of Alexandria have jurisdiction in all these, since the like is customary for the bishop of Rome also. Likewise in Antioch and the other provinces, let the churches retain their privileges. And this is to be universally understood, that if anyone be made bishop without the consent of the metropolitan, the great synod has declared that such a man ought not to be bishop . . ." (Cummings, 1957, p. 170).

Before the service of the consecration starts, the candidate is asked to publicly affirm his adherence to the orthodox faith, the church laws, the canons of the councils of Nicaea, CONSTANTINOPLE, and EPHESUS, as well as the other councils. He should also declare his constant readiness to safeguard the doctrines and rites of the Coptic orthodox church, to care for and protect the congregation, and submit to the church and her laws.

Then, following the reading from the Acts of the Apostles, the elaborate ceremony continues, including the following features: laying-on of hands; holding the divine Gospels open upon his head; making the sign of the cross thrice and giving him his ecclesiastical name; clothing him with the episcopal vestments; partaking of Holy Communion; removing the new bishop's white vestments, and clothing him with his black ones; and entrusting the episcopal staff and cross to him, while the congregation chants "Worthy, worthy, worthy."

Before the newly consecrated bishop is installed in his own diocese, he passes a certain period of time in prayer and fasting, celebrating the Divine Liturgy and communicating daily. Meanwhile his official credentials as bishop are to be drawn and preparations made for his enthronement in his own diocese. A number of bishops (three at least) accompany him on the journey. When they arrive at their destination, the clergy and congregation of the diocese usually receive them with religious chants.

Preceded by the deacons holding crosses and clergy carrying censers, the new bishop joins in a procession around the church. He then stands outside the sanctuary bowing his head, while the other bishops stand inside, and begin the proceedings, saying:

"We hereby enthrone him who has by divine grace been consecrated Abbā [Name], bishop of the holy church in the Christ-loving city of [Name], in the name of the Holy Inseparable Trinity." The congregation respond saying *"axios"* (worthy). Then standing at the synthronos (see ARCHITECTURAL ELEMENTS), he reads the Gospel (Jn. 10:1–16), and every time he utters the words, "I am the good shepherd," a Gospel is held over his head and the deacons chant *"axios"* thrice. At the end of the liturgy the new bishop distributes the *eulogia* (blessed bread) to the people. Finally, the bishops who have attended the consecration sign their names on his credentials, recording the time and place of his enthronement.

Functions and Duties

As the main spiritual leader of the diocese, the bishop assumes the responsibility of teaching and preaching in conformity with the exhortation of Saint Paul (1 Tim. 3:2; 4:11, 13, 15, 16), and in 2 Timothy 4:2, "Preach the word, be urgent in season and out of season, convince, rebuke, and exhort, be unfailing in patience and in teaching." The *Didascalia* also urges the bishop to pay particular attention to the interpretation of the scriptures and the teaching of his people (chap. 3).

The bishop ordains priests and deacons in accordance with the needs of the church after careful consideration: "Do not be hasty in the laying on of hands" (1 Tim. 5:22). Canon 9 of the Council of Antioch (341) states the following: ". . . For each bishop has authority over his own parish, both to manage it with the piety which is incumbent on every one, and to make provision for the whole district which is dependent on his city; to ordain presbyters and deacons; and to settle everything with judgment."

The bishop supervises and controls the clergy and administers discipline. "Let the elders who rule well be considered worthy of double honor, especially those who labor in preaching and teaching. . . . Never admit any charge against an elder except on the evidence of two or three witnesses. . . . In the presence of God and of Christ Jesus and of the elect angels I charge you to keep these rules without favor, doing nothing from partiality" (1 Tim. 5:17, 19, 21).

The *Didascalia* specifies Monday for the hearing of grievances and passing judgments in diocesan disputes (chap. 8). The *Constitutions of the Holy Apostles* makes similar provisions: "Let your judicatures be held on the second day of the week, that if any controversy arise about your sentence, having an interval till the sabbath, you may be able to set the controversy right, and to reduce those to peace who have the contests one with another against the Lord's day."

The bishop consecrates churches, altars, vessels needed for the liturgy, and the Holy Chrism.

The bishop provides for the needs of the clergy and the deacons, as well as of the poor, the widows, and the orphans in his diocese.

The bishop manages church finances: "Let the bishop have the care of ecclesiastical revenues and let him administer them as in the presence of God." Likewise, "We ordain that the bishop have authority over the goods of the church; for if he is to be entrusted with the precious souls of men, much more ought he to give directions about goods, that they all be distributed to those in want, according to his authority, by the presbyters and deacons, and be used for their support with reverence."

BIBLIOGRAPHY

Cummings, D. *The Rudder*. Chicago, 1957.

Habīb Jirjis. *Asrār al-Kanīsah al-Sab'ah*, 2nd ed., pp. 216–19, 223, 224. Cairo, 1950.

Ibn Sibā' Yūḥannā ibn Abī Zakarīyā. *Kitāb al-Jawharah al-Nafīsah fī 'Ulūm al-Kanīsah*, ed. Viktūr Manṣūr. Cairo, 1902. Trans. into Latin as *Pretiosa margarita de scientiis ecclesiasticis* by Vincentio Mistrīḥ. Cairo, 1966.

William Sulaymān Qelādah, ed. *Kitāb al-Disqūliyyah, Ta'ālīm al-Rusul*, pp. 63–65, 228, 263–64, 267, 839. Cairo, 1979.

ARCHBISHOP BASILIOS

BISHOP, CONSECRATION OF. In the event of a bishopric becoming vacant as a result of the death of its bishop or for other reasons, a successor is nominated by the clergy and congregation, and his name is submitted to the patriarch, together with a testimonial called a deed of election. The patriarch refers this testimonial to the Holy Synod (see SYNOD, HOLY) for approval, after which a date is set for the ceremony of the new bishop's consecration. This takes place on a Sunday and is usually held at the cathedral church of the patriarchate in Cairo.

Clothing with the Schema

On the eve of the consecration, a service is held during which the nominee is given an ecclesiastical name and is clothed with the schema, unless he has already been vested with it at the outset of his monastic life. The schema is a long plaited leather girdle adorned with crosses and is worn crosswise over the chest and the back as a symbol of strict austerity and asceticism.

At the start of the proceedings, a further verification of the unanimous agreement of the clergy and congregation on the choice of the nominee is carried out by the patriarch or his deputy. With the bishop-elect standing in front of all, they are asked three times if they consider him to be the right man, one who is capable of shouldering the serious responsibilities of the bishopric. This is done in fulfillment of the stipulation laid down in the *Constitutions of the Holy Apostles:*

And let the principal of the bishops ask the presbytery and people whether this be the person whom they desire for their ruler. And if they give their consent, let him ask further whether he has a good testimony from all men as to his worthiness for so great and glorious an authority; whether all things relating to his piety towards God be right; whether justice towards men has been observed by him . . . whether he has been unblameable in the course of his life. And if all the assembly together do according to truth, and not according to prejudice, witness that he is such a one, let them the third time, as before God the judge, and Christ, the Holy Ghost being also present, as well as all the holy and ministering spirits, ask again whether he be truly worthy of this ministry, that so "in the mouth of two or three witnesses every word may be established." And if they agree the third time that he is worthy, let them all be demanded their vote; and when they all give it willingly, let them be heard.

Pledge

The bishop-elect then reads a solemn pledge taken before Almighty God, the invisible Head of the Church; the sacred altar; the patriarch, bishops, and presbyters; the members of the Holy Synod; and the people, in which he undertakes to uphold the orthodox faith to the last breath and obey the canons of the holy apostles and the ecumenical councils of NICAEA (325), CONSTANTINOPLE (381), and EPHESUS (431), as well as the canons approved by the regional councils and the holy fathers of the church; to safeguard the rites, doctrines, and traditions of the Coptic Orthodox Church; to treat all the members of his parish with justice and without bias or favor, not condemning anyone on hearsay but affording him an opportunity to prove his innocence; to continue to lead an ascetic life, never treating the church assets as his own; and to submit to the supreme authority of the church, vested in His Holiness, the pope and patriarch of the See of Saint Mark, and in the Holy Synod.

When the bishop-elect has read the pledge, his episcopal vestments receive the sign of the cross, and his new ecclesiastical name is announced.

Sunday Procession

In the course of the celebration of the Divine Liturgy on the following Sunday morning, and immediately after the readings from the Acts and the SYNAXARION, the bishops, clergy, and deacons go to where the bishop-elect is awaiting. They bring him into the cathedral in an impressive procession, carrying crosses and lighted candles and chanting in Coptic the hymn beginning, "The Only-begotten Son, the Eternal Logos, Who for our salvation was incarnate from the THEOTOKOS, the ever-Virgin Mary, and became man, and was crucified."

Upon reaching the sanctuary, the bishop-elect kneels down and kisses the cross in the hand of the pope, before he is seated. Then the pope asks the archdeacon or a priest to read the deed of election.

Deed of Election

This testimonial is addressed by the clergy and congregation of the vacant bishopric to the pope, beginning with the honorific titles of the successor to the throne of Saint Mark. It describes the sorrowful state of the parish after the departure of its bishop and the eventual choice of a monk of a certain monastery to fill the vacancy, he being filled with virtue and piety, a man who has forsaken the world, a good teacher, eager to listen to the Gospel of Truth.

The pope descends from the throne and stands at the altar, facing eastward. With the bishops surrounding him, he offers incense and says the Prayer of Incense, while the bishop-elect kneels at the altar.

Petitions

The archdeacon says the following petitions, after each of which the congregation responds by saying the *Kyrie eleison:*

1. "Almighty God, who art in heaven, we beseech Thee, hear us, and have mercy upon us."
2. "Pray for the peace of the One Holy Catholic Apostolic Church."
3. "Pray for the life and safety of our Father the Patriarch, Abbā [name], and all the bishops, the clergy, and the Christ-loving congregation."
4. "Pray for the forgiveness of our sins and delivery from all tribulation."
5. "Pray to God to bless His inheritance and have mercy upon His people, through the intercession of the Blessed *Theotokos,* Saint Mark, and all the saints."
6. "We beseech Thee, Lord, send Thine Holy Spirit upon this elect servant of Thine [name]."

The congregation says the *Kyrie eleison* fifty times.

Laying-on of Hands

The bishops lay their hands upon the bishop-elect's shoulders and arms. Then, facing the west, the pope prays, "God Almighty, Lord of all, source of all mercy and comfort. . . . Thou art He who didst redeem us with Thy Blood. . . . Grant Thy servant [name] grace to bind and to loose. Give him wisdom to shepherd Thy flock in purity and justice, for Thine is the power and the glory, with Thy Good Father and the Holy Spirit, now and forever. Amen."

He places his right hand upon the bishop-elect's forehead, until the archdeacon has finished saying the following pronouncement: "May the Divine grace which makes good all inadequacy, heals all infirmity, and provides for the Holy Church of God, come upon [name] the servant of God, the priest and monk of the monastery of [name] in the place of [name] whom the Lord hath taken unto Him. Let us all pray, beseeching God to grant him the grace of the Holy Spirit." All then say the *Kyrie eleison*.

Looking toward the altar, the patriarch says this prayer: "Yes, Lord, make him worthy of the episcopal office, to serve Thy Name and Thy holy altar, and shepherd Thy flock in purity and truth, and be crowned with the portion of Thy Saints, through the mercies of Thy Only-begotten Son, our Lord Jesus Christ, with whom and the Holy Spirit Thou art blessed, now and forever. Amen." He looks toward the west and places his right hand upon the bishop-elect's head. The bishops lay their hands upon his arm and the pope recites the Prayer of Laying-on of Hands:

> Master, Lord God, the Almighty, Father of our Lord, God and Savior Jesus Christ, who has neither beginning nor end . . . who dwelleth in the highest and looks upon the lowly . . . do now pour Thy Holy Spirit which Thou hast granted to Thy pure apostles, give the same grace to Thy servant [name], whom Thou hast chosen bishop, that he may shepherd Thy holy flock, and become unto Thee a blameless server, and pray unto Thy goodness day and night. . . . Give unto him through Thy Christ the authority to forgive sins according to the commandment of Thy only-begotten Son, Jesus Christ our Lord, to ordain clergy, to loose all ecclesiastical bonds, to consecrate new churches and altars, and serve Thee without blame, all the days of his life, with pure, holy bloodless sacrifices.
>
> Fill him, Lord, with the graces of the Holy Spirit, grant him the grace of healing and teaching, that he may become a good guide to those who go astray, a light to those who walk in darkness and sin, a teacher to the ignorant, disclosing the word of truth rightly, following the example of the True Shepherd, our Lord Jesus Christ, ready to lay down his life for his sheep . . . that he may stand with boldness before Thy awesome throne, looking forward to the great reward which Thou hast prepared for those who labor for the preaching of the Gospel.

Then the pope turns to the east, toward the altar, and continues, "Look upon us, Lord, and upon our ministry, and purify us from all defilement. Send from above upon Thy servant [bishop's name] Thy grace of high priesthood, that he may be worthy through Thy good pleasure to shepherd Thy flock without blame, for Thou art merciful and worthy of honor and worship, Father, Son, and Holy Spirit, now and forever." Turning to the west, the pope signs the head of the bishop with his thumb three times, saying, "We ordain you [name] bishop in the holy church of the Christ-loving city of [name] and its nome, in the Name of the Father and the Son and the Holy Spirit."

Here the bishop is helped on with the episcopal vestments, while the pope says, "Glory and honor unto the All-holy Trinity, the Father, Son, and Holy Spirit; peace and edification unto the Church of God, the One Holy Catholic and Apostolic Church. Blessed be the Lord God forever. Amen." He makes the sign of the cross three times with his thumb over the head of the bishop, saying, "We ordain [name], elect of God, bishop in the One, Holy, Indissoluble Church of the Unseen and Living God, of the Christ-loving city of [name] and its nome, unto the glory and honor of the Name of the Holy Trinity, to the peace and edification of the Holy Church."

The archdeacon reads a few more petitions, and the pope says another prayer of thanksgiving and returns to his throne. At this point, the celebration of the Divine Liturgy is resumed, and the Pauline epistle is read from Hebrews 4:14 and 5:6, followed by the *Trisagion*, the Intercession of the Gospel, the Gospel reading, and the rest of the anaphora.

The pope administers the communion to the new bishop, gives him the breath of the Holy Spirit, places his right hand upon his head, saying, "Worthy, worthy, worthy, bishop [name] of the city of [name] and its nome." His liturgical vestments are changed for his black cassock, and the pope hands him his crosier and cross.

Episcopal Exhortation

Finally, the pope delivers a sermon known as the episcopal commandment, which is a compendium of precepts of virtue and godliness culled from the New Testament to serve as guidelines for the new bishop, as seen from the following passages:

> Be always humble, quiet, contented and merciful, and never lose your equanimity. Eschew the love of money, and be kind to orphans, widows, and needy strangers. Judge in all truth as though you are standing before God, avoiding bias and partiality. Follow the example of Jesus Christ, Who died for us all. Shepherd your flock and search for the stray sheep. Refrain from the pleasures of life and eating choice food. Do not accept bribes, for bribery blinds the eyes of rulers. Never expect to receive gifts in return for ordaining a priest, for this is simony. Do not be over-hasty in laying on hands in ordination, lest you should find yourself responsible for other people's misdeeds. You have received this grace free; accordingly confer it free upon whom you find to be worthy of it. . . .
>
> Be careful in dispensing church money, use it sparingly, and act as an honest and upright steward of God, allowing yourself only the food you eat and the clothes you wear. We brought nothing into the world, and we cannot take anything with us when we leave. Be charitable to orphans, the widowed, and those in want. . . .
>
> Proclaim the word of God on all occasions, convenient or inconvenient. Rebuke. Tend the flock of God whose shepherd you are, not under obligation, but of your own free will, not for gain but out of utter devotion. . . .

BIBLIOGRAPHY

Burmester, O. H. E. *The Egyptian or Coptic Church,* pp. 166–73. Cairo, 1967.

Ibn Sibā' Yūḥannā ibn Abī Zakarīyā. *Kitāb al-Jawharah al-Nafīsah fī 'Ulūm al-Kanīsah,* ed. Viktūr Manṣūr, pp. 122–25. Cairo, 1902. Trans. into Latin as *Pretiosa Margarita de scientiis ecclesiasticis* by Vincentio Mistrīḥ. Cairo, 1966.

ARCHBISHOP BASILIOS

BISHOP, TRANSLATION OF, the transference of a bishop from the see for which he was consecrated to some other diocese. This practice is forbidden by Canon 15 of the Council of NICAEA (325), which states: "On account of the great disturbance and discords that occur, it is decreed that the custom prevailing in certain places contrary to the Canon, must be wholly done away; so that neither bishop, presbyter, nor deacon shall pass from city to city. And if any one after this decree of the holy and great Synod shall attempt any such thing, or continue in any such course, his proceedings shall be utterly void, and he shall be restored to the Church for which he was ordained bishop or presbyter." This prohibition is based on the assumption that translation is motivated by ambition, which is detrimental to the proper organization of the various church parishes, both large and small.

Saint ATHANASIUS (326–373) condemned the practice of abandoning one's parish as tantamount to divorce on the part of the bishop, since his parish is his spouse.

The fourteenth Apostolical Canon allows the translation of bishops only for valid reasons: "A bishop is not to be allowed to leave his own parish, and pass over into another, although he may be pressed by many to do so, unless there be some proper cause constraining him, as if he can confer some greater benefit upon the persons of that place in the word of godliness. And this must be done not of his own accord, but by the judgment of many bishops, and at their earnest exhortation."

On this basis, Alexandrus was translated from the bishopric of Cappadocia to Jerusalem, an episode commemorated in the Coptic Synaxarion on 12 Baramūdah and 1 Baramhāt and mentioned by various church historians.

Canon 21 of the Council of Antioch (341) decrees that "a bishop may not be translated from one parish to another, either intruding himself of his own suggestion, or under compulsion by the people, or by constraint of the bishops, but he shall remain in the Church to which he was allotted by God from the beginning, and shall not be translated from it, according to the decree formerly passed on the subject."

GREGORY OF NAZIANZUS (329–389) was consecrated against his will in 372 as priest to the see of Sasima, a small village in Cappadocia. Nevertheless, he remained in Nazianzus as a suffragan to help his father, the bishop of Nazianzus, until the latter's death in 374. Gregory then retired to Seleucia, but he was called to Constantinople in 379 to support the adherents to the Nicene faith, who had neither pastor nor church. During the Council of Constantinople, he was appointed bishop of Constantinople. The Egyptian and Macedonian bishops who attended the council disputed the validity of his appointment. He resigned saying, "I will be a second Jonah. I will give myself for the salvation of our ship [the church], though I am an innocent of the storm. Let the lot fall upon me and cast me into the sea. . . . I reluctantly ascended the episcopal chair and gladly I now come down." (Schaff, 1891, Vol. 2, pp. 918–19).

PROCLUS (d. 446 or 447), patriarch of Constantinople, was consecrated bishop of Cyzicus, but the people there refused to receive him, so he remained in Constantinople as a much-admired preacher. In 434 he was enthroned by the bishops at Constantinople, and the scruples felt about translation had been removed by the letters of Celestine, bishop of Rome, to CYRIL I of Alexandria (412–444), JOHN OF ANTIOCH, and Rufus of Thessalonica on the subject of translation (ibid., p. 175). Proclus then sent both to Cyril of Alexandria and John of Antioch the usual synodical letters announcing his appointment, both of whom approved of it.

Socrates, in his *Ecclesiastical History* (7.30), explains his opinion of the validity of translations from one see to another. Defending the translation of Proclus, he lists the names of thirteen bishops who were transferred from one see to another.

K. J. von Hefele (1956, p. 33), in his comment on the fifteenth canon of the Council of Nicaea, said that "the interest of the Church often rendered it necessary to make exceptions. . . . These exceptional cases increased almost immediately after the holding of the Council of Nicaea, so that in 382, Saint Gregory of Nazianzus considered this law among those which had long been abrogated by custom."

One such was the translation of Bishop Siderius in the fourth century from his see in the villages of Palaebisca and Hydrax on the fringe of the Libyan desert to the metropolitan see of the Pentapolis. In hope of reviving the small spark of orthodoxy in Ptolemaïs, Athanasius, pope of Alexandria, promoted Siderius to that see.

This curious page of ecclesiastical history was revealed by Synesius, bishop of Ptolemaïs (c. 370–414), in his Epistle 77, to Theophilus of Alexandria (385–412), from which it is known that Siderius was a young active officer who had just come home from the army on civil duty. Orion, the bishop of Erythron, was an old man, and the inhabitants of two large villages in the diocese, Palaebisca and Hydrax, impatient with the lack of supervision, clamored for a bishop of their own and for the appointment of Siderius. Siderius was accordingly consecrated. No permission was received from the pope of Alexandria, and only a single bishop could be found to officiate, contrary to the *Apostolic Canons*, which command that a bishop be ordained preferably by three bishops but at least by two. But these were the times of the Arians (see ARIANISM), and the majority of the people were heretics. Thus, in view of the immense utility of the appointment, Pope Athanasius overlooked its irregularity, considering that in such perilous times the laws could not always be closely observed, and shortly afterward, he promoted Siderius to the metropolitan see of Ptolemaïs.

Pope KHĀ'ĪL I (744–767), said, "Sword or fire or casting to lions or exile or captivity,—these are things that trouble me not; but I will not enter into what is not lawful, nor incur my own excommunication, which I subscribed with my own hand and initiated, to the effect that no bishop shall become patriarch. For the excellent fathers excommunicated him who shall take a degree in the hierarchy by the help or favour of the government."

The only instances of translation in the Coptic church are the translation and promotion of Khā'īl, bishop of Fūwwah, to the metropolitan see of Ethiopia by Pope JOHN VI (1189–1216); and the translation and promotion of CHRISTODOULOS III, bishop of Jerusalem, to the metropolitan see of Ethiopia by Pope PETER VI (1718–1726).

In the twentieth century the Coptic church has continued to adhere to that custom, with the exception of the translations of Metropolitan Yu'annis of Beheira and Minūfiyyah to become Pope JOHN XIX (1928–1942), of Metropolitan Macarius of Asyūṭ to become pope (1944–1945), and of Metropolitan Yūsāb of Jirjā to become Pope YUSĀB II (1946–1956).

BIBLIOGRAPHY

Hefele, K. J. von. "Notes." In *A Select Library of the Nicene and Post-Nicene Fathers of the Christian Church,* ser. 2, Vol. 14, ed. P. Schaff and H. Wace. Grand Rapids, Mich., 1956.

Schaff, P. *History of the Christian Church: Nicene and Post-Nicene Christianity,* Vol. 2, pp. 918–19. Edinburgh, 1891.

EMILE MAHER ISHAQ

BISHOPRIC. *See* Eparchy.

BISHOPS, BIOGRAPHIES OF.

The ancient literary form of the biography was taken over by the Christians, as is shown by the *Panegyricus* on Constantine the Great by Eusebius and Jerome's *De viris illustribus*. From the fourth century on, the lives of saints such as the *Vita Cypriani* of Pontius and the *Vita Antonii* of Athanasius were at the center of Christian biography. The latter work, a mixture of biography and encomium, had a considerable influence in Coptic literature, with greater emphasis on the element of eulogy. The designations of these works vary between encomium and *bios*, and occasionally they are also called *politeia* (Abdel Sayed, 1984, pp. 272ff.). The first subjects of biographies or encomia were martyrs and then monks, followed by bishops. For example, an encomium on MACARIUS, BISHOP OF TKOW, is ascribed to Archbishop DIOSCORUS of Alexandria, twenty-fifth patriarch. In the early fourth century, Archbishop Alexander I, nineteenth patriarch, had reportedly written an encomium on his predecessor PETER I of Alexandria, seventeenth patriarch (see Krause, 1979, pp. 710 and nn. 171f.; further examples at pp. 710–15).

In the seventh century, when Coptic literary works were increasingly written in Coptic and no longer translated from Greek into Coptic, a biography of Bishop Pisentius of Qifṭ was written. This has been preserved in the Sahidic and Bohairic dialects and in Arabic translations (Abdel Sayed, pp. 5ff.). In each version a different author is named, although the content of the biography, apart from variations in length, agrees word for word. The Bohairic version reportedly was written by Bishop Moses, the successor of Pisentius as bishop of Qifṭ; the Sahidic, by the priest John, a disciple of Pisentius. The longer Arabic translation is said to have been composed by Theodorus of Scetis, with Moses and John as coauthors. Only in the short Arabic recension is Theodorus named as sole author. Probably, however, John was the author, and Moses may well be named as author of the Bohairic version, because in this period many Coptic bishops are known as the authors of literary works.

The biography falls into individual narratives, which in the Arabic recensions are described as miracles and enumerated. In addition to *topoi*, which are also attested in other literary works, the recensions contain so many statements about Pisentius that a biography could be worked out from them (Abdel Sayed, pp. 304ff.).

BIBLIOGRAPHY

Abdel Sayed, G. G. *Untersuchungen zu den Texten über Pesyntheus, Bischof von Koptos (569–632)*. Bonn, 1984.

Gerstinger, H. "Biographie." In *Reallexikon für Antike und Christentum*, Vol. 2. Stuttgart, 1954.

Krause, M. "Koptische Literatur." In *Lexikon der Ägyptologie*, Vol. 3. Wiesbaden, 1979.

______. "Ägypten II (literaturgeschichtlich)." In *Reallexikon für Antike und Christentum*, Supp. Vol. 1. Stuttgart, 1985.

MARTIN KRAUSE

BISHOPS, CORRESPONDENCE OF.

The inhabitants of Christian Egypt reveal a delight in writing, so far as they were able to write. Many transactions, especially those of legal content, were fixed in written form. Among the papyri and ostraca found in numerous archives and deriving from the antiquities trade, there are letters from bishops to the faithful of their dioceses, and from Christians to their bishops. It was one of the duties of the bishop to have the Easter letter from the patriarch of Alexandria read in the churches of his diocese. A companion piece to an Easter letter, from the diocese of Hermonthis, is preserved in the British Museum (Papyrus XCI; Crum, 1905, no. 464). The bishop, not mentioned by name, writes that he has sent the archpriest Apa Kyrus with the holy Easter letter of the patriarch, in order that it may be read in the churches of Djeme. There must have been similar letters in large numbers from all the Egyptian bishops.

The correspondence of two bishops from the sixth and seventh centuries in Upper Egypt particularly deserves to be mentioned.

Bishop Abraham of Hermonthis

Abraham, who resided in the monastery of Phoibammon, situated near Djeme, sent numerous letters to the Christians of his diocese, both clerical and lay. He also received letters from these persons (114 writings are dealt with in Krause, 1956, Vol. 2). Part of the correspondence was found by the excavator E. Naville in the course of pulling down the Phoibammon monastery during the excavation of the temples of Hatshepsut and Thutmose III at DAYR AL BAHRI, begun by the Egypt Exploration Fund in 1893. While some of the correspondence reached the museums of Cairo and London, another part, comprising more than 500 texts, was thrown on the excavation rubbish heaps, and was not found until the years following 1922, during the inspection of Naville's dumps by the Metropolitan Museum of Art. The discovery was divided between museums in Cairo and New York. In 1959–1960 the Metropolitan Museum sold these texts and others to Columbia University (Schiller, 1976, p. 104). In addition, texts were found during the excavation of Coptic monasteries built into pharaonic temples or anchorite settlements. Some reached museums via the antiquities trade in Luxor. Only some of the texts have been published.

While 114 texts from this correspondence were known in 1956, since then the number has grown to about 200. The existence of a large number of other writings, no longer extant, can be inferred from the texts that recapitulate the early history of transactions. For example, in Crum's *Coptic Ostraca* (CO 30) we read, "After I entreated you, you ordained me a deacon at the monastery of the holy Apa Victor." Since the bishop himself, on the evidence of his testament, could not write, he employed four scribes. It has become evident that for many transactions there were set forms, into which only the relevant personal and place names had to be inserted.

This correspondence, the most comprehensive and best-preserved on ostraca, shows the activity of an Upper Egyptian bishop around 600. It includes texts on the ordination of deacons and priests (see ORDINATION, CLERICAL, and CLERICAL INSTRUCTION) as well as documents relating to appointment to office. For these documents of appointment there was also a set form, in which clergy, for the most part deacons, were named as titular heads of churches (and monasteries). The task of these titular heads was to watch for or prevent any negligence and to instruct their subordinates, that they might walk in the fear of God. The disobedient among clergy and laity were to be excluded from communion (see EXCOMMUNICATION), until they came to the bishop. The titulars were to be punished if they overlooked any negligence.

In a letter addressed to the bishop, the writer, a cleric, pledges that he himself or his father will sleep in the church, will provide for the lamps during the night, and will hold divine service. Otherwise he is to be excluded from communion (CO 41). In another letter (*Berliner koptische Urkunden*) (BKU 69) three persons declare themselves ready to build a church by a specified time.

The bishop provides for the conduct of public worship and the celebration of communion in his diocese in circular letters and on special occasions. He commissions clergy to administer communion where temporarily there are no clergy, often because the incumbent has fallen ill. The wafers necessary for the celebration are inspected and blessed by the bishop, and he insists on the mixing of water and wine for the chalice in the correct proportions, as laid down by the Fathers. Anyone who adds more water is threatened, together with all his household, with exclusion from communion.

Anyone who does not comply with a commission to administer communion is excluded from communion (CO 53) or from the clergy (Winlock et al. [Ep.] 154; CO 485).

The bishop also makes provision for other sacraments: baptism, which takes place three times a year in Djeme (*Papyri und Ostraca in Staatsmuseum* [BP] 12501), and marriage, to which four circular letters are devoted. These repetitions show that there evidently were often infringements against the marriage laws. He quotes Luke 16:18 (CO 72) and emphasizes that only when there is unchastity can a woman be divorced from her husband. Anyone offending is excluded from communion (CO 72). In a further letter (CO 73) the bishop reiterates his position on marriage, and names various relations of kinship that stand in the way of a marriage, such as marriage to a niece and to brothers- or sisters-in-law, which is forbidden in the church canons.

The bishop also intervenes on behalf of poor people who were badly treated. Such an occurrence (CO 71) is the occasion of a circular letter, in which he compares the culprits to the evildoers of the Old and New Testaments and excludes them from communion. He uses almost the same wording in another circular (Jernstedt, no. 80), which is concerned with the hindering of poor men in their fishing. Again excommunication is threatened.

The bishop is also active in the exercise of his judicial power, AUDIENTIA EPISCOPALIS, as peacemaker and mediator. He attempts to settle a dispute (BP 8727) and to mediate between two parties (CO 49). In cases of disobedience and offenses against Christian conduct, both laity and clergy are excommunicated by him as well as by the titulars of churches and monasteries. Clergy who are disobedient or offend against the church canons are deprived of their rank. Villages and monasteries are threatened with imposition of the INTERDICT. The bishop evidently encouraged the tradition of burying the dead as mummies (see MUMMIFICATION), for he commissioned a man to buy bands, which were employed for the wrapping of the dead, and shrouds.

Bishop Pisentius of Coptos

This bishop, who came from the ranks of the monks, did not govern his diocese from a monastery except during the PERSIAN INVASION OF EGYPT. The source of his correspondence, now chiefly in the Louvre, is unknown. In contrast with those of Bishop Abraham, most of the letters are written on papyrus. Only a small part of the correspondence has been preserved, for often letters of the bishop, mentioned in answers by those addressed, have not survived.

The correspondence is concerned—like that of Abraham—with questions of ordination, problems of administration of the clergy, frequently discussed problems of betrothal and marriage, care of the poor, administration of justice, and exclusion from communion or from the clergy. In addition, a number of contemporary bishops in neighboring dioceses are named in his correspondence—for instance, Bishop Antonius of Ape and Bishop Pisrael of Kus (Qūṣ), who jointly investigated the complaints against a cleric, and Bishop Horame of Idfū.

The two sets of correspondence complement one another, and sketch a picture of church relationships in Upper Egypt in the sixth and seventh centuries such as has not yet been provided for other centuries and other regions of Egypt.

BIBLIOGRAPHY

Crum, W. E. *Coptic Ostraca*. London, 1902.

______. *Catalogue of the Coptic Manuscripts in the British Museum*. London, 1905.

______. *The Monastery of Epiphanius at Thebes*, pt. 1, pp. 223–31. New York, 1926.

Jernstedt, P. *Koptskije Teksty Gosudarstvennogo Muzeya Isobrazitelnykh Iskusstvimeni A. S. Pushkina*. Moscow and Leningrad, 1959.

Krause, M. "Apa Abraham von Hermonthis. Ein oberägyptischer Bischof um 600," 2 vols. Doctoral diss., Berlin, 1956.

______. "Die Kirchenvisitationsurkunden. Ein neues Formular in der Korrespondenz des Bischofs Abraham von Hermonthis." *Meroitica* 12 (1990):225–36.

Revillout, E. "Textes coptes. Extraits de la correspondance de St. Pesunthius, évêque de Coptos, et de plusieurs documents analogues (juridiques ou économiques)." *Revue égyptologique* 9 (1900):133–77; 10 (1902):34–47.

Schiller, A. A. "A Checklist of Coptic Documents and Letters." *Bulletin of the American Society of Papyrologists* 13 (1976):99–123.

Till, W. *Datierung und Prosopographie der koptischen Urkunden aus Theben*, pp. 168ff. Vienna, 1962.

Winlock, H. E.; W. E. Crum; and H. G. Evelyn-White. *Monastery of Epiphanius*. New York, 1926.

MARTIN KRAUSE

BISHOPS, PORTRAITS OF.

From a period unknown to us, the bishop possessed the right to a portrait. The Monophysite bishop John of Ephesus (c. 507–586) gives detailed information about this in his *Church History*, extant only partly in Syriac (ed. E. W. Brooks, CSCO 105, 106). According to John, portraits of the new bishop were hung in the churches of his diocese after his accession to office. Such a portrait of Bishop ABRAHAM OF HERMONTHIS has survived. This often-reproduced work (see Krause, p. 108 and n. 19) passed, through the antiquities trade, into the possession of the early Christian and Byzantine section of the State Museum in East Berlin. It shows the bust of the bishop, depicted full face, with *stola* and the Bible. The head is surrounded by a nimbus, and the inscription "Bishop Apa Abraham" is written in vertical lines to right and left beside it. Investigations have led to the conclusion that the portrait probably came from a small basilica west of the great arcade of the Luxor temple, which Grébaut excavated in 1893, and not from BĀWĪṬ, as was formerly thought and still is often claimed. In this excavation, part of the church treasure was also found, and this likewise bears the name of the bishop. The portrait was painted before 600, probably about 590.

From Nubia, which was under the jurisdiction of the archbishop of Alexandria and thus belonged to the Coptic church, several bishops' portraits have survived, most of them in the episcopal cathedral of FARAS, the ancient Pachoras (see Jakobielski, 1982). In contrast with the portrait of the bishop of Hermonthis, which is painted on a board and represents the bust of the bishop, the bishops' portraits from Faras are painted on the walls of the church (see the plan in Jakobielski, 1982, ill. no. 5), and show the bishop in his entirety. In addition, the bishop is often protected by a person standing behind or beside him. These protectors are Christ (no. 4), the apostle Peter (no. 60), a person who can no longer be identified (no. 75), Christ with the Madonna (nos. 69 and 122), the Madonna (nos. 57 and 5), and an archangel (nos. 58 and 3). All of the persons represented were at one time named in inscriptions. However, only in the case of four bishops is the name unambiguously guaranteed by the legend; in all other cases the names had to be deduced. The identification of the bishops represented without a surviving inscription was possible because a list containing the names of the first twenty-eight bishops of Faras, with the years of their episcopates, had survived in the church (Jakobielski, 1972, pp. 190ff.). This yielded the succession of the bishops. In addition, the gravestones of many bishops survive and give the dates of their lives.

In the church four layers of painting were identified. The bishops' portraits were found on all four layers: the last bishops' portraits on the topmost layer, the earliest on the lowest. From these facts, it is apparent that the oldest extant bishop's portrait in Faras derives from the beginning of the ninth century and represents either bishop Markos (810–826) or Chael I (826–827), while the latest portrait represents a bishop not on the list of bishops and dated to the thirteenth or fourteenth century (Jakobielski, 1982, p. 131).

From the skin color of the bishops portrayed, we can deduce their ethnic origin. Alongside bishops with a light skin color, which points to origin from Egypt, there are some with a darker complexion, which indicates an origin in Nubia.

BIBLIOGRAPHY

Golgowski, T. "Remarques sur l'iconographie de l'évêque de 'Rivergate Church.'" In *Mélanges offerts à Kazimierz Michalowski.* Warsaw, 1966.

Jakobielski, S. *A History of the Bishopric of Pachoras on the Basis of Coptic Inscriptions.* Warsaw, 1972.

———. "Portraits of the Bishops of Faras." In *Nubian Studies. Proceedings of the Symposium for Nubian Studies. Selwyn College, Cambridge, 1978,* ed. J. M. Plumley, pp. 127–41. Warminster, England, 1982.

Krause, M. "Zur Lokalisierung und Datierung koptischer Denkmäler." *Zeitschrift für ägyptische Sprache und Altertumskunde* 97 (1971):106–111.

Rahner, H. "Johannes v. Ephesos." In *Lexikon für Theologie und Kirche,* 2nd ed., Vol. 5, col. 1030. Freiburg im Breisgau, 1960.

MARTIN KRAUSE

BISŪRAH AL-ḤARĪRĪ, little-known eighteenth-century author. The manuscripts give him the title of *anbā,* which is usually applied to bishops, and more rarely to monks in the seventeenth century.

His name is given in all the manuscripts in the form Bisūrah, which at first glance suggests the reading Basūrah. G. Graf (1934) corrects this to Bistawrah or Pistauros, whereas P. Sbath (1939) simply transcribes it as Bassourah. Actually, the form Pistauros and its modifications (which correspond to Ṣalīb when Arabized) are absent from the SYNAXARION, although the name Bistawrūs is attested to in the modern period (nineteenth and twentieth centuries). However, Saint Bisūrah is commemorated on 9 Tūt in the Synaxarion (cf. Forget, vol. 47, pp. 15–16 [Arabic text]; vol. 78, p. 18 [Latin translation]), and his relics are kept in Shibīn al-Qanāṭir in the province of Qalyūb, and not in Nashīl al-Qanātir, as Basset read (Amélineau, 1893, pp. 432–33). Al-Ḥazīrī is a misreading of Graf (Graf, 1951, p. 117, last line) and does not exist.

Bisūrah's work is a collection of religious poems in very simple literary Arabic, sapient, and of moral content. The style recalls that of certain books of the Bible (Proverbs, Ecclesiasticus, etc.). The first poem or *maqālah* (treatise or discourse) suggests that the author was a monk. According to Graf, the collection contains 149 poems; Sbath says seventy. These interesting poems are not yet edited.

One manuscript from a public library containing this collection of poems (Coptic Patriarchate, Cairo, Theology 290; Graf, no. 533; Simaykah, no. 333) was copied in March 1709. It has 131 folios with eleven lines per folio (21 × 16 cm). The verses are written after the manner of prose.

There are five other privately owned manuscripts, all in Cairo. Two were bought in Cairo by Sbath before 1928. The first was given the code 1025 and is at present in the possession of his family; it was copied in 1735 on commission from the 105th patriarch, JOHN XVII (1726–1745). The second was not assigned a code and is now lost.

The three other Cairo manuscripts mentioned in the *Fihris* (index or catalog) of Sbath belonged respectively to ʿAbd al-Masīh Ṣalīb al-Baramūsī al-Masʿūdī, a well-known hieromonk; Murqus Jirjis, the bookseller who edited many ancient Arabic-Coptic texts; and Mattā Tādrus, another Coptic bookseller in Cairo.

BIBLIOGRAPHY

Amélineau, E. *La géographie de l'Egypte à l'époque copte.* Paris, 1893.

Graf, G. *Catalogue de manuscrits arabes chrétiens conservés au Caire,* p. 200 (no. 355). Vatican City, 1934.

Sbath, P. *Bibliothèque de manuscrits Paul Sbath,* Vol. 2, p. 139 (no. 1025). Cairo, 1928.

———. *Catalogue de manuscrits arabes,* Vol. 2, pp. 7–8, 27 (1260). Cairo, 1939.

KHALIL SAMIR, S.J.

BLEMMYE. *See* Beja Tribes.

BLESSING. Jesus Christ blessed with both hands, when he took the children in his arms, laying his hands upon them (Mk. 10:16); when he ascended into heaven, he lifted up his hands and blessed the apostles (Lk. 24:50, 51). The apostolic traditions are silent about a particular manner with which Jesus Christ blessed the people.

In the Coptic church the priests have used several variants for extending the benediction. The blessing with the index finger of the right hand is a typical Coptic practice. For the Copts, the one finger represents the unity of the Holy Trinity and the unity of the natures of the person of Jesus Christ as formulated by the first three ecumenical councils (325, 381, 431). Moreover, on Mount Sinai, the two tablets of the testimony were written with the finger of God (Ex. 31:18, Dt. 9:10), and it is by the finger of God that demons are cast out (Lk. 11:20).

Toward the end of the twelfth century, the blessing with the index finger became a controversial theological issue between MURQUS IBN QANBAR, who, for the sake of ecclesiastical union, attempted to introduce the blessing with two fingers, as the Melchites do, and MĪKHĀ'ĪL, bishop of Damietta. The belief was that the eternal truth of the Holy Trinity is expressed by the three joints of one finger, the fact that one joint ends in the fingernail being a constant reminder of the incarnation of one of the three divine persons. The same arguments for the use of one finger for the blessing were advanced in the thirteenth century by the author of the *Order of the Priesthood*, a work attributed to SAWĪRUS IBN AL-MUQAFFA'. Iconographical illustrations of the "one-finger blessing" by Jesus Christ are found in the altar-dome of the Church of the Holy Virgin in ḤĀRIT ZUWAYLAH, Cairo (nineteenth century), and on an icon of the enthroned Christ in the Cathedral of Saint George in Suhāj by Raghib Ayad.

In spite of the medieval condemnation of the use of two fingers for the blessing, the "two-finger blessing" with the index and the middle finger is also shown in Coptic churches in the altar-dome of the Church of Saint Mercurius (ABŪ SAYFAYN) in Old Cairo. The "two-finger blessing" was also used in the Byzantine church, and in Ethiopian and Nubian ecclesiastical art Jesus Christ is shown blessing with the index and middle finger. Coptic priests explain the mode of using two fingers for the blessing by referring to the two natures of Jesus Christ, which are, nevertheless, part of one hand. The blessing with three fingers, symbolizing the Holy Trinity, was the common blessing from the fourth century in the Eastern and Western churches. Two practices are known. The thumb, index, and middle finger are extended for the blessing as stipulated by Pope Innocent III of Rome (1198–1215), or the blessing is extended with the index, middle, and small finger while the thumb and the fourth finger are joined together, symbolizing the mystery of the Holy Trinity and the two natures of Jesus Christ.

The fact that this manner of blessing is also used by the Copts is evident from the iconographical representations showing Jesus Christ with the three-finger blessing in the altar-domes of the Church of the Holy Virgin in Bābīlūn al-Daraj, the Church of Saints Sergius and Bacchus, and the Church of the Holy Virgin in Old Cairo. Over the centuries the Copts have adopted several modes to extend the blessing.

BIBLIOGRAPHY

Assfalg, J. *Die Ordnung des Priestertums. Ein altes liturgisches Handbuch der koptischen Kirche.* Publication du Centre d'études orientales de la custode de Terre-Sainte. Cairo, 1955.

Butler, A. *The Ancient Coptic Churches of Egypt.* Oxford, 1884.

Fehrenbach, E. "Bénir (manière de)." *Dictionnaire d'archéologie chrétienne et liturgie,* Vol. 2, 1, pp. 746–58. Paris, 1910.

Graf, G. *Ein Reformversuch innerhalb der koptischen Kirche im zwölften Jahrhundert.* Collectanea Hierosolymitana, pp. 114, 115, 152–54, 192, 193. Paderborn, 1923.

Meinardus, O. "Der Segensgestus Christi im koptischen Altarziborium." *Archiv für Liturgiewissenschaft* 19 (1978):106–13.

OTTO F. A. MEINARDUS

BODMER, MARTIN (1899–1971), Swiss collector and man of letters. Bodmer was the founder in 1919 of a library of world literature, Bibliotheca Bodmeriana, first in Zürich and from 1951 in Geneva. Shortly before his death, the library won public recognition and the rights of a private institution (Foundation Martin Bodmer). The library today holds about 160,000 volumes. It includes 300 manuscripts, 65 papyri on the Egyptian Book of the Dead, Greek and Coptic biblical texts, classical and early Christian texts, 270 incunabula, including a Gutenberg Bible, and 2,000 autographs. It contains valuable collections of Shakespeare, Goethe, and Zurich and Heidelberg studies. In 1921, Bodmer established the Gottfried Keller Prize for literary works, still awarded every other year. In 1929 he started publication of the literary magazine *Corona,* which he organized and edited together with Herbert Steiner until 1943. This journal made possible numerous contacts with famous authors. In Geneva he was vice president of the International Committee of the Red Cross. He received honorary degrees from the universities of Frankfurt am Main, Bern, and Geneva. His most important publications are *Eine Bibliothek der Weltliteratur* (Zürich, 1947) and *Variationen zum Thema Weltliteratur* (Frankfurt, 1959).

HANS BRAUN

BODMER PAPYRI. *See* Appendix.

BOESER, PIETER ADRIAAN ART (1858–1935), Dutch Egyptologist and Coptologist. He studied Egyptology in Berlin under Adolf ERMAN and at Leipzig under Georg STEINDORFF. He taught at the University of Leiden (1910–1928). In 1925 he succeeded Willem Pleyte as director of the Egyptian collections in the Leiden Museum. With Pleyte, he published the museum's catalog of Coptic manuscripts, *Manuscrits coptes du Musée d'antiquités des Pays-Bas à Leide* (Leiden, 1897). Boeser then wrote *Die Denkmäler der saitischen, griechischen-römischen und koptischen Zeit: Beschreibung der ägyptischen Sammlung des Niederländischen Reichsmuseums der Altertümer in Leiden* (7 vols., 1915).

BIBLIOGRAPHY

Dawson, W. R., and E. P. Uphill. *Who Was Who in Egyptology.* London, 1972.

Kammerer, W. comp. *A Coptic Bibliography.* Ann Arbor, 1950; repr. New York, 1969.

AZIZ S. ATIYA

BOHAIRIC. *See* Appendix.

BOLLANDISTS, society of Jesuit fathers named after John van Bolland (1596–1665), who founded it on the basis of a plan conceived by Heribert Rosweyde (1569–1629), who did not live to see it materialize. The plan called for the assembling and publication of a universal register of the lives of saints from all possible original sources. The outcome of the labors of successive generations of Bollandists was publication of a multivolume work entitled ACTA SANCTORUM (still in progress). The work of the Bollandists was suspended in 1773, when the Society of Jesus was suppressed in Belgium. Their activities were resumed in 1837, when further supplements to the *Acta sanctorum* were published in the *Analecta Bollandiana,* a quarterly review devoted to hagiography and the lives of saints. It consists mainly of unpublished source material. The Bollandists' work is arranged according to the saints' days, and at present they have reached November. H. Delehaye is one of the society's most eminent editors. He is credited with sections entitled *Martyr et confesseur* (*Analecta Bollandiana* 39 [1921]), *Le calendrier d'Oxyrhynque pour l'année 535–36* (*Analecta Bollandiana* 48 [1924]), *Les martyrs d'Egypte* (*Analecta Bollandiana* 40 [1922]; also republished separately [Brussels, 1923]), *La personalité historique de St. Paul de Thèbes* (*Analecta Bollandiana* 44 [1926]), and *Une vie inédite de St. Jean l'aumonier* (*Analecta Bollandiana* 46 [1927]).

BIBLIOGRAPHY

Cross, F. L. "Bollandists." In ODCC, p. 183.

Delehaye, H. *A travers trois siècles: L'oeuvre des Bollandistes, 1615–1915.* Brussels, 1920. This appeared in English as *The Work of the Bollandists Through Three Centuries.* Princeton, 1922.

Kammerer, W. *A Coptic Bibliography.* Ann Arbor, Mich., 1950; repr. New York, 1969.

Peeters, P. *L'oeuvre des Bollandistes.* Académie royale de Belgique, Classe des lettres. Mémoires ser. 2, 39, fasc. 4. Brussels, 1942.

AZIZ S. ATIYA

BONE AND IVORY CARVING, COPTIC. Following the lead of Alexandrian art, and concurrently with its decline at the close of the seventh century, the Copts made extensive use either of ivory or of bone as a material appropriate for sculpture in relief.

When, in its beginnings, Coptic art still depended on Alexandrian art, Hellenistic themes were frequent: Greek gods or goddesses, nereids, *putti,* and dancers male and female, whose proportions in Coptic art were often sacrificed to a concern to fix the essential features. In addition, technical elements like spindle whorls and bobbins were often adorned with interesting lines or small circles marked with a point at the center, the lines being traced by incision. The heads of hairpins were carved to represent a human head or male or female bust, a bird, a fruit, or an amphora in proportional, small dimensions. Without any pretension to artistic intent, a large quantity of narrow and flat human figures, without arms or with stumps of arms and the features of the face reduced to the indispensable, were used as magic dolls by the poorest people.

But a certain group, small plaques or combs, whose style is Coptic, stands out from this somewhat mixed and sometimes rudimentary whole.

Plaques first served to form caskets, according to a tradition that was also Alexandrian. They were joined to one another according to the form intended for the object. One of the best examples is a casket in the Walters Art Gallery in Baltimore, dating from the sixth century. On it, standing personages follow one another between columns. A number of these small plaques exist separately in various museums, representing subjects such as a Parthian horseman, a dog pursuing a hare, and birds face to face. There are also Christian subjects such as a standing angel clothed in a long tunic with ascending bands rising from the bottom (Wulff, 1909, pl. 20), or a haloed Saint George, with a round head, full-face on a horse in profile, from the Mamluk period (Wulff, 1909, no. 1613) and an unequaled Virgin with Child between two angels of the ninth century, a first "Virgin of Tenderness" (*Early Christian and Byzantine Art,* no. 160).

Another type of small plaque had a vegetal decoration, the stems of which usually rose in interlacing work from a vase against the vertical rectangular background. A whole evolution of style can be observed here, from the naturalism inspired by the Coptic stone reliefs of friezes that rose in tiers inside or outside churches as at BĀWĪṬ, to a mechanical design of the seventh to the eighth centuries, in the Louvre or in the Musée des Beaux Arts in Lyons.

Comb depicting a warrior saint in a mandorla supported by two angels. Ivory. Fourth century. *Courtesy Coptic Museum, Cairo.*

Figure of a saint holding a cross. Bone. *Courtesy Coptic Museum, Cairo.*

Coptic Cross inlaid with ivory. Detail above the screen of the sanctuary dedicated to Saint George. Church of al-Mu'allaqah (Old Cairo). *Courtesy Arab Republic of Egypt.*

In combs with a handle, either inserted between two sets of teeth or commanding a single row of them, the intermediary or principal part may have been ornamented in relief with the same subjects that have been mentioned in regard to the caskets. One of the most notable examples of the second type is in Cologne (Beckwith, 1963, pl. 131). In a toilet accessory of the eighth century, a foliage of interlacing vines starts from the base and, passing the front paws of two lions placed back to back, rises above the head of each animal, separated by the space that accommodates the handle.

There are also some specimens of cylindrical boxes cut from a solid piece of material, with a cover fastened by a piece of metal. The body was covered with reliefs tracing a double row of interlacing vine branches, between two borders of flowerets; at various places a bird pecks at them (Victoria and Albert Museum, London, 136–1866). Another example is a flat case with slide-bars with Fatimid vegetal decoration.

BIBLIOGRAPHY

Beckwith, J. *Coptic Sculpture 300–1300.* London, 1963.

Early Christian and Byzantine Art. Walters Art Gallery, Baltimore, 1947.

Wulff, O. *Altchristliche und mittelalterliche Bildwerke.* Königliche Museen zu Berlin. Berlin, 1909.

PIERRE DU BOURGUET, S.J.

BOOKBINDING. The codex format—sheets of material written on both sides and attached at one edge—came into use around the beginning of the Christian era and by the fourth century had superseded the scroll. Although evidence of the structure of the codex bookblock and sewing methods survives in many earlier manuscripts, the fourth century provides the earliest examples of books actually in their bindings.

Sheets (two leaves, four pages) for these earliest papyrus codices were cut from rolls, the height of the page by twice its breadth, producing a rectangular format; the square shape of many parchment

Types of quires. *Drawing courtesy Jane Greenfield.*

Stab sewing, derived from the binding of wooden tablets. *Drawing courtesy Jane Greenfield.*

Single quire sewing. *Drawing courtesy Jane Greenfield.*

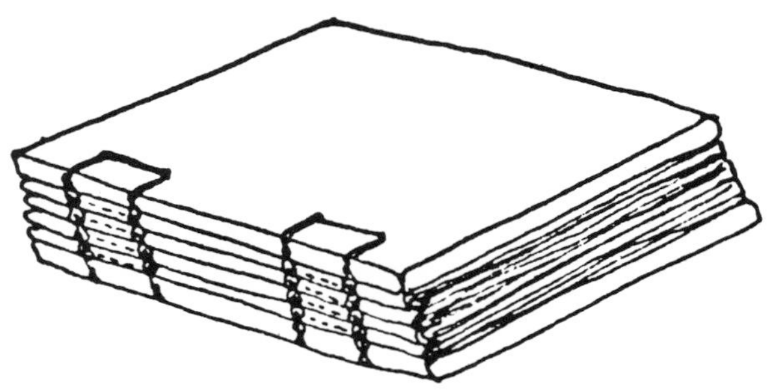

Chain stitch sewing. *Drawing courtesy Jane Greenfield.*

codices was dictated by the shape of the skin. Pagination, foliation, quire signatures, pricking, and ruling were frequently used at an early date, but quire makeup was irregular, and the arrangement of pages with like surface facing like was intermittent.

Variants of bookblock makeup were a single quire of sheets piled one on another and folded in the middle, multiple quires formed by placing folded sheets one within another, and occasionally quires of single sheets folded individually. These quires had to be attached to each other sequentially.

Stab sewing, in which the needle went through the leaves at a right angle to their plane and slightly in from the spine edge, resembled the sewing of

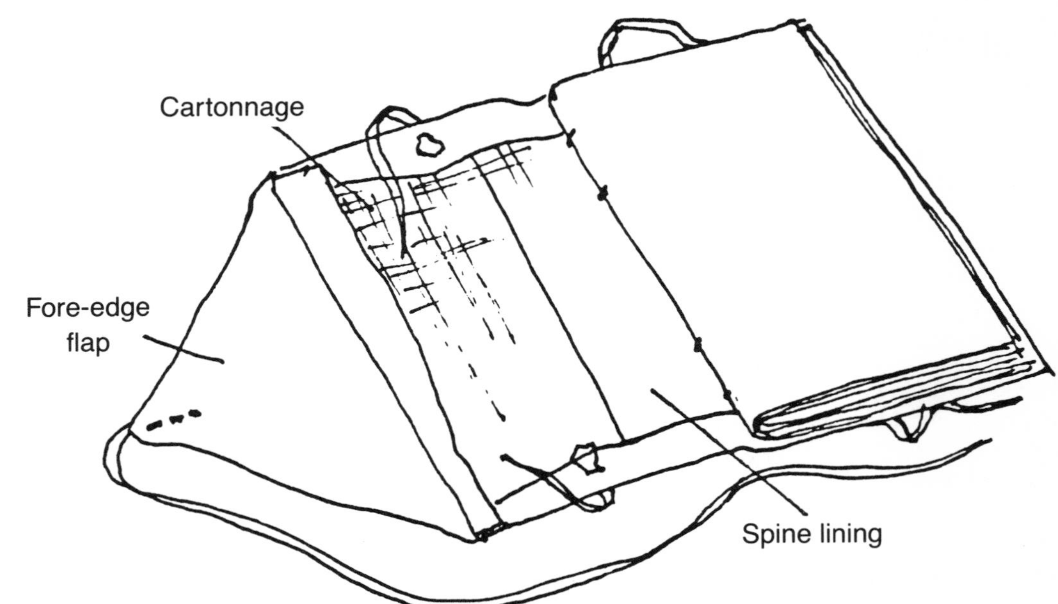

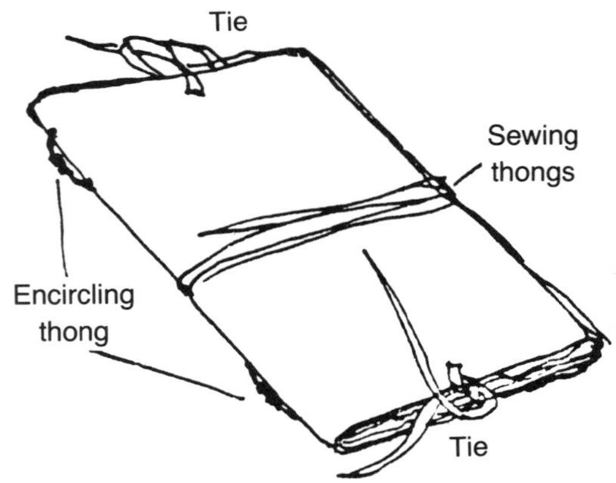

Cover components. *Drawings courtesy Jane Greenfield.*

wooden tablets and was probably loosely tied, as the tablets had to be, to allow the book to open all the way back. Sewing through the fold was usually done with two separate needles and threads. Individually folded sheets were stab sewn; single quires were sewn with two single stitches of leather or cord; multiple quires were sewn with two separate chains of stitches.

Although a few wooden boards without bookblocks are thought to be early, most fourth-century boards consisted of layers of waste papyrus *cartonnage* (paper boards) pasted inside leather covers to stiffen them. The bookblock was either sewn through the outer cover or to a spine lining of leather or parchment, which adhered to it. In some cases two papyrus boards, double the size of the book, were made. Each was folded in half, laced to either side of the book, and finally (after the book was covered) glued together to hide the attachment. The first and last leaves of the bookblock were often pasted down inside the covers to reinforce the attachment.

Goat or sheepskin, usually tan, brown, or dark red, was used for covering. Many fourth-century covers, such as the Nag Hammadi codices and the Bodmer Papyri, had one or more flaps extending from a fore-edge and were fastened with an encircling thong and small ties.

In the sixth to eighth centuries, early techniques continued in use, with the addition of cloth spine linings, sewing all along the fold, and board attachment by numerous leather tongues laced through wooden boards. Methods of fastening were elaborated and there are traces of colored, embroidered decoration (headbands) at each end of the spine.

There were few changes in structure in the eleventh and subsequent centuries; books were written on paper; braided loops attached over pegs were used for fastening. In decoration, the Coptic *horror vacui* reached its peak.

Coptic binding techniques are the prototypes of almost all those in use today throughout the Western Hemisphere and the Near East.

BIBLIOGRAPHY

Cockerell, D. "The Development of Bookbinding Methods: Coptic Influence." *The Library* 4 (1932):170–90.

Kasser, R., ed. *Papyrus Bodmer XVII, Actes des Apôtres, Epîtres de Jacques, Pierre, Jean et Jude*. Introduction, p. 7 (fastenings) and p. 8 (spine lining). Cologny-Geneva, 1961.

———. *Papyrus Bodmer XXIII, Esaie, XLVII, 1-LXVI, 24 en sahidique*. Introduction, pp. 8–15 (flaps and fastenings).

Lamacraft, C. T. "Early Book-binding from a Coptic Monastery." *The Library* 4 (1939–1940):214–33.

Petersen, T. C. "Early Islamic Bookbindings and Their Coptic Relations." *Ars Orientalis* 1 (1954):41–64.

Robinson, J. M. "The Construction of the Nag Hammadi Codices." In *Essays on the Nag Hammadi Texts*, ed. M. Krause. Nag Hammadi Studies 6. Leiden, 1975.

MYRIAM ROSEN-AYALON

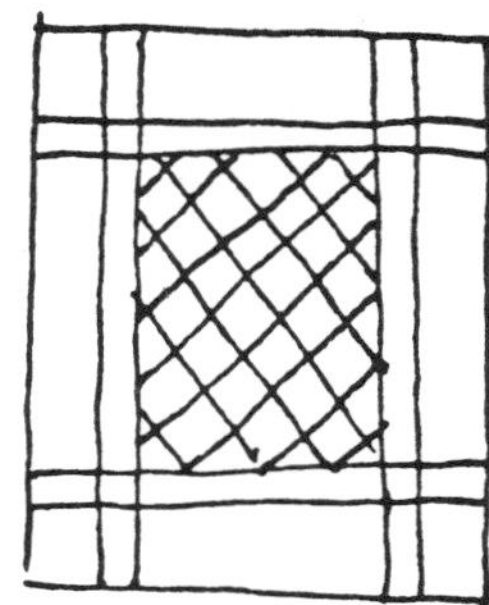

Samples of cover design. *Drawing courtesy Jane Greenfield.*

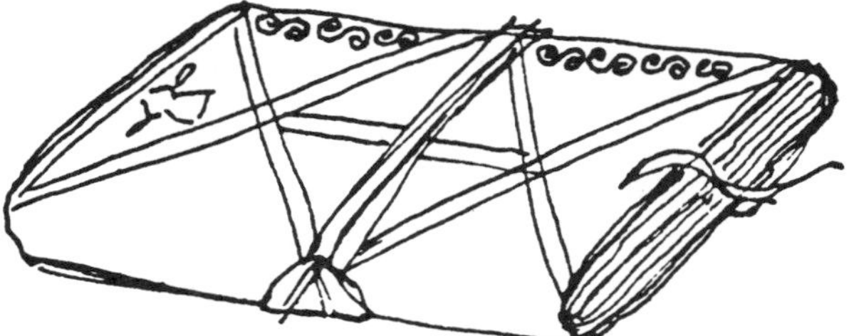

A binding from the Nag Hammadi Library. *Drawing courtesy Jane Greenfield.*

Codex cover decorated with geometrical motifs. Leather. *Courtesy German Museum of Leather, Offenbach.*

BOOK OF EPACT, treatise on the calculation of the date of Easter attributed to DEMETRIUS I, twelfth patriarch of Alexandria (189–231). We shall examine the attribution in light of the historical, liturgical, and literary Arabic traditions of the Middle Ages.

Historical Tradition

The historian Sa'īd IBN AL-BITRĪQ, Melchite patriarch of Alexandria (933–940), tells us in his *History*, "At this period, Demetrius, the patriarch of Alexandria, wrote to Agapius, bishop of Jerusalem, to Maximus, patriarch of Antioch, and to Victor, patriarch of Rome, concerning the calculation of the Easter of Christians and their fast, [so as to know] how to calculate them from the Passover of the Jews. Numerous books and epistles were composed on this subject, until the Easter of Christians was fixed, as is done today." According to A. Harnack (1893, Vol. 1, p. 330), this letter was written in the year 202.

Strangely enough SĀWĪRUS IBN AL-MUQAFFA' makes no mention of this letter in his *History of the Patriarchs*. However, the Copts' Arabic SYNAXARION, composed at the beginning of the thirteenth century, mentions it twice, on 12 Bābah and 10 Hatūr. For 12 Bābah we read,

> This day also, there fell asleep in the Lord . . . our Father Demetrius, the twelfth patriarch of the city of Alexandria. This saint was an illiterate peasant who did not know how to write. . . . He was filled with heavenly grace. He was acquainted with numerous sciences, knew the ecclesiastical books by heart with their commentaries, and spoke on many subjects and sciences. It is he who ordered the calculation of epact and that of the fast, and sent an epistle to each of the leaders of Rome, Antioch, Ephesus, and Jerusalem. When they were informed of this, they gave their approval and established it as a rule, keeping it effective until our days.

The entry for 10 Hatūr reads:

> When our Father Demetrius was made patriarch, he was a peasant who knew neither writing nor books. God illuminated his intellect by divine grace . . . and he composed the calculation of epact whereby the fast and the Resurrection are worked out. He composed it in Coptic and Greek and then sent a copy to our Father Victor, pope of Rome, one to our Father Maximos, patriarch of Antioch, and one to our Father Agapios in Jerusalem. When his letter reached the three sees, our Father Victor, pope of Rome, judged what was sent to him to be excellent, and it caused him great joy. He summoned fourteen learned bishops from dioceses of his jurisdiction and a number of wise priests. He read the calculation to them; they approved it, accepted it, and made a large number of copies of it which they sent to the other episcopal sees. Holy Lent and the glorious Easter were instituted as they are today.

Liturgical Tradition

The following *Salām* (peace) is sung in the Coptic liturgy on the feast of Saint Demetrius:

> Hail to Demetrius,
> who ordered abstinence from drink,
> and organized fasting from foods
> for the fifty days!
>
> Had this not been under the inspiration
> of the Spirit who reveals,
> how could it have been possible
> to discover and find
> the computation of the periods of time
> called epact.
> Hail to you, o priests,
> be thanked and praised
> for having come with diligence and without delay
> to the meetingplace of the assembly
> where the calculation of epact
> dictated by the Holy Spirit
> was communicated to you
> by the venerable Demetrius.
>
> Hail, o Demetrius,
> to your hands that wrote
> the computation of past epacts
> and that of future epacts.

Literary Tradition

In his history of Arabic Christian literature, G. Graf mentions no work attributed to Demetrius, patriarch of Alexandria, despite the fact he had already mentioned two of his works in his *Catalogue of the Christian Arabic Manuscripts of Cairo*. Consultation of the manuscripts gives the following results.

Demetrius is attributed authorship of a work entitled *Ḥisāb al-Abuqṭī*, (Calculation of the Epact), described as "a treatise on chronology, with tables for the finding of Easter and other ecclesiastical festivals and commemorations," and for the Passover of the Jews. This text is as yet unpublished, but it was translated into English by George Sohby from a manuscript in his personal possession. In actual fact, Demetrius' name appears only toward the end.

There are at least three manuscripts of this text, in Birmingham (Mingana Christian Arabic 11, dated

1599); in the Coptic Patriarchate, Cairo (History 60, eighteenth century); and in the George Sobhy Collection, Cairo (1768). The Birmingham manuscript is mentioned in Graf's *Geschichte der christlichen arabischen Literatur* (Vol. 4, p. 159).

In 1634 the anonymous owner of a fine manuscript of the *Book of Epact* of al-As'ad ibn al-'Assāl dated 8 July 1354 (Vatican Library, Arabic 152) wrote in a long gloss on folio 123v that at Dayr al-Baramūs there was a manuscript entitled *Kitāb al-Fāḍil* (The Remainder) of the Book of Epact composed by the Patriarch Demetrius of Alexandria. This may or may not be the same book as the one discussed here.

The Book of Epact was translated from Arabic into Ethiopian at an unknown date. M. Chaine writes, "We sometimes find attributed to Patriarch Demetrius a treatise of computation known as *Bāḥr Ḥasāb*. This work is explicitly attributed to him in the British Museum manuscript Or. 815." He mentions ten or so Ethiopian manuscripts of the same text that do not credit Demetrius and explains, "The name *Bāḥr Ḥasāb* means 'The Ocean of Computation.' It is the translation of an Arabic title which has become the title to designate any composition dealing with the calculation of chronology" (Chaine, 1925, p. 26, n. 3).

At the Syrian Catholic Patriarchate of Sharfah, Lebanon, there is a manuscript (Arabic 13/36) copied by the Copt Barṣūm al-Manfalūṭī in 1422 (or maybe in 1522) from a manuscript of the priest Ghubriyāl copied at the time of Patriarch Mark IV (1348–1363). This manuscript contains a treatise entitled *Sharḥ Karmah waḍa'ahā . . . Anbā Dīmitriyūs* (cf. Armalah, pp. 461–62; Samir, 1976, pp. 344–45). This may be the *Ḥisāb al-Abuqṭī* under a different title. Graf appears not to mention this manuscript in *Geschichte der christlichen arabischen Literatur.*

In a manuscript in the Coptic Patriarchate, Cairo (Theology 230), there is a brief text entitled "Corollary concerning the blessed New Year: the day of the year on which it occurs" (fols. 93b–94b). This may be an extract from the *Ḥisāb al-Abuqṭī*. This text is mentioned in Graf (Vol. 1, p. 354, no. 8), under the name of Demetrius, patriarch of Antioch, whereas the manuscript attributes it to Demetrius of Alexandria.

BIBLIOGRAPHY

Armalah, I. *Catalogue des manuscrits de Charfet.* Jounieh, 1936–1937.

Chaine, M. *La chronologie des temps chrétiens de l'Egypte et de l'Ethiopie.* Paris, 1925.

Graf, G. *Catalogue de manuscrits arabes chrétiens conservés au Caire.* Studi e Testi 34. Vatican City, 1934.

Harnack, A. *Geschichte der altchristlichen Literatur bis Eusebius,* 2 vols. in 4. Leipzig, 1893–1904.

Samir, K. "Ce que l'on sait de la 'Medicina moeroris et curatio doloris' de Sawīrus Ibn al-Muqaffa' (Xe siècle)." *Le Muséon* 89 (1976):339–52.

Sobhy, G. "The Coptic Calendrical Computation and the System of Epacts known as *Ḥisāb al-Abuqṭī* 'the Epact Computation' ascribed to Abba Demetrius the XIIth Patriarch." *Bulletin de la Sociéte d'archéologie Copte* 7 (1941):169–99. A translation without any analysis.

KHALIL SAMIR, S. J.

BOOK OF THOMAS THE CONTENDER,

seventh and last tractate in Codex II of the NAG HAMMADI LIBRARY. It is a revelation dialogue between the resurrected Jesus and his twin brother Judas Thomas, ostensibly recorded by Mathaias (perhaps the apostle Matthew) at a time just before Jesus' ascension. It is a literary expression of traditions native to Syrian Edessa about the apostle Jude, surnamed Thomas, the missionary to India. It was likely composed in the first half of the third century A.D. It seems to occupy a median position between the *Gospel According to Thomas,* composed around A.D. 50–125, and the *Acts of Thomas,* composed in 225. The present Coptic version was probably translated from the Greek; the existence of the text is otherwise unattested in antiquity.

The subtitle designates the work as a "book" of "Thomas the *athletes* [i.e., "one who struggles" against the fiery passions of the body] writing to the perfect," while the opening lines designate the work as "secret sayings" spoken by Jesus to Judas Thomas and recorded by Mathaias as he heard them speaking. The designation "sayings" does not really correspond to the genre of the work, which is a revelation dialogue. This type of dialogue is unlike the Platonic dialogue, in which a conversational process of statement, counterstatement, and clarification leads step by step to the birth of knowledge. It is instead more related to the literature sometimes called *erotapokriseis* ("questions and answers"), in which an initiate elicits revealed truth from a spiritual authority or revealer figure in the form of catechetical answers to topical questions. These dialogues are set at a time between the Resurrection and Ascension, when the Savior appeared on earth in his true divine form, so that both He and His sayings were available to select apostles in a form unclouded by the sort of materiality that was believed to obscure the spiritual significance of his rather parabolic earthly, pre-resurrection teaching. As the Savior's twin, Thomas had a claim to direct insight into the nature of the Savior and his teaching. By "knowing himself," Thomas would also know the "depth of the all," whence the Savior came and whither he was about to return, and thus become a missionary possessing the true teaching of Jesus.

This true teaching of Jesus turns out to be consistently ascetic. Its basic theme or catchword is "fire," the fire of bodily passions that torment the soul and its counterpart in the flames of hell: one shall be punished by that by which one sins. Around this principal theme are gathered a number of conceptual oppositions, divine light versus passionate and infernal fire, the wise man who understands the truth versus the ignorant fool who is guided by the fiery illusion of truth, as well as a Platonic opposition between the visible and invisible. The presence of the Savior as the emissary of the light serves to illumine the eyes to see invisible reality within what heretofore was only perceptually visible and thus illusory. The treatise thus evinces a Platonic dualism of a radically ascetic stripe, and may be properly considered broadly ascetic rather than Gnostic. The Gnostic myth of the creation of the world by a divine accident or evil power is neither mentioned nor apparently presupposed, and the dualism of the treatise is much more anthropological (body/soul) than cosmic (the above/below). A more appropriate designation for the doctrine of this work is Christian(ized) wisdom with ascetic application.

Finally, it is clear that the *Book of Thomas the Contender* displays the marks of a redactional history. It, or part of it, was not originally in the form of a dialogue, but rather one part was in the form of an adulterated collection of the sayings of Jesus, and another part was in the form of a didactic treatise. Whatever the form of its original sources, though, the work as a whole represents a new source for the form-critical investigation of early Christian literature and for the process by which new literary genres were adapted for Christian teaching. It also constitutes another instance in a growing body of Christian wisdom literature with its emphasis on seeking, finding, resting on, and ruling by the truth, and thus escaping the troubles of life.

BIBLIOGRAPHY

Kirchner, D., et al. "Das Buch des Thomas: Die siebente Schrift aus Nag-Hammadi-Kodex II eingeleitet und übersetzt vom Berliner Arbeitskreis für koptisch-gnostiche Schriften." *Theologische Literaturzeitung* 102 (1977):793–804.

Schenke, H.-M. "The Book of Thomas (NHC II.7): A Revision of a Pseudepigraphical Epistle of Jacob the Contender." In *The New Testament and Gnosis: Essays in Honour of Robert McL. Wilson*, ed. A. H. B. Logan and A. J. M. Wedderburn. Edinburgh, 1983.

Turner, J. D. "A New Link in the Syrian Judas Thomas Tradition." In *Essays on Nag Hammadi in Honour of Alexander Böhlig*. Nag Hammadi Studies 3. Leiden, 1972.

______. *The Book of Thomas the Contender from Codex II of the Cairo Gnostic Library from Nag Hammadi (CG II, 7): The Coptic Text with Translation, Introduction and Commentary*. Revised text and translation. Missoula, Mont. 1975.

______. "The Book of Thomas the Contender." In *The Nag Hammadi Library in English*, ed. J. M. Robinson. San Francisco, 1977.

______. "The Book of Thomas the Contender: Introduction, Edited Coptic Text, Fresh English Translation, Critical Apparatus to All Other Editions." In *Nag Hammadi Codex II, 7: Together with XIII, 2*, British Library Oriental. 4926(1) and Papyri Oxyrhynchus 1, 654, 655*. With contributions by many scholars, ed. B. Layton. The Coptic Gnostic Library, ed. with English trans., introduction, and notes. Leiden, 1988.

JOHN D. TURNER

BOOTS. *See* Costume, Civil.

BORGIA, STEFANO (1731–1804), Italian prelate and prefect of the Congregatio de Propaganda Fide. He possessed a collection of Egyptian antiquities and Coptic manuscripts that formed the basis of the collection in the Naples Museum catalogued in G. Zoega's *Catalogus codicum Copticorum manuscriptorum qui in Museo Borgiano velitris adservantur* (Rome, 1810; repr. Leipzig, 1903).

BIBLIOGRAPHY

Sauget, J.-M. "Introduction historique et notes bibliographiques au catalogue de Zoëga." *Le Muséon* 85 (1972):25–63.

MARTIN KRAUSE

BORSAI, ILONA. *See* Music, Coptic: Musical Instruments.

BOULE, town council in Egypt during Roman domination. One of the features that set Egypt apart from other Roman provinces was the scarcity of towns (in the legal sense of the term) and the peculiar status of the *metropoleis,* the nome capitals. The latter, literally "mother cities," while including the designation *polis* (city), were in fact different from the Greek *polis* as well as from the Roman *municipium* (town) at least as far as their legal status was concerned. The Egyptian *metropolis* did not enjoy the paraphernalia the traditional Greek polis had preserved even in the period of the Roman empire, among them the town council (*boule*), one of the most important and typical *polis* institutions (see GREEK TOWNS IN EGYPT). Nor did the agencies of the Egyptian *metropolis* have administrative competence over the nome territory. But the Greek cities of Egypt (Ptolemais, Antinoopolis) were there to remind the citizens of the nome capitals of their inferior status and of the desirability of a change. This change came about in 200 when the emperor Septimius Severus not only conceded the *boule* to Alexandria but upgraded the nome capitals by granting them the *boule* as well (for the chronology, see Lewis, 1982, pp. 78f.; for the *boule* of Alexandria, see GREEK TOWNS IN EGYPT).

The reasons for this move are not on record, and various explanations can be thought of. As for the prerequisites of this change, we are on firmer ground: the *metropoleis,* long considered "villages" (*komai*) by Roman law, had in fact fulfilled in the past many functions of urban centers, thus well deserving the label *metropolis,* because they were the political, economic, social, and religious focus of their respective nomes. The gap between the nome capitals and the rare Greek cities of Egypt had long been narrowed as many metropolitans had been hellenized (in some respects) in the course of the general evolution of Roman Egypt, and not least so under the influence of the metropolitan elite, the gymnasial class, which was or professed to be of Greek stock.

Notwithstanding the accretion of honor and prestige, the creation of the metropolitan *boule* proved at best a mixed blessing. The *boule* had no legislative authority; its activity was restricted to routine business and to the administrative handling of the requirements imposed by the central state authorities. Financial supervision and the collection of taxes were among the *boule*'s main attributions. As a rule, members of the *boule* (*bouleutai*) were not trained officials, a factor that, under the prevailing conditions, partly accounted for the failure of the *boule* as an administrative unit (this aspect is stressed by Bowman, 1971, p. 126f.).

We do not know whether all *metropoleis* had the same number of *bouleutai* (probably not), nor do we know the exact number of *bouleutai* in any given *metropolis* (perhaps 100 in Oxyrhynchus). Upon entrance into the *boule,* each new member had to pay a fee (the *summa honoraria*). It amounted to 10,000 drachmae, clearly an important sum only the wealthiest among the metropolitans could afford. Membership in the *boule* was for life; its presidency was limited to one year. *Bouleutai* normally were male adults, but this situation changed when the gradual reduction of the bouleutic class made it desirable to include women and to retain hold of their property for public service (see the case of Flavia Gabrielia, below). After the president, the secretary and the treasurer of the council fund were important members of the *boule.* Besides managing finances and tax collection, the town council ran the local administration, appointing and supervising the liturgical officials. In its turn, the *boule* was under the tight control of the central state authorities, represented in the first place by the nome *strategos* (general) residing virtually next door to the council's meeting place (*bouleuterion*) in the *metropolis.*

With the deterioration of general conditions in the second half of the third century (foreign wars, usurpations, economic difficulties), municipal magistracies became a heavy burden that ruined many of their holders and provoked abandonment of functions, family, and town (*anachoresis*). Toward the end of the third century, the general political and economic crisis led to a far-reaching reorganization of the Roman empire. As a consequence, state supervision increased at every level, especially in the municipalities, where the *boulai* had clearly become unable to fulfill their responsibilities. Bowman (1976, p. 166) reaches "the conclusion that an important change occurred during the first decade of the fourth century, as a result of which the councils lost much of their power; this was thereafter vested in a board of officials, the most important of whom was the *logistes* (auditor) drawn from the rank of the council but with direct responsibility to the central government. In effect this was an admission of the failure of the Severan reform, which attempted to decentralize by creating the councils in order to relieve some of the government officials of the responsibility for local administration."

In Byzantine Egypt, the *bouleutai* (actual members of the *boule*) and the *politeuomenoi* (*curiales*, members of the *ordo curialis* [curial rank] but not of the *boule* proper) became mere instruments of the state administration and above all of tax collection. Their activity encompassed the whole nome territory. The *boule* continued to exist throughout the Byzantine period and *politeuomenoi* still occurred in Egypt during the first century of Arab domination. The tendency to escape from the heavy burdens of the bouleutic class was checked by imperial decisions tying the *politeuomenoi*—that is, their property—to their status obligations (Rouillard, 1928).

The reduction of the bouleutic class led to a widening of the social gap and to cumulation of offices, as shown by a document from 553 (*Oxyrhynchus Papyri*, Vol. 36, no. 2780), in which a woman, the patrician Flavia Gabrielia, holds not only the presidency of the town council but also the positions of *logistes* (*curator civitatis*, curator of the city) and *pater poleos* (father of the city). These municipal offices had only nominal character compared with the status of the great houses (*oikoi*) and their influence on public affairs in Byzantine Egypt (see Gascou for a different view about the *oikoi*).

BIBLIOGRAPHY

Bowman, A. K. *The Town Councils of Roman Egypt*. American Studies in Papyrology 11. Toronto, 1971. This is the standard work on the subject with comprehensive bibliography of earlier research.

______. "Papyri and Roman Imperial History, 1960–75." *Journal of Roman Studies* 66 (1976):153–73.

Drew-Bear, M. "Les Archives du conseil municipal d'Hermoupolis Magna." In *Atti del XVII Congresso internazionale di papirologia*, Vol. 3, pp. 807–813. Naples, 1984. Interesting for the connection among athleticism, membership in the *boule*, and relations between Hermopolis and the outside world, not least with Rome and the imperial court.

Gascou, J. "Les Grands domaines, la cité et l'état en Egypte byzantine (Recherches d'histoire agraire, fiscale et administrative)." *Travaux et Mémoires* 9 (1985):1–90.

Jones, A. H. M. *The Later Roman Empire, 284–602. A Social, Economic, and Administrative Survey*, 2 vols. Cambridge, 1964.

______. *The Cities of the Eastern Roman Provinces*, 2nd ed., esp. pp. 327–48. Oxford, 1971.

Lallemand, J. *L'Administration civile de l'Egypte de l'avènement de Dioclétien à la création du diocèse (284–382). Contribution à l'étude des rapports entre l'Egypte et l'Empire à la fin du IIIe et au IVe siècle*. Brussels, 1964.

Lewis, N. "Notationes Legentis." *Bulletin of the American Society of Papryologists* 19 (1982):71–82.

______. *Life in Egypt Under Roman Rule*, pp. 36–64. Oxford, 1983.

Rouillard, G. *L'Administration civile de l'Egypte byzantine*, 2nd ed., pp. 62–74. Paris, 1928.

Wegener, E. P. "The βουλή and the Nomination to the ἀρχαί in the μητροπόλεις of Roman Egypt." In *Textes et études de papyrologie grecque, démotique et copte*, ed. P. W. Pestman, pp. 62–114. Papyrologica Lugduno-Batava 23. Leiden, 1985.

Work, K. A. "φενόμενος βουλευτής." *Zeitschrift für Papyrologie und Epigraphik* 30 (1978):239–44.

HEINZ HEINEN

BOURGUET, PIERRE DU, S.J. (1910–1988), professor of Egyptian and of Coptic for more than thirty years at the Institut catholique de Paris, where he also served as director of the School of Ancient Oriental Languages. In addition, he was professor of paleo-Christian, Coptic, and Byzantine art and archaeology at the Ecole du Louvre for approximately twenty years.

A chief curator at the Louvre in the Department of Egyptian Antiquities, he was in charge of the collections for the Coptic and pharaonic Lower Epoch periods, and, for a certain time, the paleo-Christian and Byzantine collections as well.

In Egypt he traveled widely to desert and oasis alike. He participated in the excavations at KELLIA and Tod, and directed the work at the site of DAYR AL-MADĪNAH.

He published in various fields, and wrote grammars of the two stages of ancient Egyptian and a grammar of Sahidic Coptic. He used the latter, which remains unpublished, as a tool in his teaching. He published widely in all the above-mentioned disciplines.

A selected bibliography of his writings includes: *Catalogue des étoffes coptes (Musée du Louvre)*, Paris, 1964; and *L'art copte*, Paris, 1968; translated into English as *The Art of the Copts*, London, 1971.

MARIE-HÉLÈNE RUTSCHOWSKAYA

BOURIANT, URBAIN (1849–1903), French Egyptologist and Coptologist. He was born in Nevers. After he became interested in Egyptology, he studied under Gaston MASPERO and became an original member of the Mission archéologique française du Caire in 1881. He was appointed assistant conservator of the Bulāq Museum in 1883 and served as director of the Mission archéologique from 1886 until 1898. He died at Vannes. His items are listed in *A Coptic Bibliography* (Kammerer, 1950, 1969).

BIBLIOGRAPHY

Bouriant, P. "Notice sur Urbain Bouriant." *Recueil de Travaux* 26 (1904):29–32 (bibliography).

Dawson, W. R., and E. P. Uphill. *Who Was Who in Egyptology,* 36–7. London, 1972.

Kammerer, W., comp. *A Coptic Bibliography.* Ann Arbor, Mich., 1950; repr. New York, 1969.

AZIZ S. ATIYA

BOUTROS GHĀLĪ (1846–1910), Coptic statesman. He was born in Kimān-al-'Arūs, a village in the province of Banī Suef. His father, the steward of the estate of Prince Muṣṭafā Fāḍil, brother of Khedive Isma'il, first sent him to the patriarchal school, which had recently been founded in Cairo by CYRIL IV (1854–1861).

He then studied Arabic, Turkish, Persian, English, and French. Endowed with a remarkable memory, Boutros had shown great flexibility in his personality. He did not seem personally to have suffered from the discrimination then rampant in favor of non-Egyptians, such as Turks and Circassians. On completing his studies, he became a teacher at the patriarchal school, headed by YA'QŪB NAKHLAH RUFAYLAH, who was later to publish a history of the Copts. In the meantime, Boutros also attended classes at the School of Languages founded by Rifā'ah al-Ṭahṭāwī. He began working at the Ministry of Justice, where he was rapidly promoted to chief interpreter; he was barely twenty-eight years old.

The post was of great importance, as the department was then concerned with establishing a modern judicial infrastructure in Egypt. This entailed, as a first step, the translation and annotation of the laws in force in Europe. He thus collaborated with Qadrī Pasha, the great jurist of the time, in setting up the national courts, designated then as "native courts" to distinguish them from the mixed courts that had been established a few years earlier. Many manuscripts written and annotated by Boutros Ghālī testify to the leading role he played in the judicial renaissance of Egypt.

The debts incurred by Khedive Ismā'īl became the pretext for foreign intervention. A commission of three delegates, English, French, and Egyptian, was formed, the Egyptian being Riyāz Pasha. His assistant was Boutros Ghālī. The *Report on the Land Tax* was presented to the commission by Boutros on 18 February 1880; it is a thorough study of the property system in Egypt, and remains an important document for the economic and financial history of Egypt.

In 1881, Boutros Ghālī was appointed undersecretary of state for justice, a position that he occupied for twelve years. During his tenure, the reorganization of the judicial system progressed. Provincial courts, district courts, and a court of appeal were established. Justice became secularized.

In 1893 he became minister of finance, and in 1895 he was appointed minister of foreign affairs, an office that he held for fifteen years until his death. The main lines of his policy remained unchanged: to preserve the legitimate authority of the khedive in face of the BRITISH OCCUPATION; to reduce the impact of the unavoidable clashes between the one and the other; and, at the same time, to modernize the country by endowing it with a liberal parliamentary regime, in order to remove the pretext for occupation.

The Anglo-Egyptian military campaign ended with the defeat of the Sudanese and the signing, on 19 January 1899, of an agreement between Egypt and England establishing a condominium or joint authority over the territory. Boutros was criticized over this issue, but it had the unanimous approval of the members of the cabinet. Egypt could not ignore the disproportion of forces while its own territory was under foreign occupation. It was probably the best that could be done in the circumstances. At least, it assured the future by preventing England from assuming total sovereignty over the Sudan.

Khedive 'Abbās II came to power in January 1892, and he soon found himself at odds with the British. It became necessary to reduce friction between legitimate authority and the power of the occupying force, and, at the same time, to protect the ruler against the threat of dethronement. In the pursuit of these aims, Boutros Ghālī showed much resourcefulness, but he sometimes became involved in initiatives that were acutely criticized, even though their final purpose was clearly to preserve the dynasty.

In 1906, as acting minister of justice in the absence of the minister abroad, he was called upon to preside over the court appointed to judge the Dinshawāy case. On a shooting trip in 1906, a group of

British officers had accidentally shot the wife of a local official at Dinshaway. During the attempted escape, two British officers and several Egyptians were wounded or killed. Four of the Egyptians were hanged and four sentenced to life imprisonment. The rest were flogged and given prison terms, as well (King, 1984, pp. 260–61). Boutros Ghālī labored very hard to reduce the number of the accused and the harshness of the sentences, but Egyptian public opinion bitterly reproached him for having accepted the leadership over this court.

In November 1908, Boutros Ghālī was appointed president of the Council of Ministers, despite British objections. His first move was to try to transform the prerogatives of the Consultative Assembly and turn it into a true parliament, before which the ministers would be responsible. However, the nationalist press, which had been unleashed against him at the time, drove him in 1909 to reinstate the 1881 law of Sherif Pasha that put restrictions on the press.

With the agreement of the British, he submitted to the assembly the proposal for a forty-year extension of the Suez Canal Company concession. The prestige of the assembly would thus be enhanced by having the opportunity to discuss the proposal. The refusal of the proposal by the assembly would bring about a final decision without running the risk of a political crisis. The proposal was, in fact, rejected by the assembly three months later.

On 21 February 1910, a month after submitting the proposal to the assembly, Boutros was assassinated by a nationalist. His death sparked serious quarrels between Copts and Muslims, lasting throughout the years before World War I. Concord and a national consensus were reached only when the Wafd party came to power.

Boutros Ghālī took an active interest in Coptic affairs. He cooperated in establishing the first COMMUNITY COUNCIL in 1874. In 1883, he obtained a khedivial decree detailing the organization and the competence of the council. He had many conflicts with the clergy and Patriarch CYRIL V (1874–1927) concerning lay participation in the administration of the church properties.

DORIS BEHRENS-ABUSEIF

BOXES AND CASKETS. *See* Bone and Ivory Carving, Coptic; Woodwork, Coptic.

BRAZIER. *See* Metalwork, Coptic.

BRECCIA, A. EVARISTO (1876–1967), Italian archaeologist. Breccia was director of the Graeco-Roman Museum in Alexandria from 1904 to 1931. He was made professor of classical antiquity and epigraphy at Pisa in 1932 and professor of ancient history three years later. He took part in many excavations in Egypt, of which the ANTINOOPOLIS excavation, which he recorded in "Le prime richerche italiane ad Antinoe" (*Aegyptus* 18, 1938, pp. 285–318), is especially worthy of mention. His significant works include "D'un édifice d'époque chrétienne à el-Dekhela et l'emplacement du Ennaton" (*Bulletin de la Société royale d'archéologie d'Alexandrie* 9, 1907, pp. 1–12); *Le Musée greco-romain 1925–1931* (Bergamo, 1932); "Dans le désert de Nitrée" (*Bulletin de la Société royale d'archéologie d'Alexandrie* 27, 1932, pp. 17–26); and *Le Musée greco-romain 1931–1932* (Bergamo, 1933).

BIBLIOGRAPHY

Barocas, C. "Breccia, Evaristo." In *Dizionario biografico degli italiani,* Vol. 14, pp. 91–93. Rome, 1972.

Calderini, A. "A. Evaristo Breccia." *Aegyptus* 46 (1966):293–96.

MARTIN KRAUSE

BRIGHTMAN, FRANK EDWARD (1856–1932), British liturgist. He was librarian of Pusey House and then a fellow of Magdalen College at Oxford. He is known above all for his *Liturgies Eastern and Western,* Vol. 1, *Eastern Liturgies* (Oxford, 1896). The second volume never appeared.

BIBLIOGRAPHY

Bate, H. N. "F. E. Brightman." *Proceedings of the British Academy* 19 (1933):345–50.

RENÉ-GEORGES COQUIN

BRITISH ISLES, COPTIC INFLUENCES IN THE. In the early Middle Ages, the fifth to the ninth century, Ireland and England were open to monastic influences from Coptic Egypt; the Irish, and to a lesser extent the Anglo-Saxons, responded favorably. There is no proof that any individual

Copt ever came into contact with any individual Anglo-Saxon or Irishman, nor is there any evidence that anyone in Ireland and England could read Coptic—only a few could even read Greek—so the influences were all secondhand. Yet the societal structures in the British Isles during that period guaranteed that Coptic influences would have more effect there than in Western areas with direct contacts in Egypt.

Western Continental Monasticism

Knowledge of the Coptic monks of Egypt and their ways reached the West through Greek churchmen, who usually favored the more structured discipline of the Western church. Even writers and church dignitaries such as the patriarch ATHANASIUS I preferred monks to be obedient to hierarchical authority; and when they praised the eremitic (solitary) life, they did so in an idealizing way, as something wonderful in the days of the primitive church. Other Greeks, such as Saint BASIL THE GREAT, strongly criticized the hermits and emphasized episcopal authority over the monks.

The conservative ecclesiastics of the West shared the Greek view. They were skeptical of hermits and fearful of wandering holy men who gained popular adulation. Gregory of Tours in the sixth century tells of a Gaul who wished to be a stylite but was talked off his pillar by the local clergy, who reminded him that he was in Gaul, not Syria, and that he would freeze in winter. Less amusing but more revealing is Sulpicius Severus' fifth-century Life of Martin of Tours, which tells how Saint Martin's eremitic life endeared him to the people but offended the hierarchy, who used his ascetic manners and appearance to discourage his elevation to the episcopate, although they did not succeed.

In the Western church, monasticism increased, but usually it was of the cenobitic (communal) rather than the eremitic type and had close connections with bishops. Bishops were frequently chosen from the ranks of monks. In the fifth century, for example, the island monastery of Lérins off the coast of southern France was virtually a seminary for Gallic bishops. Ambrose, bishop of Milan, patronized a monastic community outside the city walls and Augustine, bishop of Hippo, wrote a rule for monks. P. Rousseau demonstrated in 1971 that the hagiographers of the Western bishops depended upon monastic models.

In the sixth century the greatest of Western monks, Saint Benedict, fit into this pattern. A true Roman, he favored an orderly monastic environment with a set of offices that demanded respect—regardless of what one might think of the office-holder—and cooperation between the monks and the local bishop, who had authority over them. Although he acknowledged the existence of good hermits, Benedict really had no place for them in his system. He preferred monks to be under the control of an abbot, and he stressed the Roman virtue of *stabilitas*, envisioning that a monk would spend his life in one monastery. He had no use for the wandering monks who figure in the most primitive Egyptian accounts.

Monasticism in Ireland and England

This preference for a disciplined, organized monasticism reflected the society of the Western empire with its large urban communities and strong, often politically minded bishops. But when Christianity reached Ireland in the fifth century, it encountered a completely different society, one in which the typical Western Christian culture had little relevance. A religion that grew up in a warm, Mediterranean, urban, classical, literate environment was now entering a chilly, Atlantic, rural, barbarian, nonliterate environment. When the Anglo-Saxons conquered most of southern Britain in the fifth and sixth centuries, they created a similar world on that island. These conditions were made for monasticism, and they revivified the primitive Egyptian forms.

The Irish had no cities, and while some Anglo-Saxons took over Romano-British cities, most lived in rural areas. The episcopacy was an urban institution, but monasticism, which had begun as a flight from the cities, was rural and fitted well in England and Ireland.

As barbarians (that is, nonclassical peoples), the Irish and English lived in heroic societies that valued a man's individual qualities more than the office he held. Their heroes, such as Cuchulainn and Beowulf, were men who faced the enemy alone. The hermit, who by himself fought the world, the flesh, and the devil, fitted the image of the northern hero; bishops and cenobitic monks generally did not.

Finally, the Irish and English were converts with all the zeal of converts. The centuries-old Christian religion was as new to them in the early Middle Ages as it had been to the Jews and Romans in the apostolic age. This zeal found its outlet not in the lives of members of the settled establishment but in the lives of those who gave all for their faith, the monks.

These factors combined to make the Irish and English receptive to Egyptian monasticism, particularly that of the desert's heroic age. Eventually the romanization of both the Irish and English churches eliminated this influence, but for some years it was a potent and creative force. In Ireland, Athanasius' *Life of Antony* was known in Latin translation, as was Jerome's probably fictitious life of Paul, another Egyptian hermit. The *Sayings of the [Desert] Fathers* was translated from Greek into Latin by the Spaniard Martin of Braga in the sixth century. Contacts between Spain and Ireland were strong in the early Middle Ages, and the Irish were familiar with the *Sayings*.

Irish Saints

The great Irish monastic saints were, like Saint ANTONY, originally hermits who were forced by popular pressure to accept disciples, for example, Saint Kevin of Glendalough. Like Antony, but unlike Benedict, they were fond of wandering, and there arose in Ireland a form of spirituality called the *peregrinatio pro Christo*, a "wandering for Christ." The Irish thought that next to martyrdom, voluntary exile was the greatest sacrifice one could make. Abraham had left Ur of the Chaldees at God's call, so the practice had a biblical foundation. Both Saint Columba and Saint Columbanus went into exile in the sixth and seventh centuries. When Saint Adamnan wrote the Life of Columba in the seventh century, he not only presented the saint in Antony's mold but also included verbatim, though unacknowledged, citations from a Latin version of Antony's Life.

The Coptic monks lived in the desert. The Irish had no desert, but they did have the Atlantic Ocean. Like the Egyptian desert, it was vast and even waterless, since one cannot drink seawater. To the Irish, the wild, empty ocean appeared as lonely and forbidding as the desert had to the Egyptians. The connection was more than psychological; Irish texts, for example, spoke of the ocean as a *desertum*. The most widely read Irish book of this period was the *Voyage of Saint Brendan*. It tells the story of the abbot Brendan's departure from his homeland and his voyage on the ocean in search of the Blessed Isles, an obvious reenactment of the Egyptians' withdrawal to the desert in search of a heavenly life. Brendan wanders, meets fabulous creatures, wins contests with demons, and reaches his destination. To stress the Egyptian parallels, the anonymous author even has Brendan meet Paul the Hermit.

The flight to the desert is a symbolic return to the natural world of the Garden of Eden from the world of human beings. This is a prominent theme in Irish hagiography, in which the Irish hermits live with nature, and many of their miracles involve the animals with which they live in peace.

These literary motifs extend beyond the hagiography. Recent scholarship has established that many biblical apocrypha were known in Coptic circles—some were known only in these circles—and manuscripts of these texts date to the fourth and fifth centuries, when the hierarchical church was condemning their use. Martin McNamara has demonstrated that the Irish knew and used a great many apocrypha, including some known only from Egypt. It is virtually impossible that the Irish had direct access to Coptic works, but it is certain that they did know and appreciate those works far more than other Western peoples. Visionary and apocalyptic books were especially popular with them.

Irish Art

Artistic devices and motifs also demonstrate the contacts of the Irish with Coptic influence. The circled Irish cross may derive from the ancient Egyptian *tau* symbol, which had been turned into a cross in Egypt at least by the fifth century, as a Coptic manuscript in the Pierpont Morgan Library in New York shows (G.67, p. 215). The famous "Virgin and Child with Angels" illustration on folio 7v of the illuminated Irish manuscript the Book of Kells has been shown by F. Henry (1963) to be related to a Coptic manuscript. Henry also points out that the use of red dots surrounding a figure in order to illuminate it, a practice used in several Irish manuscripts, is of Coptic origin. Portraits of Christ in some Irish manuscripts and on Irish stone crosses bear strong resemblance to portraits of Osiris. Irish church music also shows Coptic influence. The Irish used hand bells, as did the Copts in the sixth century, but the rest of the Eastern church did not do so until the ninth.

English Saints

The Coptic influence was less strong in England because the Anglo-Saxons moved into what had been a Roman province, and there was a Roman mission to England before 600. The eighth-century historian Bede tells the story in his *Historia eccles-*

iastica. As the Romans evangelized southern England, they eventually came into contact and friction with the Irish, who had been evangelizing Northumbria. At the Synod of Whitby in 664, the Northumbrian king Oswy decided for the Roman party and guaranteed that the Anglo-Saxon church would be the ordered, stable entity so familiar in the West. Indeed, Bede himself was a Benedictine.

But the "official" triumph of Roman views was not a triumph of the heart, and old ways persisted for a while longer. One of Bede's heroes was Saint Cuthbert, a cenobitic monk of the seventh century who left his community to become a hermit. He lived on a deserted island, built a wall around himself so high that he could see only the sky, battled with demons, and performed miracles with wild animals. Only late in life was he imposed upon to accept a bishopric, an office he had previously refused (*Historia ecclesiastica* 4.27–29).

Guthlac was a monk at Repton in the seventh century but left to become a hermit on a marshy island, where he practiced strict asceticism. His biographer, Felix, in his Life of Guthlac (chap. 30), says that demons tried to tempt him by offering to teach him the way of life of "those renowned monks who dwelt in Egypt." On another occasion Guthlac routed some demons by reciting Psalm 67:2 to them, the same verse Saint Antony of Egypt had used (chap. 34).

The famous Ruthwell Cross, a large stone cross that contains verses from the poem "The Dream of the Rood," has representations of Antony and Paul engraved upon it.

The particulars relate to surface evidence, but the Coptic spirit lived on past the Synod of Whitby. Bede was a romanized Benedictine but also an Anglo-Saxon from a heroic society. His tribute to the English hermit Drycthelm exemplifies the heroism and individuality that also characterized the desert fathers (*Historia ecclesiastica* 5.12):

> This man was given a more secluded dwelling in the monastery, so that he could devote himself more freely to the service of his Maker in unbroken prayer. And since this place stands on the bank of a river, he often used to enter it for severe bodily penance, and plunge repeatedly beneath the water while he recited psalms and prayers for as long as he could endure it, standing motionless with the water up to his loins and sometimes to his neck. When he returned to shore, he never removed his dripping, chilly garments, but let them warm and dry on his body. And in winter, when the half-broken cakes of ice were swirling around him which he had broken to make a place to stand and dip himself in the water, those who saw him used to say: "Brother Drycthelm . . . , it is wonderful how you can manage to bear such bitter cold." To which he, being a man of simple disposition and self-restraint, would reply simply: "I have known it colder."

BIBLIOGRAPHY

Henry, F. *L'Art irlandais,* Vol. 1. Paris, 1963.

Kelly, J. F. T. "The Desert Fathers as Models for the Monks of the West." In *God and Charity,* ed. F. D. Costa, pp. 55–74. Brookline, Mass., 1979.

______. "The Gallic Resistance to Eastern Asceticism." *Studia Patristica* 18 (1982):506–510.

McNamara, M. *The Apocrypha in the Irish Church.* Dublin, 1975.

Ritner, R. "Egyptians in Ireland: A Question of Coptic Peregrinations." *Rice University Studies* 62, no. 2 (1975):65–87.

Rousseau, P. "The Spiritual Authority of the 'Monk-Bishops': Eastern Elements in Some Western Hagiography of the Fourth and Fifth Centuries." *Journal of Theological Studies,* n.s., 22 (1971):380–419.

Stevenson, J. "Ascent Through the Heavens, from Egypt to Ireland." *Cambridge Medieval Celtic Studies* 5 (1983):21–35.

J. F. T. KELLY

BRITISH OCCUPATION OF EGYPT. When the British occupied Egypt in 1882, the Copts were not playing any active role in Egyptian political life. The liberal wing of the nationalist movement, which developed under the influence of Christian Syrian immigrants, did not include Coptic names. The presence of Copts in the Egyptian army was too recent to be of political relevance. Although European sources of the time tend to identify xenophobic excesses that accompanied the revolt of 'Urābī with purely fanatic persecution of Christians, there is no evidence that the Copts were singled out during the riots of 1882. The Coptic historian MĪKHĀ'ĪL SHĀRŪBĪM (1900) reports on the persecutions of the *naṣārā,* or Christians, mentioning Syrians, Greeks, and British victims but no Copts in this context. E. L. Butcher (1897), who echoes the British attitude, seeing in the riots of 1882 an argument to occupy Egypt in order to secure European interests, writes that possible harm could have come to the Copts had the British not intervened at the right time by occupying the country.

In fact, there was no real antagonism between the Copts and the 'Urābī movement, which was directed first against Turkish and Circassian elements in the Egyptian army and later against European intervention in Egyptian politics. It is even reported that some Copts supported ʿUrābī. ʿUrābī, however, could not stop fanatic elements from being involved in his revolt, a factor that cost him the sympathy of Christian Syrians who first supported him. The Coptic patriarch and other Coptic notables were among the signers of a petition addressed to Khedive Tawfīq against his decision to dismiss ʿUrābī. This may have been a mere formality, but the mediating role played by BOUTROS GHĀLĪ during the ʿUrābī revolt shows that the Copts played an increasingly important role in government service.

Like the French before them, the British did not seek to favor the Copts at the expense of the Muslim majority. They preferred to rely on other Christian minorities of Egypt. Lord Cromer, the British high commissioner, held no higher opinion of the Copts than of their Muslim countrymen. He did not trust them and considered them to be opportunists. Cromer considered the Christian Syrians more modern, more emancipated, and closer to European mentality. They, with the Armenians, were in his opinion the elite of the Orient. The first impact of the British occupation on the Copts was therefore negative. In the course of modernization measures undertaken by the British, they saw themselves losing their traditional hold on the civil service. Their contempt grew as they were replaced by Syrians and Europeans. On the other hand, the Copts were accumulating wealth in land and investments under British rule. According to Coptic sources, at the turn of the century they owned one-fifth of the agricultural land of Egypt. Like the rest of the Egyptian land aristocracy, they came to enjoy great economic advantage under British rule.

The Coptic press, *al-Waṭan* (founded in 1877) and *Miṣr* (founded in 1895), strongly supported the British occupation in spite of their constant criticism about unfair treatment of the British toward the Copts in the civil service. The British tried to diminish the traditional Coptic monopoly on certain posts in order to cultivate an image of fairness toward the Muslim majority.

In 1896 a Coptic delegation presented a list of claims to the government and to Lord Cromer, asking for equal treatment with the Muslims in the civil service; for Sunday to be the holiday for the courts; for catechism for Copts in public schools; and for more opportunities to occupy high government posts.

The Coptic press stood in total opposition to the National party of Muṣṭafā Kāmil, although the party included Copts. *Miṣr* organized a petition signed by members of the Coptic community to protest any change in the political situation that could introduce new changes. This petition was met with opposition from nationalist Copts and supporters of the National party. Proposals to found a Coptic party were also made, but they did not prevail against secular tendencies within the Coptic community.

A crisis between the Coptic and the Nationalist press burst out after *al-Waṭan*, in its apologia for the British occupation of Egypt, described the Muslim conquest of Egypt as being as oppressive as any other conquest. The chief editor of *al-Liwā'*, the paper of the National party, reacted with a highly insulting and provocative article against the Copts. Because the author of the article, ʿAbd al-'Azīz Jāwīsh, was of Tunisian origin, the Copts were confirmed in their animosity toward pan-Islam.

For many modern Egyptian historians, the conflict between the Copts and Muslims at the beginning of the twentieth century was a result of the British policy of divide and rule. The nomination of Boutros Ghālī as prime minister was due to his efficiency in representing the British as well as the khedive's interests, both of which were supported by many Muslims as well. The assassination of Boutros Ghālī by a Muslim partisan of the National party brought Coptic-Muslim relations to a new crisis. Boutros Ghālī was accused by the Copts of not having addressed himself to Coptic interests while he was in government. In Asyūṭ, the city with the largest concentration of Copts in Egypt, Coptic notables decided to hold a congress to stress again their demands to the government. The government feared trouble in Asyūṭ and asked Patriarch CYRIL V to intervene and propose another location, but neither the government nor the patriarch himself managed to sway the Copts. They held a well-attended congress in March 1911, where they demanded a change in the election law according to what they felt was inadequate representation, and they requested the making of Sunday a holiday for the Copts. In his report of 1911, the British High Commissionar Eldon Gorst heavily criticized the Coptic congress, which he said was organized by a minority of rich land owners. He emphasized the great financial power of the Copts as relatively greater than that of their Muslim countrymen and at the same time made the Coptic moneylenders responsible for the misery of the poor peasants. According to him, more Coptic influence, as demanded, would make the Copts more unpopular. He accused the Copts of interpreting British impartiality between Copts and Muslims as prejudicial to the Copts.

According to official statistics of the time, the Copts held 69 percent of the posts in the ministry of interior, 44 percent in the ministry of post and railway, 30 percent in the ministry of justice, and 14 percent in the ministry of culture. According to Coptic estimates, they controlled 19 percent of the Egyptian economy while they made up only 7 percent of the population.

After the Coptic congress, public opinion turned against the Copts. The European press of Egypt as well as part of the British press supported the Coptic claims. From the Muslim point of view, the Coptic support of the British and the success of the Protestant missionary activity among the Copts since the British occupation gave enough reason for mistrusting the Copts; and even though official British policy did not favor the Copts, the missions created a common ground between British and Copts, encouraging the Copts in anti-Islamic tendencies.

The missionary activity also played an important role in the relations between the community and its patriarch and clergy. The patriarch, Cyril V, saw foreign interference as the reason for the troubles he was having with the community as it asked for lay representation in the Community Council for the rule of Coptic affairs. This conflict went as far as requesting removal of the patriarch from the chairmanship of the council in 1893 and the substitution of another church prelate in that position. In this conflict, the British sympathized with the reformers. In 1911 the Egyptian Congress of Heliopolis was held as a reaction to the Coptic Congress and to answer the Coptic demands. It was supported by Khedive ʿAbbās II and Muṣṭafā Riyāḍ, the prime minister who had always been neutral in Coptic–Muslim conflicts. The National party rejected this congress as it had rejected the Coptic congress, regarding it as a threat to national unity. Thus, they were standing on the same side as the Copts, though for different reasons.

The British attitude toward Coptic claims and their role in the conflict between clergy and community as well as the increasing Coptic conversions to Protestantism led *al-Waṭan,* which supported the patriarch, gradually to change its attitude toward the British.

The formation of a new liberal and secular trend in Egyptian nationalism slowly opened the door for the integration of the Copts into the national movement. The newspaper *al-Jarīdah* became the nucleus for the Ummah Party, one of whose members was SA'D ZAGHLŪL. *Al-Jarīdah* expressed a nationalism based on an Egyptian identity separate from pan-Islam, and managed to win Coptic sympathies. When the 1919 revolution against the British took place, it included all classes and groups of Egyptians, regardless of religion. One may say that the main achievement of this revolution was the total national unity of Copts and Muslims around Saʿd Zaghlūl and his Wafd party. The emblem of this revolution was, in fact, a crescent enclosing a cross.

The nomination of a Copt, Yūsuf Wahbah, as prime minister during the boycott of the Milner Commission's visit to Egypt in 1919 was condemned by the Coptic community as a British intrigue to embarrass the Muslims, who would fear being accused of religious fanaticism if they opposed the Wahbah government.

Saʿd Zaghlūl succeeded in attracting Coptic enthusiasm for his Wafd. Three Copts accompanied him to Paris, and Copts as well as Muslims were exiled and put in jail during the Wafd struggle for independence.

One year before the British proclaimed Egypt a British protectorate in 1913, a new law for the Legislative Assembly reserved four seats among seventeen for the Copts, among other ethnic and professional groups. The Copts were thus represented as a minority, but not as part of the professional groups of engineers or merchants. This law reflected British views and traded concessions granted to European states for the protection of foreigners in Egypt with the privilege to protect the minorities of Egypt. Lord Cromer regarded Egypt as a conglomeration of different groups without a national bond or a national identity and felt that the representative bodies should be constituted accordingly. In their declaration of 1922 of Egyptian independence, the British reserved for themselves four clauses, some of which granted them the right to protect foreigners and minorities in Egypt. These clauses were rejected by the National party as well as the Wafd party.

A lively debate on this subject took place in the entire Egyptian press, the Copts themselves being of divided opinion. A proportional representation would bar foreign interference in Egyptian affairs. Since Islam would be the state religion, a legally secured representation would make up for inconveniences caused by this fact. Since several European countries were adopting such systems to secure the rights of their minorities, this measure would not be exceptional. This idea was rejected by most political as well as intellectual personalities. Sa'd Zaghlūl felt that within a parliament only political arguments should rule. Most of the Copts also rejected special treatment for the Copts as being incompatible with the sovereignty of state. No separate interests should exist between Copts and Muslims. The result of the first parliamentary elections proved better than the law. The number of elected Coptic deputies was higher than a special status would have allowed. Independent Egypt's first cabinet under the leadership of Sa'd Zaghlūl included two Copts and a Jew. The head of the chamber of deputies was also a Copt.

BIBLIOGRAPHY

Behrens-Abouseif, D. *Die Kopten in der ägyptischen Gesellschaft.* Freiburg im Breisgau, 1972.

Blunt, W. S. *Secret History of the English Occupation of Egypt.* London, 1907.

Butcher, E. L. *The Story of the Church of Egypt.* London, 1897.

Cromer, Lord. *Modern Egypt.* London, 1908.

Mikhail, K. *Copts and Muslims Under British Control.* London, 1911.

Muḥammad Sayyid Kīlānī. *al-Adab al-Qibṭī Qadīman wa Ḥadīthan.* Cairo, 1962.

Strothman, Rudolf. *Die koptische Kirche in der Neuzeit.* Tübingen, 1932.

DORIS BEHRENS-ABUSEIF

BRUCE, JAMES (1730–1794), Scottish traveler. He studied Oriental languages and traveled in North Africa. In Egypt, where he arrived in July 1768, he visited Luxor and Karnak and excavated the tomb of Ramses III in the Valley of the Kings. In 1769 in Madīnat Hābū he acquired a Gnostic codex that was named for him, the Bruce Papyrus (Bruce Manuscript 96), and is still preserved in the Bodleian Library (cf. MacDermot, 1978). In November 1772, on the way back from Ethiopia, he visited Aswan. In 1773 he returned to England, where in 1790 he published his *Travels.*

BIBLIOGRAPHY

Dawson, W. R., and E. P. Uphill. *Who Was Who in Egyptology,* p. 41. London, 1972.

MacDermot, V. *The Books of Jeu and the Untitled Text in the Bruce Codex.* Nag Hammadi Studies 13. Leiden, 1978.

MARTIN KRAUSE

BRUGSCH, HEINRICH FERDINAND KARL (1827–1894), German Egyptologist. He became professor at Göttingen in 1868 and director of the School of Egyptology in Cairo in 1870, working in all fields of Egyptology as well as in Coptology. He founded the journal *Zeitschrift für ägyptische Sprache und Altertumskunde* in 1863. In 1881 he was given the title pasha by the ruling khedive because of his contributions to Egyptology.

BIBLIOGRAPHY

Brugsch, H. F. K. *Mein Leben und mein Wandern.* Berlin, 1893.

Dawson, W. R., and E. P. Uphill. *Who Was Who in Egyptology.* London, 1972.

Erman, A. "Heinrich Brugsch." *Zeitschrift für ägyptische Sprache und Altertumskunde* 32 (1894):69–73.

MARTIN KRAUSE

BUDGE, ERNEST ALFRED THOMPSON WALLIS (1857–1934), English Egyptologist, Coptologist, and Orientalist. He became a student at Christ College, Cambridge, where he excelled in the study of many ancient cultures. In 1893 he became keeper of the Department of Egyptian and Assyrian Antiquities at the British Museum, a post he held until 1924. Budge went to Egypt, the Sudan, and Mesopotamia many times to obtain antiquities for the British Museum. He excavated at Aswan in Egypt, at Jabal Barkal, the island of Meroë, Semna, and other sites in Nubia and the Sudan. He acquired for the museum a large number of Egyptian art objects and papyri, and numerous manuscripts in Coptic, Syriac, Arabic, and Ethiopic.

His output of published works is the largest and most astonishing of any single Orientalist, the list of his works in *Who Was Who in Egyptology* (Dawson and Uphill, 1972) being the longest recorded and numbering hundreds of books and articles on texts in cuneiform, hieroglyphic, Coptic, Syriac, and Ethiopic. His main contributions to Coptic studies include *The Martyrdoms and Miracles of St. George of Cappadocia,* Coptic text and English translation, London, 1888; *St. Michael the Archangel, Three En-*

comiums by Theodosius Archbishop of Alexandria, Severus Patriarch of Antioch, and Eustathius Bishop of Trake, Coptic Texts with Extracts from Arabic and Ethiopic Versions, edited with translation, London, 1894; *The Earliest Known Coptic Psalter,* the text in the dialect of Upper Egypt, edited from the unique papyrus codex Oriental 5000 in the British Museum, London, 1898; *The Egyptian Sudan, Its History and Monuments,* 2 vols., London, 1907; *Coptic Homilies in the Dialect of Upper Egypt,* edited from the papyrus codex Oriental 5001 in the British Museum, London, 1910; *Coptic Biblical Texts in the Dialect of Upper Egypt,* London, 1912; *Coptic Apocrypha in the Dialect of Upper Egypt,* edited with English translation, London, 1913; *Coptic Martyrdoms in the Dialect of Upper Egypt,* edited with English translation, London, 1914; *Miscellaneous Coptic Texts in the Dialect of Upper Egypt,* edited with English translations, London, 1915 (for contents, see *Coptic Bibliography,* p. 32, no. 716); *Egyptian Tales and Romances: Pagan, Christian and Muslim,* English translation, London, 1931; *Stories of the Holy Fathers . . . of the Deserts of Egypt Between 250 & 400 A.D. Circiter Compiled by Athanasius, Palladius, Jerome and Others,* Oxford, 1934; *The Wit and Wisdom of the Christian Fathers of Egypt,* the Syriac version of the *Apophthegmata Patrum* by "Anan Isho" of Beth Abha, Oxford, 1934.

In memory of his wife, Budge founded Egyptological studentships at Christ College, Cambridge, and University College, Oxford. He left his library to the former college. He died in London.

BIBLIOGRAPHY

Budge, E. A. W. *By Nile and Tigris* (autobiographical), 2 vols. London, 1920.

Dawson, W. B., and E. P. Uphill. *Who Was Who in Egyptology.* London, 1972.

Kammerer, W., comp. *A Coptic Bibliography.* Ann Arbor, Mich., 1950; repr. New York, 1969.

Smith, S. "Budge, Sir (Ernest Alfred Thompson) Wallis." *Dictionary of National Biography,* p. 121. London and Oxford, 1931–1940.

Thompson, C. "Ernest Alfred Wallis Budge." *Journal of Egyptian Archaeology* 21 (1935):68, which includes a portrait.

AZIZ S. ATIYA

BŪLUS AL-BŪSHĪ (Paul of Būsh), an Arab regarded as one of the most significant personalities in the Coptic hierarchy during the Middle Ages. There is no precise information about his birth date or his secular life as a young man before he took the monastic vow. It is possible that he was born between 1170 and 1175. This conjecture is based on the fact that Pope JOHN VI mentioned him as a possible successor in 1216, and it is known that no patriarch of the Coptic church could be nominated before the age of forty. Though he was a native of the city of Būsh north of Banī Suef in Middle Egypt, where the central office for the monasteries of Saint Antony and Saint Paul (DAYR ANBĀ ANṬŪNIYŪS and DAYR ANBĀ BŪLĀ) in the Eastern Desert was located, it is certain that he did not enroll in either of these monastic institutions. He probably joined the monastery of Anbā Ṣamū'īl of Qalamūn in the Fayyūm province, which was within easy reach of Būsh and where he resided with his friend Dawūd ibn Laqlaq, the future Patriarch CYRIL III ibn Laqlaq.

Būlus became known for his sanctity and ascetic life as well as his theological scholarship, which persuaded a group of his admirers to nominate him for the long vacated see of Saint Mark. At the time, however, Dawūd ibn Laqlaq aspired to occupy the same position at any cost. While recruiting a number of supporters, he made promises of substantial financial payments to the Muslim authorities on helping him attain the patriarchate. The only great supporter of Paul in the administration died while Dawūd kept maneuvering for the sultan's approval by all possible means, including the promise of paying 3,000 dinars for his election. In the circumstances, Paul decided to quit the pursuit of the papacy and retire to his quiet life in the monastery. In this wise Dawūd became the sole available candidate and was consequently consecrated as pope of Alexandria and seventy-fifth patriarch of the See of Saint Mark in the year 1235. The patriarchate at that date had been vacant for nearly twenty years, during which most of the bishops had died, and their seats had to be filled. This proved to be the new patriarch's opportunity to offer these episcopal seats to the highest bidders in order to collect as much money as possible by applying the *shartūniyyah* (simony—see CHEIROTONIA) to enable him to pay his own promised bribe to the Muslim administration. Cyril III actually filled forty episcopal vacancies in simoniacal fashion, which irritated both the clergy and the congregation. As a result, it was decided to elect two bishops to watch over the patriarchal actions: one permanent and the other by rotation. Būlus was the permanent candidate who was trusted for his integrity, though it is doubtful whether he preferred this task to his intellectual productivity in the seclusion of his monastic life.

In fact Būlus al-Būshī is remembered more for his writings than for his position of vigilance in the patriarchate of Cyril III. Of his surviving written works, ten codices have been known to exist, mainly in manuscript in numerous repositories, and only a few have been published. Of these, his eight *mimars* (homilies) commemorating eight events or Coptic feasts throughout the year form the best known and most widely published text. He wrote commentaries on the book of Revelation as well as on the Epistle to the Hebrews. He wrote a book on theological science and two on the subjects of confession and the Incarnation. He probably composed a special treatise on the unity of the Godhead, the Trinity, and the Incarnation of the Logos. He also compiled the sayings of the fathers on numerous theological dicta. Outside the theological field, he wrote a treatise on the age of man and on his provision, whether these are prearranged and fixed by providence or dependent on the will of free agents. He is known to have left the record of a disputation with Cyril ibn Laqlaq in the royal presence of Sultan al-Kāmil (1218–1238). According to the *History of the Patriarchs*, the Melchite patriarch Nicholas as well as the *'ulema* (Muslim learned jurists) attended this disputation, the subject of which is unknown.

The last traceable and precise date in Būlus's life was the year 1240, during which the synod that convened in the Citadel of Cairo under the surveillance of the Muslim administration decreed that Būlus should be the permanent watchdog at the patriarchate. It is not known how long he occupied that position, but we must assume that his death occurred some time after that year. According to the available sources, he must have remained a priest throughout his ecclesiastical career until the year 1240, when he was elevated to the episcopate of Miṣr (al-Fuṣṭāṭ), known to be the most important of all the Egyptian bishoprics. His life ended in this capacity, though it is impossible to provide a precise date for his death.

BIBLIOGRAPHY

Samir, K. *Maqālah fī al-Tathlīth wa-al-Tajassud wa-Ṣiḥḥat al-Masīḥiyyah.* Zouk Mikail, 1983.

AZIZ S. ATIYA

BŪLUS AL-ḤABĪS, SAINT, a Coptic monk and "new martyr" of the thirteenth century. Būlus al-Ḥabīs (Paul the Solitary) appears in the Islamic-Arabic sources as having descended from a respectable Coptic family of scribes in Cairo. Mīkhā'īl, as he was known prior to taking the monastic vows, was himself a *kātib* (scribe or secretary).

During the reigns of the Ayyubid sultan al-Malik al-Ṣāliḥ Najm al-Dīn Ayyūb and the sultana Shajar al-Durr, he served in the state chancellery in Syria. In the reign of the Mamluk sultan al-Mu'izz Aybak at-Turkumānī, Mīkhā'īl was transferred to Cairo. Thereafter he left his civil career to become a monk.

As a monk, he received the name Būlus (Paul). He spent his life from that time in a cave in the Red Mountain (al-Jabal al-Aḥmar), near Ḥilwān, south of Cairo. This retreat did not stop him from contacts with the world as a mendicant monk.

Būlus traveled widely in Upper and Lower Egypt. Besides offering people the religious and moralistic lessons of his priestly profession, Būlus provided them with concrete assistance. Regardless of a person's religious allegiance, he supported those in need and paid their debts. He freed prisoners who were held for debt or unpaid fines. He even settled immense state imposts for whole communities.

When the Dhimmis (non-Muslims: Copts and Jews) in Upper Egypt were unable to pay illegal financial demands of the government, Būlus readily produced the required cash for the tax collectors. In Alexandria, he alleviated oppression of the townspeople in the same way. Ibn Abī al-Faḍā'il, the Coptic analyst of the period, made the comment that "What Al-Ḥabīs achieved astonished the people of Alexandria."

The climax of Būlus's career occurred in 1265 when he saved communities of Copts and Jews in Cairo from imminent disaster. The Copts were blamed for reducing sixty-three houses in al-Bāṭiliyyah to rubble and ashes, while Sultan al-Ẓāhir Baybars was laying siege to the Frankish port of Caesarea in Syria. On his return, the sultan drove the chained accused Jews and Copts out of Cairo to have them burned alive. Even the Coptic patriarch JOHN VII was dragged to the scene. When the commander of the Egyptian army submitted a plea for their lives, the sultan was persuaded to spare his victims in return for a heavy fine. Būlus came forth with the whole amount and paid it on the spot.

The sultan al-Ẓāhir Baybars often mingled with his subjects in disguise, and, of course, became apprehensive of the popularity of Būlus. Likewise the *fuqahā'*, the Islamic spiritual authorities and legal scholars, felt threatened by Būlus. In particular, the *fuqahā'* of Alexandria sent formal opinions condemning Būlus to death and submitted a plea for his execution to the sultan in Cairo.

The sultan summoned Būlus to the citadel, offered him food and lodging, and asked him to reveal the source of his money. Būlus refused to disclose his secret, and insisted on continuing to use his acquired wealth for the relief of the poor and needy. Būlus may have discovered the treasure hidden by the Fatimid caliph al-Ḥākim bi-Amr-Allāh (996–1021) in the Red Mountain.

Būlus practiced passive resistance to formal state repression. But the Mamluk rulers did not tolerate anything prejudicial to the power of the Islamic state, either from the rebel Muslim *'ulema* (scholars) or from the Arab tribes, let alone the Coptic community. Būlus was condemned to death and executed.

The memory of his life and work survived for centuries after his death. Five hundred years later, the Muslim writer Ibn al-'Imād al-Ḥanbalī reiterated his story in his eight-volume biographical dictionary.

BIBLIOGRAPHY

Ibn Shākir al-Kutubī. *Fawāt al-Wafayāt,* 5 vols., ed. Iḥsān Abbās. Beirut, 1973–1974.

SUBHI Y. LABIB

BUQAYRAH AL-RASHIDI THE DEACON. *See* History of the Patriarchs.

BUQTUR. *See* Victor.

BŪRAH, older name of the town now known as Kafr al-Baṭṭīkh, in the Gharbiyyah province. The town is located in the northeast part of the Delta on the west bank of the Nile arm about five miles west of Damietta.

The earliest mention of Christianity in Būrah is found in the writings of Eutychius, who reported that a Christian named Bukam obtained permission from the caliph al-Ma'mūn (813–833) to build churches in Būrah, but as soon as the buildings had been constructed they were confiscated by the Muslims. Eutychius also mentioned that the patriarch Khā'īl was interred in Būrah, but he did not give enough information for us to determine whether this was Khā'īl II (849–851) or Khā'īl III (880–907).

The HISTORY OF THE PATRIARCHS relates that Patriarch CHRISTODOULUS (1047–1077) was from the town. When the Crusaders stormed Būrah during the patriarchate of JOHN VI (1189–1216) and occupied the town in 1218, many Copts were among those who lost their lives. This information makes it clear that there was a Christian community in Būrah until at least the thirteenth century.

BIBLIOGRAPHY

Amélineau, E. *La Géographie de l'Egypte à l'époque copte,* p. 336. Paris, 1893.

Timm, S. *Das christlich-koptische Ägypten in arabischer Zeit,* pt. 1, pp. 448–49. Wiesbaden, 1984.

RANDALL STEWART

BURIAL RITES AND PRACTICES. The act of interring the dead and laying them to rest is an old practice dating from biblical times. When Abraham died, his sons Isaac and Ishmael buried him in the cave at Machpelah, the burial place that he had bought from the Hittites to bury his wife Sarah (Gn. 23:2–20; 25:8–10). His own descendants, Isaac and Jacob, were later buried with him (see also 1 Sm. 31:13; 2 Sm. 2:5,6; 3:35; 1 Kgs. 11:43).

When Jesus Christ died on the cross, Joseph of Arimathaea and Nicodemus came and took His body, wrapped it in strips of linen with a mixture of myrrh and aloes, and laid Him in a new tomb (Jn. 19:40, 41). In Acts 7:58–8:2 we read about the burial of Saint Stephen, the first martyr.

During the apostolic age and the ages of persecution, the remains of the martyrs were gathered by believers and buried. At the death of Saint Ignatius of Antioch (c. 35–c. 107), who had been sent to Rome to be devoured by beasts, his relics were sent to Antioch for burial. Speaking of the martyrdom of Polycarp, bishop of Smyrna (c. 69–c. 155), Eusebius, bishop of Caesarea, writes, "And so we afterwards gathered up his bones, which were more valuable than precious stones and more to be esteemed than gold, and laid them in a suitable place" (*Ecclesiastical History,* 4.15.43).

As soon as the deceased dies, his next of kin closes his eyes and mouth. Then the body is washed (see Acts 9:36–40), a practice referred to by DIONYSIUS THE GREAT, bishop of Alexandria (d. 264): "The most of our brethren were unsparing in their exceeding love and brotherly kindness. . . . And they took the bodies of the saints in their open hands and in their bosoms, and closed their eyes and their mouths; and they bore them away on their shoulders and laid them out; and they clung to them and embraced them; and they prepared them suitably with washings and garments . . ." (Eusebius, *Ecclesiastical History,* 7.22.7,9).

Next, the body is anointed with spices and aromatic unguents, and wrapped in linen (Mt. 27:59; Mk. 15:46, Lk. 23:53; Jn. 19:40).

The burial service begins with the Lord's Prayer, the prayer of thanksgiving, and the prayer of incense. Psalm 50 is then read, and is followed by the intercession for the sick. After the prayer of incense to Paul, the Pauline Epistle (1 Cor. 15:1–23) is read, of which the last two verses are, "For as in Adam all die, so also in Christ shall all be made alive. But each in his own order: Christ the first fruits, then at his coming those who belong to Christ."

Next comes the *Trisagion.* The priest reads the intercession of the Gospel, followed by the Gospel reading (Jn. 5:19–29) of which verse 21 says, "For as the Father raises the dead and gives them life, so also the Son gives life to whom he will."

The priest then says the three smaller intercessions. After the Creed, the intercession of the dormant is read, then a petition and the Lord's Prayer. Finally the priest reads the absolution.

The final prayer said just before the tomb is closed contains the following petition: "We beseech Thee, our Lord God Almighty, Lover of man, on behalf of Thy servant [Name] who has relinquished his body, that Thou may graciously send Thy angel of mercy before him. . . . Bring him into the paradise of joy, into the bosoms of our early fathers Abraham, Isaac, and Jacob. And, as we continue to offer prayers for him here below, he will remember us before Thee. . . . " The priest then reads the absolution, the blessing, and the Lord's Prayer.

Commemoration prayers are offered at certain intervals that, nowadays, are usually restricted to the third and fortieth day after death and on the anniversary day. In former times, however, these intervals were more frequent.

[*See also:* Funerary Customs; Mourning in Early Christian Times.]

BIBLIOGRAPHY

Gabriel V, Patriarch. *Al-Tartīb al-Ṭaqsī* (Ritual Order), pp. 131–49. Cairo, 1964.

Ṣafī ibn al-ʿAssāl, al-. *Kitāb al-Qawānīn,* chap. 22, pp. 177–80. Repr. Cairo, 1927.

William Sulayman Qilādah. *Kitāb al-Disqūliyyah, Taʿālīm al-Rusul* (The Didascalia), chap. 34, pp. 433–34. Cairo, 1977.

ARCHBISHOP BASILIOS

BURKITT, FRANCIS CRAWFORD

BURKITT, FRANCIS CRAWFORD (1864–1935), English professor of divinity. He was active as a Syriac scholar and historian of religions. See especially his books *The Religion of the Manichees* (1925) and *Church and Gnosis* (1932).

BIBLIOGRAPHY

Bethune-Baker, J. F. "Burkitt, Francis Crawford." *Dictionary of National Biography, 1931–1940,* pp. 124–25. London, 1949.

MARTIN KRAUSE

BURMESTER, OSWALD HUGH EDWARD

BURMESTER, OSWALD HUGH EDWARD (1897–1977), British scholar of Orthodoxy and the Eastern churches. He obtained his doctorate at Cambridge University in 1933. From 1946 on, he lived in Egypt, serving first as senior lecturer in classics at the University of Alexandria and then, for over twenty years until his death, as professor at the Coptic CLERICAL COLLEGE in Cairo and librarian of the SOCIETY FOR COPTIC ARCHAEOLOGY. During that period he concentrated on Coptic studies and produced abundantly in the field of Coptology. He authored numerous books and articles in the fields of liturgy and Coptic history. Apart from numerous articles, his most important works are: *Le Lectionnaire de la Semaine Sainte,* in PO 24–25, Paris, 1933 and 1939; "Ṭuruhat of the Coptic Church," *Orientalia Christiana Periodica* 3 (1937):78–109, 505–549); *A Guide to the Monasteries of the Wadi ʿn Nāṭrūn* (Cairo, 1954); "The Coptic-Greek-Arabic Holy Week Lectionary of Scetis," *Bulletin de la Société d'archéologie copte* 16 (1962):83–137); *The Rite of Consecration of the Patriarch of Alexandria,* text according to MS 253 Lit.-Coptic Museum, Cairo, 1960; *The Egyptian or Coptic Church: A Detailed Description of Her Liturgical Services and the Rites and Ceremonies Observed in the Administration of Her Sacraments,* Cairo, 1967.

A more complete bibliography of Burmester has been compiled by O. Meinardus in *Bulletin de la Société d'archéologie copte* 23 (1976–1978):235–44.

BIBLIOGRAPHY

"In Memoriam," articles by M. B. Ghali, L. H. Rasch, O. Meinardus, and I. Ebeid. *Bulletin de la Société d'Archéologie copte* 23 (1976–1978):1–2, 3–4, 309–310, 311–13.

"In Memoriam." *Le Monde Copte* 10 (1983):56–57.

Meinardus, O. F. A. "Bibliography of Prof. Dr. O. H. E. Burmester." *Bulletin de la Société d'Archéologie copte* 23 (1976–1978):235–44.

MIRRIT BOUTROS GHALI

BURULLUS, AL-, town in Egypt located somewhere between present-day Balṭīm and al-Burj on the eastern shore of Lake Burullus in the northern Delta.

Al-Burullus had a bishop as early as the first third of the fourth century. Bishop Nonnas was in office in 339; he was succeeded by Bishop Nemesion (Munier, 1943, p. 9). Bishop Athanasius of al-Burullus attended the first Council of EPHESUS in 431 (Munier, 1943, p. 15). Among the most notable of the town's bishops was John, who lived at the end of the sixth and beginning of the seventh century (see Saint JOHN, Bishop of Parallos). As a young man John used his inheritance to build a shelter for wanderers and the sick. He later became a monk in Scetis and then bishop of al-Burullus. As bishop he had to deal constantly with sects and heretics, among whom were the followers of a monk who claimed to be inspired by the archangel Michael and to have been visited by the prophet Habakkuk. According to the SYNAXARION, John had their books burned.

Patriarch ISAAC (686–689) came from al-Burullus, which is an indication that the area came through the ARAB CONQUEST OF EGYPT in the first half of the seventh century in relatively good shape. In the next century, during the time of Patriarch JOHN IV (775–779), there lived in al-Burullus a hermit named George who possessed the gift of prophecy. When John's son, the deacon Mark, refused to become bishop of Miṣr (Cairo) and fled from the chains with which John had bound him, the patriarch wrote a letter to George complaining of his son's behavior. George told John he should not be angry with his son and he promised John that Mark (see MARK II) would become the next patriarch.

Al-Burullus remained a Coptic bishopric until at least the eleventh century, as evidenced by the attendance of Bishop Michael of al-Burullus at a synod in Cairo in 1086 (Munier, 1943, p. 28). Not surprisingly the town is mentioned in the medieval Coptic-Arabic scales and in the lists of Egyptian bishoprics (Munier, 1943, pp. 46, 53, 65).

Coptic tradition holds that the family of Jesus passed through al-Burullus on its FLIGHT INTO EGYPT.

BIBLIOGRAPHY

Amélineau, E. *La Géographie de l'Egypte à l'époque copte*, pp. 104–105. Paris, 1873.

Munier, H. *Recueil des listes épiscopales de l'église copte*. Cairo, 1943.

Timm, S. *Das christlich-koptische Ägypten in arabischer Zeit*, pt. 1, pp. 450–55. Wiesbaden, 1984.

RANDALL STEWART

BŪSH, town situated on the left bank of the Nile about 4 miles (7 km) north of Banī Suef. Nearby are the estates that supply the food for the monasteries of Saint Antony and Saint Paul (DAYR ANBĀ ANṬŪNIYŪS and DAYR ANBĀ BŪLĀ) near the Red Sea. These two estates appear to be relatively recent. The ancient texts speak only of Dayr al-Maymūn, which was situated on the right bank a little farther to the north and seems to have been replaced by Būsh toward the end of the sixteenth century. In fact, J. VANSLEB was apparently the first European traveler to mention Būsh, calling it "the farm of the religious of Saint Antony."

Formerly, one crossed the Nile at al-Maymūn to take the road for Dayr Anbā Anṭūniyūs via Dayr al-Maymūn, cited as such by d'Anglure in 1395 (1878, p. 68) and J. Coppin in 1638–1639 (1971, p. 204). But since that time, travelers cross the Nile at Banī Suef and take the road to Bayāḍ al-Naṣārā on the east bank in order to reach the monastery (Vansleb, 1677, p. 295, and 1678, p. 178; Sicard, 1982, pp. 19, 23, 46). The HISTORY OF THE PATRIARCHS (Vol. 3, pt. 3, pp. 164–268) mentions that in 1718 a delegation went to Būsh, where it seized a monk of Dayr Anbā Būlā and took him in chains to Cairo to be consecrated patriarch under the name of PETER VI.

BIBLIOGRAPHY

Amélineau, E. *La Géographie de l'Egypte à l'époque copte*, pp. 366–70. Paris, 1893.

Coppin, J. *Voyages en Egypte*, ed. S. Sauneron. Cairo, 1971.

d'Anglure. *Le Saint Voyage de Jherusalem*. Paris, 1878.

Jullien, M. *L'Egypte*, pp. 62–64. Lille, 1891.

Meinardus, O. *Monks and Monasteries of the Egyptian Deserts*, pp. 221, 371–74. Cairo, 1961.

______. *Christian Egypt, Ancient and Modern*. Cairo, 1965, pp. 252–53; 2nd ed., 1977, pp. 355–56.

Sicard, C. *Oeuvres*, Vol. 1, ed. M. Martin and S. Sauneron. Cairo and Paris, 1982.

Timm, S. *Das christlich-koptische Ägypten in arabischer Zeit*, pp. 742–47. Wiesbaden, 1984.

Vansleb, J. M. *Nouvelle relation en forme de journal d'un voyage fait en Egypte en 1672 et 1673*. Paris, 1677. Translated as *The Present State of Egypt*. London, 1678.

RENÉ-GEORGES COQUIN
MAURICE MARTIN, S.J.

BUSIR. *See* Abūṣīr.

BUSIRIS. *See* Abūṣīr.

BUTCHER, EDITH L. Very little is known about Butcher's background beyond the fact that she is the author of one of the first detailed accounts in the English language of the Coptic church, *The Story of the Church of Egypt, Being an Outline of the History of the Egyptians Under Their Successive Masters from the Roman Conquest Until Now* (2 vols., London, 1897). She also wrote *Things Seen in Egypt* (London, n.d.). She spent about twenty years researching her subject, not only from available sources of her day but also directly from all classes of the Coptic people. As the wife of a Protestant missionary, she must have lived in an atmosphere of congeniality in order to feel comfortable choosing to pursue the task she brought to completion. Since her book was published in 1897, one must assume that she went to Egypt in the 1870s. "The aim which I have set myself in writing the following pages," she says in her preface, "is a very humble one—to collect together in a readable fashion and in moderate compass all that the researches of scholars and historians have yet been able to discover about that remnant of the ancient Egyptian people popularly called the Copts, from the date of their first acceptance of Christianity until the present days."

AZIZ S. ATIYA

BUTLER, ALFRED JOSHUA (1850–1936), English historian who was educated at Oxford, becoming a fellow of Brasenose College in 1877 and receiving his doctorate in 1902. He wrote a number of works on Egypt that spanned from the Coptic era to the medieval period, including his *Ancient Coptic Churches of Egypt* (Oxford, 1884) and the acclaimed *The Arab Conquest of Egypt* (Oxford, 1902).

S. KENT BROWN

BUṬRUS, thirteenth-century Melchite bishop of Miṣr. Buṭrus is mentioned twice in an anonymous Muslim work relating the life of al-Manṣūr Qalāwūn, king of Egypt (A.D. 1279–1290), entitled *Kitāb Tashrīf al-Ayyām wa-al-ʿUṣūr* (History of Arabic Literature). In both cases, the context considers treaties of armistice between the Genoans and al-Manṣūr, following naval battles.

Both texts are written by the bishop, who signs himself Buṭrus usquf Miṣr al-Malkī (Peter, Melchite bishop of Miṣr). The Genoan emissary was Alberto Spinola, accompanied by consuls and traders. On the Egyptian side, the witnesses are four Melchites: Bishop Arsāniyūs, the abbot of the Melchite monastery of al-Quṣayr near Cairo, the deacon Mattā, and Mīkhā'īl, monk of Sinai. The agreement was concluded on 14 Ayyār *anno mundi* 6798/14 May 1290. The Genoans swore on the Gospel and the cross, "standing, with their heads uncovered." The Arabic text was published by Ḥabīb Zayyāt in 1953 on the basis of a manuscript written in Egypt at the end of the thirteenth century (National Library, Paris, Arabe 1704 [not 174 as said by the editor]), the first witnessing in fols. 338a–40b, and the second in fols. 341a–52b.

The official witnesses chosen on the Egyptian side are Melchites and not Copts, probably because the treaty was being concluded with the Genoans who, according to Muslim categories, were "Melchites."

BIBLIOGRAPHY

Ḥabīb Zayyāt. *Al-Rūm al-Malkiyyūn fī al-Islām*, Vol. 1. Ḥarīṣā, 1953.

KHALIL SAMIR, S.J.

BUṬRUS. *See also under* Peter.

BUṬRUS I. *See* Jerusalem, Coptic See of.

BUṬRUS II. *See* Jerusalem, Coptic See of.

BUṬRUS IBN ʿABD AL-SAYYID, a deacon who may have lived in Ethiopia. His name is connected with the *Fetḥa Nagast*, the Ethiopian version of the *Nomocanon* of al-ṢAFĪ IBN AL-ʿASSĀL.

According to A. Dillmann and I. Guidi, Buṭrus ibn ʿAbd al-Sayyid translated the text from Arabic into Geʿez. ʿAbd al-Samīʿ Muḥammad Aḥmad (1965), who made a detailed study of the relationship of the Arabic text with the Geʿez version, has shown that it is unlikely that Buṭrus made this translation, because numerous errors appear in the translation. The errors seem to be due to the translator's inability to read Arabic correctly, as he misplaced diacritical marks, even when the correct reading was evident; nor had he mastered Arabic style as if Arabic were his native language. Furthermore, Aḥmad shows that the word meaning "to copy" or "to translate" is used in the *Fetḥa Nagast* in the sense of "to copy."

Hence, Buṭrus copied one of the manuscripts of the *Fetḥa Nagast* for the Ethiopian priest Ibrāhīm ibn Ḥannā Naṭian, which copy was used as a basis for the manuscripts. This at least establishes that he had a good knowledge of Ge'ez.

BIBLIOGRAPHY

Guidi, I. *Il "Fetha Nagast" o "Legislazione dei Re," codice ecclesiastico e civile di Abessinia,* Vol. 2, pp. 9–10. Rome, 1899.

KHALIL SAMIR, S.J.

BUṬRUS IBN AL-KHABBĀZ, thirteenth-century metropolitan of Ethiopia and copyist of biblical texts. This priest is known from notes found in four Arabic manuscripts of Coptic origin.

1. A fourteenth-century manuscript in the Coptic Patriarchate in Cairo (Theology 220) contains ten monastic texts (Graf, 1934), or seventeen according to Simaykah and Yassa 'Abd al-Masīḥ (1942), which are found on 170 leaves. On fol. 113a–18a appears a *Collection of Pronouncements of the Fathers* comprising, among other texts, extracts of the twenty-third chapter of the book of Saint Gregory the theologian; extracts from the Wisdom of Solomon; and extracts of the thirtieth treatise of *Kitāb al-Ḥāwī* (The Comprehensive Book), an abbreviated work (*ikhtaṣarahu*) by the Muṭrān Anbā Buṭrus, known by the name Ibn al-Khabbāz.

This text is cited twice by G. Graf (1944, p. 387, concerning the *Apophthegmata;* 1947, p. 453, concerning *Kitāb al-Ḥāwī*) who mistakenly named this bishop Buṭrus al-Khabbāz. In addition, Graf considered the bishop to be the author of this work, which is now apparently lost, when in fact he was only its compiler. The reference could be to the *Pandects* composed by Antiochus of Palestine, a monk from the monastery of Saint Sabas who lived at the beginning of the seventh century (PG 89, cols. 1421–1849), whose work was known in Arabic by the title *Kitāb al-Ḥāwī* (Graf, 1944, p. 412). This composition consists of 130 homilies (actually, moral sentences drawn from the scriptures and early writers), an analysis of which appears in Ahlwardt (1897).

2. A thirteenth-century manuscript in the Ambrosian Library, Milan (C 47 Inf.) provides an Arabic translation of the four Gospels, plus a general introduction and four individual introductions, done by Al-As'ad Abū al-Faraj Hibatallāh ibn al-'Assāl from Greek, Coptic, and Syriac (Graf, 1944, pp. 162–63; 1947, pp. 407 and 484).

The manuscript was copied at the monastery of Saint Antony by Isḥāq ibn Farajallāh ibn Abī al-Faḍā'il ibn Hibatallāh ibn Abī al-Barakāt, known also as Ibn Qārūrah. He finished his work on 6 Tūt A.M. 997/6 Jumādā I A.H. 679/3 or 4 September A.D. 1280. The colophon published by Guidi (1888) indicates that the manuscript was copied from a model transcribed by Anbā Buṭrus, known as Ibn al-Khabbāz, who had copied it in turn from the autographed translation itself of Al-As'ad ibn al-'Assāl. Since the translation of Ibn al-'Assāl was completed in 1252–1253, the bishop must have transcribed his copy between that date and 1280 (see Löfgren and Traini, 1975).

3. A small manuscript of fifty-six folios in the Vatican Library (Arabic 459) contains an anonymous commentary on the book of Revelation, which, in fact, is that of BŪLUS AL-BŪSHĪ, Coptic bishop of Cairo who was invested in 1240 (Graf, 1947, pp. 358–59).

It was copied by the monk Isḥāq ibn al-Najīb at the Monastery of Saint Antony for *al-Shaykh al-Ra'īs* al-Thiqah, son of *al-Shaykh al-Ra'īs* al-Sanī (or al-Sanā', for Sanā' al-Dawlah), which he completed on 28 Baramhāt A.M. 1014/24 March 1298. Graf dated the manuscript to 1294 (1944, p. 183; 1947, p. 359, l. 9).

The colophon was published by Graf (1929), who stated that this manuscript was copied from a text written by Anbā Buṭrus ibn al-Khabbāz, the metropolitan of Ethiopia.

4. A manuscript in the Vatican (Arabic 43) containing the *Introduction to the Commentary on Paul* seems to be the only manuscript to have preserved the commentary that IBN KĀTIB QAYṢAR made on the New Testament (minus the Gospels), even though the author's name does not appear here. In the introduction (fols. 1b–22a), Ibn Kātib Qayṣar noted that he had used the Coptic version of the Pauline corpus based on a manuscript written by the priest Ya'qūb, nephew of Muṭrān Buṭrus ibn al-Khabbāz, which itself went back to a copy preserved at the Monastery of Saint Antony (Graf, 1947, p. 385, par. 2; observe, however, that fn. 2 has nothing to do with the priest Ya'qūb).

BIBLIOGRAPHY

Ahlwardt, W. *Verzeichnis der arabischen Handschriften der königlichen Bibliothek zu Berlin,* Vol. 9, pp. 552–54, no. 10185. Berlin, 1897.

Graf, G. "Arabische Übersetzungen der Apokalypse." *Biblica* 10 (1929):170–94, especially p.

179.

______. *Catalogue de manuscrits arabes chrétiens conservés au Caire,* pp. 197–98, no. 524. Vatican City, 1934.

Guidi, I. "Le traduzioni degli evangelii in arabo e in etiopico." *Memorie della Reale Accademia dei Lincei* 285 (1888):4–37, especially pp. 19–21.

Löfgren, O., and R. Traini. *Catalogue of the Arabic Manuscripts in the Biblioteca Ambrosiana; Antico Fondo and Medio Fondo,* Vol. 1, pp. 6–7, no. 6. Vicenza, 1975.

KHALIL SAMIR, S.J.

BUṬRUS IBN ṢAHYŪN AL-GHANNĀMĪ,

eighteenth-century Catholic Copt born at Akhmīm in Upper Egypt. G. Macaire, who in 1899 became the first Coptic Catholic patriarch under the name of Cyril II, says of him, "At the time of this venerable prelate [Athanasius, Coptic Catholic bishop of Jerusalem], there was living in Cairo the pious and wise Sahioun Ghannāmē, born of a family belonging to the old orthodoxy." His name was in fact Buṭrus ibn Ṣahyūn, nicknamed (*al-ma'rūf bi-*) al-Ghannāmī.

According to Macaire, he was "the author of several pious pamphlets and a remarkable treatise on the Coptic and Gregorian calendars." We now know only the latter work. He composed it in the year A.M. 1485/A.H. 1182/A.D. 1769. He entitled it *Mukhtaṣar al-Burhān al-wakīd fī ḥaqāqat 'īd* (or *yawm 'īd*) *al-Fiṣḥ al-majīd* (Summary of the overwhelming proof concerning the date of the glorious feast of Easter).

The work is composed of thirty chapters. The author wishes to prove that the Gregorian calendar is the only true one and the only one which, unlike the Julian and Coptic calendars, is in conformity with the results of astronomical science. He remarks that the present Coptic year "is not the Egyptian year of yore, but is as it was reformed by Julius Caesar a few years before Christianity." He also refutes the objections of his opponents. The work contains numerous tables of astronomical calculations, being composed to justify the Gregorian calendar introduced in Egypt by the Catholic missionaries.

Three copies of his work are known, although the present location of the third is uncertain. One is in Beirut (Oriental Library 206, nineteenth-century, 164 pages), one is in Sharfah (Syrian Catholic Patriarchate, Arabic 5/18, circa 1800, 190 folios), and the third is in Cairo and belonged to Murqus Jirjis, well-known bookseller and editor of numerous Coptic Arabic texts around 1920–1930.

Buṭrus al-Ghannāmī must have belonged to a well-to-do family in Akhmīm, which had sustained the small Coptic Catholic community from the beginning. On 4 October 1747 Jacques de Kremsier, the prefect of the Franciscan Mission of Egypt, wrote a detailed and informative report on the Coptic church in response to a questionnaire sent by the *Congregatio de Propaganda Fide.* The following reply is given in response to the fourteenth question concerning Catholic notables who could offer more assistance to the mission: "At Jirjah, a certain Buṭrus Abū Medri [Mitrī]. At Akhmīm, Sulaymān al-Ghannāmī, who gave very generous help for the fabric of our church by providing us with all the materials. At Cairo, sir Makārius Kessavi [Kīsāwī], who offered considerable help to the fathers of the Holy Land during the persecution unleashed against them by the English consul" (Trossen, p. 204).

BIBLIOGRAPHY

Armalah Isḥāq. *Al-Ṭurfah fī makhṭūṭāt al-Sharfah,* p. 353. Jounieh, 1936.

Cheikho, L. *Catalogue raisonné des manuscrits de la Bibliothèque Orientale de l'Université Saint-Joseph.* Mélanges de l'Université Saint-Joseph 7, pp. 125–26, no. 206. Beirut, 1921.

Macaire, G. *Histoire de l'église d'Alexandrie depuis saint Marc jusqu'à nos jours,* p. 353. Cairo, 1894.

Sbath, P. *Al-Fihris (Catalogue de manuscrits arabes),* Vol. 2. pp. 7, 62 (no. 617). Cairo, 1939.

Trossen, J.-P. *Les Relations du patriarche copte Jean XVI avec Rome (1676–1718).* Luxembourg, 1948.

KHALIL SAMIR, S.J.

BUṬRUS IBN SĀLIM AL-SUNBĀṬĪ,

a Melchite hieromonk from the village of Sunbāṭ, who in 1199 was living at the monastery of Saint Catherine in Sinai. Sunbāṭ is in the district of Zifta, in the province of Gharbiyyah on the Delta, and is situated 2¼ miles (about 3½ km) southwest of Mīt Damsīs. At the time of Buṭrus and in the thirteenth century, it was of considerable religious importance, especially as regards hagiography. However, no works ever mention Melchites living there.

This monk was the copyist of at least two Sinai manuscripts. One (Sinai Arabic 159, a codex of 273 sheets) contains a lectionary of the Acts of the Apostles and the Epistles of Paul for the entire year with brief commentaries; it was completed on 14 Āb 6707 of Adam/20 Shawwāl A.H. 596/14 August A.D. 1199 (cf. Atiya and Youssef, 1970, p. 312). The other (Sinai Arabic 96, 352 sheets in addition to those missing, undated) continues a manuscript (Sinai Arabic 159) giving the Gospel readings for the whole year with a commentary on each pericope (cf. Atiya and Youssef, 1970, p. 193).

Buṭrus al-Sunbāṭī wrote in a clear, pleasant hand (a specimen may be seen in Atiya and Youssef, 1970, p. 312). Although the folios are not numbered, his work was very careful. Each folio bears a title running along the top of the recto, and each fascicule (quinion) is numbered at the foot of the recto in Arabic letters (cf. Sinai Arabic 96, fols. 9, 19, 29, 39, etc.; this shows that the first forty-two folios of this manuscript have disappeared, a detail not mentioned in the catalogs). Last, each fascicule was revised, and bears at the foot of the recto of the first folio the word *qūbila*, which means that the text was rechecked against the model.

BIBLIOGRAPHY

Amélineau, E. *La Géographie de l'Egypte*, p. 415. Paris, 1893.

Atiya, A. S., and J. N. Youssef. *Catalogue Raisonné of the Mount Sinai Manuscripts*, pp. 192–93, 311–12. Alexandria, 1970.

Meinardus, O. F. A. *Christian Egypt*, p. 176. Cairo, 1977.

KHALIL SAMIR, S.J.

BUṬRUS AL-JAWLĪ. *See* Peter VII.

BUTRUS SĀWĪRUS AL-JAMĪL, thirteenth-century bishop of Malīj and first compiler of the Coptic SYNAXARION. It is not known exactly when he lived, and no details of his life are known for certain. He lived probably at the end of the twelfth century and the beginning of the thirteenth, since he comes between MĪKHĀ'ĪL, BISHOP OF DAMIETTA (d. after 1208) and CYRIL III ibn Laqlaq (1235–1243) in the author index of Abū al-Barakāt IBN KABAR.

His work is listed by G. Graf as follows. *Kitāb al-Ishrāq* (Book of the Sunrise) condemns the non-Jacobite Christian nations or parties, the Franks (Latins), Melchites, Armenians, and Syrians (Nestorians) as heretical. The exhaustive enumeration of these "heresies" makes the work interesting for the history of religious customs. There is an extensive account of the contents in Ibn Kabar.

Kitāb al-Burhān (Book of Proof) is an apology for Christianity, treating the doctrine about Christ and proving in particular the impossibility of the divinity's participating in the sufferings of the human nature of Christ. It also deals with the question of the replacement of the Mosaic law by the more perfect law of the Gospels. The Holy Scriptures, partly with sources, are interpreted thoroughly. The work uses, sometimes literally, material from the two anthologies, *al-*DURR AL-THĀMĪN (Precious Pearl) by Sāwīrus and *I'tirāf al-Abā'*.

According to Ibn Kabar, Butrus composed the Synaxarion also. This is an abstract of the lives of the saints and their histories arranged as a chronicle for each day of the liturgical year. He probably was the first compiler, arranger, and editor of the work, and laid the foundation for the Vulgate version completed later. In fact, some of its elaboration belongs to his successor, MĪKHĀ'ĪL, bishop of Atrib and Malīj, but how much is not known. That Butrus built on the works of others is evidenced by references to older sources. There is a praise of Severus of Antioch "by the author of the *Kitāb al-Ishrāq*" in a manuscript in the National Library, Paris (Syriac 238, fols. 87v–89v). Later Butrus did write a preface to the *Confession of Faith* of Severus.

BIBLIOGRAPHY

Severus of Antioch. *Confession of Faith*, ed. and trans. V. Cauvin. PO 2, pp. 308f. Paris, 1904–1975.

VINCENT FREDERICK

BUṬRUS AL-SIDMANTĪ, a monastic writer in Arabic during the eleventh century. Buṭrus came from the village of Sidmant in the district of Banī Suef. The village is known as Sidmant al-Jabal; E. AMÉLINEAU records it as Posotoment.

The precise dates of birth and death of Buṭrus are unknown beyond the fact that he lived around the middle of the eleventh century. He was primarily a biblical scholar, and his exegetic work on the Gospels stands out among his miscellaneous writings in Arabic, including biographies of some saints and a number of religious treatises. Apparently his works were known to later writers and theologians such as Abu al-Barakāt ibn Kabar and Abū Shākir Buṭrus ibn al-Rāhib, who lived in the thirteenth and fourteenth centuries. He is sometimes described as Armenian (Cheikho, 1924, p. 62), which appears to be wrong, as we know his birthplace was in Upper Egypt. A theological treatise by him dated A.M. 976/A.D. 1260 is preserved in the Vatican Library (cf. Steinschneider, no. 116, p. 135; Cheikho, 1924, p. 62).

BIBLIOGRAPHY

Amélineau, E. *La Géographie de l'Egypte à l'époque copte.* Paris, 1893.

Cheikho, L. *Al-Makhṭuṭāt al 'Arabiyah li-Katabat al-Nasrāniyah.* Beirut, 1924.

'Umar Riḍā Kaḥḥalah. *Mu'jam al-Mu'allifīn,* Vol. 3 of 15 vols. Damascus, 1957–1961.

AZIZ S. ATIYA

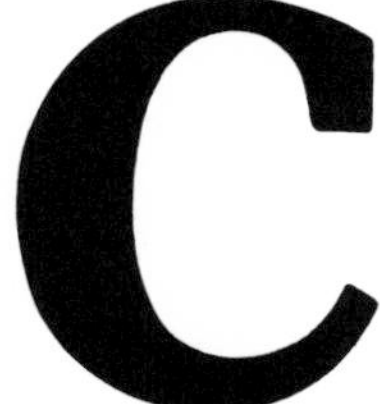

CAETANI, LEONE, Italian Orientalist, born in Rome (1869) and died in Vancouver, Canada (1935). While young, he assembled a great library of texts and studies relating to the history of Islam and a collection of photos of Arabic historical manuscripts. Then he started the collection *Annali dell'Islam* (first volume in 1905, ninth and final volume in 1926; published in Rome and Milan). His volunteering for the army in 1915 interrupted his studies, and he never resumed them. In 1924 he established the Fondazione Caetani per gli studi musulmani (still active within the Accademia dei Lincei). Three years later he left Italy, mainly for political reasons, and settled in Canada.

BIBLIOGRAPHY

Gabrieli, F. "Caetani, Leone." In *Dizionario biografico degli italiani,* Vol. 16, pp. 185–88. Rome, 1973.

TITO ORLANDI

CALAMUS. *See* Jabal Khashm al-Quʻud.

CALENDAR, COPTIC. Early Egyptian Christians, like those elsewhere, took systems of reckoning time used in the world that they knew, modified them, and adapted them to their own observances and practices. The civil day of Christians in Egypt began in the morning, as did that of the ancient Egyptians and the Romans; but their liturgical day began, then as now, at sunset, like the Jewish, Muslim, and Greek days. The seven-day week was taken over from the Jews, with its first day made the Lord's Day.

The Coptic year is the Alexandrian year, which became the civil year in Egypt in 30 or 26 B.C., shortly after the Roman conquest of Egypt. The evidence for the date of its actual introduction is ambiguous, but in any case, year 1 of the Alexandrian Era, or Era of Augustus, is reckoned as 30/29 B.C. The Alexandrian year is the ancient Egyptian solar year, coordinated with the year in the Romans' Julian calendar, which is itself the Egyptian solar year, but with a different date for the beginning of a new year and a different division of the days into twelve months. The Alexandrian year retains the ancient Egyptian division of the year into twelve months of thirty days each, plus five more days, called *epagomenai,* at its end, as well as the extra day whose intercalation at the end of every fourth year as a sixth epagomenal day was ordered by Ptolemy III Euergetes in 238 B.C., in order to rectify the old discrepancy between the calendar year of 365 days and the natural solar year.

The Alexandrian year's coordination with that of the Julian calendar, after an initial period of difficulty caused by inaccurate observance of the frequency of leap years (*anni bissextiles*) by the Romans, was rectified, so that from A.D. 5 on, the Alexandrian new year begins on the Julian 29 August, unless it is a year in which the Julian calendar will intercalate a 29 February. In that case, the Alexandrian year begins on the Julian 30 August, because in the Alexandrian system the extra day is intercalated at the very end of the Alexandrian year preceding the one in which the Julian calendar's 29 February will occur. The Alexandrian intercalary day thus falls on the Julian 29 August, with the new Alexandrian year then beginning on 30 August and that year's corresponding days in the Julian calendar continuing to be the normal ones plus 1 until the Julian year's own intercalation is made on 29 February, after which the corresponding days are those of ordinary years.

Since the fourth century the era regularly used by the Copts for reckoning the sequence of Alexandrian years has been the Era of Diocletian, in which the year of Diocletian's military election as emperor in November 284 is taken as the starting point. Among Christians, the Era of Diocletian is usually called the ERA OF THE MARTYRS, and in Western texts the abbreviation A.M. (for *anno martyrum*) conventionally indicates that a given year is so reckoned. Thus, the year A.M. 1 is the Alexandrian year running from the Julian 29 August 284 to 28 August 285. The years A.M. divisible by 4 begin on the Julian 30 (instead of 29) August, as explained above. In the colophons of manuscripts and occasionally elsewhere, the succession of Alexandrian years may also be given according to the Era of the Incarnation, or "of Christ," which is seven years (through 31 December) or eight years (from 1 January) behind the Dionysian Era of the Incarnation, or according to the Era of the World of Ammianus, with the birth of Christ placed in the year of the world 5500. If a year given according to either of these two eras is divisible by 4, it, too, like a year A.M. divisible by 4, begins on the Julian 30 (instead of 29) August. Through Coptic influence, the Alexandrian year is also used in Ethiopia, where the eras used historically by the Copts have also been followed. The Ethiopian Era ("of mercy"), regularly used in both civil and ecclesiastical calendars in modern times, is identical with the Coptic Era of the Incarnation and is thus seven to eight years behind the era used universally in Western calendars.

Although the exigencies of modern life have led to extensive use of the Gregorian calendar and of the Islamic calendar with years reckoned from the Hegira, the Coptic church also continues to observe Alexandrian years beginning on the Julian 29 August in an ordinary year, and to reckon the succession of years according to the Era of Diocletian or "of the Martyrs." For the twelve months of thirty

Comparison of Coptic and Julian Calendars

	Coptic (Alexandrian) Days and Months				Julian Days and Months
	Sahidic (forms vary)	Bohairic (forms vary)	Arabic	Ethiopic	
1–30	ⲑⲟⲟⲩⲧ (Thoout)	ⲑⲱⲟⲩⲧ (Thōout)	Tūt	Maskaram	29 (30)* August– 27 (28)* September
1–30	ⲡⲁⲟⲡⲉ (Paope)	ⲡⲁⲟⲡⲓ (Paopi)	Bābah	Teqemt	28 (29)* September– 27 (28)* October
1–30	ϩⲁⲑⲱⲣ (Hathōr)	ⲁⲑⲱⲣ (Athōr)	Hātūr	Khedār	28 (29)* October– 26 (27)* November
1–30	ⲕⲟⲓⲁϩⲕ (Koiahk)	ⲭⲟⲓⲁⲕ (Choiak)	Kiyahk	Tākhśāś	27 (28)* November– 26 (27)* December
1–30	ⲧⲱⲃⲉ (Tōbe)	ⲧⲱⲃⲓ (Tōbi)	Ṭūbah	Ṭer	27 (28)* December– 25 (26)* January
1–30	ⲙ̄ϣⲓⲣ (Mshir)	ⲙⲉⲭⲓⲣ (Mechir)	Amshīr	Yakātit	26 (27)* January– 24 (25)* February
1–4	ⲡⲁⲣⲙ̄ϩⲟⲧⲡ̄ (Paremhotep)	ⲫⲁⲙⲉⲛⲱⲑ (Phamenōth)	Baramhāt	Magābit	25–28 (26–29)* February
5–30	"	"	"	"	1–26 March
1–30	ⲡⲁⲣⲙⲟⲩⲧⲉ (Parmoute)	ⲫⲁⲣⲙⲟⲩⲑⲓ (Pharmouthi)	Baramūdah	Miyāzyā	27 March–25 April
1–30	ⲡⲁϣⲟⲛⲥ (Pashons)	ⲡⲁⲭⲱⲛ (Pachōn)	Bashans	Genbot	26 April–25 May
1–30	ⲡⲁⲱⲛⲉ (Paōne)	ⲡⲁⲱⲛⲓ (Paōni)	Ba'ūnah	Sanē	26 May–24 June
1–30	ⲉⲡⲏⲡ (Epēp)	ⲉⲡⲏⲡ (Epēp)	Abīb	Ḥamlē	25 June–24 July
1–30	ⲙⲉⲥⲟⲣⲏ (Mesorē)	ⲙⲉⲥⲱⲣⲏ (Mesōrē)	Misrā	Naḥasē	25 July–23 August
1–5	(No name for the period;	ⲡⲓⲕⲟⲩϫⲓ ⲛ̄ⲁⲃⲟⲧ (Pikougi enabot)	al-Nasī	Pāguemēn	24–28 August
6†	a day within it is [Greek] ⲉⲡⲁⲅⲟⲙⲉⲛⲏ (Epagomenē)	"	"	"	29 August†

*Dates in parentheses are those when a year A.M. is divisible by 4, that is, in the Alexandrian months preceding a Julian intercalation of 29 February.

†Epagomenal day 6 (= Julian 29 August) is intercalated only at the end of a Copto-Alexandrian year preceding a year A.M. divisible by 4, that is, on the Julian 29 August preceding a Julian intercalation of 29 February.

days, the ancient Egyptian names introduced in the first half of the first millennium B.C. are retained, in forms that are copticized or arabized. In the Bohairic dialect, the epagomenal period added at the end of the year is called "the little month." In Arabic the same period is called *al-Nasī'*, "the extension (of time)" or "postponement."

The coordination of the twelve Egyptian months of thirty days each and the five or six epagomenal days with the months and days of the Julian calendar appears in the accompanying table. The nature of the Gregorian reform of the Julian calendar makes it impossible to give Gregorian equivalences that are valid for more than a century or two. Once the Julian date is known, the corresponding Gregorian date can easily be computed according to Rule 2 below. There is no need for such conversion if the Julian date is earlier than the introduction of the Gregorian calendar on 5/15 October 1582.

To convert a Coptic or Ethiopian date (day and month) to its Julian equivalent in an ordinary year (a year A.M. or Ethiopian year not divisible by 4), add the numeral of the Coptic or Ethiopian day of the month to the day before the first day of the Julian period that corresponds to the Coptic or Ethiopian month in question (which can be found in the accompanying table). For instance, to find the Julian date corresponding to the Coptic 15 Kiyahk in an ordinary year, add 15 (the numeral of the day of Kiyahk) to 26 November (the day before the beginning of the Julian period corresponding to the month of Kiyahk in an ordinary year). Thus, 15 plus 26 November becomes 41 November, that is, 11 December.

If the year A.M. or year of the Ethiopian Era is divisible by 4, add 1 to the corresponding Julian date of an ordinary year, if the Coptic or Ethiopian date is one from 1 Tūt through 4 Baramhāt (from Ethiopian 1 Maskaram through 4 Magābit). Thus, 15 Kiyahk in a year A.M. divisible by 4 equals 11 December plus 1, or 12 December.

To convert a Julian date to its Gregorian equivalent, add to the Julian date 10 days from (Julian) 5 October 1582 through 28 February 1700, 11 days from 29 February 1700 through 28 February 1800, 12 days from 29 February 1800 through 28 February 1900, 13 days from 29 February 1900 through 28 February 2000, and so on, remembering that in the century years not divisible by 400, the Gregorian calendar has no 29 February, while the Julian calendar has it intercalated in those years just as in any other leap year.

Coptic calendar showing commemorations during the month of Misrā. *Courtesy L. Atiya.*

To convert a year A.M. to the corresponding year(s) A.D., add 283 to the year A.M. from 1 Tūt through 31 December; add 284 to the year A.M. from 1 January to the end of the Coptic year. Thus, A.M. 1700 equals A.D. 1983/1984.

To convert a year of the Ethiopian Era (or old Coptic Era of the Incarnation) to the corresponding year(s) A.D., add 7 to the Ethiopian year or Coptic year "of Christ" from 1 Maskaram (Coptic 1 Tūt) through 31 December; add 8 to the same Ethiopian or Coptic year from 1 January through the last Alexandrian epagomenal day. Thus, Ethiopian 1 Ṭer 1980 (a year divisible by 4) equals Julian 28 December 1987, whose corresponding Gregorian date, lying in the new year, is 10 January 1988.

To convert a year of the Alexandrian Era of the World (of Ammianus, rendered coextensive with the Alexandrian year beginning 29 August) to the corresponding year(s) A.D., subtract 5493 from the Year of the World from 1 Maskaram (Coptic 1 Tūt) through 31 December; subtract 5492 from the year of the world from 1 January through the last Alexandrian epagomenal day. Thus, 1 Genbot (Coptic Bashans) of the Year of the World 7155 (a date after Julian 1 January) equals Julian 26 April 1663. To convert a date in the Alexandrian Era of the World into one of the Ethiopian Era (equals Coptic Era of the Incarnation), subtract 5500 from the Year of the World. Thus, 1 Genbot 7155 equals 1 Genbot 1655 of the Ethiopian Era "of Grace."

[*See also:* Calendar, Gregorian; Calendar, Julian.]

BIBLIOGRAPHY

Bagnall, R. S., and K. A. Worp. *The Chronological Systems of Byzantine Egypt.* Studia Amstelodamensia ad Epigraphicam, Ius Antiquum et Papyrologicam Pertinentia 8. Zutphen, Netherlands, 1978.

Böker, R. "Zeitrechnung: Ägypten." In *Realencyclopädie der classischen Altertumswissenschaft,* ser. 2, Vol. 9A/2, pp. 2338–2454. Stuttgart, 1967.

Boulos, N. "Proposed Adjustment of the Egyptian-Coptic and Ethiopian Calendars." *Bulletin de la Société d'archéologie copte* 20 (1969–1970):219–38.

Chaine, M. *La Chronologie des temps chrétiens de l'Egypte et de l'Ethiopie.* Paris, 1925.

Grumel, V. *La Chronologie,* pp. 166–68, 304. Traité d'Etudes Byzantines 1. Paris, 1958.

Pestman, P. W. *Chronologie égyptienne d'après les textes démotiques 332 av. J.-C.–453 apr. J.-C.* Papyrologica Lugduno-Batava 15. Leiden, 1967.

Tables of correspondence for each day of the year, valid for the Gregorian calendar from March 1900 to February 2100, are in P. Peeters, *Bibliotheca hagiographica orientalis,* Subsidia Hagiographica 10 (Brussels, 1910), pp. xx–xxiii, and (for Ethiopia) in E. Hammerschmidt, *Äthiopische Kalendertafeln* (Wiesbaden, 1977).

AELRED CODY, O.S.B.

CALENDAR, GREGORIAN. A reform of the Julian calendar (see CALENDAR, JULIAN) was promulgated by Pope Gregory XIII in his bull *Inter gravissimas* of 24 February 1582. The commission that he had named with this in mind ultimately adopted most of the details of the project drawn up by a Calabrian astronomer, Luigi Giglio Ghiraldi (Aloysius Lilius), who had died in 1576, and the final rules were worked out mainly by a German Jesuit, Christopher Clavius. At the time of its introduction, ten days (5–14 October 1582) were dropped from the solar calendar, nine of them so that the mean vernal equinox would occur 20 March instead of 11 March, as it did at the time of the reform, and the tenth so that the calendar corrections necessary from year to year in a 400-year cycle could be diminished by one day. By placing the mean vernal equinox on 20 March, the reformers made sure that the true equinox would never occur later than 21 March, the fixed equinoctial date established in the fourth century, when Easter was defined as the Sunday after the fourteenth moon on or after (never before) the vernal equinox.

In the lunar calendar the epacts were reformed by adding three (days) to compensate for three of the five lunar equations (each necessitating new moons a day earlier thereafter) neglected in the preceding 1,400 years, and by subtracting ten to equal the ten days dropped from the solar calendar. The simultaneous addition of three and subtraction of ten amounted to an effective subtraction of seven from each epact of the series in use up to the time of the reform, and the result was a calendar date seven days later in most instances for each new and full moon in a thirty-year lunar cycle, including the paschal full moons. The beginning of the year was reaffirmed as 1 January.

In order to avoid the need for similar drastic calendar reforms in the future, the Gregorian reformers prescribed that in every century-year except those perfectly divisible by 400, the intercalary day in February indicated by the Julian calendar in every year divisible by 4 should be omitted (century years like 1600 and 2000 thus remain leap years, while those like 1700, 1800, and 1900—divisible by 4 but not by 400—are reduced to common years). In this way the reformers compensated for the accumulated overcorrection caused by the corrective intercalary days in February within the 400-year cycle. As a result, the discrepancy between the dates of the Julian calendar and those of the Gregorian calendar for one and the same solar day increases by one day in each century-year not divisible by 400.

Periodic correction of the lunar calendar was provided for by prescribing (1) the reduction of the number of each lunar epact by one at the beginning of every century-year not perfectly divisible by 400 (thereby adding one day to the new moon dates thereafter—the "solar equation" equating the advance of dates in the solar calendar caused by the omission of the February intercalary day in those years); and (2) the raising of the number of each lunar epact by one at the beginning of 1800 and of every third century-year thereafter (thereby moving new moon dates back one day—the "lunar equation" correcting the 300-year accumulation of excess of the lunar cycle over its correct value and thus keeping the maximum lag of calendar new moons behind their mean new moons from increasing beyond two days).

In century-years in which both the solar equation and the lunar equation occur, the simultaneous addition and subtraction neutralize one another, so that the epacts, and hence the new and full moon dates, remain unchanged. After 3,200 years the Gregorian solar calendar will have an accumulated need for further correction, which can be taken care of by restoring as a leap year a century-year divisible by 400 (with a corresponding solar equation in the lunar calendar), with provision for repeating that step every 3,200 years. The Gregorian lunar calendar can run for 20,000 years before needing a day's further adjustment by means of an additional lunar equation.

The Gregorian calendar was accepted as the legal civil calendar on 5/15 October 1582 by the Italian states, Spain, and Portugal. Other Catholic lands accepted it from the final months of 1582 through 1584, but the Protestant regions of northern Europe retained the Julian calendar into the eighteenth century for the most part, and the reformed calendar was not accepted as the civil calendar of the non-Catholic nations of eastern Europe until the twentieth century (Bulgaria in 1917, Greece and Rumania in 1924, Russia in 1918, Serbia in 1919, Turkey in 1927). (For the divergence between the Gregorian calendar and the Alexandrian calendar used by Copts and Ethiopians, see CALENDAR, COPTIC.)

BIBLIOGRAPHY

Archer, P. *The Christian Calendar and the Gregorian Reform.* New York, 1941.

Clavius, C. *Romani calendarii a Gregorio XIII restituti explicatio.* Rome, 1603.

Ginzel, F. K. *Handbuch der mathematischen und technischen Chronologie,* 3 vols. Leipzig, 1906–1914. See especially Vol. 3.

Kubitschek, W. *Grundriss der antiken Zeitrechnung. Handbuch der Altertumswissenschaft,* Vol. 1, pt. 7, pp. 110–12. Munich, 1928.

AELRED CODY, O.S.B.

CALENDAR, JULIAN, the Roman adaptation of the Egyptian solar calendar introduced by Julius Caesar, with the technical aid of the Alexandrian astronomer Sosigenes, in 46 B.C.; that year was extended to 445 days by intercalation in order to bring the civic year into line with the solar year. While the Egyptians divided the solar year of 365.25 days into 12 months of 30 days each, with 5, or in every fourth year, 6, intercalary days added after the last day of the twelfth month, the Romans, in their Julian calendar, retained the 31 days of March, May, Quintilis (July), and October, and the 28 days of February, as they had been in the older Roman calendar, but increased the other months, which until then all had 29 days, by one day (June, April, September, November) or two days (January, Sextilis [August], December), in order to have an annual total of 365 days. The intercalary month previously inserted periodically, at the discretion of the *pontifex maximus,* after 23 February was replaced by the intercalary day inserted every fourth year after 23 February, and in such a year the 24 February (*ante diem sextum Kalendas Martias*) was counted twice, the intercalary day being *ante diem bis sextum Kalendas Martias,* hence the expression *annus bissextilis* for "leap year." In the first thirty-six years of the Julian calendar's use, the extra day was intercalated every three years instead of every four, by mistaken interpretation of the original prescription, and in 9 B.C. Augustus prohibited the intercalation of the extra day until A.D. 8. The vernal equinox was placed on 25 March, and the year began on 1 January.

The Julian calendar remained in general use in the Western world until it was replaced by the Gregorian calendar, itself a reform of the Julian calendar, in various countries between 1582 and 1924. It is still used for the calculation of Easter and the movable feasts dependent on Easter in the Chalcedonian Orthodox churches. (For its correlation to the Alexandrian calendar used by Copts and Ethiopians, see CALENDAR, COPTIC and CALENDAR, GREGORIAN.)

BIBLIOGRAPHY

Achelis, E. *Of Time and the Calendar.* New York, 1955.

Hofmann, M. *Caesars Kalender.* Munich, 1934.

Kubitschek, W. *Grundriss der antiken Zeitrechnung. Handbuch der Altertumswissenschaft,* Vol. 1, pt. 7, pp. 99–109. Munich, 1928.

Reid, J. S. "History." In *A Companion to Latin Studies,* ed. J. E. Sandys, 3rd ed., pp. 99–101. Cambridge, 1921.

Sontheimer, W. "Zeitrechnung, II. B.a.3: Die Kalenderreform Caesars und das julianische Jahr."

In *Realencyclopädie der classischen Altertumswissenschaft,* ser. 2, Vol. 9A/2, pp. 2467–68. Stuttgart, 1967.

AELRED CODY, O.S.B.

CALENDAR, MONTHS OF COPTIC. Of all survivals from pharaonic Egypt, the calendar is the most striking. Each of the twelve months of the Coptic calendar still carries the name of one of the deities or feasts of ancient Egypt. Without doubt, this reflects the conservatism that characterizes the inhabitants of the Nile Valley, who are reluctant to set aside their traditional way of life.

The year was divided into three seasons of equal length, each comprising four months. Possibly as early as the Ramesside period, each month came to be named for an important festival that was celebrated during that period of time. Documents from around the fifth century B.C., such as the Aramaic papyri from Elephantine, indicate that the great festivals held in honor of certain divinities gave their names to the month in which that particular celebration occurred, and an inscription from Pharaoh Shebaka (700 B.C.) reveals that this certainly was the practice during the Ethiopian era (Černý, 1951, pp. 441–42).

Thanks to a hieratic ostracon in the British Museum (no. 5639a), Adolf Erman was able to identify the names of the festivals which are at the root of the names for the months of Thōout (Tūt), Paopi (Bābah), Athor (Hātūr), Mekhir (Amshīr), and Phamenōth (Baramhāt). Some years later, Gardiner, working with two papyri from Turin, added the names for the festivals of the months Epēp (Abīb) and Mesōrē (Misrā), while J. Černý, using documents from the Cairo Museum and excavations of the Institut français at Dayr al-Madīnah, found the names for the festivals of the months Pharmouthi (Baramūdah) and Paoni (Ba'ūnah). Finally, thanks to a hieratic papyrus acquired by the Cairo Museum (no. 86637), which dates from the Ramesside period and contains the so-called Calendar of Lucky and Unlucky Days, Černý (1943, pp. 173–81) was able to identify the festival for the first month of the winter season, Tōbi (Ṭūbah).

The twelve months and the origins of their names are as follows:

1. Bohairic, ⲑⲱⲟⲩⲧ; Sahidic, ⲑⲟⲟⲩⲧ; Arabic Tūt (September 11–12 to October 9–10). The first month of the Coptic year was dedicated to Thoth, god of wisdom and science, inventor of writing, patron of scribes, and "he who designates the seasons, months, and years." Thoth presided over the "House of Life," where were composed and copied all texts necessary for the maintenance and replenishment of life.

2. Bohairic, ⲡⲁⲟⲡⲓ; Sahidic, ⲡⲁⲟⲡⲉ; Arabic, Bābah (October 11–12 to November 9–10). During the second month was celebrated the "beautiful feast of Opet," whose name Paopi signifies "that of Opet." According to Erman, the "colonnade of the temple of Luxor, decorated by Pharaoh Tut-Ankh-Amon, depicts the unfolding of this great festival in all its diversity. We see Amon-Ra traveling from Karnak to Luxor to celebrate the famous festival of Opet, from which the month *Bābah* derives its name."

3. Bohairic, ⲁⲑⲱⲣ; Sahidic, ϩⲁⲑⲱⲣ; Arabic, Hātūr (November 10–11 to December 9–10). This month commemorated Hathor, a very ancient goddess, found even in predynastic times, the "Cow of Heaven," who gave birth to the sun and to all beings, gods and men. As the living soul of plants and trees, nurse to the rulers of Egypt, and mother of Horus, like Isis (with whom she was assimilated), Hathor was the "Gold of the Gods" and clothed herself in the form of a lion.

4. Bohairic, ⲭⲟⲓⲁⲕ; Sahidic, ⲕⲟⲓⲁϩⲕ; Arabic, Kiyahk (December 10–11 to January 8–9). This month derives its name from a ritual vase that was probably used for measuring incense and was very important in the celebration of the funerary feast originally known as the Union of the Ka. During this month, the great Osirian festivals were held, events of considerable importance to the Egyptian, for they represented: (1) the quest for the dismembered body of the martyred god, Osiris, pursued by the hatred of those representing the forces of evil; (2) the reuniting and reconstruction of his scattered parts into the form of a mummy; and (3) the burial of this simulacrum in the sacred cemetery. These mysteries were carried out in silence within the temple. Small statues made of wet clay mixed with seeds were fashioned in the form of Osiris and placed upon a bed. After a few days, the seeds germinated, and the figures became furry, keeping the original contours of the clay statues that had given them birth. Such are the "Vegetating Osiris," those green and virile figures, those small and holy gardens, that are occasionally found faded in the Theban tombs. A reflection of this ancient practice is found today among present-day Egyptians, who still make lentils germinate in moist cotton pads for certain religious festivals.

5. Bohairic, ⲧⲱⲃⲓ; Sahidic, ⲧⲱⲃⲉ; Arabic, Ṭūbah (January 9–10 to February 7–8). During this month a great festival known as the Swelling of the Barley was celebrated. This name is listed in the Ebers papyrus, which dates from the beginning of the New Kingdom. According to Černý (1943, pp. 173–81), the month was originally called Boṭti (Barley), but by metathesis became Tōbi.

6. Bohairic, ⲙⲉⲭⲓⲣ; Sahidic, ⲙ̄ϣⲓⲣ; Arabic, Amshīr (February 8–9 to March 9). This is one of two months (distinguished from each other as the "large" and the "small") related to fire and represented in the lists of festival objects by a brasier from which fire escapes (Parker, 1950, p. 46). This is the month of the "large fire" because it is the coldest time of year.

7. Bohairic, ⲫⲁⲙⲉⲛⲱⲑ; Sahidic, ⲡⲁⲣⲙ̄ϩⲟⲧⲡ̄; Arabic, Baramhāt (March 10–11 to April 8). This month was originally consecrated to a festival; but after the death of Amenhotep, first king of the Eighteenth Dynasty, he became the object of a particular cult and was worshiped as one of the divine patrons of the Theban necropolis. Around the Twentieth Dynasty, this cult became so popular that his name replaced that of the early festival (Parker, 1950, p. 45).

8. Bohairic, ⲫⲁⲣⲙⲟⲩⲑⲓ; Sahidic, ⲡⲁⲣⲙⲟⲩⲧⲉ; Arabic, Baramūdah (April 9 to May 8). This month was dedicated to Ermonthis, goddess of the harvest, represented as having a serpent's head and sometimes as nursing her son Kapri, the god of grain.

9. Bohairic, ⲡⲁⲭⲱⲛ; Sahidic, ⲡⲁϣⲟⲛⲥ; Arabic, Bashans (May 9 to June 7). This month took its name from the ancient festival of Khonsou, a lunar god who in very early times was integrated into the Theban theology as the son of Amon and Mut. With many qualities attributed to him, he is described as Khonsou the Magnanimous, his foremost Theban name.

10. Bohairic, ⲡⲁⲟⲛⲓ; Sahidic, ⲡⲁⲱⲛⲉ; Arabic, Ba'ūnah (June 8 to July 7). In ancient times, "the Beautiful Festival of the Valley" was celebrated during this month. Held in the Valley of the Kings and lasting some ten days, it was without doubt the most important celebration in the life of the Egyptian people. As the annual commemoration of the dead, it included "the sacrifice, the visit to the tomb, the presentation of a consecrated bouquet, and finally, the banquet given in honor of the deceased, in which relatives, dancers, and musicians participated" (Derchain, 1954, p. 86).

11. Bohairic, ⲉⲡⲏⲡ; Sahidic, ⲉⲡⲏⲡ; Arabic, Abīb (July 8 to August 6). This month was consecrated in ancient Egypt to 'Ipy, goddess of fecundity, who assumed the form of a hippopotamus. The origin of this name is obscure, but it is probably a later form of 'Ipyp, identified at Thebes with Toeris, also a goddess of fecundity who was represented as a hippopotamus. Alabaster containers, meant to hold the water for the libations poured on the ground as an offering to this goddess, also bear the name of this festival (as did objects used in the festivals for the months of Kiyahk and Amshīr).

12. Bohairic, ⲙⲉⲥⲱⲣⲏ; Sahidic, ⲙⲉⲥⲟⲣⲏ; Arabic, Misrā (August 7 to September 5). The last month of the year celebrated the birth of the sun god Ra, though originally this, the last lunar month of the year, was named for the festival honoring the heliacal rising of Sothis (Sirius). For a while, the two names were used conjointly to designate the last month of the civil calendar, but then Ra's name was accessorily applied to the first day of the civil New Year, which came to be known as the Birth of the Solar Disk during the Twentieth Dynasty and the Ptolemaic era. At Dandarah, where the two names were frequently associated with each other, the festival was called "the Festival of Ra, he who ushers in the New Year." Gardiner (1966, p. 65), seeing therein a solar festival, considered it to be a commemoration of the "moment when the sun god, at his rising, signaled the succession of the months and years." However, the first rising of Ra was also the moment of his birth (Mesōrē), the occasion of his first appearance (Parker, 1950, p. 46).

Finally, the epagomenal, or intercalary, days, called the "delayed days" (Arabic, *ayyām al-nasī*) or the "little month" (Arabic, *al-shahr al-ṣaghīr*), are five extra days that follow the month of Misrā (six during leap year). The first of these days was reserved by the ancient Egyptians for the festival honoring their most celebrated god, Osiris. Certain other great ceremonies also took place at this time.

BIBLIOGRAPHY

Černý, J. "The Origin of the Month Tybi." *Annales du Service des antiquités égyptiennes*, 43 (1943):173–81.

———. "Age of the Egyptian Month Names." *Annales du Service des antiquités égyptiennes* 51 (1951):441–42.

———. *Ancient Egyptian Religion*. London, 1952; repr., 1957.

———. *Coptic Etymological Dictionary*. Cambridge, 1976.

Chassinat, E. *Le Mystère d'Osiris au mois de Khoiak*. Cairo, 1966.

Derchain, P. *Chronologie d'Egypte*. Cairo, 1954.

Erman, A. *La religion des Egyptiens*, p. 234. Paris, 1952.

Gardiner, A. *Egypt of the Pharaohs: An Introduction.* Oxford, 1961.

Ghali, I. "Le Calendrier copte et l'ère des martyres." *Bulletin de l'Institut français d'archéologie orientale* 66 (1968):113–120.

Parker, R. *The Calendars of Ancient Egypt.* Chicago, 1950.

Wissa Wassef, C. *Pratiques rituelles et alimentaires des Coptes.* Cairo, 1971.

CÉRÈS WISSA WASSEF

CALENDAR AND AGRICULTURE. The Coptic calendar has survived not only in the liturgy of the Coptic church but also in the agricultural life of the Nile Valley, for it sets the schedule by which the farmers (fellahin) regulate their work in the fields. Many delightful maxims and aphorisms summarizing the essentials of what must be done each season to guarantee successful cultivation of crops, maintenance of good health, and protection against the weather are still heard today. Usually in rhyme, they serve as excellent mnemonic devices to remind farmers of what must be done at specific times of the year. It is possible that they derive from ancient Egypt, and were translated into Arabic as the country became arabized. The almanacs contain useful and precise directives for the months of the year—each of which has its own special traits—concerning the phases of the Nile, the winds, the crops, labors to be performed, health, and even the most intimate details of everyday life.

1. *Tūt.* The month beginning 11–12 September, when the flood reaches its maximum, and the most opportune time for irrigating the fields, as indicated by relevant sayings.

Tūt: rayy wallā fūt
("During *Tūt*, irrigate, or forgo it.")
Tūt: shiddil-ʿUntūt
("In *Tūt* pull the *ʿuntūt*" or "Get ready to work.")

(The *ʿuntūt* is a wooden peg used to fasten the yoke to a rope that loops around the neck of the cow to keep the yoke in place.)

Tūt: yiūl lil bard fūt
("Tūt says to the cold weather, 'Enter.'")

The advice inherent in these sayings was significant until the nineteenth and twentieth centuries, before the building of the Aswan Dam changed the method of irrigation. Before then irrigation was accomplished by flooding individual basins protected by dikes. The water, filled with the fertilizing silt, would stand a few months and then return to the river.

The first of Tūt marks the beginning of planting the winter crops—clover, dill, cabbage, and turnips. Colocasia, lettuce, and celery make their appearance, as well as corn and sugar cane in Upper Egypt. Onions begin to ripen, and dates grow in abundance, along with pomegranates, lemon, and quince. Cotton is harvested; beans are planted.

Advice is given in the almanac to avoid intercourse at the beginning of the month, to observe the clouds and the weather, drink no water at night, take no medicines, and dress warmly.

The fruit of the month is dates, *ruṭab Tūt.*

2. *Bābah.* The month beginning 11–12 October when the flood waters begin to subside. Some sayings warn against humidity.

Bābah: khushsh wi'fil id-darrābah
("During Bābah, go inside and pull the latch.")

The entire harvest depends on Bābah, for in this month tilling and planting begin throughout the country, as the proverbs tell:

In shaḥḥ zarʿ Bābah, ghalab-il-ūm in-nahhābah.
win khaff Zarʿ Bābah mā yib'āsh fīh walā libābah

("If the crops of Bābah are scarce they will fail the marauders, and if these crops are scant, not even a crumb will remain.")

In Bābah, the following crops are planted: clover, wheat, barley, fenugreek, peas, anise, fennel, rice, garlic, and onions. Sesame, henna, and peanuts are harvested, as well as the second crop of cotton. Fruits grow in abundance—watermelons and melons known as *Nīlī*, so-named for the Nile flood. It is the season for the first oranges. Quail also thrive.

The almanac announces the stirring of emotions at the beginning of the month, and it advises against bleedings and exposure to the fresh morning air.

The fruit of the month is the pomegranate, *rummān Bābah.*

3. *Hatūr.* The month beginning 10–11 November, named after Hatūr, goddess of gold and of sowing grains, especially wheat, as shown in this saying:

Hatūr: Abū-d-dahab-el-manṭūr
("Haṭūr, the month of scattered gold.")

This saying is particularly interesting, for it depicts the practice of pharaohs who would occasionally strew grains of wheat mixed with gold pellets through the temple.

Other maxims indicate that the farmer should take advantage of Hatūr as the most favorable time for planting.

In fātak zar' Hatūr iṣbur lammā-s-sanah tidūr
("If you miss the planting season of Hatūr, wait until the year rolls around.")

At this time wheat, safflower, coriander, lentils, and market-gardening crops are sown. After the last cotton harvest, turnips, potatoes, and corn are planted. It is the end of the planting season for lupine, fenugreek, broad beans, and chick peas. It is also the season when rice ripens, and fields turn green. Radish seeds and olives are pressed for oil; housewives begin to make butter, and the first tangerines appear.

The almanac indicates that this is the month when the bile becomes turgid. It advises exercise, and cautions against drinking water at night.

The fruit of the month is the banana, *moz Hatūr*.

4. *Kiyahk*. The month of the winter solstice and shorter days, beginning 10–11 December, as reflected in these sayings:

Kiyahk: ṣabāḥak misāk
("In Kiyahk, your morning is your evening.")

T'ūm min farshak t-ḥaḍḍar 'ashāk
("In Kiyahk, you arise in the morning to prepare your supper.")

illi ma t-rabba' barsīm fī Kiyahk, id'ū 'alayhā bil halāk ("The beast that misses its share of clover during Kiyahk, is better to perish.")

Here occurs the first agricultural forty-day period, extending from the first of Kiyahk to 11 Tūbah. During this time, the coldest and rainiest part of the year, winter planting must come to an end, the fields have to be prepared for the summer crops, and canals and ditches drained and cleaned.

The calendar specifies certain days for planting lettuce, broad beans, and apricot and plum trees. It also tells when to graft or remove trees, when to prune palm trees and vines, and, for the south, when to plant market-gardening crops. The cutting of sugar cane begins in Upper Egypt, as does the harvesting of corn and green onions. With milk abundant and of excellent quality (thanks to the clover), housewives find this the best time to prepare their yearly supply of butter.

The almanac advises people to protect themselves against the cold, and avoid drinking exposed water at night.

Kiyahk is the month when rivers abound in fish, which is the food of the month, *samak* (fish of) *Kiyāk*.

5. *Ṭūbah*. Beginning 9–10 January, the coldest month of winter, as indicated by these sayings:

Ṭūbah: abūl-bard wal'u'ūbah
("Ṭūbah, the month of cold and its consequences.")

Ṭūbah: tkhalli-s-ṣabiyyah jildah wil 'ajūzah irdah
("Ṭūbah reduces a young girl to skin and bones, and shrivels an old woman.")

Abrad min mayyit Ṭūbah
("Colder than the water of Ṭūbah.")

The Epiphany, 11 Ṭūbah, marks the beginning of the second forty-day agricultural period, which ends on 20 Amshīr. During this time the preparation of the ground for the first summer crops comes to an end, and the winter crops of Upper Egypt, broad beans and fenugreek, ripen. Also during this month, some germinate lentil and/or wheat grains on dampened pads of cotton as an auspicious beginning. The greeting most often heard is, *ij'alhā 'alaynā sanah khaḍrah*, "Please make the year green, i.e., prosperous, for us."

This is the time when the shrubs and young palm trees are transplanted; pomegranate and peach are planted, as well as tomatoes, eggplant, pepper, onions, carrots, anise, safflower, summer corn, and henna. Vines and palm trees are pruned; rice, rosemary, broad beans, and dill are harvested. Sugar cane, citrus fruits, squash, and colocasia grow in abundance.

During this month the weather is changeable. The almanac advises abstinence from broad beans and excessively salty food, and the use of pepper and spices. Ṭūbah is characterized by the fresh taste of its water.

6. *Amshīr*. The month beginning 8–9 February, of strong winds and storms known as *Zaffat Amshīr* or "Amshir's parade." Many proverbs allude to this intemperate weather.

Amshīr: abū-z-zawābi' il-kitīr
("Amshīr, the month of many storms.")

Amshīr yākhud-el-'Ajūzah we-yeṭīr
("Amshīr grabs the old woman and flies away.")

Toward the end of Amshīr, the cold weather subsides, the earth warms up, and the crops make visible progress:

Amshīr yi-ūl lil-zar'sīr bilā Ta'sīr
("Amshīr says to the crops, 'Grow with ease.'")

En kān zar'ak taḥt-il-Kōm mā-t-buṣṣ 'alayh-we-fāḍil f-Amshīr Yūm

("If your crops are still underground, don't
uncover them so long as there yet remains
one day in Amshīr.")

During the third agricultural forty-day period, which lasts from 21 Amshīr to the end of Baramhāt, winter crops are harvested, and summer crops begin. Farmers start growing cotton, first in Upper, then in Lower, Egypt. They also plant corn, sugar cane, and all kinds of fruit trees. They fertilize the palm trees, and harvest garlic, onions, and fenugreek. The first cucumbers make their appearance, the trees begin to bud, and leaves appear on the vines.

For this month the almanac advises avoiding the sun, and recommends drinking water first thing in the morning. It also warns that it is the time when emotions are aroused.

The food of the month is lamb, *kharūf Amshīr.*

7. *Baramhāt.* Beginning 10–11 March, Baramhāt is the month for abundant crops and harvesting.

Baramhāt: rūḥ il-ghayt we-hāt kull-el-ḥājāt
("In Baramhāt, go to the field and get everything.")

This is also the month of Lent for the Copts, who must abstain from all animal products at this time. Hence the saying:

*ʿĀsh-in-nuṣrānī we-māt we-nifsū yakul fūl ḥirāt
we-jibnah f-baramhāt*
("In Baramhāt a Copt lives and dies craving
for green beans and cheese.")

There are three inauspicious days in the calendar, known as *ḥusumāt* or *ayyām al-ḥusūm,* which occur at the beginning of this month. Farmers therefore refrain from cultivating their fields, and avoid all conception, both human and animal, for the life conceived risks being born abnormal. This idea probably survived from the legend of the combat of Seth, which is associated with images of storm and violence. The ancient myths maintain that Seth was the assassin of Osiris and the aggressive rival of young Horus. In the *Calendar of Lucky and Unlucky Days,* the three days singled out as unfortunate are 29 Amshīr, "At sunset on this day, do not look at anything"; 4 Baramhāt, "His voice in the heavens and on earth proclaims great disasters"; and 7 Baramhāt, "Do not leave your house when the evening sun is on the horizon, for this was . . . when . . . Horus called upon his gods to follow him; and . . . toward evening, he quarreled with them."

The cold, violent winds, loaded with dust, that blow during the first days of this month have a noxious effect on young cotton plants; so the farmers do not plant cotton at this time. However, after the spring equinox, the storms subside, and summer crops prosper in the north of the Delta. Farmers plant sugar cane, cotton, sesame, legumes, cumin, okra, and watermelons. They harvest peas, flax, onions, broad beans, and fenugreek. Also leeks begin to sprout, and the trees come into bloom.

With this being springtime, the almanac indicates that it is the best season for intercourse.

Thanks to the abundance of clover, the cow buffalos produce excellent milk, *laban Baramhāt.*

8. *Baramūdah.* The month beginning 9 April when all grains are threshed, with each farmer awaiting his turn to start threshing:

*Baramūdah: du' bil-ʿamūdah walā yib'a fil-ghayt
walā ʿūdah*
("In Baramūdah, thresh with the stake,
and not a single straw will remain in the field.")

In many regions, especially in Upper Egypt, an old custom requires that the reapers be paid in kind. During the wheat harvest, the finest ears of corn are braided into dolls that are known by the villagers as "the bride of wheat," and are hung above the doorways as a sign of good omen or placed upon piles of winnowed grain. These practices, which vary in different provinces, have doubtlessly survived from very ancient cult rituals.

During Baramūdah, the following crops are harvested: broad beans, flax, fenugreek, onions, barley, lupine, potatoes, and wheat. It is also the time for gathering honey, and for planting corn, sugar cane, rice, peanuts, henna, and indigo. Watermelons and mulberries appear, while leeks and okra are found in abundance. It is also the season of roses, from which essence is extracted and preserved.

According to the almanac, the seventh day of the month marks the beginning of a season lasting some fifty days. Rheumatism becomes widespread. Salted foods such as fish should be avoided, woolen clothing set aside, and white linen garments should preferably be worn.

The rose is the flower of the month, *ward Baramūdah.*

9. *Bashans.* The month beginning 9 May when the crops have been harvested, and nothing remains in the fields:

Bashans yikniss il-ghayt kans
("Bashans sweeps the fields clean.")

During Bashans apples, plums, melons, and apricots appear. Wheat, onions, and the last crops of clover are harvested, as are roses and the flowers of safflower. Palm trees are fertilized, and corn, sesame, rice, colocasia, and indigo are planted. This month marks the beginning of the summer crops in Upper Egypt.

The almanac states that, at the beginning of Bashans, blood runs more slowly, but that the humors are likely to become active as the summer heat sets in. It advises the partaking of refreshing drinks and abstinence from salted foods.

The fruit of the month is the *nab'* (from the jujube tree), *nab' Bashans.*

10. *Ba'ūnah.* Beginning 8 June is the month of intensive heat, generally known as *Ba'ūnah-al-ḥajar,* for the extremely hot and dry weather causes rocks to split:

> *Ba'ūnah fallā' il-ḥajar*
> ("The heat of Ba'ūnah splits rock apart.")
> *Ba'ūnah-al-ḥajar yinashshif il-Mayya fe-sh-shajar*
> ("Ba'ūnah drains the tree dry.")

During this month the following crops are sown: rice, *mulūkhiyyah* (corchorus olitorius), cucumbers, and corn. In the Fayyūm and Lower Egypt, clover is reaped, and honey is gathered. This is also the fruit season, with figs, plums, prickly pears, grapes, peaches, and apricots making their appearance, as do green beans and zucchini. Watermelons grow in abundance.

At this time the Nile is at its lowest level of the year, and its water becomes muddy and turbid. The almanac advises filtering water and recommends drinking acidulated liquids.

On 12 Ba'ūnah, the traditional, miraculous drop of water falls into the Nile, causing the waters to rise, and flooding to begin.

11. *Abīb.* The month beginning July 8 when the figs and grapes ripen.

> *Abīb: ṭabbākh il-'inab wi-t-tīn*
> ("Abīb, the cook of grapes and figs.")
> *Abīb: el-mayya f'awwiluh t-khess, we-f'akhruh t-zīd*
> ("At the beginning of Abīb, the Nile waters diminish, but at the end of the month, they rise again.")

This is the season for the flood crops known as *Nīlī* (of the Nile). Legumes, garden vegetables, and summer watermelon become plentiful. Rice and corn are sown, guava and mulberry trees are planted, and flax is put to soak.

Winds blow in from the North for fifteen days, alternating with the last hot winds of the desert. The flood waters sweep away the green, stagnating pools, and the earth is prepared for sowing the next crops.

The almanac advises a moderate intake of food. The food of the month is honey, *'asal Abīb.*

12. *Misrā.* The month of the Nile flood beginning on 7 August, when water overflows the river banks, running into the canals:

> *Misrā tijrī fīhā kull tir'ah 'iṣrah*
> ("During Misrā, the water runs into every dry canal.")

During Misrā the following crops are planted: rice, radishes, carrots, onions, tomatoes, turnips, and beets. Cucumbers, watermelon, figs, melons, and grapes are found in abundance. Green olives and sesame are harvested, as is cotton in the South.

The heat is scorching. The almanac recommends drinking fresh water first thing on arising, and eating mild foods. One must beware of insects and mosquitoes.

The fruit of the month is grape, *'inab Misrā.*

With the construction of the Aswan High Dam, the three growing seasons now partially overlap one another year in and year out. Consequently, the seasonal rhythm, inherited from antiquity, has disappeared. It survives only in the liturgy of the Coptic church.

CÉRÈS WISSA WASSEF

CALENDAR, SEASONS, AND COPTIC LITURGY. The three seasons of the Coptic calendar, a survival from pharaonic Egypt and based on agricultural activities, are commemorated by special prayers incorporated into the divine liturgies. The seasons and prayers appropriate to each, as computed according to the Gregorian calendar of the twentieth century, are as follows.

The Nile-flood season (12 Ba'ūnah–9 Bābah/19 June–19 October), during which these prayers of intercession for the water (*awshiyyāt al-miyāh*) are recited at each Liturgy:

> Priest. "O graciously, Lord, please grant Thy blessings to the waters of the river."
> Deacon. "Pray that the waters of the river may rise this year, that Christ, our Lord, may bless it, raise it to its normal level, and gladden the face of the earth; that He will help us, humankind, protect our cattle, and forgive us our sins."
> Congregation. "Lord, have mercy" (chanted three times).

In ancient times, it was believed that during the night of 11/12 Ba'ūnah, known as the "night of the droplet," when the river reached its lowest level, a miraculous drop of water fell into the Nile, and caused the waters to begin rising. This belief may have come from ancient Egyptian myths like that of Isis shedding tears of mourning for her lost husband, Osiris. One of her tears falling into the Nile caused the much desired flooding.

The sowing season (10 Bābah–10 Ṭūbah/20 October–18 January), during which these prayers of intercession for the crops are recited at each liturgy:

> Priest. "Graciously, O Lord, grant Thy blessings to the plants, the herbs, and vegetables of the fields."
>
> Deacon. "Pray for the plants, the herbs, and vegetables of the fields this year that Christ, our Lord, may grant them His blessings, that they may grow and bring forth plentiful fruit; that He may have compassion for the creatures of His hands, and forgive us our sins."
>
> Congregation. "Lord, have mercy" (chanted three times).

The harvest season (11 Ṭūbah–11 Ba'ūnah/19 January–18 June), during which these prayers of intercession for the harvest (*awshiyyāt al-thimār*) are recited at each liturgy:

> Priest. "O Lord, please grant Thy blessings this year to the winds of the sky and the fruits of the earth."
>
> Deacon. "Pray for the winds of the sky and the fruits of the earth, the trees and vines, and every fruit-bearing tree so that Christ, our Lord, may grant them His blessings, bring them to harvesting without damage, and forgive us our sins."
>
> Congregation. "Lord, have mercy" (chanted three times).

Alternatively, a common intercession may be used as a substitute for any of the preceding prayers during all seasons throughout the year:

> Priest. "Graciously, O Lord, bless the waters of the river, the vegetation, the plants of the fields, the winds of the sky, and the crops of the land this year."
>
> Deacon. "Pray for the waters of the river, the vegetation, the plants of the fields, the winds of the sky, and the crops of the land, that Christ our Lord may bless them and protect them this year, and forgive us our sins."
>
> Congregation. "Lord have mercy" (chanted three times).

BIBLIOGRAPHY

Černy, J. "The Origin of the Month Tybi." *Annales du Service des antiquités égyptiennes* 43 (1943): 173–81.

______. "Age of the Egyptian Month Names." *Annales du Service des antiquités égyptiennes* 51 (1951):441–42.

______. "Some Coptic Etymologies." *Bulletin de l'Institut français d'Archéologie orientale* 58 (1959):206–208.

Chassinat, E. *Le Mystère d'Osiris au mois de Khoiak*, pt. 1. Cairo, 1966.

Derchain, P. *Chronologie d'Egypte*. Cairo, 1954.

Dictionnaire de la civilisation égyptienne. Paris, 1959.

Drioton, E. *Pages d'égyptologie*. Cairo, 1957.

Erman, A. *La Religion des égyptiens*. Paris, 1937.

Ghali, I. "Le Calendrier copte et l'ère des martyrs." *Bulletin de l'Institut français d'Archéologie orientale* 66 (1968):113–20.

Parker, R. *The Calendars of Ancient Egypt*, p. 83. Chicago, 1950.

Wissa Wassef, Cérès. *Pratiques rituelles et alimentaires des coptes*. Cairo, 1971.

CÉRÈS WISSA WASSEF

CALENDOLOGIA, treatises comparable to those used in astrology and containing prognostications about future events, made either by correlating a given date of the year with a certain day of the week or by correlating certain atmospheric phenomena with a particular day of the week. Since they are well known in Greek, it is quite probable that the Copts derived them or simply translated them from Greek examples.

In Coptic we have the remnants of three (perhaps four) codices containing a calendologium: (1) Vienna, National Library, K1112 and 9885–9900 (ed. Till, 1936); (2) Vienna K5506 (ed. Till, 1936); (3) University of Michigan Library (*Papyri in the University of Michigan Collection*, Inv. 6590, ed. Browne, 1979); (4) (uncertain) State Museum of Berlin (see Browne, p. 56). The calendologia in the first three texts are substantially alike, each consisting of two parts: (1) the connection between 6 Ṭūbah and various days of the week, that is, if the sixth falls on Sunday, a certain prognostication will be made, but if it falls on Monday, another prediction is called for, etc.; (2) the connection between the week of 6 Ṭūbah and the wind, which may blow more or less severely during one of those days. The date of 6 Ṭūbah was chosen because it corresponds to January 1, that is, the beginning of the legal year of the Roman empire (perhaps another indication of the Greek origin of these treatises). The prognostications refer to the increase in the Nile's flow and to events concerning agricultural life. In such texts as these there were probably interpolations made by Egyptian writers.

BIBLIOGRAPHY

Browne, C. M. *Michigan Coptic Texts*, no. 13. Barcelona, 1979.

Till, W. C. "Eine koptische Bauernpraktik." *Mitteilungen des Deutschen Archäologischen Instituts, Kairo* 6 (1936):108–149, 175–76.

TITO ORLANDI

CAMOUL, SAINT, or Chamoul, a martyr under DIOCLETIAN (feast day: 16 Bashans). Lacking a first part, the text of his Passion has survived in fragments from only one Sahidic codex (British Library, London, Pap. V, ed. Winstedt, 1910, pp. 169ff.).

The action opens with Camoul in prison under the governor Pompeius. He has obviously been tortured, and has miraculously been healed; he then has a vision of Christ, who foretells his glorious end. The text is followed by various miracles performed by him in prison, further torture, and death.

Julius of Aqfahṣ (Kbehs) intervenes and has the body taken first to the martyr's hometown of Kellia, near Tarabia in the eastern Delta, and then to Peremun, where various miracles take place. The story continues with Julius in the leading role; he persuades Armenius to spare many Christians, who are then saved by the advent of Constantine after the death of Diocletian. Julius welcomes them, and they live in his house until their death.

This is a central text of the Cycle of Julius of Aqfahs, because Julius does not appear (as is often the case) simply as a witness but in a leading role. Even so, one has the impression that when it was composed, the Cycle of Julius was already well established and that the part referring to him was added to a preexisting text about Camoul. This could have taken place in about the seventh century.

BIBLIOGRAPHY

Winstedt, E. O. *Coptic Texts on Saint Theodore the General, St. Theodore the Eastern, Chamoul and Justus.* London and Oxford, 1910.

TITO ORLANDI

CANCELLI. *See* Architectural Elements of Churches.

CANDELABRUM. *See* Liturgical Instruments; Metalwork, Coptic.

CANDLEMAS. *See* Feasts, Minor.

CANDLES. Candles have been used in churches since the early days of Christianity on many occasions. According to Ibn al-ʿAssāl's *Kitāb al-Qawānīn* (Book of Canon Law) and the DIDASCALIA, candles must be lighted during all services, a reference to the words of Jesus Christ, "I have come as a light into the world" (Jn. 12:46).

Inside the sanctuary two candlesticks are placed either on the altar or close to it, one to the north and the other to the south. Likewise two candelabra stand outside the sanctuary, representing the Old and the New Testaments. During processions, bishops enter the church preceded by priests and deacons carrying lighted candles and chanting relevant hymns.

In the evening and the morning offering of incense, standing at the sanctuary door and looking eastward, his hands extended and holding in his right hand the cross with three lighted candles, the priest says the prayer of Lord, have mercy upon us. Then he turns toward the people and blesses them three times with the cross and the three lighted candles.

When the scriptures are read, the reader holds a lighted candle. When the priest or deacon reads the Gospel, two deacons, one to his right and one to his left, stand holding lighted candles. This established tradition was mentioned by Saint Jerome (c. 342–420): "Through all the churches of the east, when the Gospel is to be read, lights are kindled, though the sun is already shining; not indeed to dispel darkness, but to exhibit a token of joy; . . . and that under the figure of bodily light, that light may be set forth of which we read in the psalter, 'Thy word is a lantern unto my feet, and a light unto my paths.'"

In the performance of the Divine Liturgy the deacons serving in the sanctuary hold lighted candles, particularly at the choosing of the Eucharistic Bread; the Procession of the Lamb, crossing the oblations, the sanctification, the fraction, the confession, and the communion. During the liturgy of consecration of the holy chrism, the clergy hold candles in a procession, preceding the patriarch, who carries the myron and the oil of the catechumens to the sanctuary.

Lighted candles are carried during the performance of the church sacraments. In BAPTISM, candles are placed around the font and are also held by all persons attending. Catechumens used to be given lighted candles immediately after being baptized as a token of the inner light they had just acquired. Saint CYRIL OF JERUSALEM (c. 315–386) vividly describes the practice that illuminated the dark night during Easter celebration at the Church of the Resurrection: ". . . on the eve of the Savior's resurrection, and at the doors of the Church of the Anastasis, the white-robed band of the newly baptized was seen approaching from the neighboring baptistery, and the darkness was turned into day in the brightness of unnumbered lights." Likewise Saint GREGORY OF NAZIANZUS (329–389) refers to the symbolic meaning of these lighted candles: "The lamps which thou wilt kindle are a mystical sign of that lamp-bearing from thenceforth, wherewith we, bright and virgin souls, will go forth to meet the Bridegroom" (*Oration* 40.46, cols. 425–26).

In the celebration of the sacrament of holy unction of the sick, seven wicks and seven candles are set on a table before the sanctuary screen. Each time a priest begins to read one of the seven prayers for the sick, he lights a wick and a candle until all the prayers have been read and all wicks and candles have been lighted.

Candles are also lighted when the sacrament of Matrimony is performed, and during the ceremony of betrothal.

Candles are used in a special way on Good Friday, when the services begin in early morning and last past sunset. The sanctuary is closed, and the service is conducted in the nave of the church where candles burn only at the pulpits, where readings are conducted.

In mid-afternoon the condemnation of Christ from the Gospels is read. As the reader reaches the passage "and from the sixth hour there was darkness" (Mt. 27:45; Mk. 15:33; Lk. 23:44) the candles are extinguished. At the twelfth hour the black curtain concealing the sanctuary is drawn back to reveal candles burning again on the altar. Two icons of the crucifixion and the burial are taken in procession around the sanctuary and the church, as deacons facing the icons carry the lighted candles during the procession. The icon of the burial is then returned to the sanctuary, wrapped in white cloth and laid on the altar. Two candles symbolizing angels are placed one at the head and one at the feet of Christ.

Lighted candles are usually held during such celebrations, particularly on Easter Eve, called Saturday of light. At the Church of the Resurrection in Jerusalem, which is overcrowded with people on this occasion, when the sacred light is kindled following the circuit around the Holy Sepulcher, all candles are lighted, and the church is transformed into a blazing mass of light.

Candles are also lighted to commemorate the martyrs, "who . . . shall shine like the brightness of the firmament" (Dn. 12:3).

EUSEBIUS OF CAESAREA relates how at the funeral of Constantine the Great in 337, "his coffin was surrounded by candles burning in candlesticks of gold, presenting a marvelous spectacle, and such as no one under the light of the sun had ever seen on earth" (*Life of Constantine*, 4.66).

Candles are still burned during the various stages of funerals. It is customary to lay the body in the coffin, keeping it in state there before the church service for a few hours, for mourners to pay their last respects. Tall candlesticks with burning candles are positioned at the head and foot of the casket at home and later during the church service.

It is an old practice to light candles before the icons of Jesus Christ, the Virgin Mary, the martyrs, and the saints. In the words of Germanus, patriarch of Constantinople (c. 634–733), "Let it not scandalize some, that lights are before the sacred icons and sweet perfumes. For such rites have been devised to their honor . . ."(Labbe, 1971–1972, Vol. 7, p. 313).

The annals of the church abound in cases of individuals whose prayers were answered and requests granted through the intercession of the saints, and who light candles in the church in recognition of such favors.

BIBLIOGRAPHY

Butler, A. J. *The Ancient Coptic Churches of Egypt*, 2 vols. Oxford, 1884.

CANONICAL HOURS, BOOK OF, book containing the offices for the seven canonical hours. It includes all the prayers, Psalms, Gospel readings, and petitions to be said at the various hours by day and night, appointed in accordance with analogous points in the life and Passion of Jesus Christ. Canonical hours were appointed in conformity with Psalm 119:164 ("Seven times a day do I praise Thee because of Thy righteous judgments") and in fulfillment of Christ's commandment that prayers be offered at all times and with unflagging energy (Lk. 18:1).

Both the DIDASCALIA and Ibn al-ʿAssāl's *Book of*

Canon Law (chap. 14) set the following times for the reading of these seven prayers: early morning, before sunrise; at the third hour; at the sixth hour; at the ninth hour; at the eleventh hour; at the twelfth hour; and at midnight. It should be borne in mind here that, following the practice common at the time of Christ (Jn. 11:9), the day is computed from sunrise to sunset; thus, the third hour corresponds to nine in the morning, the sixth hour to noon, and so on. This practice had been followed by the Old Testament prophets (Ps. 5:3; 55:17; 63:1, 6; 119:62, 164; Is. 26:9) and was later maintained by the apostles (Acts 2:15; 10:3; 16:25). In adopting this approach of distributing prayer times throughout the day, stress is laid on certain analogous points in the life and Passion of Jesus Christ.

The Prayer of the First Hour, also called morning or dawn prayer, is designed to be read just before the beginning of daylight and is a reference to the coming of the True Light, which is Jesus Christ. Besides being the hour at which Jesus was arrested at Gethsemane following His betrayal by Judas Iscariot, dawn is mainly associated with the time when Christ rose from the dead.

This office is intended to offer thanks to the Almighty for having brought one safely to the morning. The tone of earnest request characterizes the opening of the Prayer of the First Hour, increasing gradually in fervor and intensity: "O come, let us worship! O come, let us request Christ our God! O come, let us worship! O come, let us beg Christ our King! O come, let us worship! O come, let us entreat Christ our Savior!" Spiritual guidance and a Christian plan of action for the day are supplied by the words of St. Paul: "I therefore, a prisoner for the Lord, beg you to lead a life worthy of the calling to which you have been called, with all lowliness and meekness, with patience, forbearing one another in love, eager to maintain the unity of the Spirit in the bond of peace. There is one body and one Spirit, just as you were called to the one hope that belongs to your call" (Eph. 4:1–5).

The Prayer of the Third Hour is a reminder of three significant events: the trial of Jesus Christ by Pilate; Christ's Ascension; and the descent of the Holy Spirit upon the disciples. Here one prays that the grace of the Holy Spirit be renewed within one, that the heart will be cleansed, and that true peace be given through the Holy Spirit, the Comforter. The absolution prayer for this hour conveys a deep sense of gratitude to God, who has called the devout to pray at this holy hour, which is that wherein He poured forth the grace of His Holy Spirit in abundance upon His blessed disciples and apostles.

The sixth hour commemorates the crucifixion and the Passion of Christ. Here one prays that the fetters of sin be torn asunder, that suffering be brought to an end by His redeeming and life-giving Passion, that through the nails by which He was nailed on the cross the mind be delivered from the recklessness of insubstantial works and worldly lusts, by the remembrance of His heavenly judgments, according to His tender mercies.

The ninth hour, at which the darkness that had pervaded the earth since the sixth hour was lifted, serves to commemorate the redemptive death of Christ in the flesh on the cross and His acceptance of the repentance shown by the thief on His right hand.

In this hour one prays that the Redeemer, who suffered death for sinners, may mortify one's carnal senses and make one a partaker of the grace of His life-giving sacraments so that, having tasted of His benefactions, one may offer Him unceasing praise.

The devout also pray that just as He received the confession of the repentant thief, He may also receive them unto Himself, when they confess His Divinity and cry out, "Remember us, O Lord, when You come into your Kingdom!"

The eleventh hour is to commemorate the act of removing Christ's body from the cross and its preparation for burial by Joseph of Arimathea and Nicodemus. It is also associated with the parable of the vineyard (Mt. 20), and so the faithful pray that they be considered worthy to be counted among the laborers who were called at the eleventh hour. They also give thanks for God's protection through the day and confess, with the Prodigal Son, that they have sinned against heaven and are not worthy to be called God's children.

The twelfth hour commemorates the entombment of Christ and is a reminder of the evanescence of human life. Mindful of their imminent standing before God and following the example of the contrite publican, the devout beat their breasts and beg forgiveness and protection through the night.

The midnight office consists of three watches, also called "nocturns," corresponding to the three stages of Christ's prayer in the garden of Gethsemane (Mt. 26:36–46). The first watch is a reminder of the necessity of being prepared for Christ's Second Coming and of having to meet Him like the Wise Virgins (Mt. 25:1–13). The second watch points to the urgency of repentance in anticipation of God's judgment. In the third watch, where stress is laid on Christ's words, "Watch and pray" (Mt. 36:41), the devout pray that when the Son of Man comes

He shall find them on the alert (cf. Lk. 12:36–38).

In addition to these hours there is another prayer called the Office of the Veil. According to the *Ajbiyah,* it is for the use of monks, but the Didascalia directs that it be read by bishops and priests as a means of examination before sleep.

In all these canonical hours the reading chosen from the Psalms, the Gospels, and the Epistles, together with the accompanying petitions and absolution prayers, are all closely related to the main theme of the relevant hour. There are, however, certain common sections that are recited at the beginning and end of each hour. The following are those which are read at the beginning:

1. In the name of the Father, and the Son, and the Holy Spirit. Amen.
2. KYRIE ELEISON, Lord have mercy, Lord have mercy, Lord bless us. Amen.
3. Glory to the Father, and to the Son, and to the Holy Spirit, both now and ever unto the ages of ages. Amen.
4. the Lord's Prayer
5. the Prayer of Thanksgiving
6. Psalm 50

Each hour concludes with the following:

1. *Kyrie eleison* (forty-one times), representing the thirty-nine scourges, the spear, and the crown of thorns
2. Holy, Holy, Holy, O Lord of Sabaoth, etc.
3. the Lord's Prayer
4. the Absolution
5. the Petition: Have mercy on us, O God, and have mercy on us. Thou who, at all times, and at every hour, in Heaven and on earth art worshiped and glorified, etc.

The principal element in the structure of the canonical hours is a selection of Psalms specially arranged to harmonize with the basic theme of the hour in question. Needless to say, the Psalms possess and impart unique spiritual dynamism and cover all the aspects of the relationship between man and God, from the depth of misery to the height of mercy, from the depth of sin to the height of grace. "In the seven Penitential Psalms we have the seven weapons wherewith to oppose the seven deadly sins; the seven prayers inspired by the sevenfold Spirit to the repenting sinner; the seven guardians for the seven days of the week; the seven companions for the seven Canonical Hours of the day" (Neal and Littledale, 1867, p. 7). It is a sublime tribute to the efficacy of the Psalms that Christ Himself frequently quoted from them—in the synod, during His temptation by the devil, at the Last Supper, and on the cross—and to note that His last words, "Into thy hands I commit my spirit," came from the Psalms.

The apostles, too, drew heavily on the Psalms in their teachings and their prayers. Saint Paul strongly urged the use of Psalms in worship (1 Cor. 14:26; Eph. 5:19; Col. 3:16).

The incorporation of such a rich heritage into Christian worship was adopted first by the church of Alexandria. The contemplative Theraputae, the Jewish Egyptian ascetics who lived in seclusion near Lake Mareotis, many of whom embraced Christianity, must have influenced, to a certain degree, the mode of worship in the emerging church.

It must also be remembered that in earlier times the Psalms that were included in the canonical hours were sung, and not just read, despite the fact that some of these hours, particularly the sixth and ninth, are associated with sorrowful events such as the Crucifixion and the death of Christ on the cross, respectively. Hence the use of the term "hymn" in the introduction preceding these hours, "the hymn of the . . . hour of the blessed day, I now offer to Christ my King and God, beseeching Him to forgive me my sins." David sang his Psalms as hymns of praise to the Almighty and the apostles were always cheerful, despite their tribulations (Acts 16:25).

Among the writings of the early fathers who described the form of worship prevalent in the Church of Alexandria is the testimony of EUSEBIUS OF CAESAREA, who quoted Philo (c. 20 B.C.–c. A.D. 55): "While one sings [the Psalms] regularly in time, the others listen in silence, and join in chanting only the close of the hymns" (Eusebius 2.17.22). Likewise, ATHANASIUS of Alexandria (c. 296–373) likened the singing of Psalms to a "balm which heals the spirit." The same point is underlined by John CASSIAN (Bk. 2, chap. 11) in his description of the practice of Psalm-singing by the Egyptians: "They do not even attempt to finish the Psalms, which they sing in the service, by an unbroken and continuous recitation. But they repeat them separately and bit by bit, divided into two or three sections, according to the number of verses, with prayers in between. . . . And so they consider it better for ten verses to be sung with understanding and thought, than for a whole Psalm to be poured forth with a bewildered mind."

With regard to the number of Psalms used in the canonical hours, the church now specifies seventy-four (i.e., one half of the total number of Psalms) to be read daily. Apparently no fixed portion was prescribed in former times, and the choice was left to the discretion of the various fathers, so long as the appointed times were adhered to.

Thanks to the relative peace that it enjoyed during the first and second centuries, the Egyptian church, long before any other church, was able to establish the pattern of these canonical hours. Each contained twelve Psalms together with a chapter from the Old Testament and another from the New.

The life story of Saint Antony the Great (251–336) bears ample evidence of this custom. When he broke his fast at sunset, he would say a Psalm before his meal and then offer twelve prayers, followed by twelve Psalms, before he retreated for a few hours of rest. At midnight he would rise to sing Psalms until dawn.

This Egyptian tradition later found its way to other corners of Christendom: it was carried to Palestine by Saint Hilarion (c. 291–371), to Mesopotamia by Saint Basil (c. 330–379), to France and Italy by Saint Athanasius the Apostolic (c. 296–373) and John Cassian. The last wrote to his disciples: "I think it best to set forth the most ancient system of the fathers which is still observed by the servants of God throughout the whole of Egypt, so that your new monastery in its untrained infancy in Christ may be instructed in the most ancient institutions of the earliest fathers."

The canonical hours of the Egyptian church were eventually incorporated into the official canons of the Second Council of Tours in 567.

BIBLIOGRAPHY

Neale, J. M. *History of the Holy Eastern Church*, Vol. 1, p. 12. London, 1847.

Neale, J. M., and R. F. Littledale. "A Help to the Spiritual Interpretation of the Penitential Psalms." In *Essays on Liturgiology and Church History*, 2nd ed., p. 7. London, 1867.

ARCHBISHOP BASILIOS

CANONICAL HOURS, HYMNS.

See Music, Coptic: Description.

CANONIZATION,

the formal declaration of a deceased person's sanctity, whereby his or her name is added to the roll of the saints of the church and commended for veneration by the faithful.

The earliest persons to be canonized were the martyrs, who submitted to death for Christ, and the confessors, who avowed their faith in Christian life and acquired a reputation for sanctity. Next were the early fathers, thanks to whom the basic doctrines and teachings of religion were firmly established, and who dedicated their lives for the proclamation of the gospel of Christ.

In the early days of Christianity, churches used to exchange news and information regarding such martyrs and confessors whose names were worthy of being mentioned in prayers. EUSEBIUS OF CAESAREA, the father of church history, records a letter sent by "the church of God which dwelleth at Smyrna to the church of God which dwelleth in Philomelium" in connection with the martyrdom of Polycarp, bishop of Smyrna (c. 69–155). The letter ends with these words, "And so we afterwards gathered up his bones, which were more valuable than precious stones and more to be esteemed than gold, and laid them in a suitable place. There the Lord will permit us to come together as we are able, in gladness and joy to celebrate the birthday of his martyrdom for the commemoration of those who have already fought and for the training and preparation of those who shall hereafter do the same."

In the Roman Catholic church the authority to canonize is the prerogative of the pope of Rome. In the Coptic church, as well as other Orthodox Churches, the power of canonization rests with the Holy Synod.

BIBLIOGRAPHY

Kemp, E. W. *Canonization and Authority in the Western Church*. London, 1948.

Naz, R. "Causes de béatification et de canonisation." In *Dictionnaire de droit canonique*, Vol. 3, cols. 10–37. Paris, 1942.

ARCHBISHOP BASILIOS

CANON LAW,

codified law governing a church. The Coptic church has no *codex juris canonici*, as the Roman church does, but it has remained closer to its sources, which it has grouped in chronological or systematic collections.

From the Coptic period, the church of Egypt was concerned with Coptic translation of the sources of church law, but these most frequently occupied a codex either by themselves or along with other works, such as biographies or sermons. Thus there are the Apostolic Canons and the Ecclesiastical Canons of the Apostles, or the DIDASCALIA and the Testament of the Lord.

A single codex has come down, the content of which forms a veritable *corpus canonum*. It was reconstructed by W. E. Crum (1915, pp. 13–14) and completed by R.-G. Coquin (1981, pp. 42–43). The law of the Copts is also known from ostraca and papyri, the data of which were collected by A. A. Schiller (1938). With profit one may also consult A. Steinwenter's small book *Das Recht*. It will thus be possible to attain, for want of direct sources, to the "law in action" of which Schiller speaks.

Coptic law is further distinguished from the law of the Roman church because since the Muslim invasion the patriarch, in his capacity as head of the Coptic nation, has exercised the functions of civil law. For this reason the documentation of the law of the Copts includes elements that in the West would be in the province of civil law—everything that concerns what is called the law of personal status, such as inheritance and marriage.

The collections that have survived may be divided into the chronological and the systematic.

Chronological collections consist of three main groups.

1. The anonymous collection in Berlin. This is preserved in a single undated manuscript, Berlin Arabic 10181, folios 51–219. An analysis of this codex is in Riedel (p. 129). Unfortunately, the end of the manuscript is missing.

2. The collection of Macarius, a monk-priest of the monastery of John Colobos in Wādī al-Naṭrūn. He compiled a collection of canons, probably in the first half of the fourteenth century, that is of the same type as the anonymous Berlin one. It has survived in eleven manuscripts, some of which are incomplete. Three are copies of ancient manuscripts made in the eighteenth century. The oldest and most complete manuscript is Paris, National Library, Arabe 251. It has been analyzed by Troupeau (1972, Vol. 1, pp. 208–209). This manuscript is dated from A.M. 1069/A.D. 1352. The collection can be divided into four major parts: (a) the pre-Nicene canons, which include the canons attributed to the apostles and those of the provincial councils; (b) the canons of the Council of NICAEA; (c) the canons of the kings (Byzantine emperors), borrowed from the Melchites and attributed by the Copts to the Council of Nicaea; (d) the canons of the medieval patriarchs—CHRISTODOULUS, CYRIL II, GABRIEL II, and CYRIL III.

3. Anonymous Jacobite collection, the name given by Riedel (1900, p. 136). It contains almost the same elements as that of Macarius, with some modifications. It is chiefly represented by the manuscripts Arabe 238–39 at the National Library, Paris (Troupeau, pp. 200–202). The manuscripts are dated by R.-G. Coquin to the fourteenth–fifteenth centuries, but some parts of the first manuscript were restored in the sixteenth century.

In systematic collections, the canons on which Coptic law is founded are arranged according to the matter with which they deal. The Coptic church very early took steps to arrange them in systematic order so as to obtain a coherent whole, easy to consult.

The first systematic collection that has survived is that of Abū Sūlḥ (or Ṣāliḥ, according to the vocalization of the name). He appears to have been concerned about translating the Coptic documentation at his disposal into Arabic in such a way as to form a legal compendium for his church. It is not known when he lived, but his work is dated to the tenth or eleventh century.

Gabriel II ibn Turayk, twelfth-century patriarch of Alexandria, is well known for his work of renovation and reform. He produced three important series of canons (Graf, 1947, pp. 324–27), a revision of two liturgical books, and, undoubtedly, biblical translations into Arabic. It is known from the testimony of Bishop Mīkhā'īl of Damietta, al-SAFĪ IBN AL-'ASSĀL, and Abū al-Barakāt IBN KABAR that he compiled a nomocanon in seventy-four chapters, to which was added as an appendix a summary of the canons of the kings. This nomocanon, which was thought lost, was rediscovered in a manuscript at the library of the Coptic patriarchate in Cairo (canon 13, no. 570 in Simaykah's *Catalogue*). Unfortunately this manuscript is incomplete at the beginning and the end, for it contains only fifty-seven chapters. The appendix with the canons of the kings is preserved in the nomocanon of Mīkhā'īl of Damietta, which reproduces it literally.

Bishop Mīkhā'īl of Damietta, twelfth-century bishop under the patriarchs MARK III ibn Zar'ah and John VI ibn Abī Ghālib, is known above all through his controversy with Mark ibn Qanbar on the subject of auricular confession. He was still alive when Mark died in 1208. Among other works, he compiled a voluminous nomocanon, probably after 1188, according to the preface of the Arabe 4728 manuscript at the National Library, Paris. The Berlin manuscript Arabic 10180 is a second recension, perhaps by Michael himself. Riedel (1968, p. 89) has given an analysis of this manuscript. The text of each canon is provided with a siglum that serves to designate it within the nomocanon.

Al-Ṣāfī ibn al-ʿAssāl, one of the three writers of the family of ibn al ʿAssāl (probably al-Safī Abū al-Faḍā'il), compiled a nomocanon that has become almost the official manual of Coptic Egypt. This nomocanon has survived in two different recensions. The author was the counselor and chief of protocol of Patriarch Cyril III ibn Laqlaq. It is believed that he had completed his work on the orders of the patriarch, who was not satisfied with it. He set to work again, and produced the second recension. It was proclaimed by the patriarch and approved at the synod of 1238. This book was also translated into Geʿez and became the official book of the civil and religious law of Ethiopia. It was edited and translated into Italian by Guidi (1897, 1899). It has been published twice in Egypt, by Phīlūthāwus Awaḍ (*al-Majmūʿ*) and by Mīkhā'īl Jirjis (*Kitāb*). All of the serious studies on the personal statutes of Coptic law are based on the nomocanon of Ibn al ʿAssāl; this is the case in particular with the work of Phīlūthāwus ʿAwaḍ, *al-Khulāṣah*.

Although it is not a canonical collection, the encyclopedia of Abū al-Barakāt, entitled *Lamp of Darkness*, should be mentioned. In the fifth chapter, "Catalogue of the Canons Received and the Councils Transmitted," Abū al-Barakāt transcribes the title and the table of the development of Coptic law from the Canons of the Apostles down to the nomocanon of Ibn al-ʿAssāl. This work was probably compiled about 1320. Since September 24, 1955, the "mixed tribunals"—tribunals of judges belonging to the different Christian communities of Egypt—have been suppressed and the Muslim judge must deliver sentences in conformity with the law of the parties to the case. For this reason the work of Ibn al-ʿAssāl remains in force.

BIBLIOGRAPHY

Abū al-Barakāt ibn Kabar. *Mīsbaḥ al Ẓulmah.* Cairo, 1971.

Coquin, R.-G. "Le Corpus canonum copte. Un nouveau complément: Le manuscrit IFAO, copte 6." *Orientalia* 50, no. 1 (1981):40–86.

Crum, W. E. *Papyruscodex saec. VI–VII der Phillippsbibliothek in Cheltenham.* Schriften der wissenschaftlichen Gesellschaft in Strassburg 18. Strasbourg, 1915.

Guidi, I., trans. *Il "Fetha nagast" o legislazione dei re,* 2 vols. Rome, 1897–1899.

Mīkhā'īl Jirjis. *Kitāb al-qawānīn.* Cairo, 1922.

Phīlūthāwus ʿAwaḍ. *Al-Majmūʿ al-Ṣafawī.* Cairo, 1908.

———. *Al-Khulāṣah al-Qānūniyyah fī al-Aḥwāl al-Shakhṣiyyah li-Kanīsat al-Aqbāṭ al-Urthudhuksiyyīn,* 2nd ed. Cairo, 1913.

Riedel, W. *Die Kirchenrechtsquellen des Patriarchats Alexandrien.* Leipzig, 1900; repr. Aalen, 1968.

Schiller, A. "Prolegomena to the Study of Coptic Law." *Archives d'histoire du droit oriental* 2 (1938):341–65.

Steinwenter, A. *Das Recht der koptischen Urkunden.* Handbuch der Altertumswissenschaft 10. Munich, 1955.

Troupeau, G. *Catalogue des manuscrits arabes,* Vol. 1. Paris, 1972.

RENÉ-GEORGES COQUIN

CANONS, APOSTOLIC, a series of eighty-four or eighty-five canons that in Greek form the concluding chapter (47) of Book 8 of the Apostolic Constitutions (Funk, 1905, Vol. 1, pp. 564–94). The Sahidic Coptic version counts seventy-one canons, the Arabic series (Book 2 of the 127 Canons of the Apostles) fifty-six only, the same as the Ethiopic version. The Greek text has often been published (e.g., by Funk, 1905; Lagarde, 1856).

We have two Coptic versions, in Sahidic and Bohairic, and several in Arabic.

Sahidic Text

This is preserved in two complete manuscripts, one in the British Library (Or. 1320, cf. Crum, 1905, no. 162), dating from A.M. 722 (A.D. 1005–1006), and an unnumbered manuscript in the Coptic Patriarchate in Cairo, dating from the eighteenth or nineteenth century. There are two editions, by P. de Lagarde (1883, pp. 209–37, upper half of the pages: British Library Or. 1320) and by U. Bouriant (1885).

Bohairic Text

According to the colophon, this translation was made from the Sahidic; it is not divided into canons but appears as the seventh book of Clement, "that is to say the completion of the eight books," as the title adds. Its text, however, is little different from that of the Sahidic. Three manuscripts are known: Staatliche Museen, Berlin (Or. quarto 519, dated to A.M. 1520 [A.D. 1803–1804]); Cairo (Coptic Patriarchate, Canons 9 and 10 [Simaykah and ʿAbd al-Masīḥ, 1942, nos. 577 and 581], dating from 1803–

1804); and a manuscript of A.D. 1854 (unpublished). There are two editions, by H. Tattam (1848, pp. 173–214) and P. de Lagarde (1883, pp. 209–37, lower half of the pages that constitute Tattam's text).

Arabic Text

At least three recensions have been listed: only the one that forms Book 2 of the 127 Canons of the Apostles has been published, on the basis of eight manuscripts, by J. and A. Périer (1912, pp. 556–61, introduction, and pp. 664–93, text and French translation). Another is contained in the Clementine Octateuch; J. and A. Périer give the text of canons 45 and 47–50 (the numbering of the Greek), which are missing from the first recension (1912, pp. 555–60); in this Clementine Octateuch these apostolic canons form Book 8 (Graf, 1944–1953, Vol. 1, pp. 581–84). A third recension appears to have been borrowed from the Melchites (Riedel, 1900, pp. 44–45, 158); it is unpublished. The parallelism between the fifty-six canons of Book 2 of the 127 Canons of the Apostles and Book 8 of the Octateuch of Clement did not escape Coptic authors, like Abū al-Barakāt (Riedel, 1900, p. 73; Samir Khalil, 1971, p. 198).

Content

The Apostolic Canons, in contrast to the ECCLESIASTICAL CANONS, deal in no particular order with the principal matters of ecclesiastical discipline, ordinations, and canonical impediments (the numbers are those of the Coptic version: 1, 2, 9, 10, 49, 54, 64, 65, 68), the Eucharist and oblations (1, 4, 5), the marriage of clergy (1, 11, 12, 18), Easter (2), simony (21, 22), the ecclesiastical hierarchy (23–33), relations with the heretics and the Jews (37, 38, 50, 58, 59), and the canonical books (71). The other canons specify various faults and the corresponding penalties, excommunication or deposition as the case may be. Some canons are duplicated. Most of the penal prescriptions have the clergy in view.

Origin

No one today defends the apostolic origin of these canons, although it was accepted in the Greek church after the Quinisext Synod of 692. It is difficult to determine at what period they were drawn up. There are two opposing opinions. On the one hand, it has been claimed that there are allusions to these apostolic canons in various synods, such as Canon 9 of Antioch (about 341) and the synodical letter of Constantinople (382) (Nau, 1932, cols. 1607–1608), from which it has been concluded that the Apostolic Canons date from the third or even the end of the second century. More recent authors think that it was the compiler of the Apostolic Canons who borrowed from the *Didascalia* and the canons of the councils of Nicaea, Antioch, Laodicea, Constantinople, and so forth. Since toward 500 Dionysius Exiguus translated them into Latin, or at least the first fifty (in the Greek numbering), these authors think that the composition of the Apostolic Canons must have been done in the fourth or fifth century. But what disturbs the critics is the allusion at the very end, in the Greek text, to "the statutes edited in eight books for you, bishops, by me Clement, which ought not to be divulged to all." This passage is missing from the Coptic and the Arabic, and could well be a later addition. Here as in other documents the Coptic-Arabic recension might well offer a state of the text prior to that transmitted by the Greek manuscripts at our disposal, since this final remark, both of the Apostolic Constitutions and of the Clementine Octateuch, is missing from the Egyptian recension.

The critics are unanimous in setting the place of origin of the Apostolic Canons in the region of Antioch, and a good number think that the Apostolic Constitutions and the Canons are by the same author. This is possible, but cannot be demonstrated; the compiler of the Apostolic Constitutions may very well have simply reworked an older document.

Characteristics of the Egyptian Recension

The Coptic and Arabic recensions (or at least that of the 127 Canons of the Apostles) differ on several points from the Greek text (which may be called the *receptus*) through the division into canons, through omissions, and through modifications of the text.

In addition to variation in number of canons, there are also some changes of order: thus Canons 6 and 7 of the Greek correspond to Canons 3 and 2 in the Coptic, 5 and 4 in the Arabic. The Coptic-Arabic recension differs also from the Greek—and Arabic versions that depend on it—by the omission of several canons. The Coptic does not have Canons 47 to 50 in the Greek, and the Arabic has also suppressed Canon 45, which forbids the clergy to pray with the heretics. The Greek Canons 47 to 50 forbid rebaptism without cause, the dismissal of a spouse and remarriage, and baptism with a heretical formula or a single immersion; some manuscripts add a trinitarian profession to Canon 50.

Canons 47 to 50, with the profession of faith, are found in the canonical collection of the Copts, which inserts the Arabic version made from the Greek; they have been edited and translated by J. and A. Périer (1912, pp. 557–59). Among the more notable modifications we may draw attention to that of Canon 67 in the Coptic (81 in the Greek, 53 in the Arabic). The Greek recension forbade the bishop or the priest to "engage in public affairs" but the Coptic version says, "We have said that it is not fitting that the bishop should sit to receive taxes." The Coptic uses here the Greek word *demosion* and the Arabic *al-kharāj* for "taxes." The Coptic translation of Canon 4 of the Council of Laodicea had modified the Greek in the same way.

The last canon (85 in the Greek, 71 in the Coptic, 56 in the Arabic) is a list of the canonical books received in the churches. It presents a certain number of variants according to the recensions and even to the manuscripts (Guidi, 1901, pp. 161–74). They all, however, distinguish between the books to be considered "venerable and holy" and those that "your children must learn in addition," that is, between the protocanonical and the deuterocanonical. The Sahidic version places Judith and Tobit among the first, the Wisdom of Solomon, Esther, the three books of the Maccabees, and the Wisdom of Sirach among the second; the Arabic omits Judith and Tobit among the first, but puts Judith in place of Esther among the second. In the list of the New Testament books, the Sahidic adds "the two epistles of Clement"; the Arabic does not. We are familiar with the list set out by ATHANASIUS in his thirty-ninth *Festal Letter* of 367 (Lefort, 1952, pp. 19–20; Greek text in CSCO 151, pp. 34–35); this too distinguishes protocanonical and deuterocanonical, and adds the *Didascalia Apostolorum* and the *Shepherd of Hermas*. In some manuscripts at least, another list follows Canon 59 of the Council of Laodicea.

The Apostolic Canons were handed down in Arabic by the medieval Coptic canonists, either in the form of the fifty-six canons of Book 2 of the 127 Canons of the Apostles or in versions borrowed from the Melchites, or perhaps from the Syrians, which have not yet been closely studied (see Riedel, 1900, p. 158). They were extensively cited, sometimes in these different recensions, by the compilers of the nomocanons, systematic collections in which the documents were grouped by subjects by GABRIEL II ibn Turayk; Michael, bishop of Damietta (composed in 1188), and al-Safī ibn al-ʿAssāl (composed in 1238; Graf, 1944–1953, Vol. 2, pp. 323–27, 333–35, 398–403).

BIBLIOGRAPHY

Bouriant, U. "Les Canons apostoliques de Clément de Rome. Traduction en dialecte copte thébain d'aprés un manuscrit de la bibliothéque du patriarche Jacobite du Caire." *Recueil de travaux relatifs à la philologie et à l'aarchéologie égyptiennes et assyriennes* 5 (1884): 199–206, 6 (1885: 97–115.

Crum, W. E. *Catalogue of the Coptic Manuscripts in the British Museum*. London, 1905.

Funk, F. X., ed. *Didascalia et Constitutiones Apostolorum*, 2 vols. Paderborn, 1905.

Guidi, I. "Il Canone biblico della chiesa Copta." *Revue biblique* 10 (1901):161–74.

Lagarde, P. de. *Reliquiae juris ecclesiastici graece et syriace*. Leipzig, 1856.

———. *Aegyptiaca*. Göttingen, 1883.

Nau, F. "Canons des apôtres." In *Dictionnaire de théologie catholique*, Vol. 2, cols. 1605–1626. Paris, 1932.

Périer, A., and J. Périer. "Les 127 canons des apôtres." PO 8, pp. 550–93. Paris, 1912.

Riedel, W. *Die Kirchenrechtsquellen des Patriarchats Alexandrien*. Leipzig, 1900; repr. Aalen, 1968.

Samir, K., S.J., ed. *Mīsbaḥ al-Ẓulmah*. Cairo, 1971.

Tattam, H. *The Apostolical Constitutions or Canons of the Apostles in Coptic*. London, 1848.

RENÉ-GEORGES COQUIN

CANONS, ECCLESIASTICAL, the name given by P. de Lagarde (1883, p. 239, n. a) to distinguish these canons from the seventy-one APOSTOLIC CANONS. In the Arabic version of the Coptic, it is the first book of the 127 Canons of the Apostles. Their superscription in Sahidic is: "These are the canons of our holy fathers the apostles of our Lord Jesus Christ, which they established in the Church" (Lagarde, 1883, p. 239), and in Arabic: "These are the canons of our fathers the apostles which they prepared for the establishment of the Church through the medium of Clement" (Périer and Périer, 1912, p. 573). This number varies to some extent: seventy-eight in Coptic and seventy-one in Arabic, with a distribution varying according to the manuscripts in Ethiopic. The final subscription in the Arabic should be noted: "Their number in the Greek is 81 canons" (Périer and Périer, 1912, p. 663), which is not what the Coptic version says. This indicates that there was at first a Greek collection in Egypt. It is further entirely remarkable that this collection of seventy-eight (or in Arabic seventy-one) ecclesiastical canons was preserved only in Egypt, and indirectly in Ethiopia.

We have at our disposal two Coptic recensions (Sahidic and Bohairic) and several in Arabic.

Sahidic Text

This has come down in three almost complete manuscripts, of which the two later ones are copies of the first, and some fragments. The manuscripts date from the early eleventh century (A.M. 722; A.D. 1005–1006) (British Library, Or. 1320, Crum, 1905, no. 162); a nineteenth-century manuscript (British Library, Or. 440, Crum, no. 163); and a manuscript from the eighteenth or nineteenth century (Coptic Patriarchate, Cairo, unnumbered). For the fragments from the White Monastery (Dayr anbā Shinūdah), see L. T. Lefort (1954). There are editions by Lagarde (1883, pp. 239–91, of British Library, Or. 1320), U. Bouriant (1884 and 1885), and G. W. Horner (1904, pp. 295–363; translation only from Lagarde's text; and pp. 459–73, Sahidic fragments edited). For Canons 31 to 62, see W. Till and J. Leipoldt (1954).

Bohairic Text

This version, based on a Sahidic recension as the colophon indicates, is sometimes called the Bohairic Octateuch or Heptateuch. It is not divided into canons, like the Sahidic and the Arabic, but into seven books with a second numbering corresponding to a division into eight books, and would resemble the Syriac Clementine Octateuch (Nau, 1913; reedited by Ciprotti, 1967). In fact, it is visibly the same text as that of the Sahidic manuscripts. Three manuscripts are known, one in Berlin (Or. quarto 519, A.M. 1520/A.D. 1803–1804); one in Cairo (Coptic Patriarchate, Canon 9 and Canon 10; Simaykah and ʿAbd al-Masīḥ, 1942, Vol. 2, nos. 577 and 581, dating from 1803–1804), and one dating from A.D. 1854. There is an edition by H. Tattam (1848). The collation with the Sahidic was done by Horner (1904, pp. 445–57) and by Till and Leipoldt (1954; see also the introduction, pp. 15–19; see also Graf, 1944–1953, Vol. 1, pp. 582–83).

Arabic Version

The manuscripts are numerous, and have been reviewed by J. and A. Périer (1912, pp. 565–71) and by G. Graf (1944, Vol. 1, pp. 576 and 584). There are two recensions, one deriving from the Coptic and another made from the Clementine Octateuch, on the basis of the Syriac or the Greek; the Bohairic manuscripts noted above are provided with a parallel Arabic version (unpublished; see, however, the remarks of G. Goeseke, in Till and Leipoldt, 1954, pp. 47–63). There are editions by Horner (1904, pp. 89–125 and 233–93) and J. and A. Périer (1912, pp. 573–663) (the Périer brothers used eight manuscripts, Horner only three). The version derived from the Octateuch is unpublished, except for two canons published by J. and A. Périer (1912, p. 560). The parallelism between the 127 Canons of the Apostles and the Clementine Octateuch was well known to Coptic authors, such as Abū al-Barakāt, in his *Misbāḥ al-Ẓulmah* ("Lamp of Darkness") (see Riedel, 1900, pp. 69–73).

Sources

These Coptic and Arabic ecclesiastical canons may be divided into three sections according to the three documents from which they derive. Canons 1–30 (Arabic 1–20) come from a document called the *Apostolic Church Order* because it was placed under different names of apostles; the canons correspond to a book entitled Aἱ *διαταγαι αἱ διὰ Κλήμεντος καὶ κανὸνες ἐκκλησιαστικοὶ τῶν ἁγίων ἀποστόλων* ("The orders established by Clement and the Ecclesiastical canons of the Holy Apostles"). It has been published several times, but reference is usually made to F. X. Funk (1887, pp. 50–73). This is a reworking of the *Didache*, and like it consists of two parts: an ethical discourse taking up the theme of the "way of life" from the *Didache*, but omitting the "way of death" (Canons 1–14; Arabic 1–12), then a series of canonical and liturgical prescriptions: the number and selection, the functions and duties of the bishop, the priests, readers, deacons, widows, deacons again, the laity, deaconesses, almsgiving (Canons 15–30; Arabic 13–20). The country of origin of this document—whether Egypt or Syria—cannot be determined with any certainty. It probably dates from the beginning of the fourth century.

Canons 31–62 (Arabic 21–47) were formerly called the *Egyptian Church Order*. This section, of which the Greek is lost except for a few fragments, has been identified with the *Apostolic Tradition* of Hippolytus of Rome since 1910 (E. Schwartz, R. H. Connolly, G. Dix, B. Botte). For the state of the question, see H. Chadwick in Dix (1968, pp. a–p). J. Magne (1975) has suggested that the *Egyptian Church Order* is not the work of Hippolytus but the *Diataxeis of the Holy Apostles* by an anonymous author. Botte (1963) has attempted to restore the original text. This section of the Ecclesiastical Canons includes an ordination ritual from the bishop down to the healer (Canons 31–39; Arabic 21–26), then a calendar of Christian initiation (Canons 40–46; Arabic 27–34), and finally various prescriptions on the liturgical or disciplinary observances of the community such as fasting, the agape, offerings, and prayer (Canons 47–62; Arabic 35–47). This part is parallel to two other documents preserved, in Arabic only, in the canonical collections of the Copts, the *Testamentum Domini* (of Syrian origin) and the *Canons of Hippolytus* (certainly of Egyptian origin, for these two texts are recastings of the original document). For Botte, this section or at least its source, the *Apostolic Tradition* of Hippolytus, was composed in Rome; for J. M. Hanssens (1965), it would derive from Alexandria. Those who hold Hippolytus for its author place the composition of the work at the beginning of the third century. Canons 63–78 (Arabic 48–71) have been called the *Apostolic Rule*. This part is parallel to book 8 of the *Apostolic Constitutions,* a compilation preserved in Greek that is dated to the end of the fourth century or the beginning of the fifth and is very probably of Syrian provenance (Funk, 1905). The concordance between our Coptic and Arabic Ecclesiastical Canons and the Greek of the Apostolic Constitutions will be found in Hanssens (1965, pp. 96–97) or in P. de Lagarde (1856, pp. XIII–XVI). After a statement about the charismata and a transition (Canon 63; Arabic 48–51), it contains an ordination ritual (Canons 64–73; Arabic 52–60) with additions relating to the first fruits and to tithes, then a calendar of Christian initiation (Canons 74–75; Arabic 61–63) and some prescriptions concerning the Christian life (Canons 75–78; Arabic 64–71).

In the Bohairic recension edited by Tattam, as in the Arabic version of the Clementine Octateuch, we may note a change of order. The calendar of Christian initiation is placed at the end. It is difficult to state precisely what is the immediate source of this third section of the Ecclesiastical Canons. E. Lanne (1960) has advanced the hypothesis that the Sahidic version of these canons derives from an Alexandrian Greek text of the *Apostolic Constitutions,* shorter than the one we know and differing also from the *Epitome of the Apostolic Constitutions* (ed. Funk, 1905, Vol. 2, pp. 72–96). Originally this Alexandrian recension also included the prayers that subsequently were omitted in the Sahidic translation of the Ecclesiastical Canons because they were already to be found in the *euchologia.*

This series of Ecclesiastical Canons (seventy-one canons), under the form and title of *First Book of the Canons of the Apostles,* was preserved in the medieval canonical collections of the Coptic church (see Riedel, 1900, pp. 121–38, collection of Macarius, anonymous of Berlin, Jacobite anonymous; and Graf, 1944–1955, Vol. 1, pp. 560–63). It was also widely used by the authors of nomocanons, or systematic collections arranged by themes: the Patriarch GABRIEL II ibn Turayk (1131–1145), Michael of Damietta (composed in 1188), and al-Ṣafī ibn al-ʿAssāl (in 1238) (Graf, 1944–1953, Vol. 2, pp. 324–27; 333–35; 398–403).

BIBLIOGRAPHY

Botte, B. *La tradition apostolique de saint Hyppolyte. Essai de reconstitution.* Liturgie wissenschaftliche Quellen und Forschungen 39. *Münster, 1963.*

Bouriant, U. "Les Canons apostoliques de Clément de Rome. Traduction en dialecte copte thébain d'après un manuscrit de la bibliothèque du patriarche Jacobite de Caire." *Recueil des travaux relatifs à la philologie et à l'archéologie égyptiennes et assyriennes* 5 (1884):199–216; 6 (1885):97–115.

Crum, W. E. *Catalogue of the Coptic Manuscripts in the British Museum.* London, 1905.

Dix, G. *The Treatise on the Apostolic Tradition of St. Hippolytus of Rome,* 2nd ed. London, 1968.

Funk, F. X., ed. *Doctrina duodecim Apostolorum.* Tübingen, 1887.

———. *Didascalia et Constitutiones apostolorum.* Paderborn, 1905.

Hanssens, J. M. *La liturgie d'Hippolyte.* Orientalia Christiana Analecta 155. Rome, 1965.

Horner, G. W. *The Statutes of the Apostles or Canones ecclesiastici.* London, 1904.

Lagarde, P. de. *Reliquiae juris ecclesiastici graece et syriace.* Leipzig, 1856.

Lanne, E. "Les ordinations dans le rite copte." *L'Orient Syrien* 5 (1960):81–106.

Lefort, L. T. *Review of Der koptische Text der Kirchenordnung Hippolyts,* by W. Till and J. Leipoldt. *Le Muséon* 67 (1954):403–405.

———. *Aegyptiaca.* Göttingen, 1883.

Magne, J. *Tradition Apostolique sur les charismes et Diataxeis des saints apôtres.* Paris, 1975.

Nau, F. *La version syriaque de l'Octateuque de Clément.* Paris, 1913. Reedited by P. Ciprotti. Milan, 1967.

Périer, J., and A. Périer. "Les 127 canons des apôtres." PO 8, pp. 550–93. Paris, 1912.

Riedel, W. *Die Kirchenrechtsquellen des Patriarchats Alexandrien.* Leipzig, 1900; repr. Aalen, 1968.

Tattam, H. *The Apostolical Constitutions or Canons of the Apostles in Coptic.* London, 1848.

Till, W., and J. Leipoldt. *Der koptische Text der*

Kirchenordnung Hippolyts. Texte und Untersuchungen zur Geschichte der altchristlichen Literatur 58. Berlin, 1954.

RENÉ-GEORGES COQUIN

CANONS OF CLEMENT, or "Letter of Peter to Clement." Under one or the other of these titles there is current among the Copts, as among the Melchites, an apocryphon containing alleged revelations of Jesus, given on the Mount of Olives before his ascension, concerning the moral life of his community and various ritual prescriptions. The order of the collection is not well established, and the whole is transmitted, as often happens (this is a certificate of authenticity!), through the medium of Clement.

The principal difference between the Coptic manuscripts and the others (Melchite or Maronite) comes from the fact that the text is here divided into forty paragraphs, while elsewhere it is not put into canonic form.

Unfortunately, there is no critical edition: Riedel (1900, pp. 166–75) gives a German translation without the Arabic text, and only the Arabic text of the Maronites, according to the version of the metropolitan David, is given in the edition of the *Kitāb al-Hudā* (1935, pp. 249–60). The text of the Copts is rather different, although it and the Melchite have no doubt a common origin; the numerous Greek words, which we find in both, lead one to posit the existence of a Greek original.

It is difficult, for lack of a study of its origin and a comparison with the related documents, to say how old the *Canons* is. Nevertheless, a good judge, F. Nau (1932, col. 1626), is of the opinion that it is a late piece. The presence of numerous Greek words simply transliterated into Arabic characters suggests placing its composition before the Muslim conquest or even before the Council of CHALCEDON in 451.

The *Canons* forms part of the *Sēnōdōs* (synod) of the Ethiopians (Riedel, 1968, p. 155, no. 18); it is given as one of the sources of the *Nomocanon* of al-ṢAFĪ IBN AL-'ASSĀL.

BIBLIOGRAPHY

Darblade, J. B. *La Collection canonique arabe des Melkites (XIIIe–XVIIe siècles).* Fonti serie 2. Harissa, 1946.

David. *Kitāb al-Hudā ou livre de la direction.* Aleppo, 1935.

Khalil, S. "Kitāb al-Hudā, Kitāb al-Kamāl and Kitāb al-Nāmūs." *Orientalia Christiana Periodica* 42 (1976):207–16.

Nau, F. "Canons des apôtres." In *Dictionnaire de théologie catholique,* Vol. 2, cols. 1605–1626. Paris, 1932.

Riedel, W. *Die Kirchenrechtsquellen des Patriarchats Alexandrien.* Leipzig, 1900; repr. Aalen, 1968.

RENÉ-GEORGES COQUIN

CANONS OF EPIPHANIUS, a set of canons prescribing moral rules concerning the clergy and the laity, promulgated by the emperor JUSTINIAN at the instigation of the patriarch of Constantinople. The Epiphanius under whose name these canons are placed is not, as one might be tempted to think, the famous bishop of Salamis in the fourth century but his namesake, the patriarch of Constantinople in the years 520–535.

There are two sets of "canons of Epiphanius," the one containing 137 canons, and the other, 45. The Melchites possess both series, whereas the Copts, who seem to have borrowed it from them, have only the short series of 45. The short series is sometimes attributed to ATHANASIUS, but this is only an error in reading, since the names Epiphanius and Athanasius could be confused in Arabic.

It is understandable that this collection of canons should be attributed to Justinian, for it reproduces the legislation of the sixth novella of the code of this emperor. On the other hand, since it is given only in the Melchite and Coptic collections, it must have an Eastern origin; moreover, given that it derives from after the Council of CHALCEDON in 451, the Copts no doubt borrowed from the Melchites.

Darblade (1946, p. 124) thinks that the larger series is earlier than the council "in Trullo," because it is not mentioned, and later than 535, since it is attributed to the patriarch Epiphanius, who died in 535. As to the shorter series, which is only a résumé of the larger one, it is not known at what period it saw the light or when the Copts adopted it. We can only say that the short series is found in the chronological collection of MACARIUS, a monk of Wādī al-Naṭrūn, in the fourteenth century and in the systematic collection of Michael, bishop of Damietta, who died at the beginning of the thirteenth century. It is mentioned by IBN KABAR in his encyclopedia *Misbāḥ al-Ẓulmah* (1971, p. 152). These texts do not appear in the Greek collections.

There is no critical edition other than the table in

Ibn Kabar's encyclopedia. A German translation will be found in Riedel's work (1900, pp. 289–94). In this Berlin manuscript, thirty-five canons are counted, and they are placed under the name Athanasius of Alexandria, a minor error due to a misreading.

There is scope for correcting the information given by G. Graf (1944, p. 621) relating to the manuscript Cairo 442 (Coptic Patriarchate, Patriarchal Library, Canon 13), which has been identified as being an incomplete manuscript of the *Nomocanon* of the twelfth-century patriarch GABRIEL II ibn Turayk, which gives us the earliest date for the use of these canons by the Copts (Coquin, 1966, pp. 287–88, where this precious manuscript is described).

BIBLIOGRAPHY

Abū al-Barakāt ibn Kabar. *Misbāḥ al-Ẓulmah*. Cairo, 1971.

Coquin, R.-G. *Les Canons d'Hippolyte*. PO 31. Paris, 1966.

Darblade, J. B. *La Collection canonique arabe des Melkites*. Fonti serie 2. Harissa, 1946.

Riedel, W. *Die Kirchenrechtsquellen des Patriarchats Alexandrien*. Leipzig, 1900; repr. Aalen, 1968.

RENÉ-GEORGES COQUIN

CANONS OF GREGORY OF NYSSA, two series of canons under the name GREGORY OF NYSSA, although we have no arguments for or against this attribution. The first series appears in the chronological collection of MACARIUS, in an anonymous chronological collection (now in Berlin), and in the systematic collection of al-ṢAFĪ IBN AL-ʿASSĀL, of which IBN KABAR gives a summary, citing Gregory of Nyssa in his *Misbāḥ al-Ẓulmah* (1971, p. 203). The second series is cited by Michael, bishop of Damietta in the late twelfth and early thirteenth centuries, in his NOMOCANON, Book 1, chapters 4 (on the subject of the construction of the church and its consecration), 7 (on the sacred bases of the altar), and 33 (dealing with the impossibility of celebrating twice on the same day on the same altar). These two series differ: in the first are given four quotations, drawn, the text says, from the works of Gregory of Nyssa; in the second, one may count only three quotations.

We may add that a manuscript that cannot be classified (Vatican Arabicus 123, fol. 20) cites, in dealing with penitence, a fifth canon also attributed to Gregory of Nyssa. The Greek collections contain five extracts purportedly from a letter by Gregory to a Bishop Letoios of Melitene. These extracts, which do not appear in the writings of Gregory of Nyssa, are, however, generally regarded as authentic (Geerard, 1974–1987, no. 3148).

So far as concerns the two series preserved in the Coptic canonical collections, there is no edition of any kind, save for what is given in the collection of Ibn al-ʿAssāl (1928, p. 10), and only a German translation by Riedel (1900, pp. 283–84), not very adequate but at least allowing one to form some idea of the content of these canons. (They are all moral precepts.)

By reason of the lack of a true critical edition of the text, one cannot know its origin and age, for without such an edition one cannot make the necessary comparison with Gregory's authentic works.

In the collection of Macarius and that of Berlin the canons are followed by a list of the patriarchal sees classed according to their order of precedence; the list is purportedly drawn from the works of Gregory of Nyssa, but in reality it appears to be extracted from the eighty-four canons placed under the name of the Council of NICAEA. According to the list, there are four ancient sees, Rome, Alexandria, Ephesus (which has been transferred to Constantinople, the texts says), and Antioch, and then three more recent ones, established at Chalcedon in 451, Jerusalem, Seleucia-Ctesiphon, and the land of the Ethiopians. (In fact, these last three are rather metropolitan sees.) An appendix gives the autocephalous church of Cyprus, which in fact has preeminence over all the other Greek metropolitan sees. The date of this text seems to be only a little later than Chalcedon, and the list is likely to have been borrowed from the Melchites, for the Monophysites, having rejected en bloc the decisions of Chalcedon, never established a patriarchate at either Constantinople or Jerusalem.

BIBLIOGRAPHY

Abū al-Barakāt ibn Kabar. *Misbāḥ al-Ẓulmah*. Cairo, 1971.

Geerard, M., ed. *Clavis Patrum Graecorum*, 5 vols. Turnhout, 1974–1987.

Joannou, P. P. *Les Canons des pères grecs* (Fonti serie 9). Grottaferrata, 1963.

Riedel, W. *Kirchenrechtsquellen des Patriarchats Alexandrien*. Leipzig, 1900; repr. Aalen, 1968.

Safī ibn al-ʿAssāl, al-. *Kitāb al-Qawānīn* (Nomocanon), ed. Murqus Jirjis. Cairo, 1928.

RENÉ-GEORGES COQUIN

CANONS OF HIPPOLYTUS, a series of thirty-eight canons peculiar to the Copts and certainly only a reworking of the famous *Apostolic Tradition* attributed, rightly or wrongly, to the antipope Hippolytus (Geerard, 1974–1987, Vol. 1, no. 1737; see also no. 1742). It would be helpful to know who the author is, an Alexandrian or a Roman, so that one could judge whether those elements of the *Canons of Hippolytus* that are additions to the text of the *Apostolic Tradition* are of Egyptian origin or not. It does seem, however, that this is not a witness to the usages proper to Egypt but simply a work of personal interpretation. But since this text has passed partially into the canonical collections, it could have influenced Egyptian practice. However, since the NOMOCANON, of al-SAFĪ IBN AL-'ASSĀL (which had and has an even greater vogue) cites the *Canons of Hippolytus* very little, their influence on Coptic practice is negligible.

It is certain that the *Canons of Hippolytus* were composed in Greek and thence translated into Coptic and finally into Arabic, the only language in which they have come down to us; only the title survives in Coptic. (It is possible that the copyist of this fragment placed it there, at the head of the *Gnōmai* of the Council of NICAEA, believing that this was the canons attributed to Hippolytus.)

A table of these canons, one that appears very ancient, has been preserved for us by IBN KABAR in Chapter 5 of his famous encyclopedia, *Misbāḥ al-Ẓulmah* ("Lamp of Darkness"), where he transcribed, along with others, the table of the canons.

After canon 1, a kind of introduction in the form of a profession of faith, this text expounds on the different orders that constitute the ecclesiastical community, from the bishop (canon 2) down to the catechumen (canons 19 and 30); then the customs of the Christian community are explained, including fasting (canon 20), observance of Holy Week (canon 22), instruction (canon 23), visiting the sick and providing care for them through the agency of a steward (canons 24 and 25), what must be done at the church (canons 26–29 and 33–37). The plan is not very rigorous, and there are some repetitions. These canons are rounded off by an Easter sermon.

The *Canons of Hippolytus* are cited by the canonical collections, both the chronological ones, such as the collection of MACARIUS (a monk of Wādī al-Naṭrūn in the fourteenth century) and the anonymous Jacobite collection, and the systematic ones, such as the *Nomocanon* of the patriarch GABRIEL II ibn Turayk, the *Nomocanon* of Michael of Damietta, and the one best known, that of al-Ṣafī ibn al-'Assāl. Thus, these *Canons of Hippolytus*, adapted to Egyptian usage, have to some extent survived in Coptic customs through the medium of the canonical collections.

BIBLIOGRAPHY

Abū al-Barakāt ibn Kabar. *Misbāḥ al-Ẓulmah.* Cairo, 1971.

Achelis, H. *Die ältesten Quellen des orientalischen Kirchenrechtes,* Vol. 1, *Die Canones Hippolyti.* Texte und Untersuchungen 6, pt. 4. Leipzig, 1911.

Botte, B. *La Tradition apostolique: Essai de reconstitution.* Liturgiewissenschaftliche Quellen und Forschungen 39. Münster, 1963.

Coquin, R.-G. *Les Canons d'Hippolyte,* pp. 273–444. PO 31. Paris, 1966.

Geerard, M., ed. *Clavis Patrum Graecorum,* 5 vols. Turnhout, 1974–1987.

Haneberg, D. B. von. *Canones S. Hippolyti arabice e codicibus romanis cum versione latina, annotationibus et prolegomenis.* Munich, 1870.

Hanssens, J.-M. "L'Edition critique des canons d'Hippolyte." *Orientalia Christiana Periodica* 32 (1966):536–44.

Riedel, W. *Die Kirchenrechtsquellen des Patriarchats Alexandrien.* Leipzig, 1900; repr. Aalen, 1968.

RENÉ-GEORGES COQUIN

CANONS OF PSEUDO-ATHANASIUS, name used to describe a canonical collection of various prescriptions touching the faithful or the clergy. The great Saint Athanasius cannot have been its author. The absence of mention of Christmas, which was introduced into Egypt among the great festivals in the middle of the fifth century, obliges one to set its composition before that date.

There are fragments in Coptic from the sixth or seventh century and a complete Arabic translation, in which the text is divided into canons, whereas the original text is continuous. The original must have been Greek. The Arabic translation does not seem to be very old, for it is not quoted in the *Nomocanon* of GABRIEL II IBN TURAYK (1131–1145), that of MĪKHĀ'ĪL, BISHOP OF DAMIETTA, or that of al-SĀFĪ IBN AL-'ASSĀL. The canons are invoked in the encyclopedia of Abū al-Barakāt IBN KABAR. The translator, or at least the man who divided the text into 107 canons, was MĪKHĀ'ĪL, bishop of Tinnis, very probably the same man who in 1051 continued for some part the HISTORY OF THE PATRIARCHS perhaps initiated by SĀWĪRUS IBN AL-MUQAFFA'. In any case, they are quoted in the spiritual work of MĪKHĀ'ĪL, bishop of Atrīb and Malīj, who lived in the thirteenth century, and in the chronological collections of the fourteenth century. As with the canons of Pseudo-Basil, one observes profound divergences between the Coptic text peculiar to Egypt and the Arabic version, when both texts are available.

The Coptic fragments and the complete Arabic version were edited and translated into English by W. E. Crum and W. Riedel (1904). New Coptic fragments were published by H. Munier (1920, pp. 238–41).

As in the other juridical compilations, the plan is not very rigorous, and one finds several repetitions. The interested reader should consult the list of these 107 canons as reproduced by ibn Kabar and translated into German by W. Riedel (1900, pp. 554–58).

BIBLIOGRAPHY

Crum, W. E., and W. Riedel, eds. *The Canons of Athanasius of Alexandria.* Text and Translation Society 9. London and Oxford, 1904; repr. Amsterdam, 1973.

Munier, H. "Mélanges de littérature copte 3: Les Canons de saint Athanase." *Annales du Service des antiquités de l'Egypte* 19 (1920):238–41.

Riedel, W. *Die Kirchenrechtsquellen des Patriarchats Alexandrien.* Leipzig, 1900; repr. Aalen, 1968.

RENÉ-GEORGES COQUIN

CANONS OF SAINT BASIL,

CANONS OF SAINT BASIL, one of the sources of Coptic church law. They appear in two series. The first, containing thirteen canons, is shared with the Melchites; the second, of 105 or 106 canons, is peculiar to the Copts.

The first series includes disciplinary sanctions with regard to priests or deacons and the prohibition against the burning of relics or of the Eucharist. These canons appear to be borrowed from the works of Saint Basil. The 105 or 106 canons are preserved partly in Coptic, but the complete text has survived only in Arabic. The original was written in Greek. As is shown by canons 15, 46, and 95, the text was composed outside Egypt. In particular, canons 46 and 95 show an ecclesiastical organization based on the metropolitan. In Egypt everything depended on the patriarch, and it was to him that the ordination of bishops reverted. For this reason the canons of Basil, which confer upon the metropolitan the right of ordaining bishops, cannot have been composed in Egypt and were probably borrowed from Syria.

We possess in Coptic an extract from canon 1 (Drescher, 1951, pp. 252, 255, 256) and canon 36 (Kahle, Vol. 1, pp. 410, 413–415, 416). Canons 14, 28–33, 38–40, 90, 93, and 94 are preserved in the Turin papyri (see Orlandi, 1974, p. 125). Canons 48–96 are in the Chester Beatty fragments, which are parchments deriving from the White Monastery (Dayr Anbā Shinūdah). The Coptic text is sometimes remote from the Arabic, to the point that the latter appears to be a reworking of the original text. It cannot be said to what extent it has been "adapted" to the Egyptian situation. As they appear in Arabic (Riedel, 1900, pp. 233ff.), the Canons of Basil include a trinitarian and Christological profession of faith (canon 1). They then speak of the two ways, of good and evil (canon 2); of marriage and its discipline (canons 3–19); penitence (canons 20–27); and the clergy (canons 38–95). They end with rules concerning the liturgy (canons 96–106). Alongside archaic prescriptions, such as those concerning *virgines subintroductae* (women living with men in spiritual marriage), they contain passages that are relevant to the Arab period (e.g., canon 86). They deserve a better critical edition.

BIBLIOGRAPHY

Crum, W. E. "The Coptic Version of the Canons of St. Basil." *Proceedings of the Society of Biblical Archeology* 26 (1904):57–62.

Drescher, J. "A Coptic Lectionary Fragment." *Annales du Service des Antiquités d'Egypte* 51 (1951):247–56.

Kahle, P. E. *Bala'izah,* 2 vols. London, 1954.

Orlandi, T. "Les papyrus coptes du Musée égyptien de Turin." *Le Muséon* 87 (1974):115–27.

———. "Les manuscrits coptes de Dublin, du British Museum et de Vienne." *Le Muséon* 89 (1976):323–38.

Riedel, W. *Die Kirchenrechtsquellen des Patriarchats Alexandrien.* Leipzig, 1900; repr. Aalen, 1968.

RENÉ-GEORGES COQUIN

CANONS OF SAINT JOHN CHRYSOSTOM,

CANONS OF SAINT JOHN CHRYSOSTOM, twelve ordered extracts from the second and, especially, the third of the six books of the treatise *On the Priesthood,* by JOHN CHRYSOSTOM.

This collection is peculiar to the Copts. It is not known at what date the Copts inserted the canons into their canonical collections. These may be divided into two groups, the chronological and the systematic. The chronological collections include the anonymous one of Berlin (colophons of the fourteenth century; Coquin, 1966, pp. 285–86), that of the fourteenth-century monk MACARIUS of Wādī al-Naṭrūn, and the anonymous "Jacobite" collection (Riedel, 1900, p. 136). The systematic collections include that of MĪKHĀ'ĪL of Damietta, who died at the beginning of the thirteenth century, and that of al-ṢAFĪ IBN AL-'ASSĀL. It was also cited by IBN KABAR in *Misbāḥ al-Ẓulmah* (1971, p. 182). It is proper to correct, or rather to state precisely, what Graf says (1944, vol. 1, p. 609). What he indicates simply by "Kairo 442" is the manuscript Coptic Patriarchate, Canon 13, which has been identified as an incomplete manuscript of the NOMOCANON of the twelfth-century patriarch GABRIEL II (Ibn Turayk), which gives us the oldest use of this text by the Copts (Coquin, 1966, pp. 287–88).

These canons will be found in a German translation in Riedel's work (1900, pp. 285–87), which may be compared with the complete text of John Chrysostom, for example, the editions of the Society for Promoting Christian Knowledge (1964) and of Sources chrétiennes (1980).

BIBLIOGRAPHY

Abū al-Barakāt ibn Kabar. *Misbāḥ al-Ẓulmah.* Cairo, 1971.

Coquin, R.-G. *Las Canons d'Hippolyte.* PO 31. Paris, 1966.

John Chrysostom. *John Chrysostom: De sacerdotio,* ed. J. A. Nairn. Cambridge Patristic Texts 4. Cambridge, 1906.

______. *Six books on the Priesthood.* London, 1964; revised version of 1906 edition, New York and London, 1978.

______. *Jean Chrysostome sur le sacerdoce,* ed. A. M. Malingrey. Sources chrétiennes 272. Paris, 1980.

Riedel, W. *Die Kirchenrechtsquellen des Patriarchats Alexandrien.* Leipzig, 1900; repr. Aalen, 1968.

RENÉ-GEORGES COQUIN

CANOPUS. *See* Metanoia, Monastery of the.

CANOPY. *See* Architectural Elements of Churches: Baldachin.

CANTICLES, BIBLICAL. *See* Music, Coptic: Canticles.

CANTOR, leader and director of the chanting of the choir and the congregation during the liturgy and other occasions such as ceremonial processions. He is usually a deacon but may also be a layman. He should have a thorough knowledge of hymnology, psalmody, and all forms of responsory, besides church ritual and traditions. His duties also include the teaching of hymns to other deacons and members of the congregation.

Cantors had a recognized position in the Old Testament. David is referred to as "the sweet psalmist of Israel" (2 Sm. 23:1). The New Testament attaches equal importance to chanting: "addressing one another in psalms and hymns and spiritual songs, singing and making melody to the Lord with all your heart" (Eph. 5:19). Likewise, "Let the word of Christ dwell in you richly, as you teach and admonish one another in all wisdom, and as you sing psalms and hymns and spiritual songs with thankfulness in your hearts to God" (Col. 3:16). In Revelation 15:2, 3, Mark 14:26, Acts 16:25, James 5:13, and 1 Corinthians 14:26, we find further reference to singing as an important form of worship throughout the apostolic age.

Considerable care is taken in the selection and training of cantors, in view of their vital role in Coptic ritual.

[*See also:* Music, Coptic: Cantors.]

ARCHBISHOP BASILIOS

CAP. *See* Liturgical Vestments.

CAPE. *See* Liturgical Vestments.

CAPITALS. *See* Architectural Elements of Churches: Column.

CARACCIOLI, CLEMENT, scribe of four Arabic manuscripts copied in Rome between 1712 and 1715. One of them (Vatican Library, Arabic 66) gives some autobiographical details (fol. 100) where the copyist wrote in Italian: "I Clement Caraccioli of Great Cairo, converted from Mohammedanism to the holy Catholic faith, wrote this blessed book in the Arabic language in Rome, in the year XII of the pontificate of our Lord Pope Clement XI Albani, may God preserve him for many years, on the 12th September of the year 1712" (Mai, 1831, p. 129).

On the same page, a note written in Arabic further states that he had lived thirty-three years in error, exercising the function of a Muslim *imām*.

Clement was a Muslim from Cairo, probably originally from Upper Egypt, as is indicated by his *nisbah* (place of origin) al-Ṣaʿīdī. He was converted at the age of thirty-three or thirty-four by the European missionaries then active in Cairo and was sent to Rome, probably around 1710, where he no doubt increased his knowledge of Christianity and copied Arabic manuscripts for the Bibliotheca Apostolica.

According to Giorgio Levi della Vida, who does not give his source, his real name was ʿAbd al-Karīm al-Ṣaʿīdī al-ʿAdawī. In the manuscripts he copied, Clement always signed his name as a neophyte, transcribing it as Klīmintī Karājillī in 1713 (in Beirut 672) and Klimanṣ Karātjillī in 1715 (in Beirut 676). His given name was probably taken on account of Clement XI (1700–1721); his surname may derive from the marquess Luigi Antonio Caraccioli, who would thus appear to have been his protector.

The following are manuscripts copied by Clement:

1. Vatican Arabic 66 (dated 9 September 1712), containing the eighty-seven homilies of JOHN CHRYSOSTOM, after the Coptic recension (cf. Graf, Vol. 1, p. 338).
2. Vatican Arabic 128 (dated 18 February 1713), containing the debate of the monk Georg (JIRJĪ AL-SIMʿĀNĪ; cf. Graf, Vol. 2, p. 79, 5).
3. Oriental Library, Beirut, 672 (dated 1713).
4. Oriental Library, Beirut, 676 (dated 25 April 1715).

BIBLIOGRAPHY

Cheikho, L. *Catalogue raisonné des manuscrits de la Bibliothèque Orientale*, Vol. 6: *Controverses*. Mélanges de l'Université Saint-Joseph 14, pp. 49–51 [409–11], nos. 672 and 676. Beirut, 1929.

Levi Della Vida, G. *Richerche sulla formazione del più antico fondo dei manoscritti orientali della Biblioteca Vaticana*. Vol. 2, n. 1. Vatican City, 1939.

Mai, A. ed. *Codices Vaticani Assemaniani*, pp. 122–29, no. 66; pp. 252–53, no. 128. Rome, 1831.

KHALIL SAMIR, S. J.

CARION OF SCETIS. *See* Zacharias of Scetis.

CARPOCRATES, an Alexandrian of the middle of the second century who was said to be a successor of CERINTHUS. Carpocrates, along with his followers, was attacked more for immoral practices than for doctrinal error. Aside from making a general charge concerning the nature of Christ and the identity of the creator of the world, IRENAEUS dwelled on the licentious practices of the Carpocratian sect, especially rejecting their opinion-based justification for such activities. In a statement disputed by recent commentators, CLEMENT OF ALEXANDRIA asserted that Carpocrates was instructed in the monadic *gnosis*. In the recently discovered letter of Clement of Alexandria to an unknown Theodorus, Clement charged Carpocrates with having obtained illegally a copy of a secret gospel of Mark (see MARK, SECRET GOSPEL OF), which he then corrupted and misinterpreted publicly. The lack of evidence in such statements and charges makes it impossible to evaluate them properly.

BIBLIOGRAPHY

Foerster, W. *Gnosis*, trans. R. McL. Wilson, pp. 34–40. Oxford, 1972.

Griggs, C. W. *Early Egyptian Christianity*, pp. 47–49. Leiden, 1990.

C. WILFRED GRIGGS

CASSIAN, SAINT JOHN, monk and author of a monastic rule. John Cassian was born around 360, no doubt in the neighborhood of the present town of Constantza, Romania. After receiving a first-rate education, John Cassian was initiated into the monastic life at Bethlehem. He soon undertook a pilgrimage to the Egyptian monastic sites, which so impressed him that he decided to stay in Egypt. He first met a number of solitaries and celebrated *hegumenoi* (leaders of monasteries) in the Nile Delta (at Thennesus, Thmuis, Panephysis, and DIOLKOS) before going to settle at SCETIS. It is very unlikely that he visited the monasteries of Upper Egypt, which included many Pachomian establishments.

The quarrels about ANTHROPOMORPHISM in 399 led him to leave Egypt. He was later at Constantinople and then at Antioch, and he took part in one or two legations from these patriarchal sees to that of Rome. At some time after 414 he was in Marseilles, where, at the request of Western monks, he undertook to put into writing the fruits of his long sojourn in Egypt. Between 420 and 430 he composed in succession *De institutis coenobiorum* (Cenobitic Institutes) and twenty-four *Conlationes* (Conferences of the Fathers), divided into three series. Before his death he participated in anti-Nestorian polemic with his treatise *On the incarnation of the Lord* (*De incarnatione Domini contra Nestorium*).

Cassian thus represents a kind of link between the Eastern and Western branches of the church at a time when they were beginning to draw apart—hence, the importance of the historical and spiritual testimony that he gave the Western monks about Egyptian monachism.

Paradoxically, the evidence from Cassian's writings is of scarcely any use for fixing the locations of the monastic settlements in Lower Egypt. The few indications he makes correspond ill with those given by other contemporary writings, and they cannot be confirmed by present topography (Guy, 1966, pp. 363–72).

As for the monks whom he visited and consulted, biographical information is fragmentary, uncertain, and sometimes nonexistent. Consideration is given only to the fourteen Egyptian monks who are spokesmen in the *Conlationes*.

The monks of Scetis include the following:

Moses (*Conlationes* I and II; cf. *Institutis coenobiorum* X 25 and, perhaps, *Conl.* XIX 9.1). A former brigand, it seems that he should be identified with Moses of Calamus in *Conl.* III 5.2 and VII 26–27. His life could not be described without reference to the parallel sources, especially *Historia Lausiaca* (see PALLADIUS) and APOPHTHEGMATA PATRUM (cf. Guy, 1963, pp. 139–45).

PAPHNUTIUS (*Conl.* III). Cassian knew him personally, and information concerning him is more precise. At first a cenobite (*Conl.* XVIII 16.7), although we do not know in which monastery, he soon sought solitude and gave himself up to it with such ardor that he was given the sobriquet *bubal*, the wild ox (*Conl.* III 1.1–3; XVIII 15.1). At Scetis he was in the school of ISIDORUS, whose successor he became after being ordained a priest (*Conl.* XVIII 15.2–8). He seems then to have acted with a special authority (cf. *Inst. coen.* V 40.1; *Conl.* IV 1.1–2; II 5.4; X 2–3). Even in his nineties, he still refused to have younger men supply him with water.

Daniel (*Conl.* IV). Unknown elsewhere, this disciple of Paphnutius was ordained priest to succeed him, but died prematurely.

Serapion (*Conl.* V). No information is given about his life; he is simply presented as a spiritual father full of discernment (*Conl.* II 10–11; XVIII 11.2–4). Perhaps he should be identified with Sarapion of Scetis, who with difficulty acknowledged the Festal Letter of Theophilus (*Conl.* X 3.1; cf. Guy, 1966, pp. 147–49).

Serenos (*Conl.* VII and VIII). No information about him is given.

Isaac (*Conl.* IX and X). No information about him is given, and nothing to locate him in relation to others known as Isaac (cf. Guy, 1966, p. 102).

The monks of the Nile Delta include the following:

Chaeremon (*Conl.* XI, XII, and XIII), at Thennesus. Cassian met him at the beginning of his stay (c. 386). Then more than a hundred years old, Chaeremon was very austere and refused to have any disciples.

Nesteros (*Conl.* XIV and XV). No information about him is given.

Joseph (*Conl.* XVI and XVII). Of noble family and a native of Thmuis, he spoke both Coptic and Greek. Perhaps he should be identified with Joseph of Panepho in the *Apophthegmata Patrum*.

Piamun (*Conl.* XVIII). He lived in the region of Diolkos, where he was the oldest of the anchorites and served them as priest (*Conl.* XVII 24.1).

John (*Conl.* XIX). After thirty years in a *coenobium* (monastery) and twenty in solitude, he returned to the *coenobium* when it became too difficult to find solitude in the desert. He is also called John of Thmuis (*Inst. coen.* V. 27–28; *Conl.* XIV 4.2). He should be distinguished from another John charged with the DIACONIA at Scetis (*Inst. coen.* V 40.1; *Conl.* XXI 1.2–3; cf. Guy, 1966, p. 116).

Pinufius (*Conl.* XX). He is known only from Cassian, who held him in special esteem (*Inst. coen.* IV 30–31). Priest of an immense *coenobium* near Panephysis, he fled from glory and went incognito to Tabennēsē. When recognized, he returned home but soon took flight again. He went to Bethlehem, where Cassian met him, but recognized once more, he returned to his *coenobium*. There Cassian met him again and heard his address on penitence and his celebrated "discourse on taking the habit" (reproduced or composed afresh in *Inst. coen.* IV 32–43).

Theonas (*Conl.* XXI, XXII, and XXIII). While still an adolescent, he was married off by his parents; but five years later an exhortation by John (perhaps of Thmuis) made him resolve to leave his wife to enter the monastery, where he succeeded John at the head of the *diaconia*.

Abraham (*Conl.* XXIV). From a well-to-do family, he lived in great solitude four miles from the Nile. He is different from the Abraham who was called "the Simple" (*Conl.* XV 4–5), and from those whose memory is preserved in the *Apophthegmata Patrum.*

Clearly, Cassian has little concern for providing his readers with historical information, even about those personages who played a large part in his work. It is Cassian's spiritual testimony that constitutes his fundamental contribution, for he was less concerned with reporting what he had seen or even the reading that he had done (notably in the Pachomian and Evagrian literature) than with organizing the whole into a coherent doctrinal corpus. Drawing on his personal experiences in the desert, his works confidently set forth the first pedagogical treatise on the experience of God as it had been gradually worked out in the concrete practice of the Egyptian monks.

According to Cassian, "spiritual combat" is not conducted haphazardly. One can only engage in it by going to school with a master or senior adept—that is to say, a man experienced in the discernment of what, beyond appearances, is in conformity with the aim of purity of heart and with the end of the monastic life, the Kingdom of God. To reach it, one must methodically pass through all the stages that lead to it, from "the formation of the outer man" (*Inst. coen.* V–XII: the eight capital vices, a theory taken over from EVAGRIUS), to the formation of "the inner man," (*Conl.* I–X), which is essentially an education in discernment and an opening up toward perpetual prayer. Only then can one enter upon the questions that relate to the "perfecting" of the inner man (*Conl.* XI–XVII and XVIII–XXIV). These concern human cooperation with the grace of God, the relation between ANACHORESIS and cenobitism, and, above all, the "spiritual science," or inward knowledge of the scriptures, thanks to which the monk will be able "to adhere to God without ceasing."

In all this, Cassian was in no way original, borrowing everything from those monks whose way of life he shared (chiefly from Evagrius). Yet he was unique in the breadth of his purpose and the vigor of his personal reflection. Under the guise of a simple compiler who might allow himself only some slight adaptations to the Western climate and context, Cassian in reality laid the foundation of the first coherent pedagogy of Christian experience, and he did so by reworking and transposing into a new culture the experiences received from the monks of Egypt.

BIBLIOGRAPHY

Cappuyns, M. "Cassien." In *Dictionnaire d'histoire et de géographie ecclésiastique* 11, cols. 1319–48. Paris, 1949.

Chadwick, O. *John Cassian: A Study in Primitive Monasticism.* Cambridge, 1968.

Chitty, D.-J. *The Desert a City: An Introduction to the Study of Egyptian Monasticism,* 2nd ed. Oxford, 1977.

Codina, V. *El Aspecto cristologico en la espiritualidad de Juan Casiano.* Orientalia Christiana Analecta 175. Rome, 1966.

Cotelier, J. B., ed. *Apophthegmata Patrum.* PG 65, pp. 71–440. Paris, 1864.

Cristiani, L. *Jean Cassien,* 2 vols. Saint-Wandrille, 1946.

Evelyn-White, H. G. *The Monasteries of the Wadi'n Natrūn,* pt. 2. New York, 1932.

Griffe, E. "Cassien a-t-il été prêtre d'Antioche?" *Bulletin de Littérature ecclésiastique* (1954):140–45.

Guy, J.-C. *Jean Cassien. Vie et doctrine spirituelle.* Paris, 1961.

———. *Le Centre monastique de Scété au IVème et au début du Vème siècle: Prosopographie et histoire.* Rome, 1963.

———. *Jean Cassien, historien du monachisme égyptien?* pp. 363–72. Studia Patristica 8. Berlin, 1966.

Heussi, K. *Der Ursprung des Mönchtums.* Tübingen, 1936.

Kemmer, A. *Charisma Maximum: Untersuchung zu Cassians Vollkommenheitslehre und seine Stellung zum Messalianismus.* Louvain, 1938.

Leroy, J. "Les préfaces des écrits monastiques de Jean Cassien." *Revue d'ascétique et de mystique* 42 (1966):157–80.

Marrou, H.-I. "Jean Cassien à Marseille." *Revue du Moyen Age latin* 1 (1945):5–26.

———. "La Patrie de Jean Cassien." *Orientalia Christiana Periodica* 13 (1947):588–96.

Marsili, S. *Giovanni Cassiano ed Evagrio Pontico. Dottrina sulla carità e contemplazione.* Rome, 1936.

Olphe-Galliard, M. "Les Sources de la conférence XI de Cassien." *Revue d'Ascétique et de Mystique* 16 (1935):289–98.

———. "Cassien." In *Dictionnaire de spiritualité, ascétique et mystique,* Vol. 2, pp. 214–76. Paris, 1932.

Pricolo, S. *L'isola dei santi: Il cenobio di Lerino e gli origini del monachesimo gallico.* Rome, 1978.

Prinz, F. *Frühes Mönchtum im Frankenreich.* Munich and Vienna, 1965.

———. "Cassiano." In *Dizionario degli Istituti di Perfezione,* Vol. 2, pp. 633–38. Rome, 1975.

Rousseau, P. *Ascetics, Authority and the Church in the Age of Jerome and Cassian.* Oxford, 1978.

Weber, H. O. *Die Stellung des J. Cassianus zur ausserpachomianischen Mönchstradition: Eine Quellenuntersuchung.* Münster, 1961.

Wrzol, L. "Die Psychologie des Johannes Cassianus." *Divus Thomas* 32 (1918):181–214, 425–56; 34 (1920):70–96; 36 (1922):269–94; 37 (1923): 385–404; 38 (1924):84–91.

JEAN-CLAUDE GUY

CASTANETS. *See* Metalwork, Coptic; Music, Coptic: Musical Instruments.

CASTRUM, Roman military camp developed from the so-called marching camp, which was constructed each evening by troops on the march in accordance with a model in force throughout the Roman empire. The uniformity of the camps enabled the soldiers to find their way about and also enabled them to react with speed in the face of danger. We are well informed on the appearance of these camps by a number of ancient descriptions (Polybius, 6. 27–32; Hyginus, *De munitionibus castrorum;* Flavius Vegetius Renatus, *Epitoma rei militaris*) and by numerous surviving monuments. As a rule, the camps have a square or slightly oblong shape within which two main streets run at right angles to each other: a wide street running across, the *via principalis* joining the two lateral gates, and the *via praetoria* running along the longer axis, but interrupted in the center by the camp forum and the principia. The latter is the sanctuary of the camp in which the standards of the legion as well as the images of the imperial family were set up. Behind it was situated the tent of the commander in chief, itself surrounded by the arsenal, the hospital, and the assembly areas of the various units. The soldiers' quarters proper were arranged in uniform blocks around these central installations. Finally the whole camp was surrounded by a rampart with an outer trench, as well as a circular road running along the inner side of the rampart, the *via sagularis.* The corners of the castrum were rounded off. The gates were located one at each end of the two main streets and were strengthened by towers erected on the inner ramparts.

The actual permanent camps, which originally functioned as winter camps, differ from the marching camps only by their more permanent design. Instead of the rampart they have a high defense wall which, from the second century, was also provided with towers projecting outward. All the buildings inside it including the men's living quarters were constructed of stone or fired bricks. The higher officers had their own houses while the commander of the legion had a large residence that served at the same time as the headquarters of the legion (*praetorium*). In the days of the empire the *principia* was combined with the forum, which originally was situated next to the *praetorium.* Outside the castrum were located a variety of workshops, brick works, baths, and often even an amphitheater. An innovation under Valentinian I (364–375) was the removal of the men's living quarters to the immediate vicinity of the wall (Petrikovits, 1967, p. 21), a practice already introduced in the eastern empire at an earlier period. Presumably this measure was due to the development of ballistics that required better protection; the area at the wall provided such better than the area situated nearer the center.

The smaller camps (*castella*) were originally planned only for the auxiliary troups, whose members did not possess Roman citizenship. After the general conferment of citizenship by Emperor Caracalla this distinction fell into disuse. The *castella* then became camps for smaller contingents of troops: the foot soldiers or the cavalry. Each of these consisted of approximately 500 or 1,000 men. In their structure these smaller camps were modeled on the large camps of the legions, only in a more simple form, although as a rule they made do with a smaller number of gates.

A considerable number of Roman military camps in Egypt are known through inscriptions and texts handed down. Very few structural remains have survived and the majority of these come from the period after DIOCLETIAN. Surviving examples follow the same plan that was adopted in the rest of the provinces of the empire. Imitations of the fort architecture of the pharaonic period are nowhere to be seen. There are several camps constructed in deserted temple enclosures.

In pagan times the military camps were each provided with a *principia,* in which the standards of the companies and also, from the third century, the images of the emperor were set up and the funds of the legion were kept. The camps laid out in the Christian period, from about the fifth century, naturally had a church. Examples of such camp churches are preserved in Egyptian camps in Abūṣīr (Taposiris Magna) and al-Tūr.

Alexandria. The legionary camp situated to the east of Alexandria near ancient Nicopolis was found in good condition up to the year 1875. In addition to the surrounding walls that were preserved almost throughout, remains of the *praetorium* and thermal installation could be seen. All the plans depict semicircular projecting bastions with square towers at the corners; however, the picture taken by T. Walsh (1803, pl. 23) shows round corner towers and rectangular towers in between, which suggest a construction probably from the final building phase in the late Roman period. In 1875 what remained of the camp fell victim to the construction of the English barracks.

Abūṣīr. For the erection in late antiquity of the camp in the precinct of the Ptolemaic temple of Osiris, use was made of materials from the temple building itself, which was probably of Doric design. The men's living quarters, which were one story high, were positioned along the wall. Remains of steps leading up to the wall coping have survived in the southeast and southwest corners (Grossmann, 1980, pp. 23–24). Within the camp near to the pylon passageway a small single-aisled church with a tripartite sanctuary was found (Ward Perkins, 1943–1944, pp. 49–51). The naos of the church was later surrounded on all sides by additional annexes.

Al-Būrdān. This was a cohort fort in the region of the coastal road to Marsā Maṭrūḥ, about 3 miles (5 km) west of the turnoff to al-Ḥammām. It measured 382 × 382 yards (350 × 350 m). Before 1970 the remains of the exterior wall as well as several indications of the inside buildings and a vaulted cistern could still be recognized. Road construction has completely destroyed them.

Babylon or Old Cairo. Situated on the border between Upper and Lower Egypt, this camp comes from the period of Emperor Trajan (89–117) and until the capitulation before the invading Arab armies in 641 it was the most important stronghold in Egypt. Significant elements of its military defenses have been preserved especially in the southwest area, as, for example, the gate facing south on the landward side and the harbor gate provided with two strong circular towers (Toy, 1937, pp. 52–78). Both gates must count among the best preserved Roman gate installations of the second century.

Scenas Mandras. Near the modern village of Mīnat al-Shurafā' (south of Ḥilwān), this is a camp from late antiquity in the southeast of a *kom* (mound) almost completely dismantled by *sabakh* (manure) diggers and lime-burners. A double exterior wall was found during the excavations, as well as several towers and the remains of house installations leaning against the inner side of the surrounding wall.

Qaṣr Qarūn. This fort of a 500-man unit of cavalry is one of the best-preserved camps from the period of Diocletian. The surrounding wall may be clearly made out with its towers and especially the living quarters and the forum shaped like a columned street, with the *principia* at the southern end. To the west of the forum were the administration building and the commandant's living quarters.

Umm al-Barakāt. The clearing of the temple of Suchos led to the discovery alongside the surrounding wall of numerous house plans of the same shape, which most probably were the living quarters of a military unit stationed here in the fifth or sixth century. The presence of these units may well have contributed to the survival of the site into the Christian period (Bagnani, 1933).

Dayr al-Dīk. The camp probably served as the military guard of the city of ANTINOOPOLIS. The surrounding wall had rounded corners but no towers. Of buildings on the inside, a number of living quarters remain on the north wall, as well as a cruciform central building on the east wall. Additional buildings go back only as far as a late medieval settlement.

Dayr al-Jabrāwī. Two parallel series of columns running approximately north–south and all made of burnt bricks could have flanked a camp forum or the *via praetoria* as in the Diocletian fort of Qaṣr Qarūn (see above).

Hiw (Diospolis Parva). The Roman fort, which was occupied by a unit the size of a cohort, coincides in size with the area of the Ptolemaic temple, whose exterior wall was repaired and equipped with a number of round towers. The buildings of the men's living quarters as well as a number of officers' residences were observed beside the north wall. This arrangement is in evidence only from the first century down to Gallienus, and accordingly does not appear to have survived the revolt under Domitianus in the third century (Flinders Petrie, 1901, pp. 54–57, pl. 24).

Luxor. The great camp housing two legions was first built in 297 under the emperor Diocletian, on the occasion of the defeat of the revolts in Upper Egypt under Domitianus, and it encompassed the whole area of the Ammon temple, which at that time was no longer in operation, although large parts of it were still standing (El-Saghir, 1986, pp. 5–31). The pylon passage was converted into the northern main gateway. Other Roman buildings

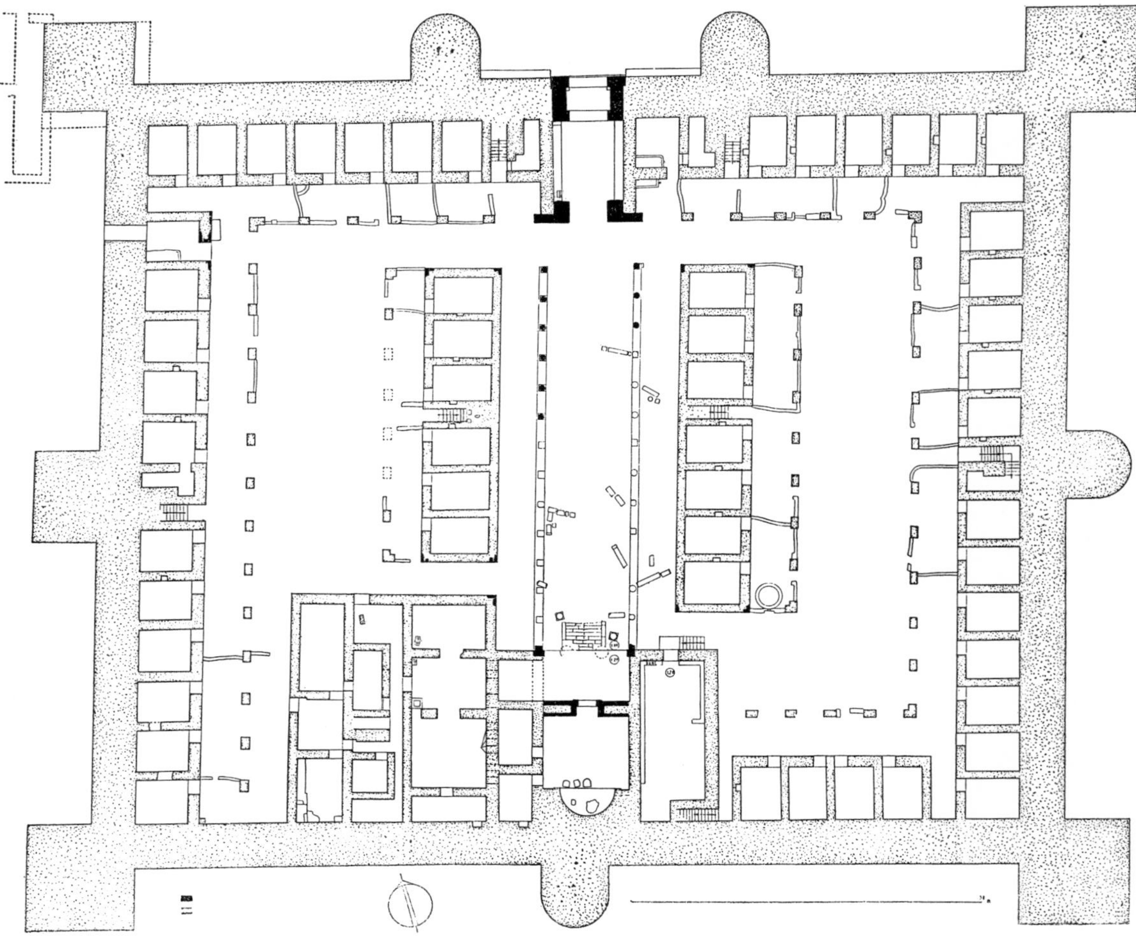

Plan of the *castrum* Qaṣr Qarūn. *Courtesy Peter Grossmann.*

have survived including the remains of the surrounding wall and above all the once richly decorated principia with its niche for the cult of the emperor (wrongly identified as a "church" in earlier times) constructed in front of the earlier barque chamber (Deckers, 1979, pp. 600–652).

Naj' al-Ḥajar. The camp of a 500-man company discovered in the 1980s, it has a gateway complex decorated with engaged columns and a number of protruding semicircular towers, probably going back to the time of Diocletian.

Aswan. Located here are extensive remains of a fortification wall that followed the line of the river, with its two square corner towers and two semicircular intervening towers. It survived into the nineteenth century and indicated the existence of the camp of a 1,000-man unit often referred to in the papyri of the fifth and sixth centuries. In the Middle Ages the camp fortification was incorporated into the city wall, and a small church was built in front of the northwest corner (Jaritz, 1985, pp. 1–19).

Elephantine. The camp built in the Roman forecourt of the Temple of Khnum was probably that of the Cohort I Felix Theodosius. The men's living quarters had a number of stories, and most of them were accommodated in the surrounding columned porticos, although a few were located within the temple area. The side entrances into the temple court appear to have been rebuilt in the form of towers (Grossmann, 1980, pp. 9–29).

Philae. This camp was not situated on the island itself, as often wrongly claimed, but lay on the west bank opposite on the former site of Shallāl, where remains of the outer ditch as well as of two towers could be seen (Grossmann, 1980, p. 27).

Dakka (Pselchis), Nubia. Roman camp of the second to third centuries, it incorporated at the same time the temple of Dakka. Up to the time of the

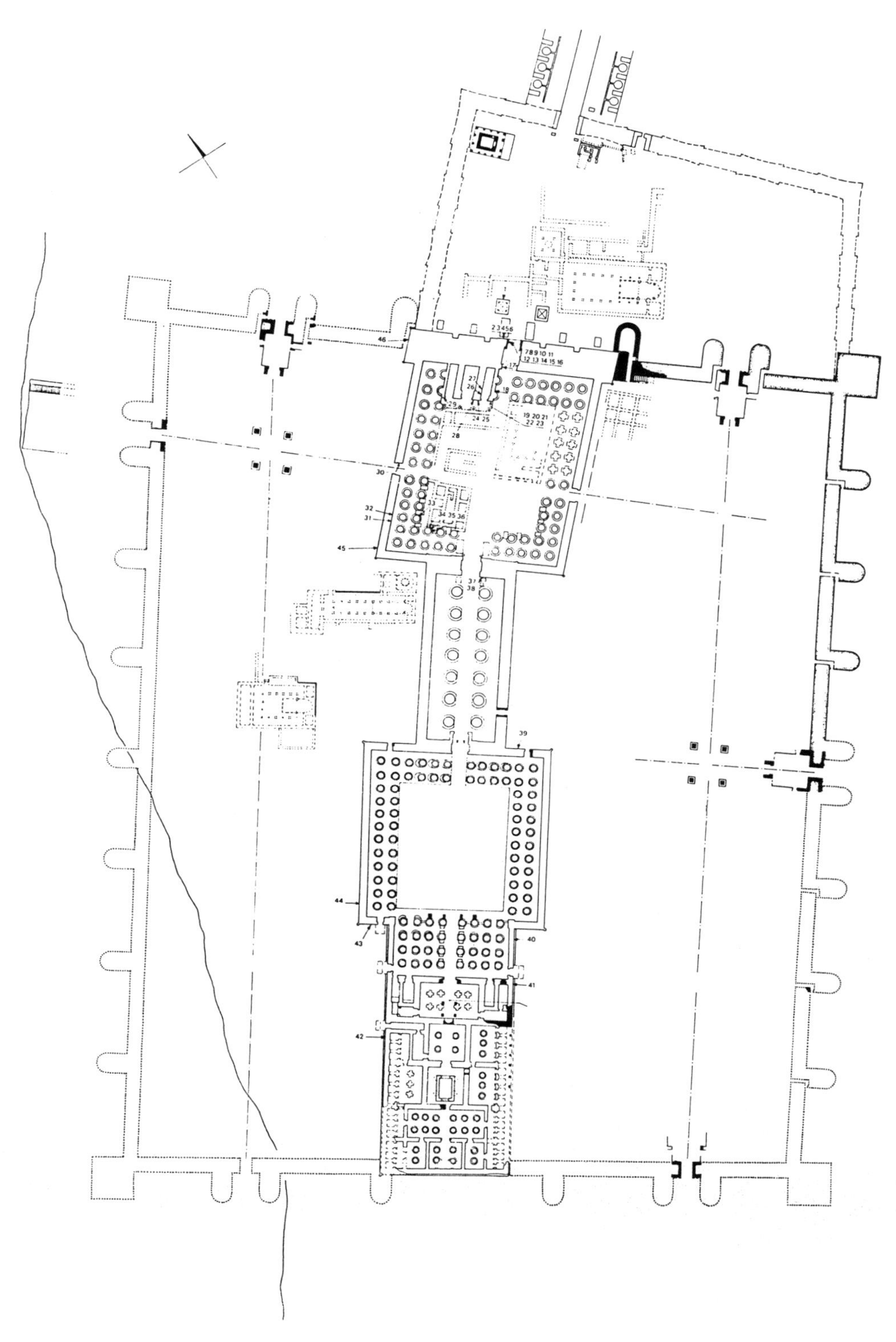

Plan of the *castrum* at Luxor. *Courtesy Peter Grossmann.*

flooding caused by the damming of the Nile, remains of the clay-brick wall, which had been repeatedly reinforced, and two gates on the southwest had survived. Both gates were flanked by protruding semicircular towers. It would appear that in the fourth century nomads occupied it and reinforced the west gate with rectangular porticos.

Al-Dayr (Oasis of Khargah). This fortified camp, probably of a cavalry detachment of 500 men, is a perfect square with semicircular protruding towers and a single gateway on the west side, which unlike the other sections was constructed of fired bricks. Curiously, the stairs are not attached to the inner wall but carved into the wall (Naumann, 1939, pp. 2–3).

Abū Sha'ār. This was a cohort fort at the coast of the Red Sea, 7½ miles (12 km) north of Hurghada, although American investigations have erroneously identified it with the site of Myos Homos. It has regularly distributed towers at the corners and at all four sides. The two gates at the northern and western sides correspond to the two inner main streets. A number of barracks are placed alongside the walls, while the rest are grouped in several blocks in the northern part of the inner area. The so-called main building, erected in the middle of the eastern part, has an inner eastern apse and probably served as the church of the fortress. To the south of it are workshops and warehouses (Sidebotham et al., 1989, pp. 127–66).

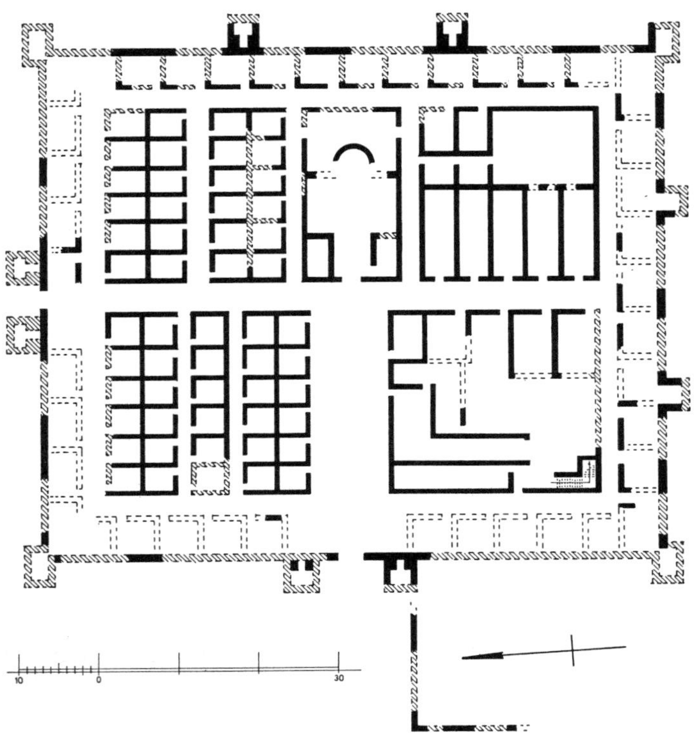

Plan of the Abū Sha'ār fort. *Courtesy Peter Grossmann.*

Tall Faramā (Pelusium). The surrounding wall with its square corner towers and numerous half-rounded bastions are all that remain of a late Roman camp that was occupied by a cavalry detachment. Since 1983 the site has been excavated by the Egyptian Antiquities Organization. The men's living quarters were sited alongside the walls, outside of which cisterns and baths were also found.

Tall Abū Sayf. This is probably to be identified with ancient Selle or Sile. Only one mud-brick wall running for 110 yards (100 m) in a north–south direction has so far been identified of the fort (Flinders Petrie, 1888, pp. 98–99, pl. 51); on the eastern border itself numerous Roman tombs were found (unpublished).

Al-Ṭūr. On the area of the Greek cemetery a few miles inland from al-Ṭūr, well-preserved remains of an extensive fortification system, with corner towers and uniform rooms laid out along the surrounding wall, were excavated by the Egyptian Antiquities Organization. It would appear that it is a late Roman fort originating perhaps in the sixth century. In the southwest section, a church of basilica design with stout square pillars and a tripartite sanctuary was found.

BIBLIOGRAPHY

Bagnani, G. "Gli scavi di Tebtunis." *Bollettino d'arte* 27 (1933):119–34.

Biernacka-Lubanska, J. *The Roman and Early-Byzantine Fortifications of Lower Moesia and Northern Thrace.* Warsaw, 1982.

Breccia, E. "Lesquier Jean—L'armée romaine d'Egypte, d'Auguste à Dioclétien." *Bulletin de la Société archéologique d'Alexandrie* 17 (1919–1920):281.

Cosson, A. de. "Notes on the Coast Road Between Alexandria and Mars Matruh." *Bulletin de la Société archéologique d'Alexandrie* 34 (1941):51–52.

Deckers, J. G. "Die Wandmalerei im Kaiserkultraum von Luxor." *Jahrbuch des deutschen archäologischen Instituts* 94 (1979):600–652.

El-Saghir, M., et al. *Le camp romain de Louqsor.* Cairo, 1986.

Flinders Petrie, W. M. *Tanis II.* London, 1888.

______. *Diospolis Parva.* London, 1901.

Grossmann, P. *Elephantine II.* Mainz, 1980.

Jaritz, H. "Die Kirche der Heiligen Psōti von der Stadtmauer von Assuan." *Mélanges Gamal Eddie*

Mokhtar. Bibliotèque d'études 97, 2, pp. 1–19.
Johnstone, S., *Late Roman Fortifications*. London, 1983.
Maspero, J. *Organisation militaire de l'Egypt byzantine*. Paris, 1912.
Naumann, R. "Bauwerke der Oase Khargeh." *Mitteilungen des Deutschen Archäologischen Instituts, Abteilung Kairo* 8 (1939):1–16.
Petrikovits, H. von. *Die römischen Streitkräfte im Niederrhein*. Düsseldorf, 1967.
———. *Die Innenbauten römischer Legionslager während der Prinzipatszeit*. Opladen, 1975.
Polybius. *Historiae*, trans. fr. text of F. Hultsch by E. S. Shuckburgh. Lake Bluff, Ill., 1987.
Schwartz, J. *Qasr Qarūn/Dionysias 1950*. Fouilles Franco-Suisses 2. Cairo, 1969.
Sidebotham, St. E., et al. "Fieldwork on the Red Sea Coast: The 1987 Season." *Journal of the American Research Center in Egypt* 26 (1989):127–66.
Toy, S. "Babylon of Egypt." *Journal of the British Archaeological Association* 1 (1937):52–78.
Walsh, T. *Journal of the Late Campaign in Egypt*. London, 1803.
Ward Perkins, J. B. "The Monastery of Taposiris Magna." *Bulletin de la Société royale d'archéologie d'Alexandrie* 36 (1943–1944):48–53.

PETER GROSSMANN

CATECHETICAL SCHOOL OF ALEXANDRIA, the first and foremost institution of theological learning in Christian antiquity. Though we first hear of it as an established school in the *Historia ecclesiastica* of Eusebius, around the year 180, its roots must be traced much further back. Its rise to prominence from humble beginnings must therefore have been a long and evolutionary process parallel to the spread of the new religion among the Jewish and pagan inhabitants of Alexandria.

Although we must repudiate the native Orthodox theory that Saint MARK was its founder, it is not inconceivable that soon after his martyrdom the newly established hierarchy became active in their missionary endeavor for gaining new converts. During the reign of the early bishops of the church, it was natural that they should start a system whereby the clergy could instruct novices and catechumens in the substance of the Gospel and the doctrines of the faith. To this purpose, study circles were held in multiple places outside the churches, led by catechists who were generally, but not necessarily, ordained presbyters. The humble origins of the school consisted of informal circles or groups of mentors and catechumens whose assured acquaintance with their new religion was a necessary condition before their admission to BAPTISM.

As a rule this operation comprised two edificatory stages. The first stage was open to all as listeners, later known in the West as *Audientes*, a term found in the writings of Tertullian and Cyprian. As they advanced in their religious knowledge, in an unspecified period they became worthy of admission to baptism as *Competentes*. As catechumens, however, they were allowed to attend the church only during the initial part of the liturgy known as Liturgy of the Catechumens (*missa catechumenorum*). Afterward they were expected to leave the church for the subsequent performance of the second phase, the Liturgy of the Faithful (*missa fidelium*), intended only for the baptized congregation.

With the progress of Christianity and the gradual disappearance of the category of the old catechumens, this primitive procedure became unnecessary. Consequently, these religious circles were transformed into regular classes with a prescribed study program, which grew in complexity beyond simple religious instruction. Ultimately this began to take the shape of a school conducted parallel to the older, pagan institution of the Ptolemaic Museion, whose famous library must have been used by the students and faculty of the emerging theological college under the protection of the church. As the theological college progressed toward maturity, the Museion began to dwindle until its liquidation after the assassination of Hypatia in 415.

Prior to the advent of PANTAENUS as the first-known head of the Catechetical School of Alexandria in the late second century, the subjects taught by catechists revolved mainly, though probably not exclusively, around religious initiation and the scripture. The discussion of the godhead, of Christ and of His virgin birth, the Cross, the burial, the Resurrection and Ascension of the Lord, the Holy Spirit, the human body and soul, the hereafter, and the Second Coming of Jesus—all these subjects constituted the themes to be clarified in school within the framework of the Bible.

When Pantaenus was appointed by the Alexandrian patriarch to the headship of the institution before 180, he is known to have reformed and organized its curriculum by extending its program beyond purely theological subjects to most branches of the humanities. Though he is sometimes described as of Sicilian origin without solid proof, the Copts simply mention him as a native of Alexandria. While introducing his reform, he has been credited with the promotion of the use of the Greek alphabet, in lieu of the difficult and antiquated demotic characters, which ultimately led to the establishment of the new Coptic language as the last phase of the ancient Egyptian. He composed certain works in Greek on exegesis, now lost. However, at some time in the course of his service as an educator, his career at the Catechetical School was interrupted by Patriarch DEMETRIUS I who elected him for a Christian mission to India. This he accepted after seeking a worthy successor to ensure the continuation of the work so auspiciously begun by him at the developing school.

His choice fell upon the most prominent of his pupils, CLEMENT OF ALEXANDRIA. Probably an Athenian of pagan birth, born about 150, Clement had become a zealous Christian theologian. He added this to his former study of Greek philosophy. He succeeded Pantaenus before 190 and retained that office until 202 or 203, when for expediency rather than fear, he decided to flee from Alexandria during the persecution of Emperor Septimius Severus. He never returned to the school and appears to have spent his later years moving between Jerusalem and Antioch, but neither the place nor the date of his death in Greater Syria is known with precision.

This is not the place to discuss the detailed biographies and work of Clement or any other head of the school. But it is necessary to outline their careers in relation to the development of the burgeoning institution of theological knowledge in the story of universal Christianity.

Clement's role in this picture is unique in one sense. His thought was solidly based on liberal principles. As a theologian and Greek philosopher at one and the same time, he labored toward the reconciliation of the tenets of his youthful religion with ancient Greek learning, where he found no incompatibility between the biblical prophets and the Greek philosophers. He was at pains trying to prove that the Greeks plagiarized Moses and the Old Testament. It is amazing how Clement sowed the seeds of Christian liberalism in the classes of the Catechetical School, when the church curia surrounding the imperious Pope Demetrius I was totally conservative in its outlook on matters of doctrine. In an age where Gnostic teachings were still rampant among Egyptian Christians, Clement, with all his traditional orthodoxy, displayed no outright hostility to the Gnostics. Though technically he was not a Gnostic, in his classes he professed that illumination in religious knowledge was the true essence of Christian perfection. Like Socrates, Clement considered ignorance as worse than sin. On the whole, Clement may rightly be regarded as one of the earliest apostles of Christian liberalism in that patristic age.

It may be sufficient here to refer to the titles of Clement's outstanding works composed during his tenure as president of the Catechetical School, leaving all analytical considerations thereof to his specific biography. Though most of his work appears to be lost, we are aware of his notable contributions including his *Exhortation to the Heathen,* an apologetic tractate; the *Pedagogus* (or *Instructor*) on Christian life and ethics; and the *Stromata,* which comprises a series of varied discourses hard to construe (*Ante-Nicene Fathers,* 1956, pp. 165–568).

After Clement, the Catechetical School remained temporarily without a head, but it kept functioning with the momentum of its great master. Finally in 215 Pope Demetrius I decided to appoint as his successor the most illustrious of Clement's pupils, ORIGEN. Under his aegis, the school appears to have reached the peak of its efflorescence.

Origen was born about 185 either in Alexandria or somewhere else in Egypt, and died an exile in Palestine around 253. His parents were ardent Christians. His mother could have been of Jewish extraction, a fact that may account for his proficiency in Hebrew. Theories about his mixed origin have been entertained, but if we believe Epiphanius of Salamis, one of his close contemporaries, Origen must be regarded as a Copt and a true son of Egypt. His very name, derived from the ancient Egyptian word Horus or Orus, should have some significance. As a child, he had lived through the anguish of his father's martyrdom for the Christian faith. As a young man, he was extremely ascetic by nature, observed the most rigorous vigils, and carried the word of the Gospel (Mt. 19:12) literally to the extent of mutilating himself, thus becoming a eunuch, a fact that contributed to his future troubles with Patriarch Demetrius I. His education was enriched by the knowledge he readily absorbed from his learned master Clement. He also studied pagan philosophy and literature under Ammonius Saccas (175–242), the real founder of Neoplatonism, whose directive influence captivated Plotinus. He must have attended the lectures of Saccas with Plotinus at the Ptolemaic School of Alexandria. He also traveled widely and became acquainted with most of the eminent scholars and prelates of his day. His wandering extended from Arabia and Syria to Greece and Rome, where he attended sermons by Saint Hippolytus. Origen was destined to become one of the world's greatest exegetical scholars of all time; his productivity was enormous beyond reason. Epiphanius of Salamis states that his bibliography reached six thousand books and treatises. The analytical survey of Origen's works is a tremendous task that belongs elsewhere. Nevertheless, a brief and panoramic reference to his accomplishments may help to reveal the stature of the school where these vast products were made.

As a biblical scholar and philosopher, his erudition was massive and his creativity colossal. There is hardly a single book in the Old and New Testaments on which he did not write a lengthy commentary. His amazing critical edition of the Old Testament, the *Hexapla,* combines in six parallel columns all the available texts in both Greek and Hebrew scripts. This he later produced in a compendium under the title of *Tetrapla* with four columns, omitting the Hebrew. These were the works used by Saint Jerome in Caesarea. His monumental exegetical commentaries entitled *Scholia* were partly put into Latin by Rufinus. Only fragments of both have survived. Origen's homilies are reputed to be among the most ancient specimens of Christian preaching. In the realm of theology, his most important work was *De Principiis,* in which he systematized the whole of the Christian doctrine in four books—on God and the celestial world, on man and matter, on free will and its impact, and on the scriptures. Though the original of that ambitious project perished almost completely, its purpose has survived in rather inadequate Latin renderings by Rufinus and Saint Jerome. In a treatise called *Contra Celsum,* Origen defended Christianity from attacks by the second-century pagan philosopher Celsus. He wrote a number of ascetic works, of which two have come down to us. The *Exhortation to Martyrdom* was composed in 235 during the persecution of Emperor Maximinus. His more extensive work *On Prayer* had a great appeal to the mind of the early Christians.

His troubles started again during his first visit to Palestine, when he was invited by the bishops of Aelia and Caesarea to preach in their dioceses. It was unthinkable in Alexandrine ecclesiastical discipline that a layman should preach in the presence of bishops. Demetrius was an authoritarian cleric, who was imperceptibly pushing patriarchal prerogative to the edge of a monarchical system unable to accept uncontrolled initiative, even if it came from so great a personality as Origen. Demetrius recalled him to Alexandria around the year 218. For twelve years he sustained the gathering storm and buried himself in writing and teaching. The "winds of wickedness" were blowing hard against him, and synods started discussing his life and dissecting his thought. Finally, the hour of deliverance came when he fled back to Palestine in 230. There he was honored and promptly ordained to the priesthood. It is said that he was even considered for the episcopate. As expected, this action provoked Demetrius, who hastened to nullify the ordination and excommunicate his unbending adversary, whom he also dismissed from the Catechetical School. Origen became an exile, and in 231 he settled in Caesarea, where a new school with more distinguished candidates arose around his person. Some of his pupils, such as Gregory Thaumaturgus, bishop of Neocaesarea in Pontus, rose to key positions in the hierarchy. He arbitrated in doubtful cases of theology inside and outside Palestine. But the real glory of his calmer moments at Caesarea was the accomplishment of his immense literary work, whose solid basis had been laid at the Catechetical School of Alexandria.

During the Decian persecution of 250, however, the great master suffered tremendously but with fortitude. He was imprisoned and tortured. Though he survived the horrors of his ordeal and regained his freedom, his health began to decline, and he died at the city of Tyre in 253 at the age of sixty-nine.

Origen, like most universal thinkers and prolific writers, was a controversial figure both in his lifetime and after his death. The term Origenism was freely accepted in the realms of theology and philosophy as a formidable institution with a supporting school of Origenists and an equally ardent school of anti-Origenists. It is impossible in these pages to embark on even the briefest analysis of Origenist theories about such subjects as the unity of God, its relation to the Trinity, the doctrine of SUBORDINATIONISM, his audacious theory about souls and their prenatal existence and destiny after death, and numerous other physical and metaphysical controversies of almost unfathomable depth. Suffice it to mention that many of the greatest names of his day and even afterward joined the fray for or against Origen. In his defense one may read Saint PAMPHILUS, Saint Athanasius the Apostolic, Saint BASIL THE GREAT, Saint GREGORY OF NAZIANZUS, DIDYMUS THE BLIND, and others. In the hostile camp are Saint Epiphanius, Bishop of Salamis in Cyprus, and both Saint Jerome and THEOPHILUS of Alexandria, who turned against Origen in later times. In the fifth century, church councils were convened solely to discuss Origen's views. After a short lull, the Origenist controversy flared up again in the sixth century, and Origen was repeatedly condemned by two councils, held at Constantinople in 542 and 553, with the connivance of the Emperor Justinian himself.

Until the discord between Demetrius I and Origen, and the decision of the latter to quit Egypt for Caesarea in Palestine, the Catechetical School of Alexandria, though closely associated with the church, succeeded in retaining at least in theory, and to a considerable extent in practice, its academic freedom and independence. After Origen's flight to Palestine and his dismissal from office at Alexandria, the school came under the direct control of patriarchal and church authority. His immediate successor was HERACLAS, his former pupil and assistant who later followed Demetrius in the patriarchate from 231 to 247. One of his first acts was to lift his predecessor's sentence of excommunication from Origen and to urge the great master to return to Alexandria, but in vain. His reign is of interest on another account. It is said that when he increased the number of local bishops to twenty, the presbyters of the church decided to distinguish him from the rest of the bishops by calling him "Papa." If this is true, then the first prelate in Christendom to bear the title of pope was Heraclas the Copt in the early part of the third century, long before it was known to Rome.

The next head of the school, another famous pupil of Origen, was DIONYSIUS of Alexandria, later surnamed the Great. He occupied that post until he became patriarch (247–264). His reign was full of troubles. In 250 the Decian persecution drove the patriarch into hiding, though he was once arrested but escaped. In 257 another persecution was conducted by the Emperor Valerian. The country was harassed from the south by barbarian tribes. In Alexandria, Aemilianus, prefect of Egypt, declared himself emperor, and the civil war that broke out ended in his capture by the imperial general Theodotus, who sent the rebel in chains to Rome. The war, however, devastated the city and depleted the population. Plague was imminent and famine was at the door. At the end of every persecution, Dionysius faced the problem of the apostates. But he was broad-minded enough to readmit them, and he forbade the rebaptism of returning heretics and schismatics. It is a wonder that he had time to compose a number of theological works, where he displayed an independent but rather controversial mind. He was accused of tritheism by his namesake at Rome, was defended by Athanasius, and opposed by Basil. In regard to the Trinity, however, he himself rejected the heretical innovations of Paul of Samosata, bishop of Antioch and wealthy procurator of Queen Zenobia of Palmyra.

At a later date Athanasius entrusted Didymus the Blind with the headship of the Catechetical School in the early decades of the fourth century, a position he held until his death toward the end of that century. He lived during the tempestuous age of ARIANISM and the Council of NICAEA (315). Among his pupils were Saint Gregory of Nazianzus, Saint Jerome, and the historian Rufinus. He was a man of erudition, but his works are almost all lost. It is said that the treatise entitled *Against Arius and Sabellius,* preserved under Gregory of Nyssa's name, was dictated by him. It is interesting to know that he cared for the welfare of the blind—he had been blind since the age of four—by promoting for the first time in history a system of embossed or engraved writing for them. After Didymus, we enter the obscure period in the history of the school. It had done its share in shaping Christian doctrine and theological scholarship in those formative years. Then the zeal and knowledge began to fade, and with them a great institution.

BIBLIOGRAPHY

Altaner, B. *Patrology,* trans. H. Graef. Edinburgh and London, 1960.

Ante-Nicene Fathers, The, Vol. 2, ed. A. Roberts and J. Donaldson. Grand Rapids, Mich., 1956.

Bardenhewer, O. *Geschichte der altkirchlichen Literatur,* 3 vols. Freiburg, 1902–1912.

Bardy, G. *Clement d'Alexandrie.* Paris, 1926.

______. "Aux Origines de l'Ecole d'Alexandrie." *Recherches de science religieuse* 27 (1937):65–90.

______. "Pour l'histoire de l'Ecole d'Alexandrie." *Vivre et penser* 2 (1942):80–109.

Burkitt, F. C. "The Christian Church in the East." In *The Imperial Crisis and Recovery A.D. 193–324,* ed. S. Coak et al. Cambridge Ancient History 12. Cambridge, 1961.

Cadious, R. *Introduction au système d'Origène.* Paris, 1932.

______. *La Jeunesse d'Origène: Histoire de l'Ecole d'Alexandrie au début du IIIe siècle.* Paris, 1935.

Catalfamo, G. *S. Clemente Alessandrino.* Brescia, 1951.

Champonier, J. "Naissance de l'humanisme chrétien." *Bulletin de l'Association G. Bude* (1947):58–96.

Faye, E. de. *Clement d'Alexandrie: Etude sur les rapports du christianisme et de la philosophie grecque du IIe siècle.* Paris, 1898.

______. *Origène—Sa vie, son oeuvre, sa pensée,* 3

vols. Paris, 1923–1928. Eng. trans. F. Rothwell, *Origen and His Work.* London, 1926.
Glocker, O., ed. *Contra Celsum.* Bonn, 1924. Eng. trans. in *The Ante-Nicene Christian Library,* Vols. 10, 23. Edinburgh, 1869, 1872.
Guerike, H. E. F. *De Scholaque Alexandriae floruit Catechetica.* Halle, 1825.
Harnack, A. von. *Geschichte der altchristlichen Literatur bis Eusebius,* 3 vols. Leipzig, 1893–1904.
Koch, H. *Pronia and Paideusis: Studien über Origenes und sein Verhältnis zum Platonismus.* Berlin and Leipzig, 1932.
Lommatzsch, C. H. E., ed. *Origenis opera omnia,* 25 vols. Berlin, 1831–1848. Superseded by newer edition by P. Koetschau in 11 vols. in *Die griechischen christlichen Schriftsteller der ersten drei Jahrhunderte.* Leipzig, 1905–1909.
Miura-Stange, A. *Celsus und Origenes: Das Gemeinsame ihrer Weltanschauung.* Giessen, 1926.
Molland, E. *The Conception of the Gospel in the Alexandrian Theology.* Oslo, 1938.
Munck, J. *Untersuchungen über Klemens von Alexandria.* Stuttgart, 1933.
Nautin, P. *Origène.* Paris, 1977. English trans. forthcoming.
Oulton, J. E. L., and H. Chadwick. *Alexandrian Christianity.* Library of Christian Classics. Philadelphia, 1956.
Quasten, J. *Patrology,* 3 vols. Utrecht and Antwerp, 1975.
Robinson, J. A., ed. *The Philocalia of Origen.* Cambridge, 1893.
Rougier, L. *Celse ou le conflit de la civilisation antique et du christianisme primitif.* Paris, 1925.
Stahlin, O., ed. *C. Alexandrinus.* Texts in *Die griechischen christlichen Schriftsteller der ersten drei Jahrhunderte,* 3 vols., ed. P. Koetschau. Leipzig, 1905–1936. Eng. trans. W. Wilson in *The Ante-Nicene Christian Library,* Vols. 4, 12. Edinburgh, 1868–1869. See also *Bibliothek der Kirchenväter,* 2nd ser., Vols. 7 (1934), 8 (1934), 17 (1936), 20 (1938).
Tollinton, R. B. *Clement of Alexandria: A Study in Christian Liberalism,* 2 vols. London, 1914.
———. *Selection from the Commentaries and Homilies of Origen.* London, 1929.
Volker, W. *Das Vollkommenheitsideal des Origenes.* Tübingen, 1931.
Westcott, B. F. "Origenes." In DCB 4, pp. 96ff. New York, 1974.

AZIZ S. ATIYA

CATECHUMEN, in the early church, a new Jewish or heathen convert undergoing a course of basic instruction and training in Christian doctrine and ritual, prior to BAPTISM and full incorporation into the body of the faithful.

Just before His ascension, Christ had entrusted to the disciples the task of propagating His teachings among all nations and baptizing them in the name of the Father and the Son and the Holy Spirit (Mt. 18:19, 20). Not long afterward at Pentecost, a large group of various nationalities living in Jerusalem were destined to be the first catechumens in the history of the Christian church. Among them were Parthians, Medes, Elamites, inhabitants of Mesopotamia, of Judaea and Cappadocia, Pontus, Phrygia, Pamphylia, Egypt, Libya, Rome, Crete, and Arabia. When the Holy Spirit came down upon the twelve disciples and they began to speak the languages of this international gathering, Peter gradually initiated them into the real meaning of the Crucifixion and the Resurrection. "So those who received his word were baptized, and there were added that day about three thousand souls. And they devoted themselves to the apostles' teaching and fellowship, to the breaking of bread and the prayers" (Acts 2:41, 42).

The Acts of the Apostles provides us with many other instances of catechumenization: the high official of Candace of Ethiopia (8:26–40), Cornelius the centurion and his household (10:1–48), and Saul of Tarsus (9:10–20). It is characteristic that in all these instances, conversion was accomplished after a relatively short period following a significant turning point in the lives of the persons involved. Yet, in the case of Saul, we are told that, following his experience on the road to Damascus, he spent three years in meditation in the Arabian desert near Damascus (Gal. 1:15–18). This last episode may account for the extension of the probationary period of the catechumenate, in many cases, to cover three years.

Catechumens were classified according to their spiritual progress and achievement in assimilating Christian doctrine. Church historians differ as to the number of these grades, but there is general agreement on the following three.

1. Those who were allowed to hear the Word of God were called listeners or hearers (*audientes*). They were admitted into the church to listen to the readings from the Epistles and the Gospel only, after which they were required to leave. Their place was therefore in the narthex, which stretched across the western end of the church.

2. Those of longer standing, who were allowed to stay and attend the sermon given by the bishop or priest and certain prayers during which they knelt, were designated as *prostrati* or *genuflectentes.* But they were not permitted to attend the liturgy. Canon 19 of the Synod of Laodicea (343–381) laid down the following restriction: "After the sermons of the bishops, the prayer for the catechumens is to be made first by itself; and after the catechumens have gone out, the prayer for those who are under penance."

3. Those who had passed the two previous stages and were considered to be sufficiently trained in the faith to receive the sacrament of baptism were called *competentes.* Throughout Lent they were thoroughly instructed in the sacraments and services of the church, with particular emphasis on the Creed, which they had to recite at baptism. The necessity for fasting, prayer, and complete continence was enjoined on all catechumens, married and unmarried alike, at this stage.

Having satisfactorily completed these three stages, and having earned the epithet *electi* or *perfectiores,* they would be entered in a special register. This took place on the second Sunday of Lent in the church of Jerusalem, and on the fourth in other churches. Catechumens were now entitled to baptism and full membership in the community of the faithful.

During the initial period of the spread of Christianity, the apostles took upon themselves the task of teaching. Later, schools and courses were systematically organized in Alexandria, Antioch, Jerusalem, Rome, and elsewhere. The CATECHETICAL SCHOOL OF ALEXANDRIA, presumably established by Saint Mark the Evangelist for the edification of catechumens, flourished at later dates under the leadership of distinguished theological scholars such as PANTAENUS, CLEMENT OF ALEXANDRIA, and ORIGEN, under whose direction the school reached its apogee.

Catechumens studied various theological works, including the *Didache* (Teaching of the Twelve Apostles), two books by Clement of Alexandria—the *Protreptikos* and the *Instructor of Children*—the *Catecheses* of CYRIL OF JERUSALEM, and *De catechizandis rudibus* of Augustine. These were compiled during the most critical and controversial periods in the history of Christianity to equip catechumens with a proper understanding of the principles of faith regarding the Trinity, the Virgin Birth, the Crucifixion, the Resurrection, the Second Coming, as well as the sacraments and ritual of the church.

Catechumens were kept under the close supervision and guidance of their catechists, and those of them who lapsed were subjected to strict disciplinary punishment. Canon 5 of the Council of Neocaesarea (315) stipulates: "If a catechumen coming into the church has taken his place in the order of catechumen, and falls into sin, let him, if a kneeler, become a hearer, and sin no more. But should he again sin while a hearer, let him be cast out."

Having completed their training, catechumens were potential recruits for the presbytery. Some showed unmistakable signs of divine grace, and, in time, became pillars of the church, such as Ambrose, bishop of Milan (c. 339–397). However, to safeguard against cases of immaturity and lack of experience, certain regulations had to be laid down, of which several may be mentioned.

Canon 80 of the Apostolic Canons reads: "It is not right to ordain a man a bishop immediately after he has joined the church and been baptized if he has hitherto been leading a heathenish life, or has been converted from wicked behavior. For it is wrong to let one without experience become the teacher of others, unless in some special case this be allowed as a matter of divine favor and grace."

According to canon 2 of the Council of NICAEA (325): "Forasmuch as, either from necessity, or through the urgency of individuals, many things have been done contrary to the ecclesiastical canon, so that men just converted from heathenism to the faith, and who have been instructed but a little while, are straightway brought to the spiritual laver, are advanced to the episcopate or presbytery, it has seemed right to us that for the time to come no such thing shall be done. For to the catechumen himself there is need of time and a longer trial after baptism, for the apostolical saying is clear, 'Not a novice, lest being lifted up with pride, he fall into condemnation and the snare of the devil.'"

And canon 3 of the Council of Laodicea (343–381) reads: "He who has been recently baptized ought not to be promoted to the sacerdotal order."

BIBLIOGRAPHY

Atiya, A. S. *A History of Eastern Christianity.* London, 1968.

Cummings, D. *The Rudder.* Chicago, 1957.

Hardy, E. R. *Christian Egypt: Church and People.* New York, 1952.

Neale, J. M. *History of the Holy Eastern Church.* London, 1854.

Schwartz, E. *Busstufen und Katechumenatsklassen.* Strasbourg, 1911.

Smith, W., and S. Cheetham. *A Dictionary of Christian Antiquities,* 2 vols. London, 1908.

ARCHBISHOP BASILIOS

CATENA, ARABIC TRADITION OF. The Monophysite Coptic chain of the four Gospels has been preserved in full in a series of Arabic manuscripts. F. J. Caubet-Iturbe has edited the part that concerns the Gospel of Matthew from nine Arabic manuscripts (Vatican Library, Arabic 452 [1214], 410 [thirteenth to fourteenth century], 411 [fourteenth century]; Göttingen, Arabic 103 [thirteenth to fourteenth century]; Bodleian Library, Hunt. 262 [sixteenth century]; Strasbourg, Arabic 4315 [sixteenth century]; Paris, Arabic 55 [1619]; Cairo, 195 [1735]; Vatican Library, Karshuni Syriac 541 [1555]; cf. Graf, 1944, p. 482).

Caubet-Iturbe's edition comprises two volumes (1969–1970). Liturgical references found in the margins of certain manuscripts have been assembled in Volume 2 (pp. 52–55).

From this abundant Arabic tradition, the manuscript closest to the Coptic model is Vatican Arabic 452. In the Arabic texts certain citations have been omitted. The identification of the citations has not yet been made for the three chains of Mark, Matthew, and John.

BIBLIOGRAPHY

Caubet-Iturbe, F. J. *La cadena arabe del evangelio de San Mateo,* 2 vols. Vatican City, 1969–1970.

MICHEL VAN ESBROECK

CATHOLICOS, term of Greek origin signifying "general," "universal," and used as a title given to high-ranking secular officials, and later as an honorary title for certain ecclesiastical dignitaries ranking below a patriarch but above a metropolitan.

On 25 June 1959, a protocol was issued in Cairo organizing the relationship between the Coptic Orthodox church and the Ethiopian church. Article 1 stipulates that the supreme spiritual head of the latter church is the pope of Alexandria and the patriarch of the see of Saint Mark, while article 4 provides for the elevation of the spiritual head of the Ethiopian church to the rank of catholicos patriarch. Bishop Basilios was raised to this rank, and was officially consecrated at the Cathedral of Saint Mark, Cairo, on 28 June 1959, by Pope CYRIL VI (1959–1971).

BIBLIOGRAPHY

Neale, J. M. *A History of the Holy Eastern Church,* Vol. 1, p. 141. London, 1850.

ARCHBISHOP BASILIOS

CEILING. *See* Architectural Elements of Churches: Ceiling.

CELADION, SAINT, ninth patriarch of the See of Saint Mark (157–167). He held the office during the reigns of emperors Antoninus Pius and Marcus Aurelius. He was laid to rest on 9 Abīb near the remains of Saint Mark in the Church of Bucalis at Alexandria.

BIBLIOGRAPHY

Atiya, A.S. *History of Eastern Christianity.* Millwood, N.Y., 1980.

AZIZ S. ATIYA

CELESTINUS OF ROME, bishop of Rome (422–432) and the authority to whom NESTORIUS, bishop of Constantinople, and CYRIL I, bishop of Alexandria, appealed during their controversy over the term THEOTOKOS (430). Celestinus sided with Cyril, and thus caused the condemnation of Nestorius at a council held in Rome. The subsequent Council of EPHESUS later deposed him. Even though the Coptic *Historia ecclesiastica* and, consequently, the Arabic *History of the Patriarchs* make absolutely no mention of Celestinus' decision against Nestorius, in the Coptic tradition he is noted precisely for this action.

From him we possess a collection of eighteen letters in Greek or Latin concerning the Nestorian question. Among the Coptic manuscripts are two homilies, as follows:

1. *Discourse of the Honored Patriarch and Residence of the Holy Ghost, Apa Celestinus, Archbishop of the Metropolis of Rome, in Honor of the Messenger of the Ages of Light, the Archangel Gabriel* was meant to be read at the Feast of GABRIEL, 22 Kiyahk. There is a single manuscript, divided between the British Library, London (Or. 7028 and Or. 6780), and the Oriental Institute, Chicago (ed. Worrell, 1923). The text comprises four sections: (1) a homiletic prologue; (2) a treatise in encomiastic form about Gabriel, who is seen as a prefiguration of Christ (here is inserted an invective against Nestorius), and who as such was chosen to announce the conception by Mary; then follows an enumeration of his appearances in the Old Testament (this section may be an elaboration of a preexisting text); (3) the narration of five miracles wrought by Gabriel; and (4) a traditional epilogue.

2. The only manuscript of the *Encomium Pronounced by the Honored Patriarch and True Master, Apa Celestinus, Archbishop of the City of Rome, in Honor of the Martyr . . . Saint Victor* is in the British Library (Or. 7022.26–59; ed. Budge, 1914). The text contains a homiletic prologue and a traditional epilogue, between which are inserted three parts: (1) a series of postmortem miracles attributed to the saint, rich in pseudo-historical episodes referring to the emperors Honorius and Constantine; (2) a moral excerpt about the wretchedness of the human condition, which is no more than an *excursus* extracted from the homily *De anima et corpore* (cf. Alexander of Alexandria), and possibly added as an afterthought; and (3) the account of one last miracle. It appears that this particular homily was supposed to accompany as a sequel a true and proper encomium of Victor, such as the one ascribed to Theopemptos of Antioch and JOHN CHRYSOSTOM.

In any event, whether these manuscripts contain original versions or later enlargements thereof, they go back to the late period in Coptic literature (seventh to eighth centuries), and were composed directly in Coptic.

BIBLIOGRAPHY

Budge, E. A. W. *Coptic Martyrdoms*, pp. 46–101. London, 1914.

TITO ORLANDI

CELIBACY, unmarried state, particularly of clergy who are so bound by a solemn vow. Although matrimony is one of the seven holy sacraments and is likened to the union between Christ and the church (Eph. 5:31, 32), ascetic celibacy is regarded as a superior state, as it relieves men from earthly attachments and prepares the soul for the coming of Christ (1 Cor. 7:26–37).

The concept of voluntary abstention from marriage is not germane to Judaic thought. Nevertheless, the highest honor is accorded to those, like Jeremiah and Daniel, who led celibate lives. Of John the Baptist, Jesus stated, "Among those born of women there has risen no one greater than John the Baptist" (Mt. 11:11).

It is in the New Testament that celibacy has its real roots, as is indicated by Christ's teachings in Matthew 19:9–12; 22:24–29; Mark 10:28–30; and Luke 20:27–36. The Apostle Paul explicitly declares his preference for celibacy over marriage, practicing it in his own life and wishing that all men could follow his example (1 Cor. 5:7–38).

In the book of Revelation, Saint John speaks of the hundred and forty-four thousand who kept themselves chaste, and had the Father's name written on their foreheads (Rev. 14:1–4).

The early fathers extolled the merits and virtues of a celibate life consecrated to the worship of God. Representative examples include Cyprian, bishop of Carthage (d. 258), to whom virginity was an angelic attribute.

Applying the parable of the talents to human life, Saint ATHANASIUS the Apostolic states, "For there are two ways in life . . . the one the more moderate and ordinary, I mean marriage; the other angelic and unsurpassed, namely virginity."

CYRIL OF JERUSALEM sees a superhuman quality in chastity: "Let us not be ignorant of the glory of chastity: for its crown is angelic, and its excellence above man. . . . Angels walking upon earth are they who practice chastity: the virgins have their portion with Mary the Virgin."

GREGORY OF NYSSA (c. 330–c. 395) admires, above all, the purity of celibacy and its freedom from corruption: "The holy look of virginity is precious indeed in the judgment of all who make purity the test of beauty; but it belongs to those alone whose struggles to gain this object of a noble love are favored and helped by the grace of God."

Similar teachings are found in the writings of CLEMENT OF ALEXANDRIA, BASIL THE GREAT, Ambrose, bishop of Milan, JOHN CHRYSOSTOM, and Saint Jerome.

The early church also publicly honored celibates by giving them precedence and priority in seating and communing.

The Coptic and other Orthodox churches require their bishops to be celibates. As to the lower ranks of the hierarchy, married candidates are eligible for ordination, but marriage is not permitted once a person has been ordained.

Celibacy is a prerequisite of the monastic life. Saint BASIL THE GREAT suggests that explicit vows be required of the postulant for admission:

"We are not cognizant of any vows of men, unless it be that some men have enrolled themselves in the battalion of those who have adopted the monastic life, if they seem to accept celibacy by silent agreement. Nevertheless, I deem it fitting that in their case too that should receive primary attention. They must be asked, and from them must be taken a perspicuous vow, so that if any of them should by any chance return to a flesh-loving and sensual life afterwards they shall be incurring the penalty attached to those who commit fornication" (Second Canonical Epistle of Basil).

BIBLIOGRAPHY

Cummings, D. *The Rudder (Pedalion).* Chicago, 1957.

Lea, H. C. *History of Sacerdotal Celibacy in the Christian Church,* 2 vols. London, 1907.

Vacandard, E. *Etude de critique et d'histoire religieuse,* pp. 69–120. Paris, 1905.

ARCHBISHOP BASILIOS

CELL. The word *cell* is very common in monastic texts, but it does not always have the sense given it in Western languages. Because monks inhabited various places, such as tombs, caves, or constructed hermitages, it is necessary to distinguish between them. We find in Greek the words *kella* (derived from Latin) and its common diminutive *kellion.* In Coptic it is translated as ⲣⲓ (ri), and in Arabic, as *qallāyah* (pl., *qalālī*), by way of Syriac. It is also known that the ascetics often made use of the tombs of ancient Egypt, which explains the use of the Greek words *taphos* (tomb) or *nekrotaphion* and the Coptic ⲙϩⲁⲁⲩ (mhaau, grave), or of caves that they fitted up. For this reason, one often finds the words to describe the habitation of a hermit in Greek or transcribed into Coptic characters as ⲥⲡⲏⲗⲓⲟⲛ (spēlion) and ⲃⲏⲃ (bēb), which designate a grotto or cavern. It is therefore proper to specify the senses that the word "cell" has received in our texts, in order to avoid possible confusion. If words like *topos* (place) or its Coptic equivalent, ⲙⲁ (ma), can be applied just as well to a Pachomian monastery as to a center of hermitages or even to a simple church, in the same way the Coptic expression ⲙⲁⲛϣⲱⲡⲉ (manshōpe, habitation) is indifferently applied to any place where monks live. It is the same with the terms *oros* (Greek) or ⲧⲟⲟⲩ (toou), which describe in the first place the mountain; then, by reason of the geography of Egypt, the desert; and, by derivation, since the monasteries were established there, a monastery. Thus, *oros tou* (followed by a proper name) designates a monastery.

It is, however, important to indicate the senses that the word "cell" has taken on in a monastic context.

The words *kellion* and ⲣⲓ (ri) designate first of all a room in a larger whole where monks live, a monastery or a prison. In this sense, it appears appropriate to the Pachomian monasteries, where each monk had the use of a "cell." The texts that show this are numerous: the texts, the Rule, and the precepts of Saint Pachomius preserved in Saint Jerome's Latin translation often speak of the *cella* of the Pachomian monk (e.g., Koch, 1933, p. 190 at the Latin *cella* or p. 185 at the Greek *kellion*). Few archaeological excavations have revealed these cells, although M. Grossmann (1986, pp. 33–40, esp. figs. 1–2 with a plan of the excavations) has discovered some on the site of the DAYR AL-BALAYZAH.

Unfortunately we do not know how these Pachomian cells were furnished, for nothing has been preserved; everything that was in wood has been carried off or has disintegrated. It is not known if niches (in Greek *thuris* or in Coptic ϣⲟⲩϣⲧ shousht) were fitted up in the walls to serve as cupboards, sometimes provided with a door. The famous *kathismation,* translated by Saint Jerome as *sellula,* which Lefort renders in French by *sellette,* small seat (1943, p. 343 and n. 56), is known to us only from the texts. Draguet comments on this *kathismation,* saying that it was a kind of chaise longue or deck chair, such that the monk occupied a position half sitting, half lying (1944, pp. 87–90).

On occasion the words *kellion* (Greek or transcribed into Coptic) and ⲣⲓ are used to describe a hermitage. But in this case its structure is better known, whether it has been built of unbaked bricks and provided with cupolas, as at ISNĀ or KELLIA, or whether the hermits have fitted up a tomb or a natural cave (Badawi, 1953, pp. 67–89). What interests us here is how the monks' quarters appeared to the visitor. It seems indeed that very early there was a room separate from that reserved for work or for sleep. This room was distinguished from the others because a niche was hollowed out in the east wall. We know that from the time of ORIGEN the Eastern Christians had the custom of praying turned toward the east—hence, this prayer niche in the east wall, which indicated the direction that the believer ought to face for prayer. This niche was often adorned, sometimes by a simple cross or a crucified Christ (Guillamont, 1968, pp. 310–25). This use of a special room for prayer is attested from the fourth century (Amélineau, 1894, p. 76, with reference to MACARIUS THE EGYPTIAN). It seems that at Isnā in the seventh century there were even two oratories, although the reason for this has not been determined (Sauneron et al., 1972, Vol. 1, pp. 15–17).

At some point, probably in the sixth century, the hermitage—or rather the lodging of a hermit—was composed of three rooms: one for prayer, one for sleep, and one for work. The last, when it was for an elder, was equipped with an acoustic tube opening in front of the door of his lodging. This was done so that, if he wished, he could keep his door bolted and yet converse with someone outside. The sleeping room had a small chamber, the silo or storeroom, in which he kept his provisions. Add to these rooms of the elder an equal number for each of his disciples, usually disposed to the south of those of the elder and also controlled by a door with a bolt. Moreover, one must take into account that the disciples might have been very numerous: one of the hermitages excavated at Kellia consisted of fifty-eight rooms.

Not all of these rooms served for the lodging of the hermits. There were a certain number of common rooms, rooms thought to have been reception rooms in front of those reserved for the elder but that perhaps served at first as workrooms. Where recent coatings of plaster have fallen, animal bones have been discovered wedged into the walls at a low height. No doubt these were intended to stretch the web for a weaving operation. We must add as common rooms the kitchens, offices, storerooms, and latrines, not to mention the courtyard, with its hydraulic installations (well, basins, and channel system for a garden). This is mentioned in texts from the fourth century on. Thus, the hermitage of EVAGRIUS was provided with a well. We are therefore far from the first sense of the *kella* of the Pachomian monk, and the sense habitually given to the word *cell.* The archaeological evidence for the hermitage as here briefly described is manifold, whether it is fitted up in a tomb or a cave (Badawi, 1953), has been constructed (as in the Kellia hermitages), or hollowed into the tufa of the plateau (as in those of Isnā; Sauneron et al., 1972).

We must mention a final sense of the Arabic-Christian word *qallāyah.* Since the bishops had to be celibate, they were chosen very early. That seems common, although not obligatory, from the period of ATHANASIUS, as his festal letters testify. A former monk or hermit who had become a bishop continued to live the cenobitic or hermit life; hence, his residence, or *episkopeion,* was quite naturally called *qallāyah.* It was the same for a patriarch. If his dwelling was called *kellion,* the name *qallāyah* came naturally to describe not only his place of residence but also the whole body of persons who formed his entourage, as one speaks of the "court" of a king. This sense appears to be attested from the tenth century but only in Arabic, not in Coptic.

BIBLIOGRAPHY

Amélineau, E. *Histoire des monastères de la Basse-Egypte.* Annales du Musée Guimet 25. Paris, 1894.

Badawi, A. "Les Premiers établissements chrétiens dans les anciennes tombes d'Egypte." In *Tome commémoratif du millénaire de la Bibliothèque patriarcale d'Alexandrie,* pp. 67–89. Publications de l'Institut d'études orientales de la Bibliothèque patriarcale d'Alexandrie 2. Alexandria, 1953.

Draguet, R. "Le Chapître de l'Histoire lausiaque sur les Tabennesiotes dérive-t-il d'une source copte? *Le Muséon* 57 (1944):54–145; 58 (1945):15–95.

Grossmann, P. "Die Unterkunftsbauten des Koinobitenklosters 'Dair al-Balayza' im Vergleich mit den Ermitagen der Mönchen vor Kellia." In *Le Site monastique des Kellia,* pp. 33–40. Geneva, 1986.

Guillaumont, A. "Une Inscription copte sur la 'prière de Jésus.'" *Orientalia Christiana Periodica* 34 (1968):310–25.

Koch, H. *Quellen zur Geschichte der Askese und des Mönchtums in der alten Kirche.* Sammlung ausgewählter Kirchen- und Dogmengeschichtlicher Quellenschriften 6. Tübingen, 1933.

Lefort, L. T. *Les Vies coptes de saint Pachôme.* Bibliothèque du Muséon 16. Louvain, 1943.

Sauneron, S., et al. *Les Ermitages chrétiens du désert d'Esna.* Fouilles de l'Institut français d'Archéologie orientale . . . du Caire 29. Cairo, 1972.

RENÉ-GEORGES COQUIN

CELSUS, anti-Christian writer and Platonist philosopher whose *Alethes Logos* (True Discourse), written about 178, is the oldest surviving literary attack on Christianity. All that is known of its author is contained in ORIGEN's reply, the eight books of *Contra Celsum,* written in Caesarea (Palestine) about 248. Celsus was most probably a Syrian, for he is best informed about Christianity in Palestine and Syria (compare Origen, *Contra Celsum* vii.9, where Celsus professes a firsthand knowledge of the ways of Christian prophets in Phoenicia and Palestine).

Origen enables a very considerable amount of the *True Discourse* to be reconstructed, and it is clear that Celsus had made himself well informed about Christianity before he launched his attack. He was acquainted with the Gospel of Matthew and probably the Gospel of John, as well as Genesis and

Exodus. He also knew of the Book of Enoch and the Book of the Secrets of Enoch, and in addition a number of apocryphal Jewish writings, such as The Life of Adam and Eve (see *Contra Celsum* vi.27; Chadwick ed., p. 342, n. 2), as well as some Gnostic and Marcionite writings. He was well aware of the division of Christianity in the second century between the "Great Church" and numerous dissident (Gnostic and Marcionite) bodies. These, while sharing the name "Christian" and refusing to be known by any other name, had nothing in common with each other (*Contra Celsum* iii.12)—indeed, they hated each other (*Contra Celsum* v.63).

Nonetheless, Christianity was a danger to the society in which Celsus lived. His principal charge against the Christians was that they formed an "illegal association" (i.1). Theirs was a secret society (i.3), born from revolt against Judaism (iii.14), that persuaded stupid individuals, by means of fear-inspiring propaganda, to desert true religion (iii.15) and give unquestioning obedience to them (i.9). Christian proselytism disrupted society and threatened the traditional authority of the pater familias over his household (iii.55), and the Christians stood aside from civic duties and gave no help to the empire (viii.69–75).

The issue of loyalty therefore lay at the heart of Celsus's attack; but to make his accusation stick, he went deeply into the origins of the Christian doctrines of God and of man, and the life and claims of Jesus. He himself believed that "there is an ancient doctrine which has existed from the beginning which has always been maintained by the wisest nations and cities and wise men" (i.14). Judaism, though in many ways repellent, had a claim to tolerance, since it was a religion based on ancient tradition (v.41). Christianity could make no such claim.

With considerable acumen, Celsus introduced a Jew into the debate for the dual purpose of demonstrating that the Jews were an ignorant and rascally people, deceived by Moses' teaching (1.23; compare iv.36), and that the Christians were even worse, being simply a rebellious offshoot from Judaism (ii.4). Celsus's Jew sought to prove that Jesus could claim neither miraculous birth (i.32) nor divine call at baptism (i.41), that he had picked up a knowledge of magic in Egypt (i.38), that his miracles were not extraordinary, and that in the end he had been unable to save himself from disgraceful punishment (ii.35, ii.39). Even his disciples did not believe him (ii.39).

To Celsus, a Platonist, it was impossible for God to come into contact with the material universe, and in no way did He behave like the angry and vengeful old man of Christian belief, roasting His enemies alive (iv.11). God was God of the whole universe, not of man only—let alone of the Christians (iv.99). The latter behaved "like frogs holding a symposium round a swamp . . . debating which of them was the most sinful, and saying, 'God reveals all things to us beforehand, and gives us warning. He forsakes the whole universe and the course of the heavenly spheres to dwell with us alone'" (iv.23). Christian teaching concerning God, man, and the universe was nonsensical.

Celsus's *True Discourse* must have had considerable success, for copies survived some seventy years after it had been written, and Origen thought it worth a great deal of time and argument to refute. Though he wrote *Contra Celsum* as an exile in Caesarea, copies of his work circulated in Egypt, and parts of books i and ii were found in the papyrus library discovered at Ṭurah, south of Cairo, in 1941 (Chadwick ed., p. 30).

Celsus's views of Egypt and its religion were more liberal than those of many of his contemporaries, such as the satirist Lucian of Samosata (c. A.D. 170). The Egyptians were an ancient people, the original inhabitants of their land (iv.36). They were to be numbered among the "wise nations" of the world (1.14); and their religion, though apparently full of mystery, superstition, and animal worship (iii.18–19), nonetheless "respected invisible ideas and not as most people think, ephemeral animals" (iii.19). On the other hand, trafficking in magic "for a few obols in the market-place" (i.69) could be charged against them, as could providing the origin of the Jewish customs of circumcision and abstinence from eating pigs (v.41). Celsus's knowledge of the Egyptians was probably no more than that of an educated provincial of his time. His attack was on Christianity in general, especially where he knew it at first hand, in Palestine and Syria. He has less to say about Egypt, and his importance in the history of Christianity there is less direct. It lies in his contribution toward shaping Origen's ideas at a mature period of his life, in the incidental light he throws on the relations between Gnostics and the "Great Church" at a time when Gnosticism in Egypt was particularly strong, and in what he indicates as the attitude of educated pagans toward Egypt and its religious practices in the latter half of the second century.

BIBLIOGRAPHY

Andresen, C. *Logos und Nomos: Die Polemik des Kelsos wider das Christentum.* Berlin, 1955.

Labriolle, P. de. *La Réaction païenne.* Paris, 1934.

Miura-Stange, A. *Celsus und Origenes.* Beiheft zur Zeitschrift für neutestamentliche Wissenschaft 4. Giessen, 1926.

Wifstrand, A. "Die wahre Lehre des Kelsos." In *Humanistiska ventenskapassamfundet, Lund. Arsberättelae 1941–1942,* pp. 391–431. Lund, 1942.

Witt, R. E. *Albinus and the History of Middle Platonism.* Cambridge, 1937.

W. H. C. FREND

CENOBITES. *See* Pachomius of Tabennēsē, Saint.

CENSER (MUMARAH). *See* Liturgical Instruments; Metalwork, Coptic.

CERAMICS, COPTIC, the pottery produced in Egypt from the late Roman to the early Islamic period. There must be no illusion about the term "Coptic ceramics." The techniques of production were in the tradition of Hellenistic and Roman techniques. Similarly, there is no marked stylistic discontinuity between the products of the Roman period and those of the Copto-Byzantine period in that both depended on pottery imported from other regions of the Mediterranean. Nor does the Arab conquest in the seventh century seem to have introduced fundamental changes in local workmanship. It is not unusual to observe the presence of "Coptic" ceramics in so-called Islamic areas until at least the tenth century.

Manufacturing Techniques

A technological study of ceramics allows one to define groups of wares according to the type of clay, the method of shaping, and the method of firing. It shows the characteristics of a workshop or manufacturing group. Such a study should begin with general comments on the materials and techniques of making ceramics in Egypt.

Raw Material. Clay is fine particles of sedimentary rock, formed from argillaceous minerals (hydrated aluminium silicates) and nonargillaceous minerals (such as quartz and calcite), which appear in varying proportions in clays in the natural state. The lamellar, crystalline structure of these minerals is modified by the addition of water, which gives the clay plasticity, and by firing at a high temperature, which makes it strong and hard. It may be supposed that the clays used by the potters of the Copto-Byzantine period were not basically different from those used in the more remote past or those still used today.

Clays may be subjected to various treatments—such as kneading, crushing, washing, and sifting—that vary according to the properties of the clay, the type of vessel to be produced, and, possibly, local customs. In order to increase the strength of the wall of a clay object, to limit plasticity, and to control porosity or shrinkage on drying, nonplastic organic and/or mineral particles called tempers are often added to the natural clay. For a more detailed study of tempers see M. Picon (1973, pp. 11ff.). For the methods of preparation of clay in pharaonic Egypt see D. Arnold (1980, cols. 399 ff.), and J. Bourriau (1981, pp. 14ff), which has a tentative classification of clays.

Pharaonic and Coptic Egypt had three basic types of clay, although in the absence of detailed systematic analyses any attempts at classification may well appear aleatory (Tobia and Sayre, 1974, p. 124; Noll, 1981, pp. 108 and 112). Potters used them separately and probably also in mixtures. *Calcareous, or marl clays* are characterized by a relatively high proportion of calcite. They have slight quantities of silica and iron oxide and a few micas (brilliant flat particles); vegetable particles are seldom present (Arnold, 1980, col. 395ff; Bourriau, 1981, pp. 14–15; Arnold, 1981, pp. 167–91).

During the Copto-Byzantine period several groups of vessels seem to have been made of calcareous clays. The first group is that of amphorae (large, two-handled jars), especially from such sites in lower Egypt as Abū Mīnā and Kellia (Egloff, 1977, type 186); they have a beige-to-yellow paste on the surface (Munsell 2, 5YR8/3, 10YR7/4), which includes many black and yellow nodules, large white particles (perhaps calcite), and some grains of quartz. Breaks are often reddish pink (Munsell 2,5YR5/7; 2,5YR5/8). The second group consists of water jugs, such as those from the fifth century at Kellia (Egloff, 1977, types 198–202); pitchers with excised, vertical fluting, perhaps from Abū Mīnā (Egloff, 1977, types 227–28); and water jugs and flasks from Isnā (Jacquet-Gordon, 1972, p. 13, pl. 4).

Siliceous clays, or silt, are characterized by high levels of silica and iron oxide. They also contain grains of quartz, micas, and organic particles (Arnold, 1980, cols. 394–95; Bourriau, 1981, p. 14). In the Coptic period such clays were no doubt the material of the "fine" (as distinct from "coarse") ceramic products of what M. Rodziewicz calls Group K (1976, pp. 50ff) and J. W. Hayes calls Egyptian B. These cooking dishes, deep bowls, and storage jars (Rodziewicz, 1976, K 35–36; Egloff, 1977, types 258–98; Jacquet-Gordon, 1972, K 1–2, 4–11, clay III) are of red to brown clays (Munsell 2, 5YR4/6; 5YR5/3). In the clays, visible to the naked eye, are fine particles of mica, grains of quartz, and frequent traces of vegetable tempers. A group of amphorae is characterized by brown, highly micaceous clays (Egloff, 1977, types 172–80; Spencer and Bailey, 1982, pp. 16ff).

Kaolinitic clays contain kaolinite, a hydrous silicate of aluminum. These clays were used for another type of "fine" ceramic ware, Group O (Egyptian A, or Coptic red slip wear, according to Hayes), which includes plates, bowls, and flasks. They are pink on the surface and in the break (Munsell 5YR7/3; 7,5YR7/4) and include, visible to the eye, micas, black nodules, and quartz grains (Rodziewicz, 1976, pp. 54ff).

Shaping. Coptic potting techniques, like those of Greece and Rome, allowed for both specialization and standardization of form. Pottery was thrown on the wheel, which was furnished with a system of propulsion permitting simultaneous production in series, varied forms, and rather elaborate finishing techniques (for the pharaonic period, see Holthoer, 1977, pp. 31–34).

An attempt to reconstruct the method of manufacture is necessary in order to grasp the morphological subtleties of each group of shapes. In the absence of an exhaustive picture, some examples may be indicated here. Open, shallow forms, such as plates, platters, and bowls, made from a ball of clay must be centered on the wheel and hollowed very exactly in order to obtain a regular rim. The rim may be thickened or flared to strengthen the structure of the vessels. For small shapes, the potter may use a clay cone. Several specimens are successively fashioned from the top of the cone by being sliced off by a string.

Large jars used for the storage of provisions, such as no. E10993 in the Louvre, Paris, may have been made in one piece after the fashion of present day *zīrs* (water jugs). Traces of cord visible on and under the maximum diameter of the body indicate that in the drying that preceded the firing, the potter wished to hold the body with a temporary support to prevent undue strain on the walls. Some lids with a beveled rim (Egloff, 1977, types 347ff.) seem to have come from the same preliminary shape as the cooking pots to which they are perfectly adapted (Egloff, 1977, types 110 and 115–16). The pot was turned as a closed shape and is thought to have been "beheaded" obliquely with a cutting tool in the upper part, thus forming the lid. The lower part, the remaining three-quarters, formed the pot (Rhodes, 1978, fig. 93, 6).

During and after the fashioning of the preliminary shape, the potters smoothed the surfaces with a blade (Rhodes, 1978, pp. 45ff.). Then they resorted to finishing. With a cutting instrument they trimmed off the walls, rim, and base (Picon, 1973, pp. 30–31). So far as bowls and plates of Group O are concerned (Rodziewicz, 1976, 0 23; Egloff, 1977, types 33–37), the helicoidal marks of tooling, quite visible on the exterior surface, constitute a veritable trademark.

On amphorae and pots, potters liked to make a network of horizontal rilling lines giving a ribbed appearance to the vessel's surface. This treatment, intended among other things to facilitate gripping the vessel, was obtained by pressure from the fingers during throwing or with the help of a cutting tool. Handles, spouts, and filters were luted (coated) with *barbotine* (liquid clay) before the final drying.

Throwing was the principal fashioning technique used in Copto-Byzantine Egypt. Molding seems to have been very rarely employed and modeling was nonexistent, except for handles and grips. A special technique, building up with a beater, seems to have been used for the construction of bread ovens, big troughs of coarse clay with thick walls (Egloff, 1977, pp. 167–69).

Firing. In spite of the rare reference to kilns in the Copto-Byzantine period, it cannot be doubted that Egypt possessed a considerable number. (On methods of firing, see Picon, 1973, pp. 55ff.) The archaeological literature refers to kilns at Maryūt (Empereur and Garlan, 1984, and Picon, 1984); at Abū Mīnā, where the specialty was figurines and *eulogia* (praise or blessing) AMPULLAE, as well as common ware; and at al-Ashmūnayn (Hermopolis Magna), where the archaeological remains are complemented by the evidence of a papyrus, dated 517, that mentions a potter's workshop in the Hermopolite nome (Spencer and Bailey, 1982, p. 17 and n. 17). In Upper Egypt, kilns have been discovered at Medamud and Tod (bibliographical references concerning these areas are collected in Egloff, 1977, p. 191, n. 2).

The structure and functioning of the kilns have never been studied in detail. The kilns at Medamud are described thus: "This kiln consists of a tower of crude bricks, with an opening at the bottom, on a level with the furnace chamber. In the tower, and restricting the stoke-hole, is a platform, perforated to make a sort of earthenware grill on which the pots to be fired were placed. The opening is below this grill. This opening served as the mouth of the furnace chamber" (Bisson de la Roque, 1931, p. 22).

Nubian kilns of Group X, or the Ballana culture, after the Meroitic period (c. 100–350), and of the Christian period (until 1350) are better known. A certain number that were situated to the north and south of Wādī Ḥalfā (West Faras, East Serra, East Debeira, Argi, Gezira, Daboro, Mugufil) generally had the form of a furnace chamber, often dug in the ground and with the help of a dome supporting a firing chamber open at the top. Access to the furnace was by a small lateral stokehole above the outside ground level. There were also in Nubia more rudimentary methods of firing (Adams, 1962, pp. 62–75).

Few analyses have dealt with the determination of the temperature of firing. In the New Kingdom it seems that siliceous clays were fired at a low temperature (500 to 800°C) and calcareous clays at a higher temperature (850 to 1000°C; Bourriau, 1981, p. 17). In the Roman period, the temperature of firing common wares ranged from 800 to 1000°C and that of terra sigillata (ware with stamped designs) between 900 and 1100°C (Picon, 1973, p. 58), the same range of temperatures at which Gaulish *sigillata* were fired.

In the present state of research, more attention should be directed to the Romanization of manufacturing techniques in Egypt and their points of contact with Copto-Byzantine ceramics, and Copto-Byzantine innovations should be identified. Further archaeological investigations, aiming at the discovery of production sites, and application of laboratory methods will undoubtedly produce a better evaluation of these problems.

BIBLIOGRAPHY

Adams, W. Y. "Pottery Kiln Excavations." *Kush: Journal of the Sudan Antiquities Service* 10 (1962):62–75.

Arnold, D. "Keramik." *Lexikon der Ägyptologie,* Vol. 3, col. 392–409. Wiesbaden, 1980.

______. "Ägyptische Mergeltone ("Wustentone") und die Herkunft einer Mergeltonware des Mittleren Reiches aus der Gegend von Memphis." In *Studien zur altägyptischen Keramik,* ed. D. Arnold. Mainz am Rhein, 1981.

Ballet, P., and M. Picon. *Recherches préliminaires sur les origines de la céramique des Kellia (Egypte). Importations et productions égyptiennes.* Cahiers de la Céramique Egyptienne 1. Cairo, 1987.

Bisson de la Roque, F. *Médamoud (1930). Fouilles de l'Institut français d'archéologie orientale, Vol. 8, pt. 1. Cairo, 1931.*

Bourriau, J. *Umm el-Ga'ab. Pottery from the Nile Valley before the Arab Conquest.* Exhibition at the Fitzwilliam Museum. Cambridge, 1981.

Brissaud, P. *Les ateliers de potiers de la région de Louqsor.* Bibliothèque d'Etude, Vol. E 78. Cairo, 1982.

Egloff, M. *Kellia. La Poterie copte. Quatre siècles d'artisanat et d'échanges en Basse Egypte.* Recherches suisses d'archéologie copte, Vol. 3. Geneva, 1977.

Empereur, J. Y., and Garlan, eds. "Recherches sur les amphores Grecques." *Actes du colloque international d'Athènes, 10–12 septembre 1984.* Supplement to *Bulletin de correspondance hellénique* 13 (1984).

Holthoer, R. *New Kingdom Pharaonic Sites: The Pottery.* Copenhagen and Stockholm, 1977.

Jacquet-Gordon, H. *Les Ermitages chrétiens du désert d'Esna,* Vol. 3: *Céramique et objets. Fouilles de l'Institut français d'archéologie orientale,* Vol. 29, pt. 3. Cairo, 1972.

Matson, F. R. "Technological Studies of Egyptian Pottery. Modern and Ancient." In *Recent Advances in Science and Technology of Materials,* Vol. 3, ed. B. Adli. New York, 1974.

Munsell Soil Color Charts (Munsell Color Company). Baltimore, 1954.

Noll, W. "Bemalte Keramiken Altägyptens: Material Rohstoffe und Herstellungstechnik." In *Studien zur altägyptischen Keramik,* ed. D. Arnold. Mainz am Rhein, 1981.

Picon, M. *Introduction à l'étude technique des céramiques sigillées de Lezoux. Centre de Recherches sur les techniques gréco-romaines, no. 2.* Dijon, 1973.

Rhodes, Daniel. *La Poterie: les formes.* Paris, 1978.

Rodziewicz, Mieczyslaw. *La Céramique romaine tardive d'Alexandrie, Alexandrie I,* trans. Z. Kiss. Warsaw, 1976.

Spencer, A. J., and D. M. Bailey. *British Museum Expedition to Middle Egypt: Ashmunein (1981).* British Museum, Occasional Paper no. 41. London, 1982.

Tobia, S. K., and E. V. Sayre. "An Analytical Comparison of Various Egyptian Soils, Clays, Shales and Some Ancient Pottery by Neutron Activation." In *Recent Advances in Science and Tech-*

nology of Materials, Vol. 3. Proceedings of 2nd Cairo Solid State Conference: 1973, Ed. A. Bishay. New York, 1974.

Decorative Techniques and Motifs

Decoration had a considerable place in Coptic ceramics. It appeared in simplified form even on articles intended for everyday use. Decorative techniques bear witness to specialization in workshops and adaptation of ornament to the type and technology of the vessel. Impressed decoration was generally associated with wares made of relatively fine clays; painting was found on wares of coarser clay. It is sometimes difficult to distinguish between the process of fabrication itself and the decorative effect that may have resulted from it, such as traces of cords on amphora and cooking pots.

Coptic decoration excelled more in its iconographic and stylistic expression than in the techniques of application. Impressed decoration was dependent on late Roman ceramics. It is in the motifs of painted decoration that Coptic ceramics seem to be distinguished from any external inspiration and present real originality. In this respect it is significant that, from the eighth century, some form of glazed (vitreous) coating was applied to painted and other Coptic wares.

Impressed Decoration and Related Techniques. A number of Coptic decorative methods show Roman influence: impressing and stamping, incising, deforming and cutting, and relief.

Decoration formed by *impressing or stamping* a carved motif on soft clay was directly inspired by late Roman "fine" ceramics, especially the *sigillata* of Late Roman B ("fine" ware from North Africa) and D, to use O. F. Waagé's terminology, taken over by M. Rodziewicz and M. Egloff. This technique was imported into and imitated in Egypt.

Fine local ceramics, particularly orange wares of Group O, were inspired by Late Roman B, as the stylistic adaptation of a dove on a vessel from Alexandria bears witness (Rodziewicz, 1976, p. 54). On wares at Kellia, there are impressions of the monogram of Christ, stars with seven branches, Maltese crosses, and a six-petaled flower (Egloff, 1977, p. 81, pls. 11, 14, 15, 1–7); and at Isnā, wares bear the monogram, rosettes, crosses, fishes, and doves (Jacquet-Gordon, 1972, p. 19). Other wares with stamped motifs were found at Armant (Mond and Myers, 1940, pls. 82–83, without specification of groups) and at Elephantine (Grimm, 1975, pp. 76–77, fig. 13). Carmine red wares of Group K, with the exception of some specimens from Kellia (Kasser, 1983, nos. 16–17 and 38), were seldom stamped, according to Rodziewicz (1976, p. 50).

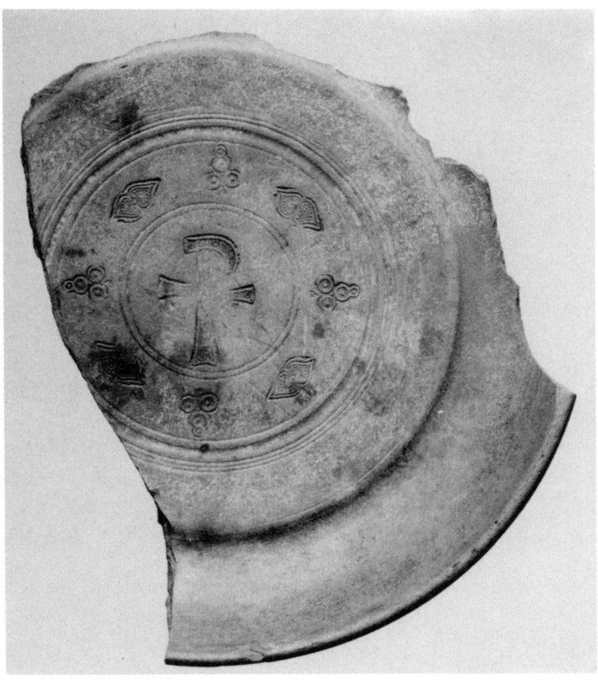

Impressed decoration on an Aswan-group bowl. *Courtesy Louvre Museum, Paris. Photo by Chuzeville.*

Terra-cotta stamps intended for imprinting decorative motifs have been found at Elephantine (Thilo, 1971, p. 235–42). Rouletted decoration, consisting of overlapping row on row of vertical or oblique incised strokes, was cut with a hard instrument. This operation took place when the vessel, after a first drying, again trued up on the moving potter's wheel. Rouletted decoration is characteristic of Group O wares (Jacquet-Gordon, 1972, p. 12, among forms D and E; Rodziewicz, types O3–O4, O22a, O24; Egloff, type 37; Grimm, p. 76, fig. 13a, c, d). Simple concentric grooves decorated the bottom of certain pieces of Group K wares (Egloff, 1977, type 63; Kasser, 1983, no. 28, 36), on the pattern of Late Roman B and D.

Another frequently found form of impressed decoration is the impression of ropes on and below the outer rim. This design might also be evidence of the manufacturing technique (Rodziewicz, types K21b, K23b, K24c).

Incised decoration is cut into the wall of the vessel with a gouge or knife to produce a line or groove. The shoulder and belly of light-colored clay pitchers at Kellia (Egloff, 1977, types 227–28), which perhaps originated in Abū Mīnā, were incised to create vertical fluting.

Water jug with stamped decoration and neck in the form of a bearded man. *Courtesy Coptic Museum, Cairo.*

Decoration by *deformation and cutting* is reserved exclusively for the rim, which is altered by pinching and pressing to make an undulation at the mouth of bowls and deep dishes (Egloff, 1977, pls. 76–79, 81; Jacquet-Gordon, 1972, forms S4; Murray, 1935, p. 7, pl. V, 4–5; Louvre, no. AF6939). The wide rim of certain plates in Group K is sometimes cut out as a slightly concave polygon (Rodziewicz, 1976, type K31; Hayes, 1976, no. 128).

Decoration in *relief* by means of appliqué or carving was uncommon. However, very large vessels such as bread ovens and basins were ornamented with pellets framed or linked by impressed rippled bands and associated with a design of impressed plants (Kasser, 1983, no. 155). The excavations of the Institut français d'archéologie orientale found some sherds from Hermitage 167 at Kellia showing such decoration. Schematic modeled faces were sometimes applied to the outer surface of vessels (Clédat, 1904, p. 102, fig. 57; Murray, 1935, pp. 2–3, pl. II, 2, III; Louvre, Archivio di filosofia 13886).

Painted Decoration. Painting clearly distinguishes Coptic pottery from the decorative techniques derived from late Roman ceramics, although the two methods of decoration were contemporaneous. Some pieces, however, juxtapose impressed motifs and painted ornamentation (Hayes, 1976, nos. 109–110).

A wide range of forms and wares could have painted decoration. Elaborate and sometimes presenting real compositions, it is present on cups, plates, wide bowls, and deep dishes. It also ornaments the shoulders of water jugs and pitchers; the permeability of their walls, preserving the coolness of the water, revived the colors. Painting was the preferred decoration for censers and pot lamps, probably for liturgical use. Reduced to simple points and quickly sketched bands and arcs, it adorns cooking pots. It is also found on storage vessels.

Decoration was not used on so-called deluxe ceramics. It appears on vessels whose material and manufacturing techniques may be mediocre, such as coarse-textured clays or sketchy finishing of rims and bases. In certain cases, the application of the decoration seems intended to conceal the technical poverty of the vessel.

The themes and techniques of painting on vases evolved until the fifth century, with Hellenistic and Roman motifs, such as garlands of flowers and designs in friezes, as the predominating influence. From the fifth to the seventh centuries, the workshops used both stylization and spontaneity in the

Large pottery jar painted with birds and saints. *Courtesy Coptic Museum, Cairo.*

treatment of motifs. They adopted the dark circle and employed a relatively limited palette of colors. They introduced a religious iconography, a wide variety of animals, and floral and geometrical combinations adapted to the demands of the form. From the eighth century the traditional character of painted ceramics persisted as much in Christian areas as in zones of Arab penetration.

Paint consisted of slip (liquid clay) colored by the addition of metallic oxides. One early technique on unglazed pottery was to coat a fired vessel with a thick layer of white slip and then paint motifs on it, as in examples of the third century from Antinoë (Antinoopolis) (Kueny and Yoyotte, 1979, nos, 198–201).

The colors used were brown and black (manganese or manganiferous hematite), red-orange (iron oxide), and white (very pure kaolin) (Neyret, 1966, pp. 40–41; Noll, p. 123). The decoration was monochrome (black/brown), bichrome (black/brown and white or black/brown and red/orange), or polychrome (black/brown, red/orange, and white). According to some experts, this technique preceded painting on a raw unfired base, but analyses of some potsherds of the Coptic period have confirmed that the painting had been fired (Noll, 1981, p. 123).

Painted decoration on a deep bowl: two men raising their right hands; ondulated rim. *Courtesy Louvre Museum, Paris. Photo by Chuzeville.*

Painted decoration on a water-jug; two hares and a vegetal motif. *Courtesy Coptic Museum, Cairo. Photo by Girgis.*

Paint was usually applied with a brush. A sketch of the figure was made in light ochre or white. Then the contours were quickly emphasized with black lines and hatching. This procedure of shading with swift, parallel strokes was probably influenced by the art of Alexandria (Badawy, 1954, p. 60). Finally the colors of the highlights were added (Neyret, 1966, p. 41; Desroches-Noblecourt and Vercoutter, 1981). Sometimes, however, the finger was used to print simple dots.

In the late Roman period, the composition of painted ceramic decoration was generally superposed friezes at the top of a vessel, as for example in the wares from Antinoopolis just cited and a vessel in the Louvre (AO.E11271), or a floral garland (*Meisterwerke altägyptischer Keramik,* 1978, no. 437). Coptic painters, however, preferred circular, centered compositions and the arrangement of motifs in metopes (square spaces in a Doric frieze). There was a close link between the form of the vessels and the composition of the ornamentation. The bodies of jars were suitable for motifs in metopes, while the insides of cups were adorned with centered designs. Lines and horizontal bands gave rhythm to the necks of water jugs, while their shoulders bore arcs encircled by pellets or lotus buds; sometimes foliage associated with fish was displayed. Geometric motifs were arranged on the wide rims of vessels and censers.

Coptic painted ceramics presented a wide range of iconography (Egloff, 1977, pp. 56–58; Mond and Myers, pls. 72–81). Painters of pottery probably drew their inspiration from the iconography of mural painting, book illumination, and textiles. Certain compositions with human figures, such as saints, appear to be veritable transpositions of scenes appropriate to wall paintings. A certain parallelism is noticeable in the treatment of forms, such as an outline delineating a motif or the hieratic aspect of a human form.

Coptic painted decoration relied to a moderate degree on the human figure. Often it was in the form of a bust, apparently derived from Egypto-Roman funerary portraits. Sometimes only the head was represented (Quibell, 1908, pl. 62, 4; Louvre, no. E10993; Bulté, 1980, no. 138, fig. p. 23). Saints in niches or saints on horseback fighting a dragon formed real little pictures (Neyret, 1966; *Hommages Serge Sauneron*, 1979, pp. 187–89; Murray, 1935, pp. 1–2, pl. I, 1, 4–5, pl. 9). The Louvre possesses a rare representation of two men raising their right hands on the fragment of a cup (Louvre, Archivio di filosofia, no. 6939).

The rich variety of beasts showed a strong preference for gazelles, lions, asses, and hares (Mond and Myers, 1940, pl. 72; Quibell, 1912, pl. 51). The volatile faun was sometimes associated with other animals (Coptic Museum, Cairo, no. 6720; Henne, 1925, pl. 21; Louvre, no. E1246/AF 4471). One painter had a liking for aquatic life (Hayes, 1976, nos. 107–108), including tortoises (Egloff, 1977, p. 53, pl. 36,2). Among the plants, the lotus and the vine were frequently depicted (Egloff, 1977, p. 49, pls. 64–65, 94; Desroches-Noblecourt and Vercoutter, 1981, no. 364).

Geometric motifs developed from the circular band into braid, plait, and scroll patterns among others (Egloff, 1977, pls. 96–98; Jacquet-Gordon, 1972, pp. 17–18). The metopes on jars were often enclosed in a lattice-work design (Coptic Museum, no. 39065/86401).

Painted mythical animal in the center of a large dish; probably from the Aswan workshops. *Courtesy Coptic Museum, Cairo. Photo by Girgis.*

In some cases the existence of schools or workshops can be distinguished, like that of the "master of Kellia" (Egloff, 1977, p. 49), as well as that of the artist who probably created two vases with similar decoration (Quibell, Vol. 4, 1912, pl. 51; Piankoff, 1942, pp. 25–29) and perhaps a third specimen (Bulté, 1981, no. 77).

Glazing. At the end of the seventh century glazing appeared, a development that has been highlighted by the work of Rodziewicz at Kom al-Dikka, Alexandria (Rodziewicz, 1978, pp. 338–45; Rodziewicz, 1983, pp. 73–75). Glaze in the form of finely powdered glass was applied to earthenware and then fired to produce a vitreous coating that would be impervious to liquid. Glaze was used with both impressed and painted decoration. Glaze was applied to vessels of Groups O and W of local fine wares (Rodziewicz, 1976, pp. 54, 61). In the eighth century, glazed specimens from Groups O and W coexisted with unglazed specimens, which disappeared in the course of the ninth century. During this second phase, local glazed ceramics continued, while glazed ceramics began to be imported from Syria, Mesopotamia (Iraq), and Persia (Iran).

On these local examples the red/orange slip coating of wares (in Group O) was covered with a clear glaze. The white slip coating of wares (in Group W) was more frequently covered with one or several layers of glaze—brown, green, or transparent. The glaze enriched the effect of the traditional red, brown, and black colors of painted decoration beneath the glaze. A green or brown glaze was also laid down over the transparent, vitreous coating. The characteristic Coptic motifs such as birds and garlands were contemporary with floral elements marked by a naturalist tendency and probably influenced by the lusterware from Samarra, Mesopotamia.

BIBLIOGRAPHY

Badawy, A. "L'Art copte. Les Influences hellénistiques et romaines." *Bulletin de l'Institut d'Egypte* 35 (1954):5–68.

Bulté, J. "La Céramique copte." *Archéologia* 138 (1980):20–25.

Clédat, J. *Le monastère et la nécropole de Baouît.* Mémoires publiés par les membres de l'Institut français d'archéologie orientale Vol. 12, no. 34. Cairo, 1904.

Desroches-Noblecourt, C. and J. Vercoutter, eds. *Un Siècle de fouilles françaises en Egypte, 1880–1980.* Cairo and Paris, 1981.

Egloff, M. *Kellia: la poterie copte. Quatre siècles d'artisanat et d'échanges en Basse Egypte.* Recherches suisses d'Archéologie copte, Vol. 3. Geneva, 1977.

Grimm, G. *Stadt und Tempel von Elephantine. Fünfter Grabungsbericht.* Mitteilungen des Deutschen Archäologischen Instituts—Abteilung Kairo, Vol. 31. Mainz am Rhein, 1975.

Hayes, J. W. *Roman Pottery in the Royal Ontario Museum. A Catalogue.* Toronto, 1976.

Henne, Henri. *Rapport sur les fouilles de Tell Edfou 1923–4.* Fouilles de l'Institut français d'archéologie orientale, Vol. 2, pt. 3. Cairo, 1925.

Hommages à la mémoire de Serge Sauneron 1927–1976, Vol. 2. Bibliothèque d'étude, Vol. 82. Cairo, 1979.

Jacquet-Gordon, H. *Les Ermitages chrétiens du désert d'Esna. Céramique et objets,* vol. 3. Fouilles de l'Institut français d'archéologie orientale, Vol. 29, pt. 3. Cairo, 1972.

Kasser, R. *Survey archéologique des Kellia (Basse-Egypte). Rapport de la campagne 1981.* Missions Suisses d'Archéologie Copte de l'Université de Genève. Louvain, 1983.

Meisterwerke altägyptischer Keramik. 5000 Jahre Kunst und Kunsthandwerk aus Ton und Fayence. Hohr-Grenzhausen, 1978.

Mond, R., and O. H. Myers. *Temples of Armant. A Preliminary Survey.* Egypt Exploration Fund, Vol. 48. London, 1940.

Murray, M. A. "Coptic Painted Pottery." *Ancient Egypt and the East* 20, June (1935):1–15.

Neyret, C. *Les Céramiques coptes du Musée du Louvre,* Mémoire, Ecole du Louvre (manuscript). Paris, 1966. We have drawn extensively on this study in regard to the painted decoration.

Noll, W. *Bemalte Keramiken. Studien zur altägyptischen Keramik,* ed. D. Arnold. Mainz am Rhein, 1981.

Quibell, J. E. *Excavations at Saqqara, II, 1906–1907.* Cairo, 1908.

———. *Excavations at Saqqara, IV, 1908–9, 1909–10: The Monastery of Apa Jeremias.* Cairo, 1912.

Rodziewicz, M. *La céramique romaine tardive d'Alexandrie, Alexandrie I.* Warsaw, 1976.

———. *La Céramique émaillée copte de Kôm el-Dikka.* Etudes et Travaux, Vol. 10. Travaux du Centre d'archéologie méditerranéenne de l'Académie Polonaise des Sciences, Vol. 20. Warsaw, 1978.

———. "Egyptian Glazed Pottery of the Eighth to Ninth Centuries." *Bulletin de la Société d'archéologie copte* 25 (1983):73–75.

Ulbert, T. "Keramikstempel aus Elephantine." *Mitteilungen des Deutschen Archäologischen Instituts, Abteilung Kairo* 27 (1971):235–42.

Waagé, O. F. *Hellenistic and Roman Tableware of North Syria, Antioch on the Orontes IV.* Princeton, N.J., 1948.

Types of Ceramic Ware

The ceramics of Copto-Byzantine Egypt are all of terra-cotta, that is, fired earthenware. They offer a varied range of shapes and manufacturing groups adapted to very specific functions. The following discussion is based largely on the few monographs on archaeological sites that deal with pottery. The classification given here must be considered tentative and intended to be revised and completed in the future. It deals with documentation generally dated from the end of the fourth to the eighth centuries A.D. inclusive.

The sites—such as hermitages at Isnā and Kellia and urban foundations at Alexandria and Elephantine—have yielded a rich collection of material completing the picture provided by museum collections. This material gives evidence of daily use of "fine" tableware, cooking pots, amphorae, and water jugs. In the hermitages, ceramic material was frequently used as a component part in building.

"Fine" Tableware. Plates and dishes were generally intended for the presentation and consumption of food. Some pieces decorated with Christian motifs may have had a liturgical role, replacing vessels in precious metal or glass.

The terminology adopted here must not be understood in the strict sense: the borderline between plates and dishes is difficult to establish; these types of vessel are also called cups and bowls. Morphological definitions seem, however, to agree on the following criteria: the diameter of the mouth is generally more than 6 to 8 inches (15–20 cm) and the objects are shallow, with a depth seldom more than one-third of the diameter.

Plates and dishes are well represented in the three groups of "fine" ceramic ware distinguished by Rodziewicz according to the clay of which they are made: Group K, Group O, and Group W (Rodziewicz, 1976, pp. 50, 54, 61), as previously noted. They were influenced by late Roman ceramics imported into Egypt, designated Late Roman A, Late Roman B: Light Sigillate D, Late Roman C, and Late Roman D: Cypriot Red Slip Ware, according to Waagé's old terminology. They are attested from the fifth to the eighth centuries and later, a period during which they evolved morphologically.

Group K (carmine red) ware is of red to brown micaceous clay; the slip is red. From the present state of our knowledge, it seems that it was especially widespread in the Delta and in Middle Egypt (Rodziewicz, 1976, pp. 50–53; Egloff, 1977, pp. 79ff., "Group 2," types 38, 40, 44–47, 50, 52–55, 57, 62, 73–77, 79).

Group O (orange) ware is of orange-pink clay. The slip, of orange-red, is brown on the rim of some specimens (Rodziewicz, p. 55). This group appears in Lower Egypt and very frequently in Upper Egypt (Rodziewicz, pp. 54–60, pl. 23–31; Egloff, pp. 79ff., "Group 1," types 32–37, 39, 41–43, 48–49, 56–59, 61, 63–66; Winlock and Crum, 1926, pp. 86–87, figs. 37, 41; Jacquet-Gordon, 1972, forms C, D, E of clays II and IIa, pp. 11–12; Gempeler, 1976, p. 109). It is widespread in Nubia and was probably made in the region of Aswan, according to W. V. Adams (Adams, 1986, pp. 538ff.).

A variant of this type, Group W (white), has light slip, that is whitish to yellow (Rodziewicz, 1976, pp. 61–62, pls. 32–33; Kasser, 1983, nos. 7 and 13).

A collection of "fine" ceramic of the fourth to fifth centuries, localized in the oases of Khargah and Dakhlah in the Western Desert, consists basically of bowls. The minerals included in the clay (small "shales") confirm the local manufacture of these products (Hope, 1981, p. 235; Rodziewicz, 1983, pp. 140–42, fig. 3a).

The typological approach to classification of pottery remains uncertain, at least for the purpose of tracing the broad outlines. Nevertheless, there are a number of plate forms with a wide flat rim whose diameter often exceeds one foot (30 cm). Other plates, of more modest size, show a thickened rim or one formed by a lip flared outward. The sides are slightly convex, sometimes with a rectilinear flaring. The base is generally formed by an annular foot.

The inner and outer surfaces of these types of vessels are coated with a matte or slightly shiny slip, in red (Group K), orange (Group O), or white-beige (Group W). Their open form makes them suitable for decoration; the inner surface sometimes carries stamped motifs, guilloches, painted decorations, and, on some late specimens, a coat of glaze. The outer surface is often decorated with guilloches, sometimes also found on the rim. Among the stamped motifs, the monogram of Christ and crosses are the most frequent (Hayes, 1976, nos. 109–110). The painted decoration is applied as a circular or centered composition. The themes are often taken from the animal and vegetable kingdoms, for example, hares running, separated by a plant motif (*Meisterwerke* 1978, no. 438, pl. 15); a central motif ornaments the bottom of dishes, sometimes a fish (Hayes, No. 107–108), a bird (Louvre, E12226; Desroches-Noblecourt and Vercoutter, 1981, no. 357), sometimes a mythical animal (Coptic Museum, no. 3374a/10271). The raised rim of plates frequently has a painted decoration of interlacing, braid, and scroll patterns (Kasser, 1983, no. 13, p. 429). The glaze that appears on certain examples of Groups O and W from Alexandria is applied over painted decorations in the Coptic tradition, such as the bird and floral themes (Rodziewicz, 1978, pls. 3–4).

The application of decoration was not a general rule: plates and dishes from Group K were generally without it, except for a few stamped impressions, imprints of cords on the outer edge, and circular grooves. It is also quite probable that the lack of painted decoration is due to the sometimes mediocre qualities of the painted layer and its poor state of preservation.

Among some typological and functional variants of "fine" tableware, some dishes for cooking, often carinated, with a broad, rounded base, should be noted. They are technologically related to wares of Group K (Egloff, 1977, types 81–97; Kasser, 1983, nos. 41ff.; Rodziewicz, 1976, types K 34–36). There are also platters with small cup-shaped depressions arranged around the rim, surrounding a central cup, which might, from their compartmentalized structure, have held several ingredients or foodstuffs. The inspiration for them could have come from silver vessels (Desroches-Noblecourt, 1982, pp. 11 and 18 and n. 11, pls. 3, 5–6; Coptic Museum, nos. 3388, 6721, 9036; for the most up-to-date

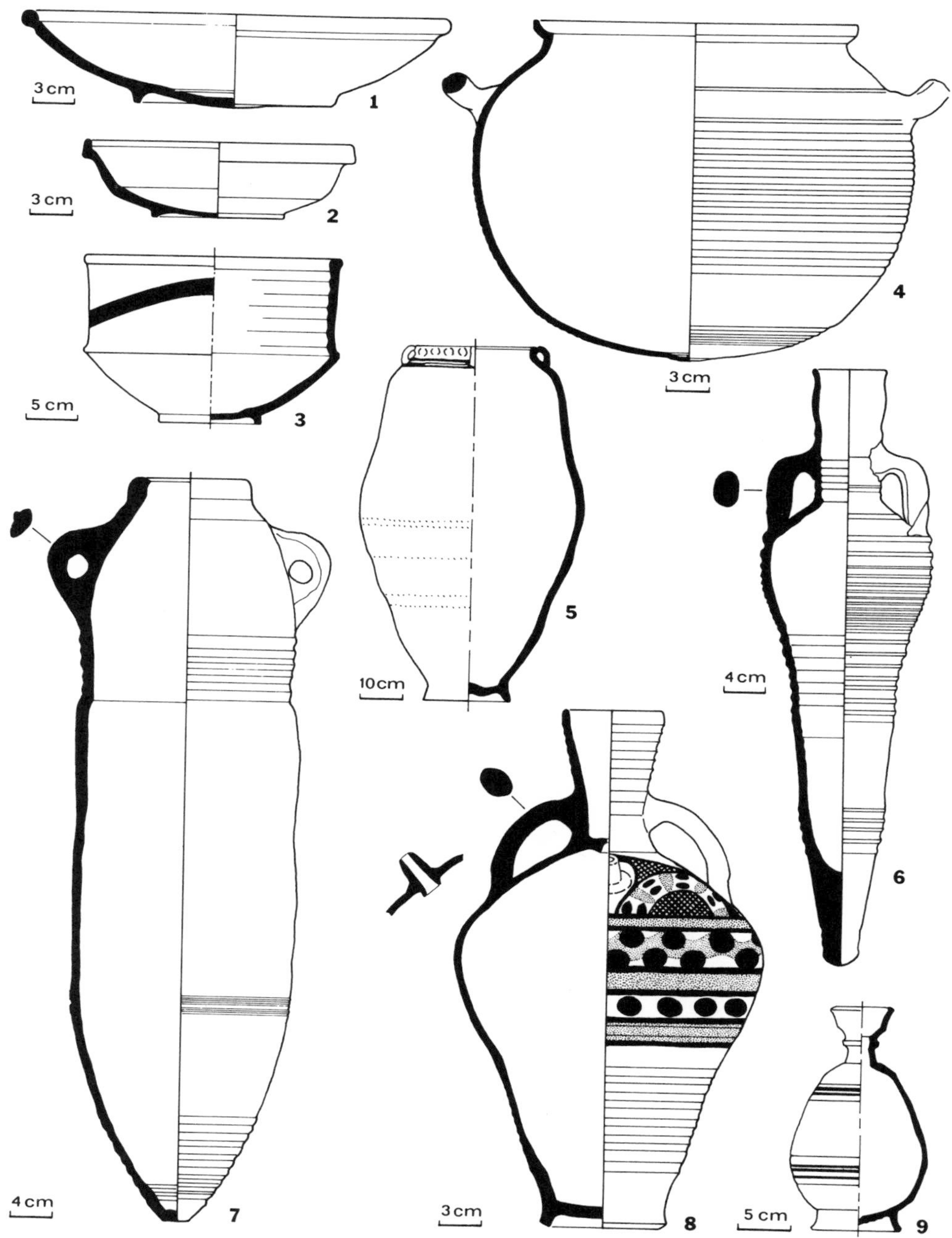

Principal pottery types and groups in Coptic-Byzantine Egypt: 1. Plate, "group K." From Kellia. Egloff, type 76. 2. Bowl, "group O." Kellia. Egloff, type 34. 3. Deep dish. Isna. Jacquet-Gordon, E11. 4. Cooking-pot. Kellia. Egloff, type 118. 5. Storage jar. Isna. Jacquet-Gordon, K2. 6. Brown "Middle Egyptian"(?) amphora. Kellia. Egloff, type 174. 7. Egyptian or Palestinian (?)"Amphore-obus," Kellia. Egloff, type 182. 8. Water-jug. Kellia. Egloff, type 204. 9. Bottle, "group O" or Aswan Ware. Isna. Jacquet-Gordon, N5. *Reproduced from Jacquet-Gordon, 1972, and Egloff, 1976, by P. Laferrière. Courtesy P. Ballet.*

discussion of these cupped platters, see Rutschowskaya, 1985).

BIBLIOGRAPHY

Desroches-Noblecourt, C. "Les Nouvelles fouilles de Tod: Résultats des quatre premières saisons de recherche. Printemps 1980-automne 1981." *Bulletin de la Société Française d'Egyptologie* 93 (1982):12.

Desroches-Noblecourt, C., and J. Vercoutter, eds. *Un Siècle de fouilles françaises en Egypte, 1880–1980.* Cairo and Paris, 1981.

Egloff, M. *Kellia: la poterie copte. Quatre siècles d'artisanat et d'échanges en Basse-Egypte.* Recherches suisses d'Archéologie copte, Vol. 3. Geneva, 1977.

Hayes, J. W. *Roman Pottery in the Royal Ontario Museum. A Catalogue.* Toronto, 1976.

Kasser, R. *Survey archéologique des Kellia (Basse-Egypte). Rapport de la campagne 1981.* Missions Suisses d'Archéologie Copte de l'Université de Genève. Louvain, 1983.

Meisterwerke altägyptischer Keramik, 5000 Jahre Kunst und Kunsthandwerk aus Ton und Fayence. Hohr-Grenhausen, 1978.

Rodziewicz, M. *La Céramique romaine tardive d'Alexandrie, Alexandrie I.* Warsaw, 1976.

______. *La Céramique émaillée copte de Kôm el-Dikka.* Etudes et Travaux, Vol. 10; Travaux du Centre d'archéologie méditerranéenne de l'Académie polonaise des sciences, Vol. 20. Warsaw, 1978.

Rutschowskaya, M.-H. "Plats à cupules d'époque copte," *Revue du Louvre* 5/6 (1985):412–15.

Deep Dishes and Bowls. Deep dishes and bowls made of brown to red clay, often black in the break, are similar to wares of Group K; however, the texture is coarser (Egloff, 1977, types 258–98; Jacquet-Gordon, 1972, E11–15, S1–4). Deep dishes are usually fairly large, generally exceeding 10 inches (25 cm) in diameter. They are characterized by a wide, often flat base, walls that widen out, and an everted lip with a broad rim decorated with pinched undulations and/or horizontal grooves on the inner surface. Bowls differ from the dishes, in general, in being deeper and having a less elaborate rim. These vessels are often decorated with painted motifs.

Cooking Vessels. Cooking vessels are found in several types of clay. They have rounded bases. Shallow dishes with flaring walls present features in common with wares of Group K, so far as clays and manufacturing techniques are concerned (Rodziewicz, 1976, K 35–36; Egloff, 1977, types 80–97; Winlock and Crum, 1926, fig. 42, A–E; Jacquet-Gordon, 1972, C 5–8). Cooking pots are often carinated (ridged) up to the lower third of their height. Some are made of Group K clays; others are of micaceous clays with quartz grains. These pots are sometimes decorated with painted dots on curved bands (Egloff, 1977, types 98–108; Winlock and Crum, 1926, fig. 42, G–K).

Other cooking pots, with a convex belly, have vertical or horizontal handles. They are made of easily recognizable micaceous clay, which in some cases includes a high proportion of quartz grains. The fine walls may reach a thickness of 4–5 mm. The outer surface carries a ribbing sometimes alternating with smooth surface.

These cooking pots form a group, very widespread in Egypt, with many morphological variations (Rodziewicz and Rodziewicz, 1983, p. 275, fig. 13; Egloff, 1977, types 112–13, dating from the end of the fourth to the fifth centuries; types 114–54, later, matching the general description of pots [above]; Spencer and Bailey, 1982, pp. 20ff., figs. 6–19, first half of the fifth to the first half of the seventh centuries; Winlock and Crum, 1926, fig. 47; Jacquet-Gordon, 1972, M 13–16, pl. CCXXV; Gempeler, 1976, p. 109, fig. 9a–b). They are generally associated with lids of similar technology (Egloff, 1977, types 347–52).

Storage Jars. Large jars were intended for storing provisions and liquids. Their dimensions (a height of about 27 to 39 inches [70 to 100 cm]) necessitated a specific method of manufacture (see the section Manufacturing Techniques above).

These receptacles have a flat base, a body with convex walls widening halfway up, a slightly marked neck, and a flanged rim. The outer surface is often ornamented with a painted design (Quibell 1908, pl. 62; Quibell, 1912, pl. 51; Winlock and Crum, 1926, fig. 46; Jacquet-Gordon, 1972, form K; Bruyère et al., 1937, pl. 39; Gempeler, 1976, p. 110, fig. 9c; Hope, 1981, p. 237, pl. 28, 9; Hayes, 1976, no. 233; Coptic Museum, Old Cairo, nos. 2994, 39065/9025, 86301). Technologically and morphologically the jars from Kellia are fairly similar to the cooking pots (Egloff, 1977, types 158–63).

Amphorae. The large jars called amphorae, which have a rounded or pointed base and two handles, were intended essentially for the transportation of provisions and liquids. There are five types.

Brown wine amphorae are of richly micaceous clay that is brown both on the surface and in the break. They have a slender form and pointed base and more or less pronounced ridges on the shoulder. The oldest examples appeared in the Ptolemaic

Storage jar ornamented with figures representing human faces. *Courtesy Coptic Museum, Cairo.*

and Roman periods (Hayes, 1976, no. 364). This group was widely distributed in Copto-Byzantine Egypt and during the first centuries of the Arab occupation.

There are three subtypes of brown wine amphorae. (1) Amphorae with a pointed base and an annular protuberance were known at Kellia from the end of the fourth to the end of the fifth centuries (Egloff, 1977, type 172). (2) Amphorae in the shape of a spinning top (Hayes, 1976, no. 365), date from the fifth to the sixth centuries, with earlier bibliographical references (Jacquet-Gordon, 1972, p. 7; Egloff, 1977, type 180; Kasser, 1983, no. 91, dating from the second quarter of the seventh century). (3) Small amphorae with a sharply defined shoulder evolved, at Kellia, from the end of the fourth century to the eighth century (Egloff, 1977, type 177, the oldest; types 173–74, common from the second half of the seventh century). They are comparable to the "Late Roman Hermopolite Amphorae B," for which D. M. Bailey's study has developed the morphological sequence according to the stratigraphy of the excavations conducted at al-Ashmūnayn (Spencer and Bailey, 1981, pp. 16ff.; see also Hayes, 1976, nos. 367–69).

Obus amphorae are of light brown micaceous clay (Egloff, 1977, types 182–83; Kasser, 1983, no. 90; Kaufman, 1910, pls. 15, 84; Bernard et al., 1937, pl. 38). They have a body shaped like a cannon shell and a barely indicated short neck. Short round handles are attached under the rim, and the surface is smooth except for some very fine grooves, traced with a comb, halfway up the body. It remains to be determined whether this group of amphorae was local or imported.

Light spheroidal amphorae of light clay are characterized by a round base and a spheroidal or baggy body with a short, narrow, cylindrical neck. Small round handles are luted on to the shoulder. The surface carries fine ribbings. These amphorae, generally dating from the seventh century onward, are principally found in the sites of the Nile Delta. Some of them might have been manufactured at Abū Mīnā (Egloff, 1977, type 186; Kasser, 1983, nos. 78–85; Jacquet-Gordon, 1972, p. 11).

Red ovoid amphorae are made of red clay with, as characteristic inclusions, vegetal particles in the form of fine, black, oblong nodules. Morphologically these amphorae are similar to the previous group. Nevertheless, their dimensions are more modest, and the shape of the body is generally ovoid. They were common at Kellia from the middle of the seventh century, as well as in the contemporary or later urban sites (such as Alexandria and al-Fusṭāṭ [Cairo]) (Egloff, 1977, type 187; Ballet, 1986); Bonnet, 1984).

Byzantine Aswan amphorae as the name implies come from Aswan (see Adams, 1986, pp. 545ff., ware U2.).

Water Jugs, Pitchers, and Bottles. A variety of forms were intended to hold liquid. Water jugs are generally made from porous clay, to preserve the coolness of the stored water by permitting constant evaporation. One group is of calcareous clay, without external coating (Egloff, 1977, types 198–200, end of fourth to fifth centuries; Winlock and Crum, 1926, p. 91; Jacquet-Gordon, 1972, clay 4, N26ff.). Another group is of reddish, micaceous clay, with the external surface coated with a slip and decorated with painted motifs (Egloff, 1976, type 204ff., from the fifth to the eighth centuries; Winlock and Crum, 1926, p. 91). Water jugs have rounded or pear-shaped bodies with varied neck forms, on the base of which a filter is luted. The foot is annular or in pedestal form; sometimes water jugs are provided with one or two handles and a spout.

Pitchers are often round-bellied. The mouth, for pouring, may be trefoil, pinched, or drawn out. Among the most easily recognizable series are

Water jug ornamented with crosses, birds, and fish. *Courtesy Coptic Museum, Cairo.*

small pitchers, often with a trilobate opening and decorated with vertical gouged lines, that were no doubt produced at Abū Mīnā and distributed in different places (Kaufmann, 1910, pls. 83–86; Egloff, 1977, types 227–28; Hayes, 1976, no. 275, which indicates an example found at Karanis). Originating also from Abū Mīnā is a collection of jugs bearing on the shoulder the inscription *eulogia* ("praise or blessing"), intended to hold the miraculous water of the sanctuary (Kaufman, pls. 85–87; for other types of pitchers and jugs, see Jacquet-Gordon, 1972, N′1-7).

Bottles (or flasks) must no doubt be recognized as the successors of the Roman *unguentaria* (ointment flasks). A certain number are related to wares of Group O in the matter of clays and slip. Among the shapes with an ovoid or pear-shaped body with a hole by way of filter, some examples seem to have contained an oily product (Jacquet-Gordon, 1972, N 1–5; of comparable shape but without trace of any kind of residue is a flask found in the Kom 167 at Kellia). Other bottles are more squat with the maximum diameter of the body greater than the height (Hayes, 1976, nos. 124–27, with parallels from Ihnāsiyah and Ballana).

Other Types of Water Vessels.

Water kegs, oval-bellied (with a horizontal axis) and short-necked, were probably used for drawing and holding water (Egloff, 1977, type 338; Hope, 1981, pp. 235–36). Widespread in the Roman period, they persisted in Copto-Byzantine Egypt.

Sāqiyah pots (qawādīs) have a wide mouth, a well-defined rim, and a base with a knob, around which a cord was tied to attach them to the *sāqiyah* (waterwheel). They were rare in Kellia (Egloff, 1977, type 256), but some were found at Thebes (Winlock and Crum, 1926, pp. 64–65, fig. 23). At Isnā, where no *sāqiyah* was found near the hermitages, they are thought to have been used as storage jars (Jacquet-Gordon, 1972, p. 7, R1–2).

Water pipes were placed either end-to-end or interlocking (Winlock and Crum, 1926, p. 92, fig. 48C–D; Ballet, 1983, pp. 2–4, fig. p).

Water keg painted with fishes. *Courtesy Coptic Museum, Cairo.*

Table of Concordances of Nomenclature of Egyptian Ceramics

RODZIEWICZ AND RODZIEWICZ, 1983	HAYES, 1972	EGLOFF, 1977	ADAMS, 1970	ADAMS, 1986
Group K	Egyptian B (pp. 397–99)	Group 2 ("sigillée égyptienne")		
Group O	Egyptian A (Coptic red slip ware) (pp. 387ff.)	Group 1 ("sigillée égyptienne")	Aswan Group A II	Byzantine Aswan wares, Group A II, R4 (pp. 543ff.)

BIBLIOGRAPHY

Adams, W. Y., *Ceramic Industries of Medieval Nubia,* Vols. 1–2. Lexington, Kentucky, 1986.

Ballet, P. "Kellia, Koms 88 et 166." *Bulletin de liaison du Groupe internationale d'etude de la céramique égyptienne* 8 (1983):2–4.

———. "Céramique tardive des Kellia et présence islamique en Egypte." In *Le Site monastique copte des Kellia. Sources historiques et explorations archéologiques, Actes du Colloque de Genève, 13–15 August 1984,* ed. P. Bridel. Geneva, 1986.

Ballet, P. and M. Picon. *Recherches préliminaires sur les origines de la céramique des Kellia (Egypte). Importations et productions égyptiennes.* Cahiers de la Céramique Egyptienne, Vol. 1. Cairo, 1987.

Bonnet, F. "Possibilitiés de datation des amphores ovoïdes, à pâte rouge, d'époque islamique, en ce qui concerne la période d'abandon des Kellia." In *Actes du Colloque de Genēve,* 13–15 August 1984.

Bruyère, B., et al. *Tell Edfou 1937.* Fouilles francopolonaises, rapports, Vol. 1. Cairo, 1937.

Egloff, M. *Kellia. La poterie copte: Quatre siècles d'artisanat et d'échanges en Basse-Égypte.* Recherches suisses d'archéologie copte, Vol. 3. Geneva, 1977.

Gempeler, R. *Stadt und Tempel von Elephantine. Sechster Grabungsbericht.* Mitteilungen des Deutschen Archäologischen Instituts—Abteilung Kairo, Vol. 32. Mainz am Rhein, 1976.

Hayes, J. W. *Roman Pottery in the Royal Ontario Museum. A Catalogue.* Toronto, 1976.

Hope, C. A. "Dakhleh Oasis Project. Report on the Study of the Pottery and Kilns. Third Season, 1980." *Journal of the Society for the Study of the Egyptian Antiquities,* 11, 4 (1981):233–41.

Jacquet-Gordon, H. *Les Ermitages chrétiens du désert d'Esna. Céramique et objets,* Vol. 3. Fouilles de l'Institut français d'archéologie orientale, Vol. 29, pt. 3. Cairo, 1972.

Kasser, R. *Survey archéologique des Kellia (Basse-Egypte). Rapport de la campagne 1981.* Missions Suisses d'Archéologie Copte de l'Université de Genève. Louvain, 1983.

Kaufmann, C. M. *Die Menasstadt und das Nationalheiligtum der altchristlichen Ägypter in der Westalexandrischen Wüste,* Vol. 1. Leipzig, 1910.

Mysliwiec, K. *Keramik and Kleinfunde aus der Grabung im Tempel Sethos' I. in Gurna.* Archäologische Veröffentlichungen, Vol. 57. Mainz am Rhein, 1987.

Quibell, J. E. *Excavations at Saqqara, II, 1906–1907.* Cairo, 1908.

———. *Excavations at Saqqara, IV, 1908–9, 1909–10: The Monastery of Apa Jeremias.* Cairo, 1912.

Rodziewicz, M. *La Céramique romaine tardive d'Alexandrie, Alexandrie I.* Warsaw, 1976.

———. *Douch. Rapport préliminaire de la campagne de fouilles de 1981.* Annales du Service des Antiquités de l'Égypte, Vol. 69. Cairo, 1983.

———. *Les Habitations romaines tardives d'Alexandrie à la lumière des fouilles polonaises à Kôm el-Dikka, Alexandrie III.* Warsaw, 1984.

Rodziewicz, E., and M. Rodziewicz. "Alexandrie 1977." *Études et Travaux* 12 (1983):275.

Spencer, A. J., and D. M. Bailey. *British Museum. Expedition to Middle Egypt. Ashmunein (1981),* British Museum, Occasional Paper 41, London, 1982. *Ashmunein (1982),* Occasional Paper 46, London, 1983. *Ashmunein (1983),* Occasional Paper 53, London, 1984. *Ashmunein (1984),* Occasional Paper 61, London, 1985. *Ashmunein (1985),* Occasional Paper 67, London, 1986.

Waagé, O. F. *Hellenistic and Roman Tableware of North Syria, Antioch on the Orontes IV.* Princeton, N.J., 1948.

Winlock, H. E., and W. E. Crum. *The Monastery of Epiphanius at Thebes,* Vol. 1. Metropolitan Museum of Art, Egyptian Expedition. New York, 1926.

Lamps. Most of the lamps in Copto-Byzantine Egypt were made of terra-cotta. They come from the areas of habitation such as Ihnāsiyah, Antinoopolis, Armant, Medamud, and Madīnat Hābū, and from religious centers that attracted pilgrims such as Abū Mīnā. The hermitages at Kellia and Isnā have furnished relatively few. The various oils used to feed lamps in Egypt, such as castor oil, palm oil, and olive oil, are mentioned by the classical authors and in the Greek papyri (Lucas, 1962, p. 329; Shier, 1978, p. 7). Vegetable fibers or strands of wool formed the wicks (Schier, 1978, p. 7).

Copto-Byzantine lamps were influenced by the technical traditions of Hellenistic and Roman lamp making. From the third century B. C. onward, saucer lamps, handmade or turned on a wheel, were progressively replaced by bivalve molded lamps. The two valves form a reservoir with a convex profile; in lamps of the Roman period the reservoir has the shape of a casserole with a cover. The upper part, slightly bulged, includes a disk or medallion, often concave, pierced by the aperture for pouring in oil, and the disk may be adorned with a decoration in relief. The lower part rests on a generally flat base, on which a maker's mark is sometimes shown. The nozzle, from which the end of the wick emerges, forms an appendage, more or less free of the reservoir. On the opposite side, a modeled handle is luted with a liquid clay. Sometimes it is molded in one piece with the upper valve. The majority of the lamps from Copto-Byzantine Egypt derived from this type of manufacture (examples of molds in Kaufmann, 1910, pl. 82, bottom of plate; Badawy, 1978, p. 345, fig. 5.50, 1 and n. 61, with earlier bibliography).

Just as with ceramic vessels, the description of lamps as "Coptic" must be viewed with caution. Certainly the iconographic scheme and the inscriptions may be used in identifying an object as Christian. However, it seems prejudicial to the study of these lamps to consider this documentation within unduly strict morphological, decorative, and chronological limits. Systematic differentiation between late Roman and Christian material, or Christian and Islamic, is the result of a procedure that neglects the reality of the technological traditions and the history of the workshops. For example, we may note the presence of dolphin and *echinus* (sea urchin) lamps, considered as late Roman, in contexts dated, respectively, in the fourth and fifth centuries and fifth and sixth centuries (Hölscher, 1954, vol. 5, p. 68, Group 3, g; Group 2, c). In the same way, the oldest lamps from al-Fusṭāṭ present the same technical and decorative characteristics as contemporary "Christian" lamps (Kubiak, 1970, pp. 3–5).

In addition, the study of lamps suffers from an almost total absence of reliable elements for dating. Either because of method or because the context did not lend itself to doing so, archaeological work has rarely furnished data capable of allowing an approach at once typological and chronological (on this question, see Hayes, 1976, pp. 93, 118). Nevertheless, we shall present here documentation generally supporting a dating between the fourth and eighth centuries, with due regard to the reservations expressed above.

The classification proposed by J. W. Hayes (Hayes, 1976, pp. 118ff.), excluding the *frog-lamps*, is based on such matters as the method of manufacture and the type of clay or slip. It attempts to discover the geographical distribution of various groups. In regard to a museum collection, the dates, established on the basis of comparison, are presented as hypotheses. This study, as well as the older one of U. Hölscher, the main lines of which we shall follow here, appears to be the most important in the present state of research.

There are four types of *mold-made lamps*. The upper part of the oval reservoir of *frog lamps* is adorned by a frog. Often there is no added handle. The frog is treated in realistic or stylized fashion. A third variant presents only the hind feet of the batrachian, the rest of the body being rendered by a square shape (Petrie, 1905, group E, "frog and corn," p. 10, pl. 64.) For the classification of the frog lamps, see studies by M. Kunze and J. Mynarczyk.

According to the majority of authors, frog lamps were particularly abundant in Egypt from the second to the fourth centuries, and they were a specially original product of the country. At Madīnat Hābū they come from levels dated probably in the third and fourth centuries (Hölscher, 1954, Vol. 5, group 4, pp. 68–69). However, their manufacture and use continued later than the fourth century. Their morphological evolution is not very well known (Shier, 1978, p. 24). Some bear Christian inscriptions or motifs (Shier, 1978, p. 24); their symbolism conjures up the themes of resurrection, immortality, and fecundity (Mlynarczyk, 1973, pp. 100ff.; Leclant, 1978, pp. 565f.).

A second type of molded lamp, akin to frog lamps in form and decoration, are lamps in other motifs called, according to F. Petrie's classification, "corn and palm," "arm," and "boss" (Petrie, 1905, Group P, pp. 10–11, pl. 65; Group A, p. 11–12, pl. 66;

Group B, p. 12, pl. 67). Often the conventional term "frog lamp" is retained, whatever the theme represented. At Madīnat Habu, some examples are dated to the fourth and fifth centuries (Hölscher, Vol. 5, p. 69, Group 5).

A third group of molded lamps is characterized by an oval body, an often carinated profile, a ribbed vertical handle, and a thick, glossy red slip. One series of these lamps are not quite oval, with a relatively large disk, often decorated with a rosette. Another series includes more elongated forms with a nozzle-channel and a small disk. Recent excavations at al-Ashmūnayn (Hermopolis Magna) have yielded an important number of these lamps. The archaeological context dates them from the fifth century to the Arab conquest. They are comparable to lamps found at Antinoopolis, which were probably manufactured in this region of Middle Egypt (Guerrini, 1974, pp. 96–98, pl. 38, 4–12 and pp. 103ff., pls. 42–43; Hayes, 1976, pp. 120–23, no. 476–91, "Middle Egyptian [questionable]. These lamps are also called red-burnished ware"; Spencer and Bailey, 1982, pp. 34–35.

A fourth group of molded lamps, generally round but sometimes oval, with larger funnels, is made of light-colored pink or orange, relatively fine clay with very small mineral elements, including micas. The clay seems identical to that of Group O (orange) ware. The slip is described as red, with rose or orange variations.

The medallion, of average diameter, is often decorated with a cross or a rose. A Greek or Coptic inscription appears on the circumference (mention of a saint or the Holy Trinity, on a lamp from Medamud in the Louvre, no. E12950 [Bisson de la Roque, 1928, no. 2024, pp. 80–81, fig. 48]). Sometimes the decoration is a floral one; rosettes, palmettes, or vine branches surround the disk. The relief of the inscriptions and motifs is very strongly marked, the molds being deeply incised.

These lamps come chiefly from Upper Egypt and Nubia and they are dated from the fifth century on (Bisson de la Roque, 1928, nos. 1850, 1913, 2024, 2025, pp. 80–81, fig. 48; Hölscher, 1954, p. 69, Group VII e and f). Hayes calls this series Early Christian Aswan Ware class, including a series deriving from Armant (Hayes, 1976, nos. 495–518, pp. 124–29). Some molds found at Elephantine indicate that this group was partly produced in this area (Ballet and Mahmoud, 1987, pp. 56–57, 64–67).

A fifth group of mold-made lamps has an oval body with a hook-like handle and is covered with light yellow slip. The decoration around the disk frequently consists of concentric semicircles in a pattern of multiple arcs, either stamped or incised. These lamps appear to have been widespread in Upper Egypt and are called "Upper Egypt yellow-slipped ware" by Hayes (1976, pp. 131–33, no. 530–39; see also Hölscher, 1954, Vol. 5, p. 69, Group 6a).

A sixth group comprises a set of oval lamps characterized by the lengthening of the reservoir, which is accentuated by a groove underlining the disk and marking off the feed-channel as far as the end of the nozzle. The decoration is varied and includes floral and geometrical designs. Inscriptions sometimes appear around the central disk. Such lamps are generally considered to be a late product from the sixth and seventh centuries and are known throughout Egypt (Petrie, 1905, p. 9, pls. 61–62, "groove lamps"). Hölscher mentions "beak-shaped lamps with grooves or without grooves" (Hölscher, 1954, pp. 69–70, Groups VIII–IX), some of which are dated by the archaeological context from the sixth to eighth centuries; some pieces of this series belong to what Hayes calls the "late buff-ware class" (Hayes, 1976, nos. 526–29, pp. 130–31).

There are two types of *wheel-made lamps.* Lamps in the shape of a teapot or juglet have pot-bellied bodies often topped by a neck. The nozzle and handle, flat or ribbed, were added after the reservoir was formed. These lamps bear no decoration (Petrie, 1905, p. 13, pl. 69, group neck; Shier, 1978, p. 49, nos. 496–99 and no. 500). They come chiefly from the upper levels of occupation of a site (Hölscher, 1954, pp. 70–71, Group 10, one example of which is dated to the fourth century, another to the fifth).

The second type is small cups or bowls. Their use for lighting is shown by the traces of the burning of the wick on the rim. These were found mainly in monasteries and hermitages (Winlock and Crum, 1926, p. 88, fig. 38; Jacquet-Gordon, 1972, pp. 7–8, pl. 228; Egloff, 1977, types 308–15, pp. 162–63, pl. 85).

Finally there are *miscellaneous* lamps such as those with multiple nozzles (*polykandilon*), which had the holes for the wicks arranged on a rectangular or circular stand. This variety, well known in the Roman period, was more rare in Christian Egypt (Badawy, 1954, p. 345, fig. 5.51). Lamps with seven nozzles may have had a liturgical function, like the modern *qandīl* (votive lamp), the seven wicks of which are lighted in succession during the ceremony of extreme unction (Badawy, 1978, p. 345 and n. 65; Viaud, 1978, pp. 44–45).

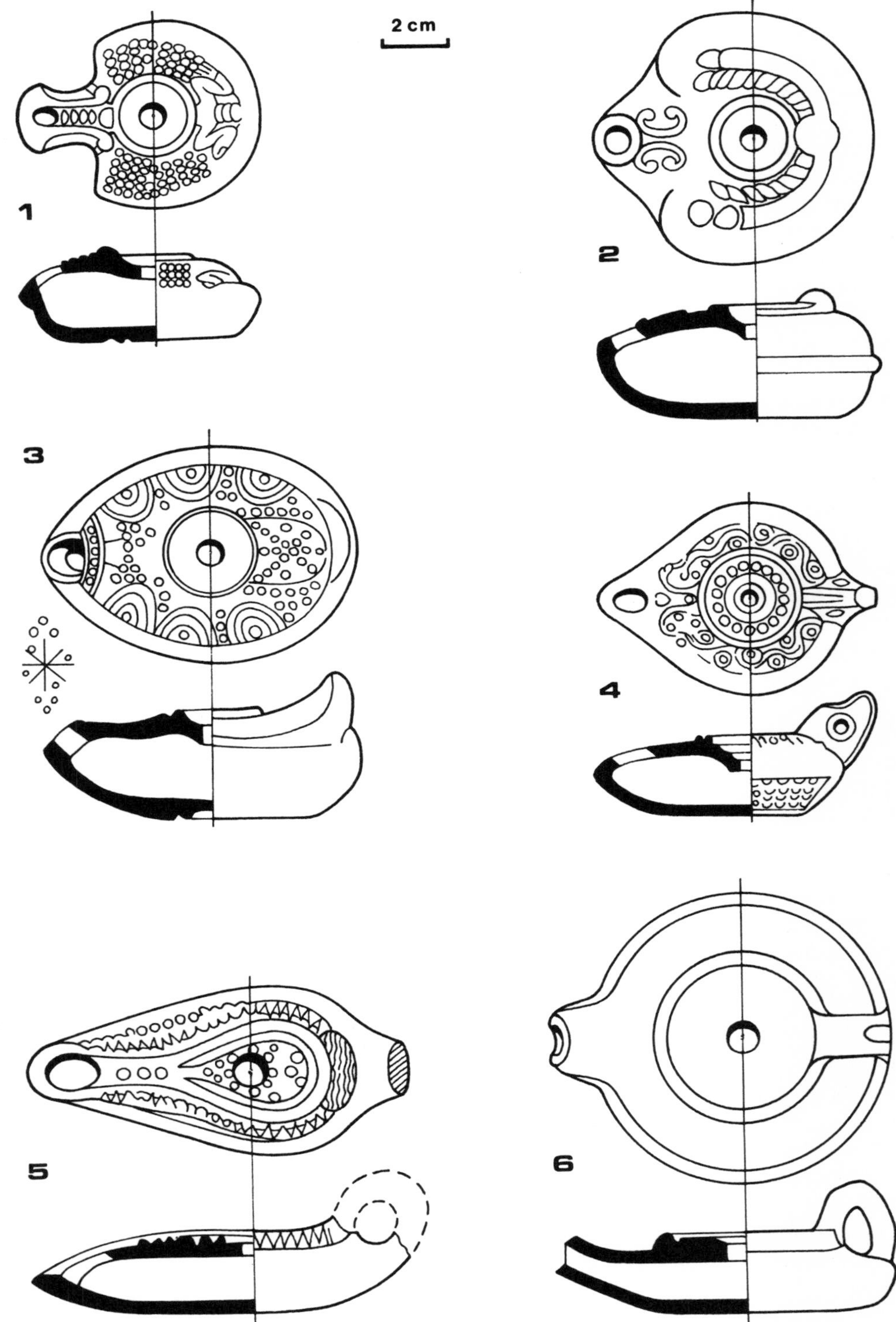

Types of terra-cotta Coptic lamps found in Madīnat Hābū: 1. "Frog and corn" type lamp. 2. Lamp derived from frog type. 3. "Upper Egypt yellow-slipped Ware," probably from the Aswan workshops. 4. "Christian Aswan Ware," probably from the Aswan workshops. 5. "Groove" lamp. 6. Wheel-made lamp. *Reproduced from Hölscher, 1954, by P. Laferrière. Courtesy P. Ballet.*

A not very common lighting device, attested at Kellia, takes the form of a large receptacle with handles. Under the inner rim, rings are fixed in the form of a funnel and serve as holders for glass chalices containing oil. The arrangement thus includes a circuit for feeding the lamp with oil and recovering any surplus. These "eternal lamps", an example of which was found at Ihnāsiyah, would have allowed more than 500 hours of lighting (Egloff, 1977, pp. 165–66, pls. 86–87, types 322–24).

This attempt at classification remains sketchy, to the extent that information about the lamps from Christian sites in the Delta, apart from Kellia, is not completely published. Those from Abū Mīnā, for example, have not been dealt with in this article. In C. M. Kaufmann's study, their photographic reproduction is matched by rare iconographical and technical commentary; however, they appear to be rather different from the lamps previously described. It is also probable that there are importations among them (perhaps from North Africa) (Kaufmann, 1910, Vol. 1, pls. 79–81).

BIBLIOGRAPHY

Badawy, A. *Coptic Art and Archaeology. The Art of the Christian Egyptian from the Late Antique to the Middle Ages.* Cambridge, Mass., 1978.

Ballet, P., and F. Mahmoud. "Moules en terre cuite d'Eléphantine (Musée Copte). Nouvelles données sur les ateliers de la région d'Assouan, à l'époque byzantine et aux premiers temps de l'occupation arabe," *Bulletin de l'Institut français d'archéologie orientale* 87 (1987):53–72.

Bisson de la Roque, F., and J. Clère. *Rapport sur les fouilles de Medamoud (1927).* Fouilles de l'Institut français d'archéologie orientale, Vol. 5, pt. 1, Cairo, 1928.

Guerrini, L. *Materiali ceramici: Antinoë (1965–1968).* Missione Archeologica in Egitto dell'Università di Roma. Rome, 1974.

Hayes, J. W. *Ancient Lamps in the Royal Ontario Museum. I : Greek and Roman Clay Lamps. A Catalogue.* Toronto, 1980.

Hölscher, U. *The Excavations of Medinet Habu. V. Post-Ramessid Remains.* Chicago, 1954.

Jacquet-Gordon, H. *Les Ermitages chrétiens du désert d'Esna,* Vol. 3: *Céramique et objets.* Fouilles de l'Institut français d'archéologie orientale, Vol. 29, pt. 3. Cairo, 1972.

Kaufmann, C. M. *Die Menasstadt und das Nationalheiligtum der altchristlichen Ägypter in der Westalexandrischen Wüste.* Leipzig, 1910.

Kubiak, W. B. *Medieval Ceramic Oil Lamps from Fustat.* Ars Orientalis: The Arts of Islam and the East, Vol. 8. Ann Arbor, 1970.

Kunze, M. "Die Tonlampen im Ägyptischen Museum." *Forschungen und Berichte* 14 (1972):97–100.

Leclant, J. *La Grenouille d'éternité des pays du Nil au monde méditerranéen.* Hommages à Maarten J. Vermaseren, Vol. 2. Leiden, 1978.

Lucas, A. *Ancient Egyptian Materials and Industries.* London, 1962.

Mlynarczyk, J. *Egyptian Types of Terra-cotta Lamps from Tell Atrib.* Etudes et Travaux Vol. 7. Warsaw, 1973.

Petrie, F. W. M. *Roman Ehnasya (Herakleopolis Magna) 1904.* London, 1905.

Shier, L. A. *Terracotta Lamps from Karanis, Egypt. Excavations of the University of Michigan.* Ann Arbor, Michigan, 1978.

Spencer, A. J., and D. M. Bailey. *British Museum Expedition to Middle Egypt: Ashmunein (1981).* British Museum, Occasional Paper no. 41. London, 1982.

Viaud, Gérard. *La Liturgie des Coptes d'Égypte.* Paris, 1978.

Winlock, H. E., and W. E. Crum. *The Monastery of Epiphanius at Thebes,* Vol. 1. New York, 1926.

Potstands. Potstands, widespread during the pharaonic period, appear relatively seldom among Coptic ceramics. Although many vessels with a rounded or pointed base, particularly amphorae, needed to rest on a stand to be balanced, they were either stuck into the ground, leaned against a wall, or laid on the earth. Monastery kitchens and storehouses at Isnā sometimes had benches or platforms that held jars (Sauneron and Jacquet, 1972, p. 19, fig. 3). Also at Isnā, a pot set in the ground might have served as a support for a larger receptacle, perhaps a water jug (Sauneron and Jacquet, 1972, p. 19). In this case, the lack of a stand is explained. Stands known in published material are rare, although Alliot states that they were numerous in the Tell Idfū houses (Alliot, 1933, p. 20).

Stands are divided into two groups. The first consists of simple forms, open at each end, with concave sides widening out toward the mouth. The relationship of the dimensions varies according to the type of receptacle placed there: There are low, wide shapes (Kasser, 1983, p. 456, nos. 147–48), those whose height is equal to the diameter (Alliot, 1933, fig. 55; Winlock and Crum, 1926, fig. 488), and tall forms (Winlock and Crum, 1926, fig. 48A). Sometimes they are decorated, like two specimens from Ṭūd ornamented with a wide, open-work design (Desroches-Noblecourt, 1982, p. 12). The second and more elaborate group is made of triple supports put together in a rectangular stand, with a flat, closed base 14 to 20 inches (36 to 50 cm) high and 24 to 39 inches (60 to 100 cm) long. Three orifices are arranged in the upper part, the middle one being lower than those on either side. Water jars were probably placed there, as is suggested by a cavity situated near the base, allowing the drainage of water exuded by porous vessels. These triple stands are decorated with zigzags, crossbars, pellets, and other motifs (Strzygowski, 1904, pp. 240–41, figs. 287–89; Bisson de la Roque and Clère, 1928, no. 2354ter, p. 59, fig. 41). They certainly constitute a simplified version of stone stands, in the shape of a table (Strzygowski, 1904, pp. 88–94; Quibell, 1912, pl. 43, fig. 1–2).

BIBLIOGRAPHY

Alliot, M. *Rapport sur les fouilles de Tell Edfou (1932)*. Fouilles de l'Institut français d'archéologie orientale, Vol. 9, pt. 2, Cairo, 1933.

Bisson de la Roque, F., and J. Clère. *Rapport sur les fouilles de Médamoud (1927)*. Fouilles de l'Institut français d'archéologie orientale, Vol. 5, pt. 1, Cairo, 1928.

Desroches-Noblecourt, C. "Les Nouvelles fouilles de Tod: Résultats des quatre premières saisons de recherche. Printemps 1980-automne 1981." *Bulletin de la Société Française d'Egyptologie* 93 (1982):12.

Gempeler, R. *Stadt und Tempel von Elephantine. Sechster Grabungsbericht*. Mitteilungen des Deutschen Archäologischen Instituts—Abteilung Kairo, Vol. 32. Mainz am Rhein, 1976.

Kasser, R. *Survey archéologique des Kellia (Basse-Egypte). Rapport de la campagne 1981*. Missions Suisses d'Archéologie Copte de l'Université de Genève. Louvain, 1983.

Leclerq, H. "Jeux et jouets." *Dictionnaire d'archéologie chrétienne et de liturgie*, Vol. 7, pt. 2. Paris, 1926.

Palanque, C. "Notes sur quelques jouets coptes en terre cuite," *Bulletin de l'Institut français d'archéologie orientale* 3 (1903):97–103.

Petrie, F. W. M. *Roman Ehnasya (Herakleopolis Magna) 1904*. London, 1905.

Quibell, J. E. *Excavations at Saqqara, IV, 1908–9, 1909–10: The Monastery of Apa Jeremias*. Cairo, 1912.

Sauneron, S., and J. Jacquet. *Les Ermitages chrétiens du désert d'Esna, Vol. 1: Archéologie et inscriptions*. Fouilles de l'Institut français d'archéologie orientale, Vol. 29, pt. 1. Cairo, 1972.

Scanlon, G. T. "Ancillary Dating Materials from Fusṭāt." *Ars Orientalis. The Arts of Islam and the East*, Vol. 7. Ann Arbor, Michigan, 1968.

Strzygowski, J. *Koptische Kunst, Catalogue Général du Caire*. Vienna, 1904.

Survey archéologique des Kellia (Basse Egypte). Rapport de la campagne 1981. Mission Suisse d'archéologie copte de l'Université de Genève. Louvain, 1983.

Winlock, H. E., and W. E. Crum. *The Monastery of Epiphanius at Thebes*, Vol. 1. New York, 1926.

Stamps. Stamps, or seals, in terra-cotta were chiefly intended to impress marks on loaves of bread used in the liturgy, the stoppers of amphorae, and ceramic vessels (for a general survey, see Badawy, 1978, pp. 345–46, figs. 5.52, 5.55, and 5.57).

The Eastern churches had the custom of impressing on liturgical loaves motifs or inscriptions relating to the rite being celebrated. It is often difficult to distinguish stamps for bread used in the Eucharist from those for *eulogia* ("blessed") bread, which was distributed to the faithful at the end of the service, on a saint's festival, on a pilgrimage, or at a funeral. The impressions were made by wood or terra-cotta stamps. The latter, preserved in greater quantity than examples in wood, are flat, often with a handle fixed on the back, or else conical. The plane surface carries the engraved motif and/or inscription. An important collection comes from Akhmīm, generally dated to the sixth and seventh centuries.

Among the motifs on the stamps for eucharistic bread are the fish and a cross inscribed ⲓⲥ ⲭⲥ ⲑⲩ ⲩⲥ ("Jesus Christ, Son of God") between the arms (Galavaris, 1970, p. 73). One type of stamp, peculiar to the Coptic church and in use down to the present day, reproduces on the eucharistic loaf a large cross formed of twelve squares within each of which a small cross is placed diagonally. Each square represents an apostle. Sometimes five holes also appear, symbolizing the wounds of Christ upon the cross (Galavaris, 1970, pp. 93f.).

The stamps intended for *eulogia* bread often carry the motif of a cross, with the ends of the arms enlarged and surrounded by an inscription such as ⲉⲩⲗⲟⲅⲓⲁ ⲕⲩⲣⲓⲟⲩ ⲉⲫ ⲏⲙⲁⲥ, *eulogia kyriou eph ēmas* ("the blessing of the Lord is upon us"). This theme, relatively widespread and uniform in Egypt, was no doubt the result of some control desired by the church (Galavaris, pp. 118f.).

Stamps were impressed upon the outer surface of the stoppers closing the mouths of jars and amphorae (discussed below). These stamps reproduced inscriptions (such as a name), animal motifs, crosses, and rosaces (circular panels enclosing rosettes). The impression was sometimes of the same type as those of the stamps for bread; it is probable that some of the stamps could have served for several purposes.

Stamps were also used to impress decoration on the inside bottom of an open shape such as a cup or plate before the piece was fired. "Fine" local wares of the Copto-Byzantine period bear stamped motifs such as the Christogram, cross, or dove after the manner of the fine imported wares, as previously discussed. Terra-cotta stamps have been found at Elephantine (Ulbert, 1971, pp. 235–42). They are either mushroom-shaped or conical. The thin end allows the stamp to be grasped. The other end, presenting a plane surface, bears a decoration incised with a pointed tool: crosses, two Christograms juxtaposed, a rose, a hare. Their presence probably attests the existence of a local workshop specializing in the production of fine ceramics.

BIBLIOGRAPHY

Badawy, A. *Coptic Art and Archaeology: The Art of the Christian Egyptians from the Late Antique to the Middle Ages.* Cambridge, Mass., 1978.

Galavaris, George. *Bread and the Liturgy: the Symbolism of Early Christian and Byzantine Bread Stamps.* Madison, Wis., 1970.

Ulbert, T. *Keramikstempel aus Elephantine.* Mitteilungen des Deutschen Archäologischen Instituts —Abteilung Kairo, Vol. 27. Wiesbaden, 1971.

Stoppers. Amphorae were closed with stoppers made generally of plaster or clay. Before the actual stopper was inserted, a preliminary stopper was pushed inside the neck; it was either a recut potsherd or, more generally, a pad of straw (Egloff, 1977, p. 180). Then the actual stopper was set in place, closing the opening of the neck. A plaster stopper, relatively flat, slightly convex in its upper part, is round and extends below the outer rim. Its inner face presents the imprint of the rim, forming a circular depression, as well as traces of straw from the first stopper. On its outer face there is the imprint of a seal in relief, most often round, which could cover almost the entire surface of the stopper.

Stoppers of unfired clay mixed with straw are conical and largely encase the upper part of the neck, sometimes even as far as the shoulder. They bear the imprint of stamps (two or more), generally round, more rarely rectangular, which seem smaller than the imprints on plaster stoppers. They are sometimes red or white, indicating that the stamps had initially been filled with colored materials before application to the stopper (Hölscher, 1954, pp. 61–62).

Stopper of brown amphora, bearing the imprint of a seal. Mud clay. *Courtesy Louvre Museum, Paris. Photo by Chuzeville.*

The imprints on plaster and clay stoppers are varied: Greek or Coptic inscriptions, often abridged, mentioning some liturgical formula or a name, monograms, crosses, roses, animals, sometimes even saints, such as Saint Menas (Clédat, 1904, figs. 6–7, 21–23, and 40–41; Strzygowski, 1904, pp. 233–40, nos. 8797–9003 and 9004–9033; Quibell, 1912, pls. 66–67; Hölscher, 1954, fig. 68; Egloff, 1977, pp. 181–83, pl. 20). These imprints probably indicate the place where the amphorae were filled and then stoppered or the name of the sender.

BIBLIOGRAPHY

Clédat, J. *Le Monastère et la nécropole de Baouît.* Mémoires publiés par les membres de l'Institut français d'archéologie orientale, Vol. 12. Cairo, 1904.

Egloff, M. *Kellia. La Poterie copte. Quatre siècles d'artisanat et d'échanges en Basse-Egypte.* Recherches suisses d'archéologie copte, Vol. 3, Geneva, 1977.

Hölscher, U. *The Excavations of Medinet Habou,* Vol. 5: Post Ramesside Remains. Chicago, 1954.

Quibell, J. E. *Excavations at Saqqara,* Vol. 4: 1908–9, 1909–10. Cairo, 1912.

Strzygowski, J. *Koptische Kunst, Catalogue Général du Caire.* Vienna, 1904.

Figurines

Small terra-cotta figures for popular use have not been much appreciated by scholars. Very few studies and archaeological publications have been devoted to them. They are at a great disadvantage because they followed Hellenistic and Roman figurines, which are infinitely richer iconographically and more elaborate technically.

Coptic figurines have been found in pilgrimage centers such as at Abū Mīnā and from sites of habitation, as may be seen from the list at the end of the article. Excavations of hermitages in Kellia and Isnā have yielded no figurines. Some female figurines were found there in a workshop and near an oven (Kaufmann, 1908, pp. 58–60 and figs. 39 and 42); Kaufmann states that the statuette of a monkey was probably produced in the local workshops (Kaufmann, 1910, p. 71, figs. 27–29). The workshops of Abū Mīnā might have supplied Alexandria with stocks of shoddy quality (Martens, 1975, p. 43; 1975, p. 75).

Manufacture. Technically, these statuettes are characterized by rough manufacturing methods. The principal techniques used were molding and modeling.

Molded figurines are fashioned from two molds, one for the front, the other for the back. The two parts thus obtained are joined with clay, leaving a hollow interior. Since the back is flat or slightly convex, only the front is detailed with the general form of the body and a simplified modeling of the face. Elements of attire and coiffure are evident on representations of women. A comparable schematization is adopted for equestrian and animal figures. Sometimes a few details were incised into the interior of the mold. The Coptic Museum has two front molds of orants, or praying figures (nos. 10125 and 10080), and one of an equestrian group (no. 10130).

Modeled figurines are made from coils of clay, crudely worked and then put together. Sometimes a piece is carved on a plaque of clay with no attempt at modeling, as in an orant in the Coptic Museum (no. 41846/10147), and a female head (no. 39232/10281).

Both procedures, molding and modeling, may have been used in the manufacture of a single figure. Some statuettes in Alexandria have a molded head and body with modeled arms and legs that have been joined to the body (Martens, 1975, p. 53; cf. also figurines at Abū Mīnā, Kaufmann, 1910, pls. 73, 1–6 and 9–20; 74, 18–26; 75, 6 and 9–11). The forequarters of some figurines of horses were shaped on the lathe (Martens, 1975, p. 53).

The statuettes are covered with white slip. Painted detail applied over the slip mitigates the inadequacies of the primitive workmanship. Strokes of black or brown paint give the face an expression defined by the encircled eyes and attire the body in a long tunic if it is human, in a harness and saddle if it is a horse.

Iconographic Types. Among the iconographic types, representations of females are the most numerous. They are generally standing, their legs joined, with variations in the position of the arms and in the coiffure. There are also some *kourotrophoi* (figures carrying children) (for Abū Mīnā, Kaufmann, 1910, pl. 73: 11 and 18; for Bāwīṭ, Palanque, 1903, p. 99, pls. 1, 4–5; for Antinoë, *Antinoë*, 1974, pl. 44:2). These female statuettes are often clothed in a long tunic, woven in a single piece and ornamented with vertical bands over the chest and back. They are adorned with necklaces and bracelets. Their protuberant, mouselike noses are modeled; their eyes, eyebrows, and mouths are indicated by strokes of paint.

Two main groups of female figures can be recognized. The first consists of figures made by mixed methods, the bodies and the heads molded, the arms and some accessories modeled. The most characteristic feature is hair arranged in melon rolls, derived from Hellenistic and Roman patterns, and encircled by a nimbus. Often, only the heads are preserved, but some complete representations of standing figures are known, with both hands positioned on or below the breast or on the hips, holding an object such as a discus, a crown, or a child. They are relatively common at Abū Mīnā (Kaufmann, 1910, pl. 73).

The second group consists of orants, with arms raised or stretched out. They are generally molded in two parts. The face, with large eyes indicated by molding or sketched in with a stroke of paint, is crowned with a triangular coiffure and pierced at the top with a hole so that the figure could be hung up. Sometimes the hair is decorated with small circles and a cross, and the triangular coiffure may be made from tufts of hair decorated with beads and bands. Two other holes at the level of the ears no doubt were created so that the figurine could be adorned with earrings (for Elephantine, see Gempeler, 1976, p. 109). A necklace, from which a cross hung on some figurines, adorns the neck.

Some sources (for example, Polaczek-Zdanowicz, 1975, pp. 136 and 149) consider the orants to be in the line of female representations of fecundity in pharaonic Egypt and closely connected with the Hellenistic and Roman Isis-Aphrodite and her fol-

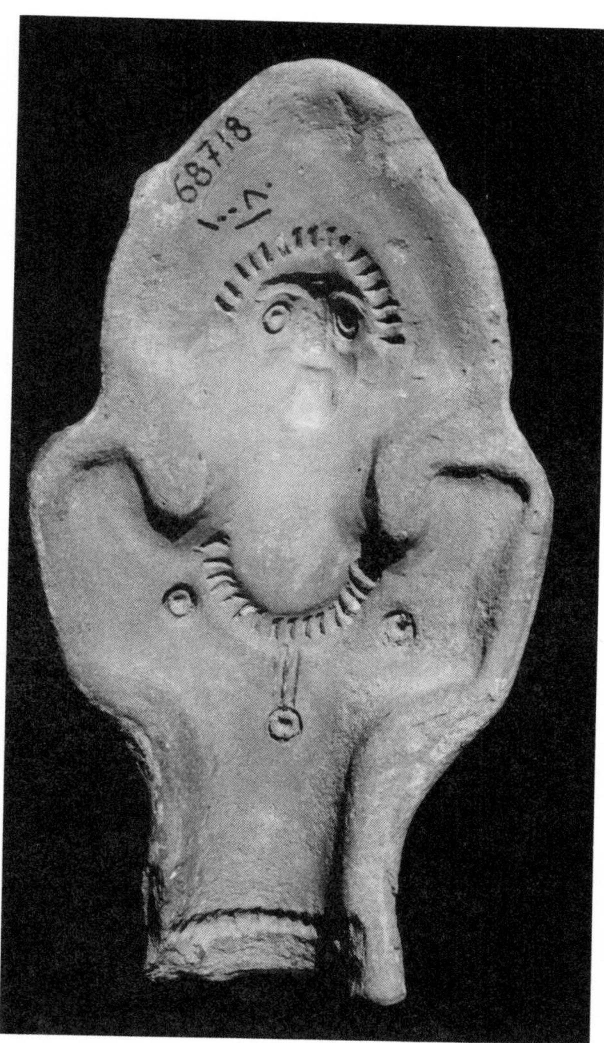

Mould of orant. Terra-cotta. Elephantine. *Courtesy Coptic Museum, Cairo. Photo by Girgis.*

lowers. The necklace of the orants recalls that of the goddess, called *periammata*. Certainly these figurines were not created *ex nihilo;* they present a definite iconographic link with some late Roman orants, probably those related to the worship of Isis (Castiglione, 1969, pp. 80–82, pl. 11). However, these statuettes also belong to the group of Coptic orants represented on funerary stelae and in other places; the presence of a cross on the coiffure or hanging from a necklace is not the least of the signs of a declared Christianity.

These two groups of female likenesses do not coexist in the same archaeological contexts. The question arises whether they are two separate productions from different periods for different functions or two separate productions from different geographical areas. Indeed, the orants are not mentioned in the publications on Abū Mīnā or Alexandria, where the first group of terra-cotta objects is predominant, but they abound in Middle and Upper Egypt. This differentiation arises perhaps from specialization in the figurine workshops and their area of diffusion. A recent discovery of molds from Elephantine partly resolves the question of the origin of the southern group of figurines (Ballet and Mahmoud, 1987, pp. 60–61, nos. 13–16).

A rare type of female figurine is represented by a flat orant from al-Bahnasā (Wessel, 1964, pp. 92–93, ill. 4, p. 95). It is characterized by earrings in

Orant. Terra cotta. Edfou. *Courtesy Louvre Museum, Paris. Photo by Chuzeville.*

glass and cornelian, as well as a tunic whose ornamentation dates from the ninth century (Du Bourguet, 1964, no. 142).

Less common than female figurines are male figurines. A group originated in Alexandria (Martens, 1975, p. 67) and Abū Mīnā (Kaufmann, 1910, pls. 74–75). In spite of an often defective state of preservation, they appear to have been attired in long robes. The hands are placed on the hips, crossed on the chest, or holding an object (Kaufmann, 1910, pls. 76: 14–16, pl. 75: 3 and 10). These figurines have the same technical characteristics as their female counterparts from Alexandria and Abū Mīnā.

It is not impossible that some fragmentary pieces of figurines may have belonged to equestrian groups, which form a fairly widespread iconographic class. Here again, both manufacturing techniques, molding and modeling, are represented (for Armant, Mond and Myers, 1940, pl. 70: 19; Coptic Museum, Cairo, no. 44720/9507; Kaufmann, 1910, 77; 1, 3; Coptic Museum, nos. 8083, 8107). In molded figurines, the anatomy and the garments of the horseman are scarcely indicated. In modeled figurines, the sense of detail is more highly developed, as seen, for example, in the pointed hat folded down in front and shield on the arm.

Among animal figurines, horses and camels are the most common. Molded pieces are more often found than modeled; the profile, mane, harness, and saddle are indicated by molding and are underlined by strokes of paint. There is evidence of the production of horses on most of the sites that have yielded terra-cotta objects. Statuettes of camels, which are less common, are often of very good technical quality. Some come from Medamoud (Bisson de la Roque, 1930, no. 4407, p. 56, fig. 52; Louvre, nos. E12781 and E14158). Sometimes they are modeled (Kaufmann, 1910, pl. 77: 4 and 7).

Abū Mīnā also offers a sampling of animals and winged creatures, among them lions, dogs, gazelles, monkeys, and cockerels (Kaufmann, 1908, pls. 77–78). These are often modeled vases, which are different from figurines because they have a narrow neck and a handle generally attached at the back. Elsewhere, examples of such varied fauna are seldom found, and it cannot be said whether this fact is due to the lack of publications or to an archaeological reality. A monkey from Medamoud is, however, to be noted (Bisson de la Roque, 1931, no. 4957, p. 84, fig. 68; Louvre, no. E14159).

Technical and Iconographic Evolution. From the published material it is scarcely possible to trace the technical and iconographic evolution of terra-cotta figurines. However, their origin and their eventual conclusion can be determined: on the one hand, late Roman figurines, those from Ihnāsiyah for example (Petrie, 1905, pls. 47–51), reflect the modifications of traditional manufacture such as the mechanical execution of folds in garments and waves in the hair and the tendency to treat figurines as reliefs. These features illustrate the transition to the sketchy type of manufacture characteristic of Coptic figurines. On the other hand, the existence of some terra-cotta specimens, modeled and looking unpolished, comparable to some examples of present-day terra-cotta, is attested at the oldest levels of al-Fusṭāṭ from the middle of the eighth to the beginning of the ninth centuries, but there is no further evidence in later archaeological remains at the site (Scanlon, 1968, pp. 2–5, pl. 1: 1a–c). Among other rare chronological benchmarks, the level of Elephantine from which orants, horses, and camels come seems to date them from the sixth century (Gempeler, 1976, pp. 111–12, and n. 191).

As for the iconographic reminiscences suggested by these representations, the idea must no doubt be abandoned that the mediocre *kourotrophoi* were influenced by the theme of *Isis lactans*. Likewise, Horus the horseman is probably not the ancestor of the equestrian figures. In general, one notes the abandonment of a syncretist iconography, such as that shown by the third- and fourth-century figurines at Ihnāsiyah. Kaufmann sees the survival of pagan beliefs, however, in the *cynocephali* (dog-headed figures) produced by the Abū Mīnā workshops (Kaufmann, 1910, p. 76).

The iconography of the figurines scarcely reveals the religious context of the period, except for some crosses incorporated in the attire of orants. What may be the deformed monogram of Christ is found on a horse from Medamoud (Bisson de la Roque, 1931, p. 82, fig. 65), as well as on the statuette of a boar (Keimer, 1943, pp. 93–101). Dating from the fourth century, it might be a blasphemous image of Christ. Collectively, these figurines were not, however, without religious intention.

Purpose. The purpose of these figurines is unclear, and several interpretations have been proposed. The figurines, including those from Abū Mīnā, and in particular the horsemen and animals, might be toys brought back to their children by pilgrims (Leclerq, 1926, "Jeux," cols. 375–76). The horsemen from Kom al-Dikka would belong to this category (Martens, 1975, p. 77). Following C. Palanque (Palanque, 1903, p. 98), H. Leclerq saw in these toys "imperfect trifles which the piety of the survivors placed near the small child taken too soon from their loving care," an argument that rests on no serious archaeological evidence (Leclercq, "Poupées," 1926, col. 2517). When the figurines are associated with a place of worship, they are no doubt votive offerings given by the faithful with a view to obtaining some benefits. The little camels of Abū Mīnā would recall one of the miracles of Saint Menas, the curing of a sterile she-camel, and would serve to obtain for the donor a benefit of the same kind (Kaufmann, 1910, p. 114 and n. 2). The female figurines might be votive offerings for cures and for fertility (Martens, 1975, p. 75). It appears, however, that most of the figurines come from residential districts, which limits their possible role in funerary furnishings and their connection with a specific religious center, unless they were brought back from a pilgrimage.

Horseman. Terra cotta. Abū Mīnā. *Courtesy Coptic Museum, Cairo. Photo by Girgis.*

Sites.

Abū Mīnā

Kaufmann, C. M. *La Découverte des sanctuaires de Ménas dans le désert de Maréotis.* Alexandria, 1908.

______. *Die Menasstadt und das Nationalheiligtum der altchristlichen Ägypter in der westalexandrinischen Wüste,* vol. 1. Leipzig, 1910.

Labib, P. "Fouilles du Musée copte à Saint Menas (première campagne)." *Bulletin de l'Institut d'Egypte* 34 (1951–1952):133–38.

Wulff, O. *Altchristliche und mittelalterliche byzantinische und italienische Bildwerke, Beschreibung der Bildwerke der christlichen Epochen,* vol. 3. Berlin, 1909.

Alexandria

Martens, M. "Figurines en terre cuite coptes découvertes à Kôm el Dikka (Alexandrie)." *Bulletin de la Société archéologique d'Alexandrie* 43 (1975):53–77.

Armant

Mond, R., and O. H. Myers. *Temples of Armant. A Preliminary Survey.* The Egyptian Exploration Society, Vol. 43. London, 1940.

Bāwīṭ

Palanque, C. "Notes sur quelques jouets coptes en terre cuite." *Bulletin de l'Institut français d'archéologie orientale* 3 (1903):97–103.

Elephantine

Gempeler, R. "Stadt und Tempel von Elephantine. Sechster Grabungsbericht." *Mitteilungen des deutschen archäologischen Instituts, Abteilung Kairo* 32 (1976):106.

Ihnāsiyah

Petrie, F. W. M. *Roman Ehnasya.* London, 1905.

Kom Ishqāw

Strzygowski, J. *Koptische Kunst. Catalogue général des antiquités egyptiennes,* Vol. 12. Vienna, 1904.

Medamoud

Bisson de la Roque, F. and J. Clère. *Rapport sur les fouilles de Médamoud (1927). Fouilles de l'Institut français d'archéologie orientale,* Vol. 5, pt. 1. Cairo, 1928.

______. *Rapport sur les fouilles de Médamoud (1929.) Fouilles de l'Institut français d'archéologie orientale,* Vol. 7, pt. 1. Cairo, 1930.

______. *Rapport sur les fouilles de Médamoud (1930). Fouilles de l'Institut français d'archéologie orientale,* Vol. 8, pt. 1. Cairo, 1931.

———. *Rapport sur les fouilles de Médamoud (1931–1932). Fouilles de l'Institut français d'archéologie orientale,* Vol. 9, pt. 3. Cairo, 1933.

Tell Idfū

Alliot, M. *Rapport sur les fouilles de Tell Edfou (1932). Fouilles de l'Institut français d'archéologie orientale* Vol. 9, pt. 2. Cairo, 1933.

Bruyère, B. et al. *Tell Edfou 1937. Fouilles Franco-polonaises,* Rapports, Vol. 1, Cairo, 1937.

Henne, H. *Rapport sur les fouilles de Tell Edfou (1921–1922).* Fouilles de l'Institut français d'archéologie orientale, Vol. 1, pt. 2. Cairo, 1924.

———. *Rapport sur les fouilles de Tell Edfou (1923–24). Fouilles de l'Institut français d'archéologie orientale,* Vol. 2, pt. 3. Cairo, 1925.

Michalowski, K., et al. *Tell Edfou 1938.* Fouilles Franco-polonaises, Rapports, Vol. 2. Cairo, 1938.

———. *Tell Edfou (1939).* Fouilles Franco-polonaises, Rapports, Vol. 3. Cairo, 1950.

BIBLIOGRAPHY

Antinoë (1965–1968). Missione Archeologica in Egitto dell'Università di Roma, ser. 21, Rome, 1974.

Ballet, P., and F. Mahmoud. "Moules en terre cuite d'Eléphantine (Musée Copte). Nouvelles données sur les ateliers d'Assouan, à l'époque byzantine et aux premiers temps de l'occupation arabe." *Bulletin de l'Institut français d'archéologie orientale* 87 (1987):53–72.

Bisson de la Roque, F. *Rapport sur les fouilles de Médamoud (1930).* Fouilles de l'Institut français d'archéologie orientale, Vol. 8, pt. 1. Cairo, 1931.

Castiglione, L. "Stele eines Kupferschmieds. Zur Deutung der römerzeitlichen ägyptischen Grabsteine." *Mitteilungen des deutschen archäologischen Instituts, Abteilung Kairo* 24 (1969):80–82.

Du Bourguet, P. *L'Art copte.* Catalogue of the Exhibition in the Petit Palais. Paris, 1964.

Gempeler, R. *Stadt und Tempel von Elephantine. Sechster Grabungsbericht.* Mitteilungen des deutschen archäologischen Instituts—Abteilung Kairo, Vol. 32. Mainz am Rhein, 1976.

Kaufmann, C. M. *La Découverte des sanctuaires de Ménas dans le désert de Maréotis.* Alexandria, 1908.

———. *Die Menasstadt und das Nationalheiligtum der altchristlichen Ägypter in der west-alexandrinischen Wüste,* Vol. 1. Leipzig, 1910.

Keimer, L. "Le Chrisme sur une statuette de porc," *Bulletin de la Société d'archéologie copte,* 9 (1943):93–103.

Leclercq, H. "Jeux et jouets." *Dictionnaire d'archéologie chrétienne et de liturgie,* Vol. 7, pt. 2, cols. 375–76. Paris, 1926.

———. "Poupées." *Dictionnaire d'archéologie chrétienne et de liturgie,* Vol. 7, pt. 2, col. 2517. Paris, 1926.

Martens, M. "Figurines en terre cuite coptes découvertes à Kôm el-Dikka (Alexandrie)." *Bulletin de la Société archéologique d'Alexandrie,* 43 (1975):53–77.

Mond, R., and O. H. Myers. *Temples of Armant: a Preliminary Survey* 63. London, 1940.

Palanque, C. "Notes sur quelques jouets coptes en terre cuite." *Bulletin de l'Institut français d'archéologie orientale* 3 (1903):97–103.

Petrie, R. F. *Roman Ehnasya (Herakleopolis Magna), 1904.* London, 1905.

Polaczek-Zdanowicz, K. *The Genesis and Evolution of the Orant Statuettes Against a Background of Developing Coptic Art.* Etudes et Travaux, Vol. 8: Travaux du Centre d'archéologie méditerranéenne de l'Académie Polonaise des Sciences, Vol. 16. Warsaw, 1975.

Rodziewicz, M. *Les Habitations romaines tardives d'Alexandrie à la lumière des fouilles polonaises à Kôm el-Dikka, Alexandrie,* Vol. 3. Warsaw, 1984.

Scanlon, G. T. "Ancillary Dating Material from Fusṭāṭ." *Ars Orientalis. The Arts of Islam and the East* 7 (1968):2–5.

Wessel, K. *L'Art copte.* Brussels, 1964.

Wulff, O. *Altchristliche und Mittelälterliche byzantinische und italienische Bildwerke. Beschreibung der Bildwerke der christlichen Epochen,* Vol. 3. Berlin, 1909.

PASCALE BALLET

CERAMICS OF THE LATE COPTIC PERIOD. It is unreasonable to posit any major changes, either in taste or technique, immediately following the Islamic conquest of Egypt. We may assume that during the late seventh and early eighth centuries, there was a shift of the better ateliers from Alexandria to the new capital at al-Fusṭāṭ (Cairo) and a somewhat less precise movement away from the patronage and taste of the religious establishments, whether Coptic or Orthodox (Melchite), to those of the Arabic governing cadres. Nowhere is this more strikingly apparent than in the employment of Arabic inscriptions on pottery, sometimes alone but more often accompanying an older medley of motifs, best seen in the bowl fragment with ducks and grapes in the British Museum (Lane, 1958, pl. 5-A). Indeed, the lengthened life of some of these motifs (Grube, 1962) against competing influences from China and Syria and Persia goes far toward proving the integrity and distinction of Egyptian wares in the broad category of Islamic ceramics.

Notwithstanding this continuity, it can hardly be gainsaid that the decisive process, one by which we can measure the popularity of "old" against "new" ceramics, was the reintroduction of glazing into Egypt, which stratigraphical tests at al-Fusṭāṭ place at the turn of the seventh century, soon after ʿAbd al-Malik's reform of the coinage in 695–696. It has been generally accepted that there had been lead glazing in the Eastern Mediterranean provinces of the Roman Empire (ca. 100 B.C. to A.D. 100) generally on cups and chalices, often with barbotine decoration, and, further, on a true clay body, as distinct from the fused frit body employed by the ancient Egyptians for their "glazed" ceramics. However, whereas the technique apparently died out in Egypt and Syria, it seems to have been practiced almost continuously in Mesopotamia and parts of Persia, certainly during the Sassanid period and through the advent of Islam in the area. When glazing does appear in Syria and Egypt, it was probably imported from Persia or made locally in imitation of these imports. Archaeology, both at Alexandria and more particularly at al-Fusṭāṭ (because there was no large-scale occupancy before the arrival of ʿAmr ibn al-ʿĀṣ in 639–640), permits us to chart the reactions of the potters to the novelty of glazing. On one front, they simply glazed certain objects that they were producing with molded or stamped or rouletted designs. This was particularly noticeable with stub-handled lamps where duplication of motifs connects the unglazed with the glazed. (The transition is thoroughly discussed in Scanlon, 1984; the archaeological verification has been published relative to Kubiak and Scanlon, 1973a, fig. 2, which is unglazed, and Kubiak and Scanlon, 1980, fig. 3, which is covered in a brown lead glaze.) It can also be noted on fragments of what M. Rodziewicz terms "céramique Romaine tardive," otherwise known as highly polished "pseudo-Samian" redwares, that were covered by a green lead glaze. Or, the rouletted designs (e.g., in Rodziewicz, 1976, type O-25, and in Scanlon, 1967, fig. 3-b) were transferred to a buff-brown clay vessel and glazed as can be seen in Figure 1, a fragment found in an eighth to ninth century context in al-Fusṭāṭ.

Though not the key to motival continuity, pseudo-Samian ware seems to have been the longest-lived of any made in Egypt; it was certainly in common use as tableware up to the threshold of the eleventh century. New shapes, unlike any surveyed by Hayes or Rodziewicz, were introduced, such as that in Figure 2, which is from the wall of a vaselike vessel with applied nodules and a rudimentary leaf and branch decoration in black slip. It can be securely dated to the ninth century. The more usual Coptic "carry-over" design (black and white slip on a pseudo-Samian standard shape) is obvious on the vessel fragment in Figure 3. It is from an eighth-century find-spot. Nor must it be forgotten that the usual rouletted, stamped, and gouged motifs continued to be employed on the polished redware without additional slip decoration or glazing.

A third response was simply to continue slip-painting vessels in the old-fashioned red-on-cream

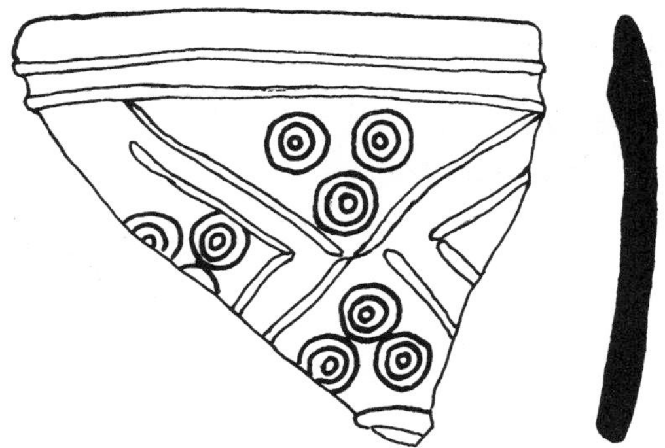

Figure 1. Fragment of green lead-glazed bowl; brown-buff clay. Eighth–ninth centuries. Location: Kelsey Museum, University of Michigan. *Drawing courtesy George T. Scanlon.*

Figure 2. Fragment of pseudo-Samian vessel; applied nodular rosettes and black-slip decoration. Ninth century. Location: American University, Cairo. *Drawing courtesy George T. Scanlon.*

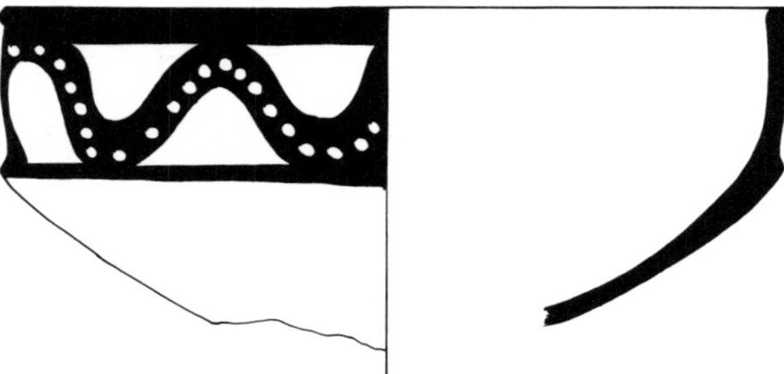

Figure 3. Fragment of pseudo-Samian bowl; slip decoration in black and white. Eighth century. Location: American University, Cairo. *Drawing courtesy George T. Scanlon.*

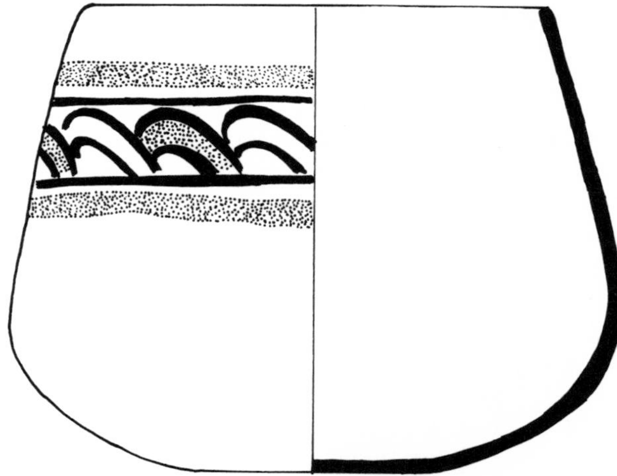

Figure 5. Food bowl; red and black design on orange-white slip external. Ninth to tenth centuries. Location: Ashmolean Museum, Oxford. *Drawing courtesy George T. Scanlon.*

slip styles of geometrics, guilloches, and plaits (Figure 4, which was found in the undisturbed pit that contained the famous luster goblet and can therefore be dated to 750–800, and Figure 5, whose design is in black and red on an orange-white wash overall slip and whose find-spot allows a dating of the ninth to tenth century). A major variant within this survival mode was the continuing utility of the Apa Jeremiah ambit of decoration. Figures 6 and 7 exhibit, albeit on a reduced scale, the interest in zoomorphic motifs. The former can be dated to the eighth to ninth century. And, though the latter is a surface find, it can be related motivally to the last period of the monastery of Apa Jeremiah, about 900. The more abstract patterns (random lines, circles, dots, and ovoid hatching) can be seen on the earliest slip-painted filter bottles (Scanlon, 1986, figs. 179, 188).

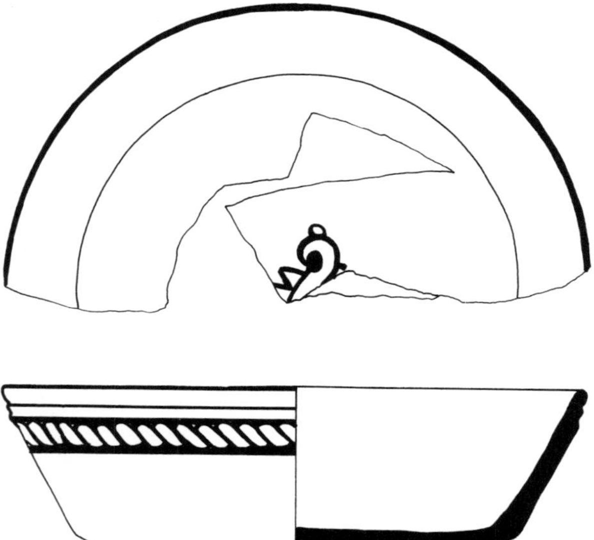

Figure 4. Shallow bowl; red-on-cream slip design external. 750–800. Location: Islamic Museum, Cairo. *Drawing courtesy George T. Scanlon.*

However interesting these efforts were toward establishing a sense of ongoingness in the realm of decorated pottery, the major response must be seen in the realm of lead-glazed wares of the eighth and ninth centuries. A wealth of motifs from the Christian period were renewed and/or modified so as to integrate both with the demands of the new technique and to satisfy a newly evolved taste. Here the key factor is the tonality of the clay, irrespective of the mode of applying the decoration. It is always of the buff-white to the buff-brown range and rather tightly potted. (Very few of the early lead-glazed pieces found at al-Fusṭāṭ were of the red clays that Rodziewicz would like to see as the link, though the pieces which do survive can be seen as experiments.) One group carried stamped and molded designs, but did not have much of a market after 900. The other, based on underglaze painting, can be found in dated contexts throughout the tenth century, which means it competed however fitfully against both Samarra luster and local imitations of Chinese imports.

The decoration was applied in one of two ways. The design was painted in slip directly on the bisque-fired vessel and then covered with a transparent glaze. After the second firing, the surface was both smooth to the touch and gritty. The designs were relatively simple and slapdash, though a certain vigor was attained through using two or

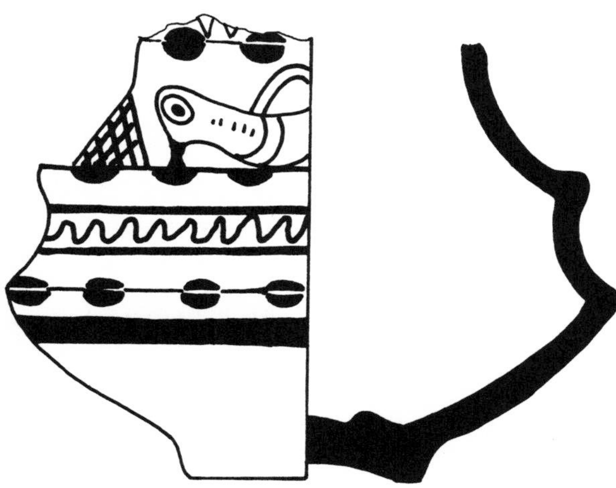

Figure 6. Base of ribbed vessel; black and reddish-brown on cream slip external. Eighth to ninth centuries. Location: Art Museum, Princeton University. *Drawing courtesy George T. Scanlon.*

Figure 7. Fragment of wall of rough redware vessel; black and buff design on white slip external. Ca. 900. Location: Kelsey Museum, University of Michigan. *Drawing courtesy George T. Scanlon.*

three colored slips. Once again there was a zoomorphic group (Figure 8) and another based on rosettes and abstract leaf patterns (Figure 9). In the somewhat later method and on larger vessels, the inner surface was covered entirely with a design painted in colored slips on an overall white slip and covered with a transparent glaze; thus it was totally smooth to the touch after the firing. The leaf and scroll design of Figure 10 echoes the lead-glazed sgraffito wares familiar from Samarra, whereas the geometrics and rosettes of Figure 11 remind us of the pottery sequences from both Apa Jeremiah and EPIPHANIUS.

Finally, there are two ceramic developments evident from the finds at al-Fusṭāṭ but absent from Alexandria, which complete the general outline of "carry-overs." From the same, undisturbed pit that produced Figure 9 there came forth a small vase with a simple external linear decoration in black slip (Figure 12). But the clay was white with a slight buffish overtone and without any covering slip other than the decorative lines in black; the surface was gritty to the touch. Both the shape and decoration prompt one to think of pre-Islamic models. This was confirmed by the more naturalistic deco-

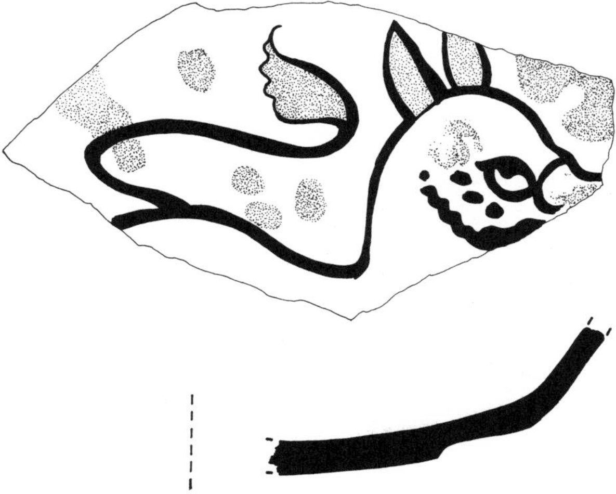

Figure 8. Fragment of bowl; zoomorphic motif: yellow, brown, and green slips under transparent lead glaze. About 800. Location: Islamic Museum, Cairo. *Drawing courtesy George T. Scanlon.*

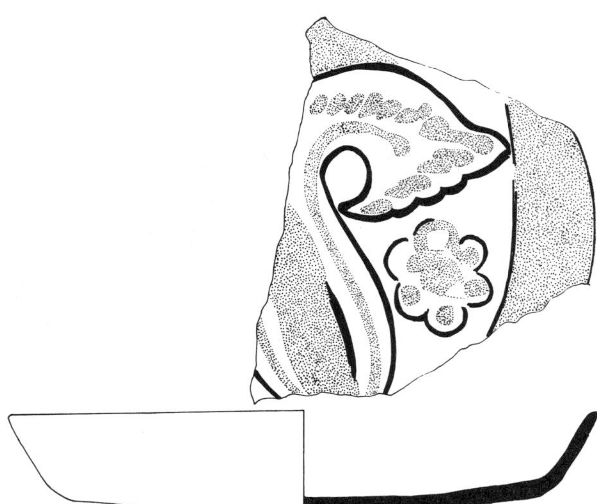

Figure 9. Matching fragments of shallow bowl; abstract leaf design in green, yellow, and purplish-black slips under clear lead glaze. Eighth–ninth centuries. Location: Ashmolean Museum, Oxford. *Drawing courtesy George T. Scanlon.*

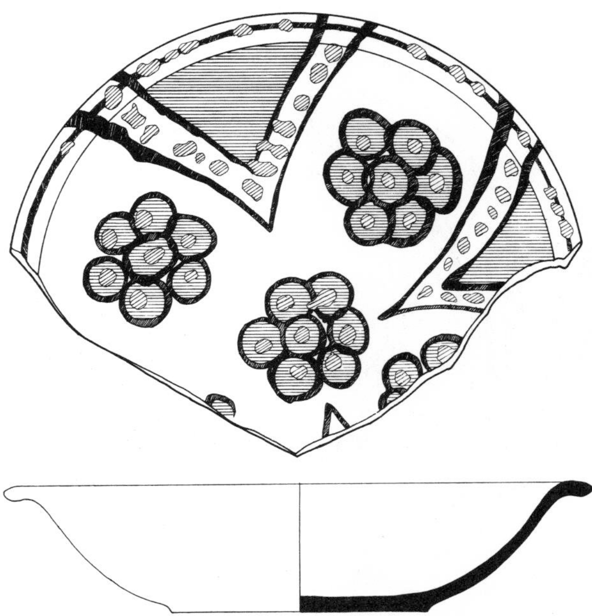

Figure 11. Fragments of bowl with flange rim; design in yellow and black on white under clear green glaze. Ninth century. Location: Kelsey Museum, University of Michigan. *Drawing courtesy George T. Scanlon.*

ration to be seen on Figure 13, made of the same white clay with black motifs of a palm-tree and an elliptical medallion containing leaf forms suggestive of the *fūl* (bean) plant. From the same find-spot another fragment of the exact same ware carried a zoomorphic motif, one similar to that seen in Figure 6, which again bespeaks a "carry-over" from the pre-Islamic Coptic range of slip-painted pottery. We know from a study of filters that an atelier in Giza produced a distinct line of vessels noted for having slip decoration; we might attribute this distinct white-ware range to the same venue. On archaeological grounds we may assume a life span from about 800 to 1000 for these kilns, and imagine them as producing nothing but slip-painted utility wares that, if decorated, were reminiscent of pre-Islamic norms and modes of decoration.

Figure 10. Fragments of rim and shoulder of deep bowl; design in yellow and black on white under clear green lead glaze. Ninth century. Location: Kelsey Museum, University of Michigan. *Drawing courtesy George T. Scanlon.*

At a second remove, a number of late classical and Christian motifs were available in Egypt on vessels imported from the kingdoms of Nubia and most particularly from Faras. Those that have appeared in al-Fusṭāṭ are from both phases of W. Y. Adams's "Classic Christian" period, which runs from about 850 to 1000 (Adams, 1962). In a later study, Adams has related most of the relevant motifs to those prevalent in Coptic art in the sixth and seventh centuries (Adams, 1981). These wares are quite distinct in color and tightness of the clay body and the tonalities of the covering and decorating slips, and cannot be confused with the purely Egyptian slip wares as exemplified in Figures 4 and 5. This is obvious in our example of what Adams calls the "connected leaves" motif (Figure 14), which can be dated immediately before 900. In Figure 15 we see a variant of this motif in the circular register of a deep bowl, which with the central motif of triangular hatching might be assigned rather to the Aswan potteries. However, from the find-spot of the various fragments which compose the vessel, we

Figure 13. Portion of body of internally ribbed vessel; decoration in black slip on gritty white clay. Eighth–ninth centuries. Location: Islamic Museum, Cairo. *Drawing courtesy George T. Scanlon.*

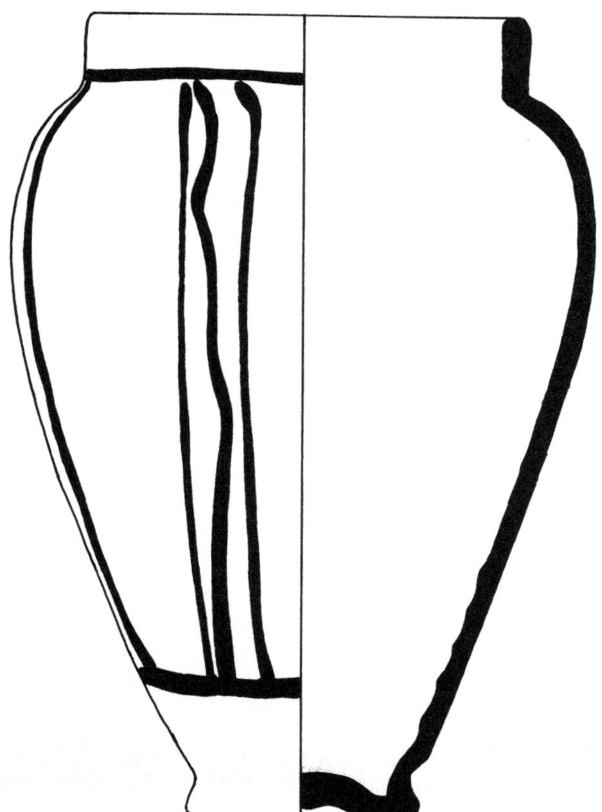

Figure 12. Vase; decoration in black slips on gritty white clay. Eighth to ninth centuries. Location: Kelsey Museum, University of Michigan. *Drawing courtesy George T. Scanlon.*

must place it also before 900. From the rather large number of fragments with zoomorphic motifs, that in Figure 16 is somewhat different in detail from those analyzed by Adams in that the collar is vertically rather than horizontally striped. It is from Faras and can be dated from the find-spot to the early tenth century.

Thus it would seem that the themes and decorative motifs of pre-Islamic pottery continued to exercise some hold on the imagination of the craftsmen and customers through the tenth century. There is little doubt that, except for the Giza factories, the personnel of those in the Greater Cairo area had become Muslim by this date. The market for slap-

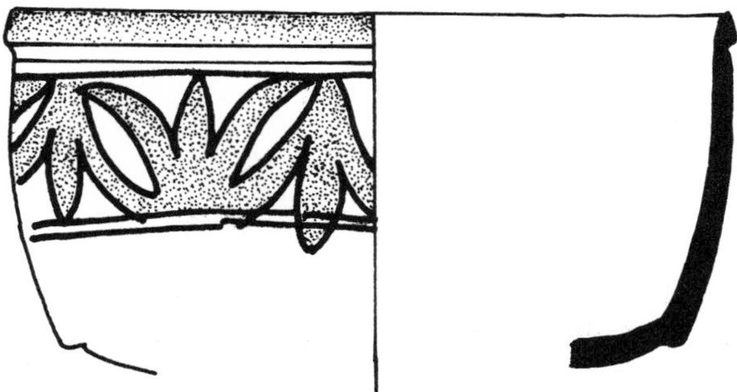

Figure 14. Portion of Nubian slip-painted bowl. Faras, Classic Christian I. before 900. Location: Art Museum, Princeton University. *Drawing courtesy George T. Scanlon.*

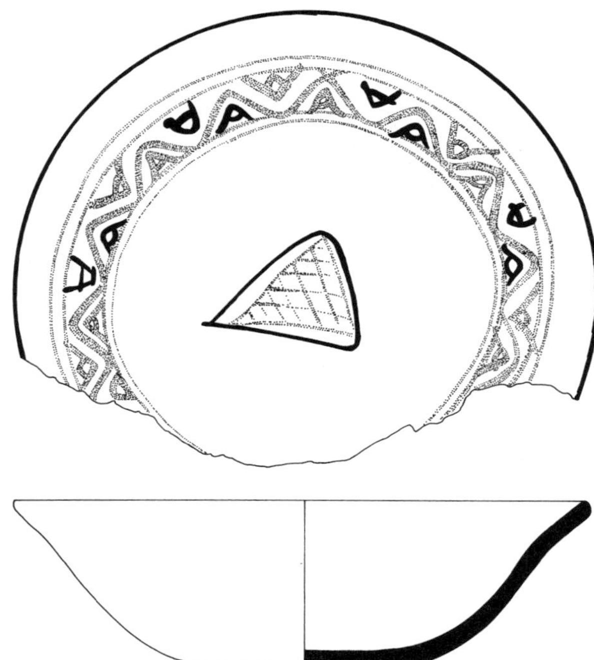

Figure 15. Matching fragments of deep bowl; internal decoration of orange and reddish-brown on overall cream slip. Possibly Aswan, Classic Christian I, before 900. Location: Islamic Museum, Cairo. *Drawing courtesy George T. Scanlon.*

Figure 16. Fragment of body of large vessel; zoomorphic decoration in brown, black, and light red on cream slip. Faras, Classic Christian I, early tenth century. Location: Islamic Museum, Cairo. *Drawing courtesy George T. Scanlon.*

dash, lead-glazed wares was practically wiped out by the appearance and plethora of newer types of pottery, for example, luster wares and underglaze sgraffito wares, imitations of Chinese celadons and splash wares, and particularly by the range of so-called Fayyūmī wares. By the middle of the eleventh century, the importing of Nubian Christian pottery had ceased. Hence the luster plate with an interior decoration of a priest with a censer (Lane, 1958, pl. 26-A) must be considered a straightforward commission rather than the reflexive expression of the Egyptian potter. A very few pieces of slip-painted, unglazed pottery have been noted from the fifteenth and sixteenth centuries, but these are proof not of a revival or of an incredible survival but simply of a genre and metier in the grip of economic and artistic poverty.

BIBLIOGRAPHY

The Preliminary Reports of the Fustat Expedition of the American Research Center in Egypt, which provide the background for this discussion, are published in the *Journal of the American Research Center in Egypt* (*JARCE*), or in collaboration with W. B. Kubiak.

Adams, W. Y. "An Introductory Classification of Christian Nubian Pottery." *Kush* 10 (1962):245–88.

______. "Medieval Nubian Design Elements." In *Studies in Ancient Egypt, the Aegean and the Sudan*, ed. W. K. Simpson and M. Davis. Boston, 1981.

Bianquis, T.; A. Watson; and G. T. Scanlon. "Numismatics and the Dating of Early Islamic Pottery in Egypt." In *Near Eastern Numismatics . . . Studies in Honour of George C. Miles*, ed. D. K. Kouymjian. Beirut, 1974.

Grube, E. "Studies in the Survival and Continuity of Pre-Muslim Traditions in Egyptian Islamic Art." *JARCE* 1 (1962):75–97.

Kubiak, W. B., and G. T. Scanlon. "Fustat Expedition: Preliminary Report 1966." *JARCE* 10 (1973):11–25.

______. "Redating Bahgat's Houses and the Aqueduct." *Art and Archaeology Research Papers* 4 (December 1973): 138–48.

______. "Fustat Expedition: Preliminary Report 1968. Part 1." *JARCE* 11 (1974):81–91.

______. "Fustat Expedition: Preliminary Report 1971. Part 2." *JARCE* 17 (1980):77–96.

Lane, Arthur. *Early Islamic Pottery.* London, 1958.
Rodziewicz, M. *La Céramique romaine tardive d'Alexandrie.* Warsaw, 1976.
———. "La Céramique émaillée copte de Kom el-Dikka." *Etudes et Travaux* 10 (1978):337–45.
Scanlon, G. T. "Fustat Expedition: Preliminary Report 1965. Part 1." *JARCE* 5 (1966):65–86.
———. "Fustat Expedition: Preliminary Report 1965. Part 2." *JARCE* 6 (1967):83–112.
———. "Excavations at Kasr al-Wizz: A Preliminary Report 1." *Journal of Egyptian Archaeology* 66 (1970):19–57.
———. "Fustat Expedition: Preliminary Report 1968. Part 1." *JARCE* 11 (1974):81–91.
———. "Fustat Expedition: Preliminary Report 1972. Part 1." *JARCE* 18 (1981):57–80.
———. "Moulded Early Lead Glazed Wares from Fusṭāṭ: Imported or Indigenous." In *Studies in Honour of Prof. Muhammad al-Nuwayhi,* ed. Arnold Green. Cairo, 1984.

GEORGE T. SCANLON

CERDON, SAINT, fourth patriarch (98–109) of the See of Saint MARK. (98–109). He held the office for ten years, nine months, and ten days during the reign of Emperor Trajan. He was laid to rest on 21 Ba'ūnah next to the remains of Saint Mark in the Church of Bucalis at Alexandria.

BIBLIOGRAPHY

Atiya, A. S. *History of Eastern Christianity.* Millwood, N.Y., 1980.

AZIZ S. ATIYA

CERINTHUS. So little is known of Cerinthus that there is nothing to place him in Egypt other than a reference to him in the *Epistula apostolorum* (Letter of the Apostles, which some believe originated in Egypt) and a statement by Hippolytus that Cerinthus was educated in the wisdom of the Egyptians. The *Epistula apostolorum* speaks of Cerinthus as a false apostle, and Irenaeus wrote of a confrontation between Cerinthus and the Apostle John in a public bath at Ephesus, but there is little else preserved of his life. Irenaeus stated that Cerinthus taught that the creation came about through a power far removed from God and that Jesus was born of Joseph and Mary. According to Irenaeus, Cerinthus taught that after Jesus' baptism, Christ descended in the form of a dove and remained with Jesus until just before the Crucifixion. This description of Cerinthian DOCETISM cannot be proved or refuted, since no Cerinthian documents or sources are known to exist.

BIBLIOGRAPHY

Duensing, H. *Epistula apostolorum.* In *New Testament Apocrypha,* ed. E. Hennecke and W. Schneelmelcher, Vol. 1, pp. 189–227, trans. R. McL. Wilson. Philadelphia, 1963.
Griggs, C. W. *Early Egyptian Christianity,* p. 47. Leiden, 1990.

C. WILFRED GRIGGS

ČERNÝ, JAROSLAV (1898–1970), Czech Egyptologist. He was born in Pilsen and studied at Charles University in Prague under František Lexa and at Berlin under Adolf ERMAN. He obtained his doctorate at Prague in 1922 with a thesis on the workmen of DAYR AL-MADĪNAH, near Thebes, whom he firmly identified as the builders of the royal tombs in the Valley of the Kings. From 1925 to 1946 he was associated as epigraphist with the excavations of the Cairo French Institute at Dayr al-Madīnah. From 1929 to 1946 he was a lecturer in Egyptology at Charles University. He published countless ostraca, graffiti, and papyri connected with the workmen's community. From 1925 he also collaborated with Sir Alan Gardiner on the publication of hieratic texts. After World War II, he held various professorships in England and the United States. His interest in Late Egyptian grammar led him into a detailed study of Coptic etymology. His bibliography in Egyptology is extensive, and his major contribution to Coptic studies is his *Coptic Etymological Dictionary* (Cambridge, 1976). His papers are now in the Griffith Institute, Oxford, while his library was left to Charles University. He died in Oxford.

BIBLIOGRAPHY

Bulletin de la Société française d'égyptologie 58 (1970):4.
James, T. G. H. "Jaroslav Černý." *Journal of Egyptian Archaeology* 57 (1971):185–89 (with portrait).
Spaull, C. H. S. "Bibliography of Jaroslav Černý." *Journal of Egyptian Archaeology* 54 (1968):3–8.

M. L. B. BIERBRIER

CHAÎNE, MARIUS JEAN JOSEPH (1873–1960), French Coptologist. He was born at Tarascon, Bouches-du-Rhône, and was trained for the priesthood and later became an abbot. He studied under Joseph Halévy at the Ecole pratique des Hautes Etudes. Among his numerous Coptic publications are *Compendium morphologiae copticae* (Rome, 1910) and *Eléments de grammaire dialectale copte* (Paris, 1933), which gave a simultaneous account of the four principal Coptic dialects, Bohairic, Sahidic, Akhmimic, and Fayyumic. Afterward he produced *Notions de langue égyptienne*, Vol. 1, *Langue du Moyen Empire*, and Vol. 2, *Langue du Nouvel Empire, le néo-égyptien, ses rapports avec le moyen-égyptien et les dialectes coptes* (Paris, 1938–1942). He also wrote *La Chronologie des temps chrétiens de l'Egypte et de l'Ethiopie* (Paris, 1925), *Les Dialectes coptes assioutiques* (Paris, 1934), *Le Verbe copte* (Paris, 1945), and *Le Manuscrit de la version copte en dialecte sahidique des 'Apophthegmata Patrum'* (Cairo, 1960). He died at the Cistercian Abbey of Sainte-Marie-du-Désert, Bellegarde-Sainte-Marie, Haute-Garonne.

BIBLIOGRAPHY

Dawson, W. R., and E. P. Uphill. *Who Was Who in Egyptology*, pp. 57–58. London, 1972.

Guillaumont, A. *Bulletin de l'Institut français d'archéologie orientale* 61 (1962):11–13.

Kammerer, W., comp. *A Coptic Bibliography*. Ann Arbor, Mich.; 1950; repr. New York, 1969.

AZIZ S. ATIYA

CHAIREMON OF ALEXANDRIA, a Stoic philosopher, Egyptian priest, and writer of the first century A.D. The exact dates of his life are not known, but he was active in a literary way from about A.D. 30 to A.D. 65. Only fragments of his works on the hieroglyphs, Egyptian history, and the comets have survived in later authors (collected and edited by van der Horst). According to the *Suda*, he was head of the school of grammarians in Alexandria and perhaps curator of the famous museum before he went to Rome as tutor of the future emperor Nero. His book on the hieroglyphs influenced later authors from CLEMENT OF ALEXANDRIA and HORAPOLLON down to John Tsetzes in the twelfth century. His works betray a syncretistic mixture of Egyptian religious ideas and Stoic philosophy as well as magical and astrological conceptions.

BIBLIOGRAPHY

Adler, A. *Sudae lexicon*, 5 vols. Leipzig, 1928–1938; repr. Stuttgart, 1967–1971.

Horst, P. W. van der. *Chairemon: Egyptian Priest and Stoic Philosopher*. The fragments collected and translated with explanatory notes. Etudes préliminaires aux religions orientales dans l'empire romain 101. Leiden, 1984.

MARTIN KRAUSE

CHALCEDON, COUNCIL OF, fourth ecumenical council, held at Chalcedon, on the Asiatic side of the Bosporus, opposite Constantinople. Convoked by Emperor Marcian (450–457) to deal with the situation caused by the acquittal of EUTYCHES and the Second (judicial) Council of EPHESUS in 449, it met in sixteen sessions from 8 October to 1 November 451. Its decisions, in particular regarding promulgation of the Christological definition of faith and its condemnation of Patriarch DIOSCORUS I of Alexandria as well as of Eutyches, alienated the great majority of Coptic Christians and mark a crucial turning point in the early history of the Coptic church and its relations with the rest of Christendom.

Preliminary: 449–451

Though the bishops at Ephesus II had proclaimed that the decisions of this council "agreed with Nicaea," the discomfiture of the papal legates, and the condemnation of Flavian of Constantinople and Domnus of Antioch, ensured that these decisions would not remain unchallenged. In the East, Theodoret of Cyrrhus wrote in desperation to Pope LEO I not a jurisdictional appeal but a letter to the one man powerful enough to correct the disasters Theodoret believed the church had suffered at Ephesus (*Letters* 113). Leo first fortified his opposition to that council through his own council of Italian bishops (29 September 449) and then proceeded through the autumn, and into the winter of 449–450, to write a series of letters (*Letters* 43–72) attempting to arouse opposition to Ephesus in Constantinople among the court, the senators, the nobility, the archimandrites opposed to Eutyches, and Emperor Theodosius II himself. Theodosius, however, was well pleased with the proceedings at Ephesus and refused to convoke a new council. Probably in April 450, he assured his cousins in Ravenna that the various disturbers of ecclesiastical peace had been removed and that "nothing contrary to the rule of faith or to justice had been done there" (Leo, *Letters* 62–64).

Opinion, however, was not universally favorable to Dioscorus. In the spring of 450 he was supported by the Egyptian, Palestinian, and Thracian bishops, but not by those in Syria, Asia, and Pontus (Liberatus, 1936, xiii.76). At court, Empress Pulcheria, Theodosius' sister, informed Pope Leo that she herself disapproved the "Manichaean error" of the council (Leo, *Letters* 60).

Alexandria, however, remained "the city of the orthodox," and Dioscorus the most powerful ecclesiastical personage in Christendom, until 28 July 450, when Theodosius died suddenly after a fall from his horse. This event resulted in a complete change in the situation. Legates from Leo, on their way to Constantinople to plead their cause with the emperor, were confronted by a court revolution in progress. Pulcheria became empress, chose a Thracian general named Marcian as her consort (25 August), and removed by exile or execution Theodosius' ministers who supported Ephesus II. Among those executed was Grand Chamberlain Chrysaphius, on whose aid Eutyches had been able to count (Theodorus Lector, 1971, p. 86, col. 165). Probably late in August 449, Flavian expired at Hypepe in Lydia, as a direct consequence of Dioscorus' violence against him at Ephesus on 8 August 449. In October, Flavian's body was brought back to Constantinople with honor, but the new patriarch, his supplanter Anatolius, was able to negotiate a deal with Leo that left him in possession of his see with what would have appeared to him only minimal concessions (Frend, 1979, p. 46). Negotiations for a new general council followed. After a postponement of the original date proposed, 23 May, due to the invasion of Nicaea by the Huns, the site was changed to Chalcedon. The council met on 8 October 451. Ephesus II had already been denounced by Leo as a *latrocinium* (robber synod) (*Letters* 95, to Pulcheria, 20 July 451), even while Theodosius was still living.

The Meeting of the Council, 8 October–1 November 451

The first session took place in the Church of Saint Euphemia. The conduct of the proceedings rested with imperial commissioners when the emperor was not present. There were nineteen of these laymen, headed by the patrician Anatolius. They symbolized the ultimate lay control of the conduct of ecclesiastical affairs in all questions except doctrinal ones, which prevailed in the Eastern Empire. The papal legates had the right of speaking first as senior delegates, but otherwise the commissioners were in control. The legates sat in a place of honor. Next to them, to the left of the commissioners, were Anatolius, patriarch of Constantinople; Maximus of Antioch; Thalassius of Caesarea in Cappadocia; and Stephen of Ephesus. On the other side of the church sat Dioscorus, Juvenal of Jerusalem, and bishops of Egypt, Palestine, and Illyricum.

The balance, however, was very soon tipped in favor of the papal legates (Paschasinus, bishop of Lilybaeum, and the presbyter Boniface) and their allies. Dioscorus had arrived early in the capital and promptly excommunicated Leo, but neither Anatolius nor Juvenal supported him. When the session opened, the legates demanded the exclusion of Dioscorus. This was refused, but Dioscorus was ordered to seat himself between the two rows of the bishops, as a defendant. At first the Egyptian bishops showed their mettle, denouncing Theodoret of Cyrrhus, who had been restored to his see by Leo, as "an enemy of God" (Mansi, 1901–1927, Vol. 6, p. 592). The imperial letter of summons, however, was followed by the reading of the minutes of Ephesus II and those of Flavian's Home Synod of 22 November 448, which had deposed Eutyches, and the mood changed. The senior bishops who had participated in Ephesus II tried to excuse themselves. Juvenal of Jerusalem rose and moved to the left side of the church, followed by most of the Illyrian bishops and four Egyptians. The move of these last foreshadowed a permanent schism in the church in Egypt and placed Dioscorus in an impossible position. He stood firm, however. He believed Flavian had been justly deposed because he had spoken of "two natures after the union." This was against the repeated statements of "the Fathers": "I accept out of the two natures one. But two natures I do not accept." By the end of the session, however, the commissioners recommended his deposition along with his principal allies: Juvenal, Thalassius of Caesarea, Basil of Seleucia, and Eusebius of Ancyra.

The second session, on 10 October, formally rehabilitated Flavian and Eusebius, bishop of Dorylaeum. The bishops then began to discuss the new definition of faith. The ground had already been prepared by the acclamation of the Formula of Reunion as part of the minutes of the Home Synod and the abject explanations and apologies of those bishops who had taken part in Flavian's condemnation. The commissioners reminded the council that the emperor upheld the decrees of Nicaea and Constantinople together with the writings of the holy fathers Gregory, Basil, and Hilary. Ambrose's writings against the Arians and the two letters of Cyril (Cyril's second and third letters to NESTORIUS) had been approved by Ephesus I. The bishops also had before them Leo's letter to Flavian condemning the teaching of Eutyches.

The Tome

The upshot was that Leo's *Tome*, with its outspokenly two-nature Christology, was accepted as orthodox. "This is the faith of the Fathers and Apostles. This is what we all believe," the bishops cried. "Peter has spoken through Leo; thus Cyril taught. Leo and Cyril teach the same. Anathema to him who teaches otherwise" (Mansi, Vol. 6, p. 972). This was quite untrue, but it indicated that the bishops intended Cyril's teaching to be regarded as the touchstone of orthodoxy, against which Leo's *Tome* would be measured. At this session there were Illyrian, Palestinian, and Egyptian bishops who were far from convinced that Leo succeeded in being orthodox when measured by Cyril's teachings.

At the third session, 13 October, Dioscorus was confronted with complaints against his tyrannical conduct by Alexandrian clergy and laity. This clinched the case against him, for it was not necessary for the bishops to condemn his doctrine. They could cite his offenses against ecclesiastical discipline. The commissioners were absent from this session, and Paschasinus presided. He had obvious pleasure in sentencing Dioscorus, in the name of "Peter . . . who is the rock of the church and the foundation of the orthodox faith," to deposition and "deprivation of all sacerdotal authority" (Mansi, Vol. 6 p. 1048). Only 185 bishops (out of a total assembly of 520) signed the sentence.

The vehemence of the opposition to the *Tome* impressed the commissioners. Patriarch Anatolius of Constantinople began a series of consultations aimed at bridging the cleavages of opinion over Christological doctrine, and on 22 October he produced a draft statement. Unfortunately, this extremely important statement has not survived. It is clear, however, that it included a series of statements emphasizing the unity of Christ's person, the definition that He was "out of two natures," and the statement that the Virgin was *Theotokos* (Mother of God). These assertions proved too much for the legates and the commissioners, but they were acceptable to the great majority of the bishops. The legates threatened to return to Rome and convene a new synod. The menace was greeted with defiance. "Let the formula stand or we depart," the bishops shouted. "These men are Nestorians, let them be off to Rome" (Mansi, Vol. 7, p. 105B; Schwartz, *Acta conciliorum oecumenicorum* (1914–1940), 2. 1.2, p. 125). In fact, had the formula "out of two natures" been accepted, the doctrinal differences between Constantinople and Alexandria would have been removed, since both Flavian and Dioscorus had subscribed to this definition, and the Monophysite schism would never have come about. But the price would have been premature schism between Rome and the Eastern patriarchates.

The incipient crisis was avoided by the wit of the commissioners. They pointed out, first, that the bishops had accepted the *Tome*, in which the phrase "in two natures" occurred; that Dioscorus had admitted that Christ was "out of two natures"; and that Leo had affirmed that there were two natures. "Which did they prefer, Dioscorus or Leo?" (Mansi, Vol. 7, p. 105c). The cry immediately went up, "As Leo we believe. Leo has expounded [the faith] rightly. He who contradicts is a Eutychian." The wisdom of the laymen prevailed. Anatolius' committee retired, to return for the sixth session on 25 October with a definition that Emperor Marcian, accompanied by Pulcheria, promulgated amid enthusiasm. The text is given below.

> Our Lord Jesus Christ is to us One and the same Son, the Self-same Perfect in Godhead, the Self-same Perfect in Manhood; truly God and truly Man; the Self-same of a rational soul and body; consubstantial with the Father according to the Godhead, the Self-same consubstantial with us according to the Manhood; like us in all things, sin apart; before the ages begotten of the Father as to the Godhead, but in the last days, the Self-same, for us and our salvation [born] of Mary the Virgin *Theotokos* as to the Manhood; One and the Same Christ, Son, Lord, Only-begotten; acknowledged in Two Natures unconfusedly, unchangeably, indivisibly, inseparably; the difference of the Natures being in no way removed because of the Union, but rather the property of each Nature being preserved, and [both] concurring into One Prosopon and One Hypostasis; not as though He were parted or divided into Two Prosopa, but One and the Self-same Son and Only-begotten God, Word, Lord, Jesus Christ.

We can see that the dominant idea was inspired by CYRIL of Alexandria. Cyril's influence may be detected in the emphasis on the unity of the Son "Self-same Perfect in Godhead, the Self-same Perfect in Manhood" (Mansi, 1798). But there is also the language of the Formula of Reunion, and acknowledgment "in two natures" recognized the orthodoxy of the *Tome*. The four adverbs, "unconfusedly, unchangeably, indivisibly, inseparably" were aimed at excluding Eutychianism and Nestorianism. It was about as good a compromise as human language of the day could achieve. It provided just enough common ground for Rome, Constantinople, and Antioch to agree; and if Cyril had kept to his Second Letter to Nestorius, Alexandria might have been included. Compromise, however, is not of the nature of religious feeling. Instinctively the Copts, as well as many Christians in Syria and Asia Minor, recoiled. Only the emperor's support won the definition as much assent as it commanded in the East.

The remaining sessions down to the sixteenth, held on 1 November, were concerned with personal and practical matters. Two bishops deposed at the Council of Ephesus II, Theodoret of Cyrrhus and Ibas of Edessa, accepted the definition and were reinstated by the council (papal restoration was not regarded as final); a quarrel between two rival claimants to the see of Ephesus was settled; a pension was agreed upon for former Patriarch Domnus of Antioch, who had accepted deposition at Ephesus II; and a dispute between the bishop of Nicaea and his metropolitan was decided.

Finally, the positions of two patriarchates were agreed. Juvenal of Jerusalem was given the dignity of a patriarch with three Palestinian provinces. Three others—Phoenicia I and II and Arabia—granted to him by Dioscorus at Ephesus II, at the expense of Antioch, were handed back to Antioch. The compromise was hammered out by Juvenal and Maximus of Antioch, and ended the long struggle by Jerusalem for recognition as a patriarchal see. More important was the twenty-eighth canon of the council, agreed upon at its final session despite the opposition of the papal legates. This confirmed canon 3 of the Council of Constantinople (381), which had accorded to Constantinople, as "New Rome," a status equal to that of "Old Rome," save only a primacy of honor retained by the latter. It took cognizance of canon 9 of Chalcedon, agreed upon the previous day, which gave appellate jurisdiction to Constantinople over ecclesiastical lawsuits involving the churches in Asia Minor, including Pontus and Thrace. Strenuous papal objections were brushed aside, and 183 bishops signed the canon.

In the months following the council, every effort was made to gain Leo's acceptance of canon 28 as well as of the definition. These foundered on the pope's uncompromising refusal even to consider according Constantinople equality of status with Rome (Leo, *Letters* 98, 104, 105, 106). On 7 February 452, however, Marcian addressed an imperial edict to the people of Constantinople: "All therefore shall be bound to hold to the decision of the sacred council of Chalcedon and indulge no further doubts." Discussion of matters of religion was prohibited (text in Schwartz, *Acta conciliorum oecumenicorum*, 2. ii.3, pp. 21–22; see also texts of Marcian's edicts of 13 March and 6 July 452 in Mansi, Vol. 7, pp. 477–80, 497–500).

To contemporaries the Council of Chalcedon was a vindication of the position of the see of Constantinople against Alexandria and, to a lesser extent, Rome. Canon 28 was henceforth to provide the title deeds for Constantinople's status in the East. The Christological definition, though making the Monophysite schism inevitable, provided Christendom with a statement of belief to which both East and West could subscribe.

In addition, the council consolidated the role of the emperor and his lay representatives in the guidance of the church, and it upheld the authority of the bishop against the growing rival charismatic authority of the monks. Not only the great assemblage of bishops that participated, but also the attempted equity of the decisions throughout the long sessions, justified its claim to be a "fair council." For the Copts, however, the deposition of Dioscorus and acceptance of the *Tome* of Leo would entail their gradual alienation from the religion of Rome and Constantinople alike.

BIBLIOGRAPHY

Altaner, B., and A. Stuiber. *Patrologia*, 7th ed., p. 249. Freiburg, Basel, and Vienna, 1966.

Chadwick, H. "The Exile and Death of Flavian of Constantinople: A Prologue to the Council of Chalcedon." *Journal of Theological Studies* n.s. 6, no. 1 (1955):17–34.

Frend, W. H. C. *The Rise of the Monophysite Movement*, 2nd ed., chap. 1. Cambridge, 1979.

Grillmeier, A., and H. Bacht. *Das Konzil von Chalkedon*, 3 vols. Würzburg, 1951–1954; Frankfurt am Main, 1973–1979.

Honigmann, E. "Juvenal of Jerusalem." *Dumbarton Oaks Papers* 5 (1950):211–79.

Kidd, B. J. *A History of the Church to A.D. 461*, Vol. 3, chap. 16. Oxford, 1922.

Leo. *Letters*. In PL 54, cols. 593–1218.

Schwartz, E. "Die Kaiserin Pulcheria und die Synode von Chalkedon." In *Festgabe für A. Jülicher*, pp. 203–212. Tübingen, 1927.

Sellers, R. V. *The Council of Chalcedon: A Historical and Doctrinal Survey*. London, 1961.

W. H. C. Frend

CHALDAEAN ORACLES, a revelatory poem, written in Greek hexameter verse, composed or edited by a certain magician named Julianus, who lived during the reign of Marcus Aurelius. Its importance is twofold: it is the last major sacred book of pagan antiquity, and it had major influence on the development of Neoplatonism from Porphyry to Psellus. Only fragments exist, although quotations are scattered in the writings of Proclus, Damascius, Psellus, and other Neoplatonists. Magical rites were based on the precepts of this purported divine revelation.

The fragments, best studied by Hans Lewy, contain much borrowed Platonism, some material common to gnosticism, and an account of the creation and the descent of the cosmic soul. Hypostases, gods, and daemons of Greco-Oriental cults are fused into a strange mass in the "Chaldaean theology." Some rituals or sacraments have been identified, including a symbolic burial, an initiation, and a purification of the soul. Although Christian writers quoted the text in collections and anthologies, there is no certain influence of the "Chaldaean Oracles" on Christian magic.

BIBLIOGRAPHY

Dodds, E. R. "Theurgy and Its Relationship to Neoplatonism." *Journal of Roman Studies* 37 (1947):55–69.

______. "New Light on the 'Chaldaean Oracles.'" *Harvard Theological Review* 54 (1961):263–73.

Lewy, H. *Chaldaean Oracles and Theurgy: Mysticism, Magic and Platonism in the Later Roman Empire*. Cairo, 1966.

C. WILFRED GRIGGS

CHALICE. *See* Eucharistic Vessels; Metalwork, Coptic.

CHALICE VEIL. *See* Eucharistic Veils.

CHAMPOLLION, JEAN FRANÇOIS (1790–1832), French Egyptologist and student of Oriental languages, including Coptic. He was educated in Grenoble. In 1806 he gave a paper at the Académie de Grenoble in which he maintained that Coptic was the ancient language of Egypt. Ten years later he published a book entitled *L'Egypte sous les Pharaons,* a description of Egypt drawn from classical and Coptic sources. His main achievement was the decipherment of hieroglyphs through the Rosetta Stone (now in the British Museum), a revolutionary discovery that inaugurated the science of Egyptology. He was appointed curator of the Egyptian Collection at the Louvre Museum in 1824.

BIBLIOGRAPHY

Dawson, W. R., and E. P. Uphill. *Who Was Who in Egyptology*, pp. 58–60. London, 1972.

AZIZ S. ATIYA

CHANCEL. *See* Architectural Elements of Churches: Cancelli.

CHANDELIERS. *See* Metalwork.

CHARISIOS. The name of this archimandrite is preserved only by some fragments of the typica preserved at Leiden (Insinger, 38a, Pleyte and Boeser, 1897, p. 182), Vienna (K 9736), and Rome (Vatican, Borgia 231; Leipoldt, 1913, p. 11).

Charisios has left no trace in the Copto-Arabic SYNAXARION; we know of his existence only from the typica of the White Monastery (Dayr Anbā Shinūdah). These merely indicate his position as archimandrite and the day of his feast, 28 Bābah, which was probably the day of his death. They do not specify the monastery of which he was archimandrite, but it is probable that it was the White Monastery itself.

At what period he lived is not known. The ostracon published by Turaev (1899, pp. 445–46) names the first abbots of Fāw and adds Shenute and Moses, but does not mention Charisios. It is therefore uncertain if he was abbot of Fāw or of Atrīb.

BIBLIOGRAPHY

Leipoldt, J. *Sinuthii Archimandritae Vita et Opera Omnia*, Pt. 4. CSCO 73. Paris and Leipzig, 1913.

Pleyte, W., and P. A. A. Boeser, eds. *Manuscrits coptes du Musée d'antiquités des Pays-Bas à Leide*, 1897.

Turaev, B. A. "Koptskiia ostraka kollektsii V. S. Golenitseva." *Bulletin de l'Académie impériale des sciences de St. Petersbourg* 10 (1899):439–49.

RENÉ-GEORGES COQUIN

CHASSINAT, EMILE GASTON (1868–1948), French Egyptologist and Coptologist. He was born in Paris and studied under Gaston Maspero at the

Ecole des Hautes Etudes and under Eugène Revillout and Paul Pierret at the Louvre. He was appointed to the Egyptian department of the Louvre in 1894 and joined the Institut français d'Archéologie orientale in Cairo in 1895. He was director of the institute from 1898 to 1911, during which time the institute's activities were expanding. Its press was inaugurated in 1898, the *Bulletin* in 1900, and the Bibliothèque d'étude in 1908. Under his direction large-scale excavations were also undertaken, including that of the Coptic monastery of Bāwīṭ. His contributions to Coptic studies included "Fragments de manuscrits coptes en dialecte fayoumique" (*Bulletin de l'Institut français d'Archéologie orientale* 2, 1902, pp. 171–206); *Fouilles à Baouit*, Vol. 1 (Cairo, 1911); *Le Quatrième Livre des entretiens et épîtres de Shenouti* (Cairo, 1911); *Un Papyrus médical copte* (Cairo, 1921); and *Le Manuscrit magique copte* (Cairo, 1955). He died in Saint-Germain-en-Laye.

BIBLIOGRAPHY

Dawson, W. R., and E. P. Uphill. *Who Was Who in Egyptology*, pp. 61–62. London, 1972.

Kammerer, W., comp. *A Coptic Bibliography*. Ann Arbor, Mich., 1950; repr. New York, 1969.

AZIZ S. ATIYA

CHEIROTONIA, the practice of simony. The biblical passage cited by the Coptic jurists condemning the practice of the *cheirotonia* or simony is recorded by Saint Luke in the Acts of the Apostles 8:14–25. As the early church moved from its sectarian structure to an all-inclusive national cult, members of the hierarchy faced new problems concerning the power structure. The temptation to sell and buy ecclesiastical privileges was a constant threat, especially since the selling and the purchasing of civic rights and privileges during the imperial age was a widespread and largely accepted practice. Saint Basil of Caesarea, aware that his suffragan bishops accepted money for the ordination of priests, addressed an open letter to the members of his clergy in which he warned them of ecclesiastical and eternal punishments if they persisted in the practice. For the Copts, the two series of CANONS OF SAINT BASIL, of which one canon (sec. 45) is specifically devoted to the condemnation of the *cheirotonia*, are authoritative.

With respect to the Coptic church, we must distinguish the motivations of this practice, whether members of the hierarchy were merely moved to increase their personal gains and prestige or practiced simony for the sheer survival of the church that was entrusted to them. In some cases—certainly not in all—the *cheirotonia* as practiced by the Coptic patriarchs, bishops, and archons was a necessary evil, comparable with such necessary evils as the "white lie" or stealing on account of need or poverty. In these cases, the end justifies an otherwise prohibited act of conduct. This principle was acknowledged by the canonical jurists of the medieval Coptic church, for example, by MĪKHĀ'ĪL of Atrīb and Malīj (Nomocanon secs. 13, 17, 24).

Similar arguments could be advanced regarding the practice of the *cheirotonia* following the ARAB CONQUEST OF EGYPT with its more or less oppressive measures against the Coptic church. For example, during the 470 years from 830 to 1300, seven patriarchs are said to have practiced the *cheirotonia*. In two cases, KHĀ'ĪL III and GABRIEL I, it is stated that they practiced the *cheirotonia* from entirely unselfish motivations and exclusively for the survival of the church. Five patriarchs, PHILOTHEUS, SHENUTE II, CHRISTODOULUS, CYRIL III, and THEODOSIUS II, were severely censured for having personally engaged in, participated with others in, or condoned the practice of the *cheirotonia*, and were therefore referred to as "lovers of money."

Four patriarchs, SHENUTE I, ABRAHAM, CYRIL II, and GABRIEL II explicitly prohibited the practice either by patriarchal order or by the issuance of ecclesiastical canons. Special condemnation for those practicing the *cheirotonia* is expressed in the canons of Cyril II and Gabriel II ibn Turayq.

BIBLIOGRAPHY

Burmester, O. H. E. "The Canons of Gabriel ibn Turaik, LXX Patriarch of Alexandria." *Orientalia Christiana Periodica* 1 (1935):5–45.

———. "The Canons of Cyril II." *Le Muséon* 49 (1936):279.

Crum, W. E. "The Coptic Version of the Canons of Saint Basil." *Proceedings of the Society of Biblical Archaeology* 26 (1904):57–62.

Meinardus, O. "The Cheirotonia among the Copts—A Necessary Evil?" *Ekklesiastikos Pharos* 59 (1977):437–49.

Reidel, W. *Die Kirchenrechtsquellen des Patriarchats Alexandrien*, pp. 231–33, 260. Leipzig, 1900.

OTTO F. A. MEINARDUS

CHENOBOSKION SHENESET. *See* Pachomius of Tabennēsē, Saint.

CHERUBIM AND SERAPHIM, celestial creatures occupying the highest order of angels, with the seraphim ranking above the cherubim.

According to Genesis 3:24, when man was expelled from the Garden of Eden, God placed the cherubim at the entrance to Paradise, with a sword whirling and flashing to guard the way to the tree of life. Likewise God commanded Moses to make an ark for the tabernacle, with two gold cherubim of beaten work at the end of the court, whose wings were outspread and pointing upward (Ex. 25:18–22). They were full of eyes "like burning coals of fire" (Ez. 28:14–16), and were also described as a tetrad of living creatures, each cherub having four faces, four wings, the hands of a human being, but the hooves of a calf (Ez. 1:5–8).

The seraphim are mentioned in Isaiah 6:2, where he saw in a vision several seraphim standing before the throne of God and ceaselessly praising Him. Each seraph had six wings, two covering his face, two his feet, and two for flying.

In allusion to Isaiah 6:2–3, the Cherubic Hymn forms an integral part of the prayer of reconciliation in all liturgies, where the celebrant priest says, "Thou art He, round whom stand the Cherubim full of eyes and the six-winged Seraphim, praising continuously, with unfailing voices, saying: [Here the congregation sings] The Cherubim worship Thee, and the Seraphim glorify Thee, proclaiming: Holy, Holy, Holy, Lord of hosts; heaven and earth are full of Thy holy glory." A similar hymn also features in the Euchologion of Serpion (d. c. 360), bishop of Tmuis.

Etymologically, the cherubim are so called because they represent profound knowledge, and the seraphim the fervor of love.

BIBLIOGRAPHY

Leclercq, H. "Anges." In *Dictionnaire d'archéologie chrétienne et de liturgie,* Vol. 1, cols. 2080–2161. Paris, 1907.

Marriott, W. B. "Angels and Archangels in Christian Art." In *Dictionary of Christian Art,* Vol. 1, pp. 83–89. London, 1876.

Strachan, J. "Seraphim." In J. Hasting, *Dictionary of the Bible,* Vol. 4, pp. 458–59. London, 1902.

Vincent, L. H. "Les Chérubins." In *Revue Biblique* 35 (1926):328–58, 481–95.

ARCHBISHOP BASILIOS

CHESTER BEATTY BIBLICAL PAPYRI. Alfred Chester Beatty, an industrialist and financier born in New York City in 1875, became one of the world's great collectors of Oriental manuscripts, specializing particularly in manuscripts of artistic merit from the point of view of miniatures and calligraphy. The collections were housed at his home in London until 1953, when, having moved to Dublin, he built a special library and exhibition gallery for his collection of Oriental and Western printed books and manuscripts.

Among the hundreds of Greek papyri in the Beatty collection, by far the most famous are the biblical texts. The acquisition in 1930 of this group of papyrus codices from Iṭfīḥ (Aphroditopolis), ranging in date from the second to the fourth century, was justly described as the greatest event in the history of the Greek Bible since Tischendorf's discovery of the CODEX SINAITICUS a century before. Portions of several of these codices were purchased separately by the University of Michigan.

The three New Testament manuscripts comprise the Gospels and Acts in one codex, dating from the third century (about one-seventh of the total text being preserved); nine of the Pauline epistles, dating from about 200; and the central portion of the book of Revelation, from the third century.

The Old Testament is represented by two separate fragmentary copies of Genesis (especially valuable, since that book is missing from both the Vaticanus and the Sinaiticus copies); substantial portions of Numbers and Deuteronomy together in one codex, dating from the first half of the second century; and portions of Isaiah, Jeremiah, Ezekiel, Esther, Daniel, and Ecclesiastes. The twelfth and last codex of the collection (dating from the fourth century) contains the closing chapters of the book of Enoch and a homily on the Passion by the second-century Christian writer Melito of Sardis.

Apart from their textual importance (for which see Kenyon, 1975), the Beatty papyri are of great significance codicologically, indicating as they do the Christian preference for the codex form of book, as opposed to the roll, which remained the favorite format in the Jewish synagogue as well as in pagan circles.

The biblical papyri (along with the Michigan portions) were edited, with complete facsimiles, by Frederick G. Kenyon (1933–). The Beatty and Michigan portions of Enoch and Melito were edited by Campbell Bonner in the series Studies and Documents, Volumes 8 and 12 (1937, 1940). The two Beatty texts of Genesis were reedited in 1977 by Albert Pietersma (American Studies in Papyrology 16), who also edited two additional (fragmentary)

Beatty papyri of the Greek Psalter, dating from the fourth century (Analecta Biblica 77 [1978]).

[*See also:* Chester Beatty Coptic Papyri.]

BIBLIOGRAPHY

Kenyon, F. G. *The Text of the Greek Bible.* London, 1975.

Pietersma, A., ed. *Chester Beatty Biblical Papyri IV and V: A New Edition with Text-Critical Analysis.* American Studies in Papyrology 16. Toronto, 1977.

———. *Two Manuscripts of the Greek Psalter: In the Chester Beatty Library, Dublin.* Rome, 1978.

BRUCE M. METZGER

CHESTER BEATTY COPTIC PAPYRI.

Second in importance only to the Beatty Greek biblical papyri (see CHESTER BEATTY BIBLICAL PAPYRI) is the large group of Coptic papyri acquired by A. Chester Beatty, some of which contain the text of lost books of the Manichaean religion (see MANICHAEISM). Large sections of these have been published, including the homilies, by H. J. Polotsky (1934), and the Psalter, part 2, by C. R. C. Allberry (1938). Other Manichaean codices were acquired by the Berlin Papyrus Collection.

Another important codex comprises portions of a fourth-century copy of the book of Joshua in Sahidic; part of the same codex was separately acquired by the Bodmer Library of Geneva. The Beatty portion was edited and translated by A. F. Shore (1963). A papyrus copy of the Apocalypse of Elijah in Sahidic (Beatty Papyrus 2018), dating from the end of the fourth or beginning of the fifth century, was edited and translated by Albert Pietersma in 1981.

BIBLIOGRAPHY

Allberry, C. R. C., ed. *A Manichaean Psalm-book,* pt. 2. Stuttgart, 1938.

Pietersma, A., ed. *The Apocalypse of Elijah: Based on P. Chester Beatty 2018 Coptic Text,* with S. T. Comstock and H. W. Attridge. Chico, Calif., 1981.

Polotsky, H. J., ed. *Manichäische Homilien.* Stuttgart, 1934.

Shore, A. F., ed. *Joshua I–IV and Other Passages in Coptic.* Dublin, 1963.

BRUCE M. METZGER

CHIFTICHI, YUḤANNA,

Coptic priest and scholar born in Cairo in the last quarter of the eighteenth century; died in France sometime after 1825. One hindrance to discovering his identity is due to the illegible spellings of his name by biographers of Champollion, to whom Chiftichi taught Coptic pronunciation. H. Hartleben (1906, Vol. 1, p. 81) writes his name "Jeacha Sceptidschy," and L. de La Brière transcribes it differently as "Icaha Scheptichi" in publishing the following letter by Champollion written in Paris to his brother, a letter of prime interest in the genesis of Champollion's discovery.

> I am going to visit a Coptic priest at Saint-Roch, rue Saint-Honoré, who celebrates Mass . . . and who will instruct me in Coptic names, and the pronunciation of Coptic letters. . . . I am devoting myself entirely to the Coptic language, for I want to know the Egyptian language as well as my own native French. My great work on the Egyptian papyri will be based on this [ancient] tongue.
> [1897; p. 69]

Chiftichi also figures in government correspondence regarding the encyclopedic *Description de l'Egypte* under the name of Youhanna only, in a letter written by the minister of the interior on 17 Floréal 10 (1802):

> Citizen, a Coptic (Cophte) priest named Youhanna, who is reputed to be very learned in Oriental languages, has been referred to me as capable of cooperating usefully in the great work upon which all the scholars recently returned from Egypt are labouring at present. I am wondering if you think he might be in a position to help with this work, and would you kindly let me know your opinion about this as soon as possible. Citizen Langlès believes that this foreigner might be put to good use. [Nouvelles Acquisitions, official letters of the Bibliothèque Nationale, Paris, Department of Manuscripts, 21937, fol. 84]

The reply is missing, but the missive of Langlès describes him as "a Coptic (Qobthe) priest named Youhanna (John)," whom he recommends for adding to the great work the "principal passages from Arabic writers regarding the antiquities and geography of Egypt."

There is no further information as to the nature and extent of Chiftichi's scientific collaboration save this note: "Apart from the four Orientalists included in the main body of the Commission of whom only one is salaried, Minister Chaptal has added to the Commission from the very beginning of the enterprise the name of the Egyptian Yuhanna Chiftichy, a refugee from Cairo. . . . He enjoys but a modest salary." On the payroll until June 1814, his name, always last on the list, and always written in Arabic as al-Shiftishī, is sometimes preceded by the word *Abūnā* (Father) Yuḥanna, or *al-Qissīs* (Priest) Yuḥanna. In other papers from the Archives du Service historique de l'armée, at Vincennes, alterations of his name appear under diverse spellings: Anna, Kassis, Anna Kassis, and Anacharsis.

In those archives that faceless name to be translated as "John the Transparent" assumes all the known characteristics of a minority Copt. In the dossier of Chiftichi in the Archives, a document dated 21 Frimaire 11 (1803) at Melun (where the Mamluks of Napoleon were stationed—see YA'QŪB, GENERAL) enumerates nine "certificates and titles being in the hands of Citizen John Chfftgy, an Egyptian born in Greater Cairo." He served under the French administration as interpreter for the province of Giza, adjudicator for tax collections, main recorder at the Tribunal of Commerce, interpreter for General Destaing, and then for Citizen Dallonville, director of rights on corporations. Later, according to the Archives, upon Fourier's recommendation, he became interpreter for the "Commission, created by General Kléber, to assemble materials for the history of the Conquest of Egypt." Finally, according to an attestation of the chief of staff, General Damas, he had been chief of the brigade, that is, colonel in the Coptic Legion. As a soldier-priest, he resumed links with the ancient tradition of the warrior-saints so popular in Egypt: Saint George, Saint Menas, and the Thebans, Maurice and Victor. Chiftichi bore a scar from a serious wound as described in a report, signed by Berthollet, Jomard, Jolliot, Duvillier, Girard, Fourier, and Delile, and addressed to the minister of the interior, 5 April 1816, in support of Chiftichi's request for French citizenship. The Archives record: "He lost his fortune and some of his closest relatives because of the events that transpired in Cairo after the departure of the French Army; and in spite of these painful losses, he has been the main support of the rest of his family since that time." In truth, he gave up half his pension to the widows and six children of his two brothers who were assassinated for being members of the Coptic Legion.

In Paris he lived in the Rue Saint-Roch when Champollion came to consult him—after lodging at the Rue de la Concorde and the Rue Royale while still continuing his ministry in the Rue Saint-Roch. He decided in 1825 to go to Marseilles in order to end his days among the Egyptian refugees there. The exact dates of his birth and death remain unknown. The destiny of Chiftichi is symbolic of the survival of Egypt through the torments of that era.

BIBLIOGRAPHY

Archives du Service historique de l'armée, Vincennes. *Orientaux: Aumôniers et interprètes,* 1 carton.

Brière, L. de La. *Champollion inconnu, lettres inédites.* Paris, 1897.

Hartleben, H. *Champollion, sein Leben und sein Werk,* Vol. 1, p. 81. Berlin, 1906.

Louca, A. "Champollion entre Bartholdi et Chiftichi." *Mélanges Jacques Berque.* Paris, 1989.

Savant, J. *Les Mamelouks de Napoléon.* Paris, 1949.

ANOUAR LOUCA

CHOIR. *See* Architectural Elements of Churches: Choir; Khūrus.

CHOREPISCOPUS, assistant to a bishop. The rapid diffusion of Christianity in the early centuries and the consequent increase in the number of churches and the duties of the diocesan bishops necessitated the appointment of assistants to these bishops, holding the title of chorepiscopus, to assume some of the pastoral duties in rural areas.

In the Eastern church chorepiscopi first appeared in the third century in Asia Minor, and before long, clergymen elevated to that dignity spread in many parts of the Christian world. The earliest known was Zoticus, chorepiscopus of the village of Comana in Pamphylia. Some chorepiscopi also attended the Council of Ancyra (314), that of Neocaesarea (315), the first Council of NICAEA (325), and the Council of EPHESUS (431). None are known to have attended the Council of CHALCEDON (451).

In the Western church chorepiscopi were first mentioned in connection with the Council of Reiz (439). Later they grew in number in various parts of Europe, especially Germany and France. By the twelfth century, however, the rank of chorepiscopus had completely vanished.

The question of determining the exact position of a chorepiscopus in the hierarchical order of the early church gave rise to much controversy. To see the matter in its proper perspective, let us consider the stipulation of such authority as was granted to the chorepiscopus by various councils. According to Canon 13 of the Council of Ancyra: "It is not lawful for chorespiscopi to ordain presbyters or deacons, without the commission of the bishop given in writing. . . ." Under Canon 14 of the Council of Neocaesarea, "The chorepiscopi, however, are indeed after the pattern of the seventy; and as fellow-servants, on account of their devotion to the poor, they have the honor of making the oblation." Finally, according to Canon 10 of the Council of Antioch (341), "The Holy Synod decrees that persons in villages and districts, or those who are called chorepiscopi, even though they may have received ordination to the episcopate, shall regard their own limits and manage the churches subject to them, and be content with the care and administration of these; but they may ordain readers, subdeacons, and exorcists, and shall be content with promoting these, but shall not presume to ordain either a presbyter or a deacon, without the consent of the bishop of the city to which he and his district are subject." It is evident from the above that the office of the chorepiscopus is inferior to that of the bishop, that his duties are mainly concerned with rural areas and the care of the poor, that he and his congregation are subject to the jurisdiction of the bishop of the city by whom he is ordained or appointed, and that he is entitled to ordain readers, subdeacons, and exorcists in the villages in his charge.

Opinion is divided as regards the ecclesiastical classification of the office of chorepiscopate: some historians consider it an episcopal rank, others a clerical one, while a third group of historians believe that some chorespiscopi were full-fledged bishops and others were only titularly so. In the Coptic and other Eastern churches, the chorepiscopate is a clerical rank accorded at times to senior priests. In larger dioceses, however, an assistant bishop may be chosen to work under a metropolitan, enjoying the prestige of a bishop, without having his name mentioned during the celebration of the Divine Liturgy. Such chorepiscopi may later be consecrated bishops, in the event of vacancies in their own or other dioceses.

BIBLIOGRAPHY

Asad Rustum. *Kanīsat Madīnat Allāh Anṭākiyah al-ʿUẓmā,* Vol. 1, p. 164. Beirut, 1958.

Ḥabīb Jirjis. *Asrār al-Kanīsah al-Sabʿah,* 2nd ed., p. 219. Cairo, 1950.

ARCHBISHOP BASILIOS

CHRISM, also known as holy myron, the sacred oil used in anointing and in ceremonies of consecration.

The tradition of using this sacred oil goes back to the Old Testament (Ex. 30) where God ordered Moses to prepare an anointing oil compounded from myrrh, cinnamon, cassia, and sweet calamus mixed with pure olive oil. It was used in anointing kings, priests, the tent of the tabernacle, the ark, the altar, and the altar vessels.

In his encyclopedic work *Miṣbāḥ al-Ẓulmah fī Īḍāḥ al-Khidmah* (The Luminary of Church Services), Abū al-Barakāt IBN-KABAR (d. 1234) devotes the whole of section nine to the subject of the holy chrism.

According to this work, in the early church the apostles continued the Old Testament practice of using the above-mentioned sacred oil, mixed with the myrrh and aloes that had been brought by Joseph of Arimathaea and Nicodemus for the burial of Christ's body (Jn. 19:38–42). The apostles consecrated this oil in the upper room (Mk. 15:15; Acts 1:13) and each one carried an adequate quantity on their evangelization mission to different parts of the world. They also gave orders that, before it was completely used up, it should be replenished by consecrating a new supply from the same ingredients added to the residual amount.

This sacred oil continued to be consecrated for use in the church according to a strict procedure kept by the patriarch. A particularly significant day was chosen to carry out this ceremony: the sixth Friday of the sixth week of Lent, this being also the fortieth day of the PASCHA and the day on which Christ baptized the disciples. The number six represented the sixth millennium after the creation of Adam, in which the Logos was incarnate for the salvation of man, and the sixth day of Holy Week, on which He was crucified. However, in the days of Pope MACARIUS I (932–952), it was agreed to have the chrism consecrated on Thursday of Holy Week. The patriarch who succeeded him, THEOPHILUS (952–956), reverted to the sixth-Friday tradition. The next patriarch, MĪNĀ II (956–974), wishing to conciliate certain monks, decided to have the ceremony of consecration performed on Maundy Thursday one year and Good Friday the next. This compromise was ended by Patriarch ABRAHAM (975–978) in favor of Thursday alone. Succeeding patriarchs have also adhered to this day.

IBN KABAR gives the following ingredients as basic components of the chrism: myrrh, sweet calamus, spring cytisus, raw amber, cinnamon, sandalwood, cassia, spikenard, saffron, cardamon, kust root, red rose petals, nutmeg, bee balm, balsam oil, and olive oil.

The concoction is performed in three stages in

which the above-mentioned ingredients are mixed together and left to filter overnight. Ibn Kabar tells us that he had consulted various manuscripts, each giving different quantities and methods. To resolve the matter, he preferred to give a description of the system used in his days by Pope THEODOSIUS II (1294–1300) at the Church of Saint Mercurius in Cairo during Holy Week 1299.

BIBLIOGRAPHY

Burmester, O. H. E. "A Coptic Tradition Concerning the Holy Myron (Chrism)." In *Publications de l'Institut d'études orientales de la Bibliothèque patriarcale d'Alexandrie* 3 (1954):52–58.

Lantschoot, A. van. "Le MS Vatican Copte 44 et le Livre du Chrême (ms. Paris arabe 100)." *Le Muséon* 45 (1932):181–234.

William Sulaymān Qelādah, ed. *Al-Dasqūliyyah, Ta'ālīm al-Rusul.* Cairo, 1979.

FUAD MEGALLY

CHRISM, CONSECRATION OF THE. The infrequent occasions on which the preparation and consecration of the chrism is performed are events of considerable spiritual joy. After concocting the prerequisite ingredients of the chrism and also of the *kallielaion* (oil of the CATECHUMENS) that is usually consecrated on the same day but in a separate service, they are placed in special vessels. Two wooden altars, covered with silk veils, are set up in the sanctuary to the right and to the left of the main altar, on which the vessels containing the chrism and the *kallielaion* are placed: the chrism on the right (southern) altar, and the *kallielaion* on the left (northern) altar.

The consecration of the chrism and the *kallielaion* is exclusively reserved to the patriarch of the church of Alexandria. The service is usually performed on Maundy Thursday, or, alternatively—though rarely—on any Sunday during the fast of Lent, and is attended by many bishops and clergy. Following the prayers of the morning service, the liturgy of the consecration proceeds as follows:

After the TRISAGION, the Lord's Prayer, the prayer of thanksgiving, and the offering of incense, the patriarch prays that God may grant him grace, blessing, and power to accomplish this sacred service.

Readings are taken from Isaiah 61, Exodus 30, and Exodus 40, all of which deal with the preparation of the holy ointment as commanded by God to Moses.

The Pauline Epistle is from Hebrews 1:5–14, the Catholic Epistle from 1 John 2:21–29, and the Acts from 8:14–40, all passages being relevant to the purpose.

The three *agios* are followed by the intercession of the Gospel, the Psalm-versicle (88:19), and the Gospel (Mk. 14:3–9) in Coptic and Arabic. Here the archdeacon calls upon the catechumens to depart.

The clergy form a procession carrying censers, crosses, fans, and candles in front of the patriarch, while the chrism and the *kallielaion* are carried by the patriarch and the bishops, all singing psalmodies. The chrism and *kallielaion* are then placed on their respective altars.

The patriarch performs the service of the blessing of the water and the foot-washing on Maundy Thursday. Then he enters the sanctuary and begins the prayer of the consecration of the chrism.

The archdeacon says, "Let us stand well," and the patriarch prays that God may sanctify the chrism. and render it fit for the holy unction.

The archdeacon says, "Bow your heads to the Lord," and the patriarch prays for the chrism to be invested with the Holy Spirit. Psalm 44:6–8 is read, followed by the three great petitions, the Creed, and two further prayers. The words of the latter prayer are accompanied with the sign of the cross while the congregation answers "Amen" each time, calling upon God to render it a phylactery of life, an indestructible seal, a breastplate of strength—against all the evil workings of the devil.

The archdeacon says, "Let us stand well," and the patriarch prays, "The love of God the Father, the grace of His holy-begotten Son, our Lord, God, and Savior Jesus Christ, and the communion and the gift of His Holy Spirit be with you," to which the congregation answers, "And with your spirit." The patriarch says, "Lift up your hearts." The congregation says, "They are with the Lord." The patriarch says, "Let us give thanks to the Lord." The congregation says, "It is meet and right."

The patriarch continues with the prayers of the holy chrism until he reaches the invocation of the Holy Spirit, which he says inaudibly, and then signs the oil various times with the sign of the cross, saying, "Holy chrism; an oil of gladness; a royal grace; a vesture of light; a garment of salvation; a phylactery of life; a spiritual grace; a purification of soul and body; a joy of grace; an eternal gladness; an indestructible seal; a repose of the faith; a breastplate of strength against every diabolic deed," the deacons following each clause with "Amen."

The archdeacon prays for the peace of the world,

for deliverance from tribulation, for forgiveness of all sins, for the priests of the church, for the sanctification of the holy chrism, the congregation answering every clause with "Kyrie eleison."

The patriarch says the prayer for the consecration of the holy chrism, to which the congregation answers, "Absolve, pardon, and forgive us, O God." Then the patriarch gives thanks to the Lord, beseeching the Almighty to send the grace of the Holy Spirit upon the holy chrism, and the congregation follows with the Lord's Prayer.

The archdeacon says, "Bow your heads to the Lord." The patriarch says the final prayer of sanctification.

The patriarch, accompanied by the clergy, the deacons, and the congregation, proceeds to the other altar to consecrate the *kallielaion*.

The vessels are then left on the two altars until Easter Day, or the following Sunday, during which period a quantity of the old chrism and the old *kallielaion* is added to the new. Then they are conveyed for preservation in the appropriate places and for distribution among the various churches which require it.

BIBLIOGRAPHY

Butler, A. J. *The Ancient Coptic Churches of Egypt*, Vol. 1, p. 337. Oxford, 1884.

Vansleb, P. J. M. *Histoire de l'église d'Alexandrie*, pp. 91, 231f. Paris, 1677.

ARCHBISHOP BASILIOS

CHRISMATORY, a small cruet, made of glass, earthenware, or metal, used as a receptacle for the holy CHRISM. It is usually kept inside a locked wooden box, and placed in the sanctuary or close to the baptismal font.

A. J. Butler describes one such chrismatory he saw in the Church of Anbā Shinūdah in Cairo: "a curious round wooden box with a revolving lid. The box is solid throughout, but has three holes scooped out inside, in each of which is deposited a small phial of oil" (1884, Vol. 2, p. 56). These three phials contained the holy chrism, the oil of the sick, and the oil of the catechumens.

BIBLIOGRAPHY

Butler, A. J. *The Ancient Coptic Churches of Egypt*, Vol. 2, p. 56. Oxford, 1884.

ARCHBISHOP BASILIOS

CHRIST, DIVINITY OF. *See* Christ, Nature of.

CHRIST, NATURE OF. Christian churches are split into two groups regarding the union of the divine and human nature in Jesus Christ. The non-Chalcedonian, including the Coptic, Syrian, Armenian, Ethiopian, and Indian Orthodox churches, reject the decisions of the Council of CHALCEDON (A.D. 451); the Chalcedonian churches, including the Roman Catholic, Greek, and Protestant churches, accept the council's decisions.

The firm position of the Coptic church, with other non-Chalcedonian churches, is that Christ is perfect in His divinity and in His humanity, which is different from saying that He is both God and man, as this statement implies a separation between His divinity and His humanity. He is the incarnate God, and in Him divinity and humanity are fully and perfectly united in essence, hypostasis, and nature. Ever since the Logos (the Word of God) dwelt inside the blessed Virgin Mary, the second hypostasis of the Holy Trinity, that is, the Son, acquired human flesh with a human soul, and was united with the humanity taken from the Virgin Mary. Thus He Who was born of the Virgin Mary is the incarnate God, one essence, one person, one hypostasis, one nature. The union of divinity and humanity in Christ is not a form of combination, commingling, or joining, but a union in the fullest sense of the word. It would then be erroneous to say that in Christ there were two natures, which is not compatible with real or genuine union. In this one nature of Christ, as a result of this union, there are human attributes and divine attributes, together without mingling, confusion, or change.

There is nothing innovative in the Coptic church's stand regarding this fundamental point, nor is there any departure from the teachings of the fathers, such as ATHANASIUS I, CYRIL I, and BASIL THE GREAT, who had formulated their views long before the subject was discussed in Chalcedon.

Until at least the middle of the fourth century, the church of Rome held the same view as the church of Alexandria, as is evident from the letters of Pope Julius (341–352) to Bishop Dionysius of Cyprus. Relying on various testimonies from the Gospel and the Epistles, he confirms that He Who was born of the Virgin Mary, and called the Only One by Whom everything was, is of one nature, one person, and adds that divinity and humanity are one, indivisible into two natures.

While the New Testament is abundantly clear on

the issue of the one nature of Christ, nowhere can we get a genuine clue to the duality of His nature.

The Gospel of Saint John speaks of the Word becoming flesh (Jn. 1:14). The verb "become" is the most unambiguous term denoting real union between the divinity and humanity of Christ. Hence He Who was born of the Virgin Mary has one nature, that of incarnate God.

The words of Jesus Christ, "No one has ascended into heaven but he who descended from heaven, the Son of Man, who is in heaven" (Jn. 3:13), do not have the slightest hint of duality.

"Before Abraham was, I am" (Jn. 8:58). The purport of these words, spoken by the human Christ, indicates divine eternity. "I am" is evidence of the unity of nature in the incarnate Logos.

Speaking to the elders of the church who met him in Ephesus, Saint Paul says, "Take heed to yourselves and to all the flock, in which the Holy Spirit has made you guardians, to feed the church of God which He obtained with his own blood" (Acts 20:28). If there is any sense of duality in the nature of Jesus Christ, how then can Saint Paul refer here to the blood which redeemed the church as God's blood?

To the Corinthians, Saint Paul writes, "None of the rulers of this age understood this; for if they had, they would not have crucified the Lord of glory" (1 Cor. 2:8), which is further confirmation that Christ, had one nature, that of the incarnate God. The Epistle to the Hebrews states, "Jesus Christ is the same yesterday and today and for ever" (Heb. 13:8). The name Jesus was given to the Logos after the Incarnation, yet the divine quality of immortality is a prerogative of the incarnate Logos.

In Revelation (1:17,18) we read, "I am the first and the last, and the living one; I died, and behold, I am alive for evermore, and I have the keys of Death and of Hades." The pronoun "I" used here cannot refer to any duality, but to real oneness, the one nature of the incarnate Son of God.

If we were to separate Christ's divinity from His humanity, the whole basis of Christianity, that is, the idea of expiation and redemption, would surely collapse. Christ's redemption is divine, not human. Hence Saint Paul's words, "who though he was in the form of God, did not count equality with God a thing to be grasped, but emptied himself, taking the form of a servant, being born in the likeness of men. And being found in human form he humbled himself and became obedient unto death, even death on a cross" (Phil. 2:6–8).

It cannot be denied that "divinity" cannot die or shed blood, but "humanity" can and did. But because of the union of divinity with humanity, such a death was divine, and such blood was divine. So was Christ's redemption.

According to the doctrine of the Coptic church, and other traditionalist churches, the Virgin Mary is the Mother of God, as defined by the holy fathers in the third Council of EPHESUS (431). This appellation can only hold good on the basis of non-Chalcedonian teaching: the perfect union of Jesus Christ's divinity and humanity, as the Virgin Mary would not be considered to have given birth only to Christ's humanity, to the exclusion of his divinity. The Virgin Mary is rightly named Mother of God, as Elizabeth said, "And why is this granted me, that the mother of my Lord should come to me?" (Lk. 1:43).

Some church historians believed that the doctrines held by Pope DIOSCORUS I (444–458) and EUTYCHES the heresiarch were analogous. The confusion arose from the fact that Dioscorus presided over the second Council of Ephesus (449), which acquitted Eutyches after his admission in writing that he concurred with the views of the traditional fathers of the church. It is possible that Eutyches reneged after his acquittal and reversed his stand. Dioscorus had consented to the acquittal only after all the other members of the council, including the bishop of Jerusalem, had acquitted him. Further evidence of the position of Dioscorus on this matter is later given by his statement in the Council of Chalcedon that if Eutyches, who had renounced the Orthodox teaching as incorporated in the document he submitted to the second Council of Ephesus, was now propagating some new ideas concerning the divinity and humanity of Jesus Christ, he deserved not merely to be punished, but to be burnt alive.

Whereas Eutyches maintained that Christ's manhood "vanished" into His divine nature and that the two became one after the union in the incarnate Christ, Dioscorus believed in the union of His divinity and humanity throughout, without mingling, confusion, or alteration.

Eutyches evaded giving a clear admission that Christ was incarnate of the Holy Spirit and of the Virgin Mary—a belief that Dioscorus vigorously defended. Eutyches denied that the humanity of Christ was consubstantial with ours. Dioscorus not only firmly acknowledged His incarnation of the Holy Spirit and of the Virgin Mary but also reiterated his views in a letter sent from his exile.

In the Council of Chalcedon, which ended by deposing him, Dioscorus spoke of his unshakable belief in the doctrine of the holy apostolic church, of his thoughts being all focused on his Creator, and of his being concerned with one thing only: safeguarding the upright faith of the church. The deposition of Dioscorus, however, occurred not because of direct theological differences, but because he had excommunicated Pope LEO THE GREAT of Rome. In his work *Histoire des Conciles* (1907, p. 53), the historian K. J. Hefele states that the archbishop of Constantinople said that Dioscorus had not been deposed because of his faith but because he had excommunicated the pope.

Nevertheless, the Coptic church held fast to its deposed patriarch who so adamantly defended its faith, not choosing a successor for Dioscorus until after his death. TIMOTHY II (458–480), the new pope, fought equally valiantly, and met with a similar fate. He was exiled by Marcian again to the island of Gangra where he remained until he was restored to his see by the new emperor, Basiliscus (475–477). He traveled to Constantinople to offer his thanks to the emperor, and there he held a council, convened by imperial summons and attended by 500 bishops. It repudiated the Council of Chalcedon and the Eutychian heresy, and reaffirmed the faith as established by the previous Councils of NICAEA, CONSTANTINOPLE, and EPHESUS.

The Coptic church has thus remained faithful to the principles that were established by the early fathers, unwilling to relinquish any of their teachings, and in the words of G. Krüger (1926, p. 814) trying "to keep to the lines marked out in the theology of Cyril. This was the case, e.g., with Timotheus Aelurus, and, above all, with Severus of Antioch."

[*See also:* Monophysitism.]

BIBLIOGRAPHY

Gregorios, Bp. *The Christological Teaching of the Non-Chalcedonian Churches.* Cairo, 1963.

Gregorios, P.; W. H. Lazareth; and N. A. Nissiotis. *Does Chalcedon Divide or Unite? Towards Convergence in Orthodox Christology.* Geneva, 1981.

ARCHBISHOP BASILIOS

CHRIST, TRIUMPH OF.

The theme of the triumph of Christ is connected to the theme of the four creatures. On 8 Hātūr the Coptic SYNAXARION commemorates the Four Bodiless Beasts that bear the throne of God. It includes references to the four six-winged creatures of Revelation 4 (a lion, a calf, a man, and a flying eagle), to the six-winged seraphim of Isaiah 6, and to the four four-headed cherubim, each with four wings, of Ezekiel 1. The Synaxarion concludes with the remark that there are also churches dedicated to them. From the juxtaposition of these three scriptural texts, it appears that the distinction among the four creatures of Revelation, the seraphim, and the cherubim is extremely vague, although we know of representations of six-winged seraphim at Isnā and of four-headed and four-winged cherubim at Abu Maqār; these were quite definitely regarded as belonging to the class of angels, the bodiless beings. In magic each of them has a name, which is also found in a related form in Nubian iconography (see below).

Because the four creatures are the bearers of God's throne (or throne-chariot, shown with wheels, which was called in ancient texts the "chariot of the cherubim"), they figure in compositions portraying Christ in majesty, in apselike niches of cells in Bāwīṭ and Saqqara (c. A.D. 700) and in apses in medieval churches. Above left is the man, below left the lion, below right the calf, and above right the eagle—in the order given in Ezekiel.

The four creatures also occur in compositions known from medieval Nubia, where they surround the half-figure of Christ, sometimes even in combination with the cross (van Moorsel, 1966, pp. 297–316). It is in this last form, too, that the Nubian version of the magic names of the four creatures has come down. Both Nubian forms, moreover, occur other than in apses. Presumably it can be concluded that there, too, the intention was to portray Christ enthroned.

Two striking variants are found in tenth-century Nubia in the church in Sonqi Tino (Donadoni 1970, pp. 209–216; van der Helm, 1985, pp. 26–27) and in about 1232–1233 in the monastery of Saint Antony (Leroy, 1975, pl. 10). In both cases the four creatures are shown upright. The threefold holy that Isaiah, Revelation, and the liturgy attribute to them is included, in several cases, as an inscription in the composition itself (as in Saint Antony), while in Bāwīṭ cells 6 and 17 it is even written on the open codex that Christ holds in his hand (van der Meer, 1938, p. 260). With regard to the role of the four creatures in Coptic angelology, a homily of Pseudo-Chrysostom (eleventh-century manuscript in the Pierpont Morgan Library, New York; tenth-century fragment from Qasr Ibrīm in Cambridge,

England) provides further information. When God condemned Lucifer, one of the four cast him down to earth, one divested him of his panoply, the third bound him, and the fourth cast him into the lake of fire. They then clothed Michael in Lucifer's panoply.

The question as to whether in the Nile Valley the four living creatures also had an allegorical meaning connecting them—for example, with the Evangelists—has not yet been resolved, although such an allegorical meaning has not been proved (de Grooth and van Moorsel, 1977–1978, pp. 233–41). Further research into the position of the four creatures in Coptic religious belief is desirable.

BIBLIOGRAPHY

Donadini, S. "Les Fouilles à l'église de Sonqi Tino," pp. 209–216. In *Kunst und Geschichte Nubiens in christlicher Zeit*, ed. E. Dinkler. Recklinghausen, 1970.

Grooth, M. de, and P. van Moorsel. "The Lion, the Calf, the Man and the Eagle in Early Christian and Coptic Art." *Bulletin Antieke Beschaving* 52–53 (1977–1978):233–41.

Helm, M. van der. "Some Iconographical Remarks on St. Michael in Sonqi Tino." *Nubian Letters* 4 (February 1985):26–27.

Leroy, J. *Les Peintures des couvents du désert d'Esna*. Cairo, 1975.

Meer, F. van der. *Maiestas Domini*. Vatican City, 1938.

Moorsel, P. van. "Une Théophanie nubienne." *Revista di Archeologie Cristiana* 42 (1966):297–316.

Muller, C. Detlev G. *Die Engellehre der koptischen Kirche*. Wiesbaden, 1959.

Nilgen, U. *"Evangelistensymbole."* In *Reallexikon zur deutschen Kunstgeschichte*, ed. Otto Schmitt. Stuttgart, 1937.

———. "Evangelisten." In *Lexikon der christlichen Ikonographie*, Vol. 1. Vienna, 1967–.

PAUL VAN MOORSEL

CHRISTIAN RELIGIOUS INSTRUCTION IN EGYPTIAN PUBLIC SCHOOLS.

Christian religious instruction in public schools was begun during the reign of the khedive Ismail (1863–1879) as part of the larger fight against illiteracy. Since the passage of a 1968 national law it has been a compulsory subject for Coptic students in all public schools, elementary and secondary. Each school district either employs a staff person in charge of Christian education or engages someone from outside the system for this purpose. All school libraries have copies of the Bible. The curriculum acquaints the students with the salient features of their Coptic heritage.

YŪSUF KHALĪL YŪSUF
SULAYMĀN NĀSĪM

CHRISTIAN SUBJECTS IN COPTIC ART

[*This entry consists of a short introduction and the following articles:*

- Adoration of the Magi
- Annunciation
- Apostles and Evangelists
- Baptism of Jesus
- Bath of the Infant Jesus
- Galactotrophousa
- Jeremiah, Saint
- Massacre of the Innocents
- Menas, Saint
- Nativity
- Orant
- Parthian Horseman
- Shenute, Saint
- Tetramorph
- Thecla, Saint
- Twenty-Four Elders
- Virgin Enthroned

For other iconographic subjects, see BIBLICAL SUBJECTS IN COPTIC ART; MYTHOLOGICAL SUBJECTS IN COPTIC ART.]

Whatever its materials and techniques—stone or wood relief sculpture, painted walls or manuscripts, textiles, metalwork, ceramics, or glass—Coptic Christian iconography retained a few rare elements of pharaonic origin and many Greco-Roman elements from Alexandrian tradition. From the fifth century on, these pagan subjects mingled with Christian motifs. The Christian subjects naturally constituted the figurative or symbolic decoration of churches and monasteries. They were readily accompanied by animal, vegetal, or geometric motifs, which themselves had a sacred symbolism. The pagan subjects were used to decorate everyday objects such as clothes, furniture, and household utensils. Their retention was not a perpetuation of paganism, for the subjects could take on a Christian meaning, as did figures of Orpheus, Cupid and Psyche, and the Good Shepherd in the Roman catacombs. The Copts extended this syncretism further to cycles surrounding Dionysis and Aphrodite or even to single figures who evoked a cycle, such as putti (cupids), dancers, Nereids, or gladiators. In the accommodation of Christian and pagan motifs, Coptic art was distinct from other art of the time and affirmed its originality.

PIERRE DU BOURGUET, S.J.

Adoration of the Magi

In the early Christian world, the theme of the adoration of the Magi was generally associated with the Nativity of Jesus. Both subjects were rarely found in Egypt. Apparently, the adoration of the Magi was never portrayed in textiles. Although D. Renner suggested that the three Magi could be recognized in three standing figures pictured upon a tunic from the Church of al-Ashmūnayn, Hermopolis Magna, dating from the seventh or eighth century (Renner, 1974, pp. 67–68), such an interpretation cannot be accepted without reservation. The theme clearly appears, however, on a censer from DAYR ANBĀ ANTŪNIYŪS, near the Red Sea (Leroy, 1976, pp. 381–90). Here, three men wearing Phrygian caps approach the Virgin, who is seated on a high-backed chair holding the Child on her lap. This same subject also appears on so-called Syrian censers, possibly made in Syria, and on a silver bracelet and a plaque of gilt silver both dating from the sixth century (Leclercq, 1931, col. 1047, fig. 7490, and col. 1051, fig. 7495).

During the Middle Ages, the motif of the Magi appeared chiefly in painting and wood sculpture. In a painting at DAYR AL-SURYĀN (Monastery of the Syrians) in Wādī al-Naṭrūn, the three Magi (an adolescent, an adult, and an old man), wearing Oriental robes and Phrygian caps, approach the Virgin, presenting her with caskets containing their gifts. Placed symmetrically on the other side of the Virgin are the shepherds (Leroy, 1982, p. 68). However, a Coptic attribution for this piece is debatable.

Not much remains from the scene decorating the sanctuary of the Church of Saint Mark at DAYR ANBĀ MAQĀR (Monastery of Saint Macarius) in Wādī al-Naṭrūn. Here the existence of embroidered clothes and gifts of the three Magi can only be deduced.

During this same period, Nativity and adoration scenes were sculpted on one of the wooden doors of the Church of Saint Sergius in Old Cairo (Zaloscer, 1974, p. 50). On the lower part of the panel, at the left, there are three shepherds accompanied by two kid goats, and at the right, three Magi. The eldest, characterized by a long beard, is kneeling. His companions—an adult and an adolescent with frizzy hair—follow him, each one bearing a gift for the Christ Child.

A panel coming from the wooden door of the Church of Sitt Maryam (Church of al-Muʿallaqah in Cairo, attributed to the thirteenth century, now in the British Museum, London), differs slightly (Beckwith, 1963, no. 142; Coquin, 1974, p. 84). The adoration of the Magi adjoins the Nativity, taking the place usually occupied by Joseph. The eldest king is kneeling and offers his gift to Mary.

After the twelfth century, the adoration and the Nativity are portrayed in illuminated manuscripts (see ILLUMINATIONS) (Leroy, 1974, p. 208). Even though examples are few, two iconographies of this theme can be distinguished. The first composition resembles early Christian representations as a whole. Here, the Nativity and adoration of the Magi constitute two distinct scenes; in the adoration, the Magi approach and bow before the Virgin, who is enthroned with the Child on her lap. It must be noted that this is how the scene was portrayed on "Syrian" censers. The second composition intimately mixes the two motifs, uniting around Mary both the Magi and the shepherds. This representation, the one most widespread in Egypt, was also found in Christian Nubia, at Faras, for example.

BIBLIOGRAPHY

Beckwith, J. *Coptic Sculpture, 300–1300.* London, 1963.

Coquin, C. *Les Edifices chrétiens du Vieux-Caire,* Vol. 1: *Bibliographie et topographie historiques.* Cairo, 1974.

Leclercq, H. "Mages." In *Dictionnaire d'archéologie chrétienne et de liturgie,* Vol. 10, pt. 1 (1931), 980–1067.

Leroy, J. *Les Manuscrits coptes et coptes-arabes illustrés.* Paris, 1974.

———. "L'Encensoir 'syrien' du couvent de Saint Antoine dans le désert de la Mer Rouge." *Bulletin de l'Institut français d'Archéologie orientale* 76 (1976):381–90.

———. *Les Peintures des couvents du Ouadi Natroun.* Cairo, 1982.

Renner, D. *Die koptischen Stoffe im Martin von Wagner Museum der Universität Würzburg.* Wiesbaden, 1974.

Vezin, G. *L'Adoration et le cycle des mages dans l'art chrétien primitif. Etude des influences orientales et grecques sur l'art chrétien.* Paris, 1950.

Zaloscer, H. *Die Kunst im christlichen Ägypten*. Vienna and Munich, 1974.

MARGUERITE RASSART-DEBERGH

Annunciation

The archangel Gabriel's visit to announce the miraculous birth of the Infant Jesus to the Virgin translates into pictorial terms the belief in the Incarnation of God and the Immaculate Conception. Despite the Monophysite denial of the dual nature of Christ (see MONOPHYSITISM), Egyptian artists frequently pictured episodes in the life of the Virgin and Child, appealing to the dogma that Mary is the THEOTOKOS (Mother of God) defined at the Council of Ephesus in 431.

The oldest known occurrence of the Annunciation in Egypt is a fragment of a fifth-century wooden relief in the Louvre, Paris. Mary is seated on the left on a high stool and is spinning wool. She looks at the viewer with an astonished expression, as the announcement is made by the angel, of whom only a leg and foot remain. The same composition was used on a gold medallion preserved in the State Museum of Berlin and on a printed fabric of the fifth or sixth century from Akhmīm in the Victoria and Albert Museum, London. As represented on the fabric, Mary is spinning and obviously flourishing her spindle, while Gabriel executes a graceful backward movement. The name Maria is inscribed between the two characters.

On the painted dome of the Chapel of Peace in the oasis of Khargah of the fifth or sixth century the Virgin Mary is standing facing the viewer. Her face is framed by her long fair hair, and the palms of her hands are open on her breast to signify prayer. The archangel Gabriel has been replaced by a dove, which is moving in the direction of Mary's face. The dove evokes the idea of the Holy Spirit descending on the Virgin to effect Gabriel's announcement, and it emphasizes the notion of the Incarnation.

In the crypt of Abū Jirjah there has survived a fragmentary picture of the Annunciation from the eighth century. It is possible to make out the Virgin's high-backed chair and the left side of her face. The angel, preserved for the most part, is shown facing forward, but the feet are in profile in a walking position emphasized by a movement of the hands in the Virgin's direction. Clothed in a cloak and a tunic decorated with two *clavi* (stripes) and woven squares, the angel makes his announcement, which appears on an inscription between the two figures. A manuscript dating from 914 in the Pierpont Morgan Library, New York, adopts exactly the same arrangement of figures, adding an inscription above that mentions the names of Mary and Gabriel.

A silk-embroidered medallion from the seventh or eighth century in the Victoria and Albert Museum shows alongside the Annunciation the scene of Mary's visit to her cousin Elizabeth. Because of the embroidered-silk technique and the style of the figures, this fabric seems to be a foreign import, probably Byzantine. Mary is seated in front of a structure crowned by a conch shell. His wings arranged asymmetrically, the angel moves forward as he raises a hand to indicate that he is the speaker. An identical composition is reproduced in a manuscript of 1180 in the National Library, Paris. The Virgin is spinning and holds the distaff in one hand, allowing the spindle to hang in front.

The painters of the Wādī al-Naṭrūn adopted other models. In an eleventh-century mural at Dayr Anbā Maqār, the angel, who is placed on the left, walks briskly on the overhang of a scoinson arch, while

Annunciation (fragment). Wood. Fifth century. Height: 28.5 cm; width: 14.5 cm; thickness: 2 cm. *Courtesy Louvre Museum, Paris. Photo by M. Seidel.*

the Virgin, seated on a background structure, indicates her surprise by a movement of her hand. In a mural of the eleventh or twelfth century at Dayr al-Suryān, the same scene, in the apse of the choir of the Church of the Virgin, is next to the Nativity. The Virgin, on the left, has assumed an upright position. Between the angel and the Virgin a dual inscription in Coptic and Syriac recalls the angel's greeting in the Gospel. The style of these late paintings is strongly stamped with Middle Eastern and Byzantine influences.

The Virgin also appears standing on a twelfth-century cedarwood panel from the Church of Sitt Maryam in Old Cairo now in the British Museum. Like the scene of the Baptism of Christ that fills the upper part of the panel, it is arranged on a background of arabesques in the purest Islamic tradition. The Virgin is holding a book, a detail characteristic of Western iconography.

A series of bronze censers in the Louvre and dating from the tenth and the eleventh centuries is decorated with episodes from the life of Christ in a style so simplistic that it is hard to recognize the scenes. The Annunciation is frequently shown, the two figures being placed alongside each other without precise details. Specimens identical to these have been found in Syria.

BIBLIOGRAPHY

Beckwith, J. *Coptic Sculpture,* p. 31 and fig. 141. London, 1963.

Bourguet, P. du. *L'Art copte,* p. 38. Paris, 1964.

Cabral, F., and H. Leclerq. *Dictionnaire d'archéologie chrétienne et de liturgie,* Vol. 6, cols. 1241–52, fig. 5191. Paris, 1903–1915.

Christentum am Nil. Koptische Kunst. Catalogue of the Exhibition in the Villa Hügel, p. 163. Essen, 1963.

Cramer, M. *Koptische Buchmalerei,* p. 65, figs. 69, 70. Recklinghausen, 1964.

Evelyn-White, H. G. *The Monasteries of the Wadi'n Natrun,* 3 vols. New York, 1926–1933.

Fakhry, A. *The Necropolis of El Bagawat in Kharga Oasis,* fig. 70. Cairo, 1951.

Kendrick, A. F. *Catalogue of Textiles from Burying Grounds in Egypt,* Vols. 1–3, pp. 64, pl. 19, and p. 57, pl. 17. London, 1920–1922.

MARIE-HÉLÈNE RUTSCHOWSCAYA

Apostles and Evangelists

In their art the Copts depicted the apostles in groups or individually. In group representations, a distinction must be made between those picturing the Twelve Apostles and those picturing only the principal ones, Saint Peter and Saint Paul.

The group of Twelve Apostles is found many times in Dayr Apa Apollo at Bāwīṭ in the lower panel of a scene showing the triumph of Christ (Clédat, 1904, Chapel 12, p. 52). To this scene must be added a group composed of Christ enthroned among his apostles, who are likewise seated.

Saint Peter, Saint Paul, and Saint Mark the Evangelist may also be depicted individually. Peter is the principal figure in a scene in the back of a chapel of the Ramessid temple of Dayr al-Sību'ah in Nubia, which unites royal pharaonic iconography and Coptic Christian motifs. In the chapel the monks had covered subjects that had been engraved in relief on the temple walls at the time of Ramses II in the thirteenth century B.C. with a layer of plaster or mud reinforced with grasses. Over the plaster, which assured the reliefs of remarkable preservation, they scattered their own Christian paintings. One pharaonic scene, however, they modified. This scene dominated by Peter originally showed Ramses offering flowers to the gods of the Temple. The monks replaced these gods with the figure of Saint Peter, represented as bowing to the pharaoh, paying an homage that had come down through millennia of pagan tradition.

Saint Paul, along with Saint Thecla, whom he is teaching, is seen in the Byzantine decoration of the Chapel of Peace at al-BAGAWĀT (Fakhry, 1951, p. 78). Saint Mark is likely the subject of a bust upon which is inscribed his name followed by the title, Evangelist (see PORTRAITURE).

BIBLIOGRAPHY

Bourguet, P. du. *Les Coptes.* Collection Que sais-je? Paris, 1988.

Clédat, J. "Nouvelles recherches à Baouît." *Comptes Rendues de l'Académie des Inscriptions et Belles Lettres,* pp. 517–526. Cairo, 1904.

———. *Le Monastère et la Nécropole de Baouît,* 2 vols. Mémoires des Membres de l'Institut français d'Archéologie orientale 12. Vol. 1 in 2 pts. Cairo, 1904, 1906; Vol. 2, Cairo, 1916.

Fakhry, A. *The Necropolis of El-Bagawāt in Kharga Oasis.* Cairo, 1951.

PIERRE DU BOURGUET, S.J.

Baptism of Jesus

The elements of the iconography of the baptism of Jesus by Saint JOHN THE BAPTIST in the Jordan are seen early in the Roman catacombs, notably that of Saints Peter and Marcellinus. The figures are generally reduced to the two earthly participants—Jesus, who appears beardless, and John the Baptist. Sometimes heavenly symbols—the divine hand and the dove of the Holy Spirit—are at the top of the scene.

The baptism is found in two wall paintings, in Chapel 30 and Chapel 17, of Dayr Apa Apollo at Bāwīṭ. They originally showed both earthly and heavenly symbols, although in Chapel 17 the hand and dove have been destroyed, leaving only traces of their former presence. The basic figures are augmented by details common in Christian iconography in the Mediterranean world in the fifth and sixth centuries—in Chapel 30 a standing angel holding a cloth, the Jordan represented as a small seated figure, and three fish; in Chapel 17 a duck. In Chapel 30 the child Jesus stands naked in an attitude of prayer. From the contrast of the forms and folds of the garments, the painting in Chapel 30 can be dated to the sixth century, that of Chapel 17 to the eighth. Although only these two complete murals at Bāwīṭ remain, traces of repetitions of the same theme, as in Chapel 27, where the Jordan is represented as a woman emerging from the water and Jesus is small and bearded with a child kneeling at his feet, suggest that there were baptism scenes in many other monasteries.

The theme also appears in three illuminations from Gospels. One is from a twelfth-century Copto-Arabic Gospel in the National Library, Paris. It retains Jesus and John but has two angels flying over the water of the Jordan. The river is covered with aquatic plants and conceals a standing, bearded Christ. The other two illuminations come from a thirteenth-century Copto-Arabic Gospel in the Catholic Institute, Paris (Leroy, 1974, p. 159), and from a seventeenth-century Copto-Arabic Gospel in the British Museum. They include Jesus, John, and the two angels but raise the level of the Jordan around Jesus and leave John and the angels on dry ground. The style is Arabic rather than Coptic.

BIBLIOGRAPHY

Bourguet, P. du. *La Peinture paléo-chrétienne.* Paris, 1965.

______. "Datation raisonnée de la peinture murale copte." In *Actes du Colloque nubiologique de 1973 à Varsovie,* pp. 40–43. Warsaw, 1976.

Clédat, J. *Le Monastère et la Nécropole de Baouît.* Mémoires des membres de l'Institut français d'Archéologie orientale 12. Vol. 1 in 2 pts. Cairo, 1904, 1906; Vol. 2, Cairo, 1916.

Leroy, J. *Les Manuscrits coptes et coptes-arabes illustrés.* Paris, 1974.

PIERRE DU BOURGUET, S.J.

Bath of the Infant Jesus

It does not seem that the bath of the Infant Jesus, a detail in the Nativity scenes that is frequent in Byzantine art, passed into Coptic art (Cramer, 1959, pp. 234–37). Although numerous paintings have disappeared, in the scenes that have survived, the bath does not appear.

A sculpture in the Coptic Museum in Cairo, however, raises a question about whether the bath was ever portrayed. The piece is not allied to any Coptic sculpture in stone or wood. It is a slab of limestone carved in relief, missing the right border and the top, which presents the greater part of the bath of an infant. The remaining framework consists of a series of meanders in which swastikas and flowerets alternate. The infant appears half-length in the center of a footbath. On his right, a person seated in profile but with head and shoulders full-face is proceeding with the washing. On his left, a woman standing full-face is taking a vase from a kind of brazier. Between her face and that of the infant are a cantharus (deep, two-handled cup) on a tripod and a fairly large object identified as a comb, with an upper and a lower series of teeth, starting from a middle band adorned with three crosses. The costumes of the two adult figures consist of a long

Bath of the Infant Jesus (?). Coptic Museum, Cairo. *Courtesy Elias Zalka.*

robe and a headdress. The low-cut robe on one figure has a wide neck marked by double lines. A light serpentine line starting from the neck ornaments a dark background. The headdress worn by the person on the left is Phrygian in form and is adorned by a cross similar to those of the object placed above the child. It is probable that the person on the opposite side wears the same headdress, which is cut off at a quarter of its height, and may have a hood under the headdress, which falls to the shoulders and hides the hair. The child and the person on the left have hair curling on each side of the face. The two adults are barefoot.

Apart from the crosses, which some (for example, Zaloscer, 1974, p. 119) think may have been added later, there is nothing to indicate that the sculpture portrays the bath of the infant Jesus. Although the scene is treated for itself without any connection with the Nativity, it is an integral part in the whole of Christian iconography. The crosses could be of the same period as the rest of the subject, without any direct connection to the life of Christ. The garments are not in any way decorated in the Coptic fashion. The tight waist of the person on the right would be achieved only by a girdle in Coptic clothing, but there is no girdle here. Finally the Phrygian cap points to an origin to the east of Egypt. J. Beckwith does not mention this piece in his book *Coptic Sculpture 300–1300*. It may be simply a scene drawing attention to the person honored or even to someone deceased.

BIBLIOGRAPHY

Beckwith, J. *Coptic Sculpture, 300–1300*. London, 1963.

Cramer, M. "Eine koptische Reliefdarstellung und ihre byzantinischen Parallelen." In *Akten des 24. Internationalen Orientalischen Kongresses*, ed. H. Franke. Wiesbaden, 1959.

Zaloscer, H. *Die Kunst im christlichen Ägypten*. Vienna and Munich, 1974.

PIERRE DU BOURGUET, S.J.

Galactotrophousa

The tender motif of the Holy Virgin giving her breast to her Son always has been so popular in Christian Egypt that some writers liked to consider it simply as a Christianized form of Isis nourishing Horus. And indeed, at least according to K. Wessel (1954–1955, p. 199) there seem to be some sculptured examples of both Isis and the Virgin in the State Museum of Berlin that could be interpreted as such. Nevertheless, there are—besides the resemblances—also some differences between the two types that make it difficult to assume a relationship (Tran Tam Tinh, 1973; 1978). Both types resemble each other in showing the same kind of eyes of the mother gazing beyond her son, while the child looks at her. They differ, however, in that since Hellenistic times Isis normally wears a garment that leaves both her breasts free, and her right hand offers her left breast to Horus. The Holy Virgin, occasionally painted with her head inclined toward Jesus, always has one breast covered, offering the other (be it the left or the right one) with her corresponding hand to Jesus. In representations from medieval Nubia she is sometimes wearing a crown and a veil. Often she is accompanied by angels, saints, or both. In the Nile Valley the motif is hardly ever seen as a genre piece but is more often depicted with dignity: in the small niches in the eastern walls of monastery cells, probably eighth century, such as Cell 42 at Dayr Apa Apollo at Bāwīṭ (Clédat, 1904–1906) and Cell 30 (Maspero, 1932), Cells A, 1725, and 1807 at Dayr Apa Jeremiah, at Saqqara; on the walls of the cathedral of Faras (four times); and in some miniatures.

Since 1965 there has been some discussion as to how the Galactotrophousa should be regarded. Did it originate on Egyptian soil, but was it aimed, because of its typically human features, at convincing the Monophysites of the human nature of Christ (Wessel, 1964, p. 234; Michalowski, 1967, pp. 91, 92, 109 and 154; Michalowski, 1974, pp. 38 and 229)? Or did it originate as a poetic motif in ancient literature too old to have come into being after the Council of Chalcedon (451), and, moreover, was it used in controversies aimed at the Docetists (who denied the humanity of Christ) and Nestorians (who refused to say God was born of a virgin), not against the Monophysites (Krause, 1970; 1978; van Moorsel, 1970)? A marble krater (jar) from the eastern part of the Roman empire, dating from 364–378 and bearing a representation of this motif—in the context of the adoration by the *Magi*—shows, however, that the *Galaktotrophousa* need not necessarily be Egyptian in origin and also that it cannot be the fruit of theological discussions about Chalcedon (Severin, 1970). The sculpture in Berlin previously cited seems, according to Wessel, also to date to before 451 (Wessel, 1978, p. 199).

BIBLIOGRAPHY

Clédat, J. *Le Monastère et la nécropole de Baouît,* 2 vols. Cairo, 1904–1906, 1916.

Krause, M. "Zur Kirchen- und Theologiegeschichte Nubiens." In *Kunst und Geschichte Nubiens in christlicher Zeit,* pp. 71–86. Recklinghausen, 1970.

______. "Bischof Johannes III von Faras und seine beiden Nachfolger; noch einmal zum Problem eines Konfessionswechsels in Faras." In *Etudes Nubiennes,* pp. 153–65. Cairo, 1978.

Maspero, J. *Fouilles exécutées à Baouit.* Cairo, 1932.

Michalowski, K. *Faras, die Kathedrale aus dem Wüstensand.* Einsiedeln, 1967.

______. *Faras; Wall Paintings in the Collection of the National Museum in Warsaw.* Warsaw, 1974.

Moorsel, P. van. "De Galaktotrophousa en de Monophysieten." In *Opstellen voor H. van de Waal,* pp. 125–36. Amsterdam and Leiden, 1970.

______. "Die stillende Gottesmutter und die Monophysiten." In *Kunst und Geschichte Nubiens in christlicher Zeit,* ed. E. Dinkler, pp. 281–90. Recklinghausen, 1970.

Tran Tam Tinh, V. *Isis Lactans.* Leiden, 1973.

______. "Du nouveau Isis Lactans (Supplément I)." In *Hommages à M. J. Vermaseren,* Vol. 3, pp. 1231–68. Leiden, 1978.

Wellen, G. A. *Theotokos.* Utrecht and Antwerp, 1960.

Wessel, K. "Eine Grabstele aus Medinet el Fajoum: zum Problem der Maria Lactans." *Wissenschaftliche Zeitschrift der Humboldt-Universität zu Berlin* IV, 1954–1955.

______. "Zur Ikonographie der koptischen Kunst." In *Christentum am Nil,* ed. K. Wessel. Proceedings Colloquium Essen 1963, pp. 233–239. Recklinghausen, 1964.

______. "Die älteste Darstellung der Maria Eleousa." *Atti del VI. Congresso Internazionale di Archeologia Cristiana,* 1962, pp. 207–213. Vatican City, 1965.

______. "Die stillende Gottesmutter." In *Studien zur altägyptischen Kultur* (Festschrift H. W. Müller), pp. 185–200. Munich, 1978.

PAUL VAN MOORSEL

Jeremiah, Saint

The name Jeremiah in Coptic tradition can refer either to the Old Testament prophet or to the founder of a monastery of that name at Saqqara, DAYR APA JEREMIAH. He is usually found in association with Enoch, also an Old Testament prophet and a monk.

Although the Greek, Latin, Coptic, Syriac, and Arabic sources do not always agree on the identification of Jeremiah as a prophet or a monk, on the location of his monastery, or on the doctrine followed by his monks, it is assumed here that the monastery ruins at Saqqara, discovered by J. E. Quibell near the pyramid of Ounas after 1904, are indeed those of Dayr Apa Jeremiah. Representations of both Jeremiah and Enoch appear there and at Dayr Apa Apollo at Bāwīṭ.

At Saqqara numerous inscriptions, essentially commemorative, follow an identical formula. After the Trinity, the Virgin (and sometimes the archangels), Apa Jeremiah, Apa Enoch, and Apa Sibylla are invoked. It is generally considered that this Jeremiah is the monk who founded the monastery, that Enoch is the Old Testament prophet, and that Sibylla is the Sibyl of Alexandria (Quibell, 1912, p. 48). Each of these names could be a conflation of personages: Jeremiah could be at once the prophet and the monk who inherited the same name; the same could be said of Enoch; Sibylla could equally well be the Christianized Sibyl of Alexandria or a simple mortal, the mother superior of a convent of nuns, which at both Saqqara and Bāwīṭ adjoined the monastery of the monks (Rassart-Debergh, 1981, pp. 201–203).

For A. Grabar, "At Saqqara . . . the local Saints Jeremiah and Enoch were inspired from certain iconographical types, almost certainly reproduced from original portraits" (Grabar, 1946, p. 129). For J. Leroy, however, "The iconography of monks has never been too realistic" (Leroy, 1975, p. 62). However that may be, at Saqqara, Jeremiah and Enoch correspond to well-defined types. They are always in the east niche of the oratory (in Cells 1807, F, D, 1719, 1724, 1727, and 1733 and Chapels F and D), sometimes head and shoulders, sometimes full-length. Their garments are identical to those of the other monks, a long tunic often knotted at the waist and a mantle covering the shoulders. It should be noted that Enoch alone has his feet covered by half-boots, instead of the monastic sandals. At Saqqara boots are a privilege reserved for the archangels, while at Bāwīṭ, archangels, the apostles, and sometimes military saints wear boots. Both figures hold some work in their hands, usually a closed codex.

The faces of Jeremiah and Enoch are individualized, as are those of Peter and Paul in early Christian art. That of Jeremiah is emaciated; the hollow cheeks are ill concealed by a rounded beard. In most representations he wears a round halo. In Cells D and 1727, he wears a square one, characteristic of a saint who is still alive. In contrast,

Enoch's face and round halo are framed by the curls of his abundant hair and by a tufted beard ending in a point.

At Bāwīṭ, Jeremiah appears both as prophet and as monk. As prophet (Chapel 12), he wears half-boots. As monk (Cells 20, 28), he wears sandals and a long dark tunic covered by a paler mantle. His face is as emaciated as at Saqqara. The inscriptions after Jeremiah the founder include Jeremias the mason, Jeremias archimandrite, and Brother Jeremias.

Where Jeremiah has a double role at Bāwīṭ, Enoch always appears as a monk clothed in a tunic and long mantle and carrying a calamus (quill pen) and scroll. He is always called Apa Enoch. His face is similar to representations at Saqqara, but his beard is shorter as if he were younger (Grabar, 1946, pp. 300–301).

BIBLIOGRAPHY

Grabar, A. *Martyrium. Recherches sur le culte des reliques et l'art chrétien antique*, Vol. 2: *Iconographie*, Paris, 1946. Photographic reprint, London, 1972.

Leroy, J. *La Peinture murale chez les Coptes*, Vol. 1: *Les Peintures des couvents d'Esna*. Mémoires de l'Institut français d'Archéologie orientale 94. Published with the collaboration of B. Psiroukis and B. Lentheric. Cairo, 1975.

Quibell, J. E. *Excavations at Saqqara (1908–9, 1909–10). The Monastery of Apa Jeremias.* The Coptic Inscriptions, ed. H. Thompson. Cairo, 1912.

Rassart-Debergh, M. "Remarques iconographiques." *Acta ad Archaeologiam et Artium Historiam Pertinentia* 9 (1980):201–203.

MARGUERITE RASSART-DEBERGH

Massacre of the Innocents

King Herod's massacre of young male children in an effort to kill the infant Jesus, an episode from the cycle of the infancy of Christ, is known in Coptic art from two examples, one at DAYR ABŪ HINNIS at Mallawī, the other at DAYR APA APOLLO at Bāwīṭ.

At Dayr Abū Hinnis the theme is found in a painted sequence in a rock-cut church. The whole sequence, which probably began with the Nativity and included the appearance of the archangel Gabriel to Joseph and the flight into Egypt, is a frieze contained between two horizontal borders. The lower one is a line of interlacing surmounting a series of variously colored rectangles. The upper one is composed of the same series of rectangles and surmounted by varied plants and flowers, rounded or pointed.

The massacre scene itself begins with King Herod, identified by his name above him. He sits on a cushioned stool, his left leg forward, his right bent back. His left arm leans on a lance, and his right hand rises toward his face (shown slightly three-quarter). He is protected by two Roman legionaries, who turn their backs behind their almond-shaped shields. The group is in a kind of tribunal with Ionic columns. In the undulating country that extends in front of them, two executioners in Iranian tunics are about their work. One is whirling a child in the air, the other lays a child on the ground. Two children lie between them, already slain, their blood flowing in streams. A third soldier threatens Saint Elizabeth, who holds her son, the young John the Baptist, on her knees. Another soldier threatens the prophet Zechariah, who, without a halo, kneels down and turns his back to the gate of the Temple, perhaps to defend it. Above the undulations rise three sanctuaries, each in the form of a tower surmounted by a kind of cupola. Between them are trees that look like umbrella pines.

The respect for the realistic proportions of the bodies, the naturalness of the movements in their diversity, the supple pose of Herod contemplating his deadly work, and the picturesque character of the backgrounds as well as of the upper decoration on the frieze indicate an Alexandrian influence that suggests a date in the fourth century. That calls into question the attribution by the excavator J. Clédat to a date later than the fifth century (Clédat, 1902, p. 47). A confirmation of the earlier date is the Christian tomb near Antinoopolis toward DAYR AL-DĪK, whose style, like that of the little bed of flowers in this scene, is close to that of the Roman catacombs of this period.

The scene of the massacre at Bāwīṭ is in Chapel 30. Clédat's description of it indicates a style approaching realism in the gestures and notes the introduction of new figures such as a group of despairing mothers.

BIBLIOGRAPHY

Bock, V. de. *Matériaux pour servir à l'archéologie de l'Egypte chrétienne*, pls. 33, 44–50. Saint Petersburg, 1901.

Clédat, J. "Notes archéologiques et philologiques." *Bulletin de l'Institut français d'Archéologie orientale* 2 (1902):44, 50.

PIERRE DU BOURGUET, S.J.

Menas the Miracle Maker, Saint

Saint MENAS THE MIRACLE MAKER was an Egyptian camel driver who was martyred in the third or fourth century. He was the object of a cult associated with miraculous life-giving waters from a sanctuary in the Western Desert or the Libyan desert (see ABŪ MĪNĀ).

Saint Menas appears in Coptic art in two iconographic types. In the older he is a young man standing in the orant (praying) position, flanked by two camels. His name is generally written nearby, but there is rarely a cross. This type is widely represented because it was used in low-relief on AMPULLAE (flasks) containing water from the sanctuary of Abū Mīnā. Saint Menas' face appears on one side of the vessel while the other side is occupied by another face, often that of Saint Thecla (see below), whose sanctuary is close to that of Menas. The model for these ampullae must have been very precise and was rather Hellenistic in style. It was perpetuated without modification by the use of molds. The first type also appears, outlined in ocher on white, in a fresco found in a seventh-century church at Kellia, now in the Louvre. Although the lower part has been destroyed, the saint's features are accentuated in the shape of the face (Daumas and Guillaumont, 1969, Vol. 2, pl. 386). This same praying figure is found in marble reliefs on stelae or on panels such as one in the Museum of the Arts, Vienna. Such reliefs belong more to Hellenistic than to Coptic art, since the Copts did not use marble.

The second iconographic type presents Menas as a centurion on horseback, often in the orant position. This type is generally seen in frescoes, notably six frescoes, probably from the eighth century, at MADĪNAT HĀBŪ (Wilber, 1940).

In Dayr Anbā Anṭūniyūs on the Red Sea, a slightly different version is found among the saints mounted on horseback in the narthex of the Old Church. It dates from 1232–1233, when the sanctuary of the church was restored. Each of these saints is depicted with head and shoulders full-face, on a horse in profile. Between the horse's hooves under the feet of the personage, a sanctuary is placed. In representations of Saint Menas, the sanctuary is evidently that of Abū Mīnā (du Bourguet, 1951, p. 43; Piankoff, 1948).

BIBLIOGRAPHY

Bourguet, P. du. "Les Monastères de Saint Antoine et de Saint Paul sur la mer Rouge." *Bulletin de la Société française d'Egyptologie* 7 (1951):37–44.

Daumas, F., and A. Guillaumont. *Kellia I, Kom 219. Fouilles exécutées en 1964–1965.* Fouilles de l'Institut français d'archéologie orientale 28. Cairo, 1969.

Drescher, J. "St. Ménas' Camels Once More." *Bulletin de la Société d'archéologie copte* 7 (1941):19–32.

Kaster, G. "Menas von Ägypten (von Cotyacum in Phrygien)." In *Lexicon der christlichen Ikonographie,* Vol. 8, cols. 3–7. Freiburg, 1976.

Piankoff, A. "Peintures au Monastère de Saint Antoine." *Bulletin de la Société d'archéologie copte* 14 (1948):159, 163.

Réau, L. *Iconographie de l'art chrétien, Vol. 3, pp. 948–50. Paris, 1958.*

Wilber, D. N. "The Coptic Frescoes of Saint Menas at Medinet Habu." *Art Bulletin* 22 (1940):36–103.

PIERRE DU BOURGUET, S.J.

Nativity

The birth of Jesus, generally associated with the adoration of the Magi, was not so popular a theme in Egypt as elsewhere in the early Christian world. It gave little inspiration to the artists who decorated the necropolises and monasteries. It may have appeared in the earliest churches, but present documentation is too sketchy to affirm this.

At Dayr Abu Hinnis, which houses the most ancient Christological cycle, it appears that the Nativity was not depicted. To be sure, A. Gayet mentioned a Nativity scene alongside an Annunciation (Gayet, 1902, pp. 272–73), but both these interpretations have rightly been refuted by H. Leclercq (1907, cols. 2326–59). However, upon considering the originality of this Annunciation, Gayet's confusion may be explained, for the angel is approaching Mary, who is half reclining upon her bed in the position she assumes for the Nativity. The two themes may have been confused, but since the paintings have disappeared, it is impossible to know.

From the tenth century, however, the Nativity was part of the decorative plan in the majority of churches and was equally important in illuminated manuscripts. It was always set amid other episodes in the lives of Mary and Christ.

The first example of a Nativity painting might be in Chapel 51 of Dayr Apa Apollo at Bāwīṭ. Here, Salome, the midwife assisting the Virgin, stands beside her. G. A. Wellen is reticent about the identification of this scene (Wellen, 1960, n. 101) as are P. Testini (Testini, 1974, p. 314, note 99), and L. del Francia (Francia 1976, pp. 221–24, pls. 13–16). There are two Nativity scenes at Wādī al-Naṭrūn, one in Dayr Anbā Maqār and the other (whose Coptic appurtenance is doubtful) in Dayr al-Suryān.

Upon the southern half-dome of the choir in the church at Dayr al-Suryān, the Annunciation and Nativity are seen side by side. The figure of Mary dominates: half-reclining upon the bed, she turns her head toward the spectator, paying scant heed to the infant asleep in a manger behind her. The Child —no longer a newborn babe—has His eyes wide open. Mother and Child stand out from a background of rock, above which angels in flight announce the good news. At Mary's feet stands a tiny white-bearded man, pensive, with his head leaning on his right hand. The inscription identifies him as Joseph. Below this principal group, the Magi (see "Adoration of the Magi," above) approach on the right, the shepherds on the left. One of the shepherds raises his hand and points to Mary and Jesus. An old man follows while a third shepherd, playing the flute, lifts his eyes toward the angels (Leroy, 1982, pp. 67–68).

The artist who decorated the sanctuary of the Church of Saint Mark at the Dayr Abū Maqār painted the arches and vaults of the octagon with scenes from the life of Christ. Although the paintings are badly deteriorated, a Nativity may still be identified. The schema reproduces the one just described at Dayr al-Suryān. Mary and the Child comprise the central element of the tableau. Above there are angels in flight, and below, a bit to the side, Joseph meditates. Magi and shepherds draw nigh to adore the Child (Leroy, 1982, p. 35).

The Nativity theme is also rare in sculpture. Only two examples in wood are known, both being panels belonging to the doors of two churches in Old Cairo, one being from Saint Sergius and the other from the Church of Sitt Maryam.

The Nativity occupies three-quarters of the ceiling of Saint Sergius. There is a disk above containing the moon and the sun, from which rays of light

Nativity. Illumination from Copto-Arabic *Tetraevangelium* (Four Gospels). Twelfth century. *Courtesy National Library, Paris.*

descend upon the sleeping babe wrapped in swaddling clothes, who lies between the donkey and the ox. Two angels watch over Him. Beside the cradle, the Virgin is lying on her bed, while opposite her, Joseph meditates, his head under his right arm (note that here Joseph is portrayed normal size). Below, on the left, are the shepherds, the oldest of whom is pointing to the scene with his hand; on the right, the Magi come bearing gifts (Zaloscer, 1974, pl. 50).

The scene is quite different and much more complex on a panel that once decorated the Church of Sitt Maryam but is now in the British Museum (Beckwith, 1963, no. 142; Coquin, 1974, p. 84). The upper third is occupied by angels in flight, singing the praises of the newborn Child. The central part presents the Nativity and the adoration of the Magi. Mary is half-reclining with her hand outstretched toward the gifts of the Magi, while the Child sleeps in the manger. Saint Joseph, below on the left, turns his head toward Mary. In the lower part of the panel is the Child's bath (see Bath of the Infant Jesus, above).

The Nativity was more popular in the minor arts, where it is relatively frequent from the sixth century. It appears on censers that are often attributed to Syria, but of which two examples, at least, derive from Egypt. One comes from DAYR ANBĀ SHINŪDAH (the White Monastery), at Suhāj (Maspero, 1908, pp. 148–49; Labib and Girgis, 1975, p. 26), and the other from Dayr Anbā Anṭūniyūs (Leroy, 1976, pp. 381–90). The Nativity is part of the Christological cycle, which unfolds on the bowl of the censer. In textiles, the Nativity scene is reduced to the principal personages: the Child, the donkey and ox, Mary, and Joseph (Francia, 1976).

BIBLIOGRAPHY

Beckwith, J. *Coptic Sculpture, 300–1300.* London, 1963.

Coquin, C. *Les Edifices chrétiens du Vieux-Caire, Vol. 1: Bibliographie et topographie historiques,* p. 84. Cairo, 1974.

Francia, L. del. "Le Thème de la nativité dans les tissus coptes, à propos d'un exemplaire inédit." In *Acts of the First International Congress of Egyptology,* pp. 221–24. Cairo, 1976.

Gayet, A. *L'Art copte.* Paris, 1902.

Labib, P., and V. Girgis. *The Coptic Museum and the Fortress of Babylone at Old Cairo,* pl. 26. Cairo, 1975.

Leclercq, H. "Antinoë." In *Dictionnaire d'archéologie chrétienne et de liturgie,* Vol. 1. Paris, 1907.

Leroy, J. *Les Peintures des couvents du Ouadi Natroun.* Cairo, 1982.

Maspero, G. "Un encensoir Copte." *Annales du Service des Antiquités d'Egypte* 9 (1908):148–49.

Testini, P. "Alle origini dell'iconografia di Giuseppe di Nazareth." *Archeologia Cristiana* 48 (1972): 271–347.

Wellen, G. A. *Theotokos, eine iconographische Studie über das Gottesmutterbild in frühchristlicher Zeit.* Utrecht, 1960.

Zaloscer, H. *Die Kunst im christlichen Ägypten.* Vienna and Munich, 1974.

MARGUERITE RASSART-DEBERGH

Orant

The orant, or praying figure, is characterized by two arms stretched out or bent. The gesture is considered to have its origin in the pharaonic hieroglyph *ka,* which indicated a being, action, or reality of a spiritual order.

It is thus not astonishing that the gesture passed into the syncretistic Egyptian stelae of the very first centuries A.D. dedicated to deceased pagans, and

Stele with two persons facing front in orant pose beneath an inscription. Seventh century. *Courtesy Louvre Museum, Paris.*

Funerary stele depicting an orant. Limestone. *Courtesy Coptic Museum, Cairo.*

from there no doubt into pagan Roman and Christian art. It finally returned to Egypt to enrich the iconography of Coptic art, whether pagan or Christian, although it was not so systematically used as elsewhere on the periphery of the Mediterranean. It spread thereafter within the still pagan Coptic stream, in two forms in particular: the funerary stelae of pagan personages and reliefs presenting a divinity, such as Daphne (see MYTHOLOGICAL SUBJECTS IN COPTIC ART).

There is a tendency to confuse this posture with that of the dancer. We can see this in relation to a dancer in a sixth-century bronze in the Louvre. But the theme also appeared in textiles, confusing Dionysian symbolism, long prevalent in the movements of dancers, with that of prayer.

As Christianity gained over paganism and then continued under Muslim domination, the significance of prayer or Christian joy replaced pagan consecrations, usually without Christian emblems, such as a cross or cruciform halo, although these were not excluded. Although the gesture disappeared in the rest of the Christian world, it was still honored in Coptic Egypt under Muslim domination, signifying the connection of important Christian personages with God. The gesture was traditional from the fourth century on in the group of Saint Menas with the camels (see AMPULLA). It was adopted in sixth-century chapel paintings at Dayr Apa Apollo at Bāwīṭ for Christ at His baptism by John the Baptist (see Baptism of Jesus, above), and in the seventh and eighth centuries for Mary in the Triumph of Christ. The gesture became typical in the ninth century, as is shown in a group of deceased Christians on a bouclé tapestry in the Abegg Foun-

Dancer with crotala, a figure easily mistaken for an orant. Bronze. Sixth-seventh century. *Courtesy Louvre Museum, Paris.*

dation in Bern, and also in Jonah emerging from the *ketos* (sea beast) on a bouclé tapestry in the Louvre. The theme was even confused with that of the exaltation of the cross, carried by a nude dancer at the end of her two raised arms, which formed the handle of a ninth-century bronze liturgical patera (saucer) in the Louvre. One cannot subscribe to the opinion of A. Grabar (1968, p. 3) that the orant in ancient Christian Egypt "is always the idealized effigy of the Christian buried at the foot of the stele."

The orant is an example of a sense of tradition that, through successive transformation of the deeper meaning of a theme without betraying it, rules out conservatism and gives expression to the very image of evolving religious life.

BIBLIOGRAPHY

Bourguet, P. du. *L'Art copte*. Paris, 1967.

———. *L'Art copte*. Musée du Louvre, Petits guides des grands musées 19. Paris, 1964.

Grabar, A. "Deux monuments chrétiens d'Egypte." In *Synthronon*, p. 3. Paris, 1968.

PIERRE DU BOURGUET, S.J.

Parthian Horseman

The Parthians ruled a huge empire that stretched from the Caspian Sea to the Indus River from 250 B.C. to A.D. 225. For them, representations of a mounted figure distinguished by a raised right arm giving a gesture of benediction with two raised fingers had a benevolent funerary significance. The theme passed to the Greeks and then to the Egyptians, because the gesture could be perpetuated by taking on new symbolism. It was prized by the Christian Copts, who used it on tapestry panels to decorate clothing and hangings from the fourth to the eleventh century.

In Coptic art the Parthian horseman commonly appears almost full-face, his right arm raised, sitting on a rearing horse shown in profile facing the viewer's right. A dog or a hare, its head sometimes looking backward, runs under the horse. In early examples of the fourth century, the forms of the horseman and his mount are still marked by movement and embellished with touches of purple-violet (Bourguet, 1964, no. A6). Gradually the forms stiffened and in the seventh century the figure was a uniform purple-violet with the features marked in white thread. By the tenth and eleventh centuries only the general silhouette survived in uniform color, rather distorted but still showing the elevated arm and hand.

Parthian horseman in an ornamented square. Tapestry. Third-fourth century. Height: 19 cm; width: 18 cm. *Courtesy Louvre Museum, Paris.*

BIBLIOGRAPHY

Bourguet, P. du. *Musée National du Louvre. Catalogue des étoffes coptes*, Vol. 1. Paris, 1964.

Picard, C. "Une Cimaise thasienne archaïque." *Monuments Piot* 38 (1941):55ff.

PIERRE DU BOURGUET, S.J.

Shenute, Saint

Saint SHENUTE was the great abbot of the Dayr Anbā Shinūdah (the White Monastery) at Suhāj in the late fourth and early fifth centuries. His iconography appears to be limited to two representations in different techniques and of unequal value, though the attributions are certain. Two others, according to J. Leroy (1974, pp. 73, 111), are much too conjectural to be accepted.

The first representation is an illumination of a sermon by the "holy prophet and archimandrite" recommending that the faithful use the church frequently. It appears in a manuscript from Hamuli now in the Pierpont-Morgan Library (M. 604). The date is probably the late ninth century, as suggested by the style of the garments and the coarse facial features and body shapes. The abbot is expressly named Shenute, and his name is preceded by the title *ho hagios,* which classes him among the saints in the Coptic calendar. His head is surrounded by a halo. He is being blessed by the right hand of Christ, who has a cruciform halo and is labeled Emmanuel in capital letters. Shenute stretches the first two fingers of his right hand toward Christ, while with his left he holds the long rod topped with a cross, the mark of his office, across his body. The two figures face the viewer, each standing under an arch. They are visually linked to each other by the position of the right arms and the direction of their sandaled feet, which are turned toward the opposite figure. The difference between God incarnate and the monk is emphasized by differences in their sizes, faces, and clothes. Christ is larger by half. The well-proportioned face of Christ has a mustache and a slight fringe of beard, while the monk's face is triangular with a pointed beard. A large cloak, which envelops Christ entirely and which he holds at the waist, allows a glimpse of the top and bottom of the tunic, which is adorned with pearls arranged in crosses on the torso and in parallel bands down to the lower edge. A cloak covers the monk's shoulders but reveals a tunic adorned with vertical lines of pearls arranged to form crosses.

The second representation of Shenute occupies a limestone stela from Dayr Anbā Shinūdah now in the State Museum of Berlin. The figure is set in an arcade whose columns are topped by capitals bearing acanthus leaves; his name, Apa Shenute, in capital letters extends across the lower band of the stela. Shenute stands full-face, his slippered feet turned to the left. His features are scarcely marked, and his rounded beard makes his head a slightly elongated oval. He is dressed in a long pleated tunic, close-fitting at the waist and covered on the shoulders and sides by a cloak of the same length. His left arm is raised toward the neck. His folded right arm rests on a long staff with a cross at its top. The absence of a halo, the use of the common monastic title *apa,* and the fact that his staff may confer on him no more than the dignity of another monastic superior of the same name in the region appear to be the reasons that impelled J. Beckwith to express doubts about the identification of the

Shenute. *Courtesy State Museum of Berlin.*

portrait with the holy archimandrite (1963, p. 55, no. 115). The doubt is not unjustified, though it is perhaps a little too strong. The veneration indicated by the arcade, and by the absence of any indication of funerary use, seems to warrant placing this rather striking piece in the iconography of the celebrated abbot of Dayr Anbā Shinūdah.

BIBLIOGRAPHY

Beckwith, J. *Coptic Sculpture, 300–1300.* London, 1963.

Leroy, J. *Les Manuscrits coptes et coptes-arabes illustrés.* Paris, 1974.

PIERRE DU BOURGUET, S.J.

Tetramorph

The tetramorphs are the four incorporeal creatures mentioned in the Bible that are the bearers of the throne of God. Revelation 4 speaks of four six-winged creatures: a lion, a calf, a man, and a flying eagle; Isaiah 6 mentions six-winged seraphim, and Ezekiel 1 speaks of four four-headed cherubim, each with four wings. From the juxtaposition of these three scriptural texts, it appears that the difference between the four creatures of Revelation, the seraphim, and the cherubim is extremely vague (although six-winged seraphim appear at ISNĀ and four-headed and four-winged cherubim are seen at DAYR ANBĀ MAQĀR, Wādī al-Naṭrūn) and that they are quite definitely regarded as belonging to the category of angels. In magic each of them has a name, which is also found in a related form in Nubian iconography (see below). The Copto-Arabic SYNAXARION commemorates them (8 Hatūr) and notes that there are churches dedicated to them.

Because the four creatures are the bearers of God's throne or throne-chariot, which was called in ancient texts the "chariot of the Cherubim" and is shown with wheels, they figure in compositions portraying Christ in majesty, in apselike niches of cells in Dayr Apa Apollo, Bawīṭ, and Dayr Apa Jeremiah, Saqqara, dating about 700, and in apses in medieval churches. Their head and neck protrude from the midst of eye-covered wings. Above left is the man, below left the lion, below right the calf, and above right the eagle—in the order given in Ezekiel.

The tetramorph also occurs in murals of medieval Nubia, where the creatures surround the half-figure of Christ, sometimes even in combination with the Holy Cross (van Moorsel, 1966, pp. 297–316). It is in this last form, too, that the Nubian version of the magic names of the four creatures has come down. Both Nubian forms, moreover, occur in places other than apses, at Faras, Tamīt, and 'ABDALLĀH NIRQĪ. Presumably it can be concluded that there, too, the intention was to portray Christ enthroned.

Two striking variants are found, first, in Nubia in the tenth-century church in Sonqi Tino (Donadoni, 1970, pp. 209–216; van der Helm, 1985, pp. 26–27) and second, in a mural of about 1232–33 in Dayr Anbā Anṭūniyūs, near the Red Sea (Leroy, 1975, pl. 10). In both cases the four creatures are shown upright. The threefold "holy" that Isaiah, Revelation, and the liturgy attribute to them is included in several examples as an inscription in the composition itself, as at Dayr Anbā Anṭūniyūs, while in Cells 6 and 17 of Dayr Apa Apollo at Bāwīṭ, it is even written on the open codex that Christ is holding in his hand (van der Meer, 1938, p. 260).

A homily of Pseudo-Chrysostom in an eleventh-century manuscript in the Pierpont Morgan Library, New York, provides further information on the role of the four Creatures in Coptic angelology. When God condemned Lucifer, one of the four cast him down to earth, one divested him of his panoply, the third bound him, and the fourth cast him into the lake of fire. They then clothed Michael in Lucifer's panoply. The question as to whether in the Nile Valley the tetramorphs also had an allegorical meaning connecting them with the Evangelists, as was common in other Christian areas, has not yet been settled (de Grooth and van Moorsel, 1977–1978, pp. 233–41).

BIBLIOGRAPHY

Donadini, S. "Les Fouilles à l'église de Sonqi Tino." In *Kunst und Geschichte Nubiens in Christlicher Zeit*, ed. E. Dinkler. Recklinghausen, 1970.

Grooth, M. de, and P. van Moorsel. "The Lion, the Calf, the Man and the Eagle in Early Christian and Coptic Art." *Bulletin Antieke Beschaving* 52–53 (1977–1978):233–41.

Helm, M. van der. "Some Iconographical Remarks on St. Michael in Sonqi Tino." *Nubian Letters* 4 (February 1985):26–27.

Leroy, J. *Les Peintures des couvents du désert d'Esna.* Cairo, 1975.

Meer, F. van der. *Maiestas Domini.* Vatican City, 1938.

Moorsel, P. van. "Une Théophanie nubienne." *Revista di Archeologie Cristiana* 42 (1966):297–316.

Müller, C. Detlev G. *Die Engellehre der koptischen Kirche.* Wiesbaden, 1959.

Nilgen, U. "Evangelisten." In *Lexikon der christlichen Ikonographie*, Vol. 1, ed. Verlag Bruder Hollinek. Vienna, 1967–.

PAUL VAN MOORSEL

Thecla, Saint

Thecla is the name of three saints in the early church. According to the apocryphal *Acts of Saints Paul and Thecla*, when the Apostle Paul was in Iconium he converted the maiden Thecla, who followed in his footsteps. She was condemned to be burnt alive for refusing to marry her betrothed but was saved by a miracle. She suffered many vicissitudes before her death in Seleucia, in Syria. Thecla of Iconium was venerated in Egypt, especially at a sanctuary in the Libyan desert near that of Saint Menas (see above). This Thecla does not seem to have passed into the Coptic liturgy, which mentions only the other two saints. A second Thecla was the mother of the martyr Apollonius. She herself was martyred along with her brother, Saint Isi, and his friend Paul. Her feast day is 4 Kiyahk. A third Thecla is associated with Saint Maqronius, who may be a double of the martyr Saint Macrobius of al-Ashmūnayn (de Fenoyl, 1960, pp. 97, 130). Her feast day is 1 Baramhāt.

Saint Thecla of Iconium is represented in a painting in the funerary Chapel of Peace at the oasis of AL-BAGAWĀT in the Western Desert. She appears alongside Saint Paul, the Virgin, and other biblical figures but is in the Byzantine style of the sixth century, which was appropriate at that time in an oasis to which Constantinople exiled undesirables. The painting should not, therefore, be considered Coptic.

Clearly Coptic are her representations in low-relief, along with those of Saint Menas, on ampullae for miraculous water from his sanctuary at Abū Mīnā. One saint occupies each side. Their association was probably due to the proximity of their two sanctuaries (Leibbrand, 1976, col. 432). Like Menas, Thecla stands in the orant position. Three of these ampullae, in the Louvre, are important for their large size, about 6 inches (15 cm) in contrast to the much smaller ampullae found along the Mediterranean, in Asia Minor, and as far away as England. Two have the common globular form, one rests on a foot (Metzger, 1981). All three present the saint standing barefoot, wearing a robe from the waist downward (except perhaps for one ampulla), her bust uncovered, and her hands (tied) behind her back. She is menaced on either side by one or two wild beasts: lion, bear, and wolves, heads of lions or forequarters of a lion or bear.

Apart from the two kinds of representation of Thecla of Iconium in association with Paul or Menas, there are representations of a Saint Thecla alone. On a stone panel in the Brooklyn Museum, the standing saint, robed only from waist to ankle, raises high a Greek cross, which she holds by the ends of the crossbar. She is attacked on one side by a wolf, on another by flames. The style is that of Coptic relief sculpture of the ninth century, with a flattened surface, sharply carved hollows, and a *horror vacui* that makes the panel resemble a printer's plate. It is a question, however, which Thecla is here portrayed. Is it Thecla of Iconium or one of the two Theclas in the Coptic liturgy? The artist either had in mind the disciple of Paul or he adapted her iconography to his portrayal of one of the other saints.

St. Thecla. *Courtesy Brooklyn Museum, Brooklyn, New York.*

BIBLIOGRAPHY

Bourguet, P. du. *L'Art copte,* pp. 50, 179. Paris, 1967.

Fenoyl, M. de. *Le sanctoral copte.* Beirut, 1960.

Leibbrand, J. "Theckla von Ikonium." In *Lexicon der christlichen Ikonographie,* Vol. 8, cols. 432–36. Rome, 1976.

Metzger, C. *Ampoules à eulogie. Musée du Louvre.* Notes et documents des musées de France 3. Paris, 1981.

PIERRE DU BOURGUET, S.J.

The Twenty-four Elders

According to the book of Revelation (4:10, 5:8, 7:11), twenty-four elders are seated on twenty-four thrones, clothed in white, holding harps, and wearing crowns of gold, which they take off when they fall down to worship God. They may have derived from an apocalyptic passage in Isaiah (24:33), or they may represent the twelve tribes of Israel combined with the Twelve Apostles. The Copts have venerated them since the seventh or eighth century and commemorate them in the Copto-Arabic Synaxarion as 24 Hatūr. Coptic folklore has adopted them for magical purposes. Their names, which correspond to the letters of the Greek alphabet, were recited for protection against the evil one.

One of the earliest representations of the twenty-four elders in Coptic art is a wall painting of the ninth or tenth century in the apse of the church in DAYR ANBĀ HADRĀ in Aswan. Each elder is identified with a letter of the Greek alphabet. Today only small fragments of the upper part of the figures on the northern wall of the apse are visible. The elders also appear in a tenth-century painting on the eastern wall of the sanctuary of Saint Takla Haymanot in the Church of Sitt Maryam (al-Mu'allaqah) in Old Cairo, but it is much damaged. Other iconographical representations include a thirteenth-century mural in the Church of Saint Antony in Dayr Anbā Anṭūniyūs, an eighteenth-century mural in the subterranean Church of Saint Paul the Theban in DAYR ANBĀ BŪLĀ (Monastery of Saint Paul), a nineteenth-century mural in the Church of the Holy Virgin in the Ḥārit al-Rūm, Cairo, and twentieth-century murals in the Upper Church of the Holy Virgin at Rod al-Faraj, Cairo, and the Upper Church of the Cathedral of Saint George, Giza. Icons (panels) of the twenty-four elders are rare. An eighteenth-century icon in the Coptic Museum, Cairo, has the names of the twenty-four elders written in Arabic. A Byzantine icon of the twenty-four elders belongs to the Church of Saint Mercurius in Dayr Abū Sayfayn, Old Cairo.

BIBLIOGRAPHY

Aescoly, A. Z. "Les Noms magiques dans les apocryphes chrétiens des Ethiopiens." *Journal asiatique* 220 (1932):87–137.

Crum, W. E. *Catalogue of the Coptic Manuscripts in the British Museum,* 505, no. 1223; 417, no. 1007. London, 1905.

Erman, A. *Ägyptische Urkunden aus den Koñiglichen Museen zu Berlin.* Koptische Urkunden, Vol. 1, no. 17, 8330. Berlin, 1904.

Evelyn-White, H. G. *The Monasteries of the Wadi 'n-Natrun,* Vol. 3, p. 95. New York, 1933.

Gaselee, S. *Parerga Coptica I. De XXIV senioribus apocalypticis et nominibus eorum.* Cambridge, 1912.

Grosjean, P. "Les Vingt-quatre vieillards de l'Apocalypse à propos d'une liste galloise." *Analecta Bollandiana* 72 (1954):192–212.

Halkin, F. "Une liste grecque des XXIV vieillards de l'Apocalypse." *Analecta Bollandiana* 84 (1966):58.

Junker, H. *Koptische Poesie des zehnten Jahrhunderts,* Vol. 2, p. 143. Berlin, 1908–1910.

Leclercq, H. "Les vingt-quatre vieillards." In *Dictionnaire d'archéologie chrétienne et liturgie,* vol. 2, cols. 3121–25. Paris, 1953.

Meinardus, O. "The Twenty-Four Elders of the Apocalypse in the Iconography of the Coptic Church." *Studia Orientalia Christiana, Collectanea* 13 (1968–1969):141–58.

Michl, J. *Die 24 Ältesten in der Apocalypse des hl. Johannes.* Munich, 1938.

OTTO F. A. MEINARDUS

Virgin Enthroned

Representations of the Virgin Mary far outnumber all other Christian themes in Coptic art. They occur in virtually every medium—painted in murals and manuscripts; sculptured in stone, wood, and ivory; and woven in wool and linen. The dominant role of the Virgin in the art of Coptic Egypt is a direct reflection of the very special character of Egyptian theology as formulated by Saint CYRIL I and confirmed by the Council of Ephesus in 431. Egyptian theologians held firmly to the dogma of the triune God. They maintained that Christ had only one nature and that he was divine from the moment of birth and that, therefore, Mary was the Mother of God—the Theotokos.

Although the cult of Mary seems to have been established in Egypt well before 431, it flourished with the rise of monasticism in the late fifth and sixth centuries. The Coptic monks were particularly devoted to her cult, and from the rubble of their long-abandoned monasteries have come the most important monuments of the art produced in her service.

Painting and Tapestry

The major works supporting a study of the Virgin Enthroned in Coptic art are the apse frescoes from the Dayr Apa Apollo at Bāwīṭ and Dayr Apa Jeremiah at Saqqara. Although none is precisely datable, the majority probably belong to the sixth century. Confirmation of this date is provided by comparison with the great tapestry, Icon of the Virgin, now in the Cleveland Museum of Art, which has been firmly dated within that century (Shepherd, 1969). In the majority of the apse frescoes, as in the tapestry, the Enthroned Virgin participates in an elaborate two-tiered iconographic program, which A. Grabar (1946, pp. 207–230) has interpreted as representing a theophanic vision. In the upper tier, Christ, in a mandorla of light, represents a vision of the Second Coming. Below, the Virgin with the Christ Child in her lap is a vision of the Incarnation.

The earliest such representation to have survived in Egypt is on one of the leaves of a pair of late fifth-century doors from the church of Sitt Barbara in Old Cairo (Beckwith, 1963, figs. 97–98). Although the details are badly effaced by time, in the lower panel it is still possible to recognize the Enthroned Virgin and Child and the flanking groups of apostles. On a panel near the top of the door, a bust of Christ is displayed in a *clipeus* (large round shield) borne by angels. Here are already the basic elements of the theophanic vision that will dominate the iconography of the apse paintings at Bāwīṭ and Saqqara in the next century.

The most usual representation of the Virgin in this context is in the slightly informal pose of the *Hodegetria* (Byzantine type of Madonna), in which she is seated frontally, relaxed with one foot slightly forward, holding the Child on her left, as in Dayr Apa Apollo, Chapels 3 and 6 (Clédat, 1904–1906, pl. 21, and Maspero and Drioton, 1931, pl. 21) and Dayr Apa Jeremiah, Chapel F and Cells 1727 and 1733 (Quibell, 1908, pl. 55, and 1912, pl. 24 and p. 22). The tapestry icon obviously derives from a similar model. Elsewhere, in Chapel 42 at Dayr Apa Apollo (Clédat, 1904, fig. 1), her role as the Mother of God is reinforced by portraying her as the Virgin *lactans* (nursing). In a third version, borrowed from imperial iconography, the Virgin displays a "portrait" of Christ in a *clipeus* in Dayr Apa Jeremiah, Cell 1723 (Quibell, 1912, pl. 24, 2).

On the Cleveland tapestry, the program in the frescoes is further enhanced by the addition of the ciborium (small columned structure) in which the Virgin's throne is placed. Its setting, seemingly suspended in infinite space, gives an illusion of timelessness. The great wreath of fruits and flowers that surrounds the whole composition evokes concepts of rebirth and salvation. It confirms the iconographic intent of the two theophanies, the Second Coming and the Incarnation, as promises of salvation.

After the Cleveland tapestry, only one other textile with this subject has so far come to light. It is a tantalizing fragment from what must have been a large hanging in looped-pile technique. It preserves only a portion of an Enthroned Virgin. The Child is seated frontally in her lap and is praying (du Bourguet, 1971, Appendix, pl. 9).

The majority of the frescoes from Dayr Apa Apollo and Dayr Apa Jeremiah belong to the two-zoned programs described above, but there are a number of autonomous representations of the Virgin Enthroned. In three instances, she is portrayed in the Egyptian tradition of the goddess *lactans,* in Dayr Apa Apollo, Chapel 30 (Maspero and Drioton, 1931, pls. 42–43) and in Dayr Apa Jeremiah, Chapel A and Cell 1725 (Quibell, 1908, pl. 41, and 1912, pl. 22). In Chapel 28 at Dayr Apa Apollo (Clédat, 1904–1906, pl. 96), the Virgin once again displays a "portrait" of Christ in a *clipeus.* Several fragments of frescoes preserving all or part of the figure of an Enthroned Virgin, apparently also autonomous representations, were found in Chapels 1, 7, 8, and 40 at Dayr Apa Apollo (Clédat, 1916, pp. 3, 51–52; Maspero and Drioton, 1931, p. 14) and in Cells 1724 and 1740 at Dayr Apa Jeremiah (Quibell, 1912, pp. 21, 23).

An illustration from a manuscript dated 895 or 898 in the Pierpont Morgan Library, New York, provides testimony to the survival, albeit crudely, of the traditional iconography of the theophany of the Incarnation. There an enthroned Virgin *lactans* is accompanied by a pair of adoring archangels.

Sculpture

Among the numerous sculptures representing the Enthroned Virgin, very few show any similarity to the theophanic iconography of the frescoes. The two finest and most developed examples are in the Coptic Museum, Cairo. In one (Beckwith, 1963, fig. 112) the Enthroned Virgin and Child are flanked by the usual pair of archangels followed by two apostles. In the other (Beckwith, 1963, fig. 111) two smaller-scale figures—apparently Peter and Paul—stand between the throne and the archangels. Both sculptures are so badly damaged that judgment of style is difficult. In general, however, comparison with the frescoes suggests a sixth-century date. A third sculpture with the Virgin and Child flanked by archangels, also in the Coptic Museum (Beckwith, 1963, fig. 113), is much more primitive in style. However, the large flanking columns recall the ciborium of the Cleveland tapestry as well as relating to the architectural forms of Coptic grave stelae. Another very fragmentary sculpture from Dayr Apa Apollo in the Coptic Museum preserves fragments from a similar composition. Finally, in the same museum (Wessel, 1965, fig. 6) is an extremely provincial version of the Virgin *lactans,* in which the flanking archangels have been replaced by tiny orants.

There are several grave stelae with simple representations of a woman, in most cases nursing, seated holding a child in her lap. These sculptures are very different from one another, but each in its own way reveals its relatively simple folk origin. None of the figures wears a nimbus and there is nothing inherent in them to justify their interpretation as Christian rather than pagan symbols. However, crosses accompanying the figures on three of the stelae, one in the State Museum of Berlin (Wessel, 1965, fig. 5) and two in the Coptic Museum, Cairo (Crum, 1902, nos. 8702, 8703), provide the needed proof that they were made for Christian graves. In these instances, however, the iconography of the *Theotokos* has apparently taken on a purely symbolic character to the extent that a mother and child, that is, *any* mother and child, could be taken as symbols of rebirth and salvation.

Two ivories, probably from the seventh century, one in the Walters Art Gallery, Baltimore, and the other in the Museum of Ancient Art, Milan (Wessel, 1965, figs. 35, 36), follow closely the iconography of the *Theotokos* in the theophanic programs described above.

BIBLIOGRAPHY

Beckwith, J. *Coptic Sculpture, 300–1300.* London, 1963.

Bourguet, P. du. *The Art of the Copts.* New York, 1971.

Brooklyn Museum. *Pagan and Christian Egypt, Egyptian Art from the First to the Tenth Century A. D.* Exhibition at the Brooklyn Museum of Art, January 23–March 9, 1941. Brooklyn, N.Y., 1941.

Clédat, J. "Recherches sur le kom de Baouît." *Comptes-rendus de l'Académie des Inscriptions, séance du 17 octobre 1902.* Paris, 1904.

______. *Le Monastère et la nécropole de Baouît,* 2 vols. Mémoires de l'Institut français d'Archéologie orientale du Caire 12. Cairo, 1904–1916.

Crum, W. E. *Coptic Monuments,* nos. 8001–8741. Catalogue général des antiquités égyptiennes du Musée du Caire. Cairo, 1902.

Grabar, A. *Martyrium,* Vol. 2. Paris, 1946.

______. *Byzantium from the Death of Theodosius to the Rise of Islam.* London, 1966.

Maspero, J., and E. Drioton. *Fouilles executées à Baouît par Jean Maspero. Notes mises en ordre et éditées par Etienne Drioton.* Mémoires de l'Institut français d'archéologie orientale du Caire 59. Cairo, 1931.

Quibell, J. E. *Excavations at Saqqara (1906–1907).* Cairo, 1908; *(1908–1909, 1909–1910).* Cairo, 1912.

Shepherd, D. G. "An Icon of the Virgin." *The Bulletin of the Cleveland Museum of Art* 56 (1969):90–120.

Wessel, K. *Coptic Art.* New York, 1965.

DOROTHY SHEPHERD PAYER

CHRISTMAS, FEAST OF.

See Feasts, Major.

CHRISTODOROS OF COPTOS,

a Christian poet in the time of Anastasius I (491–518) who was influenced by NONNOS OF PANOPOLIS (Cameron, p. 475). Between 491 and 518 he wrote a poem "On the Pupils of the Great Proclus," an epic on the Isaurian expedition (497–498) of Emperor Anastasius, poems on the history and antiquities of Constantinople and other places, an exposition on statues in the thermae of Zeuxippos in Constantinople, and epigrams.

BIBLIOGRAPHY

Cameron, A. "Wandering Poets. A Literary Movement in Byzantine Egypt." *Historia* 14 (1965): 470–509.

Stupperich, R. "Das Statuenprogramm in den Zeuxippos-Thermen." *Istambuler Mitteilungen* 32 (1982):210–35.

MARTIN KRAUSE

CHRISTODOULOS I.

See Jerusalem, Coptic See of.

CHRISTODOULOS II.

See Jerusalem, Coptic See of.

CHRISTODOULOS III.

See Jerusalem, Coptic See of.

CHRISTODOULUS,

sixty-sixth patriarch of the See of Saint Mark (1047–1077). Christodoulus, whose original name as a monk of the ENATON, west of Alexandria, was Theodore, was a native of the village of Būrah, but his date of birth is unknown. The first known event in his life concerns his castrating himself. This happened when an Arab community descended on the monastery and one of their maids tempted the monk Theodore. After yielding to her, he castrated himself in penitence and was saved from bleeding to death by the superintendent of the monastery. After that, he is said to have gone to the wilderness of Wādī Habīb and, after residing in DAYR AL-BARAMŪS for an unknown period, decided to become a solitary in a cave at the seashore near the town of Nastarūh. He is said to have resided there with a coffin containing the body of Saint Thecla the Apostolic. A disciple of Saint Paul, Thecla was martyred by being thrown to the lions, and then her body was cast into the fire at Antioch. However, her body had remained intact and worked miracles.

When SHENUTE II died in 1046, and the search was begun for a successor, it was the turn of the Alexandrians to make the choice. Their first preference was a HEGUMENOS of Alexandria, a saintly cleric by the name of Yuḥannā ibn Tirūs. But when it was learned that he was the godfather of ʿAlwān ibn Zakariyyā, an influential Copt in the Muslim administration with close ties to ʿAli ibn Aḥmad al-Jurjānī, the vizier of the Fatimid caliph al-Mustanṣir, his name was eliminated from consideration.

Then the name of Theodore the eunuch was promoted by Abū al-Malīḥ Manṣūr, known as Ibn al-ʿAlamī, a secretary of the *diwan* in Alexandria, together with a presbyter of Saint Mark's Cathedral named Simon, who later became bishop of Tanis. The secretary, accompanied by a delegation of archons from Alexandria, went to Theodore's hermitage to prevail upon him to accept the nomination. At first he refused, but with the persuasive influence of a relative of his named Zikrī ibn Marqūriyus, he accepted, though he was a poor man who possessed only 2¾ dirhams.

Thus, the delegation took him to Alexandria, where he was initially consecrated under the name Christodoulus. Later, according to established tradition, he was to be taken for another formal consecration in the ancient Church of Abū Sarjah (Saint Sergius) in Old Cairo, but he decided that this should be done in the al-Muʿallaqah church. This proved to be the beginning of a new landmark in the story of the seat of Saint Mark, which was eventually moved from Alexandria to al-Muʿallaqah, within reach of the Islamic capital, probably in response to a caliphal suggestion.

However, before leaving Alexandria, Christodoulus consecrated six churches in the city: the churches of Saint John the Evangelist, Saint Mercurius, the archangel Raphael, Saint Menas, Saint George, and Saint Mark. Moreover, he invested one person with the priesthood, appointed sixty deacons, and issued his long doctrinal ordinance covering all church traditions, the major points of which were:

1. Male and female children should not be baptized in the same baptismal font.
2. Private bread should not be mixed with the sacramental bread intended for holy communion before the liturgy.
3. Believers must drink thrice from the water used in the sanctuary and avoid spilling it on the floor.
4. The faithful should stand in awe during Sunday and feast day liturgies.
5. The faithful should refrain from talking to one another during the liturgy.
6. The faithful should listen attentively throughout the liturgy.
7. There should be no mixing of sexes in church.
8. The faithful should, in all humility, keep the fasts; and there should be no marital ceremonies during fast days.
9. No baptism or funeral rites should be allowed during the holy week; the Gospel of Intercession (*tarḥīm*) should be read for the dead, after Saint Paul's Epistle, but funeral rites should wait until Easter is over.
10. The liturgy of Maundy Thursday should be observed in silence, without the kiss or handshaking.
11. No baptism nor ordination should be performed during the fifty days' fast.
12. There should be no weeping or lamentations or speeches for the dead on Sundays, only prayer for their souls.
13. The fast of the Apostles, which is after Pentecost, should be required of the faithful, lasting until the fifth of Abīb, which is the feast day. If it falls on a Wednesday, they should break the fast, but not on a Friday.
14. If a Feast of the Illustrious Nativity falls on a Wednesday or Friday, the faithful should break the fast on those days; otherwise the fast on Wednesday and Friday is obligatory throughout the whole year.
15. Baptism is not allowed without the Eucharist; an infant could only be baptized if he fasted before the Eucharist.
16. The making of eucharistic bread at the homes of the faithful is permitted; previously it had to be prepared on the church premises.

In his ordinance, Christodoulus made clear to the bishops his firm determination to rule within his ecclesiastical prerogative, something that the bishops were not accustomed to during previous patriarchates. Eventually, they gave vent to their dissatisfaction with the pope, and a movement for finding a pretext to depose him was led by Anbā Yuḥannā, bishop of Sakhā, who was joined by Anbā MĪKHĀʾĪL, bishop of Tanis; Anbā Khayāl, bishop of Quṭūr; Iliyyā, bishop of Ṭamwayh; Anbā Jirjā, bishop of al-Khandaq; and Anbā Murqus, bishop of al-Balyanā. In addition, a number of clergymen convened in Cairo to depose the patriarch, on the basis of a technicality in which certain prayers were not recited at his consecration. However, thanks to the intercession of Shaykh Abū Zikrī Yaḥyā ibn Maqārah, the Coptic secretary and chief scribe of the caliphal office, this tempestuous movement within the church subsided.

After this, a local problem emerged when Abū Zikrī's nephew committed a felony, for which the patriarch was asked to absolve him. Despite Abū Zikrī's former support for the patriarch and his high position in the administration of the country, Christodoulus rejected the demand.

With the return to peace within the church, Christodoulus embarked on a pastoral visitation to Damanhūr, DAMRŪ, and the DAYR ANBĀ MAQĀR in the wilderness of Wādī Habīb, where he had a dispute with its monks over their habit of preserving the holy bread from the Sunday of Olives to the Wednesday of Holy Week, which he forbade after producing an ancient *mimar* (homily) supporting his theory.

Another problem of ecclesiastical significance between the sister churches of Alexandria and Antioch arose over the Antiochan use of oil and salt in baking sacramental bread. Christodoulus stood fast against this, even though the Antiochene custom was supported by so mighty a Syriac personality as Abū Bishr, the private physician of the caliphal court.

An instance of the papal fearlessness occurred in the case of a young Copt named Baghām, who, after apostatizing to Islam, recanted to his old Christian faith, an action that the Islamic state punished by death. Baghām was decapitated, and his body was left outside the church of Saint Michael. The pope courageously declared the victim a holy martyr and permitted his body to be honorably buried within the sanctuary of the church, irrespective of the position of the state.

Another problem, concerning the head of Saint Mark, was solved outside the patriarchal domain. The vizier Mi'ḍād al-Dawlah of the Fatimid administration was informed that the Byzantines were offering to pay 10,000 dinars for procuring the head, which seems to have been hidden in the house of a Copt by the name of Abū al-Fatḥ ibn Mufarrij in Alexandria. Mi'ḍād al-Dawlah arrested Abū al-Fatḥ until he could be persuaded to cede the head. In the meantime, the head was moved, and Abū al-Fatḥ denied that he possessed it. Instead, he offered the vizier 600 dinars to secure his liberty, and the situation was hushed up afterward.

A serious situation developed at Damrū, where Christodoulus was residing, involving a highly placed judge named Abū al-Ḥasan ibn 'Abd al-Wahhāb ibn 'Ali al-Ṣirafī, who hated the Christians. The judge reported to the vizier al-Yāzūrī that the patriarch had been building new churches without permission and that in Damrū alone he had seventeen churches. Consequently, al-Yāzūrī issued an order for the closure of churches in Miṣr, an order that seems to have been attenuated by the arrival of a rich Christian donation from Byzantium, including gold and silver, precious textiles, and fifty mules. This was the period of the emergence from the east of the Saljūq menace to the Byzantine empire and the Fatimid caliphate, whose united front was their only way of saving their territories.

The position of the church under Christodoulus was not altogether precarious, however. In Alexandria, the Fatimid caliph had appointed a Berber governor from the North African tribe of Kutāmah. He was sympathetic to the Copts, and the caliph gave him the keys to the closed church of Saint George established by Saint Anianus, who had succeeded Saint Mark in the first century. He even allowed the Copts, under the protection of his guards, to hold a Pentecostal procession from the Church of Saint Sergius to the Church of the Savior, a procession that had been suspended for fifteen years.

Christodoulus had to face other difficulties, which arose from within the church itself. A monk called Colluthus (Filūṭus), who solicited the episcopate and was refused by Christodoulus, who found him unfit for the dignity, started a wave of calumnious reports to the caliph about the pope. In spite of the efforts of the archons Abū al-Yumn ibn Makrāwah and Abū al-Ṭayyib al-Razāwī, as well as Abū al-Surūr Yuḥannā ibn Yūsuf al-Abaḥḥ, to dissuade him, the caliph sent his soldiers to the patriarchal residence in Damrū, where they seized Christodoulus' fortune of 6,000 dinars and arrested him. Later, he gained his freedom through the intercession of influential Coptic archons, but his money was confiscated.

The situation was somewhat improved by the murder of the vizier Nāṣir al-Dawlah, a hater of Christians, followed by the arrival of Badr al-Jamālī, an Islamized Christian of Armenian extraction. Though this seemed to offer the Copts a breathing space, the confusion within the state of Egypt, torn between the hostile armies of North Africa, the Armenians, the Turks, and the Sudanese, was worsened by the failure of the Nile to flood and the resulting famine. This situation is eloquently described by the Muslim historian of the Copts, Taqīy al-Dīn al-MAQRĪZĪ. In these calamitous circumstances, the Copts were generally victimized, and the Islamic government intensified its imposts from the church, which Christodoulus had to face with his bishops.

Other sources indicate that the Copts were numerous in the desert oases, and Christodoulus was requested to send them a special bishop. Christodoulus was aided in his relations with the Islamic administration by the Christian kingdom of Nubia, whose sovereign paid the BAQṬ, or monetary levy, to Egypt for some years.

On the international scene, Christodoulus was a contemporary of the important battle of Manzi Kert (Malāz Jard) in 1071 in the upper Euphrates, which opened the road to the west for the Saljūqs. Thus, he witnessed the root events that led to the outbreak of the Crusades from Western Europe.

After a reign lasting thirty tempestuous years, Christodoulus died on 14 Kiyahk. He was buried in the Church of al-Muʿallaqah in Old Cairo.

BIBLIOGRAPHY

Lane-Poole, S. *The Mohammadan Dynasties*. London, 1894.

———. *History of Egypt in the Middle Ages*. London, 1901.

SUBHI Y. LABIB

CHRISTOLOGY, the study of the person of Christ with special reference to the union of the divine and human natures in the one person. From the New Testament we know that the early Christians regarded Christ as both God and man, but it was the task of later Christology to express this coherently in precise theological terms. The controversies of the early Christian centuries reflect divergent approaches to this problem. Those who started from His humanity included EBIONITES and Cerinthians, who regarded Jesus as a man especially endowed by God for His mission; Adoptionists and Dynamic Monarchians, who held that Jesus was especially endowed by the Holy Spirit at His baptism; and later Nestorians (although perhaps not NESTORIUS himself) who believed in a prosopic rather than a real union of the two natures in the one person, which tended to keep the two natures separate. All of these failed to do justice to Jesus as God.

On the other side were those who started from the godhead. Among these were the Docetists, who regarded Jesus' coming in the flesh as a mere phantom appearance; Modalist Monarchians, who saw Christ as a mode of appearance of the Father; and the Apollinarians, who held that in Jesus there was a human body and soul (*psyche*) but no human spirit (*nous*), the latter being replaced by the divine Logos. All of these failed to do justice to the manhood of Christ.

Another controversy, which had important ramifications, was begun by the Alexandrian presbyter ARIUS (256–336) who, in a desire to guard the unity of the godhead, denied that the Son was truly God. Although Arius did not exclude soteriology (the doctrine of salvation), his views tended to make the Son into a demigod—neither fully God nor fully man. The Council of NICAEA (325) replied by asserting that Jesus was "of one substance with the Father," which excluded Arianism proper. Christological speculation, however, continued unabated and continued to be dominated by the division between those who approached Christ's person from His manhood and from His godhead. Theologians in Antioch (e.g., THEODORUS OF MOPSUESTIA, and Nestorius' followers) almost separated Christ into two persons, so concerned were they to preserve Jesus' human experience, while the Alexandrians (e.g., CYRIL OF ALEXANDRIA) were concerned to emphasize His divinity. The Council of EPHESUS (431) asserted that the one born from Mary was God. The orthodoxy of the term *Theotokos* was accepted, but fifteen years later EUTYCHES maintained that although there were two natures in Christ before the Incarnation, there was only one nature after. Against these views the Council of CHALCEDON (451) stated in its definition that Christ was "truly God and truly Man. . . . One and the same Christ, Son, Lord, Only-begotten, acknowledged in two natures without confusion, without change, without division, without separation." However, this statement was unacceptable to many Christians, who continued to hold that in the person of the incarnate Christ there was one single divine nature (see MONOPHYSITISM). Many variant forms of monophysitism soon developed—for instance, that of the followers of JULIAN of Halicarnassus, who taught the incorruptibility and immortality of the body of Jesus from the first moment of the Incarnation.

During the fifth and sixth centuries many efforts were made, without avail, to reconcile the Monophysites to the main body of Christians. However, by the sixth century monophysitism had consolidated itself into three great churches: (1) the Coptic (the ancient church of Egypt) and the Ethiopian branches (the latter strongly influenced by Judaism); (2) the Syrian Jacobites; and (3) the Armenians. All of these churches accept the doctrine of the church fathers prior to the Council of Chalcedon while rejecting the definition of that council. Today, with a less pronounced monophysitism, they are closer to the Orthodox churches.

BIBLIOGRAPHY

Bethune-Baker, J. F. *Nestorius and His Teaching.* Cambridge, 1908.

Chadwick, H. "Eucharist and Christology in the Nestorian Controversy." *Journal of Theological Studies* n.s. 2 (1951):145–64.

Frend, W. H. C. *The Rise of the Monophysite Movement.* Cambridge, 1972; rev. ed., 1979.

Gregg, R. C., and D. E. Groh. *Early Arianism: A View of Salvation.* Philadelphia, 1981.

Grillmeier, A. *Christ in Christian Tradition: From the Apostolic Age to Chalcedon,* trans. J. S. Bowden. London, 1965.

Grillmeier, A., and H. Bacht. *Das Konzil von Chalcedon,* Vols. 1 and 2. Würzburg, 1953–1962.

Raven, C. E. *Apollinarianism.* Chicago, 1923.

Roldanus, J. *Le Christ et l'homme dans la théologie d'Athanase d'Alexandrie.* Leiden, 1968.

Stead, G. C. The Platonism of Arius." *Journal of Theological Studies* n.s. 15 (1964):16–31.

______. *Divine Substance.* New York and London, 1977.

Wiles, M. *The Spiritual Gospel: The Interpretation of the Fourth Gospel in the Early Church.* Cambridge, 1960.

LESLIE W. BARNARD

CHRONICLES. *See* Old Testament, Arabic Versions of the.

CHRONICON ORIENTALE, chronicle of world history composed by an unknown thirteenth-century author who put events he thought important into a table of secular and ecclesiastical rulers. Its chronological bases are the Old Testament for the pre-Christian era, the Roman emperors for the period from the time of Christ to Muḥammad, and thereafter the Arab regimes in Syria and Egypt, along with a history of the caliphs to his own time (1260). It includes a section that gives an outline history of the Alexandrian patriarchs from Saint MARK (43–68) to ATHANASIUS III (1250–1261). The dates are in good order but untrustworthy as to actual calendar years.

The Copt ABŪ SHĀKIR ibn Buṭrus al-Rāhib has been taken to be the author since the *Chronicon*'s first translation into Latin was done by a Maronite, Abraham Ecchelensis (*Chronicon orientale, nunc primum latinitate donatum . . . ,* Paris, 1651; Paris, 1685). This translation was revised by J. ASSEMANI and published with four added dissertations in *Corpus Scriptorum Historiae Byzantinae* (Vol. 17, Venice, 1729).

BIBLIOGRAPHY

Cheikho, L. *Petrus ibn Rāhib's Chronicon Orientale.* In CSCO 45–46, *Scriptores Arabici,* ser. 3, 1–2. Louvain, 1955.

VINCENT FREDERICK

CHRYSOSTOM, JOHN. *See* John Chrysostom, Saint.

CHURCH, CONSECRATION OF. After a new church has been equipped with the necessary vessels, curtains, books, and icons, it has to be consecrated, that is, set apart for divine service and dedicated to a saint. The consecration of a Coptic church is a colorful, elaborate service, carried out on a Saturday evening, and is enriched with significant readings from the Old and the New Testament.

Seven new pots are filled with water into which the following seven kinds of fresh fragrant plants are placed: jasmine, basil, citron, shaddock, lemon, vine, and the tree of Mary. Leaves of garden beet are also put around the altar and the pots. Seven candles are lighted on seven candlesticks, as are seven wicks in pure olive oil.

The bishop begins by saying the thanksgiving prayer. Then he offers incense and blesses the congregation. The midnight prayer is said, followed, inaudibly, by the first 120 Psalms. The remaining thirty-one Psalms (according to the Septuagint) are to be read aloud.

The service comprises twenty-one principal lections, each consisting, as a rule, of an intercession, a lesson from the Old Testament, a psalmody or a *theotokia* sung by the deacons, and a lesson from the New Testament.

Then the deacons sing the hymn to the Virgin Mary, beginning with "The golden censer is the Virgin." This is followed by lections from Hebrews 7:26–28 and Hebrews 8; James 14–26; and Acts 7:44–56.

Then the hymn of the descent of the Holy Spirit and the *Trisagion* are chanted. A priest then recites the first intercession of the Gospel, and Psalm 67:13, 25, followed by readings from Matthew 17:1–8, Mark 9:1–8, and Luke 9:28–35.

Another priest recites the second intercession of

the Gospel, and Psalms 64:1 and 149:1, followed by John 10:12–42. Then the deacons sing a few hymns.

A priest prays the three smaller intercessions of peace, for the church, for the fathers, and for the congregation. Then the congregation recites the Creed.

Then the Bishop offers incense and says the prayer of the incense, followed by two petitions.

Seven petitions read by the archdeacon are followed by several prayers by the bishop. The bishop then prays inaudibly to the Lord after which he recites the formula for consecration of the church and a prayer of benediction.

The clergy and deacons, carrying the jars, crosses, candles, censers, censer-pots, and the gospel-book, form a procession in front of the bishop, chanting appropriate hymns, until they reach the opening in the middle of the eastern wall of the sanctuary, which the bishop sprinkles with water. They go around the four walls of the church, which the bishop sprinkles with water, saying: "For a holy consecration of the house of God."

Then he starts again at the eastern wall, this time signing with the holy oil of chrism, saying: "We consecrate this place as the church of [name of saint] in the name of the Father, and the Son, and the Holy Spirit." He continues signing all windows, corners, and pillars, saying: "Blessed is the Lord God, now and to the ages of ages, Amen."

BIBLIOGRAPHY

Burmester, O. H. E. *The Egyptian or Coptic Church,* pp. 236–45. Cairo, 1967.

Horner, G. W. *The Service for the Consecration of a Church and Altar, According to the Coptic Rite.* London, 1902.

ARCHBISHOP BASILIOS

CHURCH, LAYING THE CORNER-STONE OF. At the ceremony held to celebrate the founding of a church, the following items are placed in a receptacle: a Bible, a cross, coins in current circulation, newspapers of the day, and a document with the name of the patron saint to whom the church is dedicated, the name of the head of state, the name of the patriarch, and the names of the clergy and the notables attending the ceremony. The head priest places the receptacle in the spot designed for the purpose beneath the threshold of the middle sanctuary, saying, "We lay the blessed foundation stone of this holy church dedicated to [name of the dedicatee] in the name of the Father, the Son, and the Holy Spirit, one God, Amen. Blessed be God the Father almighty, Amen. Blessed by His only-begotten Son, Jesus Christ, our Lord, Amen. Blessed be the Holy Spirit, the Comforter, Amen."

The head priest then commences prayers saying, "Have mercy upon us, O God Father almighty. All-holy Trinity have mercy upon us. Lord God of powers, be with us, for we have no help in our tribulations and afflictions, save Thee." This is followed by the Lord's Prayer, the prayer of thanksgiving, the raising of incense for the evening, Psalm 50, and Genesis 28:10–31. A priest says the intercession for the sick, and the deacons sing the litany, "The censer of gold is the Virgin, and her sweet aroma is our Savior. She has given birth to Him; He has saved us and remitted our sins. We worship Thee, O Christ, with Thy good Father and the Holy Spirit, for Thou didst come and save us."

The epistle is taken from Hebrews 9:1–11; this is followed by the *Trisagion,* and the intercession of the Gospel, the psalm-versicle being Psalm 122:1–2: "I was glad when they said to me, Let us go into the house of the Lord. Our feet shall stand within thy gates, O Jerusalem." The Gospel is from Luke 9:28–36. The deacons sing the appropriate response, and a priest says the three greater intercessions (for the peace of the church, the fathers, and the congregation). The Creed is followed by *Kyrie Eleison* said forty-one times.

Here the head priest says a prayer incorporating an earnest request to God to establish the new church on sure foundations, imparting purity to its sanctuary where the faithful may worship His sacred name, receive the holy sacraments, and enjoy God's divine graces. The three absolutions are then said by the head priest, followed by the benediction and the Lord's Prayer.

BIBLIOGRAPHY

Bishop Athanasius, metropolitan of Banī Suef and Bahnasā. *Kitāb Tartīb Waḍ' Ḥajar al-Asās li-al-Kanā'is al-Jadidah,* pp. 3–32. Cairo, 1959.

ARCHBISHOP BASILIOS

CHURCH OF ABŪ SARJAH. *See* Babylon.

CHURCH OF ABŪ SAYFAYN (Old Cairo). In the Arabic manuscripts this church is called "church of Abū Marqūrah," and in a Garshuni manuscript (Arabic written in Syriac characters) "church of Mār Quryus" (Mercurius).

Two late Coptic manuscripts describe it thus: "Mercurius at the tetrapylon of the river." Western travelers of the seventeenth to nineteenth centuries called it "church of Mari Moncure" or "church of Saint Macarius" (probably a confusion between Marqūrah and Maqārah; Coquin, 1974, pp. 15–17).

The church belongs to the group of buildings included in the Christian enclosure of DAYR ABŪ SAYFAYN, which is situated to the north of the QAṢR AL-SHAM', near the Hilwān railway line and the mosque of 'Amr ibn al 'Āṣ in Old Cairo. Down to the late Middle Ages, when the Nile flowed more to the east than today, the river bank was in front of the church (Coquin, 1974, pp. 27–30; see also Casanova, 1919, pp. 192–98 and pl. 3). The Church of Abū Sayfayn includes the church proper, said to be dedicated to Saint MERCURIUS OF CAESAREA, and two groups of secondary chapels annexed to the church; the first to the northeast of the principal church containing three oratories on both the ground floor and the first story, and the second to the northwest above the north vestibule and the *mandarah* (reception hall).

According to some authors the church was reconstructed under the patriarch ABRAHAM (975–978) after having been destroyed and converted into a warehouse for sugarcane. It was burned down and pillaged by a Muslim mob under the patriarch MARK III (1167–1189). The chapels dedicated to Saint John the Baptist and Saint George, probably situated in the south nave of the church and its corresponding triforium (see ARCHITECTURAL ELEMENTS), were spared from the fire. An immediate reconstruction was undertaken at the expense of the *shaykh* Abū al-Barakāt ibn Abū Sa'īd Hablān, and the church was reopened in 1175. It was closed in March 1301, at the same time as all the other churches in Egypt, and reopened in 1312–1313. It underwent restorations in the course of the nineteenth and twentieth centuries carried out by the Committee for the Conservation of Monuments of Arab Art (Coquin, 1974, pp. 18–20).

In this church were consecrated Mār Basīliyus, patriarch of Antioch, in 1421–1422, as well as GABRIEL VIII (1586–1601), PETER VI (1718–1826) and JOHN XVII (1726–1745), patriarchs of the Coptic church. It has been the residence of the Coptic patriarchs from CHRISTODOULUS (1047–1077) and the place of the death and burial of subsequent patriarchs (Coquin, pp. 21–24).

An assembly of the bishops took place there to protest against the patriarch SHENUTE II (1032–1046), who practiced simony. The concoction of the CHRISM under the patriarch THEODOSIUS II (1294–1300) took place in the church (Coquin, pp. 24–25).

Anbā BARSŪM, called the Naked, lived for a long time in a crypt on the north side of the church and died during the reign of patriarch JOHN VIII (1300–1320).

The church of Saint Mercurius, the secondary chapels, and other nearby places contain numerous artistic objects. On the ground floor of the church itself is a *screen in wood* that separates the narthex from the central chapel; according to Raouf Habib, it dates from the eighteenth century (1967, p. 65). A screen of the central sanctuary is made of pine wood and composed of panels inlaid with ebony and ivory and decorated with floral motifs. The screen of the south and north sanctuaries and altar of the second is made of wood and composed of panels inlaid with ivory and ebony and representing floral designs. The first dates from 1753, while the second dates from the Fatimid period (909–1171) according to modern authors; Raouf Habib (p. 70) mentions the altar surmounted by a low ciborium (see ARCHITECTURAL ELEMENTS).

An *ambo* in marble, resting on fifteen small columns, is situated in the northeast corner of the central nave; it bears an inscription in Coptic.

The extant remains of the wall painting on the southeast column of the central nave depict according to Meinardus (1969–1970, p. 140, pl. 11, B) a horseman, probably Saint Theodorus. The wall painting in the south nave is mentioned by Raouf Habib (p. 67) as the remains of mural painting. Wall paintings on the two columns situated on each side of the door of the screen of the central sanctuary are, according to Meinardus, the surviving remnants of paintings representing on the north column Christ holding the Gospel and blessing and on the south column the Holy Virgin holding the infant Jesus (pp. 140–41, pl. 12 A–B).

In the central sanctuary, the altar is surmounted by a ciborium in wood, supported by four marble columns. The lower part of the ciborium represents Christ surrounded by the symbols of the four evangelists. The sanctuary ends in the east with an apse, the upper part of which is painted with Christ in a mandorla, supported by two angels. In the middle of the lower part and behind the episcopal chair is a niche in which Christ is painted enthroned, holding the Gospel and blessing. The twelve apostles are represented on each side. Above the arch of the niche are painted in the middle a seraph and on either side of him the angel Gabriel and the Virgin of the Annunciation.

In the time of Butler the baptismal fonts occupied the eastern part of the south nave, surmounted by a ciborium. Today they are in the south sanctuary itself, dedicated to the archangel Raphael (1884, pp. 115–16). Butler also speaks of having found in a chapel outside the principal church a chalice casket, which the priest of the church caused to be placed in the north sanctuary (1884, pp. 109–10, 117). It is a box in the form of a cube with an opening in the upper part; it is dated to 1563. The four sides of this box are covered with paintings representing Christ, the Virgin carrying the infant Jesus, the Annunciation, and the priest Zosimus giving communion to Saint Mary the Egyptian. On the walls and the beams above the wooden screens icons are suspended.

In the Chapel of Saint George on the ceiling of the south triforium and on the side of the choir one may see the remains of a sculpture in wood, described by Butler (p. 123) and dating from the thirteenth century. On the north side and a little farther forward, one sees the remains of an ambo in wood, fitted into the wall and accessible by a ladder. Raouf Habib (p. 73) dates it to the twelfth or thirteenth century. The niche fitted up in the east wall of the sanctuary contains the painting of Christ seated, holding the Gospel and blessing; He is surrounded by a mandorla. On each side are two medallions containing what may be two human busts (Meinardus, p. 139, pl. 10, A).

Mural paintings of the north triforium include a hollow in the north wall, in which a fresco represents an angel, probably the archangel Suriel according to the Coptic inscription underneath, which recalls the name of the donor. On the outside north wall one may still distinguish remains of painting (Meinardus, p. 125, pl. 7 A).

In the northeast group of secondary chapels on the ground floor the north sanctuary is consecrated to Saint James Intercisus and contains a screen in wood. Above it and on the eastern wall is an inscription in Cufic characters, dated to the tenth century. Remains of wall painting are preserved to the right of this inscription (Meinardus, pp. 139–40, pls. 10 B; 11 A). Butler (p. 118) speaks of having seen in this sanctuary the altar covered with a marble plaque in the form of a horseshoe. The central and south sanctuaries, consecrated, respectively, to Saint John the Baptist and Saint George, each have a screen that derives from the chapel of Saint George, situated in the south triforium of the Church of Saint Mercurius. According to modern authors, they date from between the tenth to the twelfth centuries. To the south of the naves is the baptistery, closed by a screen in wood of the Fatimid period, which, according to Butler (pp. 123–24), belongs to the same chapel mentioned above. The baptismal fonts are constructed of masonry.

In the naves of the first story one can distinguish the remains of wall painting, a saint blessing and holding the keys, and an inscription (Meinardus, pp. 134–35, pls. 6 A–B). The north sanctuary, closed by a screen, contains a ciborium already in ruins. In the niche in the east wall, the Holy Virgin is represented with the infant Jesus. The central sanctuary, according to Butler (p. 120), contains a remarkable screen. Its ciborium is abandoned in a corner. The south sanctuary has a screen, and the ciborium is in situ.

In the *northwest group* is the chapel dedicated to the Virgin, containing three sanctuaries that are separated from the naves by a screen in wood, above which is suspended a range of icons representing the twelve apostles. The altar is surmounted by a painted ciborium. The apse of the east wall is painted with the Ascension, deliberately damaged. In the upper register is Christ enthroned, holding the Gospel and blessing; he is surrounded by a mandorla supported by the four animals of the Apocalypse; and on each side are two angels in adoration. In the lower register the Virgin is represented in the middle, in an orant position, surrounded by twelve apostles (Meinardus, pp. 136–39, pls. 7 B; 8 A–B; 9 A). According to Butler (p. 121) the niche of the south sanctuary is decorated with the Baptism of Christ, a painting that, according to Meinardus (p. 139, pl. 9 B), must be dated to the eighteenth or nineteenth century.

The Coptic Museum possesses various pieces of woodwork deriving from this church (see Coquin, 1971, p. 35): a door of wood, composed of panels inlaid with ebony, probably from the twelfth century; a screen of wood composed of two leaves; a panel in wood representing the figure of a holy personage, sculpted in relief, dating from the twelfth century; a frame in wood composed of panels sculpted in relief, bearing an inscription in Cufic, dating from the twelfth century; and an altar plaque in pine wood, dating from the fourteenth or fifteenth century.

BIBLIOGRAPHY

Butler, A. J. *The Ancient Coptic Churches of Egypt*, 2 vols. Oxford, 1884.

Casanova, P. *Essai de reconstitution topographique de la ville d'al Foustat ou Misr.* Mémoires publiés par les membres de l'Institut français d'Archéologie orientale du Caire 35. Cairo, 1919.

Coquin, C. *Les Edifices chrétiens du Vieux-Caire,* Vol. 1: *Bibliographie et topographie historiques.* Bibliotheque d'études coptes 11. Cairo, 1974.

Meinardus, O. "The Mediaeval Wall-paintings in the Coptic Churches of Old Cairo." *Bulletin de la Société d'archéologie copte* 20 (1969–1970):119–41.

Raouf Habib. *The Ancient Coptic Churches of Cairo: A Short Account.* Cairo, 1967.

Simaykah, M. H. *Guide to the Coptic Museum and the Principal Ancient Churches and Convents I* (in Arabic). Cairo, 1930.

CHARLAMBIA COQUIN

CHURCH OF AL-'ADHRA'. *See* Balyanā, al-; Dayr al-'Adhra'; Jabal al-Tayr.

CHURCH ARCHITECTURE IN EGYPT. Only church buildings can be considered as a confessional type of structure—like the cultic buildings of pagans, Jews, and Muslims. Churches are a specifically Christian type of architecture. All other kinds of building—including funerary structures—have no confessional ties and take the same form among Christians as among people of other faiths in the same period.

Corresponding to the requirements of Christian worship, church buildings have two fundamentally different areas: (1) the sanctuary, often several rooms with the altar as the central point and the place of the actual ceremonial, placed in all extant monuments from Egypt in the east; and (2) the nave, as a rule very spacious and generally with several aisles, as the place in which the laity attend the preparatory part of the liturgy as onlookers. Generally the sanctuary consists of a central apse with side chambers disposed on either side. In simple buildings there is instead of the apse a simple rectangular cultic niche. In addition, more ample types of room like the triconch are also found.

Whatever their outward form, these cultic niches are open to the west, toward the nave, for almost their entire width. In ordinary parish churches the altar stands in front of the opening. It is surrounded in turn by a screen that projects slightly into the nave. In monastery churches the altar is frequently set up in the cultic niche itself, perhaps reflecting a primitive usage. The screen then lies in the area of the front opening.

The nave or naos (Greek, temple), the area assigned to the laity, is considerably larger than the sanctuary, and accordingly is usually constructed with several aisles. Some of the large churches, like the cathedral church of al-Ashmūnayn and the great basilica of ABŪ MĪNĀ, have a transept. The several aisles are separated by rows of columns, or pillars connected by arcades; in rare cases, they are also separated by architraves. Very often the pillars were walled up with stones and bricks. West of the area for the laity—at least in the early buildings—there is a narthex and in some cases also an atrium.

Early Christian Period

No church buildings from the fourth century A.D. have so far been discovered, with the exception of a few not yet explored. Hence from an archaeological point of view, Christian architecture in Egypt begins with the fifth century. There must have been earlier buildings, but they have perished. Presumably they were for the most part only simple buildings of mud brick which in time were replaced by new structures. Large monumental buildings were to be found in the fourth century perhaps only in the capital, Alexandria.

The oldest churches so far discovered are a few small buildings of the early fifth century from the region of the KELLIA on the western edge of the Delta. These are modest houses of prayer designed to meet the needs of monks vowed to the principle of poverty. Thus they are not representative of the architecture of this period. However, these early examples of Egyptian church building do have a sanctuary with three sections. In buildings with a single aisle the sanctuary is consequently wider than the naos. In all churches of the Kellia the altar stands in the inner part of the cultic niche, which here is rectangular.

Alongside these simple monastic churches there must have been a few more advanced buildings, for even before the middle of the fifth century some large buildings were erected at Ashmūnayn, Faw al-Qiblī (PBOW), and Suhāj; these are inconceivable without corresponding earlier buildings. They represent the highest architectural achievement of their time, and have a fully developed architectural design that was later only slightly altered. Characteristic is the basilica construction of the naos with several aisles, along with the western return aisle peculiar to early Christian building methods in Egypt, and a narthex lying to the west of it. From this at least one door leads into the naos; generally there are three. An atrium is only rarely found and, in the buildings mentioned, appears only in the cathedral church at al-Ashmūnayn (Hermopolis

Magna). All the buildings have a sanctuary with several chambers, the main chamber consisting of a cultic niche developed as an apse. In the church of DAYR ANBĀ SHINŪDAH in Suhāj the cultic niche has the form of a triconch. In addition, the churches mentioned—apart perhaps from the monastery churches in Faw al-Qiblī, still not definitively investigated—each had a gallery usually reached by a flight of steps. The two superimposed churches at Faw al-Qiblī were certainly constructed with five aisles, which elsewhere was the case only in the basilica of Armant and some smaller buildings in Madīnat Māḍī and Makhūrah. The cathedral of al-Ashmūnayn, moreover, is furnished with a three-aisle transept, the sides of which unusually end in a semicircle. This design should not, however, be confused with a triconch. In the last quarter of the fifth and the early sixth centuries a transept of this kind appears again in the church of Hawwāriyyah and in the great basilica of Abū Mīnā, the largest church building in Egyptian territory, but here the side wings have a straight termination.

While these large buildings of the fifth century have in the sanctuary a relatively extensive and complicated groundplan, perhaps resulting from the size of the space available, by the fifth century there was in the smaller buildings a canonical group of three chambers. As a rule, this group consists of a semicircular apse and two rectangular side rooms, of which at least one could be directly entered from the naos. Exceptions in which the side rooms are missing occur so far only in the area of Maryūt. In the buildings that have a cultic niche developed as a triconch, the side chambers are brought round the side conches in the shape of a gamma. In addition, it was common, particularly in Upper Egypt and evidently as early as the late fifth century, to place before the cultic niche an additional triumphal arch supported by two free-standing columns (*see* DANDARAH). With the exception of the churches in the great laura of the Kellia, the altar now always stands in front of the cultic niche and is surrounded by a low screen. In the area of the naos, the churches of the fifth century almost always have numerous niches, which are symmetrically distributed on the walls, with or without a decorative framework, and provide the reason for the often enormous strength of the walls in most Egyptian churches. This custom holds for Upper and Lower Egypt, irrespective of whether the buildings are of brick or stone. It is only in the buildings of the Maryūt region, which were evidently more strongly influenced by the general architecture of the empire, that these wall niches are not found.

In the sixth century, the form of the basilica remained roughly the same. The buildings, however, became more uniform, and no further large buildings were erected. Instead, especially in the coastal region, there are some churches with a centralized shape, which bear a close resemblance to the four-conch buildings of Syria and Asia Minor, and were probably influenced by these (Grossmann, 1977, pp. 35ff.). So far, two examples have become known from the region of Abū Mīnā. In Upper Egypt in the same period or a little later there appear a few four-pillar churches with an ambulatory (Grossmann, 1979, pp. 86ff.) that strikingly extended their influence to the architecture of Nubia in particular and there found numerous successors (see NUBIAN CHRISTIAN ARCHITECTURE).

Early Middle Ages

The early Middle Ages in Egypt began roughly with the Arab conquest of the country (A.D. 639–641) (*see* ARAB CONQUEST OF EGYPT). During this period church building showed only a continuation of the normal basilica structure, which down to the Fatimid period belonged to the type of church most frequently built, although dimensions became smaller. With the passing of late antiquity, there was an increasing tendency to enhance the division between the sacral area and that of the laity, probably because of an intensified sacralization of the liturgical ceremony. In front of the sanctuary a special room (*khūrus*) reserved for the clergy was separated from the naos, and from about the eighth century, it was divided from the rest of the nave by a high partition wall. In the middle of the wall was one wide opening that could be closed by a curtain. The room thus formed contained the altar, where all ceremony took place out of the sight of the laity. In older churches not yet equipped with a *khūrus* of this kind, it was subsequently built in, although it required strange architectural compromises. By its very nature a wide room, the *khūrus* opened in the middle of its east wall into the apse, usually covered over by a semicupola. If the side wings were given a similar form of vaulting, they could be combined with the apse into the form of a triconch, which was frequently the case. One of the earliest examples is the al-ʿAdhra' Church of DAYR AL-SURYĀN in the Wādī al-Naṭrūn, which dates from perhaps as early as the eighth century.

The High Middle Ages (Fatimid Period)

The period of the high Middle Ages, roughly contemporary with the Fatimid rule, must rank as the golden age of church building in Egypt. It was in this period that the most important buildings were constructed. In general, the arrangement of the sanctuary in these buildings corresponds to that of the preceding period, but the disposition of the rooms became tighter and more harmonious. All the chambers—including the cultic niche—were now rectangular. Moreover, since in this period all new buildings were provided with a *khūrus* from the outset, there was no need for the kind of improvisation frequently found in older buildings.

In the area of the nave, however, the development of church building took a fundamentally new direction. As in Byzantine and Islamic architecture, there was a change in Egypt from the wooden roof to vaulting. It was regarded as more economical and less flammable. That the construction of vaults was possible only in the case of smaller buildings was of no consequence, since people had already grown accustomed to smaller church buildings in the preceding period. In addition, the galleries were largely abandoned in this period.

The adoption of vaulting applied in the first place to the area of the nave. Here, strangely, Lower and Upper Egypt followed different paths. Lower Egypt preferred barrel-vaulting. It had the advantage that the directional thrust proper to the basilica remained unaffected. Upper Egypt preferred domes. Since, however, as in Lower Egypt, the ground plan of the basilica was at first retained, this led—in connection with the roofing of the central aisle—to the use of two domed areas linked for internal communication by a great arch. Further arched entries opened into the side aisles, which were themselves constructed as barrel-vaulted areas running along the domed central areas on either side. In this way a new type of building came into being—the elongated church with a domed main aisle. Examples include, among others, the monastery churches of the DAYR ANBĀ HADRĀ at Aswān, Dayr al-Shuhadā' (Isnā), and DAYR MĀR BUQṬUR (Qamulah). A building in Cairo is found in the *parekklesion* of the Menas church, while other examples can be seen even in Nubia (Tamīṭ, Faras).

In the following period the elongated, domed church went through a singular development presumably conditioned by the structural laws of domed vaulting. The two domed areas, at first regarded as of equal status, eventually became rivals, and in the course of further development this led to a stunting of the rearmost area. In the final phase, toward the end of the twelfth century, it became a small transversally oriented side room, or it entirely disappeared, with the result that this building became a central structure with a single dome.

Alongside these structures, which still stand in clear relation to the preceding basilica form, a second type of building was developed in the early Fatimid period, which was close to the Greek type of octagon-domed churches, and whose origin is probably also to be traced to Byzantine influence. This was a central building roofed over by a dome of unusually wide span (by comparison with other buildings of the period), the dome being carried by eight supports partly set into the side walls. This type is found in its present form in the church of the DAYR AL-SHAYKHAH at Aswan. Here it was developed as a double belt building with an ambulatory running around three sides. The ambulatory was matched by two chambers set at the sides of the sanctuary, which gave the sanctuary the deceptive appearance of a fivefold arrangement. The two outer chambers had nothing to do with the internal arrangement of the sanctuary. There are examples of single-belt, octagon-domed churches at Dayr al-Quṣayr (Ṭurah) and Kulb in Nubia.

Late Middle Ages and Modern Period

The last phase of Egyptian church building is represented by a simple four-pillar church, which at a cautious estimate can be identified from about the Mamluk period. Its spatial arrangement consists of nine bays of approximately the same size, usually roofed with cupolas, of which the central dome is emphasized by its richer development and greater height. This type is the result of a further development from the elongated, domed church, but it is also based upon influences from the Byzantine world. Apart from the uniform inner arrangement of the church, which is probably to be traced to Islamic influence, it shows many similarities to the Byzantine cross-in-square churches.

The program of the chambers, which in the older examples still employ a *khūrus* (*see* DAYR AL-SHAHĪD TADRUS AL-MUḤĀRĪB), rests unmistakably on Egyptian tradition. In further development, the *khūrus* gradually fell out of use, while the altar was moved back into the cultic niche, where it had already stood at one time in some monastery churches of the early period. The reason for this development was undoubtedly the frequency of masses from the Mamluk period on. Since according to the Coptic rite, it is forbidden to celebrate the mass at the same altar more than once in a day (*Nomocanon* of Michael of Damietta), there was need for a larger number of altar places, the reason for changing the side chambers of the sanctuary into additional smaller sanctuaries. With such an alteration of the traditional arrangement of the sanctuary, any understanding of the significance of the *khūrus* was also lost. The decline in the number of the faithful from the Mamluk period had the same effect. The sometimes greatly shriveled congregations felt the traditional distribution of the church building unnecessarily extravagant. So it was that toward the end of the Mamluk period the *khūrus* was eliminated. In place of the former dividing wall of the *khūrus* now appears the *ḥijāb* (iconostasis), to be set up at the entrance to the altar chamber, a form of structure that persists today.

[*See also:* Architectural Elements of Churches.]

BIBLIOGRAPHY

Bourguet, P. du. *The Art of the Copts*, trans. Caryll Hay Shaw. New York, 1971.

Clarke, S. *Christian Antiquities in the Nile Valley*. Oxford, 1912.

Grossmann, P. "Abu Mena Ailik vorläufige Berichte Kampagnen 1975 and 1976." *Mitteilungen des Deutschen Archäologischen Instituts Abteilung Kairo* 33 (1977): 35–45.

———. "Zur christlichen Baukunst in Ägypten." *Enchoria* 9 (1978):135–146.

———. *Elephantine II*. Mainz, 1979.

———. *Mittelalterliche Langhauskuppelkirchen und verwandte Typen in Oberägypten*. Glückstadt, 1982.

———. "Neue Frühchristliche Funde aus Ägypten." *Actes du XIe congrès international d'archéologie chrétienne, Lyon 21–28 septembre 1986. Vol. 2, pp. 1843–1908. Paris, 1989.*

Monneret de Villard, U. *Deyr el-Muharraqah*. Milan, 1928.

———. "Le basilica cristiano in Egitto." In *Atti del IV congresso internazionale di archeologia cristiana Città di Vaticano* (1938), Vol. 1, pp. 291–319. Rome, 1940.

Walters, C. C. *Monastic Archaeology in Egypt*. Warminster, 1974.

CHURCH ARCHITECTURE IN NUBIA.

See Nubian Christian Architecture.

CHURCH ART.

In Coptic churches, the apse rounds the *haykal* (sanctuary) off at the east, the direction the Christian faces to pray. For this reason the apse was one of the first parts of the church building to be decorated, and its iconography had specific requirements, partly inspired by the liturgy itself. Although a complete list of all the apse programs in the Nile Valley does not now exist, it can be established that a double composition that has survived in small apselike niches—probably dating from the eighth century—in monastery cells in BĀWĪṬ and Saqqara, which are also found in apses of churches, was extremely popular. In the upper part Christ is depicted seated on his throne or throne-chariot, surrounded by a mandorla, by the Four Bodiless Beasts, and by other angels, by sun, moon, and stars; the composition was inspired by Isaiah 6, Ezekiel 1, and Revelation 4. In the lower zone is His mother, flanked by apostles and angels, or by angels and other saints. The ranks of the apostles are sometimes extended to include local saints. Mary may be portrayed as orant, as an enthroned *hodigitria* (guide), as *platytera* (the one who is wider), or as *galactotrophousa* (virgin in lactation). Often the two zones were separated by a wide band in between.

There is little agreement about the meaning of this double theme. The theme has been called an ascension (Ihm, 1960, pp. 100–102), or a representation of Christ's coming again at the Last Day, or both, or of Christ enthroned and reigning in glory as Lord of the Church (Klauser, 1961). F. van der Meer (1938, pp. 255ff.) calls the upper zone a "theophany of the trishagion," but this title has met with little response, partly because it leaves the lower zone out of account. To interpret the double theme as an ascension has the disadvantage of assuming the influence of one particular feast—and a comparatively recent one—to have occupied a place of honor in the liturgical scheme. This can be regarded as an argument against an eschatological explanation as well.

A nonhistorical interpretation, on the other hand, is more likely to receive support, especially because in light of early Christian literature it appears less forced. Without specific reference to any particular liturgical feast, both Syrians (Ephraim and Jacob of Sarug) and Copts (Cyril and the *theotokia* [liturgical texts addressed to Mary]) celebrated the paradox of God's Son, who lies at Mary's breast and at the same time rules over earth and heaven, the One who in the heavens is borne by the chariot of the cherubim and here on earth by His earthly mother, Mary (van Moorsel, 1970, pp. 284–86). It has rightly been observed that this double theme appears to have been created as a conscious depiction of the orthodox doctrine of the person of Christ. But for the same writer to express amazement that this theme should be found in a monophysite setting reveals inadequate knowledge of Coptic Christology (Wellen, 1960, p. 164).

Where there was insufficient space in the apse of the church or in the niche of the cell, the double theme could be depicted in a reduced form. It already occurs in small apses at an early stage, at Saqqara, for instance; but we then still find the combination of Christ (sometimes shown as a half-figure) in the upper zone, and Mary, always flanked by angels and sometimes by saints, below. In some cases the figures in the lower zone are reduced to *imagines clipeatae* (medallion images).

Particularly in the small apses of cells, single themes are sometimes found: the Virgin and Child, flanked by angels or saints, or Christ enthroned, or Christ shown as a half-figure. The inscriptions merely give the names of the persons and personifications portrayed. Sometimes, however, one can read on the codex that Christ is holding in his hand the trisagion (van der Meer, 1938, p. 260) or the opening words of the gospel of John (Monneret de Villard, 1957, pl. 148), texts taken from the liturgy, which refer rather to a mystery than to a church feast, such as the Ascension.

BIBLIOGRAPHY

Brenk, B. *Tradition und Neuerung in der christlichen Kunst des ersten Jahrtausends.* Studien zur Geschichte des Weltgerichtsbildes. Vienna, 1966.

Dinkler, E., ed. *Kunst und Geschichte Nubiens in christlicher Zeit,* pp. 281–90. Recklinghausen, 1970.

______. "Analepsis." In *Studien zur spätantiken und byzantinischen Kunst.* Festschrift F. W. Deichmann, Vol. 3, pp. 137–41. Mainz, 1986.

Engemann, J. "Zu den Apsis-Tituli des Paulinus von Nola." *Jahrbuch für Antike und Christentum* 17 (1974):21–46.

Grabar, A. *Martyrium,* 2 vols. London, 1972.

Ihm, C. *Die Programme der christlichen Apsisma-*

Painting of the Virgin Mary holding the Christ child on her lap and flanked by the Twelve Apostles. Above Mary and the Twelve Apostles is the lower part of a scene of Christ in Glory. Bāwīṭ. Chapel XLII. *Courtesy Photographic Library of Byzantine Art, School of Applied Advanced Studies, Paris.*

lerei vom vierten Jahrhundert bis zur Mitte des achten Jahrhunderts*. Wiesbaden, 1960.

Klauser, T. Review of C. Ihm, *Die Programme. Jahrbuch für Antike und Christentum* 4 (1961):174–79.

Meer, F. van der. *Maiestas Domini.* Vatican City, 1938.

Monneret de Villard, U. *La Nubia medioevale,* Vol. 4. Cairo, 1957.

Moorsel, P. van. *Die stillende Gottesmutter und die Monophysiten.* In *Kunst und Geschichte Nubiens in christlicher Zeit,* ed. E. Dinkler, pp. 281–90. Recklinghausen, 1970.

Wellen, G. A. *Theotokos.* Utrecht and Antwerp, 1960.

PAUL VAN MOORSEL

CHURCH OF THE ASCENSION. *See* Jerusalem, Coptic See of.

CHURCH OF THE HOLY VIRGIN IN GETHSEMANE. *See* Jerusalem, Coptic See of.

CHURCH OF AL-KHANDAQ. *See* Dayr al-Khandaq.

CHURCH OF MĀR MINĀ. *See* Babylon.

CHURCH OF MICHAEL THE ARCHANGEL. *See* Jerusalem, Coptic See of.

CHURCH AND MONASTERY OF SAINT ANTONY (JAFFA). *See* Holy Land, Coptic Churches in the.

CHURCH AND MONASTERY OF SAINT ANTONY (JERICHO). *See* Holy Land, Churches in the.

CHURCH OF AL-MUʿALLAQAH (Old Cairo). This church is called in Coptic manuscripts "the church of Saint Mary, Mother of God, at Babylon in Egypt" (Amélineau, 1893, pp. 577–79). Texts in Arabic describe it as the "church of our Lady Mary, surnamed the hanging." European travelers have called it "the church of the column" or "the church of the staircase" (see Coquin, 1974, pp. 65, 74–75, 77–79).

Church of al-Muʿallaqah. Interior. *Courtesy A. Held.*

This church is situated to the south of the modern city of Cairo, at QAṢR AL-SHAMʿ (Old Cairo), occupying the south and southwest bastions of the ancient Roman fortress often called BABYLON (Coquin, pp. 65, 76–77; Simaykah, 1930, p. 20). According to some Arab historians of the fourteenth century a mosque was erected under the church of al-Muʿallaqah (Coquin, p. 77).

Church of al-Muʿallaqah (Old Cairo). Interior. *Courtesy A. Held.*

The different constructions surviving may be divided into two parts: that of the southeast, which is probably the primitive church, situated above the south bastions of the fortress and now containing a chapel and a baptistery, and that to the north of it, which is the principal church, of basilica plan.

The primitive church in the time of Butler was divided into three chapels and a baptistery (1884, pp. 224–28). The first chapel adjoining the south nave of the principal church is dedicated to the Ethiopian saint Takla Haymanot.

According to modern authors, the original part of the church of al-Muʿallaqah was built between the third and seventh centuries (Coquin, p. 66), although we have no historical source attesting the antiquity of this adaptation of the Roman bastion.

Modern authors date the construction of the principal church to the fifth or seventh century (Coquin, p. 66), while an Arab legend attributes it to Belsa (Balthasar), son of Nebuchadnezzar and a Coptic woman.

A first destruction and immediate restoration of the church is attested under the patriarch YUSĀB I (830–849). A second restoration took place under the patriarch ABRAHAM (975–978) and the caliph al-Muʿizz li-Dīn Allāh (952–975). Under the patriarch ZACHARIAH (1004–1032) the caliph al-ḤĀKIM (996–1021) had the al-Muʿallaqah church surrounded by a wall to prohibit access. Shortly afterward the church was sacked, and its closing was ordered by the Sultan al-Mālik al-Kāmil. Some modern authors mention the plundering of the church, as well as a precious chalice buried under the altar (Coquin, p. 67). The church was plundered once again under al-Ashraf Khalīl, 1290–1293). At the beginning of the fourteenth century the al-Muʿallaqah was closed anew, and reopened due to the intervention in 1301 of the emperor of Byzantium, as al-Maqrīzī and Abū al-Barakāt IBN KABAR record (see Coquin, p. 68). Later the church underwent in turn closures, burning, partial destructions, and restorations, as the Arab historians bear witness. Since the end of the nineteenth century, the Committee for the Conservation of the Monuments of Arab Art has been carrying out repairs and various works in this church.

The church of al-Muʿallaqah from the time of the patriarch CHRISTODOULUS (1047–1077) was the place of the election, consecration, or enthronement of the patriarchs of Alexandria. This lasted down to the patriarch JOHN VIII (1300–1320). It was also the patriarchal residence from the time of the patriarch MĪKHĀ'ĪL IV (1092–1102) to the reign of the patriarch THEODOSIUS II (1294–1300), and the place of burial of several patriarchs (Coquin, pp. 70–71, 79). Synods were held in this church as well as ordinations; the patriarchs from CYRIL II (1078–1092) to JOHN VIII (1300–1320) consecrated the chrism there.

The Holy Family is said to have dwelt in this church at the time of its passage to Babylon in Egypt. The relics of Saint Martin and Saint Barbara are found there.

Among the significant objects that belong, or have belonged, to the al-Muʿallaqah church are the following: The screens in wood that separate the three sanctuaries from the naves of the principal church are inlaid with ivory and composed of crosswise designs. According to modern authors they date from the eleventh to the thirteenth centuries. The wood screen of the chapel of Takla Haymanot is composed of panels inlaid with ivory and dates from the thirteenth century.

According to nineteenth-century authors, a lintel in wood from the entrance door of the principal church was still in place. It represents in relief the triumphal entry of Christ into Jerusalem on the left, and the Ascension of Christ on the right. It dates from the fourth to the sixth centuries. At present it is deposited in the Coptic Museum in Old Cairo.

Three wooden doors are composed of panels, sculpted in relief, and inlaid with ebony and ivory. They date from the eleventh to the fourteenth centuries. At present they are in the Coptic Museum in Old Cairo.

Greville Chester (1872, p. 128) noted two leaves of a door in wood in a small place situated between the central and north sanctuaries. This door contains ten wooden panels sculpted in relief and representing scenes drawn from the life of Christ. They date from the thirteenth century. They are now deposited in the British Museum in London (Dalton, 1901).

Another wooden door is situated almost in the middle of the south wall of the south nave of the principal church of al-Muʿallaqah, by which one enters the early church. It is of pine wood, inlaid with ivory, and dates from the eleventh century.

Regarding altars and their ciboria in the principal church, Greville Chester (p. 128) wrote he had seen above the altar of the south sanctuary a ciborium in wood, supported by columns in marble. Butler (1884) noted that he did not see the ancient altars, for they were already demolished. But he observed in the north sanctuary two altar tables in white marble, which would probably have belonged to the north and south sanctuaries. One of them had the form of a horseshoe, while the second had a rectangular form, in the middle of which a hole was pierced. He also says that the altar of the central sanctuary was of "the ordinary type." According to the information from the priest, the ancient altars must have been replaced by slabs upheld by small columns. The author also affirms having seen two ancient ciboria, which formerly surmounted the altars, but time and neglect had damaged the condition of the prettily painted figures. One of these altar ciboria in wood, dated to the tenth/eleventh century, is in the Coptic Museum in Old Cairo.

Describing the altars and their ciboria, modern authors must refer to those that replaced the ancient ones at the end of the nineteenth century.

Against the first column on the north side of the central nave of the principal church is placed an ambo supported by five columns. It is decorated with mosaics and crosses in relief. Modern authors attribute it to the tenth century.

Describing the altar and ciborium of the chapel of Takla Haymanot, Greville Chester (1872, p. 129) speaks of an altar covered with a circular slab, in the middle of which is carved a cross. Butler (1884, Vol. 1, p. 225) mentions the ciborium that had just replaced the old one.

Ivory inlaid screen of the sanctuary dedicated to Saint George. Church of al-Muʿallaqah (Old Cairo). *Courtesy Arab Republic of Egypt.*

Door from the Church of al-Muʿallaqah. *Courtesy Arab Republic of Egypt.*

The baptismal fonts in granite are located in a hollow in the south wall of the primitive church and surmounted by a niche adorned with mosaics.

Beginning from the narthex, on the fourth column of the row that separates the central nave from the south nave, a mural decoration depicts an angel standing, full-face, beardless, and bearing the nimbus and the diadem; his name is partially effaced.

The south sanctuary ends in an apse, the lower part of which is decorated with designs, inlaid with marble of different colors, while the upper part is decorated with designs in plaster. The niche in the middle of the apse represents a cross, inlaid with marble. Russell, 1962, p. 88, dates this niche to the twelfth century.

In the Chapel of Takla Haymanot, the flat apse in the east wall contains in two registers separated by a horizontal inscription in Coptic (Ps. 121:1–2) the following representations: in the middle of the upper register the Holy Virgin is painted in distemper, standing on a pedestal, holding Christ in her arms. On the two sides remnants survive of two figures, probably angels in adoration. In the lower register stand the twenty-four elders of the Apocalypse, seen full-face and clothed in the sacerdotal habit. Their heads are haloed, and each holds in his right hand a censer and in the left an object that cannot be identified.

In the course of work carried out in 1983 a wall painting representing the Nativity of Christ was discovered.

The library of the al-Mu'allaqah church appears to have possessed manuscripts of a theological, liturgical, and hagiographical order. These are now deposited in the Coptic Museum in Old Cairo and in the Coptic Patriarchate.

BIBLIOGRAPHY

Amélineau. E. *La Géographie de l'Egypte à l'époque copte*. Paris, 1893.

Butler, A. J. *The Ancient Coptic Churches of Egypt*, 2 vols. Oxford, 1884.

Coquin, C. *Les Edifices chrétiens du Vieux-Caire*, Vol. 1: *Bibliographie et topographie historiques*. Bibliothèque d'études coptes 11. Cairo, 1974.

Dalton, D. M. *Catalogue of Early Christian Antiquities and Objects from the Christian East in the British Museum*. London, 1901.

Meinardus, O. "The Twenty-Four Elders of the Apocalypse in the Iconography of the Coptic Church." *Studia Orientalia Christiana Collectanea* 13 (1968–1969):141–57.

______. "The Mediaeval Wall-paintings in the Coptic Churches of Old Cairo." *Bulletin de la Société d'archéologie copte* 20 (1969–1970):119–41.

Murtada ibn al-Afif. *Merveilles d'Egypte*, ed. P. Vattier. Paris, 1666.

Russell, D. *Mediaeval Cairo and the Monasteries of the Wadi Natrun: A Historical Guide*. London, 1962.

Simaykah, M. H. *Guide to the Coptic Museum and the Principal Ancient Churches and Convents I* (in Arabic). Cairo, 1930.

______. *Guide sommaire du Musée Copte et des principales églises du Caire*. Cairo, 1937.

CHARALAMBIA COQUIN

CHURCH OF THE NATIVITY. *See* Holy Land, Coptic Churches in the.

CHURCH OF QASRIYAT AL-RIHAN. *See* Babylon.

CHURCH OF QUEEN HILANA. *See* Jerusalem, Coptic See of.

CHURCH OF SAINT ANDREW. *See* Holy Land, Coptic Churches in the.

CHURCH OF SAINT ANTONY. *See* Jerusalem, Coptic See of.

CHURCH OF SAINT ANTONY (JAFFA). *See* Holy Land, Coptic Churches in the.

CHURCH OF SAINT ANTONY (JERICHO). *See* Holy Land, Coptic Churches in the.

CHURCH OF SAINT GEORGE. *See* Jerusalem, Coptic See of.

CIASCA, AGOSTINO (1835–1902), Italian Coptologist and Orientalist. Ciasca was born at Polignano a Mare, near Bari. He became prefect of the Vatican Archives and was named a cardinal in 1899. He traveled to Egypt in 1879 and acquired manuscripts for the Borgia Museum. He edited in two volumes Sahidic biblical fragments under the title *Sacrorum bibliorum fragmenta copto-sahidica Musei Borgiani* (Rome, 1885–1889; vol. 3 published by P. J. Balestri 1904, including facsimiles and atlas). Apart from this major work, he published the papyrus fragments of the same museum under the title *I papiri copti del Museo Borgiano . . . tradotti e commentati* (Rome, 1881). He died in Rome.

BIBLIOGRAPHY

Guidi, I. "Ciasca, Agostino." *Enciclopedia Italiana*, Vol. 10, p. 193. Rome, 1935–1939.

Kammerer, W., comp. *A Coptic Bibliography*. Ann Arbor, Mich., 1950; repr. New York, 1969.

AZIZ S. ATIYA

CIBORIUM. *See* Architectural Elements of Churches.

CIRCUMCISION, FEAST OF THE. *See* Feasts, Minor.

CLARKE, SOMERS (1841–1926), English architect and archaeologist. He was born in Brighton and received his training in church restoration in the office of Sir Gilbert Scott. In 1922 he retired to Egypt, where he lived until his death. There he worked with J. E. QUIBELL and Frederick W. Green in the excavations at Hierakonpolis, and later he was involved in the restoration of many temples. His main contribution in the field of Coptic studies is *Christian Antiquities in the Nile Valley* (Oxford, 1912).

BIBLIOGRAPHY

Dawson, W. P. and E. P. Uphill. *Who Was Who in Egyptology,* p. 65. London, 1972.

Kammerer, W., comp. *A Coptic Bibliography.* Ann Arbor, Mich., 1950; repr. New York, 1969.

AZIZ S. ATIYA

CLAUDIUS, SAINT. This anchorite saint (feast day, 19 Amshīr) is known from various documents: (1) the typica of Dayr Anbā Shinūdah, known as the White Monastery (Insinger, 38c–d, Pleyte and Boeser, 1897, p. 199; Oxford, Bodleian Hunt. 3); (2) a colophon (National Library, Paris, Coptic 129/19, fol. 55v, published by Van Lantschoot, 1929, no. 81), which indicates that a church was dedicated to him conjointly with Seth, abbot of the monastery situated to the south of the White Monastery; and (3) the life of Thomas of Jinjif (National Library, Paris, Arabic 263, fol. 113).

This saint is absent from the SYNAXARION of the Copts, but his name is mentioned in the calendar of the White Monastery. We know only that he was a count (Oxford, Bodleian Hunt. 3) and a contemporary of Shenute. His mention indicates that anchorites were venerated equally with cenobites by the monks of the White Monastery and that consequently the anchorite life was recognized even in Pachomian cenobitism (see MONASTICISM, PACHOMIAN).

BIBLIOGRAPHY

Lantschoot, A. van. *Recueil des colophons des manuscrits chrétiens d'Egypte.* Bibliothèque du Muséon 1. Louvain, 1929.

Pleyte, W., and P. A. A. Boeser. *Manuscrits coptes du Musée d'Antiquités des Pays-Bas à Leide.* Leiden, 1897.

RENÉ-GEORGES COQUIN

CLAUDIUS LABĪB. *See* Iqlādyūs labīb.

CLEDAT, JEAN (Périgueux, France, 7 May 1872–Bouch [Dordogne], France, 29 July 1943), French Egyptologist and Coptologist. He acquired a solid grounding in Paris (including the Ecole des Beaux Arts) and, in 1898 and 1899, published his first studies in Egyptology and Coptology that dealt with both the texts and the archaeology. Clédat arrived in Egypt in 1900 and worked there until 1914, when he was recalled to France for military service. Missions for the Egyptian Antiquities Service, the Suez Canal Company, the Institut français d'Archéologie orientale, and the Comité de l'Art Arabe took him from Middle Egypt to Elephantine Island (Aswan) and to the Delta, as well as to the Eastern Desert. They led him to alternate excavations with writing reports on pharaonic, Coptic, or Roman sites. The exposition of the results that Clédat obtained on one sector of the monastery at Bāwīṭ in 1902 and 1916 revealed its richness, and remains an indispensable reference. In 1911 he was the first curator of the museum at Ismailia. The consequences of a serious illness contracted during World War I put an end to a career already rich in accomplishment but still full of promise. The state of his health permitted Clédat to produce a few publications until 1922.

Some of Clédat's important works are: *Le Monastère et la nécropole de Baouît,* Vol. 1 issued in two parts (Cairo, 1904–1906); and *Nécropole de Qantarah* (*fouilles de mai 1914*) (Paris, 1916). He also published a number of journal articles relating to the Copts.

PIERRE DU BOURGUET, S.J.

CLEMENT, CANONS OF. *See* Canons of Clement.

CLEMENT I, SAINT, bishop of Rome at the end of the first century and the second successor to Peter. A certain number of works are attributed to him in the Greek literary tradition, works whose authenticity has been widely discussed in modern criticism. Of these, there is only one that can be cited as genuine, and this ascription can be made only with great probability, not certainty. This work is the *First Epistle of Clement* (*ad Corinthios*), which is addressed in the name of the entire Roman community and which CLEMENT OF ALEXANDRIA knew as being by Clement of Rome. It deals with many theological and moral problems, and concludes with a long prayer.

However, other works attributed to Clement are spurious, including the so-called *Second Epistle of Clement* (*ad Corinthios*). In reality this work is probably a homily, likely contemporaneous with the *Shepherd* of *Hermas,* and it can thus be dated to the first half of the second century. There are two other letters of doubtful origin ascribed to Clement, the *Epistles on Virginity.* These are known in their entirety from a Syriac translation and Greek excerpts compiled by Antiochus of Saint Saba (c. 620). These *Epistulae*, though separated, actually form one single work that may be dated to the first half of the third century. The text discusses monastic problems in general and the community life of both monks and nuns in particular. A fourth-century writing, also attributed to Clement of Rome, is the redaction of two collections: the *Homilies* and the *Recognitions*, which may be classified among the apocryphal acts of the apostles.

From the above-mentioned works, two have reached us in Coptic: an Akhmimic translation of the *First Epistle of Clement* and fragments from a Sahidic translation of the *Epistle on Virginity*. The *First Epistle* has come to us in a complete manuscript, probably from the White Monastery (Dayr Anbā Shinūdah) (Staatsbibliothek, Berlin, Or. fol. 3065), and in another, fragmentary manuscript (ed. Rösch, 1910). Carl Schmidt has prepared an edition of this translation along with a broad study that reveals its great importance and antiquity. In any reconstruction of the Greek texts for this work—in Greek there are only two manuscripts (of which one is the celebrated Alexandrinus in the British Library)—Schmidt's research should certainly be considered alongside the Latin and Syriac versions. (Such a criterion was used by Diekamp in the second edition of Funk's *Patres Apostolici*.)

For the *Epistle on Virginity* we have only fragments of a Sahidic translation from the White Monastery (ed. Lefort, 1952). This particular manuscript poses a serious problem for any critical evaluation because the attribution concerning its author is in doubt. In all probability (unfortunately we cannot be certain about this), the text was attributed not to Clement but to Athanasius of Alexandria. The situation is complicated by the fact that another fragment, *Ad Virgines*, doubtlessly assigned to Athanasius, might directly follow this epistle, although there is no way to prove any possible continuity for these two works.

Therefore, the Coptic point of view poses three possible solutions: (1) there might have existed a translation of the first pseudo-Clementine *Epistle to Virgins*, which was attributed to him directly; (2) this translation was included in a collection of ascetic texts attributed to Athanasius, and consequently was also attributed to Athanasius rather than Clement; (3) the manuscript had been collected with other ascetic texts and compiled into one single work, which as one unit was attributed to Athanasius.

It can readily be seen how any one of these diverse solutions might in turn influence the ultimate solution to the problem of the origin of the pseudo-Clementine *Epistle on Virginity* (Syriac, or perhaps Egyptian), and further, how such a solution would then affect those problems concerning the origin of other ascetic writings by Athanasius. We may never find a satisfactory solution to the problem.

BIBLIOGRAPHY

Funk, F. X. *Patres Apostolici*, 2 vols., 2nd ed. F. Diekamp. Tübingen, 1901–1913.

Lefort, L. T. *Les Pères apostoliques en copte*. CSCO 37–38. Paris, 1907.

Rösch, F. *Bruchstücke des ersten Clemensbriefes*. Strasbourg, 1910.

Schmidt, C. *Der erste Clemensbrief in altkoptischer Übersetzung*. Texte und Untersuchungen 32.1. Leipzig, 1908.

TITO ORLANDI

CLEMENT OF ALEXANDRIA (Titus Flavius Clemens), born at Athens about A.D. 150 and head of the CATECHETICAL SCHOOL in Alexandria. After wandering in many lands he settled at Alexandria as a disciple of PANTAENUS. At the CATECHETICAL SCHOOL he spent his time lecturing, studying, and writing in defense of the Christian faith. In 202 persecution forced him to flee to Palestine, and in 211 he was still there, assisting in the work of the church of Jerusalem. He may have been ordained presbyter some time before his death about 215.

Clement was the first great Christian writer to claim that all learning, whatever its source, was sacred. Faith and knowledge were not opposed but complementary, and Christians who were afraid of philosophy were "like children who are afraid of ghosts." Philosophy is the handmaiden of God, a schoolmaster to bring the Greeks to Christ. The Logos or Word of God is the divine enlightener of humanity, for "there is but one river of Truth, but many streams fall into it on this side or that." Christianity is the creation, training, and bringing back of the world to God by the Logos.

Clement had three battles to fight: (1) the battle of education within the church; (2) the battle to show that at its best, philosophy is the foe of superstition, the champion of God's unity, and a preparation for the Gospel; (3) the battle to restate the Christian position in the language of philosophy. He tended, however, to overemphasize knowledge and claimed the title "Gnostic" for Christians. He sharply distinguished between those who were "beginners" and the "true" Gnostics who had superior knowledge of love. This two-class theory is not found in the teaching of Jesus.

Clement possessed vast biblical and classical learning. His three main works were the *Protrepticos* ("Exhortation to Conversion"), the *Paedagogus* ("The Tutor"), and the *Stromateis* ("Miscellanies"). He is a difficult author to read because his style is diffuse and his thought often undisciplined. Yet he is very important, for few Christian thinkers, apart from his great successor ORIGEN, have done more to make Christianity an intelligent faith that is meant to be understood by the mind as well as the heart. He set the tone of the Alexandrian school of Christian thought, which it retained throughout its later history. This tone never lost sight of the mystical side of Christianity and the hidden work of the Logos in the whole universe as well as in the Incarnation. Clement's argument for a harmony between the best of the world's thought and Christianity led to a rapprochement between the Roman Empire and the church. In this, Alexandria was at the opposite pole to Carthage and North Africa, which had a different theology and where church and state were violently opposed. Clement's name occurs in early martyrologies, but Pope Clement VIII (1424–1429) excised it because of the alleged doubtful orthodoxy of certain of Clement's works.

BIBLIOGRAPHY

Bigg, C. *The Christian Platonists of Alexandria.* New York, 1913.

Chadwick, H. *Early Christian Thought and the Classical Tradition.* New York, 1966.

Floyd, W. E. G. *Clement of Alexandria: Treatment of the Problem of Evil.* London, 1971.

Lilla, S. R. C. *Clement of Alexandria: A Study of Christian Platonism and Gnosticism.* Oxford, 1971.

Osborn, E. F. *The Philosophy of Clement of Alexandria.* Cambridge, 1957.

LESLIE W. BARNARD

CLEMENT OF ROME. *See* Clement I, Saint.

CLERESTORY. *See* Basilica.

CLERICAL COLLEGE (Cairo). The idea of the establishment of a school for teaching Coptic theology to prepare a new generation of educated priests to assume religious responsibilities in Coptic churches goes back to the middle of the nineteenth century. Until that time the priesthood in Coptic churches held a monopoly as it was a hereditary function. A priest in a church automatically handed his religious responsibilities to one of his offspring, irrespective of how educated his successor was, beyond the reiteration of the Coptic liturgy.

The first COMMUNITY COUNCIL, established by khedivial decree in February 1874 to attend to the welfare of the Copts and the surveillance of their religious properties, conceived among its initial decisions the establishment of a clerical school for the training of educated clerics. Thus in October 1874, the council nominated PHĪLŪTHĀWUS IBRĀHĪM as the first headmaster of the new religious school to be appended to the patriarchate. This decision was endorsed by CYRIL V (1874–1927).

The new school was opened 13 January 1875 in a ceremony attended by the patriarch, the whole membership of the COMMUNITY COUNCIL, and a considerable number of Coptic dignitaries and leaders. Its establishment was hailed with great enthusiasm as the resuscitation of the CATECHETICAL SCHOOL OF ALEXANDRIA, after an interregnum of fourteen centuries since its extinction in the sixth century. The new foundation was a poor image of its distant parent, the mentor of the world of Christian antiquity. But somehow a modest beginning was made on the road of reform in a society where the very comprehension of religious worship had been declining to the edge of a formality, without real understanding of the spiritual core of the faith. The main purpose of the school was an attempt to graduate priests and bishops who were capable of conveying to the congregation a real understanding of their religious heritage. After several years the school was suspended for lack of funds and sparse enrollment, though the idea was never defunct.

In November 1893, thanks to the sustained efforts of Ḥanna Bakhūm (Bey), a member of the community council and supervisor of Coptic schools, this theological seminary was reopened and a limited numbers of candidates were accepted. He devised a viable school curriculum consisting of a balanced set of subjects from the humanities and religious matters, to be distributed over five years. Arabic and Coptic languages coupled with history, geography, and mathematics were made compulsory. But greater concentration on religious materials was the backbone of the curriculum. The subjects taught were theology, church liturgy, Coptic ecclesiastical jurisprudence, and church history and rhetoric.

The school began with an enrollment of twenty-four candidates divided into two classes, one for the younger scholars whose studies extended over five years, and the other class comprising older priests and monks who could only stay for one year of intensive work to enrich their comprehension of the standard Coptic religious traditions, before returning to their dioceses and monasteries.

In September 1918, Ḥabīb Jirjis was appointed headmaster of the school; he succeeded Yūsuf Manqariūs (Bey), who introduced a number of reforms and alterations in its program in the light of his examination of the Greek, Roman, Catholic, and Protestant curricula of various modern seminaries in Europe and America. In the 1920s, during the tenure of the new headmaster, the school became divided into two categories of students: the intermediate section drawn from the primary graduates, and the upper division in possession of the full baccalaureate, whose studies were limited to four years. In 1973, Anbā Shenouda, the bishop in charge of religious education (later Pope Shenouda III), decided to take his intermediate class to the Monastery of Our Lady, known as al-Dayr Muḥarraq in Asyūṭ. The upper division remained at Anbā Ruways and began to attract university students, while Coptic University professors replenished its academic staff on visiting assignments.

In October 1905, evening classes were established to meet the need of university students who wanted to join theological studies without discarding their regular secular education by day. In October 1959 women were admitted to the school. It appeared that the school had definitely come of age, and it assumed the deserved title of Clerical College. In its new form, its studies were classified into three categories: an intermediate division for five years, upper division for four years, and evening classes for university graduates to last three years.

A further dimension was added to the College by the enrollment of orthodox Syrian and Ethiopian monks. Its position was strengthened by a patriarchal edict to limit the priesthood to graduates of the Clerical College. One of the greater achievements of the College was the publication of the complete and authorized Bohairic-Coptic text of the Bible, in addition to other publications, including the liturgies. In this respect we must refer to the role of IQLĀDYŪS LABĪB and that of Pope CYRIL IV (1854–1861), who had previously imported the second printing press into Egypt.

An offshoot of the Clerical College in 1903 was the establishment of the School for Monks in Alexandria under the sponsorship of Anbā Yu'annis, metropolitan of Beheira, later Pope JOHN XIX (1928–1942). This expansion spread to other provincial towns, such as Tanta, Minyā, Shibīn al-Kōm, and al-Balyanā.

Another interesting by-product of the Clerical College was the attention accorded to the precentors who were mainly blind cantors taking an essential part in the celebration of the Coptic mass. These were known as *'irfān* (pl. of *'arif*) for whom a special section was established in the Anbā Ruways building. It was named the Didymus Institute for the Blind, to commemorate one of the greatest blind theologians who was selected by Pope ATHANASIUS I to preside over the Catechetical School of Alexandria, Saint DIDYMUS THE BLIND (c. 313–398).

With the foundation of the HIGHER INSTITUTE OF COPTIC STUDIES, closer relations with the Clerical College were nurtured, and many advanced graduates of the college continued their higher theological studies in that institute.

MIRRIT BOUTROS GHALI

CLERICAL INSTRUCTION. Education of the clergy of the Coptic church at a church college is a modern arrangement. In antiquity, every bishop had to provide for the education and installation of the clergy of his diocese (see ORDINATION, CLERICAL). The demands made of priests and deacons are known from the church canons (see CANONS, ECCLESIASTICAL), and from texts relating to the ordination of clergy from the correspondence of Bishop ABRAHAM of Hermonthis about 600. These texts presuppose definite attainments that the candidate was to pursue, or in accordance with which he was to act. He therefore had to be instructed about them or to acquire specific knowledge on his own. Among the latter were knowledge of the canons of the church and "professional knowledge." Sometimes the latter is more exactly described as "knowledge of the office of deacon" or "knowledge of the office of priest."

The candidate was carefully instructed in the actions of his office that should be carried out in the church and at the altar. There must also have been instruction about the prayers to be spoken by him. Since only a few clergy could read, the candidates had to learn their professional knowledge by heart. To this must be added memorization of certain biblical texts, the Gospels of Matthew, Mark, and John being named. This task had a time limit, often of two months. An examination on the memorized material took place in the presence of the bishop. It is striking that the evidence given by sources indicates that this trial did not always come before the ordination, but could occur afterward. If the text could not be recited, there was no ordination. We are not told, however, what happened when a candidate who had already been ordained failed his test.

After punishment, such as exclusion from communion (see EXCOMMUNICATION), the candidate, on being readmitted to communion, might be required to memorize further Bible texts.

BIBLIOGRAPHY

Bilabel, F., and A. Grohmann. *Zwei Urkunden aus dem bischöflichen Archiv von Panopolis in Ägypten.* Heidelberg, 1935.

Coquin, R.-G. "A propos des rouleaux coptes arabe de l'évêque Timothée." *Bibliotheca Orientalis* 34 (1977):142–47.

Krause, M. "Apa Abraham von Hermonthis. Ein oberägyptischer Bischof um 600," 2 vols. Ph.D. diss., Berlin, 1956.

Maspero, J. "Un diplôme arabe-chrétien du XIIIe siècle." *Annales du Service des antiquités* 11 (1911):177–85.

Plumley, J. M. *The Scrolls of Bishop Timotheos. Two Documents from Medieval Nubia.* London, 1975.

Steinwenter, A. "Die Ordinationsbitten koptischer Kleriker." *Aegyptus* 11 (1930–1931):29–34.

MARTIN KRAUSE

CLOISTER. *See* Architectural Elements of Churches: Atrium.

CLYSMA, ancient town a few miles north of modern-day Suez and known for its ruins. They were excavated by B. Bruyère (1966). The site (which some texts call the isle of Clysma) appears to have been inhabited by anchorites very early. It is not known exactly where these anchorites lived. The Mountain of Antony was often called the Mountain of Clysma, for contemporary texts always indicated the name of the nearest town. The following provide references to Clysma and may indicate a site more or less distant: JOHN COLOBOS, fleeing from the Maziques who had invaded Scetis in 407, went to Clysma and died there in 409 (Evelyn-White, 1932, p. 158); Sisoes, toward the end of his life, settled at Clysma, but not before 429 (Chitty, 1966, p. 79, n. 83); the Coptic version of an apothegm relating to Sisoes speaks of the "isle" of Clysma (Chaine, 1960, no. 115).

Eutychius (Sa'id ibn Batrīq) mentions that a Church of Athanasius (martyr) is said to have been built by order of Justinian at the same time as the monasteries of Raithou and Mount Sinai (1906–1909, Vol. 2, pp. 202–203). About 570, Antoninus Placentinus saw in the basilica of Clysma eighteen or more tombs of hermit holy fathers (1898, p. 188).

To the isle of Clysma is attached the legend of Mār Awjīn (Eugene), who introduced monasticism into Mesopotamia, for he is said to have served his monastic apprenticeship at Clysma (Fiey, 1962, pp. 52–81). He seems indeed to have been a historical personage; that people wished to link him with Egyptian monasticism indicates his importance.

BIBLIOGRAPHY

Bruyère, B. *Fouilles de Clysma–Qulzum (Suez).* Fouilles de l'Institut français d'Archéologie orientale 27. Cairo, 1960.

Chaîne, M. *Le manuscrit de la version copte, en dialecte Sahidique des "Apophtegmata Patrum."* Bibliothèque d'études coptes 6. Cairo, 1960.

Chitty, D. J. *The Desert a City.* London, 1966.

Evelyn-White, H. G. *The Monasteries of the Wadi'n Natrūn,* Pt. 2, *The History of the Monasteries of Nitria and Scetis.* New York, 1932.

Fiey, J. "Aonès, Awun, Awgin." *Analecta Bollandiana* 80 (1962):52–81.

Nau, F. "La Version syriaque de l'histoire de Jean le petit." *Revue de l'Orient chrétien* 17 (1912):347–89, and 19 (1914):33–57.

RENÉ-GEORGES COQUIN
MAURICE MARTIN, S.J.

COATS. *See* Costume, Civil.

CODEX, word originally meaning "block" and used for an assemblage of several wax tablets held together at one side by cords. The resulting arrangement was the model for the form of book in use today. The largest assemblage of this kind so far known contained ten tablets, of which nine are still extant (Berlin Papyrus Collection, Inv. no. 14000). When two tablets were replaced by a leaf of papyrus or parchment folded in the middle, the result was the basic form of the codex.

As a rule, gatherings were made out of single leaves, and several of these were then combined into a book-block. The format was manifold, as were the makeup, the inscribing, and the decoration. Generally the codex was protected by wrappers after the fashion of book covers, which were adorned with impressed lines and ornament. The

Codex showing the beginning of the Epistle of Paul to the Romans. Copto-Arabic manuscript, A.D. 1250. *Courtesy Coptic Museum, Cairo.*

material of the codex consisted of parchment, papyrus, or paper. C. H. Roberts and T. C. Skeat have made a fundamental contribution to our knowledge of the early history of the codex.

Although the Egyptian finds begin only with the second century A.D., Christians certainly adopted the codex form even before A.D. 100. In pagan literature, on the contrary, in the second century the codex had only a modest place compared with the traditional roll. Codices were used not only for literary works but also for memoranda and documentary texts. The parchment notebook, however, seems rather to go back to Roman origins. Palimpsests are also to be found among the codices. At present it is not possible to answer the question of whether papyrus or parchment codices were developed first, or whether we should assume simultaneous use of both materials for the manufacture of codices. From the discoveries, we can determine that there was parity between the roll and the codex about 300, but thereafter the codex prevailed. This is explained in the main by the extensive tran-

Codex showing the beginning of the Epistle of James. Copto-Arabic manuscript, A.D. 1250. *Courtesy Coptic Museum, Cairo.*

scription of literary works from rolls into codices at the beginning of the fourth century.

BIBLIOGRAPHY

Hunger, H. "Antikes und mittelalterliches Buch- und Schriftwesen." *Geschichte der Textüberlieferung der antiken und mittelalterlichen Literatur* 1 (1961):43–71.

Roberts, C. H., and T. C. Skeat, *The Birth of the Codex*. London, 1983; repr. 1985.

Turner, E. G. *Greek Papyri: An Introduction*. Oxford, 1968; 2d ed., 1980. Italian translation by M. Manfredi, *Papiri greci*. Rome, 1984.

GÜNTER POETHKE

CODEX ALEXANDRINUS, of Egyptian origin, one of the oldest known Greek texts of the Bible on vellum, the others being the CODEX VATICANUS, the CODEX SINAITICUS, and the CODEX EPHRAEMI

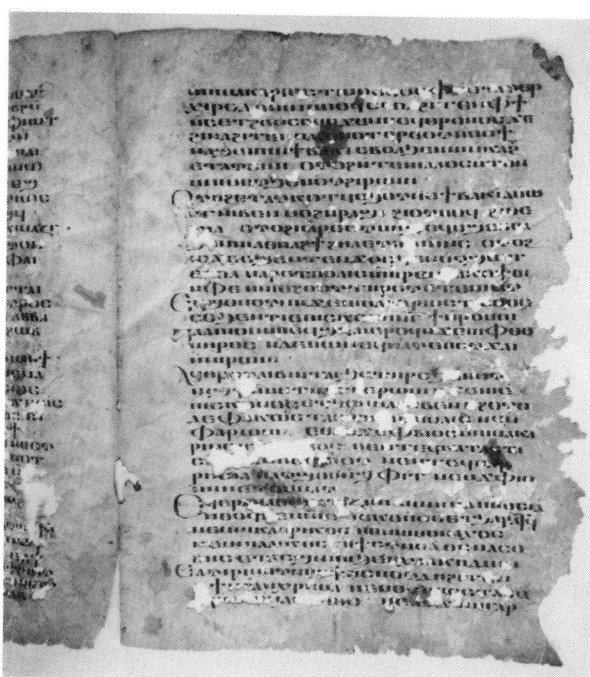

Codex showing the life of Peter the Iberian. *Courtesy The Metropolitan Museum of Art, New York.*

SYRI. Like them, it is written in simple but beautiful uncials; unlike them, it is slightly ornamented, with rubrications at the beginning of every book and its paragraphs indicated by larger capitals in the margin. But since its lines are continuous, without spaces between the words, often the initial capital of a new verse is placed at the beginning of the following line though the previous verse ends in the middle of the line. The text has few breathings and no accents. Quotations from the Old Testament are marked in the New, and sacred names are abbreviated. Colophons appear at the end of each book. Apparently the manuscript is the work of three scribes or, possibly, one scribe and two correctors. It has numerous corrections of the same style and approximately the same date.

Written a little later than both the Vaticanus and the Sinaiticus, this codex has been reasonably dated to the early part of the fifth century. While it is evident that this text coincides to a great extent with the recension of Saint Lucian of Antioch, it is also clear that it shares features with the Hesychian recension and Origen's Hexapla.

In addition to the New Testament, the codex contains two epistles of Saint Clement of Rome. An "Epistle to Marcellinus," ascribed to ATHANASIUS I, appears as a preface to Psalms along with Eusebius's summary of the Psalter. Sections of Psalms and Genesis, together with the opening folios of Matthew, are lacking and must have been lost. The Old Testament includes, besides the Maccabees of the Apocrypha, two additional Maccabee books.

The manuscript contains 773 leaves, though it is estimated that it must originally have consisted of 882. The Old Testament appears on 630 leaves and the New Testament on 143; the size of each leaf is about 12.5 inches by 9 inches (31.5 cm by 23 cm). Each page has two columns of forty-nine to fifty-one lines. The codex is composed of quires of eight leaves, and its pagination appears in three sets of numbers: one in Greek at the head of each folio, another in fourteenth-century Arabic at the outer lower corner of the verso side of the folios, and a third in relatively modern ink by Patrick Young, Charles I's librarian.

The early history of Codex Alexandrinus is obscure. Originating in Egypt, it is said to have returned to Alexandria via Mount Athos. Afterward, its journey to the Royal Library in the British Museum started from the Melchite patriarchate in Alexandria when Patriarch Cyril Lucar took it with him to Constantinople after his preferment to the ecumenical Greek patriarchate in 1621. He presented it to King James I through the British ambassador to Turkey, Sir Thomas Roe, on 30 January 1625. Sir Thomas brought it to England in 1627 and placed it in the hands of Charles I, who had succeeded James I. The king then deposited it in the Royal Library, which passed it to the British Museum in 1757.

The codex is bound in four volumes bearing the arms of Charles I. The first three contain the Old Testament and the fourth, the New Testament and Saint Clement's epistles. On the first page of Genesis, there is an inscription by a certain "Athanasius the Humble," possibly the Melchite patriarch of Alexandria at the beginning of the fourteenth century, who dedicated it to the patriarchal cell of the city of Alexandria, with a curse on anyone who might succumb to the temptation of removing it from there. His curse did not alter the course of later events.

BIBLIOGRAPHY

Burkitt, F. C. "Codex Alexandrinus." *Journal of Theological Studies* 11 (1910):603–606.

Jellicoe, S. *The Septuagint and Modern Study.* Oxford, 1968.

Kenyon, F. G. *Our Bible and the Ancient Manuscripts,* 5th ed., rev. A. W. Adams, intro. G. R.

Driver. New York, 1958.
Kenyon, F. G., and H. J. M. Milne. *The Codex Alexandrinus in Reduced Photographic Facsimile,* 5 vols. London, 1909–1957.
Metzger, B. M. *Early Versions of the New Testament.* Oxford, 1977.
Milne, H. J. M., and T. C. Skeat. *The Codex Sinaiticus and the Codex Alexandrinus.* London, 1938.
Scrivener, F. H. A. *A Plain Introduction to the Criticism of the New Testament for the Use of Biblical Students,* 2 vols., 4th ed. E. Miller. London and New York, 1894.
Swete, H. B. *Introduction to the Old Testament in Greek.* Cambridge, 1900.

AZIZ S. ATIYA

CODEX EPHRAEMI SYRI. This is one of the family of ancient codices in Greek used as a base for what is known as the Egyptian text of the Bible—the others are the Vaticanus, the Sinaiticus, and the Alexandrinus, in addition, of course, to the earlier papyri. Paleographically it is very similar to the others, except that it is written in one column and has neither accents nor breathings. Its words are continuous, without spacing. It is probably a little later than the other codices and may be dated to the fifth century. It is probably the work of two hands, but it had two correctors in the sixth and ninth centuries who added occasional marginal inscriptions. However, it must be noted that this codex is a palimpsest, that is, a work in which the vellum was reused for another text after defacing the original—which still shows. In this case, during the twelfth century a scribe who was short of vellum decided to remove the biblical text, possibly by rubbing it with pumice stone or lime or both, in order to write a new Greek version of the homilies of Saint Ephraim the Syrian, a theologian of the fourth century. The original text remained visible, however, though not always legible. The first scholar to decipher the New Testament portion, in 1841–1842, was Constantine Tischendorf, the discoverer of the Codex Sinaiticus. Only recently has Tischendorf's work been brought under serious scrutiny.

The Codex Ephraemi Syri consists of only 209 leaves—approximately 12.5 inches by 9 inches (31.5 cm by 23 cm)—from a more extensive original. Of these, 145 contain sections of the New Testament, lacking 2 Thessalonians and 2 John. The story of the manuscript goes back to the Medici family; it is known to have been in the possession of Cardinal Ridolfi of Florence. Later it was passed to Catherine de' Medici, queen of Henry II of France. She took it to Paris, where it was deposited in the National Library.

BIBLIOGRAPHY

Jellicoe, S. *The Septuagint and Modern Study.* Oxford, 1968.
Kenyon, F. G. *Our Bible and the Ancient Manuscripts,* 5th ed., rev. A. W. Adams, intro. G. R. Driver. London, 1958.
Lyon, R. W. "A Re-examination of Codex Ephraemi Rescriptus." *New Testament Studies* 5 (1958–1959):260–72.
Metzger, B. M. *Early Versions of the New Testament.* Oxford, 1977.
Scrivener, F. H. A. *A Plain Introduction to the Criticism of the New Testament,* 2 vols., 4th ed. E. Miller. London and New York, 1894.
Swete, H. B. *An Introduction to the Old Testament in Greek.* Cambridge, 1900.

AZIZ S. ATIYA

CODEX JUNG, codex containing the greater part of Codex I of the NAG HAMMADI LIBRARY. Purchased from an antiquities dealer in Belgium by the Jung Institute of Zurich on 10 May 1952, it contains pages 1–32, 37–48, 51–58, 91–136, and some fragments of the codex. The rest of the manuscript was among the Nag Hammadi texts acquired by the Coptic Museum in Cairo. The editio princeps was published between 1956 and 1975. The folios from Cairo were also used for this edition.

Codex I is composed of three quires, containing pages 1–84, 85–118, and 119–138, respectively. The pages are about 12 inches (30 cm) long and 5.5 inches (14 cm) wide. The average number of lines per page is thirty-seven or thirty-eight, with a maximum of forty-two. The two pages of the front flyleaf were inscribed when the main tractates were finished (pages A/B). Nearly the entire codex was written by one and the same hand, except the treatise on pages 43,25–50,18, which was copied by the scribe of Codex XI, tractates 3 and 4. After the completion of the editio princeps, the Codex Jung was returned to Cairo, and in the period 1975–1976 it was united with the rest of Codex I. Along with the other Nag Hammadi texts, the manuscript of Codex I can be dated to about the middle of the fourth century. It is written in the Subakhmimic Coptic dialect.

The following is a brief survey of the contents.

The PRAYER OF THE APOSTLE PAUL formally resembles the biblical psalms, but is actually the expression of the longing of a (Valentinian) Gnostic to be united with the Preexistent One, the Pleroma, from which he originated.

The APOCRYPHON OF JAMES (*Nag Hammadi Codex* I.1–16,30) is a modern title derived from the fact that the apostle James is addressing his readers and designates his writing as an "apocryphon" (I.10). James and Peter receive a special revelation from Christ after His resurrection. In a Gnostic way Christ tells His disciples that they are in emptiness and diminution, in sleep and drunkenness, which means that they are ignorant; but he promises that they will become "full" in the attainment of true knowledge. At the end Peter and James experience an ecstatic elevation to heaven. James is the leader of the disciples, whom he sends to different places (16,7–8).

The GOSPEL OF TRUTH (*Nag Hammadi Codex* I, 16,31–43,24) is named for the opening lines, which can be taken for an extended title. "Error" has taken possession of men and, spreading as a fog, has fostered ignorance of the Father. Jesus came and underwent the Passion in order to reveal the Father as true guide. The reception of *gnosis* also means that man rediscovers his real self (30,13). It is a matter of discussion whether this tractate is identical with the writing of the same name mentioned by Irenaeus (*Adversus omnes haereses,* III.11.9), or with the "occult Gospel" alluded to by Tertullian in *De praescriptione haereticorum.*

The TREATISE ON THE RESURRECTION (43,25–50,18) is the title occurring at the end of the codex. The form is a letter from a teacher of wisdom to his "son" Rheginos. He who has come to knowledge has already received the spiritual resurrection (45,40; 49,15–16). This point of view was already condemned as heretical in 2 Timothy 2:18.

The TRIPARTITE TRACTATE (51,1–138,27) is a modern designation for a tractate without title that is divided into three parts by a series of *diple* partition marks after lines 104,3 and 108,12.

I.51,1–104,3: The subject is the transcendent world of the Pleroma. The Father is described by negative predication as incomprehensible, immeasurable, and so on. The Trinity consists of Father, Son, and Church, as it is found with the Western Valentinian Heracleon. The fall of the aeon Sophia is a characteristic Valentinian theme. In this particular tractate, however, she is male and called Logos. The aeons do not yet possess the full knowledge of the Father, but will receive it through the intermediation of the Son and the Spirit. In this respect, the aeons are the prototypes of the pneumatics. The fallen Logos prepares the creation of the psychosomatic world through his progeniture of the Demiurge.

II.104,4–108,12: This part is concerned with the creation of man. Unknown to the Demiurge, the Logos inflates the spiritual element in man, which enables him to receive knowledge.

The third part of the tractate (III.108,13–138,27) deals with the three races of men and their destiny: spiritual men (the pneumatics), psychics, and material men (the hylics), a tripartition connected with contemporary philosophic anthropology, which distinguishes a noetic, a psychic, and a material element in man. The psychics are called "those belonging to the right" (for instance, the Hebrew prophets), and the hylics are designated as "those belonging to the left" (for instance, the Greek philosophers). These two lower classes originate from the passions of the fallen aeon, the Logos (Sophia). All the pneumatics will necessarily be saved through the revelation of Christ. The psychics dispose of a free will, since they are linked with the good intention, the conversion, of the fallen Logos. If they make the right choice and perform good works, they will attain a destiny not far from the Pleroma of the Father. The hylics necessarily go to perdition.

The tractate concludes with a liturgical doxology on the Father. The Tripartite Tractate can to a great extent be compared with the description of Valentinian gnosticism by Irenaeus (*Adversus omnes haereses* I,1–8). It is a characteristic document of gnostic interpretation of biblical data.

BIBLIOGRAPHY

Attridge, H. W., ed. *Nag Hammadi Codex I (The Jung Codex): Introductions, Texts, Translations, Indices,* 2 vols. Nag Hammadi Studies 22–23. Leiden, 1985.

Cross, F. L., ed. *The Jung Codex: A Newly Recovered Gnostic Papyrus. Three Studies by H. C. Puech, G. Quispel and W. C. van Unnik.* London, 1955.

JAN ZANDEE

CODEX JUSTINIANUS. Shortly after JUSTINIAN became emperor in 527, he began a major overhaul of the empire's legal code. The first step in this process was the publication of the Codex Justinianus, a revision and expansion of Theodosian's legal code. This volume was published on 7 April 529 by a commission under the direction of Justinian's legal expert, Tribonian. A second, revised edition of the Code was published on 16 November 534. Together with the Institutes (produced in 533), based on the legal text compiled by the second-century Roman jurist Gaius, and the Digest, consisting of codified excerpts of the classical jurists (published on 16 December 533), the Codex Justinianus established a single code of law incorporating all of the constitutions back to the time of the emperor Hadrian. Justinian added to, and modified, this code as necessary through more than 150 Novellae. The Code, Digest, Institutes, and Novellae are known collectively as the Corpus Iuris Civilis (1954).

BIBLIOGRAPHY

Monro, C. H. trans. *The Digest of Justinian*, 2 vols. Cambridge, 1904–1909.

Sandars, T. C. *The Institutes of Justinian*. London, 1941.

RANDALL STEWART

CODEX SINAITICUS, an ancient Greek biblical text discovered in Sinai at the Monastery of Saint Catherine by Constantine Tischendorf, and consisting of 390 vellum leaves, although the original could have been at least 730 leaves. The existing parts of the manuscript include 148 leaves of the New Testament, which is complete, and 242 leaves of the Old Testament. Its size averages approximately 15 inches (37.5 cm) in height and 13.5 to 14.25 inches (34 cm to 36 cm) in breadth, and each page has 4 columns of 48 lines each. The lines are written continuously in fine uncials without spaces between words. It has no accents and no breathings, but has some punctuation. Sacred names are abbreviated as in the CODEX VATICANUS. Apparently it was written by at least three hands, as is shown by the peculiarities of each hand, especially in the spelling. The New Testament was almost wholly written by one scribe. Numerous corrections have been made in the text, not only by the original scribes themselves but also by others from the fourth to the twelfth century. One corrector states at the end of Esdras that the book was revised in accordance with a text corrected by Pamphilus of Caesarea on the basis of Origen's Hexapla.

The manuscript has the dignified simplicity of the Codex Vaticanus in its calligraphy and, like Vaticanus, originated most probably in Alexandria. It has been thought to be one of the fifty vellum copies of the Bible ordered by Constantine in 332, although this remains open to question. Some scholars mention Caesarea (Milne and Skeat, 1938) and Rome as places of origin for this codex, but without convincing proof.

Since the Sinaiticus predates the foundation of the MOUNT SINAI MONASTERY OF SAINT CATHERINE, it is likely that a monk who came to live there brought this codex with him. It is well established that, especially during the Middle Ages, monks flocked to that monastery from many countries with their religious treasures. Even so, it is impossible to say when Codex Sinaiticus reached the monastery.

The discovery and recovery of the codex began in May 1844, when Constantine Tischendorf, one of the nineteenth-century scholars who came to the monastery's library for study, was attracted by a basket full of old parchments, of which some moldering specimens had been destroyed by fire. A closer examination revealed "a considerable number of sheets of a copy of the O.T. in Greek." He was allowed to take forty-three leaves, which he says were destined for the flames, to Leipzig, where he edited them under the title *Codex Frederico Augustanus* (1846). After an unsuccessful visit in 1853 to look for the remainder of the manuscript, he returned in 1859 with a letter from Emperor Alexander II, of Russia, but found no more until, as he was preparing for departure, the steward of the convent privately produced a bulky mess of material wrapped in red cloth. Remarkably, it included the rest of the parchments from the basket of discarded leaves in 1844. Tischendorf was allowed to take them to Cairo for further study. He finally took the lot to Europe and placed the manuscript in the hands of the Russian czar, who donated the equivalent of $6,750 to the monks in recognition of the acquisition.

The codex remained at the Russian capital until 1933, when it was sold to the British Museum for £100,000. It was delivered to the museum on 27 December. Its vellum leaves were treated, organized, and bound in two separate volumes consisting of the Old Testament and the New Testament. It is registered in the museum under the pressmark B. M. Addit. 43725.

In the second half of the twentieth century an unspecified number of the missing leaves of this codex have been found in a hoard of varied manuscripts discovered in the monastery. The exact content of this hoard is closely guarded by the monks and remains open to future identification.

BIBLIOGRAPHY

Brock, S. P., et al., comps. *A Classified Bibliography of the Septuagint.* Leiden, 1973.

Jellicoe, S. *The Septuagint and Modern Study.* Oxford, 1968.

Kenyon, F. G. *Our Bible and the Ancient Manuscripts,* 5th ed., rev. A. W. Adams, intro. G. R. Driver. New York, 1958.

Lake, H., and K. Lake. *Codex Sinaiticus Petropolitanus et Frederico-Augustanus Lipsiensis. The Old Testament . . . Reproduced in Facsimile from Photographs,* 2 vols. Oxford, 1911–1922.

Metzger, B. M. *The Early Versions of the New Testament.* Oxford, 1977.

Milne, H. J. M., and T. C. Skeat. *Scribes and Correctors of the Codex Sinaiticus.* London, 1938.

Moir, J. A. "Tischendorf and the Codex Sinaiticus." *New Testament Studies* 23 (1976):108–115.

Scrivener, F. H. A. *A Plain Introduction to the Criticism of the New Testament for the Use of Bible Students,* 2 vols., 4th ed. E. Miller. London and New York, 1894.

Tischendorf, C. von. *Bibliorum Codex Sinaiticus Petropolitanus,* 4 vols. St. Petersburg, 1862.

———. *Codex Sinaiticus. The Ancient Biblical Manuscript Now in the British Museum. Tischendorf's Story Related by Himself.* London, 1933.

AZIZ S. ATIYA

CODEX THEODOSIANUS, Roman imperial law code, published on 15 February 438 on the authority of Emperor Theodosius II, with a covering constitution addressed to the pretorian prefect of the East (*Novella Theodosiana* I). It had been approved by the Western emperor, Valentinian III, during his stay in Constantinople in October 437 when he married the daughter of Theodosius II.

The reason for the publication of the code was practical. Texts of imperial laws had become confused, repetitive, and sometimes self-contradictory. For years there had been complaints and demands for reform (see Thompson, 1979, p. 21). Lawyers were becoming ignorant of the law.

Theodosius II was interested in legal matters. On 26 February 425 he established professorial chairs for the teaching of literary sciences and law in Constantinople (Codex Theodosianus xiv.9.3). This was followed on 27 March 429 by a project aimed at updating and revising the existing Codex Gregorianus and Codex Hermogenianus (Codex Theodosianus i.1.5). The work proved impossible to carry out, and on 20 December 435 a simpler scheme was decided upon, designed to codify general enactments of Constantine (taken to mean after his defeat of Maxentius on 28 October 312). Legislation was divided into sixteen sections according to general subject, the first, for instance, relating to the emperor's decrees, the seventh to military affairs, and the sixteenth to legislation relating to the church. The emperor's hand may be seen in the tendency, wherever possible, toward conciseness and brevity. The Codex Theodosianus stands as a lasting monument to his reign and to the personal authority, sometimes underestimated, that he exercised.

There are fewer laws directed to officials in Egypt and Alexandria than might be anticipated, given the importance of the province to the empire. The code, however, provides some important information concerning social life in fourth-century Egypt. In particular, the series of laws *De patrociniis vicorium* (Codex Theodosianus xi.24.1–6) throws light on the system of landholding in force in Egypt in the fourth century, mainly comprising small to medium landholders, and the threat to this system posed by the development of patronage. Patronage laid the client open to abuses, and it also stood to deprive the state of revenue. Another series of laws defines the status and immunities of members of the Senate of Alexandria two years before the publication of the code (Codex Theodosianus xii.1.189–92, June–August 436).

BIBLIOGRAPHY

Archi, G. G. *Teodosio II e la sua codificazione.* Naples, 1976.

Gaudemet, J. "Théodosien (Code)." In *Dictionnaire de droit canonique,* Vol. 7., cols. 1215–46. Paris, 1962.

———. "Aspects politiques de la codification théodosienne." In *Istituzioni giuridiche e realtà politiche nel tardo impero,* ed. G. G. Archi, pp. 261–79. Milan, 1976.

———. *La formation du droit séculier de l'église aux ive et ve siècles,* 2nd ed. Paris, 1979.

Mommsen, T., and P. M. Meyer, eds. *Theodosiani libri xvi, cum constitutionibus Sirmondianis,* 2 vols. Berlin, 1905; repr. 1962.

Pharr, C. et al., eds. and trans., *The Theodosian Code and Novels.* Princeton, N. J., 1952.

Seeck, O. *Registen der Kaiser und Päpste.* Stuttgart, 1919; repr. 1964.

Thompson, E. A., ed. and trans. *De rebus bellicis. A Roman Reformer and Inventor.* New York, 1979.

Zulueta, F. de. *De patrociniis vicorum.* Oxford Social and Legal Studies 1. Oxford, 1909.

W. H. C. FREND

CODEX VATICANUS, one of the oldest known Bible texts of likely Alexandrian provenance, most probably written during the first half of the fourth century. Its dating is clear from its paleographical style and the absence of calligraphic ornamentation. It is written on excellent vellum, probably antelope skin, comprising 759 leaves, of which 142 are from the New Testament. The 617 folios of the Old Testament are based on the Septuagint except for Daniel, whose origin is Theodotion's version. The Old Testament version lacks passages from Genesis, 2 Samuel, Psalms, and Maccabees. In the New Testament the portion from Hebrews 9:14 on is missing.

The size of each leaf is approximately 11 inches × 10 inches (27 cm × 25 cm), and each page has 3 columns of 40 to 42 lines to the column, except in the poetical books, where the scribe resorts to the stichometric division of the lines in two columns. Its simple uncials are continuous, the words are not spaced, and the sentences have no punctuation. The manuscript has few majestic initials and a simple separation at the head of each book. Sacred names are abbreviated, and quotations from the Old Testament are presented in a special angular parenthesis (>). Apparently two scribes participated in copying the text, one for the Old Testament and another for the New Testament. A contemporary reader revised and corrected the text, and a later reader from the tenth or eleventh century also worked on the manuscript, retracing pale letters (presumably incorrect words were left without tracing), and added the breathings and accents.

This codex is known to have been in the Vatican Library before the publication both of its first catalog of 1475 and of the second of 1481, where it is cited as "Biblia in tribus columnis ex membranis in rubeo." It was taken to Paris by Napoleon during the Italian Wars (1809), and remained in the French capital until 1815, when it was returned to Rome after Napolean's defeat at Waterloo. During its sojourn in Paris, it was scrutinized by Professor Leonard Hug at Tübingen, who assessed its age and value for the first time. It was studied again in Rome in 1843 by Constantine Tischendorf, discoverer of the CODEX SINAITICUS. But its real value and importance were revealed only after its text was made accessible to biblical scholars and classicists through a complete photographic facsimile of the entire extant manuscript, published at Rome in 1889–1890. Today the manuscript is preserved in the Vatican Library (Vat. Gr. 1209).

BIBLIOGRAPHY

Jellicoe, S. *The Septuagint and Modern Study.* Oxford, 1968.

Kenyon, F. G. *Our Bible and the Ancient Manuscripts,* 5th ed., rev. A. W. Adams, intro. G. R. Driver. New York, 1958.

Metzger, B. M. *Early Versions of the New Testament.* Oxford, 1977.

AZIZ S. ATIYA

CODICOLOGY, science concerned with the externals of manuscripts in codex form, their history, and the history of manuscript collections, to the exclusion of PALEOGRAPHY.

With the first major classification of the ancient papyrus and parchment codices from Egypt, E. G. Turner reached some noteworthy codicological conclusions. Investigation of the measurements of the codex leaves and of their arrangement made it possible to recognize for specific periods scribal usages and scribal schools, knowledge of which is important for dating a codex. The same purpose is served by determining relationships between leaf size and written surface, the number of lines, and the number of columns per page. The proportions for papyrus codices do not find any exact parallel to those made of parchment because of the differing dimensions of an animal skin as compared with a papyrus roll, which had to be cut up for the production of codex leaves. For the manufacture of the codex, four leaves (quaternio) were generally folded vertically to form a quire of sixteen pages, and several quires were united into a book-block. There are, however, also other types of quire (unio, binio, ternio, quinio), and even single-quire codices. It is important to observe, in the production of the quires, the sequence of the pages with horizontal or vertical fibers in papyrus codices, or in parchment codices the sequence of hair and flesh side. In Greek manuscripts, the leaves are usually so arranged that in the open codex two hair sides or two flesh sides always lie beside one another. In the parchment leaves, punctures were frequently made on the upper, outer, and lower margins as an aid to the marking of lines. These lines, usually engraved only on the hair side, appear on the flesh side as ridges.

In addition, other methods are characteristic of particular scriptoria. Normally the leaves were inscribed before binding, and the stitching of the quires and the manufacture of the book-block were done in conjunction. Numbering of pages or of quires probably came about at the same time as the development of the codex form. The earliest example of the quire numbering belongs to the years 200 to 250 (Turner, 1977, p. 77).

The illustration of texts, particularly known from the Egyptian *Book of the Dead* papyri, was greatly advanced with the dissemination of the codex. The book form offered greater scope for artistic embellishment and for initials, ornamented rules, and flourishes.

The history of the book cover begins at the same time as the introduction of the codex. The technique for making book covers by hand has not substantially changed from the beginning to today. The Romans had used wooden protective covers for parchment notebooks, and wood was also generally the basic material for the covers of codices, which were overlaid with leather. In Egypt, instead of the wooden cover, papyrus leaves were glued together into a pasteboard and overlaid with leather (covers of the Nag Hammadi codices). The Copts, who were known for their skill in binding, adorned the leather covers with geometrical figures in low relief. Painted covers are rare. The technique and ornamentation of covers of the Byzantine period point to Coptic influence (Regemorter, 1954). Medieval bookbinding developed a great sumptuousness with the use of costly metals and precious stones.

BIBLIOGRAPHY

Hunger, H. "Antikes und mittelalterliches Buch- und Schriftwesen." *Geschichte der Textüberlieferung der antiken und mittelalterlichen Literatur* 1 (1961):43–71.

Regemorter, B. van. "La Reliure des manuscrits grecs." *Scriptorium* 8 (1954):3–23.

Robinson, J. M. "Codicological Analysis of Nag Hammadi Codices V and VI and Papyrus Berolinensis 8502." In *Nag Hammadi Codices V, 2–5 and VI,* ed. D. M. Parrott. Nag Hammadi Studies 11. Leiden, 1979.

———. *The Facsimile Edition of the Nag Hammadi Codices,* pp. 71–86. Leiden, 1984.

Turner, E. G. *The Typology of the Early Codex.* Philadelphia, 1977.

GÜNTER POETHKE

COFFER. *See* Architectural Elements of Churches.

COFFINS. *See* Wood, Uses of.

COHORT. *See* Army, Roman.

COINAGE IN EGYPT. [*This entry on Egyptian coins consists of two articles:* Pre-Islamic Period *and* Islamic Period.]

Pre-Islamic Period

In spite of its high level of civilization, Egypt lacked coinage until a relatively late date. The concept of coinage was probably introduced by Greeks, who were employed as mercenaries as early as the seventh century B.C. and later established as traders at Naucratis. After about 525 B.C., a series of hoards attests to extensive trade with the Greek world that is underscored by the almost total absence of Persian silver. Both the variety and the condition of the contents indicate a premonetary context. The most important of the hoards, which comes from Asyūṭ and dates from the first quarter of the fifth century B.C., shows a wide diversity of imported coins, many of them hacked—presumably to determine whether they were of pure silver throughout—or fragmented, as if to "make change." By the end of the fifth century, Athenian coinage, which dominated eastern Mediterranean currency, became prevalent in Egypt as well, and many large hoards have been recorded.

The famous gold stater with *nefer nub* (fine gold), certainly of Egyptian manufacture, belongs to the fourth century B.C., a period that also saw extensive imitation of Athenian silver; it has even been suggested that some coins heretofore taken as Athenian were, in fact, produced in Egypt. The regular production of official coin began at Alexandria in 326–325 B.C. with tetradrachmas of Alexander the Great, and continued when Ptolemy I assumed control of this portion of Alexander's empire. The Ptolemaic silver at first imitated the coins of Alexander, but by 305 it bore the portrait of Ptolemy I. In its latest form the portrait of Ptolemy became the invariable obverse on silver tetradrachmas; the eagle of Zeus was the reverse. The system was completed by occasional issues of large gold coins (octodrachmas, or eight-drachma pieces) and large, heavy coppers.

The Egypt of the Ptolemies was a closed economy and its coinage circulated only there and in possessions in North Africa and Cyprus; nor was foreign coin any longer found in Egypt. The Ptolemaic system survived without appreciable change until the first century B.C., when it underwent rapid debasement.

Egypt fell to Octavian (later Augustus) after the death of Cleopatra VII (30 B.C.), and from the beginning the province was treated as the private fief of the emperor. Augustus never felt compelled to produce silver, and there were several experiments with copper-based currency, which was struck only in small quantities through the first century. The regular production of the tetradrachma, a nominally silver denomination of about 25 percent fineness and perhaps equal to a denarius, began in A.D. 20. A single hoard and frequent references in the papyri show that the Roman tetradrachma was regarded as the lineal descendant of the Ptolemaic. Except for occasional interruptions, coinage was virtually annual until A.D. 296. From the time of Domitian there was substantial coinage in copper—large drachmas, hemidrachmas, diobols, obols, and chalkoi (quarter obols).

The mint, located at Alexandria, was the empire's most prolific after Rome itself. The principal elements of its coins were the imperial portrait; a legend identifying the ruler or member of his house, generally formulaic and ignoring current offices but including honorifics; the date, calculated in regnal years from 1 Tūt; and a variable reverse type. The variety in these images is reminiscent of practice at the mint of Rome, but the repertoire of types was different. Perhaps because of remoteness from the center of power, Alexandrian types seldom reflected current events; rather the types were simple and broadly conceived, embodying a mixture of Greek, Roman, and local influences. They included Hellenized versions of Roman personifications (e.g., Elpis=Spes, Eleutheria=Libertas); purely Roman deities such as Roma alongside Sarapis, Isis, and Ammon; and figures of local origin such as the Agathodaemon serpent, canopic jar, and hemhem crown. The Antonine period (138–180) displayed the widest variety of types and represented the closest the coinage ever came to artistic excellence—the large "Labors of Hercules" series was a conception worthy of Rome itself.

Taken as a whole, the coinage of early imperial Egypt owed much to its Ptolemaic antecedent in denomination and fabric, and the most frequently encountered reverse type was the very eagle that had been all but universal on Ptolemaic silver. But in 296 Egypt was integrated into the currency system that prevailed in the empire at large and that Diocletian had begun to reform elsewhere in 293; there is no good evidence for any overlap in time between the reformed coinage of Diocletian and the traditional, Greek-style coinage, which disappeared immediately from hoards. The new imperial coinage was marked by instability and frequent reform, and its vicissitudes were reflected by the coinage of Egypt. Alexandria's output consisted almost exclusively of argentiferous copper (later virtually pure copper) coins, with gold solidi being produced only rarely and silver hardly at all.

Striking of coin in Egypt, as in other provinces, slowed considerably through the fifth century, and the absence of Alexandria from the reformed mints of Anastasius (491–518) probably indicates that it had ceased to coin by 491. Byzantine currency was introduced at Alexandria under Justin I (518–527). At first it was limited to copper; and while the rest of the empire employed the *follis* (40 *noummia*) and its fractions (20, 10, 5, and occasionally 2 *noummia*) for small change, the Alexandrian system was different. The mint struck thick, dumpy coins; at its fullest the system consisted of denominations of 12, 6, and 3 *noummia*, and under Heraclius (610–641) a large coin of 33 *noummia*. The system was unique, and these coins were seldom found in company with the standard denominations of the eastern Byzantine mints, although they appeared occasionally in western Africa. It has been suggested that 12 *noummia* was the tariff of surviving base-bullion tetradrachmas, but this is only a guess; against it is the lack of evidence for survival of the third-century tetradrachma into the sixth. Their reversion to a formerly familiar shape may simply be a vestige of the earlier economic isolation of Egypt, now reinstituted; there is simply no evidence on the point. The individuality of the denominational system is reflected in the types as well: the profile bust, characteristic of the earliest Byzantine coppers at all mints, was maintained at Alexandria long after its abandonment elsewhere under JUSTINIAN (527–565).

Gold with the mint mark ΑΛΧΙΟΒ was certainly struck in or for Egypt under JUSTIN II (565–578), but other attributions are more controversial. Some coins originally identified as Alexandrian on the basis of fabric and findspot have been regarded as aberrant Constantinopolitan issues or even as barbaric productions, while others have been assigned to Cyprus, which always had close economic connections with Egypt. The most certain case is provided by solidi of the revolt of Heraclius (608–610), which are unusual in bearing indictional dates.

The seventh-century copper coinage continued

the tradition of the dodecanoummium and more rarely its fractions; the reverse continued to consist principally or exclusively of the mark of denomination and, on the dodecanoummium, a cross on steps. The obverses finally abandoned the profile bust in favor of a facing one or, later, one or more standing figures. When the Arabs took Egypt their earliest coinage seems to have consisted of crude imitations of the latest dodecanoummia.

The legacy of the Ptolemies was one of independent coinage, and except for the relatively brief interlude from 296 through the fifth century, the Egyptian coinage represented a clearly identifiable tradition, never entirely integrated into any other. It was never fully illustrative of the culture at large, but rather reflected the idiom of foreign rulers imposed on a society that remained curious and unfamiliar to them.

BIBLIOGRAPHY

Dattari, G. *Monete imperiali greche. Numi Augg. Alexandrini.* Cairo, 1901.

Grierson, P. *Byzantine Coins,* pp. 68–69, 117–19. Berkeley, Los Angeles, and London, 1982.

Kraay, C. M. *Archaic and Classical Greek Coins,* pp. 294–95. Berkeley, Los Angeles, and London, 1976.

Milne, J. G. *Catalogue of Alexandrian Coins.* Ashmolean Museum, Oxford, 1933; reprinted with additions, 1971.

Price, M., and N. Waggoner. *Archaic Greek Silver Coinage. The "Asyut" Hoard.* London, 1975.

Thompson, M.; O. Mørkholm; and C. M. Kraay. *An Inventory of Greek Coin Hoards,* pp. 225–42. New York, 1973.

Whitting, P. D. *Byzantine Coins.* New York and London, 1973.

WILLIAM METCALF

Islamic Period

When the Arabs conquered Egypt in 641 the Byzantine mint in Alexandria apparently continued to issue copper dodecanoummium coins without any essential change in appearance, except a cruder design that leads numismatists to assign them to the Arab period. There were several varieties, of which one is certainly Arab: it bears, instead of the usual A E, the mint name MACP, pronounced *Maṣr* (Miṣr), the Arabic word for Egypt and its capital al-Fusṭāṭ, indicating that the mint had been moved from Alexandria.

Byzantine-style coinage was replaced by copper *fals* coins with Arabic inscriptions sometime after the invention of Islamic coinage in Damascus (699) and surely by the time of the governor Qurrah ibn Sharīk (709–714), when Arabic glass weights for copper coins were introduced. The new Arab *fals* was not different from the Byzantine coins in weight or fabric and probably not in value, but instead of imperial portraits, crosses, and a Greek inscription it was anonymous, with brief religious inscriptions in Arabic. Starting sometime between 734 and 742, all copper issues carried the governor's name.

These coppers were the only coins minted in Egypt until 787, but imported Byzantine and Arab gold and silver coins circulated there earlier as shown by numerous references in the papyri and by the existence of Egyptian glass weights for these denominations. The Arab glass weights for coins (which are closely related to glass weights for ounces and pounds and stamped glass measuring vessels) are the most interesting feature of Egypt's eighth-century monetary history. Officially made Arab glass coin weights began during the administration of ʿAbd Allāh ibn ʿAbd al-Malik (705–709) and continued until the end of the century. They were very precisely made and show an official gold dinar standard of $4\frac{23}{24}$ grams and a series of differing silver *dirham* standards, beginning with a standard of two-thirds the weight of the dinar (2.83 grams), followed by two different standards for a "*dirham* of 13 *kharrūbas*" at 2.50 and 2.62 grams, returning to the "*dirham* of two-thirds" and ending with a "*dirham kayl*" (about 2.95 grams). Only the latter, to be assigned to the ninth century and perhaps to a different workshop from the earlier glass, approached the theoretical Islamic standard dirham of seven-tenths *mithqāl* (2.975 grams). The glass weights for copper coins, *fals,* changed even more frequently in a sequence that is not yet clear. Some of the surviving glass stamps for commodity-measuring vessels specify that the vessel was to contain "one *fals*'s worth" of the commodity named (the commodities were everyday groceries and cosmetics, not pharmaceuticals as was once thought). On some of the glass *fals* weights, the number of *kharrūbas* is specified with Coptic numerals instead of Arabic words, and other weights name Coptic artisans as the makers (the names are Khā'īl and Sāwīrus, written in Arabic script; the third name recorded is Kāmil, of uncertain ethnicity).

In the year 786–787, coinage in precious metals, gold, and silver began. Egypt immediately became a major producer of gold dinars and continued to be until the early twentieth century. From 786 until

830, Egyptian dinars bore the name of the governor: from 834 they usually had only the name of the caliph, but the Tulunid and Ikhshidid governors asserted the privilege of putting their names on the coins along with that of the caliph. Starting in 815 all Egyptian dinars are identified by the inscription "this dinar was struck in Egypt," but the Arabic word for Egypt, *Miṣr,* is also to be understood as the designation of the capital, al-Fusṭāṭ, site of the country's mint.

The earliest known silver *dirham* of Egypt is dated one year after the earliest gold, but it is likely that silver and gold coinage began simultaneously. Silver minting, however, does not seem to have caught on in Egypt, as its *dirhams* are extremely rare until the Fatimid conquest (969). Evidently, since *dirham* transactions are frequently mentioned in the papyri and hoards of foreign *dirhams* are found in Egypt, the country was able to meet its needs for silver coinage by imports.

Copper coins issued after the beginning of gold and silver minting were much smaller than previous issues and more regular in weight. Evidently the importance of copper in the currency system was much reduced. Several issues of copper took place between 802 and 827, and another followed early in the administration of Aḥmad ibn Ṭūlūn, in 871–873, the last issue of copper coins in Egypt until the thirteenth century. Small transactions were apparently carried out with cut bits of *dirhams* or by running an account with local merchants.

The Fatimid conquest of Egypt in 969 brought with it their different monetary system, developed in North Africa. The gold dinars of the conqueror, al-Muʿizz, had three concentric inscriptions on each side in place of the horizontal legends surrounded by a circular inscription that characterized the classical Abbasid Sunnī type. Each subsequent caliph had one or more distinct designs in succession, probably marking minor changes in alloy or weight standard, or perhaps only corresponding to more substantial changes in the silver coinage. In general, however, the Egyptian dinar maintained its full weight and high alloy until the end of the eleventh century. A new gold denomination, the quarter dinar or *rubʿ*, was introduced into Egypt by the Fatimids. The Fatimid gold coinage enjoyed considerable prestige in the Mediterranean world. At any given time, their coinage was substantially uniform from Sicily into Syria, and was imitated or adapted in Spain, Yemen, and Afghanistan, as well as by the Crusaders in the twelfth and thirteenth centuries.

Fatimid silver coinage in contrast was usually small and increasingly debased in the tenth and eleventh centuries, stabilizing finally at the end of the eleventh century at 30 percent silver. These little coins served as small change in place of copper coinage. Despite the low weight of the actual coins, the weight standard for a payment of a full *dirham* continued to be nearly three grams.

The Fatimids also revived official glass coin weights for dinars and *dirhams*, including fractions and multiples of the two denominations. These have been cataloged but their evolution is still not clearly understood.

Throughout the early Islamic centuries, as probably also before Islam, the relative values of gold, silver, and copper coins were not fixed but fluctuated according to the market, from day to day and place to place. The papyri and Geniza documents often refer to the exchange rate (*ṣarf*) between dinars and *dirhams*. As the early glass weights show, the weight standard of the *dirham* could change substantially and often, with five changes in the eighth century. At other periods, without the evidence of the glass weights, we can only assume that such changes were possible. These would naturally affect the normal dinar–*dirham* exchange rate as well as prices. There is also evidence for changes in the alloy of gold and silver coins. The research to support precise statements has not yet been done, but enough is known to inspire caution in comparing prices and exchange rates from the documents over long spans of time.

BIBLIOGRAPHY

Awad, H. A. "Seventh Century Arab Imitations of Alexandrian Dodecanoummia." *American Numismatic Society Museum Notes* 18 (1972):113–17.

Bacharach, J. L., and H. A. Awad. "The Early Islamic Bronze Coinage of Egypt: Additions." *Near Eastern Numismatics, Iconography, Epigraphy and History: Studies in Honor of George C. Miles,* pp. 185–92. Beirut, 1974.

______. "Rare Early Egyptian Islamic Coins and Coin Weights: The Awad Collection." *Journal of the American Research Center in Egypt* 18 (1981):51–56.

Balog, P. "Tables de références des monnaies ikhchidites." *Revue belge de numismatique* 103 (1957):107–134.

______. "The Fāṭimid Glass Jeton." *Annali dell'Instituto Italiano di Numismatica* 18–19 (1971–1972):175–264; 20 (1973):121–212.

Bates, M. L. "The Function of Fāṭimid and Ayyūbid Glass Weights." *Journal of the Economic and So-*

cial History of the Orient 24 (1981):70–81.

———. "Coins and Money in the Arabic Papyri." In *Proceedings of the Table Ronde: Documents de l'Islam mediéval: Nouvelles perspectives (March, 1988)*, ed. Yousef Ragheb (1989).

Goitein, S. D. "Money, Banking, and Finance." In *A Mediterranean Society: The Jewish Communities of the Arab World as Portrayed in the Documents of the Cairo Geniza, I: Economic Foundations*, pp. 229–66. Berkeley and Los Angeles, 1967.

Grabar, O. *The Coinage of the Ṭūlūnids*. American Numismatic Society Numismatic Notes and Monographs 139. New York, 1957.

Miles, G. C. "The Early Islamic Bronze Coinage of Egypt." In *Centennial Publication of the American Numismatic Society*, ed. Harald Ingholt, pp. 471–502. New York, 1958.

Morton, A. H. *A Catalogue of Early Islamic Glass Stamps in the British Museum*. London, 1985.

Oddy, W. A. "The Gold Contents of Fāṭimid Coins Reconsidered." In *Metallurgy in Numismatics*, Vol. 1, pp. 99–118. London, 1980.

MICHAEL BATES

COLLUTHUS, a schismatic presbyter in Alexandria during the episcopate of ALEXANDER (312–326), nineteenth patriarch of the See of Saint Mark. In 324 the council convened by Hosius to quell the growing Arian controversy deposed Colluthus for taking upon himself the episcopal function of conferring orders. Ancient sources indicate that Colluthus was not a supporter of Arius, but was himself the leader of a schismatic group. Although Philastrius stated that Colluthus erred in teaching against Isaiah 45:7 that God did not create evil, the exact nature of the beliefs of Colluthus is not known. His activities after 324 are similarly obscure.

BIBLIOGRAPHY

Salmon, G. "Colluthus (2)." In DCB, Vol. 1, p. 596.

RANDALL STEWART

COLONNADE. *See* Architectural Elements of Churches.

COLOPHON, name given to the statements at the end of a manuscript about the copyist, the readers, or other persons. Among Coptic manuscripts from the second half of the fourth century with colophons are Codex II (145.20–23; Krause and Labib, 106) and Codex VII (127.28–32; Krause and Labib, 3) from the NAG HAMMADI LIBRARY.

In collective manuscripts there are often colophons at the end of each individual book (see CODEX ALEXANDRINUS), for instance, in British Museum Oriental 7549, a Coptic Bible manuscript from the fourth century, at the end of Deuteronomy (Budge, 1912, pl. 4) and of Acts (Budge, pl. 9).

The early colophons are short; usually they contain only words of blessing for the scribe and readers and do not mention the name of the scribe. In the course of time, however, they became longer and more communicative, mentioning not only the name of the scribe but also the person who commissioned the transcription, the monastery or church for which the manuscript was intended, and often the date of its writing. In collective manuscripts it is even specified when the writing of the manuscript began and when the writing of the individual Gospels was completed (Horner, 1898, pp. xliff.). Thereby the colophons are important for Coptic paleography, because they not only date the manuscripts exactly through their naming of scribes but also provide us with knowledge of the scribal schools (see SCRIPTORIUM). They help us to reconstruct the original strength of church and monastery libraries (see LIBRARIES). and provide material for the history of the churches and monasteries that they mention. They are important for the history of piety in the period (many books were endowed for the salvation of the customer's soul) and supply abundant material for our knowledge of personalities (see PROSOPOGRAPHY). It is therefore important that the work of A. van Lantschoot, which is of value for the colophons contained in Sahidic manuscripts, be continued. Not only must the colophons of the Sahidic manuscripts, which have become known in the interval, be edited, but also those of the remaining dialects, among which the Bohairic, because of their great extent and their late drafting, promise particularly numerous insights. The later Bohairic manuscripts also contain maledictions against those who should dare to steal or damage the manuscript (see, e.g., Horner, p. cxiv).

BIBLIOGRAPHY

Budge, E. A. W. *Coptic Biblical Texts in the Dialect of Upper Egypt*. London, 1912.

Horner, G. *The Coptic Version of the New Testament in the Northern Dialect Otherwise Called Memphitic and Bohairic*, Vol. 1. Oxford, 1898.

Krause, M., and P. Labib. *Gnostische und hermetische Schriften aus Codex II und VI*. Abhandlungen des Deutschen Archäologischen Instituts Kairo,

Koptische Reihe 2. Glückstadt, 1971.
Lantschoot, A. van. *Recueil des colophons des manuscrits chrétiens d'Egypte*. Louvain, 1929.

MARTIN KRAUSE

COLUMN. *See* Architectural Elements of Churches.

COMBS. *See* Bone and Ivory Carving; Woodwork, Coptic.

COMMUNICATIO IDIOMATUM (interchange of properties), a term applied to the person of Christ by those in the early church who believed that although the human and divine natures remained separate, the attributes of the one could be applied to the other. Thus the divine Word could be described as dying on the cross and the Virgin Mary was the mother of God (*Theotokos*). The idea of *communicatio idiomatum* was anticipated by IGNATIUS OF ANTIOCH in the early second century and was taken up by the Alexandrian school of theologians: ATHANASIUS I, Apollinarius, GREGORY OF NAZIANZUS, GREGORY OF NYSSA, CYRIL OF ALEXANDRIA, and LEO THE GREAT, among others. Cyril exploited it to the fullest extent, stating, "The Word has imparted the glory of the divine operation to His own flesh, while at the same time taking to Himself what belongs to the flesh." The doctrine received conciliar authority in the *Tome* of Pope Leo I (449), accepted by the Council of CHALCEDON. There, at the sixth session, held on 25 October 451, the council drafted a Christological definition that asserted: "Our Lord Jesus Christ is to us one and the same son, the self-same Perfect in Godhead, the self-same Perfect in manhood, truly God and truly man . . . the difference of the Natures [of Christ] being in no way removed because of the Union, but rather the properties of each nature being preserved into one Prosopon and one Hypostasis." In later times, in Lutheran circles, the doctrine was understood in a way not in harmony with Leo. In Byzantium, on the other hand, the doctrine was extended to cover the relations of church and state.

Opposed to the Alexandrian idea were theologians of the Antiochene school (Eustathius, Diodore of Tarsus, and THEODORE OF MOPSUESTIA, among others). They emphasized the concrete human life of the historical Jesus. Certain thinkers held that there were two Sons—the Son of God and the Son of Man—whose union was not due to a fusion of the Word with the flesh—rather, the Word dwelt in the flesh as in a temple, much as God indwelt His prophets. The human nature of Jesus underwent real growth in knowledge and in discernment of good and evil.

MONOPHYSITISM, as held by the Coptic church, is a development of Alexandrian theology that rejected the *communicatio*, as it did Chalcedon as a whole. Now that controversies have become less pronounced, the doctrine of *communicatio idiomatum* may yet find favor in Coptic Christian circles.

BIBLIOGRAPHY

Bethune-Baker, J. F. *An Introduction to the Early History of Christian Doctrine*. London, 1949.
Boularand, E. "La théologie antiochienne." *Bulletine de Littérature ecclésiastique* 68 (1967):241–72.
Frend, W. H. C. *The Rise of the Monophysite Movement*. 2nd ed. Cambridge, 1979.
Kelly, J. N. D. *Early Christian Doctrines*. London, 1958.
Sellers, R. V. *Two Ancient Christologies*. London, 1940.

LESLIE W. BARNARD

COMMUNION, the act of partaking of the Body and Blood of Christ. Communion is given many designations in the New Testament, such as "a new covenant" (Heb. 8:8–12), "eternal life" (Jn. 6:54), a "dwelling in Christ" (Jn. 5:56; 15:5–7), and a "sharing in the Body of Christ" (1 Cor. 10:16–17).

In the early church, communion was permitted only to the faithful. CATECHUMENS who had not yet been accepted into the congregation were required to depart after the readings from the Epistles and the Gospel, that is, at the end of the Mass of the Catechumens. The sacrament was then administered to all the congregation. "All the faithful who come in and hear the Scriptures, but do not stay for the prayers and Holy Communion, are to be excommunicated, as causing disorder in the church" (*Apostolical Canon* 9).

The same penalty applied, of course, to the clergy: "If any bishop, presbyter, or deacon, or anyone in the sacerdotal list, when the offering is made, does not partake of it, let him declare the cause; and if it be a reasonable one, let him be excused; but if he does not declare it, let him be excommunicated, as being a cause of offence to the people . . ." (*Canon* 8).

The Council of Antioch (341) laid down a similar stipulation: "As for all those persons who enter the church and listen to the sacred scriptures, but who fail to commune in prayer together and at the same time with the laity, or who shun the participation of the Eucharist, in accordance with some irregularity, we decree that these persons be outcasts from the church until, after going to confession and exhibiting fruits of repentance and begging forgiveness, they succeed in obtaining a pardon . . ." (*The Canons of the Blessed and Holy Fathers*).

The so-called *consistentes* were the only group of penitents allowed to attend the liturgy to the end, but they were not permitted to partake of Holy Communion until they had been officially accepted into the body of the congregation.

In administering the Body and Blood of Jesus Christ to the communicants, the Coptic church follows as closely as possible the procedure set by Christ when He instituted this sacrament. The two species, first the bread and then the wine, are separately given. This practice was widespread among all Christian churches until about the twelfth century, when the Roman Catholic church withdrew the chalice from lay communicants.

The celebrant priest administers Holy Communion by placing the pure Body into the communicant's mouth. This manner is a modification of an earlier practice, common until the ninth century, according to which the communicant would receive the Body in his right palm while it was placed crosswise over his left palm. Reference to this older practice is made by many of the church fathers.

Female communicants were not allowed to touch the Holy Body with their own hands, and had to receive it on a mat spread over the right palm, the explanation being that after the resurrection Christ permitted men such as Thomas to touch Him (Jn. 10:26–28), while he forbade Mary Magdalen (Jn. 20:17).

When all communicants have received the Body, they receive the Blood by means of the spoon straight from the chalice. In the case of newly baptized infants, the priest dips his forefinger in the Blood, touches the Body, and inserts it into the infant's mouth.

After the oblation has been sanctified, communicants partake of it, starting with the clergy in descending order of hierarchy and then the congregation. If the liturgy is being celebrated by a bishop, he starts by communicating himself, then the rest of the clergy and the deacons, then the congregation. He may also ask a priest to administer the Blood. Should a priest be officiating alone at a service attended by a large congregation he may, to save time, ask a fully-consecrated deacon to administer the Blood to the congregation, though not to his fellow deacons.

The church has laid down certain requirements to be met before receiving communion. A communicant must ensure spiritual preparedness, by showing genuine repentance for previous sins and shortcomings. Physical cleanliness, continence, and purity is equally important, together with a liturgical fast of at least nine hours prior to communion, reckoned to be the nine-hour duration between the hour when Christ was condemned to crucifixion (9 A.M.) and his burial (6 P.M.).

BIBLIOGRAPHY

Cummings, D. *The Rudder (Pedalion)*. Chicago, 1957.

Percival, H. R. *Excursus on the Worship of the Holy Church*. In *A Select Library of the Nicene and Post-Nicene Fathers of the Christian Church*, 2d ser., Vol. 14, ed. Philip Schaff and Henry Wace. Grand Rapids, Mich., 1956.

ARCHBISHOP BASILIOS

COMMUNION OF THE SICK, a special rite by which Holy Communion is administered to a bedridden person or to a prisoner in his cell. Fasting and confession are required whenever possible.

After celebrating the Divine Liturgy in the church, and while communicating the people, the priest dips a portion of the Holy Body in the Precious Blood and places it in the *artophorion*, and then wraps it with a mat. A deacon takes a bottle of blessed water and a candle and accompanies the priest. It is necessary that the priest eats or drinks nothing after Holy Communion and observes complete silence while on his way to the sick. The priest starts by repeating the prayers of the elevation, consignation, and commixture until the conclusion of the confession. After communicating the sick person, the priest washes the *artophorion* and gives the water to the sick person to drink. Subsequently water is poured over the priest's fingers, which he drinks before he wipes the *artophorion* with the mat and wraps it up.

Should the sick person be found physically or morally unfit to receive the Eucharist, the priest should himself consume it.

The early church insisted that a dying person be communicated; according to Canon 13 of the Council of NICAEA, "Concerning the departing, the ancient canonical law is still to be maintained, to wit that, if any man be at the point of death he must not be deprived of the last and most indispensable *Viaticum*. . . ."

The thirty-sixth of the canons attributed to Saint ATHANASIUS (c. 326–373) says, "No priest shall carry forth the Mysteries and go with them about the streets, except for a sick man, when the end and death's hour of need draw nigh. And when they carry the mysteries [without], they shall suffer none but the sick to partake. And they shall not do according to favour and give unto one beside the sick, but unto the sick alone. . . ."

It seems, however, that later in the Middle Ages, the Copts ceased to take the Holy Communion to the sick outside the church for fear of any transgression on the sacraments. Instead, they probably preferred to carry the sick to take communion inside the church. Hence MĪKHĀ'ĪL, bishop of Damietta in the twelfth century, compares the Eucharist with its prototype, the lamb of the old passover, and says, "And we shall not keep it back [till the second day], and we shall not carry it out of the church, and whatsoever remains of it the priests shall eat . . . And concerning the first Eucharist, namely, the bread and the chalice which the Lord blessed and gave to His disciples, there remained nothing of it over it till the second day, and it was not carried to a house, other than the one in which it [the Last Supper] was performed."

Saint Basil, in his ninety-eighth canon says, "And we did not bring the Mystery outside the church at all to be given to a person even if he is in the distress of death."

Pope JOHN XVI (1676–1718) is considered the first Coptic patriarch to arrange the communion for the sick at home. In manuscripts in the Library of the Monastery of Saint Antony (nos. 343 and 389), it is written about that patriarch that he, "seeing the inability of the sick and bedridden to go to the holy church to partake of the Divine Mysteries H. H. arranged for the Holy Reserved Sacrament . . . to be carried to the sick and crippled and bedridden in their houses. This wise arrangement is followed until this day."

BIBLIOGRAPHY

Riedel, W., and W. E. Crum. *The Canons of Athanasius*. London, 1904; repr. 1973.

EMILE MAHER ISHAQ

COMMUNION TABLE, the fixed table standing in the middle of the sanctury (*haykal*) of the church, at which the Divine Liturgy is celebrated. It is an almost cubical structure of brickwork, stonework, or marble. In the first three centuries of the Christian era, the communion table was made of wood, partly in symbolic allusion to the wooden table at which Christ shared the Last Supper with the disciples before His crucifixion, and instituted the Eucharist; and partly to facilitate its removal when churches were subject to heathen incursions. Saint ATHANASIUS (326–373) refers to the wooden altar that was destroyed by the Arians in Alexandria. Saint Augustine (354–430) also relates how Maximianus, the Orthodox bishop of Bagai, a town of Numidia, was nearly beaten to death by the Donatists, who stripped boards of wood from the altar under which he had been hiding.

Wooden altars have not been used in the Coptic church since the fourth century. (Among the exhibits of the Coptic Museum in Cairo, there is a wooden altar that formerly stood in the Church of Abū Sarjah [Saint Sergius] in Old Cairo.) They may be used only on a temporary basis in churches that are under construction. They were banned from other churches at a later stage. In 517 the Council of Albion (Epiona) in France forbade the consecration of altars not built of stone, and toward the end of the ninth century, Patriarch John bar-Algari interdicted the use of wooden communion tables in the Nestorian church. The Ethiopian church, on the other hand, still retains the use of wooden altars. However, according to the procedure followed in the consecration of the holy CHRISM the service is invariably conducted on a wooden altar.

BIBLIOGRAPHY

Butler, A. J. *The Ancient Coptic Churches of Egypt*, Vol. 2. Oxford, 1884.

ARCHBISHOP BASILIOS

COMMUNITY COUNCIL, COPTIC, council made up of laymen to take part in the administration of community affairs. With the emergence of the Coptic church from its declining circumstances under the successive waves of persecution in the Middle Ages, its reawakening in modern times was associated with various attempts at reform. The first and most serious attempts at regeneration took place under CYRIL IV (1854–1861) who deservedly earned the title of Father of Reform. Besides reforms for the enlightenment of the clergy, he concentrated on educational and cultural projects, such as opening numerous schools, introducing Coptic and foreign languages into the curriculum, and establishing a printing press.

The development of community councils passed through various stages, following the issuance of the Sultan's *Khaṭṭ hamayūnī* (official decree) in 1856. This was a form of charter of liberties for the Christian minorities throughout the vast Ottoman empire. It authorized the establishment of special councils within the patriarchates to deal with problems of "personal status," such as marriage, divorce, and inheritance, as well as the administration of the *waqfs,* property donated to the church and the monasteries and held in trust, to be administered for ecclesiastical and charitable purposes. Such properties had been accumulating throughout the ages, and were considerably increased during the patriarchate of Demetrius II (1862–1870). On the occasion of the sultan's visit to Egypt, the sultan bestowed 1,000 *feddans* (acres) of arable land to the church, and this was supplemented by 500 *feddans* by Khedive Ismā'īl (1863–1882).

With the death of Pope Demetrius in 1870, Mark (Murqus), bishop of the province of al-Beheirah, was appointed locum tenens until a new patriarch was consecrated. Bishop Mark chose a number of notables to assist him in the administration of the financial affairs of the church. This may be considered the first nucleus of the community council. The Copts welcomed the project and decided to submit a formal application to the authorities for the foundation of a similar council to take charge of the *waqfs,* schools, benevolent societies, affairs of personal status, and other secular functions, which would relieve the clergy of such worldly concerns. The application was presented by BOUTROS GHALI to the khedive, who on 5 February 1874 approved the establishment of a council to consist of twelve members and twelve adjuncts elected by general suffrage, to meet under the chairmanship of the patriarch.

The relationship between Pope CYRIL V (1874–1927) and the elected council was not harmonious, and consequently the council was dissolved. Two councils in succession were elected, but neither could hold a profitable meeting. The first of these was again dissolved, and the second was denied access and found the doors of the patriarchate locked in 1892. When the situation was reported to the government, with Boutros Ghali as minister of finance, it was decided that both the patriarch and Bishop Yu'annis of al-Beheirah had to be removed to the Monastery of al-Barāmūs, a measure without precedent in contemporary ecclesiastical history. Khedive 'Abbās II (1892–1914) ordered the return of the patriarch on 30 January 1893, and on 1 February he arrived in Cairo amid enthusiastic public acclaim. Those who were responsible for his exile were pardoned, and two amendments to the constitution of the council were enacted. One was bylaw no. 8 of December 1908, by which the patriarch was solely responsible for the appointment of his clerical substitute in the council, and the administration of the *waqfs* would be entrusted to the patriarch and four monastic abbots. The second was bylaw no. 3 of February 1912, restricting the number of the council membership to a total of twelve, eight laymen to be elected by general suffrage and four clerics to be nominated by the patriarch. These amendments remained in abeyance for twelve years, as they were resisted by the community and consequently abolished by parliament, and the original constitution of May 1883 remained in force. In 1927, after fifty-two years as patriarch, the death of Cyril V at the age of ninety-six paved the way for the next stage.

This stage was inaugurated by Yu'annis, bishop of al-Beheirah, first as locum tenens and in 1928 as Patriarch JOHN XIX. In November 1928 the pope accepted the nomination of a committee consisting of four members of the council and two bishops under his presidency, to supervise the vast *waqf* estates. But the system faltered, and the case had to be referred to the court when the patriarch died in 1942. He was succeeded by MACARIUS III (1944–1945) after an interregnum of two years. The new pope issued a favorable letter on 22 February 1944 nominating a committee of five members of the council to be entrusted with the administration of the *waqfs,* a measure that was refused by the Holy Synod. The brokenhearted patriarch retired to the monastery of Saint Antony (DAYR ANBĀ ANṬŪNIYŪS). He died in the following year.

Anbā YŪSĀB II (1946–1956), metropolitan of Jirjā, became pope on the specific condition of his acceding to entrust the administration of the *waqfs* to the community council. This promise was circumvented after Yūsāb's consecration by his raising the abbots of monasteries to the episcopate and entrusting them with the financial administration of the *waqfs.* At this juncture, the Egyptian revolution of

July 1952 broke out, and a new council was nominated. Later, in September 1955, the ailing patriarch, who had been widely criticized for personal reasons, was relieved of his powers. A triumvirate of three bishops took charge of the conduct of patriarchal authority. On 13 November 1956, Yūsāb II died, thus closing one of the controversial chapters in the contemporary history of the Coptic church.

An interregnum of two and a half years followed his death, and the powers of the community council were drastically reduced by law, which stripped the council of its jurisdiction over personal status cases (marriage, divorce, alimony), referring them to civil courts of the state. The Coptic schools were put under the supervision of the Egyptian Ministry of Education, and all benevolent societies under the Ministry of Social Affairs. Nothing was left for the council save the solution of the material problem of the *waqfs*. This became the responsibility of the patriarchal successor, CYRIL VI (1959–1971), a solitary monk, who became the 116th patriarch on 10 May 1959.

After three-quarters of a century of strife, Cyril VI was able to find a practical solution. On 19 July 1960, the pope secured a presidential decree promulgating a law that provided for a new system to control all the Coptic *waqfs*. A joint board called the Council of Coptic *Waqfs* was formed under the chairmanship of the patriarch and comprising six bishops and six secular Coptic notables, with full authority to appoint the *waqf* trustees and supervise their administration. On 12 July 1961 Cyril VI seized the opportunity of the expiration of the five-year period of the then existing council to inform the government that he did not favor holding a new election, and the authorities approved his proposal. This led to the extension of the council elected in 1956 for the time being.

However, in 1967 the community council faced serious financial problems in funding the Theological Institutes and the administrative offices of the patriarchate. Again the solution to this problem was found by Cyril VI outside the council by his providing a committee of twelve members appointed by virtue of presidential decree, issued on 6 December 1967.

This arrangement was maintained until Cyril's death on 9 March 1971, and the succession of Pope SHENOUDA III on 14 November 1971.

After a twelve-year suspension, elections for a new council took place in August 1973. At the expiration of its five-year term in 1978, it was succeeded by another. A new round of elections was due in 1983, but this had to be canceled in the wake of the events surrounding the internal exile by President Sadat of Pope Shenouda to the Monastery of Anbā Bishoi in September 1981. Following the pope's restoration early in 1985, a new council was elected in March 1985.

The councils, however, still maintain the important role of participating in the papal elections, in their capacity as official representatives of the Coptic population. Under the church rules as recognized by the state (presidential decree of 3 November 1957), the general council has the following powers: (1) in conjunction with the Holy Church Synod, it appoints the locum tenens bishop, following the death of the pope; (2) a committee consisting of eighteen members, nine of whom are to be chosen from the general council, is authorized to select candidates for the patriarchate; (3) an electoral committee consisting of the locum tenens bishop, three clergymen, and three eminent members of the community conducts the voting process.

According to the 1883 constitution providing for the establishment of community councils, the powers they exercised were extensive. Subsequently many functions were eliminated. The council had jurisdiction of personal status cases, when the parties concerned were all of the Coptic Orthodox denomination, otherwise the case would fall within the Muslim court jurisdiction. Such cases are now to be settled by civil courts. The management of Coptic schools was originally entrusted to community councils. These schools are now under the full supervision of the Ministry of Education. The administration of the *waqfs* passed to the joint Patriarchal Laical Waqf Organization in 1960.

The 1883 constitution, slightly amended in 1927, also provided for the establishment of provincial councils in cathedral cities of Egypt, under the presidency of their local bishops. These councils assume their responsibilities within their own eparchies, and are subject to the supervision of the general council in respect to matters of particular importance. Each council consists of four members, with the exception of the council of Alexandria, which is made up of seven members under the presidency of the vicar-general.

ADEL AZER BESTAWROS

COMPLINE, the prayer of sleep instituted, according to the canonical hours, to commemorate the laying down of the body of Jesus Christ in the tomb. In churches and monasteries compline is said after vespers and before the raising of incense for the evening service. The DIDASCALIA (Qelādah, 1979) and Ibn al-'Assāl's *Kitāb al-Qawānīn* (Book of Canon Law) include compline among the seven canonical prayers.

It appears that compline was initially confined to the Egyptian church, as Saint BASIL THE GREAT does not include it in his earlier text of prayers. Instead, he divided the sext (the sixth hour) into two parts: the first preceding and the second following the evening meal, to bring the total number of prayers to seven. Later, however, Saint Basil chose to add compline after vespers, incorporating with it "At midnight I will rise to give thanks unto Thee because of Thy righteous judgment."

ARCHBISHOP BASILIOS

CONCEPT OF OUR GREAT POWER, an apocalyptic tractate dating from the mid-fourth century or shortly thereafter and influenced by Jewish speculations, biblical or apocryphal, slightly tinged with gnosticism. The aim of the text is to describe the history of the world in its fundamental stages: creation, the flood, the origin of evil, the coming of a Savior who descends into Hades to humiliate the archons, the appearance of an Antichrist who rules over the world, and finally the *apocatastasis* (second coming) and the salvation of the elect souls. This history is presented according to a scheme of three aeons—the aeon of the flesh, the psychic aeon, and the indestructible aeon. The Great Power takes the role of speaker, and communicates to his hearers a number of revelations and teachings.

The aeon of the flesh comes into being in the "great bodies" (38). During its reign the vengeance of the father of the flesh, the water, takes place. He sends the flood upon men, sparing only Noah (38.17–39.15). Then follows the reign of the psychic aeon (39.16): "It is a small one, which is mixed with bodies, begetting in the souls and being defiled." In fact during this aeon the pollution, which had already made its appearance under the aeon of the flesh, now increases, and gives birth to all kinds of evils, "many works of wrath, anger, envy, malice, hatred, slander, contempt and war, lying and evil counsels, sorrows and pleasures, basenesses and defilements, falsehoods and diseases, evil judgments" (39.20–31). The author concludes this list with an exhortation of Gnostic savor addressed to his hearers: "Yet you are sleeping, dreaming dreams. Wake up and return, taste and eat the true food. Hand out the word and the water of life! Cease from the evil lusts and desires and (the teachings of) the Anomoeans, evil heresies that have no basis" (39.33–40.9). The reference to this heresy, which was propagated during the fourth century, provides a *terminus a quo* for the dating of the text (Wisse and Williams, 1979).

A man who knows the Great Power is going to be born under the dominion of the psychic aeon (40.24–27). He will drink from the milk of the mother, he will speak in parables, he will proclaim the aeon that is to come (40.28–32). This man "spoke in 72 tongues, opened the gates of the heavens with his words, put to shame the ruler of Hades, raised the dead" (41.6–11). His coming provokes reaction from the archons. This man is Christ. By the treachery of Judas, the text tells us, the archons laid hold of him and brought him before the governor of Hades. But "the nature of his flesh could not be seized" (42.1–2). Here we have the Gnostic doctrine of docetic origin, that the Christ could not be grasped. He leaves only his outward semblance in the hands of the archons, mocks them ("he prepared himself to go down and put them to shame"), and escapes from them (cf. Nag Hammadi Library, Codex II, *Seth* 51.24–29; 52.10–14; 53.20–21; Codex I, *Apocalypse of James* 30.1–8; 31.15–21; *Apocalypse of Peter* 80.25–30; 81.3–82.17). The coming of Christ is followed by a series of signs that mark the end of the psychic aeon: "The sun set during the day; the day became dark; the evil spirits were troubled, the aeons will dissolve. But those who would know these things . . . will become blessed, since they will come to know the truth" (42.15–43.29). The signs of the end are brought on by the dissolution of the archons: the destruction of cities, the shaking of the mountains, a trembling of the earth, the death of animals (43.32–44.13) mark the transition from the realm of the archons to the kingdom of the Logos. These signs are typical of eschatological times, and are found in similar form in the Jewish pseudepigrapha of the Old Testament (Ascension of Isaiah 4 and 5; II Enoch 22; IV Esdras 5; Ascension of Moses). An imitating spirit is sent by the archons to combat a divine child come to his maturity (44.31–45.4). His coming will also be marked by signs of the end (45.31–46.5). Positive signs on the contrary will accompany the coming of the Great Power who will protect the elect, who are clothed in holy garments (46.8–24). These will return to an "immeasurable light" (46.8–9). The treatise ends with the redemption of the souls, and the fact that the elect have come to be in the unchangeable aeon.

BIBLIOGRAPHY

Wisse, F., and F. E. Williams. "The Concept of Our Great Power." In *Nag Hammadi Codices V, 2–5, and VI,* ed. D. M. Parrot, pp. 291–324 (translation). Nag Hammadi Studies 11. Leiden, 1979.

MADELEINE SCOPELLO

CONCH. *See* Symbols in Coptic Art.

CONCOMITANCE, the doctrine held in the Roman Catholic church that the Body and Blood of Christ are together and simultaneously administered in communion even when a communicant receives one of the elements only. This doctrine is meant to justify the act of withdrawing the chalice from the laity ever since the twelfth century, and giving the Body alone, the Blood being restricted to the clergy. This practice was introduced during the papacy of Paschal II (1099–1118), and the decree was confirmed at the twenty-first session of the Council of Trent on 16 July 1562.

The Eastern Orthodox churches, however, have always held that receiving both the Body and the Blood is essential for eucharistic communion, and accordingly reject the doctrine of concomitance.

ARCHBISHOP BASILIOS

CONFESSION AND PENITENCE. Sacramental confession consists in the avowal of one's sins and faults, accompanied with genuine contrition, made to a priest for the purpose of obtaining absolution.

Before Christ instituted this sacrament, He had given His disciples two relevant promises. When Peter recognized the true nature of Jesus Christ as the Messiah and acknowledged Him to be the Son of God, Christ conferred upon him the authority of loosing and binding (Mt. 16:19).

When Christ taught the disciples the proper procedure to be applied in the case of a brother who has committed a sin, that is, eventually reporting the matter to the church when other conciliatory measures have failed, He reiterated His previous promises according to which they were empowered to forgive penitents their sins or to retain them (Mt. 18:17–18).

After the resurrection, Christ breathed on His disciples, saying: "As the Father has sent me, even so I send you . . . Receive the Holy Spirit. If you forgive the sins of any, they are forgiven; if you retain the sins of any, they are retained" (Jn. 20:22–23). This authority became the prerogative of the disciples and the apostles, and was passed on to their successors in the episcopate and the presbytery.

Confession in the Old Testament

Mosaic law prescribed confession of sins with a view to expiation and atonement. When a man incurred guilt and confessed, he was required to bring a sin offering, and the priest would make expiation for him, after which he would be pardoned (Lv. 5:1–6).

The theme of John the Baptist's preaching in the Judaean wilderness, as a prelude to the coming of Christ, was the exhortation of people to repent, in view of the imminence of the kingdom of heaven. Later, the apostles, having received the authority from Jesus Christ, exercised the power of loosing and binding and urged Jews and Gentiles alike to repent and obtain forgiveness (see Acts 8:22; 17:30; 26:20). When Ananias and his wife Sapphira lied to the Holy Spirit and to Peter, they were punished with instant death (Acts 5:8–10).

Ever since the early days of the church, the sacrament of confession formed a prominent part of Christian worship. The DIDACHE stipulates: "In the church, thou shalt acknowledge thy transgressions, and thou shalt not come near for thy prayers with an evil conscience. This is the way of life" (*The Teaching of the Twelve Apostles* 4. 14).

The Apostolic Canons prohibited the clergy from denying this sacrament to any penitent: "If any bishop or presbyter does not receive him who turns away from his sin, but rejects him, let him be deposed; for he grieveth Christ who said, 'There is joy in heaven over one sinner that repenteth.'"

The APOSTOLIC CONSTITUTIONS, recognizing this God-given authority, enjoin upon the congregation the duty of honoring the priesthood: "Reverence these, and honor them with all kinds of honor; for they have obtained from God the power of life and death, in their judging of sinners, and condemning them to the death of eternal life, as also of loosing returning sinners from their sins, and of restoring them to a new life" (*Constitutions of the Holy Apostles* 3.33, 1951, p. 412). With regard to forgiveness through penitential acts the Council of Laodicea (341–381) stipulates: "They who have sinned in divers particulars, if they have persevered in the prayer of confession and penance, and are wholly converted from their faults, shall be received again to communion, through the mercy and goodness of God, after a time of penance appointed to them, in proportion to the nature of their offence" (*The Canons* . . . , Canon 2, 1956, p. 125).

The efficacy of penitence is dependent on the following elements: wholehearted contrition for having sinned against God; determination to improve one's way of life; firm belief in Jesus Christ as the sole Redeemer; and disclosure of sin or fault to the Church in the person of a priest who can grant sacramental absolution.

The church has ordained various prayers of absolution, which all refer to the authority given to the priesthood by Christ through the apostles.

Besides private confession, made by a person to his confessor alone, the early church adopted another practice, which required penitents to make a full, public confession to the congregation. This practice, entailing some measure of public humiliation, gradually disappeared, giving way to private, auricular confession, which proved to be an adequate vehicle for obtaining absolution.

Like all sacraments, confession has its outward signs and its inward graces.

The outward signs consist in the actual verbal confession, as well as the absolution given by the confessor after he has ascertained the genuine contrition of the penitent and his firm intention to make amends.

The inward spiritual grace lies in: (1) forgiveness of sin (Jn. 20:23, 1 Jn. 1:9); (2) complete effacement of the sin (Acts 3:19); (3) exculpation from guilt (Lk. 18:14); (4) salvation (Lk. 19:9, 1 Cor. 5:5); (5) release from penalty of sin (Mt. 3:7, 10; Lk. 13:3); (6) reconciliation to God (Rom. 5:1; Eph. 2:14); and (7) reaffiliation to God (Lk. 15:17–24).

According to the teaching of the Bible, all sins may be forgiven providing they have been sincerely confessed and genuinely repented. Christ, however, specified a certain sin as unforgivable, namely blasphemy against the Holy Spirit; "every sin and blasphemy will be forgiven men; but the blasphemy against the Spirit will not be forgiven" (Mt. 12:31). Likewise John the Apostle says: "All wrongdoing is sin, but there is sin which is not mortal" (I Jn. 5:17). In the view of most interpreters of Scripture, blasphemy against the Holy Spirit is condemned by Christ because it is willful opposition to the Holy Spirit. When Jesus cast out devils by the power of the Holy Spirit, the Pharisees imputed to Him the use of Satanic methods in the process. This is tantamount to substituting Satan for the Holy Spirit, and, accordingly, the Pharisees were guilty of blasphemy, which was an unpardonable sin.

As indicated earlier, a confessor must be an authorized priest, with a pious character, spiritual integrity, and a firm grasp of church doctrine. He should have insight into human nature, and show perception, discernment, and cooperation with a fellow human being who wants to make a clean breast of his personal wrongdoing. Above all he must be trustworthy, discreet, and able to command confidence. He must be willing to fast and pray for and on behalf of those who confess to him. In particular, he should treat all penitents, rich and poor, with patience, without fear or favor or expectation of material reward.

As a rule, except in cases of disability or inability to attend, confessions must be received on the church premises.

BIBLIOGRAPHY

Battifol, P. *Les Origines de la pénitence*. Etude de l'histoire et de la théologie positive 1. Paris, 1902.

Cummings, D. *The Rudder*, pp. 552–633. Chicago, 1957.

Jurgens, W. A. *The Faith of the Early Fathers*, 3 vols. Collegeville, Minn., 1970–1979.

Kelly, J. N. D. *Early Christian Doctrines*. San Francisco, 1978.

Mortimer, R. C. *The Origins of Private Penance in the Western Church*. Oxford, 1939.

Torrance, T. *The Doctrine of Grace in the Apostolic Fathers*. London, 1948.

ARCHBISHOP BASILIOS

CONFIRMATION, sacrament by which the newly baptized receives the grace of the Holy Spirit. Confirmation is a complement to the sacrament of baptism. Despite being complementary to baptism and following immediately after it, confirmation must be regarded as a distinct sacrament, with its own rites and prayers. In view of its intrinsic qualities, confirmation is also referred to as laying on of hands and anointing. Through baptism, a person is spiritually reborn; confirmation conveys special grace that strengthens the recipient for the practice of the Christian faith.

In John 7:37–39 Jesus established this sacrament: "If any one thirst, let him come to me and drink. He who believes in me, as the scripture has said, out of his heart shall flow rivers of living water. (Now this he said about the Spirit, which those who believed in him were to receive; for as yet the Spirit had not been given, because Jesus was not yet glorified." The descent of the Holy Spirit at Pentecost granted confirmation to the apostles, and, in their turn, they were able to grant it to other believers by administering this sacrament to them.

Many canons passed by various councils assert the independence of confirmation and its separateness from baptism. According to Canon 38 of the Council of Laodicea (between 348 and 381), "They who are baptized, must after baptism be anointed with the heavenly chrism, and be partakers of the kingdom of Christ."

In connection with the various categories of heretics who return to the fold of orthodoxy, Canon 7 of the Council of CONSTANTINOPLE (381) states, "Those . . . we receive upon their giving a written renunciation [of their errors] and anathematize every heresy which is not in accordance with the holy, catholic, and apostolic church of God. Thereupon they are first sealed or anointed with the holy oil upon the forehead, eyes, nostrils, mouth, and ears; and when we seal them, we say, "The seal of the gift of the Holy Ghost . . ." (*Canons of the One Hundred and Fifty Fathers*, 1956, p. 185).

The visible element in the sacrament of confirmation comprises four parts: (1) An epiclesis of the Holy Spirit upon the water; (2) the holy chrism, by which the baptized rightfully becomes a "Christian"; (3) the signing with the holy chrism—the priest anoints the baptized, using thirty-six signs of the cross, which cover almost all the members of his body; and (4) the prayers said during the process of anointing, ending with the words: "Receive the Holy Spirit and be a purified vessel of our Lord Jesus Christ."

The Coptic church, in line with other Orthodox churches, has a distinctive stand toward administering the sacrament of confirmation. Whereas in non-Orthodox churches, confirmation is the exclusive right of bishops, there is no such restriction imposed on Coptic priests, as they receive this right at ordination. Second, unlike other churches where confirmation is delayed till the age of discretion, Orthodox churches administer it together with two other sacraments, that is, preceded by baptism, and followed by holy communion. Not only is this practice based on solid historical grounds, as it was observed by all churches, Orthodox and non-Orthodox alike, until the thirteenth century, when the Roman Catholic church chose to delay confirmation until the age of discretion. It also provides the necessary precaution against the likelihood of an unbaptized and unconfirmed child's death before attaining that age.

BIBLIOGRAPHY

Jurgens, W. A. *The Faith of the Early Fathers*, 3 vols. Collegeville, Minn., 1970–1979.

Kelly, J. N. D. *Early Christian Doctrines*. San Francisco, 1978.

ARCHBISHOP BASILIOS

CONFRATERNITY. As in other Christian countries of late antiquity, confraternities, or guilds, were active in Egypt. Their members were called, in Greek, *philoponoi*, or lovers of work, and *spoudaioi*, or zealots. The term *philoponeion*, confraternity, is used in documents in reference to its legal status. (The translation "infirmary" in Lampe's *Patristic Greek Lexicon* is incorrect.) The earliest information about confraternities, in *The Letter of Ammon* (Halkin, 1932, chaps. 31–32), dates back to the times of Athanasius (i.e., the first half of the fourth century). The most recent document that mentions confraternities dates back to the end of the tenth century. There is little possibility that confraternities played a significant role after the first fifty years of Arab rule, during the period of rapid decrease of the number of Christians in Egypt.

Confraternities were characteristic of towns. We know of only one case when a confraternity was situated in the countryside, in the village of Paouore, in the district of Hermopolis (P. Oxf. [Some Oxford Papyri] 16, P. Lond. [Greek Papyri in the British Museum] III, 1080, P. Jernstedt 1).

It is not possible to establish the social composition of confraternities in Egypt, but by making analogies to other provinces, one may suppose that they included representatives of different social strata. Despite the lack of information in sources from Egypt, one may assume that confraternities included women, as happened in Constantinople.

Confraternities, founded in the atmosphere of religious tension so typical of late antiquity, attracted those people whose devotion was deeper than the average person's. They united in particular those who aspired to enter a religious order but could not do so because of family, social, or other obligations.

There were close ties between confraternities and church structures. In large towns separate confraternities were established close to churches and very often took their names. In Hermopolis, for example, there were *philoponoi* of Saint MICHAEL the Archangel, Saint VICTOR, Saint Euphemia, and the New Church. Also existing in this town was a confraternity of *agoreis,* or notaries, recorded in the Fiscal Code of Hermopolis of 590–600 (P. Sorb. Inv. 2227). It is quite possible that there were other confraternities comprising members of the same profession.

Members of a confraternity were considered a separate group in a church, along with the clergy, monks, and laymen. The activities of such confraternities included first of all frequent common prayers and religious services in churches. The Canons of Pseudo-Athanasius (Riedel and Crum, 1904, chap. 93) say, "Those that are zealous . . . go daily to the church, especially on the fourth and the sixth days, but still more on the days of Sabbath and the Lord's Day." During feasts, *philoponoi* acted as organized groups singing sacred songs, usually the Psalms. In literary works, they usually appear in such a role.

We know very little about the philanthropic activities of confraternities. In the great sanctuary of Saints Cyrus and John they worked as male nurses (*Sophronius Monachus Sophista: Narratio Miraculorum SS. Cyri et Joannis,* PG 87, pt. 3, cols. 3424–3676).

Members of confraternities belonged to a group of laymen acting at the side of the bishop and helping him in various matters. In Alexandria the patriarch used them either to exert pressure on the administration or to fight against his opponents (see Zacharias Scholasticus, *Vie de Sévère,* on events at the end of the fifth century). As an organized group of laymen, they were consulted before the election of the bishop. In Alexandria they even took part in the election of the patriarch, though their votes did not have much significance (Burmester, 1960, p. 13). Two texts, written independently, seem to suggest that the Alexandrian patriarch regularly invited the more prominent *philoponoi* to table as well as the members of his clergy (Budge, 1915, p. 825; Orlandi, 1968, pp. 46–47). The texts connect that custom to the times of Athanasius, but they probably project back into the past something that was usual in the authors' times, as hagiographic works often do. The chiefs of the *philoponoi* belonged to the town elite (Budge, 1894, p. 58).

Along with religious activities, confraternities shared a common social life, as did associations of Hellenistic and Roman times as well as the confraternities and guilds of medieval Europe. This is reflected in a Coptic text coming most probably from Hermopolis, where membership fees were paid on the occasion of a wedding, birth, or baptism (*Corpus Papyrorum Raineri* IV, 196, from the seventh century). Very likely, certain organized forms of mutual aid were employed in cases of misfortune. But unfortunately we have no confirmed records of this.

At the head of a confraternity stood a president with the title of *diadochos.* He and the members of the confraternity entered into a written agreement stating the obligations of both parties (e.g., *Corpus Papyrorum Raineri* IV, 196). Some organizational functions that are hard to define were performed by the *archigeron* (C.P.R. IV, 195; Crum, 1905, no. 1046). The function of persons called *paterion* (presumably derived from *pater*) who appeared together with *philoponoi* (C.P.R. IV, 195; Crum, 1905, no. 1013) is vague. It is possible that they constituted a group within a confraternity, but they might also have been a group of monastic character.

Confraternities were allowed to own land and houses. In the Fiscal Code of Hermopolis they also appeared as mediators between taxpayers and the fiscal authorities.

BIBLIOGRAPHY

Budge, E. A. W. *Saint Michael the Archangel: Three Encomiums.* London, 1894.

______. *Miscellaneous Coptic Texts in the Dialect of Upper Egypt.* London, 1915.

Burmester, O. H. E. *The Rite of Consecration of the Patriarch of Alexandria,* p. 13. Cairo, 1960.

Crum, W. E. *Catalogue of the Coptic Manuscripts in the British Museum.* London, 1905.

Halkin, F., ed. *S. Pachomii Vitae graecae.* Brussels, 1932.

Muszyński, M. "Les 'Associations religieuses' en Egypte d'après les sources hiéroglyphiques, démotiques et grecques." *Orientalia Lovaniensia Periodica* 8 (1977):145–74; discusses the analogies between Christian confraternities and pagan associations.

Orlandi, T. *Storia della chiesa copta,* Vol. 1. Milan, 1968.

Riedel, W., and W. E. Crum, eds. *The Canons of Athanasius of Alexandria.* London, 1904.

Sophronius Monachus Sophista. *Narratio miraculorum SS. Cyri et Joannis sapientium anargyrorum.* PG 87, pt. 3, cols. 3424–3676. Paris, 1865.

Vailhé, S. "Les Philopones d'Oxyrhynque au IVe siècle." *Echos d'Orient* 14 (1911):277–78.

Wipszycka, E. "Les Confréries dans la vie religieuse de l'Egypte chrétienne." In *Proceedings of the XII International Congress of Papyrology,* pp. 511–25. Toronto, 1970.

Zacharias Scholasticus, *Vie de Sévère,* ed. M. A. Kugener. PO 2, Paris, 1904.

EWA WIPSZYCKA

CONSECRATION, the total dedication of persons and things to the exclusive service of God. In Judaism, temples, priests, vessels, and other objects were set apart in solemn ceremonies for sacred purposes. After their exodus from Egypt, the Israelites consecrated all first-born male children to the service of God, and later redeemed them (Ex. 13; Nm. 13), and all first-born male beasts were offered as sacrifice. The tabernacle and its instruments and vessels were also sanctified (Nm. 7), as was the first temple (1 Kgs. 7, 8), the second temple (Ezr. 6), and the wall of Jerusalem (Neh. 12).

Churches have always been consecrated as places of Christian worship. In Egypt, as a result of the successive waves of persecution that restricted Christian worship to private houses and hiding places, the first church since Saint Mark's Cathedral in Alexandria was built by Pope THEONAS (282–300), the sixteenth pope of Alexandria and patriarch of the See of Saint Mark, and dedicated to the Virgin Mary by the name of The Church of the Mother of God.

The Coptic church follows established rites for the consecration of patriarchs, bishops, priests, and deacons, and of churches, altars, baptismal fonts, liturgical vessels, vestments, and icons. Ceremonies of consecration can be conducted only by bishops.

ARCHBISHOP BASILIOS

CONSTANTINE I (288?–337), Roman emperor who allowed freedom of worship in the empire, thus ending the persecution of Christians. Flavius Valerius Constantinus (Constantine) was born to Constantius Chlorus and Helena. When his father was appointed Caesar in 293, Constantine was sent to the court of DIOCLETIAN, the senior emperor, where he later distinguished himself as a military officer in the campaigns of Galerius against Persia. When Constantius died at York on 25 June 306, Constantine, who was with his father at the time, was proclaimed Augustus by the troops. On 28 October 312 he became senior ruler of the empire when he defeated his rival, Maxentius, at Rome's Milvian Bridge.

The events at the Milvian Bridge that presaged Constantine's victory have been the subject of much debate and various interpretations. Lactantius, writing shortly after the event, stated that Constantine was told in a dream to have the heavenly sign of God placed on the shields of his soldiers. In accordance with this admonition, he denoted Christ on the shields by inscribing on them an X with the upper arm bent over.

Eusebius relates in his *Life of Constantine* (1.26–40) that on the eve of the battle against Maxentius, Constantine, convinced that he would need the aid of some supernatural power to prevail in the conflict, pondered which god he should supplicate. Recalling that the emperors before him had placed their hopes in a multitude of gods and had suffered heaven-sent catastrophes, he resolved to trust in the one Supreme God of his father. He then prayed and begged this God to reveal who he was and to stand by him in his present difficulties. While Constantine was thus beseeching God, he and his army saw in the afternoon sky the cross of Christ, consisting of light, and the legend "By this, conquer." That night, after Constantine had fallen asleep while puzzling over the meaning of this epithet, Jesus Christ appeared before him with the sign that had shone in the sky and commanded him to use a likeness of the sign as protection in his encounters with the enemy. Accordingly, Constantine had workers in gold and precious stones construct a replica of the sign. The result was a gilded spear with a transverse bar topped with jewels encircling the monogram of Christ (the *chi-rho* symbol). Constantine summoned to his camp Christian teachers, by whom he was instructed in the teachings and doctrines of the God who had appeared to him.

Scholars have debated, and continue to do so at great length, what Constantine actually experienced at the Milvian Bridge. They disagree also about the appearance and possible pre-Christian significance of the sign that Constantine inscribed on his shields, or at least carried into battle. But what is clear is that Constantine acted as if he had experienced a life-changing event, and shortly thereafter he became a devoted supporter of the beleaguered Christian religion.

Early in 313, Constantine met in Milan with Licinius, his fellow Augustus. They formed an alliance, sealed it with the marriage of Constantine's half-sister, Constantia, to Licinius, and issued the decree now known as the Edict of Milan. The major thrust of the edict was to allow freedom of worship to all inhabitants of the empire and specifically to halt all persecution of Christians, as well as to restore to the church properties confiscated in earlier persecutions.

However, prohibitions against persecution from without could not guarantee peace within the church. Constantine soon found himself embroiled in the Donatist controversy, which erupted over the discipline of those who allegedly betrayed the faith during the Great Persecution under Diocletian in 303 and was destined to rack the church in North Africa for almost four centuries (see DONATISM). Though his extended and patient efforts to arbitrate the issue fairly and to establish peace between the rival factions met with failure, Constantine's response to the controversy evinced his genuine concern for the well-being of the church. When the Numidian bishops communicated to Constantine their contention that Caecilius' consecration as bishop of Carthage was invalid and that Constantine's support of the Caecilian clergy was partial and unwarranted and asked the emperor to draw up a committee of Gallic judges to decide the issue, Constantine remanded the case to the bishop of Rome, who enlisted the aid of three Gallic and ten Italian bishops. The case was heard on 2–5 October 313, and the judgment went against the Numidian faction, which had become known as Donatist, after its leader Donatus. When the Donatists appealed the decision to Constantine, the emperor once again displayed his concern for the welfare and unity of the church by convening another hearing at Arles on 1 August 314. This council confirmed the verdict of the Council of Rome. Constantine conducted his own investigation into the validity of Caecilius' consecration, and on 10 November 316 he endorsed Caecilius as bishop of Carthage and denounced the Donatists, whom he had come to see as heretics and schismatics. However, as evidenced by the fact that "heretical" Donatism remained the dominant form of Christianity in North Africa for many decades thereafter, Constantine's final verdict did nothing to heal the rift.

During the controversy the peace between Constantine and Licinius had begun to sour, eventually breaking down completely in 324. Licinius in the east violated not only the spirit of the Edict of Milan but also its specific prohibition against persecution of Christians. He expelled Christians from his court, outlawed bishops' councils, ruled that Christian men and women could not worship together in churches, and forbade meetings of Christians within the cities. There is also some evidence that Christians were martyred in the east with Licinius' compliance. Such measures and events must have been galling to Constantine, who openly supported Christianity in the western part of the empire with legislation, building programs, and an occasional special dispensation for Christian concerns. In 321 and again in 322, in an act that must have been calculated to rile his eastern counterpart, Constantine appointed consuls of his own choosing without the approval of Licinius. Then in 323, Constantine crossed into the territory of Licinius while chasing back invading Goths, who had caused much destruction in Moesia and Thrace. When Licinius' protests won him no satisfaction, war broke out between the two emperors. On 18 September 324, Licinius was defeated at Chrysopolis. Constantine spared his life, sending him to Thessalonica, but Licinius died or was executed—accounts vary—not long afterward. Some said he died in a soldier's brawl, others that he was found to be plotting against Constantine, who executed him for his perfidy, and there is some conjecture that Constantine, without any provocation except the constant fear of an eventual uprising, had him put to death.

Not long after the death of Licinius, Constantine's attention was drawn to the controversy brewing in the east between ALEXANDER I and ARIUS. Under the direction of Alexander, a council of some one hundred bishops anathematized Arius for teaching that the Son of God was posterior to the Father, was created by the Father, and therefore was not God in the same sense as the Father. Arius appealed to his friend Eusebius, bishop of Nicomedia, for aid. Eusebius responded by providing refuge for Arius and convoking a synod of bishops of Bithynia, which approved Arius and his teachings. Constantine wrote a letter to Alexander and Arius, urging them to put aside their differences and to come together in a unity of the faith. The letter is an indication of Constantine's desire for peace and tranquillity within the church, but it betrays his ignorance of the gravity of the doctrine over which the two parties were divided. Theirs was not a petty squabble over a trifling matter, as Constantine suggested. It was a major rift on an issue that was at the very heart of Christian theology and was destined to split the church.

When it was apparent that a mere letter would not suffice to quell the controversy, Constantine invited the bishops to convene in an ecumenical council at Nicaea, in Bithynia, in June 325. Socrates related that the emperor brought to the council a number of petitions addressed to him by various bishops accusing other bishops of heresy or political intrigue. Constantine burned these petitions in front of all assembled with an oath that none of them had been read and with the admonition that "Christ bids him who hopes for forgiveness forgive an erring brother." Such magnanimity, however, did not prevail at the council. Nonetheless, the council was able to agree on a statement of belief, the NICENE CREED. EUSEBIUS OF CAESAREA explained that when the first draft of the creed had been drawn up, Constantine urged all to accept it after the word "consubstantial" (see HOMOOUSION) was added to the description of the Son's relationship with the Father (Socrates *Historia Ecclesiastica* 1.8). Apparently he was concerned that the wording was capable of an Arian interpretation. The motion was carried. The council anathematized Arius and his teachings. Constantine naively believed he had squelched the Arian heresy and restored unity to the church.

Arius was reinstated in the church at a subsequent council in Nicaea in 327, but ATHANASIUS, who had succeeded Alexander as patriarch of Alexandria, refused to readmit him to the Alexandrian see, despite Constantine's urging. Arius' supporters, working through the MELITIANS, attempted to discredit Athanasius and to drive him from his bishopric. Their deceptive efforts not only came to naught but also were discovered to be fraudulent, and Constantine, now convinced that Arius' repentance and return to orthodoxy had not been sincere, issued an edict that all Arian literature was to be burned and that anyone who concealed Arian texts should be put to death.

Still, the persecution of Athanasius by his Melitian and Arian foes continued. Among other things, Athanasius was accused of acquiring his office illegitimately, of ravishing a virgin, and of killing a Melitian bishop to use his body for sorcery. When Athanasius' supporters went out and found the man alive, his detractors said he was using wizardry to fool men's eyes. Constantine, influenced, no doubt, by pro-Arians who had access to the imperial court, such as Eusebius of Nicomedia and his own sister, Constantia, scheduled a council at Tyre in 335 at which Athanasius should defend himself from the charges. However, when it became apparent to Athanasius that the council was dominated by those with pro-Arian sympathies and that his own supporters had been locked out, he fled to Constantinople. But charges were soon brought against him that he had threatened to cut off the vital grain supply from Egypt to Constantinople, and Constantine banished him immediately to Trier, where he remained until after the death of the emperor in 337.

Constantine appears to have vacillated wildly in his treatment of both Arius and Athanasius. This ambivalence is probably to be explained partly by his want of deep understanding of the theological questions at issue and partly by his zeal to mend the church and make it whole again in the easiest and quickest way possible.

In addition to his conversion to, and support of, Christianity, Constantine also left his mark on the empire by founding the city of Constantinople. Following the example of Diocletian, who had made moves to establish an eastern capital in Nicomedia, Constantine established Constantinople, the "New Rome," on the site of Byzantium. The geographical position of the old city was well suited to serve as the base for the much-needed imperial presence in the eastern portion of the empire and for a military bulwark against the incursions of eastern nomads such as the Scythians, Goths, and Sarmatae. Constantine maintained throughout his life that he had built the city in obedience to God's command. Tradition states that when Constantine was marking off the boundaries for the city's walls, one of his advisers, alarmed at how far afield the emperor was tracing the line, expressed concern to his ruler. Constantine replied that he would continue forward until the invisible guide marching before him thought it right to stop. Work on the new capital was begun in 326, and formal dedication rites were held in May 330. The city included many of the features of Rome, such as the Senate, but the predominant influence throughout was Christian; the pagan temples and shrines of the old capital were not to be found in Constantinople.

Constantine died on 22 May 337.

BIBLIOGRAPHY

Alföldi, A. *The Conversion of Constantine and Pagan Rome*. Oxford, 1969.

Barnes, T. D. *Constantine and Eusebius*. Cambridge, Mass., 1981.

Baynes, N. H. *Constantine the Great and the Christian Church*, 2nd ed. Oxford, 1972.

Doerries, H. *Constantine the Great*, trans. R. H. Bainton. New York, 1972.

Firth, J. B. *Constantine the Great: The Reorganisation of the Empire and the Triumph of the Church*. New York and London, 1905.

Keresztes, P. *Constantine: A Great Christian Monarch and Apostle*. Amsterdam, 1981; includes English translation of documents relevant to the major events in Constantine's life.

RANDALL STEWART

CONSTANTINE, sixth–seventh-century bishop of Asyūṭ. [*This entry consists of two articles:* History *and* Constantine's Writings.]

History

A summary of Constantine's life has come down complete in a unique manuscript of the Sahidic recension of the Arabic SYNAXARION of the Copts, deposited at Luxor. There also exists for the first part and identical with the above document an isolated leaf (National Library, Paris, Arabic 4895). His feast day is 11 Amshīr.

This text reports that Constantine received the monastic habit from the hands of his brother Anbā Moses, otherwise unknown, in a monastery that unfortunately is not named. Ten young men embraced the monastic life on that day. Among them, in addition to Constantine, was Rufus, the future bishop of Shuṭb (Hypselis/Shotep), and Anbā Yūsāb (Joseph), who subsequently became bishop of Isfaḥt (Apollinopolis Parva/Sbeḥt). Anbā Yūsāb is not otherwise known, but RUFUS OF SHOTEP is the author of commentaries on the Gospels, part of which is extant, and of sermons preserved in an Arabic version. His name is also cited in the second encomium of Constantine on Saint Claudius of Antioch (PO 35, p. 614).

The Synaxarion continues that Constantine memorized the New Testament, except for the Apocalypse, and the Psalms and the Prophets. Constantine was consecrated as bishop by the patriarch DAMIAN between 578 and 605. Damian also made him his vicar for Upper Egypt, and declared, "I shall consecrate as bishop only him who has with him a writing from your hand." This function of patriarchal vicar is attested by other texts for other bishops. There was one for Lower Egypt and another for the Ṣaʿīd. It seems to have been exercised above all in the confirmation of the election of new bishops, as suggested by the passage of the Synaxarion relating to Constantine. He was no longer a patriarchal vicar from the time of his elevation to the episcopate.

That Constantine was bishop in the period of Patriarch Damian is also confirmed by the HISTORY OF THE PATRIARCHS, which relates, "There were in [Patriarch Damian's] time bishops admirable for their purity and their merit. Among them, John, Bishop of Parallos [Burullus] and John his disciple, Constantine the bishop, John the Blessed, the recluse, and many others." In an encomium for the feast of Saint John of Heraclea (4 Ba'ūnah), preserved in Arabic under the name of Constantine, the author also indicates at the beginning that he received episcopal consecration at the hands of the patriarch Damian.

The notice in the Synaxarion mentions in one phrase the literary activity of the saint: "He composed sermons in great number, lives of martyrs and of saints." His pastoral acts are mentioned as well: "He strove with all his might to extirpate the roots of the Arians who were in the neighborhood of his town and in the mountains which surround it." By the term "Arians" must be understood the Melitians. The schism was born at Asyūṭ (Lycopolis) and Athanasius himself assimilated them to the Arians. For the rest, Constantine in his second encomium on Saint Claudius reproached them with a doctrine close to ARIANISM and further on added this personal detail, which the Synaxarion seems indeed to echo: "I recall what has happened since I was seated upon the [episcopal] throne, despite my unworthiness. I have suffered much from the plants which Melitius planted, and I have not been able to uproot them" (PO 35, p. 626). As for the word "mountains" in the Synaxarion, it should no doubt be interpreted as "monasteries," for the Coptic term *toou* has the two senses, and it is not unusual in the Synaxarion for the word *jabal* (Arabic, mountain) to indicate a convent. Besides, from Greek papyri and Coptic documents, as from the *History of the Patriarchs,* it is known that the Melitian schism persisted to the eighth century, in particular in the monasteries. This short life also indicates that the bishop of Asyūṭ had to contend with various forms of magic practiced in his diocese, such as astrology, sorcery, and the reading of horoscopes.

Another passage in the Sahidic recension of the Synaxarion relates, with reference to Saint Elias of Qūṣiyyah (Kos/Kussai), that at the time of the destruction of the town, probably during the Persian occupation (619–629), Constantine transferred the body of Saint Elias to Asyūṭ, which would indicate that he was still alive at that period. Finally the notice in the Synaxarion states that Constantine died "when he was [still] robust and his eyesight sound," which without doubt shows that he was not an aged man. The author then writes that he was buried "in his monastery where he lived, instead of his episcopal residence, called al-Hanādah, in the mountain of Asyūṭ." This place is known from Coptic and Arabic texts, where it is called "convent of Apa Shenute of al Hanādah in Asyūṭ." It appears that it was at Rīfah, southwest of Asyūṭ.

Constantine thus lived at the end of the sixth century and the beginning of the seventh. He played an important role in the Coptic church, particularly as vicar of Patriarch Damian for Upper Egypt. He took action, perhaps decisively, to bring back to the fold the inhabitants and monks of his diocese who remained in the schism begun by his predecessor on the throne of Asyūṭ, Melitius, in the fourth century.

BIBLIOGRAPHY

Bell, H. I., and W. E. Crum. *Jews and Christians in Egypt.* London, 1924.

Coquin, R.-G. "Saint Constantin, évêque d'Asyūṭ." *Studia Orientalia Christiana Collectanea* 16 (1981):151–70.

Crum, W. E. "Some Further Meletian Documents." *Journal of Egyptian Archeology* 13 (1927):19–26.

Garitte, G. "Constantin, évêque d'Assiout." In *Coptic Studies in Honor of W. E. Crum, Bulletin of the Byzantine Institute* 2 (1950):287–304. Republished in *Scripta disiecta 1941–1977,* Vol. 1, pp. 119–36. Louvain-la-Neuve, 1980.

______. "Constantin, évêque d'Assiout." In *Dictionnaire d'histoire et de géographie ecclésiastiques,* Vol. 13, col. 623.

RENÉ-GEORGES COQUIN

Constantine's Writings

The Coptic tradition has provided us with seven works in Arabic attributed to Constantine of Asyūṭ. To date, four of these are unknown in any other language.

1. The Arabic text of the first panegyric (encomium) of Saint Claudius the Martyr is unpublished. However, it has been translated into French by E. Amélineau (1885), on the basis of the only known manuscript of this work, in Paris (Arabe 4793 [Egypt, seventeenth century], fols. 18a–48b; for details, see CLAUDIUS OF ANTIOCH).

2. The Arabic text of the second panegyric (encomium) of Saint Claudius the Martyr is unpublished. At least two manuscripts contain it: one at Paris (Arabe 4776 [Egypt, 1886], fol. 101a–159a) and the other at Florence (Laurentiana, Oriental 204 [Egypt, 1508], fols. 69a–139b).

3. The beginning of the panegyric (encomium) of Saint George is found in Sahidic Coptic in Paris (Coptic 129/16th [twelfth century], fols. 88b–93b). Garitte published this text with a Latin translation, without referring to the Arabic version (1954, pp. 271–77).

The Arabic text is known from a single manuscript, still unpublished (Coptic Museum, Cairo, History 472 [Egypt, seventeenth century], copied by Naṣrallāh ibn Farajallāh al-Ṭūkhī; Graf no. 715/2nd; Simaykah no. 106). Folios 73a–134b contain five discourses on the miracles of Saint George, composed by Theophilus of Alexandria, Acacius of Lydda, SEVERUS of Antioch, Basil of Caesarea, and Constantine of Asyūṭ. This last discourse most probably contains the complete homily; unfortunately, the Graf and Simaykah catalogs provide no incipit, and thus the identity of the texts remains uncertain. If the Coptic and Arabic texts prove to be different, this would provide a new work to add to the list of Constantine's works in Arabic.

4. The first panegyric (encomium) of the martyr John of Heraclea has survived only in Arabic. Six manuscripts of it are known, varying considerably from each other. The first three of these were given by Garitte (1950, pp. 126–27; 2nd ed., 1980, pp. 294–95). It is intended for 4 Ba'ūnah.

The superscription of the London manuscript, given in its entirety and translated into French by Garitte (1950, pp. 127–28; 2nd ed., 1980, pp. 295–96) is of interest. It informs us that the body of John of Heraclea then rested in the town of Ḥamyūr, now the village of Umm al-Quṣūr to the north of Manfalūṭ, in the region of Asyūṭ. More important, it tells us that Constantine was consecrated bishop at Alexandria itself by the patriarch DAMIAN, that he pronounced this discourse on a Sunday, 4 Ba'ūnah, and that he arrived on the eve of the feast and spent the night in the martyrium. These details confirm the authenticity of the panegyric, despite the fact that it survives only in Arabic.

There are six manuscripts known of this text:

British Library, London, Or. 5648 (twelfth to fifteenth century; fols. 38b ff.; cf. Ellis and Edwards, 1912, p. 71; Crum, 1905, p. 363b, n. 1). The long superscription of 160 words is reproduced by Garitte, but no one gives the incipit.

Paris Arabe 4893 (Egypt, nineteenth century, fols. 2a–43a). The Arabic incipit (text in Troupeau 1972–1974, Vol. 2, p. 65), may be translated as "The sun of justice has shone forth for us, and healing is beneath his wings and in his intercession. So now hear, o people who love Christ. It came to pass, when our Father Damianos the Archbishop of Alexandria sent for me, me the wretched Constantine, and consecrated me a bishop, without my being worthy of it, for the see of the city of Assiut. . . ."

Coptic Museum, Cairo, Liturgy 85 (Graf no. 88; Simaykah 1, no. 208), copied by Marqūriyūs ibn Isḥāq the deacon, on 18 Dhū al-Ḥijjah A.H. 1130/A.M. 1435/12 November A.D. 1718, fols. 26a–35b or 183a–206b of the Coptic original. The incipit (Arabic text in Graf, 1934, p. 34) reads "The sun of justice has shone forth for us, and healing is beneath his wings. My beloved ones . . . when Anbā Damianos, the Archbishop of Alexandria, sent for me, me the wretched Constantine, and consecrated me a bishop, without my being worthy of it, for the see of the city of Assiut. . . ."

Coptic Patriarchate, Cairo, History 24 (Graf no. 445; Simaykah 2, no. 632 [Egypt, 1691–1693], fols. 224b–248a). The catalogs give no incipit.

Coptic Patriarchate, Cairo, History 80 (not in Graf; Simaykah 2, no. 621), 2nd piece, copied by the priest Yūsuf, on 7 Ba'ūnah 1345/1 June 1649; the catalog gives no incipit.

Saint Anthony, History 107, fols. 170v–210v.

5. The second discourse in honor of the martyr John of Heraclea is entitled "On the Finding of His Body and the Dedication of His Church on 4 Kiyahk [/30 November]." It survives in a single manuscript (Coptic Museum, Cairo, History 475; Graf no. 718; Simaykah 1, no. 102 [Egypt, fourteenth century], fol. 39b, then a lacuna of eight sheets, then 48a–49b).

The incipit (Arabic text in Graf, p. 275) reads: "Be attentive, o holy Fathers and brothers . . . , to my poor speech, me your spiritual father, wretched and poor." It should be noted that this *maymar* is read on 4 Kiyahk, and not on 4 Ba'ūnah, like the foregoing text.

The Coptic text is unknown, and the Arabic text is unpublished. This work is not listed by Garitte.

6. The homily *On the Fallen Soul and Its Exit from This World* is known from a sole Arabic manuscript (Coptic Patriarchate, Cairo, Theology 245 [seventeenth century], fols. 54a–68b; Graf no. 544; Simaykah no. 354). Neither of the two catalogs provides the incipit. The Arabic text is unpublished, and the Coptic text is unknown.

7. The text, panegyric (encomium) of Saint Isidorus of Antioch (or of Chios), as yet unpublished and practically unknown, is preserved in a single manuscript (Saint Anthony, History 123, fols. 3b–48a). It is intended for 19 Bashans.

The Arabic tradition lacks the two panegyrics of Saint Athanasius found in Coptic records. The one-page extract from a homily on Lent and the feast of Easter, read on the Monday before Easter at sext (published by Burmester), is probably found in the Arabic lectionaries for Holy Week, although it is not mentioned in scholarly literature.

The Arabic tradition provides the complete text of the panegyric of Saint George, the beginning of which survives in Coptic. The Arabic also contains two panegyrics in honor of the martyr John of Heraclea, the first of which has everything in favor of its authenticity, as yet unknown in Coptic. Also a homily exists on the fallen soul and its exit from this world, the Coptic version of which has not been found. Almost all the information concerning Constantine of Asyūṭ is transmitted exclusively by the Arabic tradition of the Copts. For various reasons (not excluding prejudice), none of these Arabic texts has been published to date.

BIBLIOGRAPHY

Amélineau, E. C. "Martyre d'apa Claudios d'Antioche." *Etudes archéologique linguistiques et historiques.* Leiden, 1885.

Crum, W. E. *A Catalogue of the Coptic Manuscripts in the British Museum.* London, 1905.

Ellis, A. G., and E. Edwards. *A Descriptive List of the Arabic Manuscripts Acquired by the Trustees of the British Museum Since 1894.* London, 1912.

Garitte, G. "Constantin, éveque d'Assiout." In *Coptic Studies in Honor of Walter Ewing Crum.* Bulletin of the Byzantine Institute 2, pp. 287–304. Boston, 1950. Reedited in G. Garitte, *Scripta disiecta 1941–1977* 1, pp. 119–136. Louvain-la-Neuve, 1980.

______. "Le Panégyrique de S. Georges attribué à Constantin d'Assiout." *Le Muséon* (1954):271–77.

Graf, G. *Catalogue de manuscrits arabes chrétiens conservés au Caire.* Vatican City, 1934.

Troupeau, G. *Catalogue des manuscrits arabes,* Vol. 2. Paris, 1972–1974.

KHALIL SAMIR, S. J.

CONSTANTINOPLE, FIRST COUNCIL OF, summoned by Emperor Theodosius I and convened at Constantinople in May and June 381, and recognized as the second ecumenical council. About 150 bishops from the eastern provinces of the empire attended, to which may be added thirty-six "Macedonian" bishops, mainly from western Asia Minor, whom the emperor and the council vainly tried to convince that the Holy Spirit did indeed participate fully in the godhead with the Father and the Son, and that to deny this was Arian heresy.

The "Macedonian" issue was only one reason for the summons of the council. The main reason was the emperor's determination to unite the empire on the basis of the Nicene faith. As a preliminary, immediately on his arrival in Constantinople on 24 November 380 (Socrates Scholasticus *Historia ecclesiastica* V.6), he summoned the semi-Arian bishop Demophilus and gave him the choice of accepting the Nicene Creed or deposition (25 November

380). To his honor, Demophilus chose the latter course.

There had, however, been a considerable shift in the emperor's religious outlook since the issue of the edict *Cunctos populos* on 27 February 380 (*Codex Theodosianus* xvi.i.2). In this he had stated that the religion to which he ordered his subjects to adhere was that "taught by St. Peter to the Romans: which faithful tradition has preserved and which is now professed by the priest [*pontificem*] Damasus and by Peter II, bishop of Alexandria, a man of apostolic holiness." In the autumn, during a bout of severe illness, Theodosius had accepted baptism from the strongly pro-Western Bishop Ascholius of Thessalonica (Socrates, V.6; Sozomen *Historia ecclesiastica* VII.4.2). Once arrived in Constantinople, the emperor began to move toward a more Eastern viewpoint. On 10 January 381 an edict setting out the Nicene faith made no mention of Pope Damasus or Peter of Alexandria, but simply stated that the faith asserted the "indivisible substance of the uncorrupt Trinity, which the Greeks express for those believing rightly with the term *ousia*." He had already sent for a representative of this interpretation of the faith, the leader of the Nicene party in Constantinople, GREGORY OF NAZIANZUS, and placed him on the throne of the Church of the Twelve Apostles in the city (end of 380).

The council that Theodosius now summoned was designed to ratify these decisions and unite the empire behind the emperor's policies. In Alexandria, however, Bishop Peter had played an uncertain if not a double game. In 379 he had been by no means unwilling to accept Gregory as bishop of Constantinople. But before he died on 14 February 380 he had changed his views. Using an unscrupulous adventurer named Maximus the Cynic, he set up an intrigue against Gregory and actually sent some suffragan bishops to consecrate Maximus as bishop of Constantinople (Gregory of Nazianzus, Carmen de seipso XI.844–847, 910ff.). After Peter died, his successor, Timothy (380–385), was equally hostile to Gregory, and when the council assembled in May, there were already factions. The Western group, including Ambrose of Milan, leaned toward Maximus, while the Eastern, with the exception of the Egyptian bishops, was solid in its support of Gregory.

From the outset the latter gained the upper hand. The president of the council was Meletius of Antioch, a one-time opponent of Athanasius but now honored by the emperor (Theodoret *Historia ecclesiastica* 5.7) and a firm friend of Gregory. Gregory was duly enthroned as bishop in May 381. Meletius' death, followed by Gregory's sudden resignation a month later (June 381), did not give the Egyptians any advantage. Maximus' claim to the bishopric was rejected. The senator Nectarius, a friend of Basil of Caesarea, was appointed bishop by the emperor (though he had not yet been baptized). The council's decisions were to be far from palatable to Alexandria.

The canons of the council condemned all types of Arianism, together with the "Macedonians" and Apollinarians (canon 1). Canon 2 developed the legislation of the Council of NICAEA as to the territorial jurisdiction of the major sees and added the important proviso that bishops should not interfere in the affairs of civil dioceses other than their own. In particular the bishop of Alexandria must confine himself to Egypt. As a rider to this, canon 3 ordained that Constantinople should have an honorary preeminence after Rome "because Constantinople is new Rome." Canon 4 repudiated Maximus the Cynic.

The creed that emerged from the council took cognizance of the development of Eastern theology since Nicaea. The role of the Holy Spirit was defined, and verbal changes were made in the text of the Nicene Creed that moved away from the strict Nicene standpoint championed by ATHANASIUS of Alexandria. Thus, the addition of the phrase "before all the ages" after "begotten from the Father" introduced a temporal element into the relation of the persons of the Trinity that Athanasius would have rejected (and similarly the phrase "of whose kingdom there will be no end").

The upshot was that the council was a serious reverse for Alexandria and the church in Egypt. Not only had the Nicene Creed been altered in a neo-Nicene sense but Constantinople had been granted an outright preeminence over the bishoprics of the East, and Alexandria, by implication, had been censured for interference in its affairs. Canon 3 had, however, provided no apostolic justification for the promotion of the see of Constantinople, a fact that was to unite Alexandria and Rome in opposition to it. The position of Constantinople was guaranteed finally by canon 28 of the Council of CHALCEDON. It was not until the end of the ACACIAN SCHISM in 519 that the papacy accepted the Council of Constantinople as an ecumenical council. Even then, it maintained silent reservations regarding canon 3. The First Council of Constantinople opened the period when differences among Constantinople, Alexandria, and Rome dominated the history of Christianity and led to the major division between Alexandria and the other patriarchates.

BIBLIOGRAPHY

Bardy, G., and J. R. Palanque. "Le Concile de Constantinople." In *Histoire de l'église,* ed. A. Fliche and V. Martin, Vol. 3, pp. 285–92. Paris, 1947.

Bois, J. "Constantinople (1er concile de)." In *Dictionnaire de Théologie catholique,* Vol. 3, cols. 1227–31. Paris, 1908.

Bright, W. *Notes on the Canons of the First Four General Councils,* 2nd ed. Oxford, 1892.

Gregory of Nazianzus. *Carmina de seipso.* In PG 37, cols. 961–1452. Paris, 1862.

Hanson, R. P. C. *The Search for the Christian Doctrine of God,* chap. 23. Edinburgh, 1988.

Héfele, C. J., and H. Leclercq, trans. *Histoire des conciles,* Vol. 2, pt. 1, pp. 1–48. Paris, 1907.

Kelly, J. N. D. *Early Christian Creeds.* London, 1950.

Kidd, B. J. *History of the Church to A.D. 461,* Vol. 2. Oxford, 1922.

W. H. C. FREND

CONSTANTINOPLE, SECOND COUNCIL OF, known as the fifth general council and convoked by Emperor Justinian I in May 553. It was presided over by Patriarch Eutychius of Constantinople, and attended by 165 bishops, nearly all from the eastern and Greek-speaking provinces of Justinian's empire. The main object of the council was to modify (without appearing to do so) the decisions and authority of the Council of CHALCEDON by condemning the "Three Chapters" consisting of works by THEODORUS OF MOPSUESTIA, Theodoret of Cyrrhus, and Ibas of Edessa, on the ground that they were tainted with Nestorianism. All three theologians had been vindicated at Chalcedon. The upshot was, however, the humiliation of Pope Vigilius (537–555) and a serious distancing of Eastern and Western ecclesiastical relations. In addition, the council failed to bridge the widening gulf between the Byzantine Orthodox church and the Monophysites, thus consolidating the breach between the Melchite and Coptic-Monophysite churches in Egypt.

The genesis of the council goes back to 538 with the death of SEVERUS OF ANTIOCH, whose theology had been condemned at the Home Synod of Constantinople two years earlier. The Monophysites represented too large a section of religious opinion in the East, especially in Egypt, to be ignored. Search was immediately initiated for an interpretation of the *Tome* of LEO I THE GREAT and the decisions of Chalcedon that would meet Monophysite objections while sustaining the authority of the *Tome* and the council. The first attempt, represented by ideas emanating from the Palestinian monks, tended toward Origenism, and was condemned in an edict that also condemned ORIGEN and Origenism, published in Jerusalem in February 543 (Evagrius *Historia ecclesiastica* IV.38).

However, one of the Origenist leaders, Theodorus Askidas, was befriended by Justinian and promoted to the influential bishopric of Caesarea in Cappadocia. His influence now became paramount at court, replacing that of the papal representatives. Askidas believed that religious unity could be restored in the East if the emperor could bring about the formal condemnation of the theology of Theodorus of Mopsuestia, Theodoret of Cyrrhus, and Ibas of Edessa, all representatives of the Antiochene school of theology. Ibas's letter to the Persian presbyter Maris that criticized Cyril's Christology, Theodoret's rejoinder to Cyril's Twelve Anathemas, and some outspokenly Antiochene writings of Theodorus were regarded as especially obnoxious. These comprised the "Three Chapters" that were offered for condemnation. As both Chalcedonians and anti-Chalcedonians in the East could agree on this proposition, it was hoped that unity could then be restored.

In the West, however, Askidas' plans were regarded with suspicion. To the Carthaginian archdeacon Liberatus, he was a secret Monophysite as well as the rival of the papal representative Pelagius for the emperor's favor (*Breviarium* XXIV). Liberatus found a North African ally in Facundus of Hermiana, who criticized both the theology of those who condemned the "Three Chapters" and the right of the emperor to intervene in ecclesiastical matters (*Pro defensione trium capitulorum* XII.3).

In this situation, Pope Vigilius hesitated. Personally inclined toward Justinian's views, he feared schism developing among the Western bishops if he approved them publicly. However, Justinian formally condemned the "Three Chapters" in 543 or 544. On 11 April 548 the pope followed suit. He sent his own condemnation of the "Three Chapters" to Patriarch Menas at Constantinople.

The *Judicatum,* as it was called, raised a storm of protest in the West. In 550 the Illyrian and North African bishops forced Vigilius to retract his decree. The next year, however, Justinian promulgated a new edict: a confession of faith condemning the "Three Chapters." On its acceptance by Menas,

Askidas, and other Eastern bishops, Vigilius excommunicated them (14 August 551). He had in the meantime been brought to Constantinople; now, fearing for his life, he fled to Chalcedon and refused to preside at the general council that the emperor was preparing to summon.

The council met on 5 May 553. Vigilius issued another decree, the *Constitutum* (11 May), in which he declined to condemn the "Three Chapters" or their authors. The council, however, deliberated without him. The conclusions were foregone. The chapters were condemned on the grounds that they were contradictory to the doctrines of the Council of Chalcedon. The letter of Ibas received particularly severe treatment. "It had nothing to do with Chalcedon. Anyone who does not anathematise it places himself in opposition to Chalcedon. Long live the emperor" (see Héfele and Leclercq, trans., 1909, pp. 118–20). Ibas and Theodoret had been solemnly restored to communion at Chalcedon, a fact now conveniently forgotten. Vigilius' name was erased from the diptychs (seventh session, 26 May).

Of the fourteen anathemas eventually approved by the council, the first twelve were directed mainly against the theology of Theodorus (the fourth, fifth, sixth, and twelfth explicitly), the thirteenth against Theodoret, and the fourteenth against Ibas. The positive doctrine of the council moved toward the Monophysites in permitting the acknowledgment of the Son "out of two natures," but the corollary that He was of one nature after the Incarnation was condemned (anathema 8). The term much used during the debates that there was in the Son "one divine-human energy" (*mia theandrike energeia*) anticipates the attempted Monenergist compromise of Heraclius in the next century. These concessions, however, were compromised by the council's explicit acceptance of the canonical status of the doctrine of the four previous councils (i.e., including Chalcedon). They came too late to halt the emergence of a Monophysite church with its own hierarchy, in which the majority of the Coptic bishops participated. In Egypt the division between Melchite (imperial) and Coptic churches moved toward finality.

In the West, too, the council had divisive results. Vigilius was forced to accept its decisions (December 553) and solemnly condemned the "Three Chapters" (on 23 February 554). While in North Africa there was grudging acceptance, the churches of Milan and Aquileia went into schism. Their hostility weakened the imperial position in Italy when it was confronted by the Lombard invaders in 568/569, and Aquileia did not return to communion with Rome until the end of the seventh century.

The council failed to heal the Monophysite schism while further alienating the Western churches from Constantinople. It provided Justinian with a temporary triumph but made inevitable the threefold division of Christendom into Western and papal, Byzantine and Orthodox, and Syrian and Coptic Monophysite churches.

BIBLIOGRAPHY

Bindley, T. H., and F. W. Green. *The Oecumenical Documents of the Faith*, 4th ed. London, 1950. The anathemas with a brief introduction are reprinted on pp. 151–56.

Bois, J. "Constantinople (IIe concile de)." In *Dictionnaire de Théologie catholique*, Vol. 3, cols. 1231–59. Paris, 1911.

Bréhier, L. "La lutte entre Vigile et Justinien." In *Histoire de l'église*, ed. A. Fliche and V. Martin, Vol. 4, *De la Mort de Théodose à l'élection de Grégoire le Grand*, pp. 467–82. Paris, 1948.

Duchesne, L. *L'Eglise au VIe siècle*. Paris, 1926.

Héfele, C. J., and H. Leclercq, trans. *Histoire des conciles*, Vol. 3, pt. 1, pp. 68–140. Paris, 1909.

Herrin, J. *The Formation of Christendom*, pp. 119–27. Oxford, 1987.

W. H. C. FREND

CONSTANTINOPLE, THIRD COUNCIL OF. This, the sixth ecumenical council, first met on 7 November 680 and ended its eighteen sessions on 16 September 681. The number of bishops attending was under 300, and the minutes of the last session have only 174 signatures attached to them. The council was convened by Emperor Constantine IV to settle the Monothelite controversy that had convulsed the Eastern church. MONOTHELITISM held that there was only one will in the God-man; it was designed to heal the breach between the Monophysites and the Chalcedonian Christians in the face of the Persian and Muslim invasions. In 624 a reconciling formula was drawn up that asserted there were two natures in Christ but only one mode of activity or "energy"—a formula found earlier in the writings of CYRIL OF ALEXANDRIA. The formula, however, was rejected by Sophronius of Jerusalem, and in correspondence on the subject between Sergius, patriarch of Constantinople, and Pope Honorius I the latter used the term "one will" in Christ, which soon replaced the more acceptable "one energy." The term was used in the *Ecthesis* issued by

Emperor Heraclius I in 638, which forbade mention of energy and admitted only "one will." This became the rallying cry of the Monothelites. However, the *Ecthesis* was withdrawn by Emperor Constans II in 648 and was replaced by another, less contentious document called *Typos*.

This did not solve the problem, and the doctrine of the two wills in Christ was eventually affirmed at a synod convened at Rome by Pope Agatho in 680. A letter concerning this doctrine was delivered by papal delegates to Emperor Constantine IV, who immediately called a council of the bishops of the patriarchates of Constantinople and Antioch. Although the emperor had no intention that it should be an ecumenical council, this title was assumed when the council assembled at the first session—representatives had come from the patriarchates of Alexandria and Jerusalem, then in Muslim hands. The sessions were held in the domed hall (or possibly chapel) of the imperial palace, which the acts of the council call Trullo.

The definition of faith issued by the council accepts the Chalcedonian definition and the creeds of NICAEA (325) and CONSTANTINOPLE (381). It concludes:

> Believing our Lord Jesus Christ to be one of the Trinity and after the Incarnation our true God, we say that His two natures shone forth in His one subsistence in which He both performed the miracles and endured the sufferings . . . not in appearance only but in very deed, and this by reason of the difference of nature that must be recognized in the same Person, for although joined together yet each nature wills and does the things proper to it and that without division or confusion. Wherefore we confess the two wills and two energies, concurring most fitly in Him for the salvation of the human race.

The Third Council of Constantinople, in asserting two wills and two energies in the God-man, effectively brought to an end the Monothelite controversy. It should be noted, however, that the council, while rejecting any physical unity of the two wills or energies in Christ, admitted the existence of a moral unity resulting from a harmony between the divine and human wills.

BIBLIOGRAPHY

Fliche, A., and V. Martin, eds. *Histoire de l'église,* Vol. 5, *Grégoire le Grand. Les états barbares et la conquête arabe (590–757),* ed. L. Bréhier and R. Aigrain. Paris, 1947.

Grumel, V. "Recherches sur l'histoire du monothélitisme." *Echos d'Orient* 27 (1928):6–16, 257–77; 28 (1929):19–34, 272–82; 29 (1930):16–28.

Héfele, C. J., and H. Leclercq, trans. *Histoire des conciles,* Vol. 3, pt. 1, pp. 472–538. Paris, 1909.

Schaff, P., and H. Wace, eds. *A Select Library of Nicene and Post-Nicene Fathers,* Vol. 14, *The Seven Ecumenical Councils,* ed. Henry A. Percival, pp. 325–52. Grand Rapids, Mich., 1956.

LESLIE W. BARNARD

CONSUBSTANTIATION, theological term applied by Martin Luther to the actual substantial coexistence and combination of the Body and Blood of Christ with the bread and wine of communion following the eucharistic consecration of the elements. This doctrine is rejected by the Orthodox church, which holds that the bread and wine, through a mystical transformation not easily grasped by the senses, change into the substance of the Body and Blood of Christ.

The early fathers asserted this belief in their writings. Saint Ignatius (c. 35–c. 107), an apostolic father by reason of his having been a hearer of the Apostle John, speaks of those who hold heterodox opinions on the grace of Jesus Christ: "They abstain from the Eucharist and from prayers, because they do not confess that the Eucharist is the Flesh of our Savior Jesus Christ, Flesh which suffered for our sins and which the Father, in His goodness, raised up again" (*Epistle to the Smyrnaeans* 6.2, in Jurgens, 1970, Vol. 1, p. 25). Likewise Justin Martyr (c. 100–c. 165) says, "For not as common bread nor common drink do we receive these; but since Jesus Christ our Savior was made incarnate by the word of God and had both flesh and blood for our salvation, so too, as we have been taught, the food which has been made into the Eucharist by the eucharistic prayer set down by Him, and by the change of which our blood and flesh is nourished, is both the flesh and the blood of that incarnated Jesus" (*First Apology* 66, in Jurgens, 1970, Vol. 1, p. 55).

Equally firm beliefs were expressed by, among others, Saint Irenaeus (c. 130–c. 200), CLEMENT OF ALEXANDRIA (c. 150–c. 215), Tertullian (c. 160–c. 220), JOHN CHRYSOSTOM (c. 374–407), and CYRIL OF ALEXANDRIA (d. 444). A particularly outstanding testimony is given by Saint ATHANASIUS (c. 295–373) in his sermon to the newly baptized. "You shall see the Levites bringing loaves and a cup of wine, and placing them on the table. So long as the prayers of supplications and entreaties have not been made, there is only bread and wine. But after the great and wonderful prayers have been completed, then the bread is become the Body, and the wine the Blood of our Lord Jesus Christ." And again, "Let us approach the celebration of the mysteries. This bread and this wine, so long as the prayers and supplications have not taken place, remain simply what they are. But after the great prayers and holy supplications have been sent forth, the Word comes down into the bread and wine—and thus is His Body confected" (in Jurgens, 1970, pp. 345, 346).

BIBLIOGRAPHY

Jurgens, W. A. *The Faith of the Early Fathers,* Vol. 1. Collegeville, Minn., 1970.

ARCHBISHOP BASILIOS

CONSULTATIVE COUNCIL (previously known as the High Council, the Council of the Citadel, the Khedivial Diwan, the General Assembly, the House of Commons, or the General Council), council founded by MUḤAMMAD ALĪ in 1824 to deal with all the internal affairs of Egypt not related to financial matters. The council's basic regulations were issued on 3 January 1825; in 1830 those dealing with the organization of its meetings were issued. These were followed by rules and regulations related to its organization and structure. The most important was the provision made in article 4 of the regulations issued on 1 August 1834, which read, "considering that the Council will deal mostly with matters related to the provinces, it would be appropriate that its members include some men elected from these areas."

Elsewhere the regulations state that since the council will deal with "cases which concern the Islamic Code it must include two *ʿulemas*. Also that it will have before it cases dealing with trade and supplies which calls for the presence of two merchants to deal with such matters. The High Council will also need two clerks conversant in accountancy to be entrusted with keeping accounts."

It was through this last door that a number of Copts, expert accountants, were able to join the council. But they were only a few, and by that time the council had exhausted its validity, having been replaced by other councils that took over its functions.

YŪNĀN LABĪB RIZQ

COPRES, SAINT, monk and martyr. The Greek Synaxarion gives information at two dates about a martyr-monk by the name of Copres, who is named with another monk and a soldier called Alexander. It is not said where they at first led the ascetic life, and H. Delehaye, in "Les Martyrs d'Egypte" (1922, esp. p. 90), advanced the opinion that these martyrs had been assimilated to the monks Copres and Patermuthius of Chapter 10 of the HISTORIA MONACHORUM IN AEGYPTO but without adducing proofs for his view; this is therefore only a working hypothesis.

The Copres of the Synaxarion (23 Tūt) was an Egyptian monk martyred under the emperor Julian the Apostate, which allows us to locate him chronologically. His notice in the Greek Synaxarion is banal and does not provide any noteworthy details.

The Copres mentioned for his words of wisdom in the *Apophthegmata Patrum* was a solitary of Scetis (the modern Wādī al-Naṭrūn). There is nothing to suggest attributing the three "sayings" placed under the name Copres to three distinct personages. Since he is connected with discussions relative to the identity of Melchizedek, discussions generally placed at the beginning of the pontificate of THEOPHILUS, he must have lived toward the end of the fourth century. From the words that are attributed to him, it seems that this was a man distinguished by his great simplicity and a profound humility.

The Copres of the *Historia monachorum* was met by pilgrims in Upper Egypt in almost the same period as the solitary of Scetis. He professed to be the disciple of a deceased "elder," whose deeds and exploits he recounted. He was, it seems, a priest, which was not common among the hermits, and of an advanced age (nearly ninety) when the pilgrims found him, and he was the superior of fifty other hermits. It was from him that the pilgrims learned of the existence of an elder called Patermuthius, a former thief who had been converted and had become one of the companions of the martyr mentioned above. Copres also made known the "brilliant achievements" of other solitaries, such as Sourous, Isaiah, Paul, Anoup, and Helle. Thanks to him, his visitors were able to describe in detail the life and actions, sometimes miraculous, of these "fathers of the desert." Their stories are sometimes tinged with magical practices like the "desmos" charm, a circle traced in the sand, with which Helle surrounded a place to protect it from the demons.

BIBLIOGRAPHY

Delehaye, H. "Les Martyrs d'Egypte." *Analecta Bollandiana* 40 (1922):5–154, 299–364.
Gibson, M. D. *Catalogue of the Arabic Manuscripts*

in the Convent of St. Catherine on Mount Sinai. Studia Sinaitica 3. London, 1894.
Graf, G. *Catalogue des manuscrits arabes-chrétiens conservés au Caire.* Studi e testi 63. Vatican City, 1934.
Ward, B. *The Sayings of the Desert Fathers: The Alphabetical Collection.* London, 1981.

RENÉ-GEORGES COQUIN

COPT. Defining the word "Copt" is not an easy matter. Gratuitous applications of the term in many circumstances have come together under the Coptic umbrella, resulting in a surprising mixture of connotations. A definition, therefore, that considers factual usage or acceptable conventional usage becomes necessary.

The root of the word serves as a beginning. Two etymologies have been proposed. One is based on homonymy, which connects the term with the name of the city Coptos (modern Qifṭ), situated about 25 miles (40 km) northeast of Luxor. In this city in Upper Egypt the Copts have been, and still are, more numerous than elsewhere in the country, a fact that tends to support this theory. However, today Qifṭ is largely Muslim, and in the past it was never distinguished as a center or place of Coptic activity, as was Asyūṭ or Suhāj, farther to the north in Upper Egypt. Therefore, homonymy has no historical justification that would authorize a derivation of the word in relation to the city of Coptos.

The other hypothesis sees in the word Copt the equivalent of the Greek *Aigyptos/Aigyptioi,* but reduced to the root consonants. This reduction indeed took place in Arabic administrative acts from the time of the Muslim conquest of the country in 641. The most obvious probability (still awaiting textual evidence) is that the vocable passed thus from these acts into the spoken language, as would be natural. In Arabic neither vowels nor diphthongs are transcribed. So in this manner *Aigyptos/Aigyptioi* became *kpt,* and in the subsequent pronunciation, "Copt," to designate the country and its native inhabitants.

It should be noted that the Greek words *Aigyptos/Aigyptioi* themselves seem to have been formed by the Greeks upon the name of the principal sanctuary in the north of Egypt, that of the ancient city of Memphis, dedicated to the god Ptah. This sanctuary was named *Het-ka-Ptah* meaning the divine house of the *ka* of Ptah, for which the Greeks did not transcribe the aspirated sounds and modified the vowels. No doubt the Greeks decided to designate as the geographical area that best represented the entire country and its inhabitants that well-known and most ancient Egyptian center in the north where they had first settled. Consequently it was used for ethnic and geographic purposes more than for its religious appurtenances. Had it been otherwise, the Greeks would certainly have opted for the sanctuary of Amon-Ra at Karnak in Luxor.

From the arabization of *Aigyptos/Aigyptioi,* and from the etymology reconstructed therefrom, there is reason to conclude that these words take on first of all a geographic sense, and second, a meaning that is essentially ethnic. Thus they signify none other than Egypt and the Egyptians of the period immediately following the pharaohs. The same thing, of course, must be said for the word "Copt."

Semantics and circumstances have, nevertheless, added a local religious and Christian sense to the original meaning of "Copt." In effect, the word "Copt" served to distinguish the conquering Arabs, who were Muslims, from the native inhabitants of Egypt, the great majority of whom were Christians. As a consequence, the tendency to identify Muslim with Arab spread throughout the Islamic world. It was later strengthened by a progressive conversion of Egyptian Christians to Islam under the pressure of considerable burdens, notably fiscal, which weighed upon them to the point that within three centuries only a minority remained faithful to Christian beliefs—a minority very important to this day.

It is with the elements of this minority that the Crusaders of the thirteenth century dealt. The same thing may be said for European travelers who at the end of the sixteenth century were interested in the manuscripts of the Coptic monasteries. So the term "Copt" took on, and has kept, a meaning that is inseparably ethnic and Christian.

From that time, for means of classification, modern historians have gone back chronologically and have adopted an older meaning from a time anterior to the formation and usage of the word. In effect, this complex interpretation has been affixed to all the indigenous inhabitants of Egypt and to everything concerning them over a period of history dating from the third to the middle of the seventh century—with no other distinction. Within Egypt the word "Copt" pertained to the language, social life, art, and liturgy (Christian). More extensively, outside of Egypt, it was applied to those people to whom the word seemed appropriate: the Ethiopians, for example, by reason of their ties with Christian Egypt, ties that were ecclesiastical (hierarchy and administration) and liturgical or dogmatic. The same may be said for the Syro-Jacobites and the Armenians because of their official MONOPHYSIT-

ISM. Such was the amplitude reached by the word "Copt" brought about arbitrarily by scholars. It came about in a rather natural way, since it all had to do with the people from which this minority had come and with everything connected to them. It was, however, no less an anachronism, characterized, at the same time, by a much abused generalization. The need to distinguish by this word the native Egyptians from the occupying Roman or Byzantine powers, or later the Arab conquerors, brings no justification at all. Moreover, accepting these erroneous applications and definitions causes immediate problems.

The first of these, and one that supersedes all the others, seems to have been virtually unnoticed to the present. The word "Copt" to mean "Egyptian Christian" cannot be reconciled with the characterization by modern historians of "Copt" as a period of time, from the third to the middle of the seventh century, including all the Egyptian people, not all of whom were Christian. This objection is more credible when considering that the Egyptians did not awaken to find themselves all Christian at the beginning of the third century, any more than other people. Christianity, on the contrary, did not attain a majority in Egypt until the middle of the fifth century. The majority of the people up to that time had been on the side of the pagan Egyptians, whose influence did not recede all at once. And yet these pagan Egyptians cannot be separated totally from the Christian Egyptians. For they all had in common their social status, taxes and other obligations, language, art, and, for some, a magic or gnostic literature. The attribution of the label "Copt" to this mixed society is difficult in the extreme. Under the guise of simplification, only confusion resulted.

In addition, the frequent extension in the religious sense of the word "Copt" to Christian Ethiopians, Syro-Jacobites, and Armenians makes it radically and arbitrarily empty of its essential ethnic base. Its application in these communities to the period that precedes the formation and use of the word by the Arab conquerors of Egypt makes this usage as anachronistic and unjustifiable as when used in referring to this same period in Egypt.

The label of "Copts" conferred upon Orthodox Egyptian Christians who during the nineteenth century became Catholic or Protestant—all the while keeping to the Coptic ritual—is more acceptable, in that it limits the creation of new distinctions among the Egyptian Christians. Nevertheless, it makes the usage of the word still more complex. And, to add to the confusion, the profession of agnosticism by certain contemporary Copts removes the religious value from a word that had developed an ethno-religious meaning, without clarifying it at all.

One would be tempted to cast aside the improper usages of the word and to impose upon it a definition taking into account only facts, whatever their complexity. But this would create new confusion because the anachronisms described above have become accepted, and hence make up a part of the word's meaning. It seems wiser to endorse them all with deliberation, but to offer at the same time more acceptable bases for their conventional usage. With such reckoning, the irregularities could serve scientific truth. Only the most impossible ones would be rejected, especially certain inadmissible extensions of the term.

From this perspective, the following outline can be proposed.

In Egypt or Concerning Egyptians

1. The Coptic period in Egypt lasted from the second century B.C. to the middle of the seventh century A.D. Its terminus a quo is justified by the beginning of the formation of the Coptic language, last stage of the Egyptian tongue, traced up to that point in hieroglyphs or written in hieratic or demotic. The word "Copt" has only an ethnic meaning. The native inhabitants of Egypt during this period are Copts, initially mostly pagan, then pagan and Christian, and finally Christian by a large majority. During this period the language is common to all, as is the writing; the literature and art are Coptic, either pagan or Christian according to the subject matter; the Christian liturgy is Coptic; the pagan cult of pharaonic origin, mixed together with Greek "mysteries," is also Coptic.

2. The Coptic community in Egypt lasted from the middle of the seventh century to the twentieth century. The meaning of the word "Copt" is ethno-Christian. The word "Copt" designates essentially the Orthodox Copts. By extension, it may be applied to Copts who have become Catholic or Protestant, or even agnostic (but then reverting to the purely ethnic meaning). The Coptic language remained that of the Coptic community for a short time only. By the tenth century it was supplanted by Arabic, as was their literature, which, however, remained Christian. The Coptic liturgy kept its place of honor in this community and is to be distinguished from other Christian liturgies.

Coptic art is also that of this community and is thus Christian. It lost its value as art during the thirteenth century.

Outside Egypt

The word "Copt" is to be discarded when discussing the Syro-Jacobites and the Armenians and whatever may concern them. Nor can it designate the Ethiopians, who are of a different race and language. But it may be used to describe ecclesiastical and administrative affairs such as their dogma and liturgy. Concerning Ethiopians, it is normal to speak of the Coptic hierarchy, Coptic Christians, and Coptic liturgy.

BIBLIOGRAPHY

Bourguet, P. du. *L'Art copte*. Catalogue d'exposition. Editions du Ministère des Affaires culturelles. Paris, 1964, pp. 25–27.

———. *L'art copte*, pp. 5–6. Paris, 1967.

Doresse, J. "Les Coptes." *Histoire universelle, Collection de la Pleiade*. Paris, 1970.

Lefebvre, G. "Grammaire de l'egyptien classique." 2d ed., p. 6, n. 3. Cairo, 1955.

PIERRE DU BOURGUET, S. J.

COPTIC CATHOLIC CHURCH, a distinct Eastern church in communion with Rome. Its patriarchate is in Alexandria.

Pope Leo XII of Rome (1823–1829) was falsely led to believe that the viceroy of Egypt, MUḤAMMAD 'ALĪ, wished the establishment of the Coptic Catholic patriarchate for all Copts and the appointment of the vicar apostolic Maximos Guaid (Zuwayd) as the first patriarch. On 1 August 1824, Leo XII personally consecrated as bishop Abraham Khashūr, a very young Coptic alumnus of the Propaganda College in Rome. The bishop was supposed to return to Egypt and consecrate Maximus as patriarch of Alexandria. Having acknowledged that the non-Catholic patriarchate existed actually but not de jure and having proclaimed it suppressed, in the bull *Petrus Apostolorum Princeps* of 15 August 1824, Leo XII founded the Catholic Coptic patriarchate of Alexandria. Leo XII soon recognized that he had been deceived, and the establishment of the patriarchate remained on paper only. The Catholic Copts continued to be ruled by vicars apostolic.

In September 1895, a delegation of Catholic Copts, headed by the vicar apostolic Cyril Maqār, arrived at Rome and petitioned Pope Leo XIII to form a Catholic Coptic patriarchate. Leo XIII (1878–1903), in the apostolic letter *Christi Domini* (27 November 1895), proclaimed: "We reestablish the Patriarchate of Alexandria and erect it for the Copts." In the same letter, Cyril Maqār was appointed apostolic administrator of the patriarchate. Furthermore, Pope Leo XIII stated that this Catholic patriarchate was "the only one which legitimately rules the Church founded by [Saint] Mark, the only heir of all the memories faithfully handed down from the pristine and glorious times of the Patriarchate of Alexandria." Thus, from the juridical Roman point of view, the Coptic patriarchate of Alexandria, not being in communion with Rome, was a legal fiction and canonically did not exist; thus, all the hierarchs of the Coptic church had no spiritual power or jurisdiction. This regrettable attitude overlooked the fact that Catholic Copts were a tiny minority in Egypt, and the non-Catholic Copts had a tradition reaching back to Saint Mark. Consequently, when a Coptic bishop or priest converted to Catholicism, it was presumed that he had no jurisdiction over his flock and that the Roman see had to grant him all the faculties (e.g., as Pope Benedict XIV had granted faculties to Bishop Athanasius on 4 August 1741).

In 1898, under the presidency of the apostolic administrator Cyril Maqār, the synod of Alexandria of the uniate Copts was held. It was a Latinizing event. The synod introduced Latin feasts: Corpus Christi, All Saints, the Immaculate Conception, and Saint Joseph. At the express wish of Pope Leo XIII, during the closing ceremonies of the synod Cyril Maqār dedicated the Coptic Catholic Church to the Sacred Heart of Jesus. The decrees of the synod were approved by the Roman Curia. Leo XIII also approved the introduction of Latin-rite offices and the rosary into the Coptic Catholic Church. The synod also introduced the Latin discipline of clerical celibacy. The patriarch, however, could grant a dispensation to married priests converting to Catholicism. The same synod introduced the FILIOQUE into the creed and theological thought, and accused the orthodox Copts of "having followed external doctrines." Furthermore, the synod tried to prove that the Greek fathers had come close to the *filioque* and presented witnesses of the Egyptian tradition allegedly tending toward the *filioque*. This synod was a classic example of uniatism; it was a very rapid Latinization of the Eastern canonical Christian discipline, liturgy, theological thought, and spirituality.

On 19 June 1899, the apostolic administrator of the patriarchate, Cyril Maqār, was appointed patriarch of Alexandria by Leo XIII; he was to be known as CYRIL II, recognizing Cyril the Great (412–444) as CYRIL I. This, of course, was not accepted by the

Coptic community, whose patriarch bearing the name Cyril II lived in the eleventh century. Soon great difficulties emerged, especially with respect to the financial dependence of the patriarchate on Rome, and in 1908 the patriarch was suspended. A great number of uniate Copts returned to the Coptic Orthodox Church. Cyril II published a pamphlet against the papal primacy but again subjected himself to Rome in 1912 and died in 1922 in Beirut as a titular archbishop at peace with the Roman Curia. Cyril II had been a great scholar; note his *L'Eglise copte, sa foi d'aujourd'hui comparée avec la foi de ses pères* (Cairo, 1893); *Histoire de l'église d'Alexandrie depuis St. Marc jusqu'à nos jours* (Cairo, 1894); *La Constitution divine de l'église* (Bern, 1922).

The Catholic patriarchal see remained unoccupied until 30 December 1927, when Bishop Markos Khuzām was named as administrator. Only after a probationary period of twenty years, on 9 August 1947, was he permitted to occupy the Catholic patriarchal see as Mark II (Mark I being the Evangelist). On 2 February 1958, Mark II died, and on 10 May 1958, Stephanos I Sidarūs was appointed patriarch. In 1965 he was created the first Coptic cardinal.

The erection of the Catholic patriarchate contributed greatly to the growth of the Coptic Catholic Church: in 1895, it had 5,000 communicants; in 1907, 14,576; in 1931, 35,365; in 1950, 57,556; in 1959, 80,580; and in 1975, 107,500. Besides the patriarchal eparchy of Alexandria (with residence in Cairo) there are the eparchies of Asyūṭ, Minyā, and Luxor. The Catholic patriarchate is ruled by the patriarch with his synod, which includes all the bishops. In the patriarchate there are preseminaries in Ṭahṭā and Alexandria, and minor and major seminaries in Cairo. The official Arabic bulletin of the Catholic patriarchate is *Al-Ṣalāḥ;* the second periodical is *Ṣadīq al-Kāhin.*

BIBLIOGRAPHY

Attwater, D. *The Christian Churches of the East.* Vol. 1, *Churches in Communion with Rome,* pp. 128–37. Milwaukee, Wis., 1961.

Colombo, A. *Le origini della gerarchia della chiesa copta catolica nel secola XVII.* Oriens Christianus Analecta 140. Rome, 1953.

Metzler, J. "Matta Righet: Apostolischer Vikar der Kopten und Vertrauensmann der S.C. de Propaganda Fide (1747–1821)." *Euntes Docete* 13 (1960):358–407.

______. "Das apostolische Vikariat der Kopten." *Euntes Docete* 14 (1961):36–62; and 15 (1962): 70–105.

Sacra congregatione per le chiese orientali. *Oriente cattolico: Cenni storici e statistiche,* pp. 91–104. Vatican City, 1974.

Scaduto, M. "La missione di Cristoforo Rodriguez al Cairo (1561–1563)." *Archivum Historicum Societatis Iesu* 27 (1958):233ff.

Trossen, J. P. *Les Relations du patriarche copte Jean XVI avec Rome (1676–1718).* Luxembourg, 1948.

Vries, W. de. *Rom und die Patriarchate des Ostens.* Munich, 1963.

PETRO B. T. BILANIUK

COPTIC CONGRESS OF ASYŪṬ (6–8 March 1911), meeting attended by 1,150 delegates acting on behalf of 10,500 Copts, with Bushrā Ḥanna as chairman, and Tawfīq Doss as secretary.

The congress was convened against a background of controversy and contrary to the wishes of Patriarch CYRIL V (1874–1927), as well as the moderate elements in the community. The government reluctantly granted permission for the meeting to be held, providing that members refrained from any action that might lead to a breach of the peace.

Cyril V expressed his concern in a statement on 2 March, "Whilst it gives us pleasure to see that a number of Copts have agreed to work together for the welfare of the community at large, we would ask our beloved children to refrain from building up a huge gathering in Asyūṭ, which could result in agitation and render them liable to criticism. We would therefore urge everybody to exercise extreme prudence, wisdom and circumspection."

The metropolitan of Asyūṭ, Bishop Macarius, held a different view. "With all respect and obedience to Your Holiness," he said in a telegram to the patriarch, "I would assure you that there is no cause for concern. No personal or public damage is likely to result, the main objective of the Congress being the forging of stronger ties among all Egyptians through the safeguarding of the legitimate rights of Copts. I do not feel the slightest apprehension of its being held in Asyūṭ."

This anxiety was also reflected by the choice of the congress chairman and its speakers. Bushrā Ḥannā was chosen in preference to the extremist Akhnūkh Fānūs; and the speakers were mostly nationalist figures such as Murqus Ḥannā, Sinot Ḥannā, and Fakhrī ʻAbdelnour. Even Akhnūkh Fānūs, known for his inflammatory articles in the *Miṣr* and *al-Waṭan* newspapers, showed remarkable restraint in his speech. To emphasize this sense of nationalism, the inaugural session started with the national anthem, and the Egyptian flag flew on the top of the building.

Article 10 of the statute drawn by the General Assembly stated that "speakers may not raise political or religious issues. Should they do, they shall first be cautioned, and, if they persist, shall be dismissed from the Assembly."

This fear for unrest was due partly to the sectarian character of the meeting and partly to the state of tension prevalent in the wake of the assassination on 21 February 1910 of BOUTROS GHĀLĪ, the only Christian prime minister to date. With such sensitive topics eliminated, the congress proceeded to discuss matters of mainly social and financial character. This found apt expression in the words of Murqus Ḥannā: "Members of the Coptic community have gathered here in as much as members of the medical or legal profession would gather together —because they have something in common to discuss, and a desire to strengthen their bonds and deepen their sense of nationalism."

The main questions discussed by the Congress were:

1. Allowing Coptic students and civil servants a holiday on Sunday. Akhnūkh Fānūs suggested that if government employees worked an additional 45 minutes each day, offices could be closed on Sunday. Equally if students stayed a full day on Thursday, schools could be closed on Sunday.

2. That ability should be the only criterion in filling posts. Tawfīq Doss asked for the removal of restrictions banning or limiting the number of Coptic employees in certain government posts. (*Al-Mu'ayyad,* a Muslim newspaper, of 12 March 1911, argued that although Copts formed only 6 percent of the population, the number of Muslim employees in the Post Office, the Railways, and the Ministry of Finance did not exceed 10 to 20 percent, and that Copts had an overwhelming majority in key positions in the provinces.)

3. Murqus Ḥannā called for proportionate representation in parliament, referring to the Belgian system that enhanced the rights of minorities by allowing two votes to citizens paying higher taxes and three votes to holders of higher qualifications. Religious considerations, he argued, should be totally disregarded in the election of parliamentary candidates.

4. Ḥabīb Doss recommended that village schools be open to all Egyptians, Muslims, Copts, and Jews alike, without discrimination, or alternately, that the 5 percent tax levied for this purpose on Copts be used in financing private schools for Copts. The latter recommendation was opposed by Murqus Fahmī, as it would lead to a split in national unity.

5. Murqus Fahmī called for equal financial treatment by the treasury for Coptic and Muslim amenities, and urged for the establishment of personal status courts for the Copts.

BIBLIOGRAPHY

Ṭāriq al-Bishrī. *Al-Muslimūn wa-al-Aqbāṭ fī Iṭār al-Jamā'ah al-Waṭaniyyah,* p. 726. Cairo and Beirut, 1982.

SAMIRAH BAHR

COPTIC EVANGELICAL CHURCH, a Presbyterian national church founded through the efforts of the United Presbyterian Church in North America in 1854. The first Presbyterian missionaries to Egypt emphasized bible teaching and preaching. The Evangelical churches are about 250 in number besides having another 200 meeting centers for prayers, with a community of 250,000. These churches have 340 pastors, most of them having earned their B.D. degree in theological sciences from the Evangelical Theological Seminary at Cairo established in 1863. Some serve in educational areas, others in social services. Some deal with youth and others work in various administrative capacities. The majority are pastors.

On 5 February 1863, the Egyptian Presbytery decided to establish a theological school to prepare the national Evangelical pastors. It started with nine students. Among those students was Tadrus Yusuf, the first Egyptian Evangelical pastor, who completed his studies in 1871. In 1885, the theological school was located in Cairo. The present seminary building was founded in 1927. Up to that time, 520 pastors were graduated from the theological seminary. In 1967, the evening department started, and through it lay men and women were able to join the seminary. The first woman graduated in 1970. There is a specialized library of about 20,000 books.

The Evangelical work spread from Egypt to the Sudan, and the first Egyptian pastor who went there was Jabrā Ḥannā. He established the Evangelical Church in the Sudan in 1900. The Presbytery of the Sudan was part of the Synod of the Nile of the Evangelical Church in Egypt until 1965, when it became independent. The Synod of the Nile sent to

South Sudan the first Egyptian missionary, Dr. Suwāylim Sidhum.

The administrative structure of the church consists of the basic unit that is "the local church," the Synod of the Nile comprising eight presbyteries. The moderator of the Synod is elected annually, and the secretary of the Synod is appointed for three years.

The activities of the Evangelical church include bible publishing, education (sixty schools), social work, health care (hospitals in Cairo, Ṭanṭā, and Asyūṭ), and Sunday schools. The church owns the largest Christian publishing house in the Arab world. The Evangelical church has been a member of the World Council of Churches since 1963 and the Middle East Council of Churches since 1974.

SAMUEL HABIB

COPTIC LANGUAGE, SPOKEN. Coptic was the spoken language of ancient Egypt until the ARAB CONQUEST OF EGYPT in the seventh century. It was recorded first in the hieroglyphic (sacred) script, the earliest form of Egyptian pictorial writing, and succeeded by the hieratic (priestly), which was the simplified running script, and the demotic (from "demos," meaning people), which became the popular form of Egyptian writing. Later, during the reign of the Ptolemaic dynasty, approximately in the third century B.C., instead of the still complicated demotic script, Egyptians began to adopt the Greek alphabet, which became distinguished as Coptic. Because the Greek alphabet could not cope with all the Egyptian sounds, it became necessary to add seven letters from the demotic script to express the full range of the Coptic language. These were, of course, the final seven letters of the new Coptic alphabet, that is, ϣ (*shai*), ϥ (*fay*), ϧ (*khay*), ϩ (*houri*), ϫ (*janja*), ϭ (*tchima*), and ϯ (*ti*). It should be noted, however, that the letter ϧ (*khay*) existed only in the Bohairic dialect, not in the Sahidic, and that the Akhmimic dialect used the form B to express the sound of the letter ϩ (*houri*). In the meantime, the new script was the only form that comprised the vowels unknown in the other ancient Egyptian writings. Consequently, the Coptic script expressed, for the first time, most of the sounds of the hitherto unknown vowels in the ancient Egyptian language.

The influence of the Greek vocabulary on Coptic began with Alexander's conquest of Egypt in 332 B.C., when the government administration adopted Greek terminology. In the meantime, the government employees learned the Greek language, as did most classes of society in Lower Egypt. This led to the progressive incorporation of Greek words into the local demotic, ending up with the establishment of what is known as Proto-Coptic. This was mainly spoken Egyptian written in Greek characters. The Papyrus Heidelberg 414 from the third century B.C. is the oldest document known to represent this phase in the development of Coptic. The next stage is known as Old Coptic. In Roman times, from the third to the second century B.C., we find stelae as well as mummy labels and even papyrus documents containing Egyptian demotic names written in Greek letters interspersed with demotic signs beyond the seven aforementioned letters. They were mainly the product of pagan mystic signs, symbols, and horoscopes. Since the Alexandrian population was conversant with Greek as well as with Coptic, many Greek theological terms were used in all attempts to translate the scripture into Coptic. With the spread of Christianity among the inhabitants of the Delta and Upper Egypt where people were not conversant with Greek and only knew the native tongue, it became necessary to translate the scripture into Coptic with fewer Greek influences.

We must assume that the purely Coptic version of the scripture, as well as the liturgies, must have emerged in the course of the third century A.D. Saint Antony, who was himself totally illiterate in Greek, was influenced by the Coptic Gospel dictate to sell all one's possessions and distribute them among the poor (Mt. 19:21). A Coptic translation must have instructed the native followers of Saint Pachomius. However, the full translation of the scripture from Greek into Coptic must have been completed only in the course of the fourth century A.D. After the Council of CHALCEDON in 451, the Copts lost their interest in Greek and concentrated on their native tongue.

With the Arab conquest of Egypt in the seventh century, use of the Arabic language began to appear among the Egyptians. However, Copts started writing their own theological treatises in Arabic in the thirteenth century. Coptic as a spoken language of the country folk persisted in numerous regions of Upper Egypt to the end of the sixteenth century and the beginning of the seventeenth.

The factors at work in the gradual disappearance of the Coptic language may be enumerated as follows:

1. The decision in 706 of ʿAbd-Allāh ibn ʿAbd al-Malik, the Arab viceroy of Egypt, to use Arabic as the only language of the administration. To keep their places in the administration, the Coptic functionaries learned the language of the rulers and this led to the appearance of bilingual documents at first, ultimately giving way to Arabic as the sole mode of expression in the government.

2. The gradual apostasy of the Copts to Islam as a result of the successive waves of financial pressures and religious persecution. The change was accelerated by the promise of promotion to all Islamized members of the community and the desire to escape from the imposition of a progressively heavy capitation tax known as JIZYAH on those who clung to the old faith and resisted apostasy to Islam.

3. The excessive persecutions of the natives, notably by al-ḤĀKIM BI-AMR ILLĀH (996–1020) who issued an order to stop the use of Coptic not only in public places and offices but also at homes and in private circles. Those caught conversing in Coptic were liable to have their tongues cut. Consequently, the Copts were forced to screen their places of worship where religious offices were celebrated in Coptic. Nevertheless, the ruling class did not hesitate to attack these places of worship and to punish all Coptic worshipers without mercy. It is said that the establishment of mills at the entrance of churches in those days was intentionally done to drown out the sound of Coptic hymns within, as a means of deluding the government forces from without.

4. The decadence of the monastic institutions, which hitherto had been fortresses of strength for the Christian faith. The monks were subjected to heavy imposts, and it is said that in 710 those who paid the taxes were marked by cauterization of their hands. Consequently, monks unable to show their cauterization were subjected to the most sordid persecution. In 732 a group of such monks had their hands amputated, and some died while their churches were pillaged.

5. The introduction of the Arabic language in the churches to cope with the gradual failure of the congregation to understand the Gospels and the liturgies in Coptic. This change was authorized by Pope GABRIEL II in the twelfth century, and the arabization of the church offices has continued until the present.

The use of Arabic instead of Coptic in religious literature is best exemplified in the *History of the Patriarchs* compiled by Sāwīrus, bishop of Ashmunayn in the tenth century. Again in the thirteenth century, the famous work on the story of churches and monasteries, ascribed wrongly to ABŪ ṢĀLIḤ THE ARMENIAN, and authored by ABŪ AL-MAKĀRIM, appeared in Arabic. At this time, however, numerous treatises appeared bilingually in Coptic and Arabic. To this period also belongs the composition of the works known as SULLAM (pl., *Salālim*), that is, the Scala (glossary, vocabulary), which consisted of Coptic vocabulary rendered into Arabic. Abū Isḥāq ibn al-ʿAssal is responsible for one such work entitled *Al-Sullam al-Muqaffā wa al-Dhahab al-Muṣaffā* (Rhymed Glossary). His brother, Abū al-Faraj ibn al-ʿAssal, wrote a famous introduction in Arabic on the rules of the Coptic language (see AWLĀD AL-ʿASSĀL). Al-Samannūdi, the pen name of Anbā Yuʿannis, bishop of Samannūd, wrote another *Sullam*, the vocabulary of which is derived from the Gospels, the Epistles, the Psalms, and the liturgical works. He also composed an introduction on the Coptic Bohairic dialect, as well as other works on the Sahidic dialect. Ibn Kātib Qayṣar wrote *Kitāb al-Tabṣirah* (Guide Book) and al-Qalyūbī wrote another similar work entitled *Al-Kifāyah* (Sufficiency). Ibn al-Duhayrī, otherwise known as Anbā Christodoulos, archbishop of Damietta, wrote a work in which he criticized the works of former grammarians.

In the fourteenth century, Shams al-Riyāsah al-Quss ibn Kabar (d. 1324) wrote his *Al-Sullam al-Kabīr* (Major Glossary), a Coptic lexicon classified in subjects. Anbā Athanasius, bishop of Qūṣ, wrote a work entitled *Qilādat al-Taḥrīr fī ʿIlm al-Tafsīr* (The Art of Interpretation), another introduction to the Bohairic and Sahidic grammars.

In the fourteenth century, a remarkable work entitled *Triadon*, a didactic poem in Sahidic Coptic, appeared by an anonymous writer, possibly an Upper Egyptian monk. The original poem was in 734 verses, of which only 428 survived, with an Arabic translation that is somewhat artificial and not always clear. It was an attempt to glorify the moribund Coptic language and eulogize biblical personalities and Coptic saints.

In the fifteenth century, the Arab historian al-MAQRĪZĪ (d. 1441) points out in his famous work *Al-Khiṭat wa-al-Athār* (On History and Geography) that women and children in Upper Egypt knew almost no other tongue for communication but Sahidic Coptic (Vol. 2, p. 507). Again in the same work (Vol. 2, p. 518), while discussing the region of Durunkah in the province of Asyūṭ, he mentions that the inhabitants of the Upper Egyptian Christian villages were all conversant with the doctrines of their faith, as well as with the Coptic language.

In the sixteenth century, according to statements

made by the famous Egyptologist J. MASPERO in 1909, the Copts still spoke Coptic. During the reign of Louis XIV (1643–1715), it is tradition that a priest and an old Coptic woman were introduced to a seventeenth-century French tourist as the last Egyptians who were thoroughly acquainted with Coptic as a spoken language. Afterward, Coptic survived only as the language of the liturgy. Moreover, the Dominican traveler J. M. VANSLEB points out in the account of his travels in Upper Egypt in 1672–1673 that Anbā Yu'annis, archbishop of Asyūṭ, introduced to him a certain Mu'allim Athanasius, who was the last Copt to be conversant with the Coptic language as a speaking medium in the country. Nevertheless, the English writer James E. Quibell reports in the year 1901 that the Reverend David Strang of the American mission at Banī Suef informed him that when he first came to Egypt some three decades before that date, Coptic had been spoken in Upper Egypt within living memory. As a concrete example, a certain Jam Estephanos, an old man from Qūṣ, stated that he remembered as a boy hearing his parents converse in Coptic, which was probably true of the inhabitants of both Qūṣ and Naqādah (Worrell, 1942, p. 306). W. H. Worrell quotes an oral tradition about Coptic in the village of Ziniyyah, a village in the same neighborhood. A carpenter by the name of Isḥāq is credited with the importation from Asyūṭ of Coptic to Ziniyyah. One Ṭanyōs, a Coptic-speaking person, came to Ziniyyah from Naqādah, where he died a centenarian around the year 1886. Another by the name of Muḥārib, who also spoke Coptic, came from Naqādah at the age of eighty. Khalīl abū Bisādah, who knew spoken Coptic from his parents at Ziniyyah, is said to have been taught written Coptic by both the aforementioned Ṭanyōs and Muḥārib. He continued to live at Ziniyyah until his death around the year 1910. From Naqādah again, a certain Mityās came to share the teaching of Coptic at Ziniyyah with Khalīl Abū Bisādah. At Farshūṭ in the nineteenth century, the cantors and priests spoke only Coptic within the church sanctuary. Yassā 'Abd al-Masīḥ, who died in 1959, reported that his grandfather used only Coptic within the church. The Ziniyyah tradition of the use of Coptic as a speaking medium does not mean that Coptic had survived in Egypt as a spoken language that late, but only that it was employed in spots for the glorification of a defunct institution (Worrell, 1942, pp. 301–304). Strictly speaking, the survival of Coptic appears in the vocabulary and sentence construction of the modern spoken or colloquial Arabic of Egypt (see EGYPTIAN ARABIC VOCABULARY, COPTIC INFLUENCE ON). It must also be stated that liturgical Coptic has been preserved within the church as an established tradition, though the use of Arabic has been growing.

In fact, the discovery of the Coptic ecclesiastical heritage and the revival of the study of the Coptic language appears to have been made in modern times by Western scholarship in Europe. The first work to be published in the West in this field was written by the Jesuit priest Athanasius Kircher, and was entitled *Prodromus Coptus sive Aegyptiacus* (1636). He also created a grammar of the Coptic language entitled *Lingua aegyptiaca restituta* (1643–1644). In 1659, T. Petraeus published Psalm 1 in Bohairic Coptic supplemented by phonetic Latin characters under the title *Psalmus Primus Davidis, Coptice, Arabice et Latine* (London, 1659). Since then, several other Coptic grammars have appeared —by Blumberg (1716), Christian Scholtz (1778), and the Catholic Coptic scholar Rūfā'īl al-Ṭūkhī (1778)—together with the first Coptic lexicon by Lacroze (1775). In Egypt itself, the study of Coptic in schools was sponsored by CYRIL IV (1854–1861), who insisted on the use of Coptic in churches as the official liturgical language. Outside the church, Iqlādiyūs Labīb became a champion of the use of Coptic among the laity as a spoken language. In the meantime, Cyril IV entrusted the HEGUMENOS Takla with the teaching, on a scientific basis, of the Coptic language, liturgy, and hymnal to priests. He was succeeded in this capacity by Mu'allim 'IRYĀN JIRJIS MUFTĀḤ. Unfortunately, the latter was responsible for departing in his system from the old Coptic phonology to the modern Greek. This took place with the assistance of a teacher of the Greek language at the 'Abīdiyyah School in Cairo. This new system was unopposed by the church authority and soon spread among the younger generation of the modern Coptic priests. Among its strong supporters was the great champion of the Coptic language, Iqlādiyūs Labīb, who was himself a pupil of Mu'allim 'Iryān Muftāḥ.

In the late twentieth century, a new trend has been encouraged by SHENOUDA III. Emile Maher Ishaq, as head of the Coptic language section in the Cairo Clerical College, is promulgating the return to the original Coptic phonology and the elimination of the Greek influence that is foreign to traditional Coptic.

BIBLIOGRAPHY

Blumberg, C. G. *Fundamenta linguae copticae in gratiam eorum conscripta*. Leipzig, 1716.

Ishak, E. M. *The Phonetics and Philology of the Bohairic Dialect of Coptic, and the Survival of Coptic*

Words in the Colloquial and Classical Arabic of Egypt, and of Coptic Grammatical Constructions in Colloquial Egyptian, 2 vols. D. Phil. thesis, Oxford, 1975.

Jirjis Phīlūthāwus ʿAwaḍ. *Dhikrah Muṣliḥ ʿAẓīm.* Cairo, 1911.

———. *Al-Lughah al-Qibṭīyyah.* Cairo, 1916.

Kircher, A. *Prodromus Coptus sive Aegyptiacus.* Rome, 1636.

Lacroze, M. V. de. *Lexicon aegyptiaco-latinum ex veteribus illius linguae monumentis summo studio collectum et elaboratum.* Oxford, 1775.

———. *Lingua aegyptiaca restituta.* Rome, 1643.

Petraeus, T. *Psalmus Primus Davidis, Coptice, Arabice et Latine.* London, 1659.

Quatremère, E. M. *Recherches critiques et historiques sur la langue et la littérature de l'Egypte.* Paris, 1808.

Rūfā'īl al-Ṭūkhī. *Rudimenta linguae coptae sive aegyptiacae.* Rome, 1778.

Scholtz, Christian. *Grammatica aegyptiaca utriusque dialecti.* Oxford, 1778.

Sobhy, G. *Kiṭāb qawāʿid al-lughah al-Miṣrīyah al-Qibṭiyah.* Cairo, 1925.

Vansleb, J. M. *The Present State of Egypt, or, a New Relation of a Late Voyage into that Kingdom Performed in the Years 1672 and 1673.* London, 1678.

Walters, C. C. *An Elementary Coptic Grammar.* Oxford, 1972.

Worrell, W. H. *Coptic Texts.* London, 1942.

———. *A Short Account of the Copts.* Ann Arbor, Mich., 1945.

EMILE MAHER ISHAQ

COPTIC LEGION. *See* Yaʿqūb, General.

COPTIC MUSEUM, museum founded in Cairo in 1902. The first exhibition of Coptic art in Egypt took place sometime at the end of the nineteenth century in the Bulāq Museum, the precursor of the actual Museum of Egyptian Antiquities. The collection was exhibited in a hall called "La Salle copte" before it was moved to the new museum founded in 1902. In 1908 the collection was moved to a permanent home in the Coptic Museum, which was established in the suburb of Cairo now known as Old Cairo. It remained in the hands of the Coptic church until 1931, when it became a national museum under the jurisdiction of the Egyptian Department of Antiquities.

The site chosen for the museum was the area of the fortress of BABYLON, which had been founded by Emperor Trajan (98–117) and whose walls can still be seen from the entrance of the museum.

Coptic Museum (Old Cairo). Courtyard. *Courtesy Coptic Museum, Cairo.*

The nucleus of the Coptic collection consisted of a number of historic items assembled from Coptic homes, old Coptic churches, and ancient monasteries, as well as from a number of archaeological sites. With the support of Patriarch CYRIL V (1874–1927) it was possible to acquire some painted ceilings, marble columns, mosaic floors, and fountains, as well as a few samples of elaborate carved woodwork from old palaces and private residences. With the transfer of the museum ownership from the church to the Department of Antiquities, the collection was further enriched by moving the considerable Coptic objects of archaeological distinction accumulated in the Egyptian Museum to the newly established Coptic Museum.

Initially the museum consisted of a relatively small wing that was later extended by a substantial modern building inaugurated in 1947 by King Fouad I, thus providing the needed space for the increasing archaeological and artistic collections. It was therefore possible to devote certain halls to special collections such as stonework, woodwork, metals, and textiles.

The library proved to be the pride of the museum, since it contained a rich collection of Coptic sources. In addition to published materials, a vast number of Coptic manuscripts were assembled from the ancient churches and monasteries. An enormous collection of Coptic ostraca and rare documentary objects were housed in it. The unique Gnostic papyri collection known as the NAG HAMMADI LIBRARY was deposited among its treasures. Significant private collections were also acquired, such as that of the Coptic historian MĪKHĀ'ĪL SHARŪBĪM. Some of its contents were cataloged by Henri Munier and Walter Crum, as well as Murqus Simaykah and Yassā Abd al-Masīḥ. A vast accumulation of Coptic and Arabic manuscripts of all ages are available to qualified scholars. The library holds Old and New Testaments, lives of saints, horologia, apocryphas, language books, and dictionaries, in addition to a number of scientific and medical treatises. Most recently it acquired the oldest known codex of the Psalms, dating from the fourth century.

In 1984, the museum was partly renovated and the collection redisplayed. An inventory of the vast holdings in storage is underway, as is a new catalog for the displays.

A rough inventory of the contents of the museum is indicative of the extent of the monuments on display in its halls. Though steadily increasing from new discoveries in Coptic excavations, the collection to date numbers more than 14,000 items. The following is a list of the contents of each category as of 1985:

2,568	items of stone and marble sculpture
486	frescoes
196	icons
112	ivory objects, plus 248 bones, 6 mother of pearl, 4 horn, and 1 amber
1,500	Coptic textiles
1,470	metal objects including gold, silver, bronze, iron, copper, and lead
1,274	pieces of carved woodwork
1,534	pieces of pottery and glazed ceramic
93	glass items

Coptic Museum (Old Cairo). Hall of Apa Jeremiah (Saqqarah). Columns discovered in 1907. Pulpit at the far end is one of the oldest yet found. *Courtesy Coptic Museum, Cairo.*

BIBLIOGRAPHY

Crum, W. E. *Coptic Monuments* (*Catalogue général des antiquités égyptiennes du Musée du Caire*). Cairo, 1902.

Gabra, G. *The Project. "Catalogue Général du Musée Copte."* In *The Greek Presence in Ancient Egypt: Symposium, Delphi: March 17–20, 1988,* ed. L. Marangou and P. Nearchou. Forthcoming.

______. *Das Projekt "Catalogue Général du Musée Copte": Stand der Arbeiten bis Dezember 1988.* In *Proceedings of the Fourth International Congress of Coptic Studies (Louvain La Neuve, 5–10 September 1988),* ed. J. Ries. Forthcoming.

Munier, H. *Manuscrits coptes* (*Catalogue général des Antiquités égyptiennes du Musée du Caire*). Cairo, 1916.

Murqus Simaykah. *Guide to the Coptic Museum.* Cairo, 1932.

______. *A Brief Guide to the Coptic Museum and to the Principal Ancient Churches of Cairo.* Cairo, 1938.

Pahor Labib. *The Coptic Museum.* Cairo, 1950.

______. *The Coptic Museum and the Fortress of Babylon at Old Cairo.* Cairo, 1953.

______. *Coptic Gnostic Papyri in the Coptic Museum at Old Cairo.* Cairo, 1956.

______. *Das koptische Kairo. Koptische Kunst Christentum am Nil,* pp. 92–94. Essen, 1963.

Raouf Habib. *The Coptic Museum, General Guide.* Cairo, 1967.

Su'ād Māhir and Ḥishmat Messiha. *Coptic Textiles in the Coptic Museum.* Cairo, 1957. In Arabic.

Strzygowski, Josef. *Koptische Kunst* (*Catalogue général des antiquités égyptiennes du Musée du Caire*). Vienna, 1904.

MUNIR BASTA

COPTIC REFORM SOCIETY, founded around 1907–1908 by Akhnūkh Fānūs, a lawyer and journalist of British education. After the attempts by some Copts to establish a Coptic political party were rejected by a majority who preferred not to link Coptic interests with political activity, the Reform Society was founded as an organization to defend Coptic interests. Most members were employees of the Egyptian State Railways or school teachers.

They demanded equal opportunities to be afforded to Coptic applicants for administrative government posts, a major grievance of the Copts under British control. They accused both the British and

Egyptian authorities of restricting access of Copts to those posts. However, according to British statistics and statements, the Copts were already overrepresented in administrative posts.

BIBLIOGRAPHY

Muḥammad Sayyid Kīlānī. *Al-Adab al-Qibṭī Qadimān wa Ḥadīthān.* Cairo, 1962.

DORIS BEHRENS-ABUSEIF

COPTIC RELATIONS WITH ROME. In antiquity, the pope and Church of Alexandria stood in close and friendly relations with the pope and Church of Rome. Quite often both churches formed an alliance against New Rome (Constantinople) and its patriarch. The early synods of Alexandria were recognized by Rome: DEMETRIUS I against ORIGEN (231); PETER II against MELITIUS of Lycopolis (306); ALEXANDER I against ARIUS (318 or 321); ATHANASIUS I against the ARIANISM of the Eusebians (339); Athanasius, who clarified the terminology of *ousia* and *hypostasis,* thus initiating the reconciliation of the Semi-Arians (362); CYRIL I against NESTORIUS (430). However, in rejecting the Council of CHALCEDON (451) the Copts (in the Synod under TIMOTHY II Aelurus, and under PETER III MONGUS) initiated a complete break with Rome. This lasted until the time of the Crusades when unsuccessful negotiations for reunion were attempted under the Coptic pope CYRIL III (1235–1243). The reunion of the Copts with Rome during the Council of Florence in 1442 and its acceptance by the Coptic pope JOHN XI (1427–1452) found no support among the Coptic people. Occasionally until 1582, Rome did consider the Church of Alexandria as Uniate (see FLORENCE, COPTS AT THE COUNCIL OF).

Between the Council of Florence (1439–1445) and the end of the nineteenth century, the Roman church held a rigorous doctrine on the unity and unicity of the church: the nature of schism as the separation from the Church of Rome, and the union as the full and unconditional subjection to the pope and the Holy Roman Apostolic See. Thus, for example, on 20 April 1590, Pope Sixtus V wrote to the Coptic Pope GABRIEL VIII of Alexandria that "he and his flock were separated from the unity of the Holy See as a branch which has lost all its sap . . . and could not bear fruit which would be worthy of eternal beatitude," and therefore he would have to bring his flock to obedience and subjection to the Roman pontiff, who is the Vicar of Christ. Sometimes the popes of Rome preferred to designate the Eastern churches as "nations" (e.g., Pope Innocent XII in his *breve* to the Coptic Patriarch JOHN XVI, 3 March 1697).

In 1560, two Coptic priests went to Rome as delegates of the Coptic church to negotiate terms of reunion. Then Pope Pius IV (1559–1565) sent two Jesuits, Christoforo Rodriguez and Giovanni Battista Eliano, to the Coptic Pope GABRIEL VII (1525–1568). This mission brought no positive results, for the Roman representatives demanded of the Copts and their pope unconditional subjection to the pope of Rome with all that was implied at the time. The Copts refused this type of subjection, for it was alien to their understanding of church unity.

In 1582, another attempt at reunion with Rome was made by the Coptic pope JOHN XIV (1570–1585) whose intentions were sincere and serious. He requested Pope Gregory XIII (1572–1585) to send legates from Rome to negotiate the terms of reunion. When the two papal legates, Giovanni Battista Eliano and Francesco Sasso, arrived, he convoked a synod of the Coptic church to discuss the matter. However, when John XIV died suddenly in mysterious circumstances, the two legates were imprisoned by Turkish authorities as foreign spies. They were released only after a ransom of 5,000 gold pieces was paid. Eliano negotiated with the new patriarch, GABRIEL VIII (1586–1601), a profession of faith that did not include a formula of "the two natures in Christ"; this seems to have found no support in Rome. However, he assumed a very rigorous and negative position with respect to the Coptic rites, in which he found many "superstitions."

On 15 January 1595, Clement VIII, in the presence of twenty-four cardinals, received in audience five representatives of Gabriel VIII. In his name they made a profession of faith (the formula of Gregory XIII) professing obedience to the pope of Rome and abjuring "all they held until now which was opposed to the rite of the Holy Roman Church." On 28 June 1597, the representatives of Gabriel VIII returned with ratified documents of reunion and were granted an audience with Clement VIII. The documents of this reunion did not grant the Coptic church sufficient autonomy and demanded of the Coptic patriarch a promise of obedience to the pope of Rome. In a letter of 7 October 1602 to Gabriel VIII (who had died on 14 May 1601) Clement VIII demanded "due obedience," for the Alexandrian Church of Saint Mark was of Petrine origin and therefore had to be especially closely tied to Rome. The union of 1595–1597 remained ineffective.

In 1576, Pope Gregory XIII had established the

Greek College in Rome with the stipulation that the students be instructed in Greek language, literature, theology, and ecclesiastical rites, and he prohibited the use of Latin. All this was soon ignored, and the Greek College became a tool of the Latinization of the Greeks and other Eastern Christians, including the Copts. In 1602, Pope Clement tried to organize an "Egyptian College" in Rome, but this plan did not materialize.

Under the Coptic popes MATTHEW IV (1660–1675) and JOHN XVI (1676–1718) discussions concerning reunion with Rome continued but without results. The numerous negotiations with the Coptic popes concerning reunion in the sixteenth and seventeenth centuries remained fruitless. The Copts wanted reunion in love and rejected both strict legal subjection to Rome and the demand that they give up traditions not exactly consonant with Roman customs. In one instance, the Congregation for the Propagation of the Faith decided in a 1625 decree that the Sunday observance laws for attendance at the Liturgy also applied to the Copts. However, this was unknown in the Coptic customs and tradition.

In 1623, Pope Urban VIII (1623–1644) wanted to reestablish contact with the Coptic church and sent Franciscan missionaries headed by Father Paulo di Lodi to work among the Copts. Then in 1630, the Capuchin father Joseph of Paris established several missions in the Levant, among them one in Cairo under the successful direction of Father Agathangelo of Vendôme. The Coptic pope Matthew III (1634–1649) opened all his churches to the friars, and Agathangelo gave spiritual conferences in the Coptic monasteries of the Lower Thebaid. The greatest obstacle to reunion was the immoral conduct of the Catholics residing in Egypt, especially those of the French Consulate ("synagogue of Satan"). Both the complaints of Matthew III that "the Roman Catholic Church in this country is a brothel" and the appeals of Agathangelo to the prefect of the Propaganda Congregation to excommunicate the offenders remained fruitless. Agathangelo departed to Ethiopia and to martyrdom.

In 1697, the Friars Minor of the Observance were placed in charge of the Apostolic Prefecture of Upper Egypt. Only after 1720 did the Coptic mission have modest success. On 9 August 1739, Athanasius, the Coptic bishop of Jerusalem (vicar general of the Coptic pope with residence in Cairo), secretly made a Catholic profession of faith before RŪFĀ'ĪL AL-ṬŪKHĪ and Justus Marāghī, two Uniate Coptic priests educated in Rome. Al-Ṭūkhī brought Athanasius' profession of faith to Rome; and on 4 August 1741, Pope Benedict XIV granted Athanasius jurisdiction over all the Catholic Copts (about 2,300). Athanasius hardly used these faculties, and then returned to the Coptic church.

On 3 June 1744, the pope Benedict XIV appointed Justus Marāghī as vicar general, who died in 1748. Then the prefect of the Latin Rite Reformed Franciscans received jurisdiction over the Uniate Copts, a circumstance that considerably undermined the Uniate cause. In 1758 the Coptic archbishop, Anthony Fulayfil, became Catholic, and in 1761 Rome appointed him the first Coptic vicar apostolic. Rome ruled the Catholic Copts through apostolic vicars until the second erection of the Coptic Catholic Patriarchate of Alexandria in 1895.

The eighteenth century was characterized by confusion marked by lack of understanding. During the first half of the eighteenth century, Franciscan missionaries in Egypt demanded that the Catholic Copts burn their books, and many missionaries actually ridiculed and misrepresented the Eastern rites, tradition, and customs. An extreme case occurred when the prefect of the Reformed Franciscans bluntly told the Coptic Catholic priests that their "prayers were going to the devil and not to God" (26 September 1805; Metzler, 1960, p. 377). However, during this period the Uniate Copt Rūfā'īl al-Tūkhī (d. 1787) was editing and printing Coptic liturgical books in Rome, and he was appointed the ordaining bishop for Coptic seminarians in Rome.

The popes of Rome generally had no knowledge of the particular customs and laws of the Copts, and usually followed either Latin or Byzantine practices and canons in their dealing with the Catholic Copts. For example, Pope Benedict XIV, in the Apostolic Instruction *Eo quamvis tempore* (4 May 1745) to the Catholic Copts, relied on Greek sources, and so thought that Oriental clergy could marry before but not after ordination as deacons—but the Coptic custom and tradition permitted ordained deacons to marry.

Furthermore, the Congregation for the Propagation of the Faith always kept the Catholic Copts in strictest obedience and dependence, much more than any other Eastern Catholic church. This is illustrated by the fact that after their return to Egypt, the Coptic priests educated in Rome were usually given faculties for three years only "in order to keep them in a stricter dependence" (Decree of 1736). The Roman Catholic missionaries (and possibly also the Uniate clergy) hoped to win over the Coptic pope JOHN XVII (1726–1745) and his successor MARK VII (1745–1769) to the cause of union. They were unsuccessful because joining the union was considered becoming a "Franc" (i.e., an alien with French culture). However, several of the clergy did make a secret profession of Catholic faith, the value of which was questionable. On 15 March 1790, the Congregation for the Propagation of the Faith fortified the decree of 1729, which prohibited the Coptic Catholic priests from having intercommunion with the non-Catholics. In the same decree, the Congregation stipulated that absolution could be granted to converts to the Catholic church only after they abjured errors and they professed the faith of Urban VIII. This definitively settled the thorny question of intercommunion that had been under discussion among the missionaries.

The creation of the Coptic Catholic Patriarchate in 1824 increased the tensions and hostilities between the Coptic and the Roman churches. (On the establishment of the Patriarchate and subsequent events in the nineteenth and twentieth centuries up to 1971, see COPTIC CATHOLIC CHURCH.)

After the death of the Coptic pope CYRIL VI on 9 March 1971, SHENOUDA III became the patriarch and pope of Alexandria on 14 November 1971. In May 1973, he visited the Vatican and met with Pope Paul VI. They issued a common declaration that ended fifteen centuries of quarrels: the doctrine of the two natures in Christ was agreed upon (*Acta Apostolicae sedis* 65, 1973, pp. 299–301; cf. also pp. 314–22). On this occasion, Shenouda III brought part of the relics of Saint Athanasius to Rome for the sixteenth centenary of the saint. This was a gesture graciously following upon the 1968 gift of relics of Saint Mark from Rome to Egypt. In 1974, a commission for dialogue was established at Cairo between the Vatican and Orthodox Copts. In June 1974, Shenouda III established the Marseille-Toulon and Paris eparchies in France for Coptic French nationals. On 2 June 1979, Pope John Paul II received legates of the Coptic Orthodox Church and encouraged them to work toward reunion—praying "with my brothers the bishops and the faithful of the Catholic Churches in Egypt" for full ecclesial communion.

BIBLIOGRAPHY

Arbanites, A. K. "Koptike Ekklesia." *Threskeutike kai Edike Egkuklopaideia*. Athens, 1965.

Atiya, A. S. *A History of Eastern Christianity*. London, 1968.

______. *The Copts and Christian Civilization*. Salt Lake City, Utah, 1979.

Attwater, D. *The Christian Churches of the East.* Vol. 1, *Churches in Communion with Rome*, pp. 128–37. Milwaukee, Wis., 1961.

Burmester, O. H. E. *The Egyptian or Coptic Church*, pp. 303–311. Cairo, 1967.

Chauleur, S. *Histoire des Coptes d'Egypte*. Paris, 1960.

Columbo, A. *Le origini della gerarchia della Chiesa copta catolica nel secolo XVII*. Orientalia Christiana Analecta 140. Rome, 1953.

Cramer, M. *Das christlich-koptische Ägypten einst und heute. Eine Orientierung*. Wiesbaden, 1959.

Cramer, M., and W. Till. "Kopten." In *Lexikon für Theologie und Kirche*, Vol. 6, pp. 538–46. Freiburg, 1957–1965.

Faivre, J. "Alexandrie." In *Dictionnaire d'histoire et de géographie ecclésiastique*, Vol. 2, cols. 289–369. Paris, 1914.

Jugie, M. A. A. "Monophysite, Eglise copte." In *Dictionnaire de théologie catholique*, Vol. 10, pt. 2, cols. 2251–2306. Paris, 1929.

Meinardus, O. F. A. *Christian Egypt: Ancient and Modern*. Cairo, 1965.

______. *Christian Egypt: Faith and Life*. Cairo, 1970.

Metzler, Josef. "Matta Righet: Apostolischer Vikar der Kopten und Vertrauensmann der S.C. de Propaganda Fide (1747–1821)." *Euntes Docete* 13 (1960):358–407.

______. "Das Apostolische Vikariat der Kopten." *Euntes Docete* 14 (1961):36–62; 15 (1962):70–105.

Roncaglia, M. *Histoire de l'église copte*, 2 vols. Beirut, 1966, 1969.

Sacra Congregatione per le Chiese Orientali. *Oriente Cattolico: Cenni storici e statistiche*, pp. 91–104. Vatican City, 1974.

Scaduto, M. "La missione de Cristoforo Rodriguez al Cairo (1561–1563)." *Archivum historicum Societatis Iesu* 27 (1958):233ff.

Spuler, B. *Die morgenländischen Kirchen*. Leiden, 1964.

Trossen, J. P. *Les relations du patriarche copte Jean XVI avec Rome (1676–1718)*. Luxembourg, 1948.

Viaud, G. *La liturgie des Coptes d'Egypte*. Paris, 1978.

Vries, S. de. *Rom und die Patriarchat des Ostens*. Freiburg and Munich, 1963.

Wakim, E. *A Lonely Minority: The Modern Story of Egypt's Copts*. New York, 1963.

PETRO B. T. BILANIUK

COPTIC STREET, Bloomsbury district, Borough of Camden, London, W.C.1, a small street in central London opposite the British Museum. It was formed during the building boom following the Great Fire of London in 1666 and called Duke Street after the Dukes of Bedford, who owned it. It was renamed in 1894 to end confusion with other Duke Streets in the capital. The new name was inspired by an important collection of manuscripts from the Coptic church, which had been acquired by the British Museum during the previous year.

FUAD MEGALLY

COPTIC TESTAMENT OF ISAAC, a pseudepigraphal book possibly dating from the fourth or fifth century. Two Coptic versions of the *Testament of Isaac* have survived: the Sahidic, edited by K. H. Kuhn (1957), and the Bohairic, edited by I. Guidi (1900). The former has been translated into English by its editor (Kuhn, 1967), the latter, by S. Gaselee in an appendix to *The Testament of Abraham* (Box, 1927). M. R. James mentions also an Arabic and an Ethiopic version of this work (James, 1892). The Sahidic is, no doubt, the earlier of the extant versions; the Bohairic was translated from Sahidic, although it does not always agree with it. This relationship is suggested not only by a number of Sahidicisms in the Bohairic version but also by the general development of Coptic literature (see LITERATURE, COPTIC). Guidi rightly observes that the *Testament of Isaac* and the *Testament of Jacob* are imitative of the *Testament of Abraham,* although the *Testament of Isaac* introduces a new element–the moral and religious teaching attributed to Isaac (Guidi, 1900, p. 223). Guidi is on less safe ground when he goes on to argue that they were composed originally in Coptic. Although the philological evidence is inconclusive, the possibility of a Greek original of the *Testament of Isaac* must be considered, even if no Greek version has been preserved. P. Nagel (1963) is certain that the Sahidic *Testament of Isaac* was translated from the Greek and that the work can be dated between 380 and 410. There is, however, too little evidence on the genesis of the work to permit its dating except in a most tentative way. In its present form, the *Testament of Isaac* is certainly Christian, but it contains Jewish legendary material. The explicitly Christian elements may have been superimposed, for they appear to be easily detachable.

A brief summary of the contents of the work follows. As an old man, Isaac is visited by the angel who attends his father, Abraham, in heaven and is told of his own impending death. Isaac expresses concern for his son Jacob but is reassured by the angel and instructed to pass on the teaching that he himself has received. Jacob then arrives, and Isaac comforts his grieving son, speaking to him of the inevitability of death, which is confirmed by the experience of Old Testament characters, except for Enoch. A short prophetic passage describes the life of Jesus and refers to the Eucharist. Isaac's household assembles around him, but his death is delayed and he continues to live an ascetic life. He pronounces a series of ethical exhortations addressed to priests, monks, and laymen. The angel reappears and takes him to heaven, whence he looks down on the terrible fate that is in store for sinners. Tormentors, whose chief is Abdemerouchos, mete out a variety of cruel punishments to all those who have sinned. Isaac is then led to his father, Abraham, and through him is instructed by the Lord on the conditions necessary for entry into the kingdom of God. After the Lord commands the archangel Michael to assemble the angels and all the saints, they repair to the deathbed of Isaac, who takes leave of Jacob and intercedes for him with God. Then Isaac's own soul, white as snow, is taken to heaven upon the chariot of the Lord.

BIBLIOGRAPHY

Box, G. H. *The Testament of Abraham,* pp. 55ff. (appendix by S. Gaselee). London, 1927.

Charlesworth, J. H. *The Pseudepigrapha and Modern Research,* pp. 123ff. Missoula, Mont., 1976.

Delcor, M. *Le Testament d'Abraham,* pp. 78ff. Studia in Veteris Testamenti Pseudepigrapha 2. Leiden, 1973.

Guidi, I. "Il Testamento di Isacco e il Testamento di Giacobbe." *R. Accademia nazionale dei Lincei, Rome. Classe di scienze morali. Atti. Rendiconti,* ser. 5, 9 (1900):223ff.

James, M. R., ed. *The Testament of Abraham,* pp. 6f. Cambridge, 1892. Repr. 1967.

Kuhn, K. H. "The Sahidic Version of the Testament of Isaac." *Journal of Theological Studies* 8 (1957): 225–39.

______. "An English Translation of the Sahidic Version of the Testament of Isaac." *Journal of Theological Studies* 18 (1967):325–36.

Nagel, P. "Zur sahidischen Version des Testamentes Isaaks." *Wissenschaftliche Zeitschrift der Martin-Luther-Universität Halle-Wittenberg* 12, nos. 3–4 (1963):259–63.

K. H. KUHN

COPTO-ARMENIAN RELATIONS. *See* Armenians and the Copts.

COPTO-ETHIOPIAN CHURCH NEGOTIATIONS. *See* Ethiopian Church Autocephaly.

COPTOLOGIA, international journal of Coptic thought and Orthodox spirituality inaugurated in January 1981. The journal seeks to encourage the use of Coptic Orthodox piety to stem the increasing influence of secularism in the Western world, with a concentration on Alexandrine theology and desert monasticism.

FAYEK ISHAK

COPTOLOGICAL STUDIES. Coptological studies may be divided into several periods. The oldest began in the first Christian centuries, when the Greek alphabet with the additional letters from demotic was used to elevate the spoken Egyptian language into a written language. This made it possible for many Egyptians to read the Old and New Testaments or Gnostic writings. The inventor of this Coptic alphabet is unknown. The glosses in magical texts are probably to be regarded as further preliminary stages. After the invention of the alphabet, rules had to be created for the translation of these writings from Greek into Coptic. Bilingual Greco–Coptic word lists were prepared, and later trilingual lists including Latin. In addition, bilingual manuscripts of the Old and New Testaments were written. The translation of Coptic literature from one dialect into another—for example, the translation of Sahidic literature into Bohairic—also began at this time, as did the effort that can be detected in Bohairic to replace Greek loanwords with Coptic words. As a result of bilingualism, Greek documentary formulas in the realm of law were translated into Coptic.

A new phase in Coptological studies began after the ARAB CONQUEST OF EGYPT, when Coptic was gradually superseded by Arabic as the colloquial language and the language of literature and business. To preserve the knowledge of the Coptic language, including Bohairic as the language of the church, Coptic–Arabic word lists (*scalae*) and grammatical summaries were prepared, which were to be of the greatest importance for the next phase of Coptological studies. Arabic versions were added to the Coptic literary texts, especially the Old and New Testaments, and many literary writings were translated into Arabic. The Bohairic dialect remained the language of the church.

A new phase began in the sixteenth or seventeenth century, when European travelers brought Coptic manuscripts from Egypt to Europe, and scholars concerned themselves with the deciphering of these manuscripts. The first one we know to have possessed Coptic manuscripts was the Arabist Giovanni Battista Raimondi (1540–c. 1610). About 1600 the French bibliophile N. C. F. de Peiresc (1580–1637) obtained Coptic manuscripts from Coptic monasteries through travelers in Egypt, and stimulated Claude Saumaise to Coptological studies. In 1626 the Italian traveler Pietro della Valle returned from Egypt with Coptic manuscripts, among which was a *scala* written in the year 1319. The Italian Franciscan Thomas Obicini occupied himself with this manuscript (Vat. Copt. 71) until his death in 1632. Anastasius Kircher, who next studied this manuscript, published it in the year 1643.

In the following period as well, the influx of Coptic manuscripts from Egypt into European collections continued the interest in the Coptic language. A large number of scholars in many lands devoted themselves seriously to this language and culture, Kircher, through his untenable statements about the Egyptian hieroglyphs, had brought his correct Coptic researches into discredit. Theodor Petraeus (1630–1672) brought the first Coptic manuscripts to Germany.

Robert Huntington's Coptic manuscripts, bought in Egypt, are now in the Bodleian Library in Oxford. Joseph Simon Assemani, who had been sent to Egypt by Pope Clement XI, returned with Coptic manuscripts to Rome in 1715.

Johann Michael VANSLEB, who traveled in Egypt in 1664, 1672, and 1673 and collected Coptic manuscripts there, laid the foundation for the Paris collection, and Cardinal Stefano Borgia (1731–1804) did the same for the important Coptic collection in Naples. Bernardino Drovetti (1776–1852) sold Coptic manuscripts at Turin. J. Bruce brought the Gnostic codex named after him from Luxor to the Bodleian Library at Oxford, and Robert Curzon also returned to England from his journey with manuscripts. Henry Tattam came home from Egypt in 1838–1839 with Coptic manuscripts that were housed in English collections. Konstantin von Tischendorf bought manuscripts for Leipzig.

In the course of the eighteenth century these Coptic manuscripts were copied and studied by a large number of scholars, of whom only a few need be mentioned: P. E. Jablonski copied manuscripts in Paris, Leiden, and Oxford; C. G. Woide, the Paris and Oxford manuscripts; C. Scholtz, the Berlin Coptic manuscripts. Such manuscript copies, along with the first printed Coptic texts, formed the basis for the earliest Coptic grammars and dictionaries. Thus, for his Coptic dictionary La Croze used manuscript copies of the New Testament by Jablonski and the first Psalm published in 1663 by Petraeus. This dictionary was frequently copied before its publication in 1775. D. Wilkes's edition of the Coptic (Bohairic) New Testament in 1716 was based on transcripts of texts in Oxford, Rome, and Paris. In 1799 Woide printed Oxford Sahidic manuscripts. In the nineteenth century Tattam and M. G. Schwartze in particular were editors of New Testament writings. No less important were the reports that travelers in Egypt, such as R. Pococke and R. Curzon, wrote about their journeys.

In the eighteenth century the Uniate Copt RŪFĀ'IL AL-ṬŪKHĪ went from Egypt to Rome, where he brought out in print—even though defectively—a Coptic grammar and several Coptic liturgical books with an Arabic translation: the Anaphora (1736), Horologion (1750), Pontifical (1761–1762), and Ritual (1763).

In addition to the scholars who pursued their Coptological studies out of interest in the content of the Coptic texts or in the Coptic language, other scholars concerned themselves with the Coptic language in order to decipher the hieroglyphs with its aid. They started from the correct assumption of some relationship between the Coptic language and the Egyptian hieroglyphs. Only the three most important among many scholars need be mentioned: the Swedish diplomat and Orientalist Johann David Akerblad (1763–1819), the English doctor Thomas Young (1773–1829), and the Frenchman Jean François CHAMPOLLION (1790–1832), who finally deciphered the hieroglyphics.

The nineteenth century marks further progress in Coptological studies, insofar as the increasing specialization within the known scientific disciplines led to the development of new disciplines.

In 1845 Schwartze was named extraordinary professor of Coptic language and literature at the University of Berlin. Coptology thus became an independent scientific discipline at a German university, even though limited to Coptic language and literature, the areas in which Schwartze worked. Schwartze died just three years after the establishment of Coptology in Berlin. Colleagues in related disciplines published manuscripts he left after his death.

In Berlin, Coptology was replaced by Egyptology, also a newly founded discipline. K. R. Lepsius was its first representative. His successor, A. Erman, founded the "Berlin school," which investigated the early Egyptian period as well as the Coptic language, and published Coptic literary and nonliterary texts. The Berlin school, through its representatives at the University of Berlin—K. H. Sethe, H. Grapow, and F. Hintze (b. 1915)—held fast to this tradition and also exercised a great attraction for many scholars. In addition to the German Egyptologists who devoted themselves to Coptological studies we may mention above all W. E. CRUM, who on Erman's advice specialized in Coptology. Many of Erman's pupils later worked in disciplines related to Egyptology—above all, C. Schmidt, who earned his living as a theologian but was the leading German Coptologist of his time.

Erman's pupil G. Steindorff founded the Leipzig school, from which came J. LEIPOLDT and S. MORENZ. Erman himself was a pupil of Georg Ebers (1837–1898), professor at Leipzig, as well as of Lepsius. He also trained Coptologists, including O. von Lemm.

In France, G. Maspero formed a school similar to that of Erman in Berlin. Many of his pupils devoted themselves to Coptological studies, including Amélineau, Bouriant, Chassinat, Daressy, Gayet, Lacau, Lefebvre, Piehl, and Spiegelberg. Maspero was a pupil of Mariette, who, like Champollion, the decipherer of the hieroglyphics, concerned himself with Coptology.

In England only a few Egyptologists at the universities in London, Oxford, and Cambridge were active in Coptology. The most important was F. L. Griffith at Oxford. The last Oxford Egyptologist who also worked as a Coptologist was J. W. B. Barns. The Egyptologists E. A. W. BUDGE and H. R. H. HALL, who held posts in the British Museum, were active in Coptology. It was regrettable for Coptology that the leading Coptologist, Crum, could not exercise any public activity in a university or a museum, and therefore was not able to establish Coptology at an English university. Fortunately for him, he possessed sufficient financial means to devote his full powers to Coptological research. His friend H. F. H. Thompson, who in addition to his own labors supported him in his work on the *Coptic Dictionary*, likewise lived as a private citizen. A hopeful new beginning for Coptological studies in the person of C. Allberry, who was charged with the edition of the Chester Beatty Manichaean manuscripts, came to a sudden end in World War II.

More numerous are the scholars who taught in theological faculties, or were active as parish ministers or members of the clergy, and who in their researches devoted themselves to the Coptic Old and New Testaments, church history and the history of dogma, or confessional and liturgical studies.

Besides the Egyptologist Griffith, the classical archaeologist MICHALOWSKI has gained a reputation in connection with the young discipline of Nubiology. Murad Kamil became the preeminent scholar in Ethiopic studies and the relations between the Coptic and the Ethiopian church.

In the realm of legal history, A. A. Schiller and A. Steinwenter have won lasting credit for their research into Coptic law, while in the history of medicine the Egyptologists Grapow and Erichsen should be mentioned.

In Egypt, Coptic laymen were mindful of their glorious past, and in the second half of the nineteenth century began, with the aid of the printing press, to make Coptic (Bohairic)-Arabic grammars and dictionaries available to their countrymen. Liturgical books and other works that previously had been reproduced only by transcripts were printed by them. Iqlādyūs Labīb should especially be mentioned. In the twentieth century the number of Copts pursuing Coptological studies has increased. Among them are Murqus Simaykah, the founder of the Coptic Museum, his collaborator Yassa ʿAbd al-Masīḥ, and Georgy Sobhy, as well as such professors in the Egyptian universities as Sami Gabra and Murad Kamil.

The beginning of the newest phase in Coptological studies cannot be clearly identified. It began at the latest in 1930 with the discovery of the Manichaean codices, to which were added in 1946 the finds of the Gnostic library at Nag Hammadi and the biblical manuscripts and other Coptic writings that later found their way to the Chester Beatty and Bodmer libraries (see BODMER PAPYRI) and to other collections (see PAPYRUS DISCOVERIES).

These finds awoke the interest of wider circles in Coptology, and prompted scholars in disciplines bordering on Coptology to cooperate in the publication of these important manuscripts. In Egypt the new interest was demonstrated by the foundation of the Société d'Archéologie copte in 1934 and by its subsequent activities, such as the publishing of the first Coptological journal and several series of Coptic and Arabic source documents, the building of a Coptological library, and the excavation of a monastery.

Later, scholars founded the Institute of Higher Coptic Studies, which, in addition to Coptological research, was intended to serve the further development of the Copts. The education of the Coptic clergy was improved in a newly founded theological faculty of the Coptic patriarchate.

The increasing interest in Coptic works of art found expression in art exhibitions: in 1941 in Brooklyn, in 1944 in Cairo, and in 1963 at the Villa Hügel in Essen. This last exhibition traveled via Zurich and Vienna to Paris. The exhibitions also exercised an influence through scientific catalogs and symposia.

In Egypt, ruined Coptic sites were excavated, for instance, the pilgrim town of Abū Mīnā. The many excavations carried out in Nubia by teams from many nations between 1959 and 1963, as a rescue operation prior to the flooding of the country through the new high dam, yielded such rich finds, especially from the Coptic period, that they led to the founding in 1972 of the International Society for Nubian Studies. There was discussion between excavators and theorists at the international congresses of Nubiologists (the sixth took place at Uppsala in 1986). The Christian period with its rich finds—we need only recall the wall paintings in FARAS and the discovery of numerous manuscripts at QAṢR IBRĪM—occupied a large place in these congresses. After the completion of the campaigns in Nubia, excavations of Coptic ruins in Egypt were carried out in increasing numbers; of these we should mention above all the excavations in the KELLIA.

The work of the International Committee for the Nag Hammadi Codices led, after its conclusion, to the formation of the International Association for Coptic Studies in 1976 and the First International Congress of Coptologists in Cairo. The fourth congress was held at Louvain in 1988. In addition to the holding of congresses, the association coordinates the work on the Coptic sources. It supports scholars in their labors, and also sets in motion the accomplishment of such major tasks as the new edition of the Coptic New Testament and the first edition of the Coptic Old Testament.

Since the 1960s an increased interest in Coptology aroused by the discoveries, exhibitions, and excavations mentioned above has been apparent in universities. There are now professorships of Coptology or of Coptic language and literature at a number of European universities: Geneva, Halle, Münster, and Rome. In other universities (such as Yale and Paris) Coptologists have been called to professorships of theology, the history of religions, or the Christian Orient.

In Cairo the COPTIC MUSEUM has been enlarged both in personnel and in space, a center for Coptic studies has been created, and a start has been made on assembling on an international basis a general catalog of the contents of the museum. By no means least to be mentioned is the international collaboration on the present *Coptic Encyclopedia*.

Alongside the increasing interest in Coptological studies and their development, we must, unfortunately, report some setbacks. The increasing specialization in the scientific disciplines has caused the concern with areas of Coptology in many of the disciplines bordering on Coptology to abate. This can be established above all in Egyptology, where the Egyptologist to an increasing extent is no longer concerned with Coptological problems, and often no longer even teaches the Coptic language. In addition, it frequently happens in English and American universities that the posts of Coptologists, on the death or retirement of the holder, are not filled by Coptologists, but are devoted to other scientific desciplines. The latter threatens not only the development but also the existence of Coptological planning in universities and research institutes (such as the international archeological institutes in Cairo), as well as the continuance of scientific undertakings.

BIBLIOGRAPHY

Gravit, F. W. "Peiresc et les études coptes en France au XVIIIe siècle." *Bulletin de la Société d'archéologie copte* 4 (1938):1–22.

Irmscher, J. "Die Entwicklung der koptologischen Studien an der Martin Luther Universität." In *Koptologische Studien in der DDR*, pp. 6–29. Wissenschaftliche Zeitschrift der Martin Luther Universität Halle-Wittenberg, Sonderheft. Halle-Wittenberg, 1965.

______. "Die Anfänge der koptischen Papyrologie." In *Graeco-Coptica. Griechen und Kopten im byzantinischen Ägypten*, ed. P. Nagel. Martin Luther Universität, Halle-Wittenberg, Wissenschaftliche Beiträge 1984/48, pp. 121–36. Halle, 1984.

Kammerer, W. *A Coptic Bibliography*, pp. 2–5. Ann Arbor, Mich., 1950.

Kasser, R. "Centre d'études coptes en Suisse." *Bulletin de la Société d'archéologie copte* 20 (1971):211–14.

Munier, H. "Gaston Maspero et les études coptes." *Bulletin de l'Association des amis des églises et de l'art coptes* 1 (1936):27–36.

Myszor, W. "L'état actuel des études coptologiques en Pologne." *Enchoria* 8 (1978):25–28.

Nagel, P. *Bibliographie zur russischen und sowjetischen Koptologie*. Arbeiten aus der Universitäts- und Landesbibliothek Sachsen-Anhalt in Halle 23. Halle/Saale, 1978.

Petersen, H. "Coptic Studies in the United States of America." *Bulletin de la Société d'archéologie copte* 19 (1970):249–75.

Quatremère, E. *Recherches critiques et historiques sur la langue et la littérature de l'Egypte*. Paris, 1808.

Rykmans, G. "L'Orientalisme à Louvain avant 1936." *Le Muséon* 79 (1966):13–33.

Schiller, A. A., and W. Worrell. "Tentative Directory of Persons Interested in Coptic Studies." *Aegyptus* 12 (1932):393–401.

Schwartze, M. *Koptische Grammatik*, pp. 16–32. Berlin, 1850.

Segelberg, E. "Coptic Studies in Sweden." *Bulletin de la Société d'archéologie copte* 20 (1971):215–18.

MARTIN KRAUSE

COPTOLOGY, a scientific discipline in Oriental studies that investigates the language and culture of Egypt and Nubia in the widest sense: literature, religion, history, archaeology, and art. Its range extends from late antiquity to the Middle Ages, or even down to the present. It touches on and intersects with a number of neighboring disciplines.

The greater part of its vocabulary connects it with Egyptology, as which it is still reckoned in many countries, because Coptic is the last branch of the Egyptian language: about four-fifths of the Coptic words derive from Egyptian, as their etymologies show (see J. Černý, *Coptic Etymological Dictionary* [Cambridge, 1976]). The reproduction of the vowels in Coptic is important to the Egyptologist for the reconstruction of the vowels that were not written in Egyptian, and for the investigation of verbal accent, syllable structure, and metrics in Egyptian.

In terms of content, a continuity can be observed between the ancient Egyptian and the Christian period in the survival of ancient Egyptian elements (concepts, ideas, and usages), particularly in religion, literature, and art, but also in Coptic medicine.

Coptology is linked with classical philology by the stock of Greek and Latin loanwords in the Coptic language; the Greek, accounting for about 20 percent, far surpass the Latin. Their examination, which has begun, will experience a new florescence when all the loanwords have been collected.

In addition there are texts preserved in Coptic that were originally composed in Greek, but whose Greek version either has not survived or exists only in fragments or in a Latin translation. Here Gnostic and Hermetic writings from the Nag Hammadi discovery especially should be mentioned.

In association with Byzantine studies, Coptology investigates the Byzantine period in Egypt.

Work on the examination of Coptic codicology and paleography connects Coptology with papyrology. In addition to a few scrolls, early Coptic codices in particular have been preserved; they are roughly contemporary with the Greek. While Greek paleography has been well investigated, the Coptic has not advanced beyond preliminary work. Only with the appearance of COLOPHONS do we find ourselves on firm ground. Collaboration with the Greek papyrologists is necessary because Greek and Coptic documents often belong to the same ARCHIVES.

The Coptic nonliterary texts are important sources for the history and the cultural and economic developments of late antiquity. Especially from the sixth century on, they take their place alongside the Greek sources, later replace them, and are then the only sources.

The same holds good for epigraphy: gravestones, inscriptions on buildings, and graffiti are couched in Coptic as well as in Greek. In the forms used we can often demonstrate the translation of Greek models. While Greek inscriptions in Egypt became fewer after the sixth century, in Nubia they alternated with Coptic for another five hundred years.

In association with the history of religions, Coptology examines the Gnostic, Hermetic, and Manichaean texts, which often are preserved only in Coptic translation and have long been lost in their original language. The Coptic magical texts and spells also belong here.

The work of the Coptologist intersects with various theological disciplines (Old and New Testament, church history and history of dogma, confessional lore, and liturgics). Here reference should be made above all to the work on editions of the Coptic Old and New Testaments, to work in textual criticism, and to the editing of apocryphal and pseudepigraphical writings of both Testaments.

In church history, the origins of Christianity in Egypt, its history beyond the split from the imperial church after the Council of CHALCEDON, and the theological disputes that were dealt with at the early Christian councils are all the objects of Coptological research. A special investigative task force is at work on monasticism in Egypt and the hagiography of Coptic Christianity. The investigation of local Egyptian church history is still in its beginnings.

The confessional historian, in association with the Coptologist, examines the history of the Coptic church and its dogmas after its separation from the imperial church.

We thus come to the period that extends from the ARAB CONQUEST OF EGYPT down to the present. Here there are connections with Arabic studies and with the study of Islam. The Coptic language gradually lost its significance as a colloquial and literary language and was replaced, except as the language of the church, by Arabic. The Copts translated their literary works into Arabic, and prepared Coptic-Arabic word lists, the *scalae*, and grammatical summaries, in order to preserve the knowledge of their language. Part of the Coptic literature is preserved only in Arabic translation. The Coptic language had previously influenced Egyptian Arabic in its phonology, and Coptic words had been accepted into Arabic as loanwords. The relations between Copts and Moslems are also a subject for research in both disciplines.

Along with classical, early Christian, and Byzantine archaeologists, those concerned with provincial archaeology, and historians of architecture, Coptologists are concerned with the study of Coptic art, iconography, and architecture. Here, on the one hand, they have established a survival of Egyptian building tradition in Coptic architecture, for instance, at the White Monastery in Suhāj (DAYR ANBĀ SHINŪDAH), which Shenute had built at the beginning of the fifth century in the style of an Egyptian temple. Pictorial themes from late antiquity appear, above all on Coptic textiles.

Coptology is linked with Nubiology, a discipline only a few decades old, in the investigation of Nubia in the Christian period, which spans a period of more than a thousand years. The Christian epoch in Nubia came to an end only in the sixteenth century. Like the Ethiopian church, the Nubian was dependent on the patriarch of the Coptic church. The excavations carried out in Nubia before the building of the dam at Aswan have brought to light abundant source material (written and archaeological), which also sheds new light on the relations between the Coptic and the Nubian churches.

Research into the relation between the Coptic church and the Ethiopian church links Coptology with Ethiopic studies. The Ethiopian patriarch was an Egyptian Copt until Emperor HAILE SELASSIE broke with this ancient usage. Coptic literature was translated from Arabic into Ethiopic.

The field of Coptology also intersects with the study of the Christian East (see ORIENS CHRISTIANUS) which is concerned with the languages and literature of the Eastern Christian churches, including the Coptic.

We may link the investigation of the Coptic language with linguistics, which is still in its infancy, since it is only in recent years that linguists, following H. J. Polotsky, have concerned themselves with this task.

Coptology is connected with the history of law through investigation of Coptic law or of the law of the Coptic documents. So far only some of the sources, Coptic nonliterary papyri and ostraca, have been published. The older publications need to be replaced by new ones, since they no longer correspond to the requirements of modern text editions.

The investigation of the Coptic medical texts links Coptology with the history of medicine. Although ancient Egyptian medicine was treated in nine volumes by H. Grapow and his collaborators, many texts in the Greek and Coptic languages still await treatment.

BIBLIOGRAPHY

Krause, M. "Die Koptologie im Gefüge der Wissenschaften." *Zeitschrift für ägyptische Sprache und Altertumskunde* 100 (1974):108–125.

______. "Die Disziplin Koptologie." In *The Future of Coptic Studies*, ed. R. McL. Wilson, pp. 1–22. Coptic Studies 1. Leiden, 1978.

MARTIN KRAUSE

COPTS IN LATE MEDIEVAL EGYPT. Individuals identified by the word *Qibṭ* figure prominently in the Arabic biographical literature of medieval Egypt, and especially during the Mamluk period (1249–1517). The term referred to persons of Coptic lineage. Virtually all individuals recorded in these biographical sources, however, were practicing Muslims—as were their fathers and often their grandfathers. Yet they were still regarded as "of the Coptic people." They were routinely depicted as having a natural aptitude for accounting and administration, but also as having an inclination toward treachery, dishonesty, guile, and, above all, spiritual ambiguity. Several writers of the Mamluk era claimed that a Muslim of Coptic descent was potentially a false Muslim. Even worse, he was suspected of converting to the majority faith, admittedly often under duress, in order to aggrandize his own position at the expense of his "genuine" Muslim colleagues. Indeed, such a person was frequently accused of converting in order to blaspheme against Islam and to lead true believers astray. Such a false Muslim was always, it was alleged, on the verge of retrogressing to Christian practices.

The Copts who succeeded in Cairo during the Middle Ages unquestionably found themselves in a delicate situation. They professed Islam, yet were not widely accepted as true believers. How many of them were actually backsliders is difficult to assess. Most did retain some ties with their religious past, and many continued to interact with Coptic social groups. This contact was the subject of wide discussion, and was viewed as a sign of indifferent adherence to the true faith. Yet Muslim Copts apparently had little choice in the levels of society open to them, since all the indicators point to a state of partial segregation from the various elements of the orthodox *'ulamā'* class (learned interpreters of Islamic Law). Had they been willingly accepted, these people might have been assimilated into its ranks.

They were not accepted, however, and the range of activities they pursued implies the limited extent to which their contemporaries were disposed to allow their penetration into the Mamluk power structure—or their participation in the Islamic establishment. The Mamluks were prepared to recruit Muslim Copts to their service, and it is likely that they promoted propaganda hostile to Copts in order to bind them more tightly. Indeed, only the Mamluks stood between the Copts and the potentially dangerous masses of the population; no acts of persecution could occur without their acquiescence. Individual Copts who realized that they stood to lose in any contest with a legitimate Muslim were ready to accept the ambivalent conditions of service imposed by their Mamluk overlords, who alone opened the doors of influence and wealth. That Mamluks provided security to Copts largely because they were of use to them did not instill feelings of mutual affection. But whatever the motives, security in return for service was better than no security at all.

The Mamluks appointed Muslim Copts to several of the highest executive offices of the state, where they often administered the fiscal and procedural affairs of the imperial court and the households of the great amirs. Copts were occasionally rewarded for exceptional assistance in times of crisis with the honorary rank of amir. But they were not permitted to engage in any military activities, which remained the exclusive prerogative of the Mamluks, especially those of the first generation. Copts were encouraged to infiltrate several levels of the governmental bureaucracy. They staffed many segments of the secretarial class. They were appointed to financial controllerships expressly to amass substantial fortunes that they were to share with their patrons. Yet only one individual held the post of controller of pious endowments in a Muslim religious institution, and his social status deviated considerably from the usual. In general, Copts appeared consistently in controllerships directly associated with *diwans* of the regime, and did not administer funds of Muslim institutions, even though they professed the faith. The evidence points, in fact, to the exclusion of Copts from offices involved with the functions of the Islamic community. They were rarely appointed as official scribes in either the civil courts or the governmental bureaus, and few ever attained the pivotal office of secretary of the chancellery.

Throughout the later Middle Ages, the Muslim Copts do not seem to have gained access to offices endowed with the authority to make decisions affecting the spiritual lives of legitimate Muslims. Their role in the bureaucracy was primarily financial and procedural. Few appeared among the stewards who managed the mundane operations of mosques, colleges, and hospitals. There were no Muslim Copts who were court notaries, because the *shāhid* was first a lawyer trained in the *sharīʿah* and second a bureaucrat. Persons of Christian ancestry were not widely regarded as suited to study Islamic law. Above all, they were not considered legitimate arbiters in legal questions concerning Muslims. Muslim Copts held no legal offices in the sample derived from the biographical literature of this period. Not a single case was reported for any aspect of the judiciary. Since the legal profession was a fundamental component of the *ʿulamā'* class and its most authoritative element, the absence of Muslim Copts from its ranks underscores their marginal status.

This hypothesis of marginality is reinforced by the virtual absence of Muslim Copts from the scholarly and religious categories. They tended neither to pursue advanced studies in the Islamic sciences nor to minister to the spiritual needs of the Islamic community. Since they were Muslims, many would presumably have wished to do so, and one must therefore conclude that they were denied the opportunity. Biographical compilers did not explain why Muslim Copts pursued few studies in the Islamic curriculum. They simply did not record any such studies, as they did so meticulously for persons they considered to be true believers.

In summary, the Muslim Copts emerge from the biographical accounts of the fourteenth and fifteenth centuries as a highly specialized group, channeled by both the military and the civilian elites into fiscal and administrative tasks. There they were useful to the Mamluks, who, although rarely averse to extorting money by any available means, nonetheless displayed little interest—or finesse—in the bureaucratic techniques required by a *diwan* post. Moreover, a Mamluk could not justify such doings to the extent his clients could, especially if they were not held accountable to Islamic principles, as he was. The Mamluks proclaimed themselves defenders of the faith, pledged to guard the community of believers from its enemies. In practice, they found the Copts ideal agents for unobtrusive infiltration into the revenue-yielding processes. The appearance of the same individuals holding multiple offices suggests that certain persons effectively monopolized these procedures.

Military-Executive Offices

Officials in this category wielded some measure of authority over procedural administrators or advisers. In the Mamluk state, most of these posts were held by members of the military elite. Yet the appearance of Muslim Copts in this category suggests that adroit members of the minority group could aspire to offices normally closed to civilians in general. Virtually all persons in this category had developed client ties with one or more influential Mamluks; a majority were associates of sultans.

Amīr: Mamluk officer. When the title was bestowed on a civilian, it granted him honorary status and privileges usually reserved for the military elite. Given in recognition of service to the sultan in the fiscal bureaus, it was a rare distinction for a Copt.

One position, less than 2 percent of fifty-nine total:

Zayn al-Dīn Yaḥyā ibn ʿAbd al-Razzāq al-Qibṭī al-Miṣrī al-Qāhirī, known as al-Ashqar, b. 800/1397–1398 (*Manhal* III, f. 402b; Wiet 2633).

Amīr al-mashwarah: Officer of (royal) consultation. Rare: title appeared only in this case. Presumably a civilian member of the sultan's advisory council with executive responsibilities.

One position, 100 percent of one total:

Saʿd al-Dīn Ibrāhīm ibn ʿAbd al-Razzāq al-Skandarī al-Miṣrī al-Qibṭī, known as Ibn Ghurāb, d. Rajab 808/December 1405–January 1406 (*Ḍaw'* I, p. 65).

Amīr mi'ah: Commander of 100, official military rank in the Mamluk hierarchy. One of the highest honors ever bestowed on any civilian in the state, recognizing exceptional service to the sultan. The appearance of this title in a civilian's career list proves that the Mamluk military system was not totally exclusive and that Muslim Copts who had shown extraordinary talent were singled out by the regime for co-optation at the highest levels.

One position, 3 percent of thirty-one total:

The preceding Ibn Ghurāb, but position noted only in *Manhal* I, f. 23; Wiet 47.

Dawādār: Executive of the imperial court in Cairo (in the Citadel); literally, bearer of the sultan's pen box or inkstand. Responsible for carrying out the sultan's commands, and thus an intermediary between the throne and senior bureaucrats. Presenter of petitions submitted during audiences, arranger of the sultan's daily schedule, assigner of documents to appropriate *diwans,* and securer of the royal signature and/or seal on edicts. Usually a Mamluk grand amir and therefore distinguished among Muslims of Christian background.

One position, less than 3 percent of thirty-six total:

Nāṣir al-Dīn Muḥammad ibn ʿAbd al-Razzāq, d. Muḥarram 881/April–May 1476 (*Ḍaw',* VIII, p. 55, no. 70).

Kāshif: Inspector. Provincial official sent out from Cairo or based locally (more rarely) to supervise upkeep of public works (roads, canals, dikes, toll stations, and guardhouses). A senior inspector was appointed as governor of the Delta (*al-wajh al-Baḥrī*), Upper Egypt (*al-wajh al-Qiblī*), and of the Fayyūm and Bahnasā. The latter were military posts restricted to higher officers, but Copts appeared in the fiscal and administrative ranks.

Three positions, 16 percent of nineteen total:

Fakhr al-Dīn ʿAbd al-Ghanī ibn ʿAbd al-Razzāq al-Armanī al-Qibṭī, d. Shawwāl 821/November 1418 (*Manhal,* II, f. 336; Wiet 1442) (twice).

Karīm al-Dīn ʿAbd al-Karīm ibn ʿAbd al-Razzāq al-Qibṭī al-Miṣrī, known as Ibn Kātib al-Munākh, d. Rabīʿ II 852/June–July 1448 (*Manhal,* II, f. 345; Wiet 1461).

Muqaddam: Commander. Usually an office restricted to the most senior Mamluk amir. Significant here is that an individual from the Coptic minority received this title, which conferred military status, if not powers.

Two positions, 2 percent of 104 total:

Saʿd al-Dīn Ibrāhīm ibn ʿAbd al-Razzāq al-Skandarī al-Miṣrī al-Qibṭī, known as Ibn Ghurāb, d. Rajab 808/December 1405–January 1406 (*Ḍaw'* I, p. 65; *Manhal,* f. 23; Wiet 47) (twice).

Nā'ib: Representative of the Sultan. In the Mamluk military hierarchy, representative of the sultan in the Egyptian or Syrian provinces. In this context, a Copt served as assistant to senior Mamluk officers.

One position, less than 1 percent of 151 total:

Nāṣir al-Dīn Muḥammad ibn ʿAbd al-Razzāq al-Armanī al-Qibṭī, d. Muḥarram 881/April–May 1476 (*Manhal,* III, f. 180; Wiet 2187).

Naqīb al-jaysh: Adjutant of the army. Responsible for guaranteeing the presence of amirs and officials whose services were required by the sultan. Royal guard during processions, ceremonials, trips. Caller of the roll during the troop reviews. Under the chamberlain (*ḥājib*), served as a chief of police and local security, especially in the Circassian period. Open to bribery. That Muslim Copts held this office, formally the exclusive domain of the military caste, suggests the regime's preparedness to appoint trusted bureaucrats whose reliability was proven.

Three positions, 25 percent of twelve total:

Nāṣir al-Dīn Muḥammad ibn ʿAbd al-Razzāq, d. Muḥarram 881/April–May 1476 (*Ḍaw'* VIII, p. 55, no. 70; *Manhal* III, f. 180; Wiet 2187) (three times).

Shādd: Superintendent of a royal bureau or of a royal monopoly, treasury, repository, or customs station (often in a provincial capital).

One position, 7 percent of fourteen total:

Karīm al-Dīn ʿAbd al-Karīm ibn ʿAbd al-Razzāq al-Qibṭī al-Miṣrī, known as Ibn Kātib al-Munākhāt, d. Rabīʿ II 852/June–July 1448 (*Ḍaw'* IV, p. 313, no. 848).

Shādd al-khāṣṣ: Superintendent of the private fund reserved for costs of military expeditions, which could not be routinely predicted or budgeted from the state treasury. Uniforms for royal Mamluks, robes of honor, and expenses for state festivals were also paid out of the fund. This official usually served in a provincial capital; his counterpart in Cairo was the *nāẓir al-khāṣṣ.*

One position, 50 percent of two total:

Zayn al-Dīn ʿAbd al-Qādir ibn ʿAbd al-Ghanī al-Armanī al-Qibṭī al-Qāhirī, known as Ibn Abī al-Faraj, d. 833/1430 (*Manhal* II, f. 338; Wiet 1445).

Ustādār: Majordomo, literally *ustādh-dār* (master of the house). Overseer of a sultan's or amir's household, supervisor of supplies for the royal family and palace Mamluks. During the Circassian period (1382–1517), he often combined several offices (supplanting the *wazīr*) to assume control over all state finances. Usually conferred on a grand amir who was a working associate of the current sultan, this office marked the highest level to which a civil bureaucrat might aspire. The frequency of arrests and dismissals accompanying the office, however, suggests that its prestige was counterbalanced by its risk.

Nineteen positions, 26 percent of seventy-three total:

Fakhr al-Dīn ʿAbd al-Ghanī ibn ʿAbd al-Razzāq al-Armanī al-Qibṭī, known as Ibn Abī al-Faraj, d. Shawwāl 821/November 1418 (*Manhal* II, f. 336; Wiet 1442) (twice).

Karīm al-Dīn ʿAbd al-Karīm ibn ʿAbd al-Razzāq al-Qibṭī al-Miṣrī, known as Ibn Kātib al-Munākhāt, d. Rabīʿ II 852/June–July 1448 (*Ḍaw'* IV, p. 313, no. 848).

Zayn al-Dīn ʿAbd al-Qādir ibn ʿAbd al-Ghanī al-Armanī al-Qibṭī al-Qāhirī, known as Ibn Abī al-Faraj, d. 833/1429–1430 (*Manhal* II, f. 338; Wiet 1445) (twice).

Tāj al-Dīn ʿAbd al-Razzāq ibn Ibrāhīm al-Qibṭī, known as Ibn al-Hayṣam, d. Dhū al-Qaʿdah 834/August–September 1431 (*Ḍaw'* IV, p. 191, no. 485).

Taqī al-Dīn ʿAbd al-Wahhāb ibn ʿAbd-Allāh al-Miṣrī al-Qibṭī al-Ḥanafī, d. Dhū al-Qaʿdah 819/December 1416–January 1417 (*Manhal* II, f. 359b; Wiet 1487).

Saʿd al-Dīn Faraj ibn Mājid al-Qibṭī al-Miṣrī, known as Ibn al-Naḥḥāl, d. Jumādā II 865/March–April 1461 (*Ḍaw'* VI, p. 169, no. 570; *Manhal* II, f. 345; Wiet 1461) (twice).

Saʿd al-Dīn Ibrāhīm ibn ʿAbd al-Razzāq al-Skandarī al-Miṣrī al-Qibṭī, known as Ibn Ghurāb, d. Rajab 808/December 1405–January 1406 (*Ḍaw'* I, p. 65; *Manhal* I, f. 23; Wiet 47) (twice).

Nāṣir al-Dīn Muḥammad ibn ʿAbd al-Razzāq al-Armanī al-Qibṭī, d. Muḥarram 881/April–May 1476 (*Ḍaw'* VIII, p. 55, no. 70; *Manhal* III, f. 180; Wiet 2187) (three times).

Manṣūr ibn al-Ṣafī al-Qibṭī, d. Shawwāl 870/May–June 1466 (*Ḍaw'* X, p. 170, no. 716).

Sharaf al-Dīn Mūsā ibn Yūsuf al-Būtījī al-Miṣrī al-Qāhirī al-Qibṭī, known as Ibn Kātib Gharīb, d. Ṣafar 882/May–June 1477 (*Ḍaw'* X, p. 192, no. 810).

Zayn al-Dīn Yaḥyā ibn ʿAbd al-Razzāq al-Qibṭī al-Qāhirī, known as al-Ashqar, d. Rabīʿ I 874/September–October 1469 (*Ḍaw'* X, p. 233, no. 983; *Manhal* III, f. 402b; Wiet 2633) (three times).

Ustādār al-dhakhā'ir wa-al-amlāk: Overseer of the sultan's treasures and munitions, responsible for inventories of supplies and armaments held in reserve for military campaigns. Also accountable for supervising the sultan's private estate. Rare: the office appears only in this case.

Two positions, 100 percent of two total:

Taqī al-Dīn ʿAbd al-Wahhāb ibn ʿAbd-Allāh al-Miṣrī al-Qibṭī al-Ḥanafī, known as Ibn Abī Shākir, d. Dhu al-Qaʿdah 819/December 1416–January 1417 (*Ḍaw'* V, p. 102, no. 384) (twice).

Ustādār al-mustaʿjarāt: Overseer of state leases and rents. Based in the Egyptian provinces, or holding accountable subordinate officials who were locally responsible for collecting rents from government properties. Rare: office appeared only in this case.

One position, 100 percent of one total:

The preceding Ibn Abī Shākir.

Ustādār al-waqf: Overseer of pious trust foundations. To be distinguished from the *nāzir al-awqāf* or controller of such endowments, this was a state official directly tied to the Mamluk regime. Responsible for monitoring exchanges, replacements, sales, and alienations of *awqāf*. In practice, involved with government confiscation of pious endowments. That this office appeared only in the career of an eminent Copt is not coincidental.

One position, 100 percent of one total:

The preceding Ibn Abī Shākir.

Wakīl: Commissioner, fiscal agent of the government. Without complement, an official overseeing the state treasury or the special fund.

Two positions, 13 percent of sixteen total:

Saʿd al-Dīn Ibrāhīm ibn ʿAbd al-Karīm al-Qibṭī al-Miṣrī al-Shāfiʿī, known as Ibn Kātib Jakam, d. Rabīʿ I 841/September–October 1437 (*Ḍaw'* I, p. 68).

Ṣalāh al-Dīn Muḥammad ibn Ibrāhīm, d. Rajab 895/May–June 1490 (*Ḍaw'* VI, p. 283, no. 949).

Wālī: Governor of a town or district, usually chief of police. A military office with direct ties to the local populace. Usually held by an amir of secondary or tertiary rank. Prerogatives often used to extort bribes or to oversee government confiscations of property.

Two positions, 13 percent of sixteen:

Fakhr al-Dīn ʿAbd al-Ghanī ibn ʿAbd al-Razzāq al-Armanī al-Qibṭtī, known as Ibn Abī al-Faraj, d. Shawwāl 821/November 1418 (*Manhal* II, f. 336; Wiet 1442) (twice).

Forty-two positions, 8 percent of 538 total reported in this category in the two dictionaries, were held by persons of Coptic ancestry.

Bureaucratic Offices

Officials in this category served as procedural administrators or consultants in the fiscal and diplomatic bureaus of the Mamluk state. A majority of such bureaus were located in Cairo, the imperial capital, although lesser bureaucracies of similar hierarchical organization were maintained in the Syrian provincial capitals as well. The statistics for personnel in these positions contrasted markedly with those for the military-executive category, dominated as it was by members of the military caste. In the Mamluk state, bureaucrats were rendered dependent on their Mamluk patrons as a matter of royal policy, so as to maximize their service as procurers of information and collectors of revenue. Accordingly, we find high percentages of foreigners (mostly Syrians) and minorities (mostly Muslim Copts) appointed to these posts. The range of offices reported for Copts in the following list attests to their significance in the *diwan* networks of medieval Egypt.

ʿĀmil: Factor or collection agent usually of the *jizyah* (poll tax paid by non-Muslims), or in a religio-academic institution. Subordinate to the supervisor of this department. The title also appears in the literature in connection with other *diwans* involved with revenue accorded to certain groups. The *naqīb al-ashrāf* (syndic of the Prophet's descendants) employed factors in his service. However, the single occurrence of this term without complement suggests its initial meaning.

One position, 100 percent of one total:

Manṣūr ibn al-Ṣāfī al-Qibṭī, d. Shawwāl 870/May–June 1466 (*Ḍaw'* X, p. 170, no. 716).

ʿĀmil al-awqāf: Factor or collection agent serving under either the *nāẓir al-awqāf* or, more likely, the overseer (*ustādār*) of pious trust foundations as a government official. The position appeared only in this case, and was tied to the *waqf* of a grand amir.

One position, 100 percent of one total:

Manṣūr ibn al-Ṣafī al-Qibṭī, d. Shawwāl 870/May–June 1466 (*Ḍaw'* X, p. 170, no. 716).

Kātib (pl.: *kuttāb*): Secretary or scribe in a fiscal *diwan*. A processor of records and balancer of accounts. Secretaries in Mamluk Egypt, in contrast with *muwaqqiʿīn* (clerks, who had the notarial right of *tawqīʿ*, formal signature), were confined to archival or administrative tasks. But in their sphere of information gathering, including military intelligence and local spy networks, they wielded influence far in excess of their procedural duties. The large bureaus, particularly the *dīwān al-inshā'* (chancellery), which combined the functions of an archive, foreign ministry, and intelligence office, represented the ultimate goals of *kuttāb*. Despite its influence, this office remained an object of scorn and belittlement to many civilian notables. This lack of esteem certainly contributed to the large proportion of Copts, most of whom were at least nominal Muslims, who held the office. Indeed, persons designated as *kuttāb* who claimed Coptic ancestry seem to have been less professionally mobile in a relative sense than other officials in the bureaucratic category. (See Qalqashandī, *Ṣubḥ* I, 9, 13, 130–35, 140, 175–80; II, 4, 13, 33, 52, 97, 118, 339, 441–43; III, 150; V, 452; VI, 41.)

Twenty-four positions (without complement), 29 percent of eighty-two total:

Shams al-Dīn Abū al-Faraj ʿAbd-Allāh al-Maqsī al-Qibṭī, d. Shawwāl 755/August–September 1354 (*Manhal* III, f. 506b; Wiet 2809).

Amīn al-Dīn ʿAbd-Allāh ibn Rīshah al-Qibṭī al-Aslamī al-Miṣrī, d. 790/1388 (*Manhal* II, f. 277b; Wiet 1343).

Tāj al-Dīn ʿAbd al-ʿAẓīm ibn Ṣadaqah al-Qibṭī al-Aslamī, no death date (*Ḍaw'* IV, p. 240, no. 620).

Majd al-Dīn ʿAbd al-Ghanī al-Qibṭī al-Miṣrī, d. Shaʿbān 813/November–December 1410 (*Ḍaw'* IV, p. 245, no. 638).

Karīm al-Dīn ʿAbd al-Karīm ʿAbd al-Razzāq al-Qibṭī al-Miṣrī, known as Ibn Kātib al-Munākhāt, d. Rabīʿ II 852/June–July 1448 (*Ḍaw'* IV, p. 313, no. 848) (twice).

Karīm al-Dīn ʿAbd al-Karīm ibn Barakah al-Qibṭī al-Miṣrī, known as Ibn Kātib Jakam, d. Rabīʿ I 833/November–December 1249 (*Ḍaw'* IV, p. 308, no. 833).

Karīm al-Dīn ʿAbd al-Karīm ibn Fakhīrah al-Qibṭī, d. Rajab 855/July–August 1451 (*Ḍaw'* IV, p. 231, no. 879).

Tāj al-Din ʿAbd al-Razzāq ibn ʿAbd Allāh al-Qibṭī, known as Ibn Kātib al-Munākh, d. Jumādā I 827/April 1424 (*Manhal* II, f. 316b; Wiet 1409).

Tāj al-Dīn ʿAbd al-Razzāq ibn Ibrāhīm al-Qibṭī al-Miṣrī, known as Ibn al-Hayṣam, d. 834/1430–1431 (*Manhal* II, f. 315b; Wiet 1407).

Tāj al-Dīn ʿAbd al-Wahhāb ibn Naṣr-Allāh al-Qibṭī al-Aslamī, known as al-Shaykh al-Khaṭīr, no. death date (*Manhal* II, f. 364b; Wiet 1498).

Saʿd al-Dīn Abū al-Ghālib Ibrāhīm al-Qibṭī, known as Ibn ʿAwīd al-Sarrāj, d. Rabīʿ II 856/April–May 1452 (*Ḍaw'* XI, p. 120, no. 375).

Saʿd al-Dīn Ibrāhīm ibn ʿAbd al-Wahhāb al-Qibṭī al-Maymūnī, known as Ibn al-Najīb, d. 795/1392–1393 (*Manhal* I, p. 99, no. 51; Wiet 51).

Saʿd al-Dīn Ibrāhīm ibn ʿAbd Al-Razzāq al-Qibṭī al-Muslimī al-Skandarī al-Miṣrī, known as Ibn Ghurāb, d. Rajab 808/December 1405–January 1406 (*Ḍaw'* I, p. 65).

Burhān al-Dīn Ibrāhīm ibn Bariyyah al-Qibṭī al-Muslimī, no death date (*Ḍaw'* I, p. 33).

ʿAlam al-Dīn Abū al-Faḍl Jallūd al-Qibṭī, d. Dhū al-Qaʿdah 872/May–June 1468 (*Ḍaw'* XI, p. 163, no. 515).

Fakhr al-Dīn Mājid ibn ʿAbd al-Razzāq al-Qibṭī al-Aslamī al-Skandarī, known as Ibn Ghurāb, d. 811/1408–1409 (*Manhal* III, f. 71b; Wiet 1949).

Fakhr al-Dīn Mājid ibn Abī al-Faḍā'il al-Qibṭī, known as Ibn al-Marzūq, d. Rajab 833/March–April 1430 (*Ḍaw'* VI, p. 235, no. 812).

Majd al-Dīn Mājid ibn al-Naḥḥāl al-Qibṭī al-Aslamī, d. Dhū al-Ḥijjah 843/May–June 1440 (*Ḍaw'* VI, p. 235, no. 813) (twice).

Khayr al-Dīn Muḥammad ibn Yaḥyā al-Qibṭī, known as Ibn Fakhīrah, d. 899/1493–1494 (*Ḍaw'* X, p. 72, no. 245).

Sharaf al-Dīn ibn Yūsuf al-Būtījī al-Miṣrī al-Qāhirī al-Qibtī, known as Ibn Kātib Gharīb, d. Ṣafar 882/May–June 1477 (*Ḍaw'* X, p. 192, no. 810) (twice).

Sharaf al-Dīn Yaḥyā al-Qibtī al-Qāhirī, known as Ibn Ṣanīʿah, d. Muḥarram 882/April–May 1477 (*Ḍaw'* X, p. 268, no. 1061).

Kātib al-dawālīb: Secretary in the bureau of royal (sugar) mills and presses; accountant of inventories in the state workshops. The position appeared only in this case.

One position, 100 percent of one total:

ʿAbd al-ʿAẓīm ibn Dirham wa-Nuṣf, d. 879/1474–1474 (*Ḍaw'* IV, p. 241, no. 622).

Kātib al-dīwān: Secretary in a fiscal bureau of the government, specifically the *dīwān al-dawlah* (see under *nāẓir al-dawlah*). This position was similar to, and may have been an alternative title for, the *mustawfī al-dawlah* (accountant of finances under the *nāẓir* or *wazīr*).

Three positions, 43 percent of seven total:

Karīm al-Dīn ʿAbd al-Karīm ibn Barakah al-Qibṭī al-Miṣrī, known as Ibn Kātib Jakam, d. 833/1430 (*Manhal* II, f. 343; Wiet 1457).

Manṣūr ibn al-Ṣafī al-Qibṭī, d. Shawwāl 870/May–June 1466 (*Ḍaw'* X, p. 170, no. 716).

Sharaf al-Dīn Mūsā ibn Yūsuf al-Būtījī al-Miṣrī al-Qāhirī al-Qibṭī, known as Ibn Kātib Gharīb, d. Ṣafar 882/May–June 1477 (*Ḍaw'* X, p. 192, no. 810).

Kātib (dīwān) al-jaysh: Secretary in the department of the army, accountant of receipts from land allotments (iqṭāʿāt) in the Egyptian and Syrian provinces used to support the royal Mamluk amirs.

Two positions, 29 percent of seven total:

Muwaffaq al-Dīn ʿAbd-Allāh ibn Ibrāhīm al-Qibṭī al-Qāhirī, d. Rabīʿ I 877/August–September 1472 (*Ḍaw'* V, p. 4, no. 7).

Khayr al-Dīn Muḥammad ibn Yaḥyā al-Qibṭī, known as Ibn Fakhīrah, d. 899/1493–1494 (*Ḍaw'* X, p. 72, no. 245).

Kātib dīwān al-Mamālīk: Secretary in the bureau of Mamluks; accountant of funds used to maintain the royal barracks in Cairo (several located in the *Qalʿah* or Citadel, others on Rawḍah Island or Raydāniyyah) and the provincial capitals.

Four positions, 33 percent of twelve total:

Muwaffaq al-Dīn ʿAbd-Allāh ibn Ibrāhīm al-Qibṭī al-Qāhirī, d. Rabīʿ I 877/August–September 1472 (*Ḍaw'* V, p. 4, no. 7).

Karīm al-Dīn ʿAbd al-Karīm ibn Abī al-Faḍl al-Qibṭī al-Miṣrī, known as Ibn Jallūd, d. Rajab 881/October–November 1476 (*Ḍaw'* IV, p. 316, no. 860).

Tāj al-Dīn ʿAbd al-Razzāq ibn Ibrāhīm al-Qibṭī, known as Ibn Kātib Jakam, d. Dhu al-Ḥijjah 834/August–September 1431 (*Ḍaw'* IV, p. 191, no. 485).

Saʿd al-Dīn Faraj ibn Mājid al-Qibṭī al-Miṣrī, known as Ibn al-Naḥḥāl, d. Jumādā II 865/March–April 1461 (*Ḍaw'* VI, p. 169, no. 570).

Kātib dīwān al-mufrad: Secretary in the sultan's special bureau that funded monthly payments to his Mamluk troopers, purchase of their uniforms and equipment, fodder for their mounts, and so forth. In general, this bureau collected revenues from urban properties, markets, port tolls, tariffs, and a variety of taxes—rather than from land allotments, proceeds of which supported amirs and were under the jurisdiction of the *dīwān al-jaysh.*

One position, 100 percent of one total:

Manṣūr ibn al-Ṣafī al-Qibṭī, d. Shawwāl 870/May–June 1466 (*Ḍaw'* X, p. 170, no. 716).

Kātib dīwān al-murtaja'āt: Secretary in the bureau of reclamation, responsible for assessing and collecting income from estates of Mamluk amirs who died, or were dismissed and/or demoted before the end of the accounting year. This bureau was initially known as the *dīwān al-sulṭān* (sultan's department), but the title dropped out of use with the expansion of the *dīwān al-jaysh* and the office of *ustādār* in the later Mamluk period.

One position, 100 percent of one total:

'Alam al-Dīn 'Abd al-Wahhāb ibn Qasīs al-Qibṭī al-Qāhirī, d. Muḥarram 791/December 1388–January 1389 (*Manhal* II, f. 365b; Wiet 1499).

Kātib al-lālā: Secretary to the *lālā*, an honorific title (literally "radiant") held by a eunuch amir in the royal household, a guardian of the princes. The position appeared only in this case.

One position, 100 percent of one total:

Shams al-Dīn Abu al-Manṣūr Naṣr-Allāh al-Qibṭī al-Qāhirī, known as Ibn Kātib al-Warshah, d. 850/1446–1447 (*Ḍaw'* X, p. 200, no. 854).

Kātib al-sirr: Confidential secretary, head of the *dīwān al-inshā'* (royal chancellery). Serving as foreign minister (responsible for informing the sultan about classified state and diplomatic matters) and as senior scribe (responsible for presenting official correspondence to the ruler and supervising the drafting of replies to such correspondence; bearer of the royal seal and securer of the sultan's signature or emblem; director of the royal post and messengers). He also attended the sultan during audiences in the Palace of Justice (Dār al-'Adl), receiving petitions from the *dawādār* and working closely with the four chief judges in appeals heard by the throne. One of the most influential civil officials in the realm (the office was duplicated in the provincial capitals and was subordinate to the viceroy or *nā'ib al-sulṭān*). More foreigners (usually Syrians) held this post than native Cairenes during the fifteenth century, due to the sultan's wish to keep a dependable agent in charge of intelligence. A distinction for a person of Coptic ancestry. (See Qalqashandī, *Ṣubḥ* I, 19, 104, 110, 137; III, 487; IV, 19, 29, 30; V, 464; VI, 206–07; XI, 114.)

Three positions, 3 percent of one hundred total:

Karīm al-Dīn 'Abd al-Karīm ibn 'Abd al-Razzāq al-Qibṭī al-Miṣrī, known as Ibn Kātib al-Manākhāt, d. Rabī' II 852/June–July 1448 (*Ḍaw'* IV, p. 313, no 848; *Manhal* II, f. 345; Wiet 1461) (twice).

Fakhr al-Dīn Mājid ibn Abī al-Faḍā'il al-Qibṭī, known as Ibn al-Marqūq, d. Rajab 833/March–April 1430 (*Ḍaw'* VI, p. 235, no. 812).

Kātib al-umarā': Secretary to the Mamluk amirs, presumably in the dīwān al-Mamālīk, bureau of Mamluks (see above).

One position, 100 percent of one total:

Sa'd al-Dīn Ibrāhīm ibn Fakhr al-Dīn al-Qibṭī, d. Rajab 864/May 1460 (*Ḍaw'* I, p. 183).

Milk al-umarā': Accountant of properties held by Mamluk amirs (presumably as *iqṭā'*). All three references to this post occurred in the careers of Muslim Copts, underscoring the sultan's policy of granting reliable clients supervisory powers over his amirs' estates.

Three positions, 100 percent of three total:

Karīm al-Dīn 'Abd al-Karīm ibn 'Abd al-Razzāq al-Qibṭī, known as Ibn Kātib al-Munākhāt, d. Rabī' II 852/June–July 1448 (*Ḍaw'* IV, p. 313, no. 848; *Manhal* II, 345; Wiet 1461) (twice).

Nāṣir al-Dīn Muḥammad ibn 'Abd al-Razzāq al-Qibṭī, d. Muḥarram 881/April–May 1476 (*Ḍaw'* VIII, p. 55, no. 70).

Mubāshir: Steward, intendant. Serving in a wide range of bureaucratic settings, the *mubashir* worked under the authority of a *nāẓir* or *kātib* to process accounts and generally to maintain institutional functions. Also appears in the sources on occasion as a courier and a precursor who cleared the streets for important officials. Although a subordinate post, the majority of individuals holding it were Muslims of proven lineage. Muslim Copts rarely received the position, attached as it often was to religio-academic institutions as well as the regime's *diwans.*

One position, 1.5 percent of sixty-six total:

Tāj al-Dīn 'Abd al-Razzāq ibn 'Abd-Allāh al-Qibṭī, known as Ibn Kātib al-Munākhāt, d. Jumādā I 827/May 1423 (*Ḍaw'* IV, p. 194, no. 495).

Mubāshir al-dīwān: Steward in the fiscal bureau, specifically the *dīwān al-dawlah* (see under *nāẓir al-dawlah*).

Two positions, 13 percent of fifteen total:

Karīm al-Dīn 'Abd al-Karīm ibn Barakah al-Qibṭī

al-Miṣrī, known as Ibn Kātib Jakam, d. Rabī' I 833/November–December 1429 (*Ḍaw'* IV, p. 308, no. 833).

Fakhr al-Dīn Mājid ibn 'Abd al-Razzāq al-Qibṭī al-Skandarī, known as Ibn Ghurāb, d. Dhu al-Ḥijjah 811/April–May 1409 (*Ḍaw'* VI, p. 234, no. 811).

Mubāshir dīwān al-jaysh: Steward in the army bureau that oversaw revenues yielded by land allotments to support the sultan's Mamluk amirs and their retinues.

One position, 100 percent of one total:

Sa'd al-Dīn Ibrāhīm ibn 'Abd al-Wahhāb al-Qibṭī al-Maymūnī, d. 795/1392–1393 (*Manhal* I, p. 99, no. 51; Wiet 51).

Mubāshir dīwān al-khāṣṣ: Steward in the special bureau supervising a fund maintained to cover the costs of military expeditions and other related expenses (sometimes translated as the "privy fund").

One position, 100 percent of one total:

Abū al-Ghālid al-Qibṭī, d. Rabī' I 899/February–March 1489 (*Ḍaw'* XI, p. 120, no. 376).

Mubāshir istifā' al-mufrad: Steward in the accounts department of the sultan's special bureau disbursing payments to his Mamluk troopers.

One position, 100 percent of one total:

Tāj al-Dīn 'Abd al-Razzāq ibn 'Abd-Allāh al-Qibṭī, known as Ibn Kātib al-Munākhāt, d. Jumādā I 827/May 1423 (*Ḍaw'* IV, p. 194, no. 495).

Mustawfī: Accountant in a fiscal bureau of the government or a religio-academic institution.

Three positions, 75 percent of four total:

Amīn al-Dīn 'Abd-Allāh ibn al-Tāj al-Qibṭī al-Aslamī, d. 740/1339–1340 (*Manhal* II, f. 262; Wiet 1310).

Tāj al-Dīn 'Abd al-Razzāq ibn 'Abd-Allāh al-Qibṭī, known as Ibn Kātib al-Munākhāt, d. Jumādā I 827/April 1424 (*Ḍaw'* IV, p. 194, no. 495).

Burhān al-Dīn Ibrāhīm ibn Bariyyah al-Qibṭī al-Muslimī, no death date (*Ḍaw'* I, p. 33).

Mustawfī al-dawlah: Accountant in the fiscal bureaus; originally under supervision of the *wazīr*, subsequently answerable to the *nāẓir al-dawlah*.

Two positions, 100 percent of two total:

Sharaf al-Dīn 'Abd al-Wahhāb ibn Faḍl-Allāh al-Qibṭī al-Aslamī al-Qāhirī, no death date (*Manhal* II, f. 362; Wiet 1492).

Jamāl al-Dīn Ibrāhīm al-Qibṭī al-Aslamī al-Qāhirī, known as al-Kaffāt, d. 745/1344–1345 (*Manhal* I, f. 45; Wiet 96).

Mustawfī dīwān al-jaysh: Accountant in the army bureau, which oversaw revenues yielded by land allotments to support the sultan's Mamluk amirs and their retinues.

One position, 100 percent of one total:

'Alam al-Dīn Shākir al-Miṣrī al-Qibṭī, known as Ibn al-Jī'ān, d. 790/1388 (*Manhal* II, f. 170; Wiet 1162).

Mustawfī al-khāṣṣ: Accountant in the sultan's special bureau administering a fund reserved to cover costs of his military campaigns and related expenses incurred by his Mamluks. All references to this post occurred in the careers of Muslim Copts, indicating the prominence of this minority in activities securing the ruler's fiscal solvency and capacity to wage war.

Four positions, 100 percent of four total:

'Abd al-Ghanī ibn al-Hayṣam al-Qibṭī, known as Ibn al-Hayṣam, no death date (*Manhal* II, f. 335b; Wiet 1441).

Karīm al-Dīn 'Abd al-Karīm ibn Fakhīrah al-Qibṭī, d. Rajab 855/August–September 1451 (*Ḍaw'* IV, p. 321, no. 879).

Tāj al-Dīn 'Abd al-Razzāq ibn 'Abd-Allāh al-Qibṭī, known as Ibn Kātib al-Munākh, d. Jumādā I 837/April 1424 (*Manhal* II, f. 316b; Wiet 1409).

Majd al-Dīn Rizq-Allāh ibn Faḍl-Allāh al-Qāhirī al-Qibṭī al-Aslamī, d. 740/1339–1340 (*Manhal* II, f. 97b; Wiet 1031).

Mustawfī al-khizānah: Accountant in the royal wardrobe of the treasury. Responsible for allotting funds to pay for production of robes of honor distributed by sultans during ceremonials recognizing exceptional service or formal promotions (given to both Mamluks and civilians). Robes also were bestowed upon ambassadors and other visiting dignitaries. The position occurred only in this case.

One position, 100 percent of one total:

The preceding Majd al-Dīn Rizq-Allāh.

Mutkallim al-awqāf: Official in the bureau of pious trust foundations, presumably trained in the law of *waqf* with expertise in matters of sale, replacement, or transfer.

One position, 6 percent of seventeen total:

Nāsir al-Dīn Muḥammad ibn 'Abd al-Razzāq al-Qibṭī, d. Muḥarram 881/April–May 1476 (*Ḍaw'* VIII, p. 55, no. 70).

Mutakallim al-dīwān: Official in the financial bureau, specifically the Dīwān al-Dawlah (see under *nāẓir al-dawlah*). Duties similar to those of the *mubāshir* but empowered to decide procedural legal matters concerning collection and expenditure of revenues.

One position, 100 percent of one total:

Tāj al-Dīn ʿAbd al-Wahhāb ibn Naṣr-Allāh al-Qibṭī al-Aslamī, known as al-Shaykh al-Khaṭīr, d. Dhu al-Qaʿdah 865/August–September 1461 (*Ḍaw'* V, p. 114, no. 408).

Mutakallim al-mukūs: Official in the bureau of tolls, imposts, and market dues.

One position, 100 percent of one total:

ʿAbd al-Bāsiṭ ibn ʿAbd al-Wahhāb al-Qibṭī, known as al-Kātib al-Maysam, d. Shaʿbān 892/July–August 1487 (*Ḍaw'* IV, p. 28, no. 86).

Muwaqqiʿ: Clerk, scribe. In contrast with the *kātib,* this official had the prerogative of *tawqīʿ*, the official right of signature, seal, or other insignia legally certifying documents. This prerogative was granted only to individuals who had received formal training in the Islamic sciences. A distinction for persons of Coptic ancestry.

Three positions, 2.6 percent of 116 total:

Amīn al-Dīn Ibrāhīm ibn ʿAbd al-Ghanī al-Qibṭī al-Miṣrī, known as Ibn al-Hayṣam, d. Rabīʿ II 859/March–April 1454 (*Ḍaw'* I, p. 67).

Sharaf al-Dīn Yaḥyā al-Qibṭī al-Qāhirī, known as Ibn Ṣanīʿah, d. Muḥarram 882/April–May 1477 (*Ḍaw'* X, p. 268, no. 1061) (twice).

Muwaqqiʿ al-dast: Scribe of the royal bench in the Palace of Justice (Dār al-ʿAdl). Responsible for composing and sealing in the sultan's presence edicts, deeds, letters of appointment, and correspondence.

One position, 4 percent of twenty-eight total:

Majd al-Dīn Faḍl-Allāh ibn ʿAbd al-Raḥmān al-Miṣrī al-Qibṭī al-Ḥanafī, known as Ibn Makānis, d. Rabīʿ II 822/April–May 1419 (*Ḍaw'* VI, p. 172, no. 581).

Muwaqqiʿ dīwān al-inshā: Scribe in the imperial chancellery.

One position, 8 percent of thirteen total:

The preceding Ibn Makānis.

Nāẓir: Fiscal controller, supervisor. This office evolved from the overseer of revenues yielded by charitable trusts (*awqāf*) to fiscal administrator of a government bureau or budget director of a religio-academic institution such as a mosque, *madrasah* (school), or Ṣūfī hospice in the Egyptian Mamluk period. Relatively few persons of Coptic ancestry held posts in the latter capacity, but they appeared frequently in the former. The supervisory powers of a *nāẓir* over a fiscal bureau enabled him to process large revenues. In virtually all cases, he was to siphon a percentage of such monies into a private fund reserved for his patron, the sultan or grand amir who had appointed him. Most *nuẓẓār* were compelled to share their authority with a cosupervisor, often titled *ṣāḥib* and usually of Mamluk origin, who checked to see that he was performing his clandestine function to his employer's satisfaction. (See Qalqashandī, *Ṣubḥ* V, 465; IX, 257–58.)

Three positions, 2 percent of 169 total:

Shams al-Dīn Inbrāhīm ibn ʿAbd-Allāh al-Qibṭī, known as Kātib Arnān, d. Shaʿbān 798/May–June 1396 (*Manhal* I, p. 57, no. 31; Wiet 31).

Saʿd al-Dīn Ibrāhīm ibn ʿAbd al-Razzāq al-Skandarī al-Miṣrī al-Qibṭī, known as Ibn Ghurāb, d. Rajab 808/December 1405–January 1406 (*Ḍaw'* I, p. 65).

Fakhr al-Dīn Mājid ibn ʿAbd al-Razzāq al-Qibṭī al-Skandarī, known as Ibn Ghurāb, d. Dhu al-Ḥijjah 811/April–May 1409 (*Ḍaw'* VI, p. 234, no. 811).

Nāẓir al-aswāq: Supervisor of markets, specifically the horse and slave markets. Distinct from the *muḥtasib* or inspector of weights and measures in the markets, to which no person of Coptic background was appointed in this survey. The latter was a legal official, selected from the persons of proven Muslim lineage and formal training in the *Sharīʿah.* The former was a revenue collector in state employ and subordinate to the executive secretary (*dawādār*) and the *wazīr.*

One position, 33 percent of three total:

ʿAlam al-Dīn Yaḥyā al-Qibṭī al-Miṣrī, d. Rajab 835/March–April 1432 (*Manhal* III, f. 508; Wiet 2813).

Nāẓir al-awqāf: Supervisor of pious trust foundations. Appointed in Cairo by the sultan, in the provincial capitals by the viceroy (*nā'ib al-sulṭān*). This official regulated expenditures made by budget supervisors of local charitable institutions, heard appeals contesting their practices, and arbitrated disputes between staff and descendants of donors. Even though his duties were often more symbolic than real, this official was regarded as especially prone to corruption and bribery. Therefore his character was to show no blemish, his religious convictions no deviance whatsoever. Accordingly, only devout believers were appointed, and this single reference to a Muslim Copt, attached to a specific foundation (Sarghatmishiyyah Madrasah), proves that few converts or their descendants held the post.

One position, 2 percent of fifty-two total:

Ibrāhīm ibn Fakhr al-Dīn al-Qibṭī, known as Ibn al-Sukkar wa-al-Laymūn, d. Rajab 864/May 1460 (*Ḍaw'* I, p. 183).

Nāẓir al-bandar: Supervisor of the port. The post first appears for the port of Alexandria, but after the monopolies imposed by Sultan Barsbāy (825–841/1422–1437), the official appears in the Red Sea ports controlled by the regime.

Three positions, 100 percent of three total:

Karīm al-Dīn 'Abd al-Karīm ibn 'Abd al-Razzāq al-Qibṭī al-Miṣrī, known as Ibn Kātib al-Munākhāt, d. Rabī' II 852/June–July 1448 (*Manhal* II, f. 345; Wiet 1461) (twice).

Sa'd al-Dīn Ibrāhīm al-Qibṭī al-Nāṣirī al-Muslimī, known as Ibn al-Mar'a, d. Rabī' II 844/August–September 1440 (*Ḍaw'* I, p. 184).

Nāẓir dīwān al-dawlah: Supervisor of the financial bureaus, in theory he shared authority with the *wazīr* and cosigned all fiscal directives with him; in practice he gradually superseded him. This individual directed an umbrella department overseeing the other fiscal bureaus, all of which had to report their accounts at regular intervals. Also, royal instruments of appointment to fiscal offices were composed here; and the department paid out annual, monthly, and daily stipends to officials in the other government bureaus as well as the civil judiciary. (See Qalqashandī, *Ṣubḥ* IV, 29; XI, 117.) Holders of this office were among the most influential bureaucrats of the Mamluk state, but they competed with their counterparts in the *dīwān al-khāṣṣ* or *dīwān al-mufrad,* unless the sultan allowed one individual to take them over jointly. Muslim Copts held a majority of these posts.

Twenty-one positions, 62 percent of thirty-four total:

Shams al-Dīn 'Abd-Allāh al-Maqsī al-Qibṭī, d. Sha'bān 755/August–September 1354 (*Manhal,* f. 506b; Wiet 2809).

Amīn al-Dīn 'Abd-Allāh ibn Rīshah al-Qibṭī al-Aslamī al-Miṣrī, d. 790/1388 (*Manhal* II, f. 277b; Wiet 1343).

Amīn al-Dīn 'Abd-Allah ibn al-Tāj al Qibṭī al-Aslamī, d. 740/1339–1340 (*Manhal* II, f. 262; Wiet 1310).

Karīm al-Dīn 'Abd al-Karīm ibn 'Abd al-Razzāq al-Qibṭī al-Miṣrī, known as Ibn Makānis, d. Jumādā II 803/January–February 1401 (*Ḍaw'* IV, p. 312, no. 846).

Karīm al-Dīn 'Abd al-Karīm ibn Barakah al-Qibṭī al-Miṣrī, known as Ibn Kātib Jakam, d. Rabī' II 833/December 1429–January 1430 (*Ḍaw'* IV, p. 308, no. 833; *Manhal* II, f. 343; Wiet 1457) (twice).

Fakhr al-Dīn 'Abd al-Raḥmān ibn 'Abd al-Razzāq al-Qibṭī al-Ḥanafī al-Qāhirī, known as Ibn Makānis, d. Dhu al-Ḥijjah 794/October–November 1392 (*Manhal* II, f. 290; Wiet 1370).

Tāj al-Dīn Faḍl-Allāh al-Ramlī al-Qibṭī, d. Ṣafar 826/January–February 1423 (*Ḍaw'* VI, p. 173, no. 585; *Manhal* II, f. 521; Wiet 1795) (twice).

Fakhr al-Dīn ibn al-Sukkar wa-al-Laymūn al-Qibṭī, d. 875/1470–1471 (*Ḍaw'* XI, p. 164, no. 520) (twice).

Sa'd al-Dīn Faraj ibn Mājid al-Qibṭī al-Miṣrī, known as Ibn al-Naḥḥāl, d. Jumādā II 865/March–April 1461 (*Ḍaw'* VI, p. 169, no. 570).

Jamāl al-Dīn Ibrāhīm al-Qāhirī al-Qibṭī al-Aslamī, d. 745/1344–1345 (*Manhal* I, f. 45; Wiet 96).

Sa'd al-Dīn Ibrāhīm al-Qibṭī al-Nāṣirī al-Muslimī, known as Ibn al-Mar'ah, d. Rabī' II 844/August–September 1440 (*Ḍaw'* I, p. 184).

Amīn al-Dīn Ibrāhīm ibn 'Abd al-Ghanī al-Qibṭī al-Miṣrī, known as Ibn al-Hayṣam, d. Rabī' II 859/March–April 1455 (*Ḍaw'* I, p. 67; *Manhal* I, p. 93, no. 49; Wiet 49) (twice).

Sa'd al-Dīn Ibrāhīm ibn Barakah al-Miṣrī al-Qibṭī, known as al-Bashīrī, d. Ṣafar 818/April–May 1415 (*Ḍaw'* I, p. 33).

Shams al-Dīn Naṣr-Allāh al-Qibṭī al-Aslamī, known as Ibn al-Najjār, no death date (*Ḍaw'* X, p. 200, no. 855) (twice).

Zayn al-Dīn Yaḥyā ibn 'Abd al-Razzāq al-Qibṭī al-Miṣrī al-Qāhirī, known as al-Ashqar, d. Rabī' II 874/September–October 1469 (*Ḍaw'* X, p. 223, no. 983; *Manhal* III, f. 402b; Wiet 2633) (twice).

Nāẓir al-iṣṭabl: Supervisor of the royal stables, responsible for distributing revenues designated to maintain the royal cavalry housed in the Citadel complex (near the Maydan al-Rumaylah). He administered purchases of fodder and harness, as well as payment of wages to grooms and stable attendants.

Nine positions, 41 percent of twenty-two total:

Amīn al-Dīn ʿAbd-Allāh ibn Abī al-Faraj al-Qibṭī al-Miṣrī, known as Ibn Tāj al-Dīn Mūsā, d. Jumādā II 844/October–November 1440 (*Ḍaw'* V, p. 41, no. 155; *Manhal* II, f. 256; Wiet 1297) (twice).

Tāj al-Dīn ʿAbd al-Wahhāb ibn Naṣr-Allah al-Qibṭī al-Aslamī, known as al-Shaykh al-Khaṭīr, d. Dhu al-Qaʿdah 865/August–September 1461 (*Ḍaw'* V, p. 114, no. 408; *Manhal* II, f. 364b; Wiet 1498) (twice).

Saʿd al-Dīn Faraj ibn Mājid al-Qibṭī al-Miṣrī, known as Ibn al-Naḥḥāl, d. Jumādā II 865/February–March 1461 (*Ḍaw'* VI, p. 169, no. 570).

Fakhr al-Dīn Mājid ibn Abī al-Faḍā'il al-Qibṭī, known as Ibn Marzūq, d. Rajab 833/March–April 1430 (*Ḍaw'* VI, p. 235, no. 812).

Shams al-Dīn Abū al-Manṣūr Naṣr-Allāh al-Qibṭī al-Qāhirī, d. 850/1466–1447 (*Ḍaw'* X, p. 200, no. 845).

Zayn al-Dīn Yaḥyā ibn ʿAbd al-Razzāq al-Qibṭī al-Qāhirī, known as al-Ashqar, d. Rabīʿ I 874/September–October 1469 (*Ḍaw'* X, p. 233, no. 983; *Manhal* III, f. 402b; Wiet 2633) (twice).

Nāẓir al-jaysh: Supervisor of the army bureau administering the grant of, and receipts collected from, all military land allotments in Egypt and Syria. An exceedingly influential official because of his discretionary powers over personnel (Mamluk amirs) who received land in return for service, and who often attempted to transfer it to their own heirs, in defiance of the state's right of alienation upon their death, dismissal, or retirement. The prominence of Muslim Copts placed in this office suggests the ruler's concern about bribery and corruption over distribution of the royal fisc. He sought to appoint individuals who were dependent upon him for their security and professional advancement. (See Qalqashandī, *Ṣubḥ* IV, 17, 30, 190 [relationship with trust properties in Damascus]; VI, 61; XI, 89, 93.)

Fifteen positions, 18 percent of eighty-two total:

ʿAlam al-Dīn ʿAbd-Allāh ibn Aḥmad al-Qibṭī al-Miṣrī, d. 755/1354–1355 (*Manhal* II, f. 257; Wiet 1301).

Saʿd al-Dīn Ibrāhīm ibn ʿAbd al-Razzāq al-Skandarī al-Miṣrī al-Muslimī, known as Ibn Ghurāb, d. Rajab 808/December 1405–January 1406 (*Ḍaw'* I, p. 65; *Manhal* I, p. 85, no. 47; Wiet 37) (four times).

Jamāl al-Dīn Ibrāhīm al-Qibṭī al-Aslamī, known as Jamāl al-Dīn al-Kaffāt, d. 745/1344–1345 (*Manhal* I, f. 45; Wiet 96).

Fakhr al-Dīn Mājid ibn Abī al-Faḍā'il al-Qibṭī, known as Ibn al-Marzūq, d. Rajab 833/March–April 1430 (*Ḍaw'* VI, p. 235, no. 812).

Nāṣir al-Dīn Muḥammad ibn ʿAbd al-Razzāq al-Armanī al-Qibṭī, no death date (*Manhal* III, f. 180; Wiet 2187).

Fakhr al-Dīn Muḥammad ibn Faḍl-Allah al-Naṣrānī al-Qibṭī al-Qāhirī al-Aslamī, d. 732/1331–1332 (*Manhal* III, f. 240b; Wiet 2311).

Shams al-Dīn Mūsā ibn ʿAbd al-Wahhāb al-Miṣrī al-Qibṭī, d. 771/1369–1370 (*Manhal* III, f. 373; Wiet 2554) (twice).

Sharaf al-Dīn Mūsā ibn Yūsuf al-Karakī al-Qibṭī al-Shawbakī, no death date (*Manhal* III, f. 379; Wiet 2571) (three times).

Jamāl al-Dīn Yūsuf ibn ʿAbd al-Karīm al-Qibṭī al-Shāfiʿī, known as Ibn Kātib Jakam, d. Dhu al-Ḥijjah 862/October–November 1458 (*Manhal* III, f. 459; Wiet 2710).

Nāẓir al-khāṣṣ (dīwān al-): Supervisor of the sultan's special bureau administering a fund reserved to cover costs of military campaigns and other related expenses incurred by his Mamluks. This official assumed many of the duties of the *wazīr*. Its incumbent was usually a close associate of the ruler, and he recommended the names of candidates for high-level bureaucratic posts to his patron. He also supplanted the supervisor of the royal repository (*nāẓir al-khizānah*) from the reign of Barqūq (784–801/1382–1399). But during the Circassian period, his responsibilities were reduced as the *nāẓir al-mufrad* and the *ustādār* enlarged their spheres of influence. Ultimately, the *nāẓir al-khāṣṣ* was responsible primarily for supplying robes of honor for court ceremonials. (See Qalqashandī, *Ṣubḥ* IV, 30; VI, 44, 200–01, 216; VIII, 231; XI, 89, 93, 316.)

Twenty-seven positions, 50 percent of fifty-five total:

ʿAlam al-Dīn ʿAbd-Allāh ibn Aḥmad al-Qibṭī al-Miṣrī, known as Ibn Zunbūr, d. 755/1354–1355 (*Manhal* II, f. 257; Wiet 1301).

Fakhr al-Dīn ʿAbd-Allāh ibn Mūsā al-Qibṭī al-Miṣrī, known as Ibn Tāj al-Dīn, d. 776/1374–1375 (*Manhal* II, f. 276b; Wiet 1340).

ʿAbd al-Ghanī ibn Hayṣam al-Qibṭī, known as Ibn al-Hayṣam, no death date (*Manhal* II, f. 335b; Wiet 1441) (twice).

Majd al-Dīn ʿAbd al-Ghanī ibn Ibrāhīm al-Qibṭī al-Miṣrī, d. Shaʿbān 813/November–December 1410 (*Ḍaw'* IV, p. 245, no. 638).

Karīm al-Dīn ʿAbd al-Karīm ibn Barakah al-Qibṭī

al-Miṣrī, known as Ibn Kātib Jakam, d. Rabīʿ I 833/November–December 1429 (*Ḍaw'* IV, p. 308, no. 833; *Manhal* II, f. 343; Wiet 1457) (twice).

Karīm al-Dīn ʿAbd al-Karīm ibn ʿAbd al-Razzāq, known as Ibn Makānis, d. Jumādā II 803/January–February 1401 (*Ḍaw'* IV, p. 312, no. 846; *Manhal* II, f. 344; Wiet 1460) (twice).

Taqī al-Dīn ʿAbd al-Wahhāb ibn ʿAbd-Allāh (Mājid) al-Qibṭī al-Miṣrī al-Ḥanafī, known as Ibn Abī Shākir, d. Dhu al-Qaʿdah 819/December 1416–January 1417 (*Ḍaw'* V, p. 102, no. 384; *Manhal* II, f. 359b; Wiet 1487) (twice).

Sharaf al-Dīn ʿAbd al-Wahhāb ibn Faḍl-Allāh al-Qibṭī al-Aslamī al-Qāhirī, no death date (*Manhal* II, f. 362; Wiet 1492).

Jamāl al-Dīn Ibrāhīm al-Qibṭī al-Aslamī, known as Jamāl al-Kaffāt, d. 745/1344–1345 (*Manhal* I, f. 45; Wiet 96).

Amīn al-Dīn Ibrāhīm ibn ʿAbd al-Ghanī al-Qibṭī, known as Ibn al-Hayṣam, d. Ṣafar 859/January–February 1455 (*Manhal* I, p. 93, no. 49; Wiet 49).

Saʿd al-Dīn Ibrāhīm ibn ʿAbd al-Karīm al-Qibṭī al-Miṣrī, known as Ibn Jakam, d. Rabīʿ I 841/September–October 1437 (*Ḍaw'* I, p. 68; *Manhal* I, p. 96, no. 50; Wiet 50) (twice).

Saʿd al-Dīn Ibrāhīm ibn ʿAbd al-Razzāq al-Skandarī al-Miṣrī al-Qibṭī al-Muslimī, known as Ibn Ghurāb, d. Rajab 808/1405–1406 (*Ḍaw'* I, p. 65; *Manhal* I, p. 85, no. 47; Wiet 47) (four times).

Fakr al-Dīn Mājid ibn ʿAbd al-Razzāq al-Qibṭī al-Skandarī, known as Ibn Ghurāb, d. Dhu al-Ḥijjah 811/April–May 1409 (*Ḍaw'* VI, p. 234, no. 811; *Manhal* III, f. 71b; Wiet 1949) (twice).

Fakhr al-Dīn Mājid ibn Qarwīnah al-Qibṭī al-Aslamī, d. Jumādā I 768/January–February 1367 (*Manhal* III, f. 72b; Wiet 1951).

Shams al-Dīn Mūsā ibn ʿAbd al-Wahhāb al-Miṣrī al-Qibṭī, d. 771/1369–1370 (*Manhal* III, f. 373; Wiet 2554) (twice).

ʿAlam al-Dīn Yahyā al-Qibṭī al-Miṣrī, d. Rajab 835/March–April 1432 (*Manhal* III, f. 508; Wiet 2813).

Jamāl al-Dīn Yūsuf ibn ʿAbd al-Karīm al-Shāfiʿī al-Qibṭī, known as Ibn Kātib Jakam, d. Dhu al-Ḥijjah 862/October–November 1458 (*Manhal* III, f. 459; Wiet 2710).

Nāẓir al-khizānah (al-kabīr): Supervisor of the royal repository of robes in the Citadel. His duties were gradually supplanted by the *nāẓir al-khāṣṣ*.

Two positions, 33 percent of six total:

Amīn al-Dīn ʿAbd-Allāh ibn Abī al-Faraj al-Qibṭī al-Miṣrī, known as Ibn Tāj al-Dīn Mūsā, d. Jumādā II 844/October–November 1440 (*Ḍaw'* V, p. 41, no. 155).

Shams al-Dīn Mūsā ibn ʿAbd al-Wahhāb al-Miṣrī al-Qibṭī, d. 771/1369–1370 (*Manhal* III, f. 373; Wiet 2554).

Nāẓir al-mufrad (dīwān al-): Supervisor of the special bureau established to support the sultan's Mamluks, responsible for paying their stipends and ordering their clothing, fodder, and so on. Revenues set aside for this department were collected from tolls and market taxes in provincial towns, plus several customs duties. The department became prominent during the sultanate of Barqūq (784–801/1382–1399), who purchased large numbers of Mamluk troopers. A majority of those posts were held by Muslim Copts.

Eighteen positions, 75 percent of twenty-four total:

Tāj al-Dīn ʿAbd al-ʿAẓīm ibn Ṣadaqah al-Qibṭī al-Aslamī, d. 844/1440–1441 (*Ḍaw'* IV, p. 240, no. 620; *Manhal* II, f. 333; Wiet 1437) (twice).

Karīm al-Dīn ʿAbd al-Karīm ibn ʿAbd al-Razzāq al-Qibṭī al-Miṣrī, known as Ibn Kātib al-Munākhāt, d. Rabīʿ II 852/June–July 1448 (*Ḍaw'* IV, p. 313, no. 848; *Manhal* II, f. 345; Wiet 1461) (twice).

Tāj al-Dīn ʿAbd al-Razzāq ibn ʿAbd-Allāh al-Qibṭī, known as Ibn Kātib al-Munākhāt, d. Jumādā I 827/April 1424 (*Ḍaw'* IV, p. 194, no. 495; *Manhal* II, f. 316b; Wiet 1409) (twice).

Tāj al-Dīn ʿAbd al-Razzāq ibn Ibrāhīm al-Qibṭī, known as Ibn al-Hayṣam, d. Dhu al-Ḥijjah 834/August–September 1431 (*Ḍaw'* IV, p. 191, no. 485; *Manhal* II, f. 315b; Wiet 1407) (twice).

Taqī al-Dīn ʿAbd al-Wahhāb ibn ʿAbd-Allāh (Mājid) al-Qibṭī al-Ḥanafī, known as Ibn Abī Shākir, d. Dhu al-Qaʿdah 819/December 1416–January 1417 (*Ḍaw'* V, p. 102, no. 384; *Manhal* II, f. 359b; Wiet 1487) (twice).

Fakhr al-Dīn ibn al-Sukkar wā-al-Laymūn al-Qibṭī, d. 875/1470–1471 (*Ḍaw'* XI, p. 164, no. 520).

Saʿd al-Dīn Ibrāhīm al-Nāṣirī al-Qibṭī al-Muslimī, known as Ibn al-Mar'ah, d. Rabiʿ II 844/August–September 1440 (*Ḍaw'* I, p. 184).

Amīn al-Dīn Ibrāhīm ibn ʿAbd al-Ghanī al-Qibṭī al-Miṣrī, known as Ibn al-Hayṣam, d. Rabīʿ II 859/March–April 1455 (*Ḍaw'* I, p. 67).

Manṣūr ibn al-Ṣafī al-Qibṭī, d. Shawwāl 870/May–June 1466 (*Ḍaw'* X, p. 179, no. 716).

Sharaf al-Dīn Mūsā ibn Yūsuf al-Būtījī al-Misrī

al-Qāhirī al-Qibṭī, d. Ṣafar 882/May–June 1477 (*Ḍaw'* X, p. 192, no. 810).

Zayn al-Dīn Yaḥyā ibn 'Abd al-Razzāq al-Qibṭī al-Qāhirī, known as al-Ashqar, d. Rabī' I 874/September–October 1469 (*Ḍaw'* X, p. 233, no. 983; *Manhal* III, f. 402b; Wiet 2633) (three times).

Ṣāḥib al-dīwān: Intendant of a fiscal bureau, sharing authority with a supervisor or *nāẓir*. Title undesignated but presumably the department of the army (*jaysh*).

One position, 50 percent of two total:

Fakhr al-Dīn 'Abd-Allāh ibn Mūsā al-Qibṭī al-Miṣrī, known as Ibn Tāj al-Dīn, d. 776/1374–1375 (*Manhal* II, f. 276b; Wiet 1340).

Ṣāḥib dīwān al-ashrāf: Intendant of the bureau for revenues accruing to the Prophet's descendants. An individual appointed to this office served as a supervisory agent of the regime, sharing his authority (as a regulator) with the *naqīb al-ashrāf*, who was more autonomous although also appointed by the sultan. This department was open to bribery due to the claims persons with proven Ḥāshimī genealogies could make on the state treasury. Forgeries were inevitable, and the *ṣāḥib* was responsible for calling the *naqīb* to account, since the latter identified with the *'ulamā'*. No Muslim Copt held the latter office, but the only reference to the former occurred in a Copt's career.

One position, 100 percent of one total:

Muwaffaq al-Dīn 'Abd-Allāh ibn Ibrāhīm al-Qibṭī al-Qāhirī, d. Rabī' I 877/August–September 1472 (*Ḍaw'* V, p. 4, no. 7).

Ṣāḥib dīwān al-jaysh: Intendant of the Army Bureau. Technically subordinate to the supervisor (*nāẓir*) of this department, in practice the *ṣāḥib* acted as a regulator of the former and was answerable directly to the regime for revenues yielded by land allotments granted by the sultan to support his Mamluk officers. From a fiscal perspective, this was one of the more important offices in the bureaucratic hierarchy.

One position, 25 percent of four total:

Fakhr al-Dīn 'Abd al-Ghanī al-Qibṭī, known as Ibn Bint al-Mulkī, d. Rajab 848/October–November 1444 (*Ḍaw'* IV, p. 251, no. 653).

Wazīr: During the Abbasid period, prime minister after the caliph, his alter ego, supervisor of the tax bureaus and chancellery. Under the Fatimid caliphs and Ayyubid sultans of Egypt, this official enjoyed similar sweeping powers, subordinate only to the ruler. But under the Mamluk sultans, and especially from the reign of al-Ẓāhir Barqūq (d. 801/1399), the position gradually diminished, and was no longer ranked as "office of the sword" (and thus rarely devolved on a Mamluk amir). Various former functions were progressively assumed by fiscal intendants (*nuẓẓār*) who now directed the financial bureaus (Dīwān al-Māl, Dīwān al-Dawlah) and a special fund established for the sultan's military expenses (Dīwān al-Khāṣṣ). The *wazīr*'s previous chancellory prerogatives were assumed by a confidential secretary (*kātib al-sirr*), and his former close association with the autocrat was now maintained by a majordomo (*ustādar*), usually a Mamluk grand amir and colleague of the sultan. Thus, by the later Middle Ages, the vizierate in Egypt was restricted largely to collection of certain specific taxes and duties—a procedural rather than an executive office. As the vizierate declined in authority, the percentage of Copts appointed to it steadily increased. The resultant burgeoning of references to Copts therefore parallels a progressive erosion of the office's authority while also suggesting the officeholder's rising dependence on the regime's autocratic powers to perform his duties. Later Mamluk sultans were prone to place Copts in lucrative but vulnerable positions to assure a flow of revenues directly to their coffers through confiscation and other pressure tactics. The rate of arrest for persons holding the vizierate exceeded 50 percent during the fifteenth century, according to biographical records. (See al-Maqrīzī, *Khiṭaṭ* II, 58, 223–26; Qalqashandī, *Ṣubḥ* IV, 28–33.)

Forty-nine positions, 53 percent of ninety-two total:

Shams al-Dīn 'Abd-Allāh al-Maqsī al-Qibṭī, d. Sha'bān 755/August–September 1354 (*Manhal* III, f. 506b; Wiet 2809).

'Alam al-Dīn 'Abd-Allāh ibn Aḥmad al-Qibṭī al-Miṣrī, d. 755/1354–1355 (*Manhal* II, f. 257; Wiet 1301).

Fakhr al-Dīn 'Abd-Allāh ibn Mūsā al-Qibṭī al-Miṣrī, known as Ibn Tāj al-Dīn, d. 776/1374–1375 (*Manhal* II, f. 276b; Wiet 1340).

Karīm al-Dīn 'Abd-Allāh ibn Shākir al-Qibṭī al-Miṣrī, known as Ibn al-Ghannām, d. Shawwāl 823/October–November 1420 (*Ḍaw'* V, p. 21, no. 73).

Amīn al-Dīn ʿAbd-Allāh ibn al-Tāj al-Qibṭī al-Aslamī, d. 740/1339–1340 (*Manhal* II, f. 262; Wiet 1310).

Fakhr al-Dīn ʿAbd al-Ghanī ibn ʿAbd al-Razzāq al-Armanī al-Qibṭī al-Qāhirī, d. Shawwāl 821/November 1418 (*Manhal* II, f. 336; Wiet 1442).

Karīm al-Dīn ʿAbd al-Karīm al-Qibṭī al-Miṣrī, d. 784/1382–1383 (*Manhal* II, f. 349b; Wiet 1465).

Karīm al-Dīn ʿAbd al-Karīm ibn ʿAbd al-Razzāq, known as Ibn Makānis, d. Jumādā II 803/January–February 1401 (*Ḍaw'* IV, p. 312, no. 846; *Manhal* II, f. 344; Wiet 1460) (twice).

Karīm al-Dīn ʿAbd al-Karīm ibn ʿAbd al-Razzāq al-Qibṭī al-Miṣrī, known as Ibn Kātib al-Munākhāt, d. Rabīʿ II 852/June–July 1448 (*Ḍaw'* IV, p. 313, no. 848; *Manhal* II, f. 345; Wiet 1461) (three times).

Fakhr al-Dīn ʿAbd al-Raḥmān ibn ʿAbd al-Razzāq al-Qibṭī al-Ḥanafī al-Qāhirī, known as Ibn Makānis, d. Dhu al-Ḥijjah 794/October–November 1392 (*Manhal* II, f. 290; Wiet 1370).

Tāj al-Dīn ʿAbd al-Razzāq ibn ʿAbd-Allāh al-Qibṭī, known as Ibn Kātib al-Munākhāt, d. Jumādā I 827/March–April 1425 (*Ḍaw'* IV, p. 194, no. 495; *Manhal* II, f. 316b; Wiet 1409) (twice).

Tāj al-Dīn ʿAbd al-Razzāq ibn Ibrāhīm al-Qibṭī, known as Ibn al-Hayṣam, d. Dhu al-Ḥijjah 834/August–September 1431 (*Ḍaw'* IV, p. 191, no. 485; *Manhal* II, f. 315b; Wiet 1407) (twice).

Muwaffaq al-Dīn Abū al-Faraj ʿAbd al-Wahhāb al-Qibṭī al-Miṣrī al-Aslamī, d. Rabīʿ II 796/February–March 1394 (*Manhal* III, f. 506b; Wiet 2810).

Taqī al-Dīn ʿAbd al-Wahhāb ibn ʿAbd-Allāh (Mājid) al-Qibṭī al-Miṣrī al-Ḥanafī, known as Ibn Abī Shākir, d. Dhu al-Qaʿdah 819/December 1416–January 1417 (*Ḍaw'* V, p. 102, no. 384; *Manhal* II, f. 359b; Wiet 1487) (three times).

Tāj al-Dīn ʿAbd al-Wahhāb ibn Naṣr-Allāh al-Qibṭī al-Aslamī, known as al-Shaykh al-Khaṭīr, d. Dhu al-Qaʿdah 865/August–September 1461 (*Ḍaw'* V, p. 114, no. 408; *Manhal* II, f. 364b; Wiet 1498) (twice).

ʿAlam al-Dīn ʿAbd al-Wahhāb ibn Qasīs al-Qibṭī al-Qāhirī, known as al-Kātib al-Sayyidī, d. Muḥarram 791/December 1388–January 1389 (*Manhal* II, f. 365b; Wiet 1499) (twice).

Tāj al-Dīn Faḍl-Allāh al-Ramlī al-Qibṭī, d. Ṣafar 826/January–February 1423 (*Ḍaw'* VI, p. 173, no. 585).

Fakhr al-Dīn ʿAbd-Allāh ibn Mūsā al-Qibṭī al-Miṣrī, d. 776/1374–1375 (*Manhal* II, f. 276b; Wiet 1340) (three times).

Saʿd al-Dīn Faraj ibn Mājid al-Qibṭī al-Miṣrī, known as Ibn al-Naḥḥāl, d. Jumādā II 865/March–April 1461 (*Ḍaw'* VI, p. 169, no. 570).

Shams al-Dīn Ibrāhīm ibn ʿAbd-Allāh al-Qibṭī, d. Shaʿbān 798/May–June 1369 (*Manhal* I, p. 57, no. 31; Wiet 31).

Amīn al-Dīn Ibrāhīm ibn ʿAbd al-Ghanī al-Qibṭī, known as Ibn al-Hayṣam, d. Ṣafar 859/January–February 1455 (*Manhal* I, p. 93, no. 49; Wiet 49) (twice).

Saʿd al-Dīn Ibrāhīm ibn ʿAbd al-Karīm al-Qibṭī al-Miṣrī, known as Ibn Kātib Jakam, d. Rabīʿ I 841/September–October 1437 (*Ḍaw'* I, p. 68; *Manhal* I, p. 96, no. 50; Wiet 50) (twice).

Saʿd al-Dīn Ibrāhīm ibn ʿAbd al-Razzāq al-Skandarī al-Miṣrī al-Qibṭī al-Muslimī, known as Ibn Ghurāb, d. Rajab 808/December 1405–January 1406 (*Ḍaw'* I, p. 65; *Manhal* I, p. 85, no. 47; Wiet 47) (twice).

Saʿd al-Dīn Ibrāhīm ibn Barakah al-Miṣrī al-Qibṭī, known as al-Bashīrī, d. Ṣafar 818/April–May 1415 (*Ḍaw'* I, p. 33; *Manhal* I, p. 44, no. 23; Wiet 23) (twice).

Fakhr al-Dīn Mājid ibn ʿAbd al-Razzāq al-Qibṭī al-Skandarī, known as Ibn Ghurāb, d. Dhu al-Ḥijjah 811/April–May 1409 (*Ḍaw'* VI, p. 234; *Manhal* III, f. 71b; Wiet 1949) (twice).

Fakhr al-Dīn Mājid ibn Qarwīnah al-Qibṭī al-Aslamī, d. Jumādā I 768/January–February 1367 (*Manhal* III, f. 72b; Wiet 1951).

Manṣūr ibn al-Ṣafī al-Qibṭī, d. Shawwāl 870/May–June 1466 (*Ḍaw'* X, p. 170, no. 716).

Shams al-Dīn Naṣr-Allāh al-Qibṭī al-Aslamī, known as Ibn al-Najjār, no death date (*Ḍaw'* X. p. 200, no. 855).

Saʿd al-Dīn Naṣr-Allāh al-Qibṭī al-Aslamī al-Qāhirī, known as Ibn al-Baqarī, d. Jamādā II 799/March 1397 (*Manhal* III, f. 383; Wiet 2568) (twice).

ʿAlam al-Dīn Yaḥyā al-Qibṭī al-Miṣrī, d. Rajab 835/March–April 1432 (*Manhal* III, f. 508; Wiet 2813).

Sharaf al-Dīn Yaḥyā al-Qibṭī al-Qāhirī, known as Ibn Ṣanīʿah, d. Muḥarram 882/April–May 1477 (*Ḍaw'* X, p. 268, no. 1061) (twice).

Jamāl al-Dīn Yūsif ibn ʿAbd al-Karīm al-Qibṭī al-Shāfiʿī, known as Ibn Kātib Jakam, d. Dhu al-Ḥijjah 862/October–November 1458 (*Manhal* III, f. 459; Wiet 2710).

In this category 228 positions, 22 percent of 1,039 total reported in the two dictionaries, were held by persons of Coptic ancestry.

Artisan-Service Occupations

In contrast with their prominence in the *diwans* of the Mamluk regime, relatively few persons of Coptic origin engaged in the myriad crafts or manufacturing trades reported in the biographical literature of the later Middle Ages (fourteenth and fifteenth centuries). Their representation among the mercantile networks of Cairo also was surprisingly minimal, especially in light of the regime's sporadic attempts to place the transfer of luxury foreign products, such as spices from south Asia, under state monopoly. More than two hundred references to merchants appeared in the survey (cf. Petry, pp. 242–46). One kind of occupation that Copts sought frequently involved personal service (*khidmah*), either in a bureau of the government or in the household of a grand amir or other eminent official.

Bazzāz: Draper, cloth merchant. Dealing primarily in apparel items rather than elaborately embroidered decorative pieces designed for ceremonials or uniforms.

One position, 5 percent of twenty-two total:

Ibrāhīm ibn Mubārak al-Dhahlī al-Shaybānī al-Qibṭī, born 839/1435–1436 (*Ḍaw'* I, p. 118).

Khādim (pl. khuddām): Servant. One usage suggests domestic employment in a bureau or household with no designation of literary training. The other implies some degree of skill in accountancy, especially when preceding *al-dīwān*. Usually an initial position, mentioned at the beginning of an individual's career. The specialized usage of *khādim* tied to a religious institution (such as *khādim al-jāmi'* or *khādim al-masjid*), indicating status as a pilgrim or Ṣūfī mystic, does not apply to these cases, none of which were associated with religious service.

Eleven positions, 5 percent of 224 total:

Karīm al-Dīn 'Abd al-Karīm ibn Barakah al-Qibṭī al-Miṣrī, known as Ibn Kātib Jakam, d. 833/1429–1430 (*Manhal* II, f. 343; Wiet 1457).

Sa'd al-Dīn Ibrāhīm al-Qibṭī al-Nāṣirī al-Muslimī, known as Ibn al-Mar'ah, d. Rabī' II 844/August–September 1440 (*Ḍaw'* I, p. 184).

Shams al-Dīn Ibrāhīm ibn 'Abd-Allāh al-Qibṭī, known as Kātib Arnān, d. Sha'bān 798/May–June 1396 (*Manhal* I, p. 57, no. 31; Wiet 31).

Sa'd al-Dīn Ibrāhīm ibn 'Abd al-Razzāq al-Aslamī al-Qibṭī al-Skandarī, known as Ibn Ghurāb, d. Rajab 808/December 1405–January 1406 (*Manhal* I, p. 85, no. 47; Wiet 47) (twice).

Sa'd al-Dīn Ibrāhīm ibn Barakah al-Miṣrī al-Qibṭī, known as al-Bashīrī, d. Ṣafar 818/April–May 1415 (*Ḍaw'* I, p. 33) (twice).

Majd al-Dīn Mājid al-Qibṭī al-Naṣrānī al-Aslamī, d. Dhu al-Ḥijjah 843/May–June 1440 (*Ḍaw'* VI, p. 235, no. 813; *Manhal* III, f. 73; Wiet 1952) (three times).

Shams al-Dīn Naṣr-Allāh al-Qibṭī al-Aslamī al-Qāhirī, known as Ibn al-Najjār, no death date (*Ḍaw'* X, p. 200, no. 855).

Khādim al-dīwān (pl. al-dawāwīn): Servant in a financial bureau, presumably the *Dīwān al-Dawlah* or bureau of revenues (see *nāẓir al-dawlah*). This was an entry-level position suggesting apprenticeship in bookkeeping and secretarial skills.

Three positions, 75 percent of four total:

Sa'd al-Dīn Ibrāhīm al-Qibṭī al-Nāṣirī al-Muslimī, known as Ibn al-Mar'ah, d. Rabī' II 844/August–September 1440 (*Ḍaw'* I, p. 184).

Shams al-Dīn Ibrāhīm ibn 'Abd-Allāh al-Qibṭī, known as Kātib Arnān, d. Sha'bān 798/May–June 1396 (*Manhal* I, p. 57; Wiet 31).

Shams al-Dīn Naṣr-Allāh al-Qibṭī al-Aslamī, known as Ibn al-Najjār, no death date (*Ḍaw'* X, p. 200, no. 855).

Khādim al-dīwān al-sulṭānī: Servant in the "Sultan's Department," referring to the Bureau of Reclaims responsible for collecting income from estates of Mamluk amirs who died, or were dismissed and/or demoted before the end of the accounting year (see *Kātib dīwān al-murtaja'āt*). The position occurred only in this case.

One position, 100 percent of one total:

Karīm al-Dīn 'Abd al-Karīm ibn 'Abd al-Razzāq al-Qibṭī al-Miṣrī, known as Ibn Makānis, d. 803/1400–1401 (*Manhal* II, f. 344; Wiet 1460).

Tājir lil-awlād: "Merchant to youths"; in this context, a dealer in children's garments (*farārīj*), as his father had been. Subsequently involved in the East-West trade in spices, the holder of this title was prosperous and founded a *madrasah*. Whether the term *awlād* connoted dealings with the *awlād al-Nās* (descendants of Mamluks) is unclear from the biography.

One position, 100 percent of one total:

Badr al-Dīn Ḥasan ibn Suwayd al-Miṣrī al-Qibṭī al-Mālikī, known as Ibn Suwayd, d. Ṣafar 829/December 1425–January 1426 (*Ḍaw'* III, p. 101, no. 406).

Tājir al-firanj: "Merchant of the Franks." Dealt with European merchants in the import-export trade of luxury goods. In this case, the individual served as a customs inspector in the port of Ṭarābulus, regulating tariffs on cotton sold to Europeans. That this single reference to such a position appeared in a Muslim Copt's career is noteworthy.

One position, 100 percent of one total:

Sa'd al-Dīn Ibrāhīm al-Nāṣirī al-Qibṭī al-Muslimī, known as Ibn al-Mar'ah, d. Rabī' II 844/August–September 1440 (*Ḍaw'* I, p. 184).

Zi'baqī: Dealer in mercury (R. Dozy, *Supplément aux dictionnaires arabes* I, pp. 576–77).

One position, 100 percent of one total:

Ibrāhīm ibn Mubārak al-Dhahlī al-Shaybānī al-Qibṭī, born 839/1435–1436 (*Ḍaw'* I, p. 118).

Nineteen positions, 7 percent of 254 total in this category reported in the two dictionaries, were held by persons of Coptic ancestry.

Literary, Scholarly, and Religious Offices or Titles

Positions in this category, along with specialists in revealed law (*Sharī'ah*), constituted the foundation of the *'ulamā'*, the civil literary elite of premodern Egypt. Since few persons of Christian origin held offices or received titles in this broad field, and none in the legal disciplines, representation of Muslim Copts among the learned establishment of Mamluk Egypt (1250–1517) was insignificant. In theory, Islam is an egalitarian faith with no provision for discrimination among believers, regardless of previous confessional orientation or heritage. But in practice, Coptic converts to Islam or their descendants seem to have been largely excluded from the mainstream of Muslim intellectual life under the Mamluk regime. Yet the occurrence of the following examples, sparse as they may be among the myriad religious and scholarly offices reported in the sources, does prove that entry into the *'ulamā'* class was possible for a few members of the Muslim Coptic community.

Adīb: Man of letters. Connotes accomplishment in the literary arts similar to the title *shā'ir*. The tenth form usage of this root, *ista'daba*, to take on someone as a preceptor (R. Dozy, *Supplément aux dictionnaires arabes* I, 14), did not appear in this case.

One reference, 5 percent of nineteen total:

Fakhr al-Dīn 'Abd al-Raḥmān ibn 'Abd al-Razzāq al-Qibṭī al-Ḥanafī al-Qāhirī, known as Ibn Makānis, d. Dhu al-Ḥijjah 794/October–November 1392 (*Manhal* II, f. 290; Wiet 1370).

Muqri' al-shubbāk: Literally, "reciter of the grid" or "reciter of balustrade" (surrounding a sepulcher); Qur'ān reader in an elevated oratory or gallery of a religious foundation, usually the dome (*qubbah*) of an endowed tomb (in this case, Baybarsiyyah Khāniqāh in Cairo). Though it was a distinction for a Muslim of Coptic ancestry, this was the only reference to an individual of such background in the entire religious category of occupations, according to a survey (cf. C. Petry, *The Civilian Elite of Cairo*, pp. 262–67). Total references to *muqri'īn* alone (without complement) approached two hundred positions. (See also R. Dozy, *Supplément aux dictionnaires arabes* [Leiden, 1927], I, 723, II, 329; G. Makdisi, *The Rise of Colleges*, p. 215.)

One position, 100 percent of one total:

Fakhr al-Dīn ibn al-Ghannām al-Qibṭī al-Ṣūfī, d. Jumādā II 895/April–May 1490 (*Ḍaw'* XI, p. 164, no. 521).

Mutaṣawwif: Specialist in principles/doctrines of mystic (*Ṣūfī*) belief and ritual practice. This individual was probably an instructor (*mudarris* or spiritual guide of novices; in Sa'īd al-Su'adā' and Baybarsīya Khānqāhs). However, the overall number of references to professorships (endowed teaching posts) in all disciplines or without complement approached six hundred in this survey (cf. Petry, *The Civilian Elite of Cairo*, pp. 250–53).

One position, 14 percent of seven total:

Fakhr al-Dīn ibn al-Ghannām al-Qibṭī al-Ṣūfī, d. Jumādā II 895/April–May 1490 (*Ḍaw'* XI, p. 164, no. 521).

Shā'ir: Poet, recognized master of verse. In traditional Muslim societies, a title granted to persons regarded as accomplished in the highest literary art.

Three titles, 2 percent of 186 total:

Fakhr al-Dīn 'Abd al-Raḥmān ibn 'Abd al-Razzāq al-Qibṭī al-Ḥanafī al-Qāhirī, known as Ibn Makānis, d. Dhu al-Ḥijjah 794/October–November 1392 (*Manhal* II, f. 290; Wiet 1370).

Majd al-Dīn Faḍl-Allāh ibn 'Abd al-Raḥmān al-Miṣrī al-Qibṭī al-Ḥanafī, known as Ibn Makānis, d. Rabī' II 822/April–May 1419 (*Ḍaw'* VI, p. 172, no. 581; *Manhal* II, f. 520b; Wiet 1794).

Ibrāhīm ibn Mubārak al-Dhahlī al-Shaybānī al-Qibṭī, born 839/1435–1436 (*Ḍaw'* I, p. 118).

Six references, 2 percent of 213 total reported in these categories in the two dictionaries, were held by persons of Coptic ancestry.

BIBLIOGRAPHY

All references to persons are from the following biographical dictionaries, both compiled in the fifteenth century (but the second listing individuals from the fourteenth): al-Sakhāwī, *Al-Ḍaw' al-Lāmiʿ fī Aʿyān al-Qarn al-Tāsiʿ*, 12 volumes (Cairo, 1934; *GAL* II, 43, no. 1; *GAL Supp.* II, 31–32); and Ibn Taghrī-birdī, *Al-Manhal al-Ṣāfī wa-al-Mustawfī baʿd al-Wāfī*, Vol. I in print (Cairo, 1956), remainder in manuscript (National Library of Cairo, 1113; National Library, Paris, fonds arabe, 2068–73; *GAL* II, no. 4); summary of biographies in G. Wiet, "Les biographies du Manhal Safī," *Mémoires de l'Institut d'Egypte* 19, 1932. Although no practicing Christians were included in these works, the statistics they provide are the most complete available for Coptic officials in the medieval period. Figures listed under specific offices refer to totals reported in the two dictionaries.

M. Perlmann, "Notes on Anti-Christian Propaganda in the Mamluk Empire," *Bulletin of the School of Oriental and African Studies* 10 (1940–1942), 843–61, and "Asnāwī's Tract Against Christian Officials," *Ignaz Goldhizer Memorial Volume*, Vol. 2, pp. 172–208 (Jerusalem, 1958).

For the literature on the subject of deterioration of Dhimmi status in Egypt during the Mamluk period, see G. Wiet, "Ḳibṭ," *Encyclopaedia of Islam*, 1st ed., Vol. 2, pp. 990–1003. See also C. Bosworth in the general bibliography and E. Ashtor-Strauss, "The Social Isolation of the Ahl al-Dhimma," *Etudes orientales à la mémoire de Paul Hirschler*, O. Komolos, ed. (Budapest 1950).

The abbreviation GAL stands for Brockelmann, C. *Geschichte der arabischen Literatur*, 2 vols., 2nd ed. Leiden, 1949. 3 supp. vols. Leiden, 1936–1942.

Arabic sources

ʿAynī, al-. "*ʿIqd al-Jumān fī Tārīkh Ahl al-Islām.*" MS Dār al-Kutub, Tārīkh 1044. *GAL*, Vol. 2, p. 65; Supp. 2, p. 51.

Dimashqī, al-. *Kitāb al-Ishārah ilā Maḥāsin al-Tijārah.* Cairo, 1900–1901.

Ibn Ḥajar al-ʿAsqalānī. *Al-Durar al-Kāminah fī Aʿyān al-Miʾah al-Thāminah*, 4 vols. Hyderabad, 1929–1931. *GAL* 2, p. 83.

———. *Inbāʾ al-Ghumr bi-Anbāʾ al-ʿUmr*, 3 vols. Cairo, 1969–1973. *GAL*, Vol. 2, p. 83.

Ibn Iyās. *Badāʾiʿ al-Zuhūr fī Waqāʾiʿ al-Duhūr*, 5 vols. Istanbul, Cairo, Wiesbaden, 1931–1963.

Ibn Taghrī-birdī. *Al-Nujūm al-Zāhirah fī Mulūk Miṣr wa-al-Qāhirah*, 12 vols. Berkeley, Calif., 1915–1960. *GAL*, Vol. 2, p. 51, no. 1.

———. *Ḥawādith al-Duhūr fī Madā al-Ayyām wa-al-Shuhūr*, 4 vols. Berkeley, Calif., 1930–1931. *GAL*, Vol. 2, p. 52, no. 6.

Jāḥiẓ, al-. *Al-Tabaṣṣur bi-al-Tijārah.* Cairo, 1935. *GAL*, Vol. 1, pp. 152–53; Supp. 1, p. 244.

Jahshiyārī, al-. *Kitāb al-Wizārah wa al-Kuttāb.* Leipzig, 1926.

Khalīl al-Ẓāhirī. *Zubdat Kashf al-Mamālik wa-Bayān al-Ṭuruq wa-al-Masālik.* Paris, 1884.

Māwardī, al-. *Kitāb al-Aḥkām al-Sulṭāniyyah.* Cairo, 1928.

———. *Kitāb Qawānīn al-Wizārah.* Cairo, 1929.

Qalqashandī, al-. *Ṣubḥ al-Aʿshā fī Ṣināʿat al-Inshāʾ*, 14 vols. Cairo, 1914–1928.

Ṣafadī, al-. *Al-Wāfī bi-al-Wafayāt.* Istanbul, 1949, 1953; Damascus, 1959; Wiesbaden, 1962—.

Sakhāwī, al-. *Al-Tibr al-Masbūk fī Dhayl al-Sulūk.* Cairo, 1896–1897. *GAL*, Vol. 2, p. 48, no. 3.

Suyūṭī, al-. *Ḥusn al-Muḥāḍarah fī Akhbār Miṣr wa-al-Qāhirah*, 2 vols. Cairo, 1909. *GAL* 2, p. 157; Supp. 2, p. 196.

Secondary Sources

Ashtor, E. *A Social and Economic History of the Near East in the Middle Ages.* Berkeley, Calif., 1976.

Atiya, A. "Ḳibṭ." In *Encyclopaedia of Islam*, 2nd ed., Vol. 5, pp. 90–95.

Ayalon, D. "The Circassians in the Mamluk Kingdom." *Journal of the American Oriental Society* 69 (1949):135–47.

———. "Studies on the Structure of the Mamluk Army." *Bulletin of the School of Oriental and African Studies* 15 (1953):202–238, 448–76; 16 (1954):57–90.

———. "The System of Payment in Mamluk Military Society." *Journal of the Economic and Social History of the Orient* 1 (1957):37–65; Orient 1 (1958):257–96.

———. "Discharges from Service, Banishments and Imprisonments in Mamluk Society." *Israel Oriental Studies* 2 (1972):25–50.

———. "Aspects of the Mamluk Phenomenon." *Der Islam* 53, no. 2 (1976):196–225; 54, no. 1 (1977):1–32.

Babinger, F. "Wazīr." In *Encyclopaedia of Islam*, 1st ed., Vol. 4, pp. 1135–36.

Björkmman, W. "Beiträge zur Geschichte des Staatskanzlei im islamischen Ägypten." *Hamburgische Universität, Abhandlungen aus dem Gebiet der Auslandkunde*, ser. B, 16 (1928).

Bosworth, C. E. "Christian and Jewish Religious Dignitaries in Mamluk Egypt and Syria: Qalqashandī's Information on Their Hierarchy, Titulature and Appointment." *International Journal of Middle East Studies* 3 (1972):59–74, 199–216.

———. "Recruitment, Muster and Review in Medieval Islamic Armies." In *War, Technology and Society in the Middle East,* ed. V. Parry and M. Yapp, pp. 59–77. Oxford, 1975.

———. "Protected Peoples (Christians and Jews) in Medieval Egypt and Syria." *Bulletin of the John Rylands Library* 62 (1979):11–36.

Cheikho, L. *Les Vizirs et secrétaires arabes chrétiens en Islam 622–1577,* ed. Camille Hechaïmé, S. J. Al-Turāth al-'Arabī al-Masīḥī II. Lebanon and Rome, 1987. Text in Arabic. Title pages in Arabic and French. Introduction in Arabic and French.

Escovitz, J. H. "Vocational Patterns of the Scribes of the Mamluk Chancery." *Arabica* 23 (1976):46–62.

Gril, D. "Une émeute anti-chrétienne à Qūṣ au début du VIIIe–XIVe siècle." *Annales islamologiques* 16 (1980):243–74.

Krenkow, F. "Kātib." In *Encyclopaedia of Islam,* 1st ed., Vol. 2, p. 819.

Labib, S. *Handelgeschichte Ägyptens im Spätmittelalter (1171–1517).* Wiesbaden, 1965.

Lapidus, I. *Muslim Cities in the Later Middle Ages.* Cambridge, 1967.

Little, D. P. "Coptic Conversion to Islam Under the Baḥrī Mamlūks." *Bulletin of the School of Oriental and African Studies* 39 (1976):552–69.

Makdisi, G. "Madrasa and University in the Middle Ages." *Studia Islamica* 32 (1970):255–64.

———. *The Rise of Colleges, Institutions of Higher Learning in Islam and the West.* Edinburgh, 1981. Extensive bibliography.

Perlmann, M. "Notes on Anti-Christian Propaganda in the Mamluk Empire." *Bulletin of the School of Oriental and African Studies* 10 (1940–1942):843–61.

———. "Asnāwī's Tract Against Christian Officials." *Ignace Goldziher Memorial Volume,* Vol. 2, pp. 172–208. Jerusalem, 1958.

Petry, C. "Geographic Origins of Dīwān Officials in Cairo During the Fifteenth Century." *Journal of Economic and Social History of the Orient* 21 (1978): pt. 2, pp. 166–84.

———. *The Civilian Elite of Cairo in the Later Middle Ages.* Princeton, 1981.

Popper, W. *Egypt and Syria Under the Circassian Sultans.* Vols. 15–16 of University of California Publications in Semitic Philology. Berkeley, 1955–1957. Indices of offices.

Rabie, H. *The Financial System of Egypt, A.H. 564–741/A.D. 1169–1341.* Oxford, 1972.

Richards, D. "The Coptic Bureaucracy Under the Mamluks." In *Colloque international sur l'histoire du Caire,* pp. 373–81. Cairo, 1969.

Sourdel, D., with R. Sellheim. "Kātib." In *Encyclopaedia of Islam,* 2nd ed., Vol. 4, pp. 754–57.

———. *Le vizirat 'abbaside.* Damascus, 1959.

Strauss, E. "The Social Isolation of the Ahl al-Dhimma." In *Etudes orientales à la mémoire de Paul Hirschler,* ed. O. Komlos. Budapest, 1950.

Tritton, A. *Materials on Muslim Education in Medieval Times.* London, 1957.

Wensinck, A. "Khādim." In *Encyclopaedia of Islam,* 2nd ed., Vol. 4, p. 899.

Wiet, G. "Ḳibṭ." In *Encyclopaedia of Islam,* 1st ed., Vol. 2, pp. 990–1003.

———. "Les secrétaires de la chancellerie (*kuttāb-al-sirr*) en Egypte sous les Mamlouks circassiens (784–922/1382–1517)." In *Mélanges René Basset.* Paris, 1925.

———. "L'Egypte arabe." In *Histoire de la nation egyptienne,* ed. G. Hanotaux. Paris, 1937.

CARL F. PETRY

CORNELIUS, one of the prominent "ancient brothers" of the Pachomian *koinonia* (community). He belonged to the second group of disciples who came to PACHOMIUS around 324 (Lefort, Sahidic-Bohairic 24; Halkin, 1982, Greek, recension 1, 26), and he was appointed by him as father of the Monastery of Tmoushons shortly after it was received into the *koinonia* (Lefort, Sahidic-Bohairic 51.59; Halkin, Greek, recension 1, 54.61). He is mentioned among the elders at the time of Theodorus' appointment as father of Tabennēsē in 336–337 (Halkin, Greek, recension 1, 79), as well as at the time of the great trial of Theodorus around 344 (Halkin, Greek, recension 1, 106). He died in 346 during the same plague that carried away Pachomius and many others among the early Pachomian brothers (Lefort, Sahidic-Bohairic 119; Halkin, Greek, recension 1, 114).

According to the witness of Pachomius (Lefort, Sahidic-Bohairic 91; Halkin, Greek, recension 1, 111), Cornelius struggled to acquire all the fruits of the Holy Spirit and had therefore purified his heart to the point of not having any distraction during communal prayer. He was also a man of wisdom capable of answering the questions of some philosophers from ASHMŪN (Lefort, Sahidic-Bohairic 55; Halkin, Greek, recension 1, 82). With SOUROUS, he was one of the two persons with whom Pachomius exchanged letters in a cryptic language.

[*See also:* Monasticism, Pachomian.]

BIBLIOGRAPHY

Halkin, F. *Sancti Pachomii vitae graecae.* Subsidia Hagiographica 19. Brussels, 1982.

Lefort, L. T. *S. Pachomii vita bohairice scripta.* CSCO 89. Louvain, 1925, 1953.

______. *S. Pachomii vitae sahidice scriptae.* CSCO 99, 100. Louvain, 1933–1934. Repr. 1952.

ARMAND VEILLEUX

CORPUS HERMETICUM. *See* Hermes Trismegistus.

COSMAS I, forty-fourth patriarch of the See of Saint Mark (730–731) (feast day: 30 Ba'ūnah). He was a native of the town of Banā, near Samannūd in the Gharbiyyah Province. Little is known about his secular life before he took the monastic vow in the wilderness of Anbā Maqār.

Cosmas had a monastic life distinguished by sanctity, humility, and self-denial. When the Coptic archons unanimously decided to nominate him for the patriarchate, he was reticent to accept their invitation and protested that he was unworthy of occupying the throne of Saint Mark. Nevertheless, the community of the faithful forced him to accede to their wishes, and he was consequently consecrated patriarch.

His accession, however, came at a time when the political and economic circumstances of the Umayyad empire were precarious, and this had dire repercussions for the Coptic community in Egypt. In spite of the lenient position of Caliph Hishām ibn 'Abd al-Malik (724–743), who issued a special circular to his agents in al-Fusṭāṭ (Cairo) not to pressure their subjects and to permit the church legally to pursue its tradition without disturbance in conformity with the COVENANT OF 'UMAR, the governors of the country did not waiver in imposing economic sanctions beyond the normal KHARAJ (community tax), not only on the Copts in general but also on the church and even the monasteries. Cosmas had no way to ease the hardships of the imposts except by common prayers to fortify the morale of the community, without incurring the use of force that had marked the reign of his predecessor, Alexander II. Thus, his short reign of fifteen months was concluded peacefully in spite of the economic hardships.

BIBLIOGRAPHY

Atiya, A. S. *History of Eastern Christianity.* London, 1968.

Cambridge History of Islam, 2 vols. ed. P. M. Holt, A. K. S. Lambton, and B. Lewis. Cambridge, 1970.

Hitti, P. K. *History of the Arabs.* London, 1946.

Lane-Poole, S. *History of Egypt in the Middle Ages.* London, 1901.

SUBHI Y. LABIB

COSMAS II, fifty-fourth patriarch of the See of Saint Mark (851–858). A native of Samannūd, Cosmas joined Dayr Anbā Magar as a deacon and then became a presbyter. He was still there when he was summoned by the bishops, the clergy, and the archons of the city of Alexandria to occupy the throne of Saint Mark. His enthronement was hailed by the community of the faithful. It is said that people from adjacent villages and towns came in crowds to Alexandria to render homage to the new patriarch and to offer their pious dues to the church. But in the harangue that followed, fighting broke out between the congregated parties and one person was accidentally killed. The governor of Alexandria at the time, Aḥmad ibn Dīnār, on hearing of the unfortunate incident, held the patriarch responsible and put him under house arrest. The governor requested that the patriarch yield to the Islamic administration all the offerings collected, thus leaving him without capital while retaining him under arrest. Two Coptic archons, Maqārah ibn Yūsuf and Ibrāhīm ibn Sāwīrus, both secretaries at the central administration in al-Fusṭāṭ (Cairo), were able to prevail upon the governor of Egypt, 'Abd al-Wāḥid ibn Yaḥyā, who held the title of vizier, to summon the patriarch to al-Fusṭāṭ ostensibly to pay the KHARAJ (community tax) but actually to free him from incarceration at Alexandria. While they helped him to raise the tax, they decided that Cosmas should leave Alexandria and reside in the Christian town of DAMRŪ, east of Miṣr (HISTORY OF THE PATRIARCHS, Vol. 2, p. 3), which for the first time became the seat of the patriarchate instead of Alexandria. At Damrū the patriarch worked hard on developing the local churches and sent, with two of his bishops, his synodical epistle to the patriarch of Antioch, John (Yuḥannā). The Abbasid caliph at Baghdad at the time was Ja'far al-Mutawakkil (847–861), and apparently both patriarchs suffered much persecution at his hands. According to the *History of the Patriarchs* (Vol. 2, pt. 1, p. 6), Egypt seems to have fared the worst, for the caliph appointed a Pharisee named al-Ghayr 'Abd al-Masīḥ ibn Isḥāq, a curious name, probably of an Islamized Eastern Christian, as overseer of the taxes and as governor, with explicit orders to give the Copts no respite on his extraordinary financial imposts.

Consequently, a fierce wave of oppression was inaugurated in Egypt. This was not confined to unusual financial demands but also extended to religion and the social order. In matters of religion, all crosses were to be broken, and the ringing of bells was forbidden. Christian prayers were virtually silenced, and the sale of wine was prohibited in order to deprive the priesthood of the use of sacramental wine. In response, Christians would procure grapevines, soak them in water, and press them for juice as a substitute to the wine in the celebration of the liturgy. Even prayers for the dead were forbidden and "He [al-Ghayr ʿAbd al-Masīḥ] became even as Diocletian, and his deeds were as his" (*History of the Patriarchs,* Vol. 2, pt. 1, p. 7). Profane images of devils and pigs were nailed on the entrances of churches, and a movement toward destruction of churches was begun. To humiliate the Christians socially, people were prohibited from riding horses, and they were ordered to wear their dresses dyed in black to distinguish them from Muslims. Matters were made worse by the issuance of a caliphal decree to dismiss all Copts from the government administration and to replace them with Muslims or Islamized Christians. As a result, many of the Christians, to save themselves from humiliation and utter poverty, apostatized to Islam. These included even prominent Copts, such as Stephen (Uṣṭufān) ibn Andūnah, a noted scribe, who converted to Islam with the rest of his children and his family.

However, not long after the replacement of Copts by Muslims in the administration, the finances of the country began to suffer ostensible depletion. Even wealthy Muslims, such as Ibn Saʿīd al-Asfahānī, were victimized by Muslim functionaries. Apparently the poll tax (JIZYAH), which had been two dinars, now became as high as fifteen dinars. Living in the country became almost intolerable, and many Copts preferred to abjure their faith to save their skins, while the helpless patriarch looked upon the sordid situation in tears. A new functionary, al-Ḥārith ibn Miskīn, proved to be even worse than his predecessor, and the persecution of the Copts continued.

At that time, Byzantine raiders attacked and pillaged the city of Damietta, and the governor employed Coptic slave labor to reinforce the walls of that city as well as other vulnerable cities, such as Alexandria, Rosetta, Burullus, and other coastal towns.

Eventually the authorities became aware of the need to restore the Copts to the administration in order to salvage the depleted economy. Also, the Copts were employed in shipbuilding and manning the fleet, and in the manipulation of seafaring craft. These were badly needed by the Muslims in defense of their coastal fortifications, as well as for launching counterraids on Byzantine shores and islands. Thus, it appears that, at the end of the reign of Caliph al-Mutawakkil, the worst pressures on the Copts in Egypt were partially lifted. More attention was given to constructive projects, such as the dredging of the Alexandrian harbor to encourage the travel of foreign merchant ships to promote international commerce and to improve agriculture. This explains the return of relative prosperity to the country during the closing days of the patriarchate of Cosmas II, who died during his construction of a church at the village of Danūshar in the diocese of Sakhā on 21 Hātūr. Apparently he was buried in that church.

BIBLIOGRAPHY

Lane-Poole, S. *History of Egypt in the Middle Ages.* London, 1901.

Muir, W. *The Caliphate: Its Rise, Decline and Fall.* Edinburgh, 1924.

Weil, G. *Geschichte der Chalifen,* 5 vols. Mannheim, 1846–1862.

SUBHI Y. LABIB

COSMAS III, fifty-eighth patriarch of the See of Saint Mark (920–932). Cosmas apparently succeeded GABRIEL I without complications about his selection. His life is treated very briefly in the HISTORY OF THE PATRIARCHS, despite his relatively long reign of twelve years. Nothing on his internal relations with the Islamic administration is cited in his biography, and the only item of an international character that is cited concerns his nomination of a certain Buṭrus as archbishop for the diocese of Ethiopia.

It is said that the Ethiopian monarch entrusted Buṭrus with caring for his two sons after his death and that Buṭrus gave the crown to the younger son, who seemed more suitable for running the affairs of the kingdom. Later, a monk by the name of Mīnā, of Dayr Anbā Antūniyus, and a companion came to Ethiopia and requested funds from the archbishop, who refused. They conspired against him by submitting false letters from the patriarch to the older son. The letters stated that Mīnā was the real appointee to the Ethiopian diocese and that Buṭrus was an impostor. Consequently, the older son mustered an army and, with the new pretender, defeated the younger brother, seized the crown, and exiled Buṭrus.

Later, Mīnā and his companion quarreled over the episcopal treasure, and their trick was exposed. The disagreement ended in their dismissal and an appeal was made for the return of the rightful dignity. But Buṭrus had died in the interval, and the Ethiopian diocese remained vacant during the reign of five successive patriarchs. Meanwhile, the new sovereign had Mīnā killed and invested the assistant of Buṭrus with the duties of his master's office, despite the fact that he was not properly consecrated by Cosmas. Cosmas died on 3 Baramhāt.

SUBHI Y. LABIB

COSMAS AND DAMIAN, SAINTS, two doctors and brothers who suffered martyrdom at the time of the Diocletian persecutions (feast day: 22 Hātūr). They were called *anargyroi* (silverless) because they did not ask money from the sick whom they cured. The Byzantine church, however, gradually came to distinguish *three* pairs of brothers named Cosmas and Damian, who suffered, respectively, in Arabia under the emperor Hadrian, at Rome under Carinus, and finally in Asia after Diocletian. Such was the opinion of the patriarch Methodius in the ninth century.

It has become clear that all three groups derive from Pheremma, a place near Cyr in Cilicia. The cult of the *Anargyroi* spread with extraordinary vigor because, as healing saints, they gradually supplanted their pagan predecessors Castor and Pollux, the Dioscuri. Numerous collections of cures were added to the many forms of the legend.

The shortest account, from Asia, is scarcely a martyrdom. Cosmas and Damian practice medicine without charge at Pheremma. One day Damian, for fear of hurting the feelings of a poor woman named Palladia, accepts three eggs. Cosmas tells him that henceforth they will always work together but that after death they should be buried separately. Damian dies first. Cosmas thereafter heals a camel with a broken foot. Cosmas also dies, and at the moment of his burial the people hesitate to comply with the brothers' request. But the camel announces in a human voice that the brothers are not to be separated in the tomb. This meager report presupposes the tomb at Pheremma and the commemoration on 1 November at Constantinople.

This story was taken up by Simeon Metaphrastes. It exists in Latin, Georgian, and Arabic versions, and is generally followed by accounts of miracles. In Greek, fifty-seven different arrangements have been counted for sixty-two miracles. Some of them occur in Georgian or in Arabic.

The second group may be called Roman. The feast day is 1 July. The doctors are denounced before the emperor Carinus, who has them brought to Rome. At the time of their interrogation, the *Anargyroi* threaten the emperor with a stiff neck, and in fact, the emperor suddenly has his head inverted on his shoulders. Bewildered, he cries for mercy and proclaims the true God. He is then cured and decrees an edict of tolerance throughout the empire. Returning to their own country, the doctors are the victims of an ambush by a jealous colleague, who kills them by guile in the mountains. There are no miracles associated with this legend. But already in the Syriac version one fifth- or sixth-century witness relates the episode of the eggs, attaching it to a persecution of Kurinos and to the emperor's stiff neck. The two forms were thus not distinguished in Syria. What is more, the historian Malalas knew the story in the sixth century. Far from traveling to Rome, the brothers cured Carinus at the time of his campaign against the Persians to avenge his brother Numerian. When the emperor leaves the region of Cyr, their jealous colleague ambushes the saints. In spite of an interchange of Carinus and Numerian effected by Malalas, this version eliminates every difference between the Asiatic and the Roman groups.

In the third group, the Arabic, there is a Passion of the classic type in which the five brothers Cosmas, Damian, Anthimus, Leontius, and Euprepius are indicted before the tribunal of Lysias at Aegae in Cilicia. At the time of their examination they declare that they are natives of "Arabia." They undergo drowning, scourging, fire, and the cross, and then are beheaded. The feast is on 17 October.

What appears in Coptic and Arabic is a combination of two legends, of which the substance is as follows. Under Diocletian and Maximian, the widow Theodotē lives with her five sons in the castle called Son of God (the name Theodotē does not occur elsewhere, save in the Asiatic group). The two eldest sons, Cosmas and Damian, are doctors. The stories of the eggs and the camel appear in this account. Next it is explained how Diocletian, who apparently recognized this hospital of the Son of God, turned against the Christians. The bishop of Antioch agreed to hold the son of the shah of Persia as a hostage on the emperor's behalf. Seduced by rich gifts from the shah, the bishop sets the hostage free. When Diocletian comes to reclaim him, the bishop says that he is dead and hands over another body, swearing by all that is most sacred in Christianity that this is the corpse of the shah's son. But Diocletian produces the young man, whom he had captured alive, and subjects the bishop and all Christianity, by which he had sworn, to the most wretched persecution. Cosmas and Damian are then summoned to Antioch and suffer torture under the prefect Lysias. They come from Arabia, from the city of Dabarma (an Arabic corruption of the Coptic *tpherema* for Pheremma). The three other brothers are subsequently called to suffer the same fate. The archangel Michael heals them, and Lysias is replaced by Claudius. After a fruitless attempt to drown the brothers, they are cast into the fire in the middle of the great theater at Antioch. But the pillar to which they are bound falls to the ground and the whole earth begins to tremble. Theodotē their mother is executed. Victor, son of Romanus, has the courage to bury her. That is why he is banished to Egypt, where he will become a famous martyr. The story is followed by seven miracles, of which three are unknown among the sixty-two Greek miracles.

This text combines the Asiatic and the Arabic groups, and excludes the Roman. Two features connect this legend with the Coptic literature: the presence of Victor and the attitude with regard to the events at Antioch as a whole. The son of the shah of Persia appears in a series of other Passions, but there he bears the name of Nicomedes: the Passions of Claudius, Basilides, John and Symeon, Justus, Epimeus, and also the eulogy of Theodorus. This is the cycle of Basilides, in which the martyrs are artificially united into a family. But the very name of Nicomedes is no accident. It was at Nicomedia that ARIANISM chiefly flourished. The memory of Paul of Samosata, the bishop of Antioch shortly before the coming of Diocletian, is not strange to the presentation of this legend. Paul of Samosata was deposed for corruption before Diocletian came to power. Elsewhere the memory of emperors favorable to Christianity is probable.

The group of seven miracles has been preserved in Coptic at the beginning of a manuscript in the Pierpont Morgan Library (Codex 586, dated from 844, fols. 8–15). Mutilated though it is at the beginning, it preserves some interesting details. At the time of the miracles, the five martyrs are all called twice by their names. The martyrdom of the brothers is fixed on 22 Hatūr and 10 Ba'ūnah. This last date is explicitly proclaimed as the day of the victory of Constantine, who is said to have taken part on this occasion in a eucharistic liturgy on the day when the bones of the saints were gathered from the dust for burial at Pheremma. The text continues that this was the day on which the icon of the Son of God, which Diocletian had torn down, was set up again. This last detail is clearly linked with the exordium of the Coptic-Arabic Passion, in which Constantine repairs what a genuinely deceived Diocletian had destroyed.

The astonishing thing about this legend is that, apart from its elements of fiction at Antioch, it rather coincides with the Latin Passion, which serves as the basis for the inauguration of the cult at Rome under Pope Felix IV toward 530. In no Passion is the need to explain Diocletian's *volte-face* more perceptible than in the Copto-Arabic form of the legend of the *Anargyroi.* The real opposition between the groups of *Anargyroi* is between the Roman group known to Malalas and the Coptic Arabic group, which both go back to the tradition of Pheremma, near Cyr. The cycle of the king of Persia's son, Nicomedes, could have its roots in the justification of Diocletian, who at first was favorable to the *Anargyroi.* This favor might even be a consequence of Carinus' edict of tolerance. But the fact remains that the ambush by the jealous rival is irreconcilable with the martyrdom of the five brothers, except in their final conjunction well after the persecutions under Constantine.

The Coptic documents on the Passion are very widely scattered. They have in part been collected by W. Till (1935; this includes a leaf from Naples, one from Berlin, and three from Paris, to which must be added the leaf, now burnt, used by Lefort, 1940, pp. 40–41. This page immediately precedes the Coptic 102, 8 in the National Library, Paris. The mutilated series of the miracles are in the Pierpont Morgan Library, manuscript MS 586).

The Copto-Arabic Passion would be difficult to reconstruct without the help of the parallel Arabic versions. An Arabic version has been published by Yuḥannā Sulaymān (1926; cf. Graf, 1947, p. 501). But more numerous witnesses are extant:

Mingana Syriac manuscript 367 (Garshuni, thirteenth century), fols. 98–114
Oxford, Hunt 470 manuscript (1577)
Oxford, Bodleian, manuscript 3266, Selden 54 (fourteenth century)
British Museum, Oriental 4723 (seventeenth century), fols. 1–13
Paris, Arabic manuscript 4776 (1896), fols. 33–59
Paris, Arabic manuscript 4879 (nineteenth century), fols. 54–111 and 111–21, four miracles
Mingana Syriac manuscript 240 (1686), fols. 25–41 and 41–48. These texts present a group of seven miracles that are also found in the Cairo

manuscript 712 (fourteenth century), fols. 339–47 (Graf, 1934, p. 266).

Mingana Syriac manuscript 562 (1815), fols. 219–28

Paris, Arabic manuscript 154 (seventeenth century), fols. 38–53

Mingana Syriac manuscript 22 (1527), fols. 4–29

as well as in manuscripts inadequately described, such as Sharfet 11/6 (twelfth century), Beirut 625 (seventeenth century), and Gotha 2882, fols. 97–104. The fragment in Paris 258, fols. 250v, contains the third miracle of Rupprecht's Greek series (Bibliotheca Hagiographica Graeca 373b). But the Arabic tradition has also inherited texts from the other collections which have still hardly been studied.

In the Asiatic group, we have the Sinai Arabic manuscript 540 (twelfth century), fols. 40 and 534 (thirteenth century), fols. 293. For the miracles, Sinai Arabic manuscript 540 contains a collection of twenty stories in fols. 42–104.

In the uncontaminated Arabic group, the Arabic version (Bibliotheca Hagiographica Graeca 378) will be found in two manuscripts in the British Museum: Or. 5019 (eleventh century) and Sinai Arabic manuscript 534 (thirteenth century); for the Passion, see Bibliotheca Hagiographica Graeca 379, on 17 October, Sinai Arabic codex 540, fols. 33–40).

BIBLIOGRAPHY

Esbroeck, M. van. "La Diffusion orientale de la légende des saints Cosme et Damien." *Hagiographie, cultures et sociétés IVe–XIIe siècles*, pp. 61–77. Collection Etudes augustiniennes. Paris, 1981.

Graf, G. *Catalogue des manuscrits arabes chrétiens conservés au Caire*. Vatican City, 1934.

Malalas, J. *Joannis Malalae Chronographia*, ed. Ludwig A. Dindorf. Bonn, 1831.

Till, W. *Koptische Heiligen- und Märtyrerlegender*, Vol. 1, pp. 156–63. Rome, 1935.

Yuḥannā Sulaymān, *Tuḥfat al-zamān fī sīrat al-fārisayn Quzmān wa-Damyān*. Cairo, 1926.

MICHEL VAN ESBROECK

COSMAS INDICOPLEUSTES, the name given to an anonymous Nestorian author of the twelve-book *Christian Topography*, written a few years before the Second Council of CONSTANTINOPLE (553). Cosmas was an Egyptian merchant, probably from Alexandria, who plied his trade in Alexandria, the Red Sea port of Adulis (Sawākin), and Ceylon (Sri Lanka), calling at the island of Socotra and the ports of the Malabar Coast of south India on the way. He had probably sailed as far north as the Somali Coast (Zingion) (II.30).

Cosmas was a man of his time, one for whom interest in theological questions took precedence over those of topography and animal life, with which he was also profoundly and intelligently concerned. He eventually became a monk. Though he had never studied theological questions systematically, he claimed to be a follower of the Nestorian catholicos Mār Aba (540–552) (II.2). The Nestorian tendency of his biblical exegesis is shown by the influence of works of Diodorus of Tarsus, THEODORUS OF MOPSUESTIA, and SEVERIAN OF JABALAH (especially the last named), all representatives of the Antiochene theological school, at a time when this school was increasingly under threat of condemnation by Emperor JUSTINIAN (527–565) and his advisers. At the same time, Cosmas made use of the festal letters of Athanasius, the writings of SEVERUS OF ANTIOCH, and writings of the Monophysite patriarchs of Alexandria, TIMOTHY III (517–535) and THEODOSIUS I (535–567; died in exile in Constantinople in 567), if these appeared (whether inadvertently or not) to support his two-nature theology and belief in man's destiny to dwell with Christ in heaven after the Resurrection. Also of interest is Cosmas's knowledge of Alexandrian, pagan, and anti-Jewish writers, such as Manetho, Apollonius Molon, and Apion, who demonstrated, to Cosmas's approval (XII.4), that Moses was the leader of a scurvy band of beggars who revolted against Egypt and formed the Jewish nation.

The *Christian Topography* was written over a period of years: the first five books were compiled for a friend, Pamphilus, and the remainder as occasion arose: partly to answer critics of the original books, partly to provide evidence from earlier writers for the truth of his understanding of scripture, and (bk. XI) to describe the animals and other curiosities he had encountered in his travels, especially to the island of Taprobane (Ceylon).

The first concern of Cosmas, however, was theology. He aimed at proving, contrary to prevailing Greek and some Christian theories, that the universe had the same shape as Moses' tabernacle (see III.51), that it was in the form of a cube and not a sphere. The earth was a flat, oblong table, 12,000 miles long and 6,000 miles wide, surrounded by ocean (II.24, 47, 48) beyond which was Paradise, where Adam and Eve had lived (cf. II.43). The whole area was surrounded by high, perpendicular mountains on which the vault of heaven rested. Between heaven and earth lay the firmament, dividing the universe into two stages. God and the just dwelt on the upper level, to which man would be admitted after the Resurrection; on the lower was humanity in this life.

The geographical descriptions that Cosmas provides are therefore incidental to his main purpose, but they are nonetheless very accurate. As a young man he was in Adulis at the outbreak of the war between the kingdom of Axum and the Himyarites of southern Arabia (522), and he describes monuments set up long before, by Ptolemy III Euergetes (246–221 B.C.) in that port (II.56–63). He also refers to numerous Alexandrian traders established there. His work is valuable for the evidence it provides of the spread of Christianity down the Nile Valley, to Socotra, to south India, and to Ceylon. He refers to the kingdom of Meroë and the cataracts of the Nile (VI.6), but—perhaps significantly—there is no description of the Nubian kingdoms to which Justinian and Theodora were sending missions about the time Cosmas was writing. For Meroë and ideas about the sources of the Nile he relies on current tradition.

Cosmas shows how by the middle of the sixth century the discoveries concerning the physical universe made in previous ages were being superseded by others that were more fanciful, based on what was believed to be the meaning of the literal text of the Bible. Cosmas, however, retains his interest through his meticulous descriptions, often illustrated, of what he saw during his travels. In particular, he provides evidence for the continuance of Alexandria as a major trading center for goods imported into the Byzantine Empire from the countries bordering the Indian Ocean.

BIBLIOGRAPHY

Cosmas Indocopleustes. *Christian Topography.* In PG 88, cols. 52–476. Paris, 1864.

Leclercq, H. "Kosmas Indicopleustès." *Dictionnaire d'Archéologie chrétienne et de liturgie,* Vol. 8, cols. 820–49. Paris, 1928.

Peterson, E. "Die alexandrinische Liturgie bei Cosmas Indicopleustes." *Ephemerides liturgicae* 46 (1932):66–74.

Winstedt, E. O. *The Christian Topography of Cosmas Indicopleustes.* Cambridge, 1909.

Wolska-Conus, *Cosmas Indicopleustes—Topographie chrétienne.* Sources chrétiennes 141, 159, 197. Paris, 1968–1973.

W. H. C. FREND

COSTUME, CIVIL. Fabrics preserved in public collections are very often in fragments, whether because they were discovered in a poor state of preservation or because a single garment was divided at the end of the excavation. The dating of these textiles is generally agreed to be a sensitive matter, since they most frequently come from clandestine excavations. Their classification therefore depends on the style and not the archaeological context. Some official excavations, such as those at Akhmīm, the Fayyūm, and Antinoë (ANTINOOPOLIS), have enriched the museums. Most often, unfortunately, these discoveries have not been published or are mentioned only in passing in the publications (excavations of Clédat at Bāwīṭ), or are not reproduced in photographs. Finally, certain important collections have regrettably not yet been published systematically (Coptic Museum, Cairo; Metropolitan Museum, New York).

Comparing preserved remains and representations of clothed personages is also helpful in analyzing Coptic civilian costume. Stelae and reliefs treat garments in rather summary fashion, but they are richer in information when painted details have survived. Wall paintings, generally more precise, portray civilians only rarely. Some textiles depict clothed figures, and may thus be used to determine the arrangement of the pieces that composed the costume.

Finally, the clothes in use in Egypt in the first centuries of the Christian era are abundantly represented by portraits, masks, and funerary cloths.

Headdresses

The custom of Coptic women wearing a headdress was respected from the beginning of the Christian era until well after the Arab conquest. This custom, common to the peoples of the Mediterranean basin, had a symbolic significance in Christian eyes, according to CLEMENT OF ALEXANDRIA, since it represented the power of man over woman (*Paedagogus* 3.11). Hence in paintings and on stelae, women are always depicted with their heads covered and are generally draped in a large shawl or veil. Pieces of clothing specially intended for the head were also manufactured by the Copts.

If they appear only rarely in paintings or on stelae, bonnets are frequently mentioned by the archaeologists (Quibell at Saqqara, Gayet at Antinoë), who describe their material (linen, wool, or silk) and their decoration. These bonnets, put together from several parts, may according to the wealth of their owner have been cut from coarse linen cloth or decorated with a subtle combination of colored ribbons sewn on a background of linen of extremely fine texture (fragmentary mummy head, Louvre). Others are adorned with chenilles of colored wool or tapestry motifs.

Corresponding, no doubt, to the period during which discriminatory measures were taken against the Copts by the caliph Hārūn al-Rashīd, some bonnets carry a sewn decoration of two stripes that form a cross (Louvre, TC 2479). It was from the tenth century on that bonnets of multicolored silk were manufactured for women as well as children. Their use, obviously reserved for the highest classes in the population, continued beyond this period. There are only very few bonnets in the collections, and they are generally fragmentary (Louvre, 8241).

Museums do possess numerous head bands (fillets) executed in a plaiting often given the name *sprang* in unbleached linen and colored wool. Such textiles were often called "net," "lace," or "*filet de dentelle*." Their use is mentioned by Gayet, who says he has even discovered some worn under a bonnet. If the fillets of conical form indisputably belong to this category of headdress (Louvre, TC2486, TC2483, TC2474; Victoria and Albert Museum, 32, 142, 143, 144; Musées Royaux d'Art et d'Histoire, Brussels), it is more difficult to classify the numerous rectangular fillets whose form, like their technique and decoration, may lead to some confusion with headbags.

If fillets and bonnets do not appear in pictorial evidence, a feminine fashion widespread in the Byzantine period is attested by plaster statuettes, which show women wearing a thick pad surrounding the head and knotted at the nape of the neck or under the chin. This arrangement is confirmed by the tombs of women discovered at Antinoë by Gayet and then Donadoni. Some pads consist of tufts of multicolored wool threaded on a cord (Louvre, AF6258). Others, executed in fabrics either plaited or in the *sprang* style, are stuffed with horsehair or wool (Louvre, 868, B149); others again, stuffed in the same way, are made of a thick web of discarded pieces of material (Louvre, no. C350).

According to archaeological evidence, these pads could be worn over head fillets. If these pads seem to be a survival of the crown of justification deposited on the mummies in the pharaonic period, it is more probable in the Coptic period that the head pad was a simple piece of civilian dress. In fact, women are depicted in numerous paintings dressed in a shawl bulging out on the forehead, as if this part of the head was upholstered with a pad. Moreover, some pads have been found sewn to a small shawl. This fashion could have been introduced into Egypt from Palmyra, where it was much in favor, as witnessed by the female funerary busts found at this site. It is more difficult to determine the use of small leather pads with openwork and gilded decoration, which have been discovered at the neck of some mummies and whose dimensions are sensibly smaller than those of the fabric examples (Louvre, X4852; British Museum, 26563).

Shawls

The shawl, together with the tunic, is the piece of clothing best represented in the collections, and its almost systematic use is confirmed both by the pictorial evidence and by the archaeologists. Different types of shawls seem to have been in use. One most frequently represented consists of a large rectangular piece of fabric draped around the shoulders and the waist (covering the head when it is worn by women), leaving one arm free. This arrangement is reproduced on a painting from Antinoë representing the deceased Theodosia in her tomb and on a number of mummy cloths. This type of shawl could equally be used as a blanket, as is shown by several Coptic terms employed indiscriminately in the sense of "outer garment." This practice should be compared with the Greek habit of using the *himation* (outer garment) in the same manner. However, all Coptic shawls are not of the same impressive dimensions, and some of more modest size seem to have been more readily worn by women. They were simply placed on the head, with the two sides crossed over in front and thrown back behind the shoulders, or folded diagonally and knotted on the breast.

The mantle appears to have enjoyed only little success among the Copts down to the Muslim period, since they preferred to wear the large draped shawl. The mantle and shawl were never worn at the same time. If a mummy cloth (Metropolitan Museum, 08.181.8) perhaps shows a woman clad in a mantle, it is from the eighth century and later that this garment is portrayed. There were two types in existence at the same time. The first and more common was a rectangular piece of fabric, without sleeves, large enough to cover the arms about 3¾ to 5 feet (1.15 to 1.50 m), but not falling much lower than the knees. An opening for the head was contrived by a momentary interruption of the weaving, and hence appears as a simple horizontal slit (stela in the Coptic Museum, Cairo, 8705). The other is longer and provided with sleeves woven at the same time as the body of the garment. It is equipped with a hood formed by a rectangle folded in two and sewn to the slit at the neck (Louvre, H183; Bode-Museum [former Kaiser-Friedrich-Museum], Berlin, 17521).

The decoration of these mantles was patterned on that of the tunics and underwent a parallel evolution. It consists of *clavi* (vertical bands framing the neck opening on back and front), edgings to the sleeves, and eventually *orbicula* (medallions placed at the shoulders, and at the knees in front and behind) and horizontal bands running along the lower edge of the mantle and going up at a right angle on the sides (Louvre, G205). From the tenth century, the use of the mantle became general to the point of rivaling that of the shawl, which tended to disappear.

In parallel with the tunics, we may note the increasing use of wool both for the background (instead of linen) and for the decoration, and by way of consequence the extension of the technique of tapestry and of color to the background of the garment. At the same time, a very clear taste asserts itself for ornamental overlay and the use of decoration selvages (Louvre, 2051, 2057). It is difficult to decide whether we should classify a curious garment reproduced on certain stelae as a mantle (British Museum, 1523; Coptic Museum, Cairo, 8689). It comes to a point on the front of the body, which might indicate that, being circular in form (whereas all woven Coptic garments were basically rectangular or square, since they were woven to shape and not cut from a piece of fabric to be sewn up afterward) and without any slit for the arms, it could be thrown back on the shoulders to allow greater freedom of movement.

Scarves

From the discoveries made in the cemeteries, it is known that both men and women wore scarves. This is confirmed by numerous mummy cloths, stelae, and even fabrics (one deriving from Akhmīm and preserved at the Abegg Stiftung). Long, narrow, and often ending in fringes, these scarves were most often carelessly thrown over the shoulders or round the neck. Sometimes they were draped in a fairly complex manner, like large shawls (stela in the Coptic Museum, Cairo, 8687). While many scarves discovered are of wool of plain color, the majority of those preserved in the museums carry a decoration placed at the extremities, which consists of simple stripes (Louvre, MG738; stela in the British Museum, 1533), squares, medallions, stars, or flowers (Louvre, MG1260), always executed in tapestry. Some are entirely covered with registers of tapestry: decorations of animals passant, or of geometrical or floral motifs, with subtle variations of color at the heart of a single motif, effected by gradually lightening of the colors (Musée des Beaux Arts, Orléans, 54; Louvre, MG426, MG449, MG730). Some techniques appear to have been used less.

Mantle, chestnut-colored background with red neckline and shoulder band decorated with motifs in ecru and red. Tapestry. Ninth century. Length: 1.15 m; width: 1.50 m. *Courtesy Louvre Museum, Paris.*

End of a shawl (or shoulder band) with octagons on a yellow background and four dancers in red or dark blue, alternately. Tapestry. Twelfth century. Length: 0.40 m; width: 0.58 m. *Courtesy Louvre Museum, Paris.*

That of weaving a bouclé decoration is very rarely seen, although it was a technique familiar to the Coptic weavers (Louvre, MG613). In other cases, lines of color traced by using warp and woof of different colors marked out squares on the background of the material. This technique was employed well after the Arab conquest for some tunics. Finally, the technique, used exceptionally for the decoration of Coptic materials, of printing with a stencil plate is attested for a scarf found at Antinoë by Gayet and now preserved in the Musées Royaux d'Art et d'Histoire in Brussels (44).

Tunic decorated with embroidered designs and four personages who wear long-sleeved tunics with distinctive bands, necklines, and belts. Textile. Late Middle Ages. Length: 1.08 m; width: 0.80 m. *Courtesy Louvre Museum, Paris.*

Tunics

The tunic is the piece of clothing most often represented, as well as the one of which the largest number are found in the collections. This abundant documentation is explained by the fact that this garment was in use among the Copts from the beginning of the Christian era until long after the Arab conquest. Furthermore, the discoveries made at the time of the official excavations testify that civilians were often buried with several tunics one on top of another. This is not a specifically funerary custom, since wall paintings, like portraits, masks, and mummy cloths, frequently depict persons wearing at least two tunics. In fact, it is usual to notice two series of *clavi* at the level of the neck opening, or again to see a longer tunic extending beyond the outer tunic.

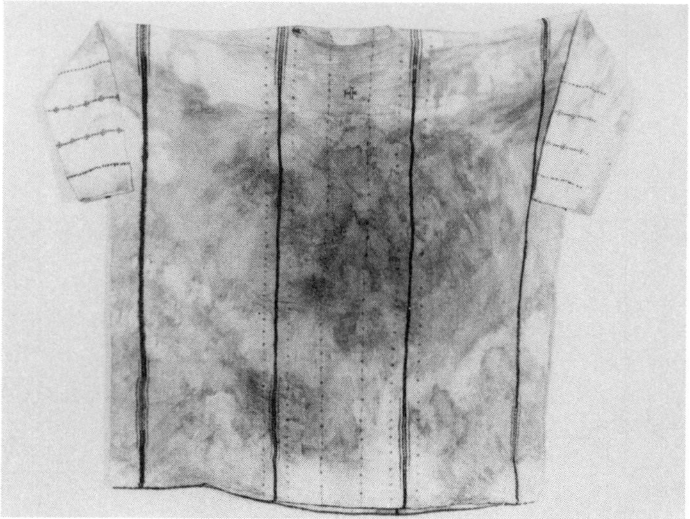

Tunic with sleeves, decorated with vertical embroidered lines of alternating flowerets and crosses. Embroidered textile. Length: 2.30 m; width, including the sleeves: 2.66 m. *Courtesy Louvre Museum, Paris.*

The form of Coptic tunics is constant until the tenth century. They form a T with sleeves, and are woven of a single piece, beginning with a sleeve, the decoration being executed at the same time (*orbicula, tabula, clavi,* sleeve-bands, decoration at the neck or the bottom of the garment). Whether they are long—reaching to the ankles—or short—stopping at the knees—all had an impressive breadth of shoulder compared with the narrowness of the sleeves. The excess fabric fell back on the arm at the level of the elbow (as is shown by a painting from the tomb of Theodosia at Antinoë), and the fullness of the garment was caught in at the waist by a belt. It is for this reason that many tunics had a stitched fold at the waist. Decorated tunics were worn both by women and by men, and children were dressed like adults. These precious garments were manufactured by specialists, and it is common to find a used tunic decoration employed again as an economy measure and sewn on a new tunic.

Child's tunic with hood, decorated with rows of dark animals and plants. Tapestry. Eleventh century. Length (excluding the sleeves and hood): 0.40 m; width: 0.48 m. *Courtesy Louvre Museum, Paris.*

Undergarments

Some tunics, particularly fine and almost transparent, have been found by archaeologists as having been worn under thicker tunics, in female tombs (Antinoë, Saqqara). Their form is in no way different from that of the outer tunics. The decoration, however, is characteristically a series of flowers or floral buttons arranged at the edge of the sleeves, of *clavi*, or of *orbicula*, and sometimes enriched with large triangles filled with the same motifs placed at the neck opening or at the bottom near the edge (Louvre, F189, F190).

Whether from an excess of modesty or negligence, archaeologists do not mention other undergarments, although their use is attested both by the vocabulary and by some pictorial representations. For example, Saint Thecla is portrayed on stela no. 8693 in the Coptic Museum in Cairo with her loins draped in a linen cloth. This is no doubt the *perizōma* mentioned in the Coptic martyr narrations. It must have consisted of a rectangular piece of fabric simply draped, unless it was formed by a triangular loincloth in the manner of those found in Nubia in certain monastery cemeteries. In addition to this, women wore a linen cloth swathing the breasts. The only references to undergarments are by Gayet and Quibell. These are pantaloons worn by women, which probably correspond to a rather late date. In fact, by the complexity of their execution (they are composed of several parts put together by an expert set of seams) as well as by the materials used (silk and cotton), the examples preserved (Louvre, AF6093; Musées Royaux d'Art et d'Histoire, Brussels, 425) indicate a very advanced stage in the evolution of Coptic civilian dress.

Belts

We have seen that the use of belts was rendered indispensable by the great width of tunics. Archaeologists mention different kinds of belts found during excavations, and it is possible to compare with their descriptions several fragments of fabric cataloged as "galloons" in the museums; these might just as well have served as belts as braid sewn on a garment. Some are simple twisted or plaited belts, sometimes in two colors (Louvre, MG1120); others are regular galloons woven to patterns or stitched (Louvre, MG45, MG368; F21, MG594). Finally, Gayet at Antinoë and Quibell at Saqqara have discovered belts of multicolored knitting (Louvre, AF6027.)

Handbags

On a few stelae (Coptic Museum, Cairo, 8705) and in certain paintings (Wādī Sarjah), people are depicted carrying a handbag of approximately rectangular form, the surface of which is decorated with geometrical motifs. During the excavations at Antinoë Gayet in fact discovered some bags that had been made in the *sprang* style, in wool of different colors, or in unbleached linen. While some pieces of network preserved in the museums may, by their form, their decoration, and their close-woven texture, have been used as handbags (Louvre, E12599; Victoria and Albert Museum, no. 477), this is not the case for the majority of those preserved, since their mesh is much too large for this purpose. We must therefore consider them as head fillets, inasmuch as this item of Coptic dress is much more frequently attested by the discoveries of the archaeologists than handbags.

Socks

The use of socks by the Copts is confirmed both by the excavations carried out at Antinoë or Bahnasā and by some mummy cloths, generally representing women (Louvre, AF6440; Metropolitan Museum, 08.181.8). To judge from the specimens preserved in the museums (Victoria and Albert Museum, 592, 2085) and the archaeological evidence, these socks were of wool worked in knit stitch. Unlike our modern socks, they were shaped in such a way as to isolate the great toe from the other toes, no doubt to make room for sandal laces. These socks are most often colored, and some were adorned with stripes. At Antinoë, Gayet found some socks with top and heel of a different color from that of the main body. The description he gives and the fact that they were discovered in very rich tombs prompt one to think that these were socks worn by the members of the Byzantine administration stationed at Antinoë. In addition, Gayet mentions stockings of wool and socks of stitched cloth, of which no example is preserved in the public collections.

Sandals and Shoes

The use of sandals, frequent in pharaonic Egypt and in particular from the New Kingdom on, was maintained in Coptic Egypt. The Copts, however, diversified the categories of footwear and employed leather almost exclusively, whereas in ancient Egypt vegetable fibers were preferred. Coptic sandals, like their more ancient prototypes, were always provided with a strap separating the big toe from the others. However, instead of being fastened directly to the sides of the sandal, as in the simpler models (Romans Museum, 176), this thong may have been attached to one or more transverse bands, which may have been richly decorated (Romans Museum, 173). Sometimes a strap passing behind the heel was added (Romans Museum, 171).

Shoes properly so called are mentioned much more often than sandals by the archaeologists, and appear in larger numbers in the collections. The sole was always composed of several layers, while the upper and the sides may have been either of one piece (Louvre, B294) or in three pieces (Louvre, D1335). The heel was always reinforced by a semicircular piece of leather. The upper may be rounded (Louvre, C740, D1747, B130), straight (Louvre, B217), or pointed (Louvre, C740, C342, D942). More rarely, laces were knotted around the ankle (Louvre, D942, C342; Romans Museum, 180; Coptic Museum, Cairo, stela no. 8685). The decoration, generally rather rich, played on the contrast between the background color—red (Louvre, B130, C740), black, or more rarely white (Louvre, C342, C352)—and that of the bands sewn on the periphery of the shoe.

Gilding was frequently employed as a decoration either for the band or in the form of motifs in cutwork sewn on the upper. This decoration consisted most often of squares (Louvre, C352, B130) or circles (Romans Museum, 177), sometimes set

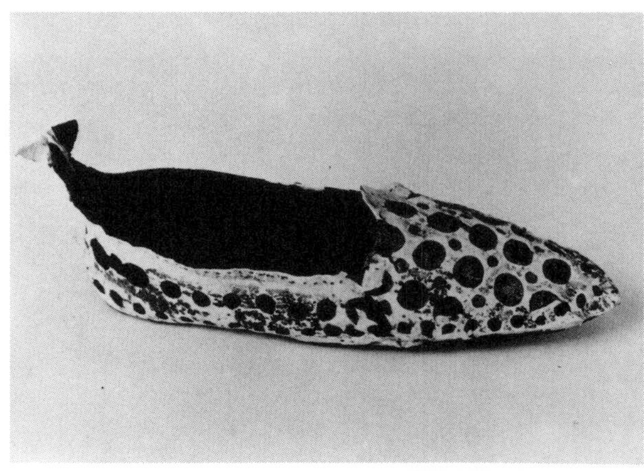

Decorated shoe. *Courtesy German Museum of Leather, Offenbach.*

off as a free-hanging decoration on the point of the toe or at the heel (Romans Museum, 175 and 177). Some mummy cloths (Cairo Museum, 33281) present shoes laced upward, which is confirmed by the discoveries made by Gayet at Antinoë. It should, however, be noted that no shoe of this type is preserved in the collections.

Finally, Clédat at Bāwīṭ and Gayet at Antinoë have found boots, generally worn by men. An example in the Romans Museum (1886b) shows that boots, like shoes, were made of several parts sewn together and that they ended with a pointed toe curved upward as well as at the top of the boot. Like the shoes and sandals, the boots have no heels; the use of heels appears to have been totally unknown in Coptic Egypt.

From the beginning of the Christian era to the

Two ornamented shoes. Leather. *Courtesy Museum of Israel, Jerusalem.*

twelfth century, Coptic civilian costume varied little in its components. It is, however, possible to detect that in the course of time some elements formerly in fashion fell into disuse. Thus it is that the large shawl of the early centuries was replaced by the small shawl, itself later rivaled by the mantle. It is the permanence in the use of these different garments that attracts attention when one studies the Coptic civilian dress. We note during several centuries the custom of putting tunics (normally two or three) on top of one another and covering them sometimes with a shawl, sometimes with a mantle. The use of headdresses for women is also a constant. It must be stated that, on the whole, the Arab conquest does not seem in any way to have overturned the habits of the Copts in matters of dress. These appear to have been modified only well after the conquest under pressure from Muslim fashion, after which the Coptic community was considerably diminished. It is not possible at present to determine with any precision the fluctuations of fashion among the Copts and their impact on this or that piece of Coptic dress. The documents are too often lacking, and our ignorance of the archaeological context of the pieces preserved means that it is possible only for the tunics and shawls to trace a chronological evolution supported by study of the materials, the techniques, and the decoration.

[*See also:* Textiles, Coptic.]

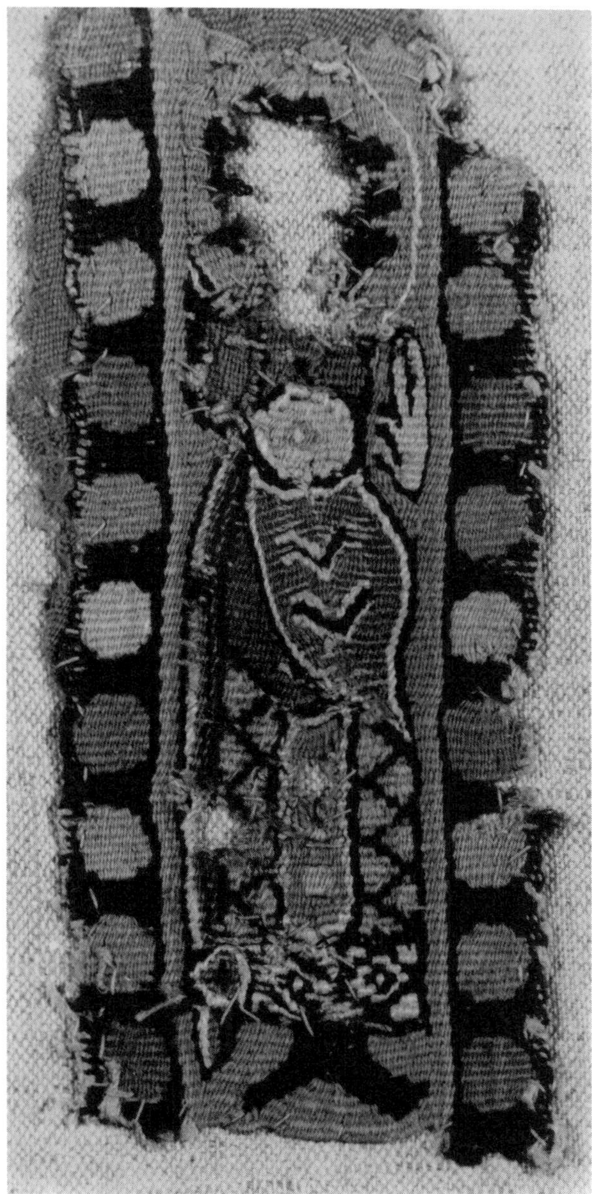

Woman wearing a tunic crossed diagonally by a lozenge-shaped decoration called *thorakion*. Detail of a shoulder-band from a woman's robe. Tapestry. End of tenth century. Length: 18 cm; width: 20 cm. *Courtesy Louvre Museum, Paris.*

Dalmatic

The origin of the dalmatic is not very well known. The word itself seems to indicate that it is a garment deriving from Dalmatia, a province of the Roman Empire from the second century B.C. But at present, we do not know any example of the ancient Dalmatian costume. The only documents at our disposal are Latin and Greek texts in which the word "dalmatic" is used and some graphic representations in which certain personages wear a costume close to the literary descriptions. Unfortunately, there is no tangible proof of the concordance of these sources; no inscription on the frescoes of the Roman catacombs affirms that the orants are clothed in dalmatics, and conversely no ancient text offers a diagram of the vestment. Caution is therefore required.

The dalmatic was a long white garment falling to the feet. It could be woven in wool, silk, or linen. It was adorned with two *clavi* (bands) of purple-red (the intensity of which varied with the dye employed) descending on either side from the neck to the lower part of the garment. It was worn without any waistband and was provided with long full sleeves.

It was adopted by the Romans from the second century A.D., when the habit of wearing garments of foreign origin was introduced, and the emperors themselves (for example, Commodus and Heliogabalus) often set the example. But at this period the wearing of the dalmatic was considered the act of men of peculiar and effeminate habits. This was no longer the case two centuries later, and the Edict of the Maximum, proclaimed by the emperor DIOCLETIAN in A.D. 301 to resolve an economic crisis, gives a list of prices for dalmatics for men and women.

The dalmatic was finally adopted by the Christian clergy. According to the *Liber Pontificalis,* it is said to have become an ecclesiastical vestment in the fourth century A.D., in the pontificate of Pope Sylvester (314–335), who made it the official vestment of deacons. According to the *Vita Sylvestri,* however, the dalmatic became a liturgical vestment only under Liberius (352–366). In fact, it was probably in the course of the fifth century A.D. that it became a mark of the Roman deacons, although the pope sometimes accorded the right of wearing it to clergy of other churches.

From the third century A.D. we find in the Roman catacombs (cemetery of Saint Agnes, cemetery of Saint Priscilla, cemetery of Saints Peter and Marcellinus) frescoes representing male and female orants clothed in a white garment adorned with purple-red *clavi* and with very full sleeves (about half the total length of the garment); here we may recognize the dalmatic described by the texts. It should be mentioned, however, that some of these dalmatics are in color, and that the majority of them have one or two bands of purple-red at the wrist, although the texts speak only of a white garment adorned with *clavi.*

This same term "dalmatic" has been used to describe the tunics brought to light in excavations carried out since the nineteenth century in the necropolises of Egypt (at Saqqara, Bāwīṭ, and Antinoë), but that is a misuse of the term.

Toward the middle of the third century A.D. the mode of burial in Egypt was completely changed. The dead no longer underwent mummification. They were buried dressed in their finest garments, sometimes with three or four tunics one on top of another. Thanks to the exceptional climate of the country, these textiles have survived to our own day. These tunics, most often with long sleeves—and making a real break with the traditional loincloth of the pharaonic period and the Rameside robe—were sufficiently long and full for the term "dalmatic" to come at once to mind. But a simple description proves that they are completely different: their *clavi* are most often linked together by a yoke edging the opening for the neck; they are wider, no longer self-colored, and end in a circular or spear-shaped decorative motif. Finally, they generally stop in the middle of the chest. Alongside them appear the *orbicula,* circular or square medallions, plain or decorated, set on the shoulders and at the level of the knees. A decorative band on the lower part of the garment sometimes picks up, in the opposite direction, the arrangement of the *clavi* and the yoke that links them. These Coptic tunics seem to be shorter, although we do not know the exact stature of their owners.

The Coptic tunic, as just described, has thus nothing in common with the dalmatic. On the other hand, it is identical with the design worn at the same period throughout the Mediterranean basin, of which the mosaic of the great hunt at Piazza Armerina (Sicily) furnishes numerous examples. Moreover, it presents some similarities with the tunics found at Palmyra, metropolis of the desert of Syria—to which R. Pfister (1932) traces the origin of the Coptic garment—and from there with Persia.

One point, however, remains obscure: the presence at Akhmīm (ancient Greek Panopolis) of two tunics identical with the Roman dalmatic. One is mentioned by A. S. Cole (1881–1895); the other is in the Victoria and Albert Museum in London (description by Kendrick, 1920). A third example is the dalmatic in the Louvre (TC2463), the provenance of which is unknown (perhaps Antinoopolis). Akhmīm and Antinoopolis sheltered a Greco-Roman population, and Akhmīm was a great textile center, known throughout the civilized world of the period. Did these imported dalmatics or Coptic dalmatics imitate the Roman pattern? Were they reserved for the use of the Greco-Roman population, or were they equally worn by the Copts? We do not know. But we have concrete proof of the existence of the garment of which the ancients tell us and of which the frescoes of the Roman catacombs provide the first picture.

BIBLIOGRAPHY

Bourguet, P. du. *Catalogue des étoffes coptes du Musée du Louvre,* Vol. 1. Paris, 1964.

Burmester, O. H. E. *The Egyptian or Coptic Church.* Cairo, 1967.

Cabrol, F., and F. Leclerq, eds. "Dalmatique." In *Dictionnaire d'archéologie chrétienne et de liturgie.* Paris, 1920.

Cole, A. S. *On the Art of Tapestry-making and Embroidery.* Society for the Encouragement of Arts, Manufactures, and Commerce, Cantor Lectures, Vol. 2. London, 1881–1895.

Combefis, F. *Vita beati Silvestri* (*Illustrium christi martyrum. Lecti triumphi*), p. 265. Paris, 1660.

Crum, W. E. *Coptic Dictionary.* Oxford, 1962.

Daremberg, C., and E. Saglio. "Dalmatica." In *Dic-*

tionnaire des antiquités grecques et romaines, Vol. 2, pt. 1. Paris, 1892.

Duchesne, L. *Liber Pontificalis,* Vol. 1, p. 171. Paris, 1886–1892.

"Edictum Diocletiani et collegarum de pretiis rerum venalium." In *Inscriptiones Asiae Provinciarum Europae Graecarum, Illyrici Latinae,* ed. T. Mommsen, 5 vols. *Corpus Inscriptionum Latinarum,* Vol. 3, pt. 2, pp. 824–84. Berlin, 1873–1902.

Gayet, A. J. *Catalogues des objets recueillis à Antinoë pendant les fouilles de 1898 à 1907,* ed. E. Leroux. Paris, 1898.

Inscriptionum orientis et Illyrici Latinarum. Supplement, pt. 1, ed. T. Mommsen, O. Hirschfeld, and A. Domaszewski (*Corpus Inscriptionum Latinarum,* Vol. 3, supplement), pp. 1942–51. Berlin, 1902.

Kendrick, A. F. *Catalogue of Textiles from Burying-grounds in Egypt,* Vol. 1, *Graeco-Roman Period.* Victoria and Albert Museum. London, 1920.

______. *Catalogue of Textiles from Burying-grounds in Egypt,* Vol. 2, *Period of Transition and of Christian Emblems.* Victoria and Albert Museum. London, 1921.

Lampridius, A. "Antoninus Heliogabalus." In *Héliogabale; raconté par les historiens grecs et latins,* ed. G. Duviquet. Paris, 1903.

Lauffer, S. *Diokletians Preisedikt.* Berlin, 1971.

Pfister, D. "Le Costume civil copte, ses composantes et son évolution." *Mémoires de l'Ecole du Louvre* (1981).

Pfister, R. "La décoration des étoffes d'Antinoë." In *Revue des Arts asiatiques,* Annales du Musée Guimet, pp. 215–43. Paris, 1928.

______. *Les débuts du vêtement copte.* Etudes d'Orientalisme, Mélanges Linossier, Vol. 2. Paris, 1932.

______. *Textiles de Palmyre.* Paris, 1934.

Quibell, J. E. *Excavations at Saqqara. 1905–1906.* Cairo, 1907.

______. *Excavations at Saqqara 1908–1909, 1909–1910—The Monastery of Apa Jeremias,* Vol. IV, p. 1912. Cairo, 1912.

Vycichl, W. *Dictionnaire étymologique de la langue copte.* Louvain, 1983.

DOMINIQUE PFISTER
DOMINIQUE FLAMM

COSTUME, MILITARY. Since the Copts lived under foreign occupation or domination, which reduced them to a tolerated community, one might think that military service would not be accessible to the Copts. Nevertheless, it is known that Saint PACHOMIUS served in the army for a time in the reign of Constantine, although he was soon discharged. Moreover, even posts of high command, and consequently subordinate posts, were entrusted to Copts at the end of the Byzantine occupation.

A statuette that belongs to the Coptic collections of the Louvre gives concrete form to this historical datum. This statuette, about 19 inches (0.47 m) high and made of limestone painted in red ochre, with the pupils of the eyes in black, portrays a standing man holding a buckler. At his belt he carries a sheathed dagger. He is dressed in a tunic that stops at the knees, and his torso is covered by a cuirass of scales, surmounted by a large plastron. Just above the belt there appears on the cuirass a gorgon's head, full-face. This was intended to strike fear into the enemy. The two legs and the feet are enveloped in breeches of coarse latticework, perhaps of leather, since there is no footwear. The head is remarkable for its expression, with almond eyes in antique style on chubby cheeks and a short nose above closed lips in a rounded face typical of the Copts. The flat hair is drawn close to the top of the forehead, such as we see in Roman art from the end of the third century or beginning of the fourth. The model was probably a Coptic veteran who had himself portrayed for posterity. It is possible that he

Coptic auxiliary of the Roman army. Limestone statuette painted in red ochre. End of third century. Height: 0.47 m; width: 0.18 m; thickness: 0.12 m. *Courtesy Louvre Museum, Paris.*

attained the rank of centurion, which his accoutrements seem to indicate, although he does not bear a sword. Whether he was an auxiliary or a junior officer, his representation supplies an important document for the military costume of the period. But his bearing especially and the striking realism of his face with its wide opened eyes under thick arching eyebrows show a rare technique in Coptic art. This is the sole known example of military statuary of the period.

The last type of representation of military figures —and, in consequence, of the uniform—encountered in Coptic iconography includes biblical figures, like those of Saul or David, and persons whose function or activity is of some special interest. An episode from the cycle of David that adorns Chapel 3 of the monastery of Bāwīṭ (Clédat, 1904, p. 20, pl. 17) catches him at the moment before he confronts Goliath, when he is armed under the direction of Saul. The king is enthroned between two guards, one holding a lance but neither presenting any other identifying mark. David, according to Clédat's commentary, wears a cuirass and under it, stopping at the knees, a tunic of metal over a tunic of rose material with darker vertical lines. He is shod with boots to the knees. The left arm is bent under a round buckler adorned with spirals, and the right arm brandishes a sword.

Finally, in the scene of the Massacre of the Innocents at DAYR ABŪ ḤINNIS and at Bāwīṭ, the soldiers of Herod wear the Persian tunic with three pointed flaps.

Of these representations, only the military costume of the Louvre statuette emerges as an authentic witness to a state and a period. Amid general uncertainty about Roman usage in this regard, the monuments that present it are too badly damaged to contribute to the documentation so far as the imperial period is concerned, and the Louvre piece is unique and precious. The other uniforms mentioned here do not seem to correspond to the periods to which the personages belong. Thus, they seem to be conventional and merely indicative of functions exercised, as happened later in medieval illuminations of Christian manuscripts, Western and Eastern.

BIBLIOGRAPHY

Bourguet, P. du. "A propos d'un militaire égyptien de la période romaine." *Bulletin de la Société française d'Egyptologie* 68 (1973):11–16.

Burmester, O. H. E. *The Egyptian or Coptic Church.* Cairo, 1967.

Clédat, J. *Monastère et la nécropole de Baouît,* Vol. 1. Cairo, 1904–1906.

Crum, W. E. *Coptic Dictionary.* Oxford, 1962.

Vycichl, W. *Dictionnaire étymologique de la langue copte.* Louvain, 1983.

PIERRE DU BOURGUET, S. J.

COSTUME OF THE RELIGIOUS, the dress of hermits, monks, and secular clergy. When Christianity appeared in Egypt, the earliest converts, for the most part from a Jewish milieu, did not dress differently from their coreligionists. Jesus did not modify the dress of his disciples. He gave them only the injunction reported in Matthew 10:9–10: "Take no gold, nor silver, nor copper in your belts, no bag for your journey, nor two tunics, nor sandals, nor a staff. . . ." Jesus opposes the custom of the traveler or the wandering philosopher, requesting an even greater deprivation. But this appeal of Jesus does not appear to have been actually put into practice in the later Christian setting.

In both Jewish and Christian environments, there were several distinctive customs in matters of dress. Women, young girls, or widows who lived in community, took the veil as a sign of modesty and virginity. The polemics surrounding this custom were numerous. Tertullian even devoted a whole work to it. The Essenes, for their part, chose the white baptismal robe to signify to the world their purity and their "baptism of life." In the desert, the prophets of all ages clothed themselves in a cloak of camel's hair and a loincloth of skin. In the course of the fourth and fifth centuries, a new ethic of clothing arose around PALLADIUS, Saint John CASSIAN, and EVAGRIUS PONTICUS, rooted in the prophetic example in the context of the desert and of eremitism. To the ideal hermit were attributed the *mēlotē* (mantle of animal skin), symbol of mortification; the *skhēma* (a garment like a scapular marked with a cross, which recalled the cross of Christ); the *Koukle* (a hood, cowl, or cap), symbol of the grace of God and a witness to the childlike spirit of the follower of Jesus, His simplicity and His innocence; the *girdle* (leather belt worn by soldiers), which kept the Christian from impurity and was an attribute of the soldier of Christ; the sleeveless *tunic,* symbol of renunciation of the world; and *sandals,* which rather than shoes gave nimbleness for running the spiritual course.

This costume, however, was not worn in any rigorous fashion in the different ascetic centers. Anchorites and cenobites exhibited various and sometimes whimsical forms of dress, at least in early times. They drew upon local forms of dress, adapting them as closely as possible to the basic ideal scheme. Considerations of the level of asceticism, the material resources, and personal preferences were also taken into account. Also it was possible to distinguish one group of monks from another by variations in their dress.

An important evolution toward a more uniform style of dress took place under the influence of the political, economic, social, and religious progress of Egypt. The state had something to say, and popular fashions—Egyptian, Greco-Roman, Syrian, Byzantine, or Arab, to mention only the most important—influenced even the religious. These conditions produced in Egypt a very changing and subtle style of dress, for these fashions were more or less fixed according to the regions, the levels of population, and the zones of immigration. This evolution can be traced through six periods.

Third Century

Egyptian asceticism in the third century passed through a period of extreme poverty and solitude. Some hermits wore nothing at all and possessed nothing, not even a garment. Without even a loincloth, they covered themselves only with their long hair or their beard if they could grow one. Some used their mats as clothing as well as for sleeping. Others plaited tunics for themselves from the fiber of palm, papyrus, or some other fibrous and coarse plant. Simple long white tunics of linen, without sleeves or decoration, were also used. Some ascetics wore the *klaft* (cap), which was like the cap of very small children. Some covered themselves in cool weather or on journeys with the *balot* (cloak of sheepskin or goatskin), which on occasion served as a pouch if the ends were knotted. Some girded themselves with the *mojh* (leather cincture characteristic of soldiers), on which was hung a purse for small change. The most valiant ascetics lapped over themselves, front and back, the *skhēma*, or Arabic *marcnah* (scapular of tanned leather, made of bands passed over the shoulders and attached to the *mojh*).

Although these garments constituted the basic model of religious dress, the complete costume was practically never worn at this period.

Alongside these garments of Egyptian origin, a whole range of clothing brought in from abroad was gradually established with the great periods of immigration. The Greek *kentonarion* was a "patchwork" garment of various fabrics, which gave it a multicolored appearance. Two tunics, the *kolobion*, from Greece or Syria, and the *lebitōn*, are often confused. The first was of brown wool, the second of white linen and originally worn by the Levites (hence the name), straight in form and without sleeves or seams. In the same way the plebeian cloaks of Greece and Rome, the *lodix* and the *mēlōtē*, were found among the monks of Egypt. The *lodix* was very shaggy, of wool woven with all its fleece, either sheep wool or goat hair; it served both as a greatcoat and as a rug or blanket for covering animals. The Greek *mēlōtē* (mantle) was made of sheepskin or goatskin with its white fleece. It was knotted on the chest, and was akin to the *balot*. In Rome it was also fastened with a fibula.

Person with a cane wearing a long tunic. Wood. *Courtesy Louvre Museum, Paris.*

The *mēlōtē* generally came down to the level of the knees. It is often portrayed in representations of Moses and Elijah.

In Romanized contexts, the *analabos* replaced the *skhēma*. The *analabos* was similar to suspenders, shoulder-straps, or bands of woven wool, which, like the *skhēma*, crossed over on the back and on the chest, passing over the shoulders and attaching to the belt. This kind of crossed sash had the immediate advantage of holding the ample tunics in fashion close to the body so as not to hinder movement, especially during work.

The ascetics who originated from Syria brought with them the *akēs*, a simple loincloth of linen, wool, or some vegetable fiber crudely worked.

Fourth Century

A rather important change took place in the fourth century when the first rules for monastic life, including clothing, were enacted, and in a very specific manner, first by ANTONY (toward 310) and then by PACHOMIUS (315). The latter rule, taken up and encouraged by ATHANASIUS I of Alexandria, affected also the secular clergy and liturgical usage. Other rules followed, which we do not always know, since they probably remained in the domain of oral tradition and are consequently lost. The directives issued by Antony and Pachomius had better fortune, for they were immediately translated and disseminated in the West. It is probable that at this period each monastery of any importance had its own usages, following the basic model more or less strictly. It was thus that the number of the garments worn by the religious grew. In addition to those known in the preceding century we may note the *cacitōn* (tunic), of coarse linen, hemp, or jute, made of two pieces of cloth joined at the shoulders and rectangular in form; the *pork* (Bohairic, *phōrk*), (cloak), of dark color and woven of fleecy wool, reserved for divine service; the *hōōk* (leather belt or plastron that soldiers also wore); the *auleou* (loincloth) of horsehair; the *hboos* (perhaps a liturgical tunic of linen); and finally the *rahtou*, of tanned goatskin or sheepskin, which was akin to the *skhēma* but perhaps corresponded to the triangular aprons of the Shenutian monks; found on the mummies of several monks, it symbolized a very high degree of asceticism.

Other garments, of Greco-Roman origin, made their appearance in the milieus of the Coptic religious. Such were the *zōnē*, a belt of leather that gathered the tunic to the body and held in the *analabos*, and the *lention*, without any ornament, a symbol of mortification, which could serve as a turban just as well as for linen or loincloth.

For the liturgy, there was a whole array of garments. The principal item was the *sticharion*, a tunic made of linen and falling to the feet, with sleeves stitched and tapered at the wrists. In early times this tunic was always white. Sometimes it was adorned with *clavi* or with motifs embroidered on the lower part. Other vestments included the *kamassion*, also a tunic of linen for the use of deacons and priests, closely resembling the long liturgical tunic; the *epōmis*, made of two pieces of linen joined at the shoulders and white in color, put on by priests and deacons at the moment of communion; the *katanouti*, a small cloak for the liturgy, which recalled the woolen *pallium* of the Romans; the *maphorion*, which was in origin a woman's cloak, worn around the neck and shoulders among men, as among the monks in the Christian period, and resembling the Latin *ricinum*, a kind of shawl edged with fringes; and the *ballin*, a long double band of wool passing round the head, then crossing behind the back and fastened in the girdle.

Fifth Century

The fifth century was the great period of the *koukoullion* or *koukle*, the *kolobion*, the *lebitōn*, and the *akēs*, while the *lention*, *kentonarion*, *lodix*, *maphorion*, and *katanouti* seem to have been abandoned. The *koukoullion* was originally a simple piece of material of small dimensions, or even a bag, attached at the back to cover the head in times of rain or cold. It thus took the place of a hood on thick cloaks. Peasants, artisans, and travelers were the first to wear it, then the slaves and the monks. In 382 it was officially authorized. The Roman army in Gaul adopted it for the winter, which leads one to think of a garment properly Gaulish. Small children were muffled up in hoods of identical form.

Some typically Egyptian garments also disappeared, to be replaced by others. This was probably due to a stricter application of the rules in the monastic communities. Thus the monks wore only the tunic, *shtēn*, and *cacitōn*, the *klaft*, the *mojh*, and probably the *pork* and *hboos*; though we have no evidence of these certainly dating from this century, they definitely survived into the following centuries.

Sixth Century

During the sixth century, there were scarcely any changes from the preceding one. The *klaft* was perhaps less frequent, or restricted to liturgical usage, as was the *kolobion.* But the *thouraji* began to appear. This was made of leather, and represented the armor against evil for both men and women. It was a kind of *analabos* of leather, which recalled the *telamōn* (baldric, or ornamental shoulder belt) of the Greeks and Romans as well as the Greek *thōrakion.* The *thouraji* was one of the consecrated vestments handed over in the course of the vesting ceremony for monks and nuns at a later period.

Seventh Century

There were profound modifications in Egypt at the time of the arrival of the Arabs, and clothing was no exception. The features of the monastic habit were sharply transformed, first, because Egypt turned in upon itself in a period when it sought to eliminate foreign customs that were too pressing or burdensome. The only garments of Greco-Roman or Byzantine origin that were preserved were used for the liturgy. A second cause of transformation was the Coptic church's very quick adoption of Greek rituals. In the monastic centers, where the forms and rules became blurred once more as in the beginning, the *thalis, sak, and jōlh* were current.

The *thalis,* of rough hairy material, was a rectangle twice as long as it was wide, cut in strictly rectilinear fashion with a hole at the center. It was worn folded in two. Archaeologists have found on the walls of a monastery at DAYR AL-MADĪNAH instructions relating to the *thalis,* according to which there were two possible sizes, small and large. But we should also note that the *thalis* was also a simple sacks for onions and other merchandise, and that it sometimes had the color of an onion.

Reliquary plaque depicting St. Simeon Stylites. Enchased silver. Syria. Sixth century. Height: 0.30 m; width: .26 m. *Courtesy Louvre Museum, Paris.*

The *sak* was similar to the *thalis.* It, too, was originally a common sack, with which the Hebrews in particular clothed themselves as a sign of mourning after rending their garments. The *sak* afforded a very coarse tunic in goathair or horsehair, of a quite straight form. Among the Christians, it symbolized mourning and penitence and became assimilated to the various haircloth garments dear to the ascetics.

The little known *jolh* was no doubt a very simple cloak, of which again there were two standard sizes, small and large.

With the arrival of the armies of ʿAmr and the conquest of Egypt, new clothing appeared. People began to wear the *qalansuwah,* a long woolen garment ending in fringes, which the monks rapidly adopted to replace that other hooded cloak, the *birrin* (or Latin *birrus*). The monks continued to follow the ancient ideal of Palladius and Cassian in assigning symbols to garments, even if the evocation of martyrdom and the arena became less pronounced. The clothing of this period was always marked by a lively desire for wandering and solitude, poverty and penitence, which in former times the prophets proclaimed. This, in fact, has always been characteristic of the ascetic spirituality of Christian Egypt. This period also assigned a special designation to the civil dress of the cleric or monk, *kosmikon,* which signified "of the world" or "of the clergyman."

Eighth Century and After

The evidence relating to the costume of the religious in later times is scanty. Some sources still mention the *epōmis* in the eighth and ninth centuries; the *ballin,* the *rahtou,* and the *koukle* in the ninth century; the *qalansuwah,* the *koukle,* and the *klaft* in the twelfth; the *qalansuwah* again in the fourteenth; and finally, the *jibab* and the *mizzar* in the seventeenth century.

The *jibbab* was a long tunic of brown wool, the sleeves of which did not reach the wrists and which was closed in front. The *mi'zar* was a large lined cloak, black on the outside and white on the inside.

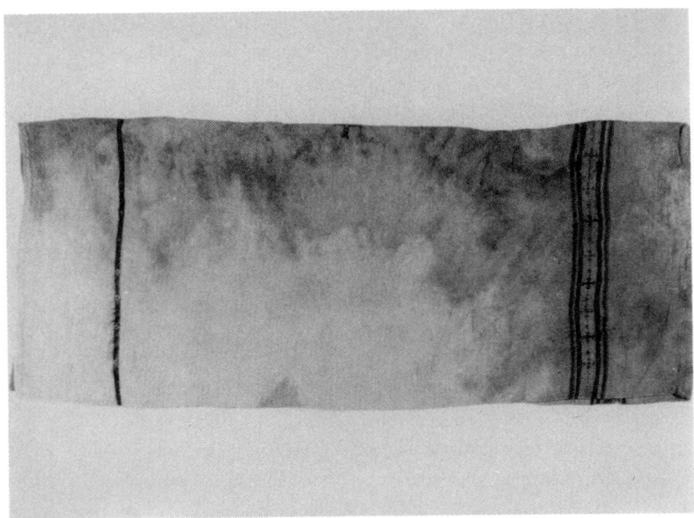

Lower part of a tunic (detail) showing embroidered vertical rows of alternating crosses and flowerets. *Courtesy Louvre Museum, Paris.*

It was generally reserved for traveling.

In fact, though the reforms in clothing during the Arab period introduced many new things, they did not replace the original clothing. Even now the religious of Coptic Egypt call to mind the ancient model and its symbolism, even if sometimes they have forgotten the first significance or the origin of their dress.

This brief survey of the religious clothing of Egypt is by no means exhaustive. A more thorough study of Coptic clothing reveals, in fact, many other articles of clothing, about which we have only very few details and no dating. Thus we know that in early times people continued to wear the *shenti,* a loincloth, unless this is the Roman *cento;* that some wrapped themselves in shrouds or funerary cloths; that there was a cloak, the *sholbi,* and a woolen tunic, the *jōouni,* among the monks. The latter also borrowed from the Greco-Roman wardrobe the *talaris* tunic, the *stolē,* the cloaks *palis, birrus,* and *phelonion,* as well as the *telamōn* (baldric). In the milieus of Syrian origin, the fleecy tunic *counac (kaunakēs),* the *ephod* (of the high priest), and the headgear *sidarin* continued to be worn. For the liturgy, clergy such as the cenobites kept the vestments consecrated to the Basilian and Cyrillic rituals in the Eastern church: the *ōmophorion* (scarf), the *epitrachelion* (sash), the *morphōtakion* (robe), and the *onarion* (sash) (cf. Burmester, 1967, pp. 29–30, 183). Arab customs introduced at various periods the *tunyah,* the *ʿabā,* and the *shamass* as tunics. As mantles there appeared the *burnus,* the *shamlah,* and the *taylasān;* as headdress, the *caük,* the *kaslet,* the *turban,* while some mantles (*burnus, qalansuwah*) had a hood attached. As a belt for the liturgy, the religious adopted the *hyassah* and the *minṭakah,* with the *baṭrashīl* as a ornament; and for footwear the *markūb* (footwear) and *tāsūmāh* (sandal). The poorest clothed themselves in *muraqqaʿ* or rags. There were also pantaloons, which were worn by the religious at a late date, but for which we have only vague iconographic evidence.

Despite this multiplicity in matters of clothing, an underlying continuity kept alive the direct heritage of the first religious, Antony and Pachomius; costume was accommodated to the religious domain, and a continuing heritage was very definitively established in a land watered with the blood of the earliest martyrs. Throughout all the changes, the ancient values persisted, through an ingenious concern for adaptation that was able, for example, to transpose the Greek *sticharion* into the Arabic *istikhārah,* the *kamassion* into *qamīṣ* or *shamas* (pen-

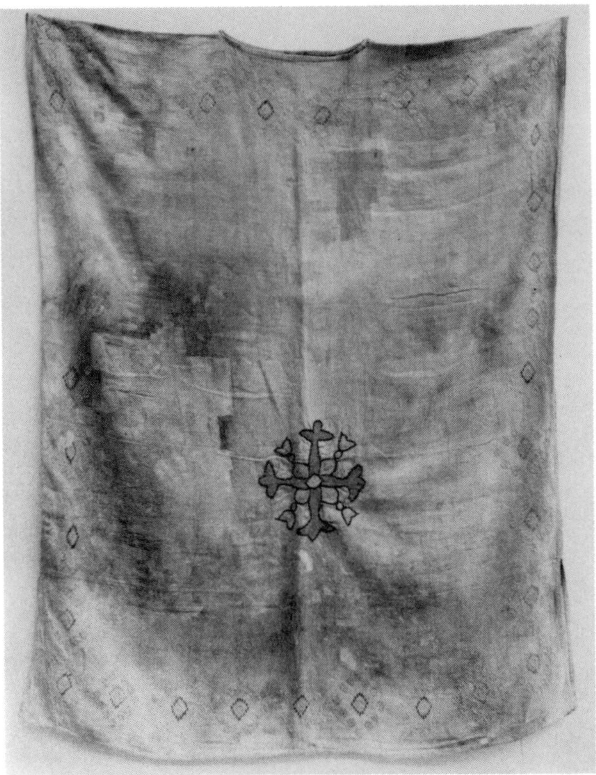

Back of a tunic showing a Byzantine cross in the center. Textile. Late Middle Ages. Length: 1.08 m; width: 0.8 m. *Courtesy Louvre Museum, Paris.*

dant), the *sak* into *shuqqah,* the *zonē* into *zunnār,* and the *skhēma* into *iskīm,* though the origins of these garments might be forgotten.

[*See also:* Liturgical Vestments.]

BIBLIOGRAPHY

Benigni, U. "Lexici ecclesiastici coptici." In *Bessarione,* ed. Emanno Loescher, fasc. 61, 1907; fasc. 62, 1901.

Burmester, O. H. E. *The Egyptian or Coptic Church.* Cairo, 1967.

Butler, A. *The Ancient Coptic Churches,* Vol. 2. Oxford, 1884.

Crum, W. E. *A Coptic Dictionary.* Oxford, 1939; reissued 1962–1972.

Dozy, R. P. A. *Dictionnaire détaillé des noms de vêtements chez les arabes.* Amsterdam, 1846.

Muyser, J. "Vie d'Amba Harmim par Hor de Preht." *Bulletin de la Société d'archéologie copte,* Vol. 9:1, pt. 2. Würzburg, 1863.

Renaudot, E. *Ritus Orientalium Coptorum, Syrorum et Armenorum,* Vol. 1, pt. 2. Würzburg, 1863.

Vycichl, W. *Dictionnaire étymologique de la langue copte.* Louvain, 1983.

NICOLE MORFIN-GOURDIER

COTTON. *See* Textiles, Coptic: Yarns.

COVENANT OF ʿUMAR, ascribed to the second Orthodox caliph, ʿUmar ibn al-Khaṭṭāb (634–644), and regarded as a document of primary importance in regulating the relations between the Muslim conquerors of the Middle East and their Dhimmi subjects, that is, the Jews and the Christians, including the Coptic nation in Egypt. The situation of the Copts vis-à-vis the Arab conquerors under the leadership of ʿAmr ibn al-ʿĀṣ was, however, a peculiar one. Egypt had been under the Byzantine yoke at the time of the advent of the Arabs. Since the Council of CHALCEDON in 451, the Byzantine lords in Egypt were of the Melchite creed, which the Copts disregarded as heretical. Cyrus al-Muqawqas, the Byzantine ruler at the time of the Conquest, persecuted the Monophysite Copts as heretical; the Copts in return accused him of heresy and loathed the subjugation of their country to the Byzantine empire.

The result of this anomalous situation was that in 641 the Copts did not care who invaded their country, for their position could be no worse than under the Byzantine rule. Therefore, they stood aside during the progressive struggle between the Arabs and the Byzantine defenders of their Egyptian colony. All they knew about the newcomers was that they were monotheistic in their religion, which sounded somewhat like their own Monophysite creed. So it did not matter to them very much who won the ensuing battles. The triumph of the Arabs at the battle of Heliopolis (641) was followed by the fall of numerous cities in the Delta, including Atrīb and Minūf. The terror inflicted on the inhabitants could be matched only by the Byzantine persecution in the prior decade. According to bishop JOHN OF NIKIOU, the eminent chronicler and eyewitness of these events, people "began to help the Muslims," at least by carrying fodder and provisions (Butler, 1978, p. 236), which they sorely needed in their struggle. The next decisive step for the Arabs was the capture of the fortress of Babylon, wherefrom the Byzantine masters conducted their firm rule of the Delta in the north and Upper Egypt in the south. This is not the place to discuss the details of the ensuing siege and warfare leading to the surrender of the formidable fortress on Good Friday, 6 April 641 (Butler, 1978, pp. 258–74). The fate of Egypt was sealed with the fall of the capital city of Alexandria in the next year and the flight of Cyrus to Constantinople after signing the treaty of 8 November 641. According to John of Nikiou (Butler, 1978, pp. 320–21), the stipulations of that momentous treaty were as follows:

1. payment of a fixed tribute to the Arabs
2. eleven months of armistice, ending in the Coptic month of Paope on 28 September 642
3. cessation of hostilities on both sides, including operations against Alexandria
4. departure by sea of the Roman garrison of Alexandria with its treasure, but Romans within the country to be subject to payment of tribute on leaving
5. no Romans to attempt recovery of Egypt in the future
6. Muslims to desist from church seizure and interference with Christians
7. Jews to be permitted to stay in Alexandria
8. Roman hostages numbering 150 officers and 50 civilians to remain for the execution of the treaty.

The estimate of the tribute in article 1 amounted to 12 million dinars (Butler, 1978, p. 321). The main item of the treaty consisted of the safeguarding of the churches and the security of the Christian population.

Parallel to this treaty, the Arabs seem to have issued the famous Covenant of ʿUmar. The early Islamic historians such as ʿAbd al-Ḥakam, Kindī, and Balādhurī do not have any record of this covenant, which led some scholars to consider the covenant fictitious or apocryphal. Nevertheless, its detailed citation by al-Qalqashandī (1355 or 1356–1418), even at that late date, leaves no chance for doubting the veracity of the situation as a whole, if not in its minute details. Here is a summary of al-Qalqashandī's account of the Covenant (1913, pp. 381–87), which runs in perfect parallel to the Treaty of Alexandria, in its varied stipulations and conditions. First, the JIZYAH, or poll tax, was to be paid by all Dhimmis, that is, protected non-Muslim subjects. Second, Dhimmis were required to offer free hospitality to all Muslim soldiers for three days in their churches. Third, they were to be loyal subjects to their Muslim rulers. Furthermore, they were permitted to ride only donkeys and they were to ride them sideways. They were required to rise in the presence of Muslims, and they were to wear vestments that were distinguishable from those of their Muslim compatriots. Dhimmis were not to raise their voices in prayer, and they were not to hold ostentatious processions with their censers and scriptures. Their church bells were to be rung in low tones. This special stipulation could be fictitious, since bells appeared in the Eastern churches only in modern times, and certainly not before the seventeenth century, according to the Jesuit C. Sicard (Tager, 1951, p. 54, n. 1). Under these conditions, the Christians, including the Copts of Egypt, were allowed to retain their established churches without interference. However, they were not allowed to restore ruined churches or build new ones.

The covenant also stipulated that Dhimmis were not permitted to be employed in the service of Muslims or the Muslim state in accordance with the dictates of the Qur'ān. This principle, however, proved to be utterly impractical for the simple reason that the Copts, who were the accountants, were the only functionaries who could help with the levy of the KHARAJ, or general taxation. The rulers had no other means of levying taxes but through the good offices of their Coptic subjects. Some rulers occasionally dismissed the Copts from office, resulting in the collapse of the economy and the ultimate return of the Copts to rectify the financial position of the state. Nevertheless, jurists such as Ibn al-Naqqāsh continued to uphold this system, at least in theory, in their *fatwā* (juridical consultation) issued before 1362 (Belin, 1851, p. 419).

The restrictions imposed on the Dhimmis were reinstated by caliphs from time to time. Abū Yūsuf Ya'qūb, a contemporary Muslim judge of the time of Caliph Hārūn al-Rashīd (786–809), states that these conditions were fully recorded in his *Kitāb al-Kharāj* (Book of Taxation). The same Abū Yūsuf also says, on the authority of ʿAbd-al-Raḥmān ibn Thābit ibn Thūbān, that ʿUmar ibn ʿAbd-al-ʿAzīz wrote to one of his representatives confirming the substance of ʿUmar ibn al-Khaṭṭāb's covenant (Ye'or, 1985, p. 169). In spite of these protestations, financial and political conditions left the Copts in office. Even in the early days of ʿAmr ibn al-ʿĀṣ, the Coptic patriarch BENJAMIN I emerged at Alexandria. Previously, he had spent most of the years of his reign a fugitive moving from one desert monastery to another for fear of arrest by the Byzantine ruler Cyrus al-Muqawqas. Benjamin I was honored by the Muslim victors, who permitted him to occupy numerous churches previously appropriated by the Melchites while the Coptic foundations remained secure under the terms of the Covenant of ʿUmar.

BIBLIOGRAPHY

Abdur Rahman I. *Non-Muslims under Shariʿah.* Brentwood, Md., 1979.

Bat Ye'or. *The Dhimmis, Jews and Christians under Islam.* London and Toronto, 1985.

Belin, M. "Fetoua relatif à la condition des Zimmis, et particulièrement des chrétiens en pays Musulmans depuis l'établissement de l'Islamisme jusqu'au milieu du VIIIe siècle de l'hégire." *Journal asiatique,* ser. 4, 18 (1851):417–516.

Butler, A. J. *The Arab Conquest of Egypt.* Oxford, 1902; repr. 1978.

Lane-Poole, S. *A History of Egypt in the Middle Ages.* London, 1921; repr. New York, 1969.

Qalqashandī, al-. *Ṣubḥ al-Aʿshā,* Vol. 13, pp. 383ff. Cairo, 1913.

Tager, J. *Aqbāṭ wa-Muslimūn.* Cairo, 1951.

AZIZ S. ATIYA

CRAMER, MARIA (1898–1978), German Coptologist. She was a pupil of Hermann RANKE and Hermann JUNKER. Though she was working as a schoolteacher, she published several books and articles on Coptic paleography, book illumination, inscriptions, liturgy, and hymns. Some of her works related to Coptic studies are: *Koptische Inschriften im Kaiser-Friedrich-Museum zu Berlin* (Cairo, 1949);

Koptische Buchmalerei; Illuminationen in Manuskripten des christlich-koptischen Ägypten vom 4. bis zum 19. Jahrhundert (Recklinghausen, 1964); *Koptische Paläographie* (Wiesbaden, 1964); *Koptische Liturgien* (Trier, 1973).

MARTIN KRAUSE

CRONIUS OF NITRIA, SAINT. *See* Antony of Egypt, Saint; Paul the Simple, Saint.

CROSBY SCHØYEN CODEX (earlier names: Crosby Codex, Mississippi Coptic Codex I, and Savery Codex), a single-quire papyrus codex in Sahidic Coptic that came to light as part of a major manuscript discovery made by Egyptian peasants in 1952 near the base of the cliff Jabal Abū Mannā some 7½ miles (12 km) east of the discovery site of the NAG HAMMADI LIBRARY. The manuscript collection, known locally as the Dishnā Papers (after the nearby town of Dishnā), included remains of some thirty-eight books (rolls and codices) among which are classical texts, biblical and apocryphal manuscripts, mathematical exercises, and letters of Pachomian monks. The inclusion of the Pachomian material has led James M. Robinson to suggest that the entire collection derives originally from a Pachomian library (Robinson, 1986, pp. 1–25). The Pachomian monastic system, headquartered at nearby Pbow (modern Fāw al-Qiblī), included some eleven monasteries in Upper Egypt.

The Crosby-Schøyen Codex, which measures 15.2 × 14.7 cm, is composed of a single quire of thirty-five sheets or folded pairs of conjugate leaves. Its original total of 136 pages has been diminished through loss of material from the beginning and end. Pages 25–126 are in excellent condition and relatively complete, and one-half of pages 23–24 survives. Some minor additional text appears on the remnants of pages 10–22 and 127–28. In addition, forty-one fragments are preserved in the Rare Book Room of Perkins Library at Duke University (P. Duke inv. C 125).

The surviving pages of the codex preserve five distinct tractates. These include MELITIUS OF SARDIS's *On the Pascha* (pp. 7–51; pp. 23–51 extant), The Jewish Martyrs, a translation of 2 Maccabees 5:27–7:41 (pp. 52–74), 1 Peter (pp. 75–107), Jonah (pp. 107–124), and an unidentified text (pp. 124–26). An additional tractate may have existed on lost pages 3–6 (assuming a front fly leaf, pp. 1–2). Since the final pages of the codex are lost, one has no way of knowing whether the last unidentified text continued to the end of the codex. This final text appears to be an early Christian homily that advises the need for action and preparedness alongside of belief. The selection of these five tractates for inclusion in a single codex has led to the speculation of the codex's use as a paschal lectionary, "a reader's book used at the observance of Christ's death and resurrection—and *ipso facto* at a baptism" (Cabaniss, 1961, pp. 70–72).

The single scribe who copied the codex wrote in black ink with a coarse pen. The hand is careful, large, and bold (Willis, 1961, p. 388). Later corrections to the text may be the work of a second scribe. With the exception of the final unidentified tractate, the codex was written in double columns of varying length (11–19 lines). The final tractate is written in a single column. Coptic pagination is present though not continuous for the entire codex. The scribe began new enumeration with the first page of 1 Peter (p. 75) and the first page of Jonah (p. 107). The Coptic dialect throughout is Sahidic, though various dialectical peculiarities are to be found.

The date of the codex has been variously estimated from the latter half of the second century to the sixth century, though a third century date is most often cited (Willis, p. 389; Cabaniss, p. 71; E. G. Turner, 1977, p. 137; Hall, 1979, p. xlv and xvii n. 8).

The Crosby-Schøyen Codex was originally acquired by the University of Mississippi in 1955 through a donation of Lucius Olen and Margaret Reed Crosby (Willis, pp. 382–83). It was labeled by the university as Mississippi Coptic Codex I: the Crosby Codex. Work toward publication was begun immediately, but circumstances resulting from the desegregation of the University of Mississippi caused delay and in the end failure of these efforts. The codex remained in the University of Mississippi library until 1981 when it was deacquisitioned and sold. It has since remained in private hands. It was acquired in the early 1980s by the Pax ex Innovatione Foundation under the leadership of Winsor T. Savery. While owned by the foundation, the codex bore the name Savery Codex ("The Savery Codex in Claremont," pp. 4–5). The codex was purchased at auction in December 1988 (Checkland, 1988) by Martin Schøyen of Norway and relabeled Crosby-Schøyen Codex, Manuscript 193 in the Schøyen Collection. A critical edition, the *editio princeps,* prepared under the auspices of the Institute for Antiquity and Christianity in Claremont, California, is forthcoming.

BIBLIOGRAPHY

"Bible Scripts Bought. Two Rare Collections Are Gifts to University of Mississippi." *The New York Times*, Nov. 27, 1955, p. 135.

Cabaniss, A. "The University of Mississippi Coptic Papyrus Manuscript: A Paschal Lectionary?" *New Testament Studies* 8 (1961):70–72.

Checkland, S. J. "Medieval Texts Fetch 2.5m for Museum." *The London Times*, Dec. 7, 1988, p. 5.

Hall, S. G. *Melito of Sardis. On Pascha and Fragments.* Oxford Early Christian Texts. Oxford, 1979.

Metzger, B. "Recent Discoveries and Investigations of New Testament Manuscripts." *Journal of Biblical Literature* 78 (1959):15–16.

Robinson, J. M. "The Discovering and Marketing of Coptic Manuscripts: The Nag Hammadi Codices and the Bodmer Papyri." In *The Roots of Egyptian Christianity*, pp. 1–25.

"The Savery Codex in Claremont." *Bulletin of the Institute for Antiquity and Christianity* 12 (1985):4–5.

Turner, E. G. *The Typology of the Early Codex.* Philadelphia, 1977.

Turner, J. S. "A Codex of Coptic Christianity." *Humanities* 10 (1989):10–11.

Willis, W. H. "The New Collections of Papyri at the University of Mississippi." In *Proceedings of the IX International Congress of Papyrology*, pp. 381–92. Oslo, 1961.

JAMES E. GOEHRING

CROSS. *See* Symbols in Coptic Art.

CROSS, MANUAL. *See* Liturgical Instruments.

CROSS, PECTORAL. *See* Liturgical Insignia.

CROSS, PROCESSIONAL. *See* Liturgical Insignia.

CROSS, SIGN OF THE, symbolic sign of the crucifixion. The writings of the church fathers and the oldest liturgies clearly indicate the use of the sign of the cross as an integral part of the service or the sacrament. "Unless the sign of the cross is made either on the foreheads of the faithful, or on the water itself wherewith they are regenerated, or on the oil with which they are anointed with chrism, or on the sacrifice with which they are nourished, none of these things is duly performed" (Saint Augustine, Homily 118 on Saint John 19:24).

The sign of the cross takes various forms, each having its own interpretation. It may be made with the right thumb when crossing oneself, and the right forefinger when crossing other people or things. This can be interpreted as a sign of the oneness of God, or a reference to Christ's saying, "But if it is by the finger of God that I cast out demons, then the kingdom of God has come upon you" (Lk. 11:20). It may also be taken as a reference to the system of purification according to Mosaic law, in which the priest used his finger (Lv. 14:16); to the two tablets of the testament written by the finger of God (Ex. 31:18); or to Jacob's ladder (Gn. 28:12) symbolizing the cross on which Jesus Christ rose to heaven.

Using three fingers indicates the Holy Trinity, and five fingers indicates the five wounds suffered by Jesus Christ on the cross.

The form of the sign of the cross has developed since the early days of Christianity, when it used to be made on the forehead once or thrice; then on the forehead, the heart, and the arm. "The sign of the cross is on our brow and on our heart. It is on our brow that we may always confess Christ, on our heart that we may always love Him, on our arm that we may always work for Him" (Ambrose, *De Isaac et Anima* 8). Later it became customary to make the sign on the forehead (in the name of God), the mouth (in the name of Jesus Christ the Word of God), and on the heart (in the name of the Holy Spirit).

From the sixth century onward the sign of the cross settled in the form now common to us, that is, with the thumb crossing the forefinger of the right hand, we touch the forehead, the chest, the left shoulder, and the right shoulder.

ARCHBISHOP BASILIOS

CROSS, TRIUMPH OF THE, a subject of rich Christian significance and the theme of a tapestry in the collection of Coptic textiles in the Louvre. About 4 feet (1.20 meters) high and 6.8 feet (2.10 meters) long, it was created in the technique of "looped" fabric, which produced a relief effect.

Triumph of the Cross. Detail of the center. *Courtesy Louvre Museum, Paris.*

Triumph of the Cross. Detail of the right: Jonah. *Courtesy Louvre Museum, Paris.*

This tapestry has suffered some damage, though the highly colored essentials of the subject have not been affected.

The tapestry sets the glorious exaltation of the cross in an Old Testament context. The design is divided horizontally into two registers. The lower register is a full-length picture of Eden. At the sides, on either side of two bushes, wild and domestic animals play together (Is. 11:6), leaving room in the center for the Iranian tree of life. The tree is on the same axis as a *crux ansata*—descended from the pharaonic sign of life (ANKH)—in the center of the upper register. The loop that surmounts the two crossed branches of this emblem is conceived as a crown of laurel, dotted with precious stones and containing a star formed of two intersecting squares. On either side a decorated column separates the tree from two scenes oriented toward it. On the left, very incomplete, is a donkey advancing toward a peacock, from whose beak hangs a small *crux ansata;* the scene suggests the prophecy of Balaam (Nm. 24:17), which would be confirmed by the star integrated into the central *crux ansata.* On the right, Jonah, duly identified by an inscription above his head and rising as an orant from the *kētos* (sea creature) under the trunk and fruit of the castor tree, is the manifest sign of the resurrection of Christ (Mt. 12:40).

Triumph of the Cross. Detail of the left: Prophecy of Balaam. *Courtesy Louvre Museum, Paris.*

The tapestry thus depicts the Triumph of the Cross, arising out of the entire Old Testament history of salvation and, through the tree of life in the earthly paradise, linking it to the heavenly Jerusalem, just as by its form it transports the whole of the pharaonic past heavenward.

BIBLIOGRAPHY

Bourguet, P. du. "Deux pièces coptes de la fin de la période ommeyade." *Revue du Louvre et des Musées de France* 19, 2 (1969):101–105.

PIERRE DU BOURGUET, S. J.

CROSS, VENERATION OF THE. Through the crucifixion of Jesus Christ, the cross, which had previously been a method of punishment, humiliation, and disgrace, became a symbol of glory, honor, and spiritual joy. Matthew (24:30) calls it the sign of the Son of Man. Hence the veneration that Christians came to feel toward it, using it as their distinguishing emblem and deriving courage, endurance, and fortitude from it. They blessed themselves with its sign; they wore it round their necks; they decorated their buildings with it; they erected it over the graves of their dead. It also became an object constantly in the hands of their priests.

The Coptic church designates two days for the Holy Cross: 17 Tūt, to commemorate the discovery of the cross by Empress Helena, mother of Emperor CONSTANTINE I the Great, in 326, and 10 Baramhāt, to commemorate its restoration to Jerusalem in 628 following the defeat of the Persians by Emperor HERACLIUS, who released the cross and liberated Patriarch Zachariah of Jerusalem.

The veneration of the cross, by bending the knee, bowing down before it in reverence, and kissing it, is a mark of respect and homage to the Savior's cross, not in worship but in veneration.

Christians honor the cross for various reasons: (1) it is their own sacred emblem; (2) it is the symbol of redemption; (3) it was on the cross that God revealed Himself to us in the person of the crucified, enabling us to witness God's consummate love, His perfect sanctity, His boundless mercy, His superior justice, His sublime wisdom, and His transcendent authority over nature and the entire creation; (4) it is the symbol of unity and peace, which broke down "the dividing wall of hostility" (Eph. 2:14–16); the cross has brought about full reconciliation, not only between God and man, but also between man and men.

The essential significance of the miracle of the Crucifixion is summed up in the words of Saint ATHANASIUS: "It was fitting for the Lord to spread out His hands . . . that with the one He might draw the ancient people, and with the other the Gentiles, to unite both in Him."

BIBLIOGRAPHY

Daniélou, J. *A History of Early Christian Doctrine,* Vol. 1, chap. 19. London, 1964.

ARCHBISHOP BASILIOS

CROSSES. *See* Metalwork, Coptic; Woodwork, Coptic.

CROSS-IN-SQUARE, also called quincunx, the most important type of church building of the middle and late Byzantine periods of the Byzantine empire. It characteristically consists of an approximately square room, the naos, from which is cut out an internal cross-shaped unit by erecting four columns at the center and joining them by means of arches to the outer walls. The central area, again square, always carries a pendentive dome, while the cross arms extending outward from it are barrel-, cross-, or sail-vaulted. The small corner sections outside the cross arms are likewise covered with cross- or sail-vaults. In the East this naos, organized in such a way, is joined to a normal sanctuary consisting of three chambers, each of which is usually furnished with a little eastern apse, which is, as a rule, encased on three sides on the east outer wall. At the west end a simple, equally vaulted narthex is mostly attached. In addition, this type of building may be provided with an ambulatory.

The cross-in-square type presumably was realized for the first time around A.D. 880 in the so-called Nea, the new palace church of Emperor Basil I (867–886) in Constantinople. This edifice has not been preserved, but it is adequately known from some contemporary descriptions and numerous succeeding buildings. The earliest examples are the north church of the monastery of Lips (Fenari Isa Camii) from 907 and the church of the Myrelaion (Bodrum Camii) from 920. Also well known are the Panagia ton Chalkeon (1028) from Thessalonica and the Theotokos church of Hosios Loukas at Stiris in Phocis, whose date is a still unsettled problem.

Until the end of the late Byzantine period Byzantine church architecture was dominated almost exclusively by the cross-in-square type. The changes it underwent in the course of time in no way affected the basic principle of the type. This is the case even with the reduced version that appears from the late eleventh century, in which the eastern cross arm coincided with the central chamber of the sanctuary. The pair of columns at the front was thereby rendered superfluous.

On the other hand, in Egypt the cross-in-square can be found only in a few isolated instances, which for the most part have reached us in a state of irreparable later distortion. The buildings in question are some hall churches from the Mamluk period, such as the church of Dayr al-Shahīd Tādrus al-Muḥārib at MADĪNAT HĀBŪ, and the church of Amir Tādrus at Old Cairo, which in its present form presumably dates from the eighteenth century. Since all the bays have been uniformly covered with sail-vaults, which are not very flexible in their proportions, the examples mentioned do not display a spatial accentuation of the center. Only the dome over the central bay is taller. Unlike the Byzantine cross-in-square they are, moreover, provided with a *khūrus,* which is a normal feature of Egyptian churches even into the Mamluk period.

In Nubia the situation is substantially different. As a result of the general decline in population in the thirteenth century and the decline of Christianity accompanying it, the existing churches were not transformed through rebuilding. Consequently, several churches comparable to the Byzantine cross-in-square have been preserved there. Characteristic examples are the church of Archangel Raphael at TAMĪT, the church at Faqīrdīb, and presumably also the north church at 'ABDALLĀH NIRQI. Unlike the Byzantine edifices, columns were never applied in these buildings for easily explainable reasons. The supports are pillars built up using rubble or mud bricks, and in order to achieve greater stability, they very often also have a cruciform cross-section. Furthermore, here one finds that the spatial accentuation of the center that is essential to the type is only very negligently observed. A beautiful example of a reduced cross-in-square from Nubia is provided by the cemetery church at Tamīt.

[*See also:* Architectural Elements of Churches.]

BIBLIOGRAPHY

Adams, W. Y. "Post-pharaonic Nubia in the Light of Archaeology II." *Journal of Egyptian Archeology* 51 (1965):160–78.

Bresciani, E. "Le chiese." In *Tamit (1964). Missione archeologica in Egitto dell'Università di Roma,* pp. 27–37. Rome, 1967.

Clarke, S. *Christian Antiquities in the Nile Valley.* Oxford, 1912.

Grossmann, P. *Mittelalterliche Langhauskuppelkirchen und verwandte Typen in Oberägypten.* Glückstadt, 1982.

Krautheimer, R. *Early Christian and Byzantine Architecture.* Harmondsworth, 1965.

Mango, C. *Byzantine Architecture.* New York, 1976.

Megaw, A. H. S. "The Original Form of the Theotokos Church of Constantine Lipa." *Dumbarton Oaks Papers* 18 (1964):279–98.

Millet, G. *L'Ecole grecque dans l'architecture byzantine,* 2nd ed. London, 1974.

Millingen, A. van. *Byzantine Churches in Constantinople,* 2nd ed. London, 1974.

Monneret de Villard, U. *La Nubia medioevale,* Vols. 1–4. Cairo, 1935–1957.

Rice, D. T. "Excavations at Bodrum Camii 1930." *Byzantion* 8 (1933):151–74.

PETER GROSSMANN